MACROECONOMICS
The Dynamics of Theory and Policy

William J. Boyes
Professor of Economics
College of Business Administration
Arizona State University

Published by

H70 **SOUTH-WESTERN PUBLISHING CO.**

CINCINNATI   WEST CHICAGO, ILL.   DALLAS   PELHAM MANOR, N.Y.   PALO ALTO, CALIF.

Copyright © 1984

by

SOUTH-WESTERN PUBLISHING CO.
Cincinnati, Ohio

ISBN: 0-538-08700-5

Library of Congress Catalog Card Number: 83-60389

Cover photograph: © Joel Gordon, 1982

1 2 3 4 5 D 8 7 6 5 4

Printed in the United States of America

PREFACE

In 1983 a number of significant and dramatic economic events caught the attention of the media and the American public.

- The U.S. economy began to recover from its eighth postwar recession.
- The stock market turned without warning into a raging bull then fluctuated wildly on rumors of Federal Reserve actions and speculations over the possible reappointment of its chairman Paul Volcker.
- The international monetary system raised eyebrows in many concerned nations as Third World debt was scrutinized and U.S. deficits were criticized.
- On June 5, the 100th birthday of the founder of macroeconomics, John Maynard Keynes, was celebrated as modern Keynesians were attempting to provide a stronger theoretical underpinning for the Keynesian system and for activist discretionary policies.

Students come to a macroeconomics course wanting to study and discuss these and other topics of current interest, such as recessions, inflation, stagflation, and policy issues. They are not, on the other hand, particularly interested in spending a semester examining and exhausting the implications of abstract theories.

The Dynamic Interaction of Theory and Policy

The purpose of this book is to satisfy student demand. To meet this demand, the framework of this book has been dictated by the following two overriding objectives:

1. To provide a theoretical understanding of the most recent developments in macroeconomics, such as the rational expectations hypothesis, the contract and information based theories of business cycles, supply-side economics, the debate over the exchange rate regimes, and Third World debt
2. To provide a historical foundation for current theories and policies

The dynamic interaction of theory and policy forms the basis of the text. The theories generate implications that, when applied as policies, affect the development of the economy and generate new theories or addenda to existing theories.

A question asked throughout the text is, How can we understand the current policies, controversies, or theories without understanding what went before? Why, for example, did the Reagan administration adopt the particular policies that it did? How can we understand the Great Inflation of the 1970s without understanding how the connection between balanced budgets and political success was broken? Economic theory, therefore, is not developed in an ivory tower isolated from events in the real world. Nor are economic events independent of economic theory. Macroeconomics should not be studied as an ivory tower abstraction. What would have happened had Keynes not written his *General Theory*? Would the world's economies have succumbed to political pressures and fallen into rampant inflation in the 1970s? Similarly, would monetary policy have been the same had Milton Friedman not questioned many of the postulates of Keynesian economics?

Contemporary Interactions of Theory and Policy

Currently the field of macroeconomics is involved in sifting through the dust after the collapse of the Keynesian system to determine whether only parts of the system are worth saving or whether the system itself will rise again like the phoenix. This makes the study of macroeconomics exciting. It also makes writing a text difficult because, with publication lags, it is impossible to capture all the newest theoretical suggestions and the newest policy applications. The framework of this text, however, provides a theoretical foundation for considering whatever new suggestions and policy applications do come about. That is what makes this text exciting.

Features of This Text

Albert Einstein once said that everything should be made as simple as possible but not more so. This book has been written with that rule in mind. The length, coverage, and writing style of the book have been dictated by many years of teaching at state universities. The typical state university class on intermediate macroeconomics includes a wide range of student interests and talents. In such classes the desire to spend 550 pages on theoretical development prior to considering recent issues may not be universal. In this book current issues are discussed as soon as possible. Policy issues are examined throughout the text, and the most current theoretical issues are reached very quickly. The complete theoretical framework, including expectations formation processes, is developed by Chapter 8. Since the first two chapters are introductory, only six chapters are required to fully develop the theoretical framework.

Structure of the Chapters

At the beginning of each chapter an overview of material to be covered is presented in a boxed section titled *What to Expect*. The graphs used throughout are made as easy to read and interpret as possible by a consistent use of color to distinguish important points, such as supply from demand curves and *IS* from *LM* curves.

Review questions and exercises appear at the end of each chapter along with a list of suggested readings. Typically, the readings include academic articles as well as current events articles from business publications and news magazines. The questions are structured in such a manner that the first questions will help the reader to review the material covered in the chapters while the latter questions require the reader to extend the material covered.

Several of the chapters include appendices that are more technical than the text. I have attempted to take as many of the algebraic derivations as possible out of the chapter text in order to make the chapter material flow more smoothly. While the material in these appendices is instructive, its inclusion in a macro course depends solely on instructor and student desires. I encourage, however, all classes to at least peruse the second appendix to Chapter 8. This appendix lays out the transition from the static presentation of price levels and money supply changes to that of inflation and monetary growth rates. It is placed in an appendix only because it is not necessary in order to understand the remainder of the text material.

Chapter-by-Chapter Organization

Chapters 1 and 2 are introductory and provide an overview of macroeconomics and of the measurement of macroeconomic variables. Chapter 3 is devoted to the Keynesian framework. In Chapters 4 and 5 the *IS-LM* model is developed and the beginning of the classical economic counterrevolution is discussed. The Friedman-Phelps alternative is examined in Chapter 6, and the complete aggregate demand-aggregate supply model is developed in Chapters 7 and 8. The remainder of the text is devoted to refinements of the theory and examinations of policy implications. In Chapters 9 through 12 current controversies over tax policy, investment, consumption, the formulation and implementation of monetary policy, the condition of the budget, and the question of whether the deficit is a burden are discussed. In Chapter 13 the framework of the earlier chapters is utilized to examine the Great Stagflation of the early to middle 1970s and to discuss the rules versus discretion debate. In Chapter 14, economic policies and developments since the Great Stagflation are examined. Issues such as problems with Social Security, declining productivity, fundamental tax reform, and supply-side economics are considered. Chapter 15 is a concluding discussion of current issues in stabilization policy focusing primarily on theoretical controversies. The current debates between modern Keynesians and nonactivists are explored and placed in a theoretical perspective. In addition, some of the interactions between policy applications and theory, such as the idea that the political process itself generates fluctuations in economic activity, are further developed. Chapter 16 presents an overview of open economy macroeconomics—the study of the interaction among national economies.

Glossary

Important terms are included and placed at the end of the book for easy student reference.

Instructor's Manual

The instructor's manual contains suggested answers to the review questions and thirty multiple-choice questions for each chapter. It is available to adopters upon request.

Acknowledgements

Many people contributed to this text, and I apologize in advance for names I fail to mention. First, the recognition of a need for the text and the way in which the material is presented is due to the students I have taught at California State University, Long Beach and at Arizona State University. In particular, I want to thank Jalal Ahmad, Nancy Roberts, Keith Ugone, Mark Kinsey, Robin Dunn, Stephen Russell, Bill Barchilon, John Williamson, and untold others for working through drafts of the manuscript and providing comments and questions. The following friends and colleagues provided suggestions and guidance:

Art Blakemore, Arizona State University
James Fackler, the University of Kentucky and the Federal Reserve Bank of New York
Paul Smith, University of Missouri
David Smyth, Wayne State University
Wolf Mayer, University of Cincinnati
Ryan Amacher, Clemson University
Rich Hart, Miami University of Ohio
Brian Stanhouse, Notre Dame University
Don Schlagenhauf, Arizona State University

Their comments have aided significantly in the structure and exposition of the text. Finally, the project would not have been completed without the support of my wife Susan, my parents, and, of course, Kessa.

William J. Boyes

TABLE OF CONTENTS

The ideas of economists, both when they are right and when they are wrong, are more powerful than is commonly understood. Indeed, the world is ruled by little else. Practical men, who believe themselves to be quite exempt from any intellectual influences, are usually the slaves of some defunct economist. Mad men in authority, who hear voices in the air, are distilling their frenzy from some academic scribbler of a few years back.

John Maynard Keynes, 1926

The first two chapters of the book are introductory and are intended to lay the foundation for the remainder of the book. In the first chapter, a brief overview of the United States economy since the 1920s is presented. Then a summary discussion of some important schools of economic thought is provided. The chapter concludes with a consideration of why different economists sometimes offer contradictory policy advice.

Chapter 2 is devoted to an explanation of important economic variables underlying the study of the aggregate economy. First, the structure of the national income and product accounts is explained. Then three important types of price indices are presented and their use in measuring inflation compared. The chapter then turns to a consideration of various ways of assessing labor market conditions. Finally, the balance of the chapter reviews some techniques for measuring monetary and fiscal policy.

CHAPTER 1.

An Introduction and Overview

For the study of political economy you need no special knowledge, no extensive library, no costly laboratory; you do not even need textbooks or teachers, if you will but think for yourselves.

Henry George
Lecture at the
University of California,
March 9, 1877, Works,
Vol. III (1904), p. 139.

This book will take you from a principles level of knowledge about macroeconomic theory to an understanding of the current frontiers of macroeconomic research. In addition, after completing the book you should have a grasp of the controversies that surround economic policy. This first chapter is intended to provide the following:

- An introduction to macroeconomics

- An outline of the development of macroeconomic theory and the leading schools of thought

- A brief examination of the primary issues on which economists disagree

- An introduction to the questions that macroeconomics seeks to answer

Introduction

Since World War II the United States economy has experienced eight recessions averaging over nine months in length and with an average 4.5 percent drop in output. Prices, relatively stable for more than 200 years before 1960, (see Figure 1-1) doubled then doubled again and even once again during the decades of the sixties and seventies. While federal government budgets remained relatively balanced until the 1960s, there has been only one year since then in which the government ran a surplus. The three years 1980, 1981, and 1982 saw total deficits equal to the total of the previous 12 years. The deficits projected for 1983 and 1984 total more than those for the previous 17 years. The money supply grew at a relatively constant 5 percent rate during the 1950s and 1960s, but soared at more than a 12 percent rate at times during the 1970s. The stock market surged after August, 1982, after having been motionless for more than a decade. The dollar became less valuable to other countries during the 1970s but at the same time oil revenues collected by the OPEC countries were invested in the U.S. As other countries inflated while the United States fell into recession in the early eighties, the dollar once again climbed in value. Unemployment rose during the seventies even as inflation rose and hit near record levels in 1979.

Why? What accounted for these movements in economic variables? It seems that each time economists believe they have the answers to these questions (that is, that they have the world figured out) something occurs

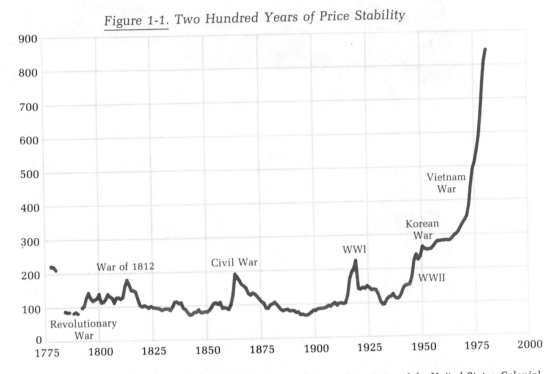

Figure 1-1. Two Hundred Years of Price Stability

Sources: U. S. Bureau of the Census, *Historical Statistics of the United States, Colonial Times to 1970*, bicentennial ed. (Washington, D. C.: 1975), Series E-82; *Economic Report of the President* (1983), Table B-57.

This graph presents us with several questions. (1) Why have prices tended to rise during war periods? (2) What happened in the late 1950s and early 1960s to lead to a continued increase in prices after 200 years of price stability? And (3), what causes prices to rise or fall?

to generate even more questions. During the 1920s optimism was the order of the day. The economy was booming, stock prices were soaring, reflecting as well as adding to America's optimism regarding the future. Most people believed growth and prosperity would continue forever. We know what happened.

After having lived through the Great Depression of the 1930s and souring on existing theories, economists turned to the ideas of John Maynard Keynes believing them to be panaceas. The early 1960s were the heydays of what is known as *Keynesian economics*. During this period economists pronounced the business cycle dead and devoted their attention to "fine tuning" the economy. Through appropriate use of fiscal and monetary policy it was believed that the rate of growth of the economy, and inflation and unemployment could be set at virtually any level, given the existing structure of the economy. While this approach appeared to be successful in the early 1960s, it fell apart in the late 1960s.

Following World War II, it was believed that whenever inflation fell, unemployment would rise and vice versa. The 1970s proved this belief wrong. In March 1951, the Federal Reserve was given its independence—separated from control by the Treasury, in what was called the *Accord*. In 1982 there were eight bills introduced in Congress, all of which aimed to reduce the independence of the Federal Reserve. Tax increases, commonly believed to slow down consumer spending failed to work in 1968. Similarly, tax cuts were thought to increase spending but failed to do so in 1981.

All these surprises, misforecasts, mistakes, and learning experiences have brought forth new or revised approaches to economics: Keynesianism, monetarism, supply-side economics, rational expectations, Reaganomics, Tiponomics, and others have emerged.

Theories, or as they are often called, paradigms, useful in one context were altered or totally redeveloped to have validity in another context. For example, during the 1940s the economy was improving but still suffering from the Great Depression. After the experience of unemployment rates near 25 percent, it is no wonder all thoughts were on the collapse of the economy and on policies that would keep the economy from falling into depression in future years. During the 1970s, on the other hand, the economy was suffering from what we might call the *Great Inflation* and all thoughts were on the causes, consequences, and cures of inflation. Theories developed during the 1940s were revised in order to have relevance to the 1970s.

To study macroeconomics appropriately one must study the evolution of particular paradigms and be aware of the economic environment from which each explanation emerged.[1] In this book we focus on current issues in the theory and policy of macroeconomics. We do so by developing a general theoretical framework in which the various paradigms of the forties, fifties, sixties, seventies, and eighties can be discussed and by considering the circumstances that led to each revision or adaptation of the paradigms. The theoretical framework used throughout this book is the demand and supply analysis familiar from microeconomics. Since most issues in macroeconomics can be thought of as having an effect on, or being affected by, either the demand or the supply side of the economy, this dichotomy is particularly useful for the study of macroeconomics.

In the next section of this chapter we will provide a brief overview of the evolution of the field of macroeconomics using the demand/supply dichotomy. In the final section we consider the question of why economists disagree.

---

[1] This is not to say that a new theory should be developed for each event. In fact, scientific methodology would argue for just the opposite—a logical system that can be used in any environment. This is just where the field of macroeconomics is headed toward today.

An Overview

Macroeconomics did not become a separate area of study in economics until the 1930s. Prior to the 1930s, the aggregate economy was examined from the perspective of a system of individual markets in a branch of study called general equilibrium theory. The main problem in general equilibrium theory was proving that an economy consisting of a large number of individual, perfectly competitive markets would have a general equilibrium, that is, simultaneous equilibrium in each of the individual markets. In addition, much attention was focused on the question of whether this equilibrium was stable; that is, whether or not the economy would move back into equilibrium following a disturbance.

Although market structures such as monopoly, oligopoly and duopoly had entered the economist's vocabulary, perfect competition was the only market structure examined in the study of general equilibrium. It was shown that under the assumption of competitive markets with flexible prices and where individuals have complete knowledge of market developments, a general equilibrium would exist. This equilibrium would occur automatically; prices would adjust to excess demands or supplies so as to drive the economy toward equilibrium. Most economists, therefore, worked from the premise that markets would clear—that the quantities producers were willing and able to supply would equal the quantities purchased. There could be temporary aberrations from general equilibrium, but these aberrations would be just that, temporary. This premise applied to all markets, including the labor market. These economists, known as *classical economists* (see Figure 1-2), maintained that the economy would always be at full employment except for those temporary aberrations. As a result, the classical economists asserted that the proper role of the government is to allow the market system to operate—not to interfere with it.

According to the classical economists, unemployment did not exist, except very temporarily, and inflation was an easily explained phenomenon. Using the accounting relationship known as the *equation of exchange*, inflation was due simply to an increase in the money supply. The equation of exchange can be written as follows:

$$MV = PQ$$

Where M is the stock of money, V is the velocity of money (the average number of times a year that the money stock is used in making payments for goods), P is the price level, and Q is the level of real output. We have already noted that the classical economists believed that the market mechanism would generate an output level consistent with full employment. In other words, they believed Q to be constant or fixed at the full-employ-

Figure 1-2. The Schools of Thought

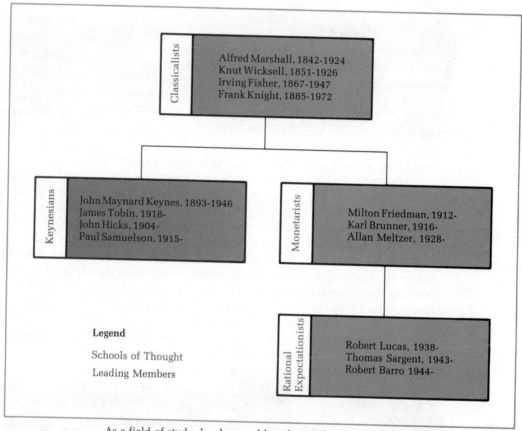

As a field of study develops and broadens, it becomes increasingly difficult to classify scholars into a particular school. Yet, while those leading members of the various schools of economic thought since the late 1800s may be classified into more than one school, the development of the field of macroeconomics shown in this figure is essentially accurate.

ment level of production. In addition, the velocity of money was assumed fixed. We will explain the reasons for this belief in later chapters. As a result of V and Q being fixed, the equation of exchange indicates that the price level will change whenever the stock of money changes. Hence the money supply is the only variable important in explaining the price level, and it acts as a veil over the real or physical output of the economy.

In the 1930s, fluctuations in the output of the economy began to be considered as something other than temporary aberrations from equilibrium. Q could no longer be considered fixed at the full-employment level. In 1936, John Maynard Keynes's book, *The General Theory of Employment, Interest and Money* altered the approach economists had been taking. Keynes developed a theoretical approach directed toward demonstrating that unemployment could last for a very long time (that is, a general equilibrium could occur at less than full employment) and that, therefore, it is necessary for government to alter its spending and taxing programs so as to move the economy toward full employment.

The Keynesian theoretical apparatus was born during the worst recession in modern American history, called the *Great Depression*. The unemployment rate in the United States went from 1.8 percent in 1926 to 25 percent in 1933 and remained near 17 percent for almost ten years. Prices fell nearly 50 percent from 1924 to 1933 and did not reach 1929 levels again until 1941. Understandably the Keynesian framework focused on the determinants of real output, real income, and unemployment and did not devote much attention to inflation.

The impact of the Great Depression was enormous. It was the type of event that affects a nation's behavior for many years. People who lived during the depression have never forgotten it. It also dictated economic thinking for at least the next two decades. Those trained in the Keynesian tradition were given a pervasive belief in the effectiveness of government spending and taxing and cared little about whether or not the flow of money increased or decreased. Furthermore, their academic training was based on the premise that either there is no general equilibrium at full employment or, if there is, that the economy will not be automatically driven toward it.

The Keynesian theoretical apparatus was directed toward determining the equilibrium level of output and, consequently, the equilibrium level of unemployment. If that level differed from the level desired by policymakers, Keynesian theory offered a prescription for changing the existing equilibrium to the desired level. This prescription involved changing the level of aggregate demand through government spending and taxing. As the Keynesian theoretical framework became the accepted paradigm of aggregate economics, economists began to direct their attention toward determining the best policies of government intervention or activism.

From the end of World War II until the early 1970s, the U.S. economy experienced unprecedented prosperity. Output grew at about 4 percent per year, the unemployment rate averaged less than 4 percent and the inflation rate averaged only 1.6 percent per year. Fine tuning the economy using Keynesian policies seemed to be the perfect answer. It was only during periods in which Keynesian prescriptions were not followed that the economy had any troubles (for example, the Eisenhower years, 1954 and 1958). Thus, the apparently successful application of Keynesian principles to economic policy that occurred in the U.S. (in the 1960s in particular) was an event of incomparable significance. Keynesian principles had led to a set of simple relationships between government spending and taxing policies and economic activity. It was an economics whose success was difficult to argue against at least until the decade of the 1970s when the U.S. economy underwent the first major recession since the 1930s. Yet, this time, in contrast to the 1930s when prices dropped, the inflation rate actually accelerated.

From 1974 to 1981, the U.S. economy experienced an average inflation rate of over 9 percent and even reached rates as high as 13 percent. In contrast to the predictions of Keynesian theory, massive government deficits and high rates of monetary expansion did not significantly reduce the unemployment rate. Instead, unemployment hit 8.5 percent in 1975 and was still over 7 percent in 1978. It remained at that level through 1980, and climbed again during 1981 and 1982 to near 11 percent.

The cause of the 1970s' stagflation was (and is) a topic of heated debate. Some economists attributed the problem to events in other parts of the world; e.g., a large decrease in protein sources due to a dislocation of the anchovy population, an increase in petroleum prices, and the OPEC oil embargo. Other economists pointed to the rapid rate of growth of the U.S. money supply as the villain. Still others noted that the basic policy approach suggested by the Keynesian framework was faulty. They drew an analogy with a football game. Suppose the Chicago Bears are playing against the Tampa Bay Buccaneers. Chicago would be like a Keynesian economist if, based on previous game films where Tampa Bay was noted to line two defensive backs on the right and two on the left, Chicago decided to line all its players on the right side, assuming that Tampa Bay would not change its defensive setup.[2] The purpose of this analogy was to point out that Keynesian policy changes assumed that individuals and businesses would not alter their behavior in response to governmental policy changes.

Whatever the reason, the Keynesian prescriptions seemed to have failed. As a result economists began to sift through the remarkable intellectual event called the *Keynesian Revolution* to determine what should be retained and what should be discarded. It is this sifting process that we are involved in when we study macroeconomics today. The issues are not resolved, nor are the answers readily apparent. Economists disagree about the appropriate explanation of economic events and, hence, over the appropriate policy or approach to economic problems. This uncertainty or ambiguity creates an exciting environment in which to study macroeconomics. It puts a premium on economic intuition and logic and for a textbook it requires the development of a framework in which the many issues can each be readily analyzed. The framework used in this book is the demand-supply one familiar from microeconomics. The approach taken here is to keep this framework as uncluttered and simple as possible and yet be able to capture the various theoretical developments.

---

[2] Thomas Sargent used this analogy in a workshop presentation on October 25, 1982. A member of the audience who was raised in St. Louis suggested that perhaps Chicago would not change—perhaps Sargent's analogy should have included another team.

The U. S. Economy since
1940: the Demand Side

Rapid growth in aggregate demand is one of the most prominent characteristics of the post-World War II period. Aggregate demand may most easily be thought of as "final sales" and can be closely measured as real Gross National Product (real GNP) less inventory changes. Since 1947, GNP has grown at nearly twice the rate of the 1923-1947 period. Another related feature is the stability of GNP—the size and number of fluctuations were substantially smaller from 1947 to 1973 than before, although the 1974-1975, 1980-1981, and 1981-1982 recessions changed this pattern. This is shown in Figure 1-3.

Economic instability can be thought of in terms of a demand curve shifting along a stable supply curve, as shown in Figure 1-4. What causes

Figure 1-3. *The Rate of Growth of Real GNP, 1910 to 1982*

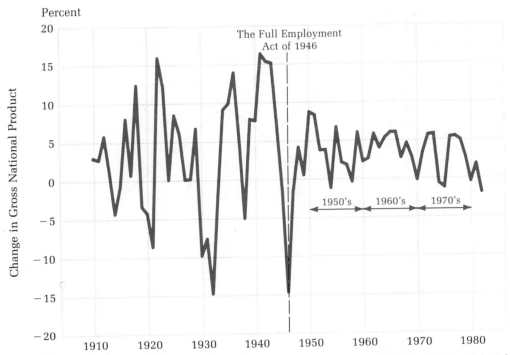

Sources: U. S. Bureau of the Census, *Historical Statistics of the United States, Colonial Times to 1970,* bicentennial ed. (Washington, D. C.: 1975), Series F-31; *Economic Report of the President* (1983), Table B-2.

Real GNP has fluctuated widely and frequently since 1900. Economists thought they had solved the problem of these fluctuations when, during the 1960s, they fine tuned the economy. Then came the 1970s and the 1980s, and the fluctuations increased. The business cycle had arisen from the dead.

What causes

the aggregate demand curve to shift? According to Keynesian explanations, economic instability was caused by the *autonomous components of demand*, those parts of demand not dependent on the condition of the economy. In other words, demand shifts originated from unpredictable changes in the behavior of individuals or firms. Consumption spending by households was considered to be primarily endogenously determined; that is, dependent on the condition of the economy. Hence, it was stable and predictable. The villain was business spending or investment. Investment could change according to the nonpredictable whims and expectations of businesses, referred to as *animal spirits*. Such a change would shift the demand curve and then, through consumption's multiplier effect amplifying the initial change in demand, lead to fluctuations in output or real GNP.

Figure 1-4. *Demand Induced Changes in Real Output and Prices*

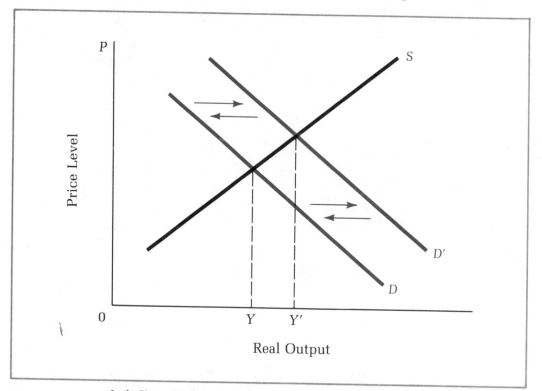

In the Keynesian framework it is aggregate demand shifts along a stable aggregate supply curve that lead to fluctuations in output. The demand shifts are caused by the unpredictable behavioral changes on the part of households and, primarily, businesses.

The erratic growth path of nonresidential fixed investment in the pre-1947 period provided the rationale for the Keynesian beliefs discussed previously. From 1920 to 1929, investment grew at a rate of 4.5 percent per year. It declined at a -1.7 percent rate between 1929 and 1941, and rose at nearly a 9 percent rate from 1941 to 1947. From 1950 to 1973 nonresidential fixed investment grew at a relatively stable 4 percent per year. Since 1973 its growth rate has fallen to about 2 percent per year.

The other component of autonomous demand is government expenditures. In the Keynesian scheme, government expenditures were seen as a way to offset the erratic fluctuations in investment. Interestingly, since the early 1950s, it has been government expenditure that has been the most unstable component of aggregate demand. In contrast to the 1930s and early 1940s when expanding government expenditures helped make up for the collapse of investment, the experience since the late 1940s, especially during the Korean and Vietnam War periods, has been one of instability caused by expanding government expenditures.

As will be thoroughly treated in Chapter 12, the growth of government is not as evident at first glance as we would think. The ratio of government spending to GNP has remained relatively constant since 1947. It is through transfer payments that the growth in the government's role in the economy becomes apparent. *Transfer payments* refer to the collection of taxes from one sector of the economy to be given to another sector. They include items such as social security, unemployment compensation, aid to families with dependent children, and many other programs. As a fraction of GNP, transfer payments have risen from less than 1 percent in the 1920s to more than 10 percent today. Government purchases, combined with transfer payments, as a proportion of GNP, have risen from 9 percent in the 1920s to over 30 percent in the 1980s.

In the past fifteen years the emphasis on the money supply in explanations of aggregate demand behavior has grown tremendously. The reason for this shift of opinion away from the animal spirits explanation can be attributed to the work of Milton Friedman. During the 1950s and early 1960s the money supply grew at a relatively constant 5 percent per year. But the growth exploded to nearly 9 percent per year beginning in the late 1960s. Furthermore, the growth rate fluctuated widely during the 1970s, reaching very high rates for one or two months only to drop to virtually no growth for the next couple of months. Friedman was tireless in pointing to the connection between economic instability and changes in the money supply.

The evils ascribed to a growing government and to erratic and expansive money supply growth have brought about a new emphasis on the supply side of the economy. In fact, the policies of the Reagan Administration initiated in the early 1980s have been called supply-side economics.

The U. S. Economy since
1940: the Supply Side_____

The interest in the supply side of the economy is understandable in light of the economic experiences of the late 1960s and 1970s. Very simply, the demand curve was shifting out much more rapidly than the supply curve. Policymakers and economists frustrated with failures of slowing the demand shifts began to ask why the supply curve could not be shifted out more rapidly. Whereas during the 1940s to 1960s economists viewed economic problems as being caused by deficient demand, during the 1970s to 1980s they were focusing on the lack of supply.

In the 1950s and 1960s policymakers set their primary goal as one of full employment and attempted to expand demand whenever unemployment fell below full employment. In the late 1960s Milton Friedman warned policymakers that this demand management approach was not only inappropriate but dangerous. Friedman indicated that there was an equilibrium unemployment rate that was outside of the control of aggregate demand and independent of the inflation rate. Friedman's label for this equilibrium was the *natural output level* or *natural unemployment rate*.

The natural output level can be represented by the vertical aggregate supply curve shown in Figure 1-5. The inevitable conclusion that comes from the economic structure represented by Figure 1-5 is that the natural output level must grow—the supply curve must shift out—to offset any demand increases. Without this growth, attempts to expand demand would only cause inflation. The growth of natural real GNP has fluctuated, but in a fairly narrow range, rising at an annual rate of 2.5 percent in the 1920s, at a 3.5 percent rate during 1967-73, and at a much lower rate since 1973. Actual real GNP grew somewhat more slowly than the natural rate during the 1923-47 period and slightly faster from 1947 to 1973. Real GNP has grown slowly in the years since 1973.

The declining rate of growth of actual real GNP reflects a decline in the rate of growth of labor productivity—output per worker. From 1947 to 1965 productivity grew at a 3.5 percent per year rate. It declined to a 2.0 percent rate during 1965-73, and dropped to a 0.5 percent annual rate since 1973. Much of the focus of economic analysis in the late 1970s and early 1980s has been on the causes of this productivity slowdown. Several possible explanations have been offered—the growth of government, increased rates of taxation, and the misallocation of investment. The last explanation, the shift in investment from long-lived capital such as buildings and equipment to short-lived capital such as automobiles and trucks during the 1970s, focused on one of the most serious problems. Since the shift was due to tax effects and not economic efficiency, the relative shift in investment was believed to be detrimental to the econ-

Figure 1-5. *The Natural Output Level*

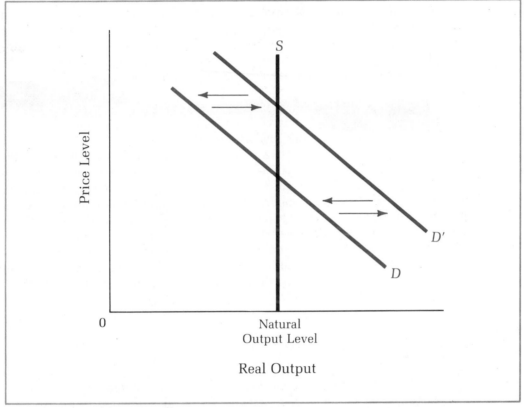

According to the natural rate hypothesis, changes in demand can only cause prices to change. Real output cannot be altered unless aggregate supply is changed.

omy's productive ability. The ratio of nonresidential fixed investment to GNP has remained fairly constant since the 1960s. However, long-lived investment has declined steadily while short-lived investment has increased.

The Reagan administration was swept into office in 1980 on the promise of less inflation, less government, and more freedom. Much of the administration's rhetoric and action was directed toward the supply side of the economy. The Capital Cost Recovery Act of 1981 attempted to alter the allocation of investment spending toward longer-lived projects. But the Reaganomics' approach went further than only stimulating long-lived investment. It attempted to implement the policies of Professors Art Laffer and Robert Mundell and Congressional representatives Kemp and Roth. Their thesis was that a reduction in taxes, a massive reduction, would stimulate increased work effort by employees and would, therefore, strongly stimulate the economy.

Few economists would disagree with the idea that economic policy was misplaced in interfering with investment and the supply side of the economy over the past twenty years. Yet this might be the only thing about which they would agree. Very few would align themselves with the ideological view of supply-side economics as propagated by Laffer, Mundell, Kemp, and Roth. Perhaps even fewer would support these views as implemented in the Reagan economic program. The tax cut, designed to take place over three years, 1981, 1982, and 1983, coupled with a tight monetary policy and increased government expenditures drove the economy into a tailspin. Many economists had warned that the supply-side policies would not work instantaneously.

As the elections of 1982 were taking place, the Laffer-type supply-siders were claiming that their ideas were never implemented correctly and the recession was not a fair conclusion about their theses. Others were blaming all the economy's woes on the supply-side approach. Whatever the truth, it is obvious, probably more now than ever, that economists do disagree. The old joke that if all economists were lined up head to toe around the world they would never reach a conclusion and Harry Truman's dictum that he would like to see a one-handed economist because he was so tired of their "on the one hand this and on the other hand that" were back in vogue.

Why Do Economists Disagree?

Economists are supposed to be scientists, schooled in seeking and testing truth. Even if their science is dismal it is still reputed to be a science. How then can their disagreements be so sharp?[3]

First, economists often make different assumptions about the time period to which their conclusions apply. When one economist asserts that lower tax rates will stimulate the economy and another argues that they will depress the economy, the first might be assuming a short-range period of time and the other a longer period of time.

Second, economists tend not to emphasize the extent of their ignorance, even though ignorance is formidable in the domain of macroeconomics. For example, the interactions among monetary policy, tax policy, government spending, and regulatory programs depend on people's expectations. It is no longer possible to believe that people will fail to alter their behavior in response to governmental monetary and fiscal policies. And it is simply not possible to predict with certainty how people will alter their behavior.

---

[3] Charles Wolf, Jr., "Why Economists Disagree," *Newsweek* (November 21, 1981), p. 21 is a very good discussion of this topic. Also, read Don Conlon's speech to NABE (Seattle, Washington: September 22, 1982).

Finally, we must recognize that economists have differing values and these values creep into macroeconomics quite easily. When, for instance, John Kenneth Galbraith or Walter Heller decry cuts in social security benefits, they are speaking more from a personal distaste for reducing this program than from the economic effects of the cuts.

However, as Charles Wolf, Jr., Dean of Rand Corporation's Graduate Institute stated: "Perhaps economics doesn't look so bad if it's compared with medicine. Recently I had occasion to consult consecutively with three orthopedic surgeons about a ligament injury: one recommended immediate surgery; the second suggested a cast for six weeks and then surgery, maybe; the third proposed rest and rehabilitation."[4]

In this book we will not shy away from controversies. Instead, it is important that the student come away with a feeling for the state of flux in the field of macroeconomics. The emphasis throughout this text is on macroeconomic policy. The economic environment in which policies were proposed, the pros, the cons, and the results of the policies are discussed. But policies are very seldom universally approved of by economists. Controversies over economic issues are more common than agreement. There are seldom simple, straightforward answers. In this text we provide the basis upon which analyses of economic issues can be formulated. From this base the student will be able to understand why one economist says one thing and another says just the opposite.

In the following chapters an attempt is made to provide the reader with two lessons: first, an appreciation of, and facility in the use of, the macroeconomic framework employed today; second, an understanding of why economists and policymakers took the paths they did at the times they did. The macroeconomic framework has evolved and continues to evolve in response to actual economic events. On the other hand, economic events are influenced or caused by the application of the macroeconomic framework. To understand why Professors Thomas Sargent, Robert Lucas, and others advocate certain policies based on rational expectations it is important to understand what went before. To know why Keynes proposed his *General Theory* it is necessary to understand what went before. Similarly, to understand many of the economic problems of the 1970s it is necessary to know what policymakers proposed and implemented in the 1960s and to understand on what foundation they based their proposals.

These ideas dictate the structure of this text. While it looks quite traditional in its structure, moving from the Keynesian framework to recent innovations, the material is not presented in a traditional manner. An effort has been made to provide the historical setting for the macroeconomic theories and policies that developed. In addition, we will

---

[4] Wolf, loc. cit.

attempt to arrive at an analysis of current events and issues as quickly as possible. By the time Chapter 8 is reached, the reader will be current with the macroeconomics of the eighties.

To summarize briefly, there are several major questions of interest in macroeconomics. The following are examples:

1. What causes inflation?
2. What causes unemployment?
3. What determines the level of real GNP?
4. What causes fluctuations in the level of real GNP? Can policy be designed to eradicate these fluctuations?

Over the years attempts to answer these questions have led to the emergence of several schools of thought. Some of the most prominent current schools are

1. Classical
2. Keynesian
3. Monetarist
4. Rational Expectations
5. Supply-Side

These questions and the answers provided by the various schools of thought are the subjects of this book. We begin in the next chapter with an introduction to several important economic variables.

SUGGESTED READINGS

Inflation is not a new phenomenon, as illustrated in

Anna J. Schwartz, "Secular Price Change in Historical Perspective," *Journal of Money, Credit, and Banking*, Vol. 5 (February, 1973), pp. 243-269.

For a discussion of the schools of thought look at

Douglas D. Purvis, "Monetarism: A Review," *The Canadian Journal of Economics*, Vol. 13 (February, 1980), pp. 96-112.

Economists define their roles in various ways. Some differing interpretations are given in the following:

Robert B. Carson, *Macroeconomic Issues Today* (New York: St. Martin's Press, 1980), Chapters 1-3.

Don Conlon, "In this Autumn of our Discontent, A Word to the Wise, Otherwise. . . ." (Presidential Address to the National Association of Business Economists, September 22, 1982.) Reprinted in *Business Economics*, Vol. 18, No. 1 (January, 1983), pp. 10-14.

George J. Stigler, "Economists and Public Policy," The 1982 Warren G. Nutter Lecture in Political Economy. American Enterprise Institute.

Charles Wolf, Jr., "Why Economists Disagree," *Newsweek* (November 21, 1981), p. 21.

For a more extended overview of issues discussed in this chapter read

Robert J. Gordon, "Postwar Macroeconomics: The Evolution of Events and Ideas," *The American Economy in Transition*, Martin Feldstein, ed. (Chicago: University of Chicago Press, 1980).

CHAPTER 2.

Measurement of Macroeconomic Variables: Output, Inflation, Unemployment, and Monetary and Fiscal Policy

If you don't know where you're going, any road will do.
                    Wise Old Saying

Misunderstandings about macroeconomic terminology often add confusion to debates over economic issues. In this chapter we discuss methods of measuring macroeconomic variables and define much of the terminology used throughout the text. Answers to the following questions will be covered in this chapter:

- *How is output measured?*

- *What does it mean when the Consumer Price Index increases?*

- *What does the unemployment rate actually measure?*

- *When is monetary policy or fiscal policy expansionary or contractionary?*

Introduction

King Canute achieved such power in eleventh century England that his followers told him he was capable of controlling all events by his mere command. Wise Canute responded by taking his advisers to the beach, where he ordered the ocean tide not to come in. Of course, the tide made its customary surge oblivious to monarchical command. Recently the United States economy, like the tides, seems to be running its course oblivious to the commands of Congress and the president. Responding to accelerating inflation, rising unemployment, declining productivity, declining stock market values, and worsening trade relations with other countries, the administration of Ronald Reagan, elected in 1980, undertook a dramatic attempt to turn the economy around. Taxes were cut, increases in government spending on goods other than military items were vigorously resisted, governmental regulations and restrictions were reduced, and the Federal Reserve Board undertook a restrictive monetary policy.

The intended outcome was a reduction of inflation, interest rates, and unemployment, and an increase in economic growth, personal incomes, business profits, and stock market values. However, as of the middle of 1982, although the inflation rate had declined, interest rates remained at very high levels, unemployment had actually risen, and economic growth had slowed. This dismal performance induced many people to argue that the administration was as powerless to control the course of the economy as old Canute had been with the tide. Still others asserted that while Reagan should be applauded for his attempts, in reality his programs were simply on too small a scale to be effective. Moreover, monetary and fiscal policy were not restrictive and the tax cuts were only illusionary.[1] Finally, some compared the economy in mid-1982 to an ocean liner in the process of changing directions.[2] The person at the helm turns the wheel but appreciable time will elapse and considerable distance will be covered before the ship settles into its new course.

How do we evaluate these statements? Which assertion is correct? How do we determine whether monetary or fiscal policy is restrictive? What interest rates should we watch? How do we know whether the economy is actually growing or not? The purpose of this chapter is to answer these questions.

The chapter is divided into four major sections and an appendix. First, we briefly discuss the national income accounts. In this discussion we will define output, production, and demand. We then turn, in the second section, to an examination of price indices and inflation rates. Third, measures of labor market activity (i.e., employment and unemployment) are considered. In the last section we are concerned with the measurement of fiscal and monetary policies. The chapter is followed by an appendix that provides a reference for locating various economic statistics.

Measures of Output and Income

In most economies, a multitude of goods and services are produced in a variety of market structures. It is, therefore, a very complex undertaking to attempt to explain or predict the impact of events on the economy. It would be virtually impossible to predict overall impacts on the economy by examining each individual market in succession. Macroeconomists have simplified their analyses by aggregating all markets into one, combining all goods and services into a single good, and deriving the demand for and supply of this composite good.

Although it is unambiguous to state that the quantity of output in a single market has increased 5 percent or that the price of the product has risen 3 percent, it is not clear what is meant when it is stated that the total output of the United States has risen 5 percent or that the price of total output has risen 3 percent. If the output of every product rose by 5 percent then it would be obvious that total output had risen by 5 percent. But, more typically, output in some industries rises while in others it falls.

---

[1] "The Tax Cut Illusion," *Federal Reserve Bank of Minneapolis: Annual Report* (1979).
[2] William Allen, *The Midnight Economist* (January, 1982), p. 59.

How do we combine a 6 percent decrease in auto production, an 8 percent increase in housing construction, a 5 percent increase in the quantity of golf balls produced, and the variations in innumerable other outputs in the economy, so as to be able to speak of a 5 percent increase in total output? Similarly, how can we combine the price of every single item so as to be able to speak of the price of total output? The remainder of this introduction and the first section are devoted to answering these questions.

We will begin by discussing the accounting scheme known as the *national income and product accounts* (NIPA), with which the adding up of goods and services is accomplished. Besides providing a measure of output, these accounts supply a conceptual framework for relating output, income, and spending to one another.

The National Income and Product Accounts

To combine the multitude of goods and services into one aggregate product we must look for a common unit or common denominator in which all goods can be expressed. Then we may simply add up the units. Apples plus oranges plus golf balls sum to what? The common unit for every good sold in the United States is dollars. Hence, we can measure the total production of each good by summing the market value of that good; that is, the total quantity of the good that is produced multiplied by its market price. We can then add the total market value of all goods and services to derive a measure of output (the total production of our one good) of the economy. This measure is called Gross National Product (GNP). The formal definition of *GNP* is the market value of all final goods and services produced in the economy for a given period.[3]

The following are questions to answer when defining GNP:

1. What is meant by market value?
2. What are final goods and services?
3. Why are only those goods produced during a given period included?
4. Are purely financial transactions included?

The definition states that goods and services included in GNP are measured in market prices. However, market prices often include sales and excise taxes which means the price paid by the consumer is not always the price the seller actually receives. As we shall discover, this point is important when output is related to income. The valuation of GNP at market prices also means that GNP values cannot be unambiguously compared from year to year. Changes in GNP could be the result of price changes rather than changes in the quantity of goods produced. And,

---

[3] It is important to note that GNP is a flow measured as so many dollars per period of time—a year, for example.

finally, perhaps the most important implication of valuing output at current market prices is that any good that does not have such a value is excluded.[4] For example, the goods or services produced by a homemaker are excluded.

Another aspect of the definition of GNP is that only final goods and services are counted. A *final good* or *service* is one that is not resold in order to be used in the production of another product. *Intermediate goods*—those goods used in the production of a final product—are not counted as part of GNP. For example, the construction of an automobile starts with the purchase of inputs such as steel. Suppose these inputs cost $100, but that once the automobile is produced, it is sold to a dealer for $175. Finally, the dealer sells this car to a consumer for $200. If the three sales were added, output would be measured at $475. However, $475 overstates the value of production in the economy because the purchase of steel—an intermediate good—is included more than once. It was counted in the original purchase of steel, in the sale to the automobile dealer, and again in the sale to the consumer. This double-counting problem is avoided by employing the value of the final sale of $200 as the measure of current production.

An alternative approach that avoids the double-counting problem is to sum only the value added at each stage of production. The value added to a good at a particular stage of manufacturing is equal to the value of the good sold minus the cost of the intermediate materials. In terms of the automobile example, the value added by the automobile producer ($75) and by the automobile dealer ($25) is added to the price of steel ($100), to find a measure of current production. Clearly the value-added approach, although much more difficult to calculate, yields the same value as the final sales price.

The third aspect of the definition of GNP that needs to be clarified is that only currently produced goods are included. Hence, sales of old baseball cards, used cars, and existing homes are not included. These goods were included in the value of GNP at the time they were originally produced. To include them again would be to overstate GNP in the present period.

Finally, any transaction in which only money is transferred is excluded. Therefore, transfer payments such as social security, unemployment benefits, and welfare benefits are not included in GNP. As the NIPA framework is developed, the reader will see that these financial transactions are merely transfers from one account to another which leave the

---

[4] There is one exception to the valuation at market prices. Government services have no market price. Because of the importance of these services, they cannot be excluded from GNP. Therefore, these items are valued at their cost which usually means the wages of the government employees who produce them.

total value of output unchanged. Moreover, transfer payments are not compensation for current production.

The NIPA include much more than a measure of GNP. These accounts provide measures of various income concepts as well as a framework for relating these measures to one another. It should be added that these accounts are quite complex and detailed. Entire books have been devoted to national income accounting.[5] Here, however, we present only a brief overview.

One of the most important relationships in macroeconomics is that between the value of output and the income that is generated in producing that output. Intuition suggests that the two should be equal since the receipts from the sale of output must accrue to someone as income. For businesses to produce goods, factors of production—land, labor, capital, and entrepreneurship—must be employed. In return, the owners of the factors of production receive payments—respectively: rents, wages, interest, and profits—the sum of which is known as national income.[6] Is national income equal to the value of output or GNP? No, since in generating GNP, no allowance is made for the fact that some of the capital stock in the economy is worn out and must be replaced. The allowance for replacing this capital is referred to as either *depreciation* or the *capital consumption allowance* (CCA). Since the CCA does not create income, the fact that it is still included in GNP means the value of the output measure exceeds the value of the income measure. If depreciation is subtracted from GNP, *net national product* (NNP) is derived. Thus,

$$NNP = GNP - CCA$$

However, NNP is also not equal to national income (NI). The value of goods and services in NNP are still measured by their market prices. As we have explained, these prices include sales tax and excise taxes—*indirect business taxes* (IBT)—which are not income. If the IBT are subtracted from NNP, we arrive at a measure of income accruing from current production.

$$NI = NNP - IBT$$

Economists typically refer more to personal income than to national income. Personal income is a measure of the flow of income to the

---

[5] An excellent book on this topic is John Kendrick's *Economic Accounts and their Uses* (New York: McGraw-Hill Book Company, 1972).

[6] The calculation of national income by adding up the factor payments is often called the factor share approach. Formally, national income is equal to the sum of compensation of employees (wages), net interest, rental income, and profits. Profits are frequently segmented into corporate profits and proprietors' income.

household sector whereas national income includes income flows to the business sector that are not passed on to households. To derive personal income we must subtract corporate profits, net interest (interest paid less interest earned), and contributions for social insurance from national income. Although part of corporate profits—dividends—and part of interest payments—personal interest income—are paid to the household sector, these items are not subtracted from national income. In addition, any transfer payments to the household sector must be added on. Carrying out these calculations, as summarized in the following equation, generates personal income:

$$\text{Personal income} = \text{National income} \begin{array}{l} -\text{Corporate profits} \\ -\text{ Net interest} \\ -\text{ Contributions for social insurance} \\ +\text{ Transfer payments} \\ +\text{ Personal interest income} \\ +\text{ Dividends} \end{array}$$

The actual amount of income available to the household for spending is less than personal income since taxes are taken out of personal income. *Disposable personal income* or simply *disposable income* is personal income less personal tax payments. It is out of this income that the household can choose to spend (consume) or save. That is,

$$\text{Disposable income} = \text{Personal income} - \text{Taxes}$$

and

$$\text{Disposable income} = \text{Consumption} + \text{Personal savings}$$

In Table 2-1, the structure of the national income and product accounts is presented for 1982. So far we have discussed the national income accounts from the fifth line in Table 2-1 down. Let us now complete the discussion by examining the first four lines in Table 2-1. Note that the sum of personal consumption expenditures, gross private investment, government purchases of goods and services, and net exports of goods and services is equal to GNP.

$$\text{GNP} = \text{Consumption} \begin{array}{l} +\text{ Gross private domestic investment} \\ +\text{ Government purchases} \\ +\text{ Net exports} \end{array}$$

These four items represent the major uses of the value of production and together are called *aggregate demand*. Since terms like *consumption* and *investment* will be referred to frequently in this book, we will spend a moment defining them.

Consumption refers to the purchase of goods and services by households for their own use. This component of demand includes purchases of durable goods, such as an appliance that lasts more than one year; of

Table 2-1. *The Structure of the National Income*
and Product Accounts for 1982 (in billions of dollars)

Personal consumption expenditures	1,972.0	
Gross private domestic investment	421.9	
Government purchases	647.1	
Net exports	16.5	
Equal:		
Gross national product		3,057.5
Less:		
Capital consumption allowances	356.8	
Equals:		
Net national product		2,700.8
Less:		
Indirect business taxes and other	264.3	
Equals:		
National income		2,436.5
Less:		
Corporate profits	161.1	
Net interest	265.3	
Social insurance contributions	253.7	
Plus:		
Government transfers to persons	360.8	
Personal interest income	371.8	
Dividends	67.0	
Business transfer payments	13.7	
Equals:		
Personal income		2,569.7
Less:		
Personal tax and nontax payments	397.2	
Equals:		
Disposable personal income		2,172.5

Source: Economic Report of the President (1983).

nondurable goods, such as clothing or food, which are usually used up during the year; and of services, such as haircuts, which must be consumed at the time of purchase.

Business firms also purchase goods and services that are not resold to consumers or other firms. These goods, which firms keep for themselves and which thus add to the economy's stock of income-yielding assets, are known as *gross private domestic investment*.[7] Included in this compo-

---

[7] It is important to note that investments do not include the purchase of a bond or stock in some business. Even though the financial press describes such activity as investments, we restrict this term to additions to the physical stock of capital.

nent are fixed investments, such as the purchase of a machine and a newly produced building; residential investments, for example, the construction of a house or apartment; and inventory investments. Inventory changes, including changes in business firms' holdings of raw materials, components, and finished goods, are included as part of investment, since they are assets that will eventually yield income. The term gross domestic signifies that depreciation has not been deducted from the investment spending by domestic business.

The final two forms of demand are government purchases of goods and services, and the net exports (exports minus imports) of goods and services. Government purchases include federal, state, local, and municipal spending. These purchases add to demand for domestic production, as do foreign purchases of domestic goods. However, at first glance it might not be clear why the purchase of foreign goods by United States residents should be subtracted from exports. The reason is that the other components of demand do not distinguish spending by where the good was produced. Investment spending is business spending on capital goods and is a component of demand irrespective of where that capital was produced. It is left up to net exports to take account of where a good was produced.

The components of the demand for goods for various countries in 1981 are presented in Table 2-2. For all countries the major component of

Table 2-2. Allocation of GNP over Components of Aggregate
               Demand across Countries in 1981

Country	$\dfrac{\text{Consumption}}{\text{GNP}}$	$\dfrac{\text{Investment}}{\text{GNP}}$	Government Purchases/GNP	$\dfrac{\text{Exports}}{\text{GNP}}$	$\dfrac{\text{Imports}}{\text{GNP}}$
France	63.3	23.3	15.5	21.0	23.0
Germany	55.2	24.8	20.5	28.9	29.1
Japan	58.2	32.7	10.0	15.2	16.1
United Kingdom	60.1	16.0	21.5	28.0	25.7
United States	64.4	15.6	20.8	10.2	11.0

Source: International Monetary Fund, International Financial Statistics (December, 1982).

demand is consumption spending. In the United States in 1981, approximately 65 percent of output was allocated to consumption. Other than consumption spending being the dominant component across countries, the allocation of GNP over the other components varies substantially. This variation is important because it yields insights into the economic performance of countries. For example, the ratio of imports to GNP is often thought to reflect the importance of international economic relations, or what an economist would call the "openness" of a country.

Clearly, France, Germany, and the United Kingdom are more open than the United States. This fact indicates why countries such as Germany are so concerned with other countries' economic performances and policies.

Another important fact that appears in Table 2-2 is that both the United Kingdom and the United States allocate a smaller portion of output to investment than the other countries. Many economists believe this explains the relatively slower economic growth rate of these countries in the last decade.

Real and Nominal GNP

One of the reasons for measuring output is to evaluate the state of the economy. Frequently this means comparing the values of income and output at different points in time. For example, in 1975, GNP was $1,549.2 billion while in 1974 it was $1,434.2 billion. Can we say we were better off in 1975 than in 1974?

Recall that, since goods are valued at current market prices in calculating GNP, there are three ways in which GNP can increase over time. More goods can be produced at the same prices, or the same quantity of goods can be produced at higher prices. Or there can be some combination of higher prices and larger quantities. As an example, consider a country that produces one good—golf balls. Suppose this economy produced 1,000 golf balls in 1973 and 2,000 golf balls in 1983. If the price of golf balls remained at $1 a ball, GNP in this country would have increased from $1,000 to $2,000. On the other hand, if this economy produced the same quantity of golf balls in 1983 as it did in 1973, but the price of golf balls increased from $1 a ball to $2 a ball, we would again find that GNP had doubled. Price increases may inflate our measure of output and thus make comparisons of GNP measured in current prices—nominal gross national product—invalid.

In order to compare measures of output at different points in time, changes in physical output in the economy between different time periods must be isolated from price changes. Real GNP is a measure of these physical output changes. In each period the nominal value of every good produced and the price at which each good is sold are known. Hence, the physical quantity of each good produced in any period can be derived by dividing the nominal value by the price. Real GNP is then calculated by adding the physical output of every good valued at the price at which each good sold during some base period. Real GNP is currently measured in 1972 prices.

The behavior of nominal and real GNP since 1960 is traced out in Figure 2-1. Note that real and nominal GNP are equal in 1972. This is due to the fact that real GNP is evaluated in 1972 prices. Perhaps the most important fact that can be seen in this figure is the tremendous divergence between nominal and real GNP since 1972. This reflects the inflation experienced during the 1970s. Another interesting observation is that physical output has increased in all but three periods. During 1970 real GNP fell 0.2 percent, and from 1973 to 1975, it dropped 1.81 percent. It also fell during the recession which began in 1981. Interestingly, nominal GNP actually increased from 1973 to 1975, illustrating the problem of comparing nominal and real values.

Figure 2-1. Real and Nominal GNP

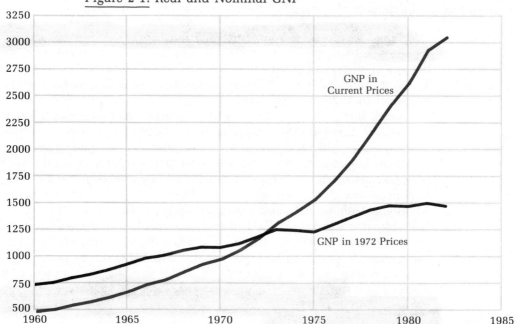

Since 1960, both nominal and real GNP have generally increased each year. The exceptions are the fall of real GNP during 1970 and during the recessions that occurred from 1973 to 1975 and 1981 to 1982 despite the fact that nominal GNP increased during these periods. Real and nominal income were equal in 1972 since this is the base year. From that year on, the path for nominal GNP is above the path for real GNP. This reflects the inflation experienced during the 1970s.

Potential Output

The national income accounts provide a measure of output at current prices. Price indices allow this value to be converted into a measure of production or real output. However, many economists believe a measure of what output could have been had the economy been operating at full capacity is necessary in order to properly evaluate the performance of the economy. The measure constructed with this purpose in mind is known as *potential output.*

Potential output is not observable and must, therefore, be approximated. The basic idea behind the construction of the series is quite simple. Suppose that in 1973 the economy was fully employed at a GNP level of $1,235.0 billion. In addition suppose the growth rate of the economy's capacity to produce is assumed to be 4 percent each year. Potential output for 1974 would simply be $1,235.0 billion times (1 + 0.04), or $1,284.4 billion.

Unfortunately, the determination of potential GNP is not quite this straightforward. There are disagreements about the definition of full employment and about the growth rate of potential output. Prior to 1976, full employment was somewhat arbitrarily defined by many economists as 4 percent unemployment, and the growth rate of potential output was estimated to be 3.9 percent per year. However events of the 1970s—changes in composition of the labor force, oil price shocks, and the slowdown of productivity growth—forced the Council of Economic Advisors to revise upward the definition of full employment to a rate in excess of 5.0 percent. In addition, the growth rate of potential GNP has been revised downward.

In Figure 2-2, the actual and potential GNP series are presented for the period 1960 to 1982. Notice that potential output exceeded actual output

Figure 2-2. Actual and Potential Gross National Product

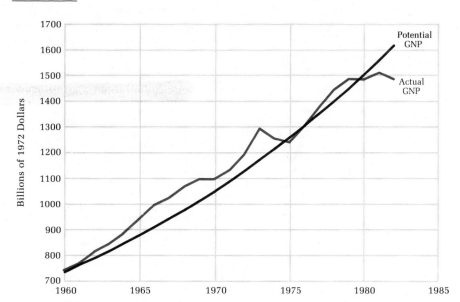

Real GNP measures the value of current output in constant prices; potential GNP measures output when the economy is operating at full capacity. During the last half of the 1960s, real GNP exceeded potential GNP indicating the economy was "overheated." However, since 1974 potential GNP has often exceeded real GNP. This reflects the well-known stagnation that has plagued the U.S. economy.

during the recessions of 1960-61, 1975-76 and 1980-82. The difference between these two variables is known as the *GNP gap*, and is a measure of economic slack. For example, note the size of the GNP gap during the 1975-76 recession and compare it to the boom period from 1964 to the middle of 1969 when the economy was actually operating beyond capacity.[8]

Measures of Inflation

Inflation—defined as a sustained upward movement in prices—became the major economic problem in the United States during the 1970s. The Consumer Price Index rose 13.3 percent in 1979, 12.4 percent in 1980, and 8.9 percent in 1981. The Implicit Price Deflator rose 8.6 percent in 1979, 9.3 percent in 1980 and 9.4 percent in 1981. Why do these measures of inflation differ? Which should we rely on?

There are three price indices typically relied on as measures of inflation—the Consumer Price Index (CPI), the Producer Price Index, and the Implicit GNP Price Deflator.[9] Perhaps the most closely followed price index is the CPI. The reason for this attention is that the CPI is designed to be a measure of the cost of a given basket of goods for urban consumers.[10] Annual percentage changes of the CPI are presented for the period 1948 to 1982 in Figure 2-3. With the exception of the years immediately after the Korean War, the CPI rose relatively modestly from 1950 to 1965 (2.0 percent yer year). Between 1965 and 1972 the CPI suggested a more rapid inflation rate of 4.6 percent. The CPI has averaged an annual percentage increase of 9.25 since 1972.

Another major price index is the Producer (formerly Wholesale) Price Index (PPI). In contrast to the CPI which focuses on the cost of a basket of

---

[8] Professor William Fellner, a former member of the Council of Economic Advisors, and a member of *The Wall Street Journal's* Board of Contributors, has argued that the concept of potential output should not be used as a basis for policymaking. According to Fellner, policymakers have reacted to a GNP gap with an overly expansionary demand management policy reflecting the idea that the economy can make up for output losses. This approach totally ignores the fact that resources not utilized during one time period will not necessarily be available in future time periods. In other words, potential GNP in any particular time period, if it has any value at all, is simply a guide to what output could have been in that time period. William Fellner, "Structural Problems behind Our Measured Unemployment Rates," in *Contemporary Economic Problems* (Washington, D.C.: American Enterprise Institute, 1978).

[9] The Federal Reserve Bank of Richmond has published an interesting pamphlet dealing with the theory of price indices. The reader interested in learning more about price indices is referred to this pamphlet which is entitled *Measuring Price Changes: A Study of Price Indexes.*

[10] Prior to 1978, the CPI was designed to reflect the expenditure patterns for urban wage earners and clerical workers. The revision of the CPI broadens the coverage of the index so that 80 percent, rather than 45 percent, of the total noninstitutional population is included.

Figure 2-3. Inflation Rates in the United States (Year to Year Percentage Change in Price Indices)

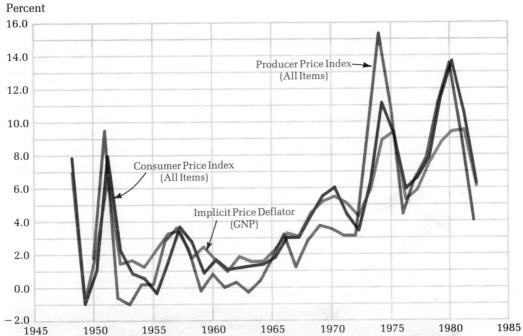

In the United States, three aggregate price indices are available to measure aggregate price change. If these indices are converted into percentage changes, measures of inflation are obtained. As can be seen, the percentage change of all three price indices have generally been rising which indicates inflation. While all three measures are generally consistent, there are differences. For instance in 1976, the CPI measured the inflation rate at 5.8 percent while the PPI and the implicit deflator suggested that the inflation rate was 3.7 and 5.2 percent respectively. The different measures of aggregate price change are due to the way the indices are constructed.

goods to consumers, the PPI measures the cost of a basket of goods at the level of the first significant commercial transaction. This means the prices of raw materials and semifinished goods are included in the index. The PPI had the same general trends as the CPI during the period 1947 to 1977. That is, between 1950 and 1965, 1965 to 1972, and 1972 to 1978, the percentage increases were 1.4, 3.2, and 11.0, respectively. The major difference, however, was that the PPI increased at a considerably faster rate during the 1972 to 1978 period than the CPI, as can be seen in Figure 2-3.

If there were only one good in the economy, the construction of a price index would be an extremely straightforward task. For example, suppose the only good in the economy is a McDonald's hamburger and that the price of this hamburger for three consecutive years is as follows:

Year	Price	Price Index (Base = Year 2)
1	$0.25	62.5
2	0.40	100.0
3	0.50	125.0

Since a price index compares prices over time, one year must be chosen as the basis of comparison. This year is called the *base period*. Although the selection of the base period is arbitrary, it is important that the base period be normal in the sense that extremely high or low prices did not occur. In our one-good economy, we will choose Year 2 to serve as the base year. Then, a price index for Year 3 is constructed by dividing the price of hamburgers in Year 3 by the price level in the base year. That is, the price index is 0.50 ÷ 0.40 or 1.25. It is traditional to multiply 1.25 by 100 so as to get rid of the decimals, which makes the price index 125. In general, the formula for calculating the price index for Year i is as follows:

$$I_i = \frac{\text{Price in Period } i}{\text{Price in the Base Period}} \times 100$$

Notice that the price index for the base year is 100. Why?

The presence of a multitude of commodities means that some way of combining them so that the overall rate of price change can be measured must be found. The method used to calculate the CPI and the PPI is to weight the various items by the quantity of each good purchased in the base year. This method assumes that the quantities purchased in the base year are the quantities purchased in all years. The assumption allows us to focus on how much it would cost the consumer in a given period to purchase exactly the same mix of items that was purchased in the base period. This type of price index is known as a *Laspeyres Index*, and is calculated as follows:

$$\text{Price Index}_t = \frac{\Sigma p_t^i q_0^i}{\Sigma p_0^i q_0^i} \times 100$$

Where $p_t^i q_0^i$ is the quantity of Good i purchased in the base year times the price of this good in Period t, and $p_0^i q_0^i$ is the expenditure on Good i in the base year.

An example may be helpful in understanding the theory used in constructing an aggregate Laspeyres price index. Suppose only five goods are consumed—hamburgers, beer, bread, gasoline, and automobiles. These goods would constitute the market basket of goods. The prices and quantities of these goods must be measured. In addition, one period must be selected as the base year. In Table 2-3, the prices and quantities of the goods in our market basket in the base period (Year 1) and a later period (Year 2) are presented. As can be seen, a total of $193.70 was spent on

Table 2-3. Price Index Data

GOOD	Base Year (Year 1)		
	P_1 PRICE	Q_1 QUANTITY	P_1Q_1 EXPENDITURE
Hamburger	$ 0.65/lb	60	$ 39.00
Beer	1.65/pack	10	16.50
Bread	0.35/loaf	52	18.20
Gasoline	0.40/gallon	50	20.00
Automobile	100.00	1	100.00
Total	103.05		193.70

GOOD	Base Year (Year 2)		
	P_2 PRICE	Q_2 QUANTITY	P_2Q_2 EXPENDITURE
Hamburger	$ 0.70/lb	62	$ 43.40
Beer	1.95/pack	15	29.25
Bread	0.40/loaf	50	20.00
Gasoline	1.00/gallon	48	48.00
Automobile	110.00	1	110.00
Total	114.05		250.65

these goods in the base year. If the same quantity of goods was purchased in the later period, they would cost $250.65. The price index for our five goods in Period 2 is

$$\text{Price Index}_2 = \frac{\Sigma p_2 q_1}{\Sigma p_1 q_1} \times 100$$

$$= \frac{\$250.65}{\$193.70} \times 100 = 129.40$$

This indicates that a basket of these five goods costs almost 30 percent more in the second period.

The Implicit GNP Price Deflator is another aggregate price measure. This measure is very different from the other two we calculated. The price deflator is calculated by dividing the nominal GNP by real GNP. Recall that *nominal GNP* is the value of expenditures for a given period in current prices whereas *real GNP* is the value of expenditures for a given period using prices from a base year. This suggests that the ratio of nominal to real GNP will yield a price measure for a given period. For instance, since nominal and real GNP in 1982 were $3,057.5 billion and $1,475.5 billion, respectively, the implicit price index for 1982 was 2.072 (i.e., $3,057.5 billion ÷ $1,475.5 billion).

Both nominal and real GNP reflect expenditures on goods and services made in a particular period. Therefore, the GNP deflator reflects the cost of the actual quantity of goods and services purchased in a period in terms of the base year prices.[11] In contrast, both the CPI and PPI measure the cost of a given basket of goods purchased in some previous period in terms of current prices.

Figure 2-3 shows the behavior of the Implicit GNP Price Deflator in relation to the CPI and PPI. As would be expected, all three indices increased over the period reflecting the fact that aggregate prices have been rising. However, the actual measure of price increase depends on the price index employed. During 1981 the CPI suggested that the inflation rate fell to 8.9 percent from the 12.4 percent change that occurred in 1980. In contrast, the GNP deflator measured inflation at 9.4 percent in 1981 which was an increase of 0.1 percent over the 1980 inflation rate. This difference is directly attributable to the different commodity baskets actually purchased during the two years.

For example, by assuming that goods and services are purchased in the same quantities they were in the base year, as is the case of the CPI, important biases in the index can develop. The CPI is biased upward in periods of rising prices because the consumer is assumed to not adjust purchases. This is a serious defect since a basic fact of economics is that as the relative price of an item increases, the quantity of that item demanded decreases, *ceteris paribus*. Housing costs provide a good example of this upward bias. Approximately 6 percent of homeowners bought new houses in the base period of 1972 and that same percent is assumed to hold today despite extremely high mortgage interest rates and housing prices that no doubt lowered the percent of homeowners buying new houses.[12]

The assumption of a fixed market basket of goods becomes even more tenuous over time as new products are introduced into the economy and old products disappear. Quality changes, furthermore, are not fully ac-

---

[11] The use of current period purchases as a weighting method is known as a *Paasche Price Index*, and the general formula for such an index is

$$\text{Price Index}_t = \frac{\Sigma P^i_t q^i_t}{\Sigma P^i_o q^i_t} \times 100$$

As an illustration of how this formula can be applied consider the example presented in Table 2-3 once again. The price index in this case would be 124.23 for Year 2 because the value of the base year expenditure is $193.70 and the base year value of the second year expenditure is 201.75.

[12] For an interesting article on the treatment of housing in the CPI, see Alan S. Blinder, "The Consumer Price Index and the Measurement of Recent Inflation," *Brookings Papers on Economic Activity*, Vol. 2 (1980), pp. 539-565.

counted for.[13] However, it should be pointed out that indices such as the implicit price deflator are not free of biases either. They do not recognize that relative commodity prices change over time.

In addition to the problems associated with the weighting of goods, price indices are subject to sampling and measurement problems. In calculating the value of a price index, it is too costly (and practically impossible) to measure every item and every consumer. Hence, a sample must be used and, of course, the design of the sample critically affects the quality of the index. Even a correctly designed sample is susceptible to sampling error. This is why the Bureau of Labor Statistics often cautions that a small change in an index may merely be a statistical artifact.[14] Mismeasurement of variables used in the construction of a price index will adversely affect the index. The actual measurement of prices is frequently pointed out as a trouble area. In principle, the actual prices at which transactions are made should be used in the construction of the index. However, the Bureau of Labor Statistics uses the list price. The transactions price may actually be less due to discounts, special offers, and price shading. To the extent that list prices are used when actual transactions prices are less, the price level will be overstated. Some economists argue that using the fairly downward rigid list price imparts a downward rigidity to price indices that is, in fact, not there.

Labor Market Measures

The labor market comprises transactions between buyers and suppliers of labor services. It is in this market that the level of employment and wage rates are determined. In this section we examine two measures of labor market conditions, the unemployment rate and the employment ratio.

The Unemployment Rate

Perhaps the most frequently used statistic to measure labor market conditions is the unemployment rate. This statistic is supposed to indicate the extent of utilization of available (rather than potential) labor

---

[13] Because of the rapidity of technological progress in the United States, quality changes have been a major problem in constructing price indices. In the United States, the Bureau of Labor Statistics estimates the additional cost associated with producing the change in quality by evaluating manufacturing costs and adding the established markup. This cost is then adjusted out of the new price.

[14] The Bureau of Labor Statistics estimates that the Consumer Price Index may have a sampling error of approximately 0.1 percent. This means a report of an increase of 0.1 percent in the CPI over the last month may be due to sampling error rather than an actual price increase.

resources. In addition, the unemployment rate is often used to assess the hardship experienced by workers who are willing to work and are available for work but who are unable to find jobs.

If asked how to define the unemployment rate, an individual might guess that it is simply the number of individuals unemployed divided by the total number of workers available. In principle, this is a correct response. When this seemingly straightforward definition is applied, however, several questions arise. For instance, in order to calculate the unemployment rate, the number of workers available for work must be known. Is the number of workers available equal to the population or to the number of workers actively seeking work? If the latter, then what does it mean to be *actively* seeking work? Are children or senior citizens to be counted as part of the labor force?

The Bureau of Labor Statistics (BLS) calculates the unemployment rate using surveys taken around the middle of each month. According to the BLS, individuals are *employed*

> if they are 16 or older and (1) are in the armed forces; (2) did any work at all as paid employees in the survey week; (3) worked at their own business or farm; (4) worked fifteen hours or more during the survey week as unpaid workers in an enterprise run by a family member; or (5) spent the survey week absent from work because of illness, bad weather, vacation, or some personal reason.

Unemployed individuals are defined as ones who

> are 16 or over, did not work at all during the survey week, were available for work, and were (1) looking for work during the last four weeks, (2) waiting to be called back to a job from which they had been laid off, (3) had a job to which they were going to report within thirty days, or (4) would have been actively looking for work if they had not been ill.

The sum of the number of employed and unemployed workers yields the total labor force—the number of individuals available for work. Then, the formula for the unemployment rate can be written as follows:

$$\text{unemployment rate} = \frac{\text{number unemployed}}{\text{number in labor force}}$$

$$= \frac{\text{number unemployed}}{\text{number unemployed} + \text{number employed}}$$

For example, in December, 1979, the BLS reported that the number of civilian workers employed was 97,912,000 while 6,087,000 workers were unemployed. The unemployment rate for that month was 5.85 percent.

Frequently, unemployment rates for demographic subgroups such as teenagers or females are reported. The same formula used for calculating the overall unemployment rate is used to calculate subgroup unemployment rates. The BLS just uses the number unemployed and employed in the subgroup under consideration.

The postwar unemployment rate for the United States is presented in Figure 2-4 along with the growth rate of real output. Notice that during the 1960s, the unemployment rate seemed to follow a declining trend while, in contrast, the trend in the 1970s seemed to be rising.

Figure 2-4. *Employment and Unemployment Measures*

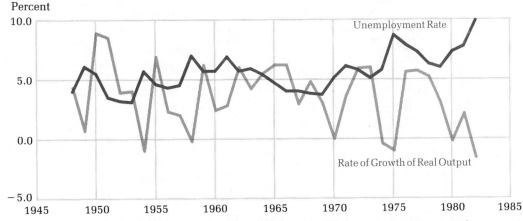

Two of the important measures of labor market conditions are the unemployment rate and the employment ratio. The unemployment rate measures the percentage of the labor force that is unemployed. As can be seen, the unemployment rate is closely related to the percentage increase in real output. During the 1970s, real income increased at a lower average rate compared to other decades and the average unemployment rate was higher. The employment ratio measures the proportion of the noninstitutionalized population that is employed. The employment ratio recognizes the fact that the labor force participation rate may change whereas the unemployment rate does not recognize that fact.

Furthermore, notice that although there do appear to be trends, the unemployment rate has fluctuated a good deal. Periods where real GNP rises rapidly (as was the case in the 1960s, 1971-73, and 1976-77) are times when the unemployment rate declines while recessionary periods (such as 1974-75 and 1979-80) show increases in the unemployment rate.

Problems with the Unemployment Rate

Economists have recently questioned the usefulness of the unemployment rate as an index of the hardship experienced by workers who are willing to work, but unable to find jobs.[15] Many believe the unemployment rate does not measure hardship precisely enough. When the rate is calculated, an individual is counted as employed if any work was done as a paid employee during the survey week. This means the unemployment rate does not distinguish between full- and part-time work. For example, a dishwasher working only twenty hours a week is as fully employed as a dishwasher working forty hours a week. The failure to distinguish between full-and part-time work means the unemployment rate is misleading. The fact that the percentage of the labor force engaged in part-time work increased during the recession of 1981-82, as seen in Table 2-4, supports this point.

Table 2-4. Trends in Part-Time Employment

YEAR	PART-TIME EMPLOYMENT FOR ECONOMIC REASONS	PERCENTAGE OF CIVILIAN LABOR FORCE
1976	3,334,000	3.6
1977	3,369,000	3.4
1978	3,298,000	3.2
1979	3,373,000	3.2
1980	4,064,000	3.8
1981	4,499,000	4.1
1982	5,852,000	5.3

Source: *Economic Indicators* (March, 1983).

Another problem that stems from the formal definition of employment is the underemployment problem. Consider a trained physicist who is working as a janitor since this is the only job available. No consideration is given to the worker who is employed but has skills for a higher level job. To the extent that underemployment exists, the unemployment rate understates the amount of hardship.

---

[15] For an interesting discussion of this point, see S. Smith's "An Examination of Employment and Unemployment Rates," *Quarterly Review* (Federal Reserve Bank of New York, Autumn, 1977).

The formal definition of an unemployed individual can also result in the unemployment rate being a somewhat misleading measure of hardship. Frequently, after a number of months, or even years, of looking for a job, a worker becomes frustrated and simply stops looking. This individual is not counted either in the number of workers employed or in the labor force since he or she is not actively seeking work. Labor economists describe this worker as a discouraged worker. Since the discouraged workers are not counted as being unemployed, the unemployment rate can be thought of as understating the amount of hardship. This problem is especially apparent in a prolonged recession during which the average duration of unemployment increases.

The discouraged worker effect is essentially a result of the fact that the labor force participation rate—the percentage of the population in the labor force—varies over the business cycle. It increases during upswings in economic activity as individuals enter the labor force in response to their perception that job opportunities have improved. It falls during downturns in economic activity as unemployed workers become discouraged and give up their search for jobs.

Perhaps the most important problem in using the unemployment rate as a measure of labor market conditions concerns institutional changes that occur. Recent secular changes in the labor participation rate is a case in point. Figure 2-4 indicates an upward trend in this rate since the mid-1960s. This trend suggests a basic structural alteration in the pattern of choice among work in the labor market, work at home, and the amount of leisure. Specifically, the rates at which women and teenagers have entered the labor force have increased. For instance, the percentage of the labor force that was female was 38 percent in 1972 while the teenage percentage of the labor force was 9.2. However, five years later the percentages were 41.0 for women and 9.5 for teenagers. These facts have led many economists to assert that the unemployment rate has increased simply because some of these women and teenagers are first time labor force entrants and do not have the experience and job skills required by employers.

Several economists argue that the biggest drawback to the use of the unemployment rate as an indicator of hardship is the increase in unemployment benefits. To be eligible to receive these benefits, individuals are required to register as being unemployed with the United States Employment Service or to register for manpower training. These individuals are counted among the unemployed. However, because high levels of unemployment compensation enable longer periods of search, or simply more time to enjoy leisure-time activities, much of the measured unemployment may be voluntary.[16] If this is true, the unemployment rate will

---

[16] Ronald Ehrenberg and Ronald L. Oaxaca, "Do Benefits Cause Unemployed to Hold Out for Better Jobs?" and Martin Feldstein, "Unemployment Compensation—Its Effect on Unemployment," both in *Monthly Labor Review* (March, 1976).

overstate hardship—voluntary unemployment should not be reflected in the statistics.[17]

Employment Ratio

Economists have been putting more emphasis on the employment ratio as an indicator of labor market conditions because of the problems surrounding the unemployment rate. The *employment ratio* is defined as the proportion of the noninstitutionalized population that is employed.[18] It is, therefore, independent of the labor force participation rate, which is not the case for the unemployment rate.

In Figure 2-4, both the unemployment rate and the employment ratio are presented for the period 1948 to 1980. Notice the behavior of these two measures in 1975-76. The unemployment rate, although declining, was still at levels that suggested historically slack conditions or an excess supply in the labor market. On the other hand, the employment ratio suggested a relatively tight labor market—it reached levels above its long-run average. These two measures seemed to conflict with one another. An explanation of this conflict is found in the behavior of the participation rate.

Changes in the labor force participation rate affect the unemployment rate but do not affect the employment ratio. If both the labor force participation rate and the number of people employed are rising, then the employment ratio will more correctly reflect labor market conditions. If the participation rate is rising faster than the number of people employed, the unemployment rate would rise simply because more people are seeking jobs and not because the condition of the economy is deteriorating. For instance, consider the labor market conditions in the U.S. prior to the 1976 Presidential election. This was a period in which the economy was beginning to recover from the recession begun in 1974. The labor force participation rate was increasing. During his campaign, Jimmy Carter attacked President Gerald Ford for being insensitive to the poor. Carter pointed to the unemployment rate then hovering around 8.0 percent. Ford's response was that more people were employed than ever before. Although, to the public, this appeared to be a poor response, if President Ford would have examined the employment ratio he would have found evidence of an improving labor market, evidence that might have convinced the public. Although the employment ratio does not solve all the

---

[17] Clarkson and Meiners estimate that the current overall unemployment rate has been inflated by as much as 2.1 percentage points because of the work registration eligibility requirements. This result can be found in K. W. Clarkson and R. E. Meiners, "Government Statistics as a Guide to Economic Policy, Food Stamps and the Spurious Increase in the Unemployment Rates," *Policy Review* (Summer, 1977).

[18] If the employment ratio were defined as the proportion of the civilian labor force that is employed, it would simply be the mirror image of the unemployment rate.

problems the unemployment rate has, it appears to be a substantial improvement.

Monetary and Fiscal Policy

Measures of output, prices, and employment are extremely important if we are to have some idea how the economy is performing in attaining society's goals of low inflation, low unemployment, and a rapid growth in output. However, equally important, and perhaps just as frequently mentioned in the news media, are the policy variables used to attain these goals. In this section, we will examine the ways in which monetary and fiscal policy are measured.

Measures of Monetary Policy

Monetary policy is the control of the supply of money for the purpose of influencing economic performance. Economists have disagreed and continue to disagree over how monetary policy should be measured. Some argue that changes in monetary aggregates should be used, while others assert that changes in interest rates should be the indicator. At this point, a complete discussion of this debate is premature. We will delay that until later chapters. Here we will simply examine what monetary aggregates and interest rates measure.

Let us first consider the measurement of monetary aggregates, or what may more commonly be known as measures of, and measures related to, the money supply. The 1983 *Economic Report of the President* reported four measures of monetary aggregates, two of which have traditionally been followed more closely—M-1 and M-2. The measure that has become known as M-1 is supposed to measure the quantity of financial assets in circulation that are immediately accepted as a means of payment. For years this measure was defined as the amount of currency and coin in circulation plus the amount of demand deposits at commercial banks other than interbank deposits and float.[19] However, over the last decade, a number of major financial changes (or as they were called, innovations) have occurred. New types of checkable deposits arose and new ways to earn market interest rates were offered to consumers. As a result, in early 1980 the Federal Reserve Board broadened M-1 to include demand deposits at mutual savings banks, travelers' checks at nonbank issuers, negotia-

---

[19] *Interbank deposits* refer to the deposits of one bank held by another bank. *Float* refers to the checks or drafts in the process of collection. For example, if you write a check on your account in the First Interstate Bank of California to your mortgage company, First Federal Savings of Oregon, several days will elapse before the Oregon institution sends the check to the California institution for collection. The funds in process are said to be in float.

ble order of withdrawals (NOW accounts), automatic transfer service accounts at banks and thrift institutions, and credit union share drafts. *NOW accounts* are essentially interest-bearing checking accounts, while *automatic transfer service accounts* allow funds from savings accounts to be automatically transferred to checking accounts.

Some economists believe that M-1 is not a broad enough measure of the money supply, since many assets can be converted into money in a relatively short period of time. For instance, banks usually allow individuals to convert time deposits into cash immediately. Therefore the Federal Reserve defines another monetary aggregate. This is *M-2* which is the sum of M-1 plus small denomination time deposits at all depository institutions, overnight repurchase agreements at commercial banks, overnight Eurodollar deposits of U.S. nonbank residents, and money market mutual fund shares. M-1 might be thought of as transactions funds while M-2 measures liquidity. Hence, the two measures provide different information regarding the money supply. *Repurchase agreements, or RPs,* are agreements between a bank and a business that enable the bank to borrow the businesses' funds overnight. In this way the business earns interest on idle funds and the bank has use of funds overnight. *Eurodollars* are U.S. currency circulating in Europe (or Nassau or other locations) that banks can use overnight much like the RPs.

There are measures of the money supply that are even broader than M-2. The *M-3 measure* adds large-denomination time deposits at all depository institutions and term repurchase agreements at commercial banks and saving and loan associations to M-2. The other measure, known as *L* (to symbolize liquidity) augments M-3 by including other liquid assets held by U.S. residents.

Figure 2-5 yields some important insights about the relation of M-1 and M-2. Both M-1 and M-2 show an upward trend. However, what is particularly interesting is that since 1975 M-1 and M-2 have quite different growth paths. In fact, there is a period of time during which the growth rate of M-2 was increasing while the growth rate of M-1 was declining.

Another closely watched financial variable is the interest rate. But which interest rate? There are many. A reference to a particular interest rate is usually a reference to one of three rates—the prime rate, the federal funds rate, or the three-month Treasury bill rate. The *prime rate* is the interest rate charged on very short-term loans to business customers with the highest credit ratings. This rate is important because other lending rates are scaled upward from the prime rate. The federal funds rate is determined in the federal funds market. This is a market involving the borrowing and lending by commercial banks to and from each other, typically for periods of one day. Therefore, the federal funds rate is considered to be a measure of the yield on the most liquid of financial assets. The *Treasury bill rate* or *T-bill rate* is the interest rate on 90-day

Figure 2-5. *Measures of Monetary Policy*

Growth Rates

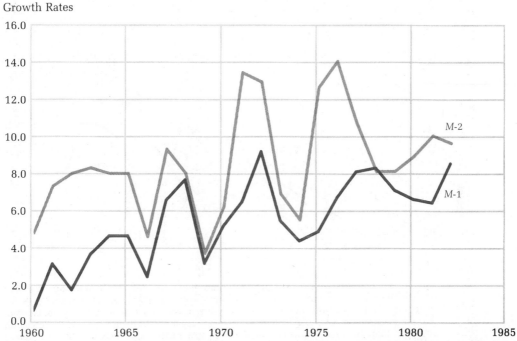

Two of the more frequently used measures of monetary policy are M-1 and M-2. M-1 might be thought of as a measure of transactions funds while M-2 measures liquidity. These two measures have quite different growth paths since 1975. During the period 1976 to 1980, the percentage change in M-1 was declining while M-2 was increasing.

securities issued by the Treasury for the purpose of financing the government debt. The Treasury issues many types of securities, but the 3-month T-bill is considered to be one of the best indicators of short-term fluctuations in the money and credit markets.

The federal funds rate is presented along with the growth rate of the money supply (M-1) and the inflation rate in Figure 2-6. The federal funds rate shows an upward trend over the last twenty years with a large degree of short-term variability. For example, in 1974, the federal funds rate was 10.51 percent and one year later was down to 5.82 percent. Two additional insights can be found by carefully examining Figure 2-6. The general upward trend in interest rates and prices points out the relationship between nominal interest rates and inflation. In addition, there is some indication that an inverse relationship between the money supply and interest rates exists. Around 1970, the percentage increase in the money supply was positive. For the same period, the interest rate on federal funds was declining. Again, between 1973 and 1974, the money

Figure 2-6. Money Market Rates

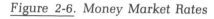

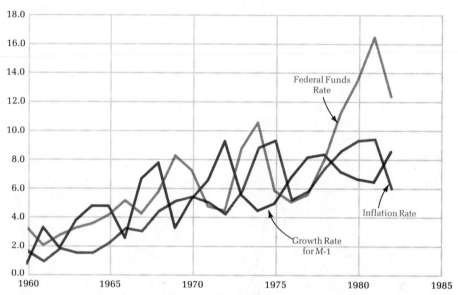

Interest rates have been extremely high in recent periods. A measure of the one and only interest rate does not exist for our economy since many interest series are available. A series frequently used to measure short-term interest rates is the federal funds rate. As can be seen, the trend in interest rates has been positive since 1960 as has been the trend in prices. In addition, there is some indication that an inverse relationship between the percentage change in the money supply and interest rates exists.

supply increased while the interest rate fell. A theoretical explanation for this inverse relationship will be presented in Chapters 4 and 5. We will also find in later chapters of the book that this inverse relationship is only a short-run relationship. In the long run the relation between a change in the growth of the money supply and a change in nominal interest rates is positive due to the change that the money supply brings in the expected rate of inflation. The positive trends in the money supply growth rate and the interest rate shown in Figure 2-6 seem to support this point.

Not only are there several interest rates, but there is also a distinction between real and nominal interest rates. In the financial markets, any reference to an interest rate is to a nominal interest rate. However, in microeconomic theory the *interest rate* is the rental price per year for the use of a dollar of capital—a real interest rate. An example may be helpful to illustrate the relationship between real and nominal interest rates. Suppose you wish to borrow $100 for one year and must pay $110 at the end of the year. The interest rate then, is 10 percent. This is the *nominal interest rate* because it has not been adjusted for inflation. Suppose you expect the inflation rate to be 9 percent. Then, you are expecting that the constant purchasing power or real value of the money you must pay back will be 9 percent less than if there had been no inflation. You actually repay purchasing power of $101. Thus, the real interest rate is 1 percent. The relation between nominal and real interest rates can be shown in the following equation:

$$r^* = r - \pi^e$$

Where:

π^e = the expected inflation rate; $(\Delta P \div P)^e$
r = the nominal interest rate
r^* = the real interest rate

If individuals expect inflation to occur, then the nominal interest rate will exceed the real interest rate. The difficulties involved with measuring price expectations have led observers of financial markets to speak of real interest rates as nominal interest rates less the actual inflation rate ($r^* = r - \pi$). This relationship is shown in Figure 2-7. Keep in mind that it is the real interest rate on which people make decisions about whether to borrow or lend, to invest or save, to hold cash balances or long-term financial assets. Hence, whenever π^e is not zero; that is, whenever expected inflation is not zero, it is the real rate that is important.

Figure 2-7. *The Real Interest Rate*

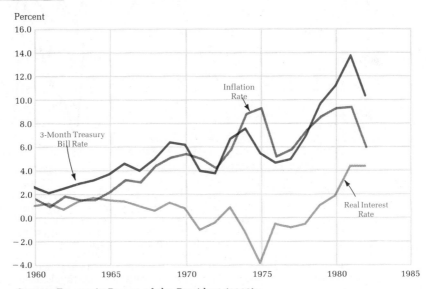

Source: *Economic Report of the President* (1983).

The nominal interest rate less the rate of inflation provides a measure of the purchasing power of the return on a loan. This is termed the *real interest rate*. In reality the real interest rate is the actual nominal rate less the expected rate of inflation. The actual and expected inflation rates may differ and this may account for the negative real interest rate shown here.

Measures of Fiscal Policy

Fiscal policy is the use of government expenditures and tax rates to influence economic performance. The difference between government expenditures and tax revenues is often used as a measure of whether fiscal policy has been stimulative or restrictive. Since spending adds to demand and taxes subtract from demand, a deficit is considered expansionary or stimulative and a surplus (taxes greater than spending) restrictive. In Figure 2-8, actual budget deficits since 1955 are presented. An examination of Figure 2-8 yields a few important facts. Prior to 1968 major deficits occurred only over the periods 1940 to 1946 and 1952 to 1954—times of world conflict. Smaller deficits occurred in nonwar years mostly as the result of business downturns. When the economy improved the deficits disappeared. In other words, prior to the late 1960s the federal budget appeared to be balanced over the business cycle.

Figure 2-8. The Actual Budget and the High-Employment Surplus

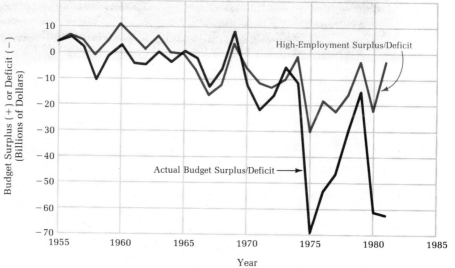

Source: *Survey of Current Business* (April, 1982).

Fiscal policy is often measured by the government budget where deficits suggest an expansionary policy stance. Large peacetime deficits are a phenomenon originating in the 1970s. Prior to this period major deficits occurred only in times of world conflict. Smaller deficits were the result of business downturns and disappeared when the economy improved. The use of the government budget situation to measure fiscal policy has been criticized because the actual deficit is the result of both the structure of the budget and the current level of economic activity. As a result, the high-employment surplus measures a given fiscal program as if output was at full employment. In 1962 the budget situation suggested an overly expansionary fiscal policy. However, when account was taken of the economic climate, the high-employment surplus indicated that fiscal policy was contractionary.

Since the late 1960s, these general relationships have changed. The federal budget has continually been in deficit. Projections of future federal budgets predict additional deficits. Yet, these have been peacetime periods. This budgeting pattern has led many individuals to ask whether the federal budget, and, thus, fiscal policy, is out of control.[20]

While a detailed answer to this question will be delayed until later, we must point out that there are pitfalls in using the deficit to judge fiscal policy. A deficit is the result of both the structure of the budget and the current level of economic activity. A budget deficit, for example, could occur with a nonexpansionary fiscal policy if business activity was depressed. Therefore, in order to measure the impact of fiscal policy, the concept of a high-employment surplus or full-employment surplus *(HES)*, was developed. The adjustments made to obtain the high-employment budget remove from actual receipts and expenditures the effects of cyclical fluctuations in the economy. Consequently this budget shows the surplus or deficit as it would be if the economy were moving smoothly along its potential growth path.[21] The criterion for determining whether a given fiscal program is expansionary is based on whether a deficit would occur if output was at its full-employment level. If a deficit would occur even at full employment, then the fiscal program is judged to be expansionary.

For example, suppose as shown in Figure 2-9, that there are two possible fiscal programs denoted with the letters *A* and *B*. Program *A* indicates that the deficit run at employment levels below 96 percent will move toward surplus more slowly as employment increases than would the deficits under Program *B*. Consider the output levels consistent with employment rates of 93 and 94 percent and the corresponding deficits under fiscal Programs *A* and *B*. If the level of economic activity generates an output level consistent with an employment level of 94 percent, the conclusion reached from Figure 2-9 is that the two programs are equally expansionary. On the other hand, if the level of economic activity is consistent with an employment rate of 93 percent, fiscal Program *B* would be judged as being more stimulatory than Program *A* as the resulting deficit from *B* is larger. To avoid this definitional problem, the *HES* suggests that fiscal policy should be measured at full employment. The problem with this concept is in the definition of full employment. What level of unemployment is considered to be full employment? The Council of Economic Advisors, who report the *HES*, defines full employment as unemployment of 5.3 percent.

---

[20] *Economic Report of the President* (1981).

[21] For a more detailed definition, see pages 50 and 51 of the 1980 *Economic Report of the President.*

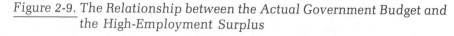

Figure 2-9. *The Relationship between the Actual Government Budget and the High-Employment Surplus*

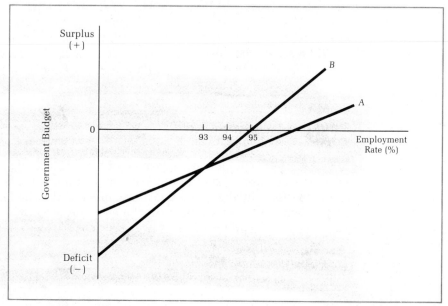

The actual deficit may not accurately reflect fiscal policy. Suppose two different fiscal programs are being considered. At the employment rate of 93 percent both programs would be associated with deficits. Since a larger deficit would occur under Program B, this program would be judged more expansionary. However, assume full employment is an employment rate of 95 percent. In this case, Program A would be labeled as more expansionary. Since the actual budget situation depends on the state of the economy, the proper way to judge fiscal policy is to evaluate it at some fixed employment ratio such as the employment ratio associated with full employment. This is the idea behind the high-employment surplus.

Figure 2-8 presents both the *HES* and the actual deficit for each of the years 1940-80. As can be seen, the year 1970 was a watershed year. Prior to 1970 the high-employment budget was in surplus virtually the entire time, while it has been in deficit since.

Conclusions

Although we have covered a great deal of ground, we could ask the reader to put his feet up on the desk, prop his eyes open, and read on for there are literally hundreds of additional economic variables and statistics that would be worth discussing. We will not do that because we have examined the variables of primary interest for the study of macroeconomics. Moreover, with our analysis of the National Income and Product Accounts we have provided a foundation upon which the study of macroeconomics can proceed.

As we traverse the history of macroeconomics and examine various macroeconomic theories we will constantly be referring to the variables discussed in this chapter and to the NIPA framework. The reader will probably find it useful to refer back to specific sections of this chapter to refresh his or her memory regarding some economic variable. If additional details are desired, the reader may find the sources listed in the appendix to this chapter useful.

PROBLEMS AND EXERCISES

1. In the 1980 *Economic Report of the President* (page 117) it was stated that

   > regulation which diverts capital and labor from the production of steel, automobiles, or clothing to the production of environmental cleanliness, workers' safety, or other goods whose values are difficult to measure, entail a loss in measured productivity. This is not necessarily a matter for concern, since it stems primarily from the limitation of what can be captured in national income statistics.

   Explain.

2. According to the estimate of potential output in 1977, the U.S. economy fell short of potential output by 5.3 percent. Given that potential output would grow by 3.5 percent during 1978, some argued that policies should be instituted so that actual output would increase by approximately 9 percent from 1977 to 1978. Discuss the appropriateness of using the potential GNP series in this manner.

3. Consider the following table which contains data for a hypothetical economy:

ITEM	AMOUNT
Indirect business tax (IBT)	215
Government purchases of goods and services (G)	625
Disposable income	2,000
Net private domestic investment	175
Business transfer payments	10
Personal income taxes	400
Capital consumption allowances (CCA)	225
Corporate profits and inventory valuation adjustments	140
Compensation of employees	1,625
Net exports of goods and services (NX)	-5
Personal consumption expenditures (C)	1,750

Calculate the values of gross investment, GNP, net national product, national income, and personal income.

4. The following table contains prices and quantities of the three goods produced in an economy in three different years:

Commodity	1979		1980		1981	
	Price	Quantity	Price	Quantity	Price	Quantity
Food	$1.00	10	$1.50	5	$0.50	15
Movies	4.00	10	4.00	10	4.25	9
Gasoline	1.15	50	1.30	48	1.50	45

Compute a Laspeyres price index from the foregoing table. Use 1980 as the base year.

5. Why does an index like the implicit price deflator understate price changes?

6. Consider the following table which suggests general trends in employment and unemployment:

	E/P	U/NW	L^F/P	U/L^F	U/P
Total Population					
1956	57.5	5.8	60.0	4.1	2.5
1973	57.8	7.0	60.8	4.9	2.9
1981	58.3	13.5	64.3	7.6	4.8
Adult Men					
1956	84.6	19.3	87.6	3.4	3.0
1973	78.7	12.3	81.3	3.2	2.6
1981	74.0	23.7	79.0	6.3	5.0
Adult Women					
1956	34.9	2.4	36.4	4.2	1.5
1973	42.2	3.7	44.4	4.8	2.1
1981	48.6	7.4	52.1	6.8	3.6
Teenagers					
1956	45.3	10.4	50.9	11.1	5.7
1973	46.0	14.4	53.8	14.5	7.8
1981	44.6	24.4	55.4	19.6	10.9

Source: *Monthly Labor Review* (February, 1983).
Where: E = Employed
              U = Unemployed
              L^F = Labor force
               P = Civilian noninstitutional population
           NW = Nonworkers

Two general trends appear in this data. First, the employed percentage of the population shows an upward trend. Second, the unemployed percentage of the population shows an upward trend as does the unemployment rate in the conventional sense. Is there a contradiction between these two trends? Why, or why not?

7. Assume the monetary aggregates were not redefined in 1980; what would be the implications for monetary policy?

_SUGGESTED READINGS

For light discussions of measurement issues, read

The Wall Street Journal (April 5, 1982). p. 1.

Federal Reserve Bank of Minneapolis, "The Tax Cut Illusion," *1979 Annual Report.*

Various pieces in William Allen, *The Midnight Economist* (Quarterly issues).

The following are good sources on employment measurement problems:

Ronald Ehrenberg and Ronald L. Oaxaca, "Do Benefits Cause Unemployed to Hold Out for Better Jobs?" and Martin Feldstein, "Unemployment Compensation—Its Effects on Unemployment," *Monthly Labor Review* (March, 1976).

William Fellner, "Structural Problems behind Our Measured Unemployment Rates," *Contemporary Economic Problems* (Washington, D. C.: The American Enterprise Institute, 1978).

S. Smith, "An Examination of Employment and Unemployment Rates," *Quarterly Review* (Federal Reserve Bank of New York, Autumn, 1977).

U. S. Department of Labor, BLS, *How the Government Measures Unemployment* (Washington, D. C.: U. S. Government Printing Office, 1977).

The measurement of potential output is discussed in the following:

E. F. Denison, "Changes in the Concept and Measurement of Potential Output in the United States of America," *General Series Report 367* (Washington, D. C.: Brookings Institution, 1981).

Arthur Okun, "Potential GNP: Its Measurement and Significance," *Proceedings of the Business and Economic Statistics Section of the American Statistical Association* (1962).

General discussions of economic variables are presented in Economic Report of the President, Annual issues.

_APPENDIX. Important Macroeconomic Data Sources_____

Often there are questions such as, What is happening to interest rates? or, How does the inflation rate in the United States compare with the rate in the United Kingdom? A superior in a company may desire a forecast for next year's GNP. While we have defined many macroeconomic variables, discussed how to calculate certain variables, and in some cases presented data series, we have not discussed where to locate these data if the need arises. In this appendix, a short annotated list of important macroeconomic data sources is presented.

General Data Sources

1. *Economic Report of the President* (Washington, D.C.: U.S. Government Printing Office), various issues.

   This report is available in January of each year. In addition to including the annual reports of the president and of the Council of Economic Advisers which are presented to Congress, the last half of the report contains statistical tables relating to income, employment, production, prices, and finance. Annual historical postwar data series are presented for many variables. Data in quarterly or monthly form are presented only for the previous two years of that report.

2. *Economic Indicators* (Washington, D.C.: Council of Economic Advisers).

   This is a monthly publication. The most recent data on total output, unemployment, prices, money, federal finance, and international statistics are presented. Historical series are not available from this source.

National Income Account Sources

1. *Survey of Current Business* (Washington, D.C.: U.S. Department of Commerce).

   The U.S. Department of Commerce publishes monthly the most recent national income data and general business statistical data. Articles summarizing some aspects of the current business situation also appear.

2. *Historical Statistics of the United States, Colonial Times to 1970* (Washington, D.C.: U.S. Department of Commerce).

   This source provides a wide range of historical statistics. Besides national income account data, data ranging from population statistics to agricultural statistics can be found.

Labor and Employment Data Sources

1. *Monthly Labor Review* (Washington, D.C.: U.S. Bureau of Labor Statistics).

   This is a monthly publication of the U.S. Department of Labor. In addition to articles summarizing various developments in the U.S. labor market, detailed monthly labor and productivity data are published. Data on hours worked, labor turnover, unemployment rates, employment status, and earnings are presented for various categorizations.

2. *Handbook of Labor Statistics* (Washington, D.C.: U.S. Bureau of Labor Statistics).

   The U.S. Bureau of Labor Statistics annually prepares a volume that contains the major historical series that it produces. Much of the data published in the *Monthly Labor Review* is historically compiled in this source.

Money Stock, Credit, and Finance Data Sources

1. *The Federal Reserve Bulletin* (Washington, D.C.: Board of Governors of the Federal Reserve System).

   This is a monthly publication of the Board of Governors of the Federal Reserve System. Detailed data on variables such as monetary aggregates, interest rates, financial position of commercial banks and federal finance are presented. Unfortunately, a historical time series of relevant variables is only available by using various issues of this publication.

2. *Monthly Trends* (St. Louis, Mo.: Federal Reserve Bank).

   The Federal Reserve Bank of St. Louis publishes this summary of current financial trends monthly. This publication is available free of charge from the Bank.

International Economic Data Sources

1. *International Financial Statistics* (Washington, D.C.: International Monetary Fund).

   This is a monthly publication that is a standard source of international statistics on all aspects of domestic and international finance. It shows for most countries of the world current annual, quarterly, and monthly data needed in the analysis of problems of international payments and of inflation; i.e., data on exchange rates, international liquidity, money and banking, trade, prices, and some income account data.

2. *Main Economic Indicators* (Paris, France: Organization for Economic Cooperation and Development).

    The OECD compiles and publishes monthly data on national accounts, production, deliveries, stocks and orders, labor, wage, prices, home and foreign finance, and international trade and payments. In addition, the OECD occasionally creates historical series of the data published in *Main Economic Indicators* and publishes them in *Historical Statistics*.

Price Data Sources

1. *Monthly Labor Review,* and *Handbook of Labor Statistics.*

2. *CPI Detailed Report* (Washington, D.C.: U.S. Bureau of Labor Statistics).

    This is a detailed monthly report on consumer price movements, including statistical tables and technical notes. The report covers two indexes, the consumer price index for all urban workers and the consumer price index for wage and clerical workers.

PART TWO.   The Basic Macro Model
Chapters 3 - 8

Money was wonderfully plenty. The trouble was, not how to get it—but how to spend it, how to lavish it, get rid of it, squander it. . . . All of a sudden, out went the bottom and everything and everybody went to ruin and destruction! The wreck was complete. The bubble scarcely left a microscopic moisture behind it. I was an early beggar and a thorough one.

Mark Twain, Roughing It

The classical economists, those preaching, teaching, and writing during the 1800s and early 1900s, relied on the efficiency of markets and the flexibility of wages and prices to equate demands and supplies, to give jobs to all those wanting them, and to maintain secular growth. Their models and theories can be characterized using the basic demand and supply curves familiar from microeconomics. The intersection of these curves determines equilibrium price and quantity. Shifts in either curve are met immediately by price changes so that demands and supplies are continually equated.

The Great Depression of the 1930s spurred many economists to ask questions that had been implicit at least since the major recession of 1907. How could the economy fall into a recession and how could unemployment rise and remain high for months or even years, if the classical model was appropriate? Why didn't prices adjust to keep demands and supplies equal? In 1936 John Maynard Keynes published a major study in which he attempted to demonstrate what he thought were the errors, weaknesses, and incorrect assumptions of the classical model. In short, Keynes's model argued that the upward sloping supply curve of the classical model should be replaced by a horizontal line during periods of recession because prices were not flexible, particularly in a downward direction. Moreover, Keynes asserted that the intersection of the downward sloping demand curve and the horizontal supply curve could take place at less than full employment. In other words, in the Keynesian model unemployment could exist for very long periods of time unless the demand curve was shifted outward through the use of government policies.

The Keynesian analysis profoundly affected economic theory. But more importantly, it dictated how economic policy would be carried out for the following forty years. Moreover, it changed the negative perception legislators and individuals had had toward deficits, a development that continues to have impact today. As Keynes had pointed out, the ideas of economists are more powerful than is commonly understood.

The purpose of Part II is to develop the Keynesian model and then to examine the reason for its collapse.

Chapters 3 through 5, in particular, focus on the Keynesian theory.

In large part, the Keynesian model seems most relevant for an economy in deep recession. With the prosperity experienced in the United States following World War II, it became apparent that the model was less generally applicable than had previously been thought.

Chapters 6 and 7 are an introduction to the erosion of the Keynesian framework; the beginning of the end for Keynesian macroeconomics. Chapter 8 completes the job of dismantling the Keynesian model.

CHAPTER 3.

Aggregate Demand and Equilibrium Output: An Explanation of the Great Depression

It is not an overstatement to say that had the Republican principles of balancing the budget been accepted in 1931 and 1932, the final stone in the foundation of permanent recovery would have been laid three years ago.

Herbert Hoover, 1935

Most people greatly underestimate the effect of a given emergency expenditure, because they overlook the multiplier.

John Maynard Keynes, 1934

WHAT TO EXPECT

The Great Depression caused economists to rethink their views on how output is determined. The result was Keynesian economics—a theory that stressed the role of aggregate demand in determining output. The Keynesian view of the economy is examined in this chapter. Some of the important questions addressed are

- *Why does GNP take on a given value?*

- *What does equilibrium output mean?*

- *How can unemployment exist when an economy is in equilibrium?*

- *What is a multiplier?*

- *What is fiscal policy?*

- *Are budget deficits a necessary outcome of fiscal policy?*

Introduction: The Great Depression, 1929-1941

The 1920s was a period of generally high prosperity and economic growth. Gross National Product in constant dollars increased by 42 percent between 1920 and 1929. Construction was booming. The automobile was revolutionizing lifestyles. Everyone seemed optimistic and prosperous as was reflected in clothing styles and the popular dance—the Charleston. Soaring stock prices mirrored America's optimism regarding the future. Popular opinion was that growth and prosperity would continue forever.

This euphoric atmosphere came to an abrupt end with the economic crash that began in October, 1929. Black Thursday, October 24, 1929, was the beginning of the end for many. Stock market speculation turned into panic and, subsequently, into bank failures. The economy simply collapsed. The contraction from 1929 to 1933 was the most severe business cycle downturn in recent U.S. history.

Table 3-1 documents the extent of the collapse. GNP in constant dollars fell by 29 percent between 1929 and 1933. Consumption expenditures fell by 18 percent, construction declined 78 percent, and for all practical purposes the investment component of demand did not exist in 1933. Unemployment rose to such an extent that at its peak approximately one quarter of the labor force was without a job.

Table 3-1. *Some Important Statistics of the Great Depression*

YEAR	GROSS NATIONAL PRODUCT (BILLIONS	CONSUMPTION OF 1929	GROSS INVESTMENT DOLLARS)
1929	104.4	79.0	16.2
1930	95.1	74.7	10.5
1931	89.5	72.2	6.8
1932	74.6	66.0	0.8
1933	74.2	64.6	0.3
1934	80.8	68.0	1.8
1935	91.4	72.3	8.8
1936	100.9	79.7	9.3
1937	109.1	82.6	14.6
1938	103.2	81.3	6.8
1939	111.0	85.9	9.9

YEAR	CONSTRUCTION (BILLIONS OF) (1929 DOLLARS)	STOCK MARKET INDEX	UNEMPLOYMENT RATE (PERCENT)
1929	8.7	83.1	3.2
1930	6.4	67.2	8.7
1931	4.5	43.6	15.9
1932	2.4	22.1	23.6
1933	1.9	28.6	24.9
1934	2.0	31.4	21.7
1935	2.8	33.9	20.1
1936	3.9	49.4	16.9
1937	4.6	49.2	14.3
1938	4.1	36.7	19.0
1939	4.9	38.5	17.2

Sources: Cols. 1, 2, 3, and 4: Peter Temin, *Did Monetary Forces Cause the Great Depression?* (New York: W. W. Norton & Co., Inc., 1976), Table 1; Col. 5: *Security Price Index Record* (Standard & Poor's Statistical Service, 1978); Col. 6: Michael Darby, "Three and a Half Million U.S. Employees Have Been Mislaid: Or, an Explanation of Unemployment, 1934-1941," *Journal of Political Economy* (February, 1976).

The Great Depression, beginning in 1929 and lasting throughout the 1930s, had far reaching effects on the economics profession and on popular opinion. Prior to the thirties the economics profession viewed the economy as self-correcting. Problems of excess demand or supply would quickly be solved by free enterprise's competitive response. Hence, there was simply no need for the government to intervene. The experience of the thirties seemed (and given the advantage of looking back some fifty years we stress the word *seemed*) to call for an alternative view—a call answered by John Maynard Keynes.

It was during the thirties that Keynes refined his views on output and employment and offered an alternative to the existing economic theory— classical economics. Keynes's ideas were published in 1936 in *The General Theory of Employment, Interest, and Money.* The Keynesian approach not only appeared to explain the crash and other economic developments, but it suggested a way in which economic stability could be guaranteed. The Keynesian framework essentially ignores the role of prices, as would be expected given the deflationary experiences of the 1930s, focusing instead on real output and employment. Special attention is devoted to fluctuations in investment spending—the paths of real output and employment are stable or unstable depending on the stability of investment.

If the data for this period are examined, the focus on investment spending changes would be clearly understandable. From 1920 to 1929 investment had grown at 4.5 percent per year although it had dipped below that rate during the 1923 and 1927 downturns. From 1929 to 1933 investment completely collapsed, falling 97 percent. In fact, the recovery from 1933 to 1938 and from 1939 to 1941 was not enough to offset the declines of 1929-1933 and 1938-1939.

The economic events of the 1930s and the essence of Keynesian economics can be explained in terms of simple demand and supply analysis. The state of the economy in 1929 can be represented by the intersection of the aggregate demand and aggregate supply curves, as shown in Figure 3-1, where the demand curve for 1929 is D_{1929}. The Keynesian approach of assuming prices to be constant is represented by the assumption that the price level is fixed no matter the output level. This is translated into a horizontal supply curve. The large decrease in investment spending between 1929 and 1933 caused demand to fall. The demand curve shifted back and towards the left. The result was a new equilibrium level of output, Q_{1933}, with lower production and employment.

Notice that only demand changes cause output and employment to change. Supply has no role. Hence in the Keynesian view an understanding of how output is determined, and why it fluctuates, requires a careful description of demand and the factors that cause demand to change. The three primary components of demand are the purchase of goods and services by households, by business, and by government. To understand what causes output to be a particular amount or what causes it to change requires knowledge of consumption, investment, and government spending.

In the Keynesian scheme the investment component of demand is very volatile, causing large swings in demand and, subsequently, in output. The policy implication of this is straightforward. Government

Figure 3-1. *A Demand and Supply Interpretation of the Great Depression*

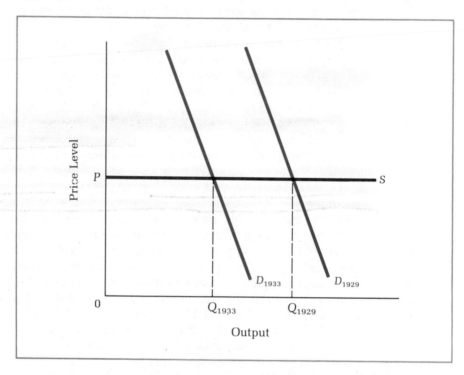

Simple demand and supply analysis can be used to illustrate the developments of the early 1930s and the essential ideas of Keynesian economics. The intersection of the demand curve for 1929 (D_{1929}) and the supply curve (S) determines output. The supply curve is horizontal due to the Keynesian assumption of constant prices. Between 1929 and 1933, private investment declined from 16.2 billion to 0.3 billion. This large drop in demand caused the demand curve to shift back and to the left so that the curve for 1933 is denoted as D_{1933}. Equilibrium output declined to Q_{1933}. Clearly illustrated is the fact that demand changes cause output and employment changes. This indicates the importance of the components of demand in the Keynesian view.

spending and taxing policies should be used to offset investment spending changes so that demand, output, and employment will be stabilized. We will examine these points in detail in the remainder of this chapter. To simplify the analysis, we assume that GNP is equal to national income, thereby ignoring the capital consumption allowance (CCA) and indirect business taxes (IBT).

A Simple Model of Output Determination

In order to focus on the essential concepts of the Keynesian model, we will assume initially that there is no government spending. This is in line with the situation in the United States prior to the 1930s when government spending was less than 2 percent of GNP. Hence, demand is generated, and output determined, by the purchase of goods and services by households and businesses.

Before proceeding with the analysis, it is important to understand the basic approach economists take when examining issues. It is called *comparative statics* and involves the comparison of one equilibrium point with another. For example, in Figure 3-1, the demand curve shifted inward leading to a new, lower output level. The comparison of the two equilibrium points, Q_{1929} and Q_{1933} is a comparative statics approach. It is obviously comparative. It is static because it is the final position of the economy after adjustments have taken place that is being compared with the original position. Using Figure 3-1 as an example again, note that we did not attempt to describe the path the economy took from Q_{1929} to Q_{1933}. We simply compared the equilibrium in 1929 to the equilibrium in 1933.

The Consumption Function — determined by income level

The first component of demand to be studied is consumption demand. The basis for consumption (C) is really quite straightforward as can be observed by asking yourself the following question: What determines the amount that I spend or consume? Most likely you've come up with the answer that the amount you earn; that is, your income (Y), determines the amount you spend. Thus, your theory of consumption is that an individual's consumption demand is determined by his income level. This is very similar to the theory of consumption postulated by Keynes. In fact, Keynes claimed that "as a rule and on the average, as income increases, consumption will increase, but not by as much as the increase in income."[1]

Consider an individual who is contemplating how much consumption to undertake over a period of one week. Let us carry out an experiment with this individual by providing her with various income levels and finding out how much she chooses to consume. For example, with no income, how much will she consume? Your initial reaction might be that with no income she could buy nothing. But this is not correct. Even if she believes that during the forthcoming week her income will be zero, she still must eat to stay alive. This means she is consuming. The fact that consumption can be positive when income is zero comes about because individuals can borrow or use part of their saving to stay alive for the week. This behavior is called *dissaving*. Therefore, when our individual replies that her consumption will be $100 even though her income is zero, we should not be surprised.

---

[1] John Maynard Keynes, *The General Theory of Employment, Interest, and Money* (New York: Harcourt, Brace and World, Inc., 1935), p. 96.

Now suppose instead that the individual anticipates that her income over the week will be $500. She reasons that better quality products can be consumed (i.e., steaks instead of beans), and some new desires can be fulfilled. Therefore, perhaps all of the five hundred dollars will be consumed. Consider one other income level. Suppose anticipated income over the week is six hundred dollars. The individual satisfied most desires with five hundred dollars. Thus, perhaps one of the more important additional desires that can be satisfied at an income above $500 is to save for a rainy day, for a period of reduced or even zero income. Thus, perhaps when income is $600 per week, only $580 is spent for consumption, and $20 is saved.

We could continue this process for a large number of income levels. The result would be the formulation of a specific consumption schedule, such as the one presented in Table 3-2. An examination of this consumption schedule renders two important insights beyond the observation that consumption increases as income increases. First, notice that for each additional $100 of income, consumption increases by $80. The relationship between the additional income (change in income) and the additional consumption (change in consumption) is known as the *marginal propensity to consume* (MPC). In our example, the MPC is a constant (0.8).

A second important insight can be found by examining the fraction of income that is consumed at various income levels. This fraction is known as the *average propensity to consume* (APC). At the income level of 100, the APC is 1.80; when income is 400, the APC falls to 1.05. Therefore, the APC falls as income increases. This relationship is due to the fact that as income increases, people save a larger share of their total income.

In Figure 3-2, the relationship between consumption and income is presented graphically. The relationship shown in this figure is known as the *consumption function*. In algebraic form this relationship can be written as

(3-1) $C = C_0 + c_y Y$

C_0 is described as the intercept of the consumption graph. We have already discussed that for our individual the intercept, or C_0, represents the amount that will be spent on consumption when income is zero. Since this amount of consumption does not depend on income, it is referred to as *autonomous* or *exogenous consumption*; that is, consumption that is determined by factors other than income.

The other part of the consumption function is the term $c_y Y$. This portion of consumption spending varies with income. In mathematics, c_y is known as the slope coefficient and is calculated by dividing the change in the variable measured on the vertical axis by the change in the variable

Table 3.2. Consumption and Saving Schedule

Income (Y)	Consumption (C)	Saving (S)	ΔC	ΔY	$MPC = \dfrac{\Delta C}{\Delta Y}$	$APC = \dfrac{C}{Y}$	$MPS = \dfrac{\Delta S}{\Delta Y}$	$APS = \dfrac{S}{Y}$
$ 0	$100	$-100				—		—
			80	100	0.80		.20	
100	180	-80				1.80		-0.80
			80	100	0.80		.20	
200	260	-60				1.30		-0.30
			80	100	0.80		.20	
300	340	-40				1.13		-0.13
			80	100	0.80		.20	
400	420	-20				1.05		-0.05
			80	100	0.80		.20	
500	500	0				1.00		0.00
			80	100	0.80		.20	
600	580	20				0.97		0.03
			80	100	0.80		.20	
700	660	40				0.94		0.06
			80	100	0.80		.20	
800	740	60				0.92		0.08
			80	100	0.80		.20	
900	820	80				0.91		0.09
			80	100	0.80		.20	
1000	900	100				0.90		0.10
			80	100	0.80		.20	
1100	980	120				0.89		0.11
			80	100	0.80		.20	

Note: The columns point out the essential features of the Keynesian consumption function. Consumption increases, but not by as much as income increases. The MPC is constant. The APC declines as income increases. MPC plus MPS and APC plus APS each sum to 1.0.

measured on the horizontal axis (the "rise" over the "run"). In terms of the consumption function, the slope is the change in consumption divided by the change in income. But recall, this is also the definition of the marginal propensity to consume. In other words, the slope of the consumption function is the marginal propensity to consume. In summary, then, the consumption function consists of two parts, autonomous consumption and the consumption that is induced by (depends on) income, called *endogenous consumption*.

Is it necessary that the consumption graph be a straight line? A straight line consumption graph says that no matter the level of income,

Figure 3-2. *The Consumption and Saving Functions*

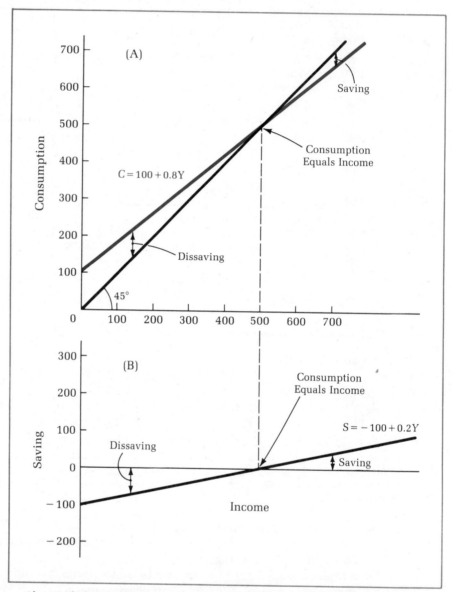

Along with the upward sloping consumption line, a 45-degree guideline is presented in the upper panel which can be thought of as representing points at which the variable measured along the horizontal axis equals the variable measured on the vertical axis: in this case, all points where income equals consumption. Since the 45-degree line and consumption cross at an income level of 500, we know that this is the only income level at which all income is consumed. At income levels higher than 500, saving occurs, while at lower income levels dissaving or borrowing takes place. The vertical distance between the consumption and 45-degree line measures the amount of saving or dissaving, as shown in the lower panel.

an additional dollar induces individuals to consume a certain fixed percent of that dollar. In other words, is the MPC constant? Keynes thought not. He felt that the MPC did change and that the consumption curve changes shape over the business cycle. He stated that

> The MPC is not constant for all levels of employment, and it is probable that there will be, as a rule, a tendency for it to diminish as employment increases; i.e., when real income increases, that is to say, the community will wish to consume a gradually diminishing proportion of it.[2]

However, it has become traditional to represent the Keynesian consumption function as a straight line or with a constant MPC.

The theory of consumption demand has been developed so far without clearly distinguishing whether this theory was concerned with the nominal or the real value of goods and services. Failure to distinguish between nominal and real values is not a problem as long as prices are assumed fixed, since the nominal value is equivalent to the real value. However, if the fixed price assumption is dropped, as we will eventually do, it is important to understand whether the basic consumption relationship is developed in real or nominal terms.

Consider the following simple example. Suppose your income increased by 10 percent, from $20,000 a year to $22,000 a year while at the same time the price level rose by 10 percent, from 1.0 to 1.1. Would your consumption increase as suggested by the MPC? Notice that your income cannot buy any more goods and services at $22,000 than it could at $20,000. In each case your purchasing power, or real income, is $20,000. Will your consumption increase? The nominal value of your consumption will increase, but the real value will not. To see this, suppose that we live in a world in which there is only one good. If a consumer decides to purchase one unit at a price of $10, nominal consumption is $10 and real consumption is 1.0. Now, suppose the price increases to $20. Nominal consumption will increase to $20 while real consumption remains at 1.0. Real consumption depends on real disposable income.[3]

The Saving Function

In the model with households and businesses, there are only two things that income can be used for—consumption and saving. Saving is, simply, not spending one's income on goods and services. Thus, $Y \equiv C + S$, where the symbol "$\equiv$" means by definition is identical to. Since $Y \equiv C + S$, then $S \equiv Y - C$. This simple manipulation is quite important for it

---

[2] Ibid., p. 20.
[3] The assumption that prices are fixed means we need not distinguish between real or nominal variables. However, it is important to understand that this relationship would be developed in real terms if prices were allowed to vary.

tells us that once we know the consumption function we know the saving function. We do not have to formulate an independent explanation of saving behavior.

Reconsider Table 3-2. At the zero income level, consumption is 100. This spending can only come from borrowing or the drawing down of savings. Thus, saving is a −100 when income is zero. At the income level of 500, consumption is 500, and so saving must be zero. Other saving levels can be found by using the fact that saving plus consumption must equal income.

Just as the examination of the consumption-income relationship yielded some important insights, so also does an examination of the saving-income relationship. The most obvious relationship is that the saving level increases as income increases. More specifically, each additional $100 of income results in a saving increase of $20. The relationship between the additional income (or change in income) and the additional saving (change in saving) is known as the *marginal propensity to save* (MPS). In our example, the marginal propensity to save is 0.2. Notice that the marginal propensity to save and the marginal propensity to consume (0.8) sum to one. The MPC and the MPS will always sum to one no matter the value of the MPC.[4] The *MPC* is defined as the fraction of an additional dollar of income spent on goods and services. The *MPS* is defined as the fraction of an additional dollar of income not spent on goods and services. Since an additional dollar of income must either be spent on goods and services or not spent, the MPC and MPS must sum to unity.

Another important relationship can be found by examining the proportion of total income that is saved at various income levels, referred to as the *average propensity to save* (APS). The APS increases as income increases. This should make sense because as income rises, most people save a higher percentage of their income. This is pointed out in the column for the APC and the column for the APS in Table 3-2. They sum to one.[5] Therefore, if the fraction of income that is consumed falls as income

---

[4] We have just stated that the MPC and the MPS sum to unity. A little algebra can be used to prove this. Recall that income, in this two-component model, can be used for either consumption or saving. That is, $Y \equiv C + S$. If income can be used for consumption or saving, then a change in income will change either consumption or saving. Algebraically, we write this as, $\Delta Y \equiv \Delta C + \Delta S$. Then,

$$\frac{\Delta Y}{\Delta Y} \equiv 1 = \frac{\Delta C}{\Delta Y} + \frac{\Delta S}{\Delta Y}$$

Recalling the definitions of MPC and MPS, we see that $1 = MPC + MPS$.

[5] The relationship between the APC and APS can also be simply proved. Again, use the income identity that $Y \equiv C + S$. Now divide both sides of this equation by Y. The result is

$$\frac{Y}{Y} \equiv 1 = \frac{C}{Y} + \frac{S}{Y}$$

But $C/Y = APC$ and $S/Y = APS$, therefore, $1 = APC + APS$.

increases, then the fraction of income that is saved (i.e., the remainder) must increase.

A diagram representing the relationship between saving and income levels is presented in Figure 3-2 B. This relationship is called the *saving function*. The intercept is referred to as the level of *autonomous saving* and the slope of the saving line is known as the MPS.

The relationship between the saving and consumption functions can be seen by examining Figure 3-2 A and Figure 3-2 B together. In order to simplify the explanation, a 45-degree line is added to the consumption function diagram. Any point on this line represents equal distances along the axes. Therefore, any point on the 45-degree line is a point where consumption and income are equal. Consider the income level $700. At this income level consumption is $660. Therefore, saving must be $40. Forty dollars is precisely the amount of the vertical distance between the consumption function and the 45-degree line at the income level $700. At a lower income level, say $100, consumption is $180. In this case, the vertical distance between the 45-degree line and the consumption line represents the amount of dissaving, $80. Thus, the vertical distance between the consumption line and the 45-degree line at each income level measures saving. If this distance is plotted on a diagram with saving and income on the axes, the saving function is traced out, as in Figure 3-2 B.

The Aggregate Demand Curve and Equilibrium Output

The other component of demand is business desired investment demand. For the desired, or planned, investment component of demand we initially use the simplest model by assuming that businesses choose their level of investment independently of the output or income level. In other words, we are assuming planned (desired) investment spending to be autonomous or exogenous—it does not depend on sales or income. Diagrammatically, the investment demand curve will simply be a horizontal line at the desired investment level in Figure 3-3. We emphasize the words *planned* or *desired* since business firms employ people and buy other inputs on the basis of their anticipations. When sales fall below anticipated sales, firms lay off workers, sell off machines, and cut back production. Hence, it is the plans that are most crucial in determining a firm's demands for goods and services.

To obtain aggregate demand (AD) we just add the business sector's demand (investment) and the household sector's demand (consumption). At an income level of zero, desired consumption is $100 and desired investment demand is also $100. Thus total *autonomous demand* (demand when income is zero) is $200. When income is $100, we know that desired consumption is $180, while desired investment demand remains at $100. Therefore, at the $100 output level, total (aggregate) demand is

AD = business sector's demand + household's sector's demand
          INVESTMENT   Consumption

Figure 3-3. The Aggregate Demand Curve and Equilibrium Output

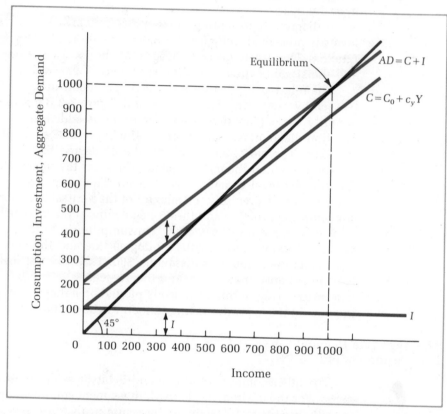

In this model, only households and business firms demand current production. The consumption function represents household demand and the investment function denotes business demand. The latter is drawn as a horizontal line to indicate that investment is autonomous. The aggregate demand curve is derived by vertically adding the consumption and investment lines. For instance, at the income level $100, desired consumption is $180 and desired investment is $100 generating aggregate demand of $280. Equilibrium occurs at the point where aggregate demand intersects the 45-degree line. Only at this point is aggregate spending equal to output.

$280. In a similar manner, we can derive AD for other levels of output. Carrying out this exercise we obtain the results presented in Table 3-3 and graphed in Figure 3-3. Notice the intercept of the AD curve is $200, total autonomous demand, and the slope of the AD curve is 0.8, the sum of the slopes of the consumption and investment curves.

Now that we have derived AD, we should be able to graphically determine the specific quantity of output that will be produced in this economy. A 45-degree line is introduced to Figure 3-3. Recall that a 45-degree line shows all points at which the variables measured on the two axes are equal. Thus, in Figure 3-3 the line shows all points at which

Table 3-3. Aggregate Demand Schedule

Y	C	I_p	$C + I_p \equiv AD$	S
0	100	100	200	-100
100	180	100	280	-80
200	260	100	360	-60
300	340	100	440	-40
400	420	100	520	-20
500	500	100	600	0
600	580	100	680	20
700	660	100	760	40
800	740	100	840	60
900	820	100	920	80
1,000	900	100	1,000	100
1,100	980	100	1,080	120

The two-component model of the economy shows aggregate demand, consumption, and investment increasing as income increases. Yet aggregate demand (AD) and income (Y) are equal at only one income level. At this income level, saving and investment are also the same.

the value of output (the variable measured on the horizontal axis) is equal to AD (the variable measured on the vertical axis). The AD curve intersects the 45-degree line at only one point. This point, where output (income) is equal to $1,000, is the only point at which aggregate spending is equal to output.

The Leakage and Injection Approach to Equilibrium

If an individual decides to save, the value of factor payments (income) generated from the production of goods and services will not all be spent on goods and services and will, therefore, imply a demand that is less than the value of output. Only if this reduction in demand is met by an increase in another component of demand will production remain at its current level. In the simple model used in the previous section, this alternative form of demand is desired investment. Therefore, the value of output and AD will be equal only at the income level at which saving, the "leakage" from spending, is equal to investment, the "injection" to spending.[6]

Again, examine Table 3-3. If we can find an income level at which saving and planned investment are equal, it will be the equilibrium income level. In our example, saving and investment are each $100 when

---

[6] This equilibrium condition can be derived directly from the equilibrium condition $Y = C + I$. Subtract C from both sides of the equation, then $Y - C = (C + I) - C$ or $S = I$.

income is $1,000. The $1,000 income level is the same equilibrium value that was discovered using the *AD* curve. Table 3-3 is shown diagrammatically in Figure 3-4.

Figure 3-4. Saving, Investment, and Equilibrium Output

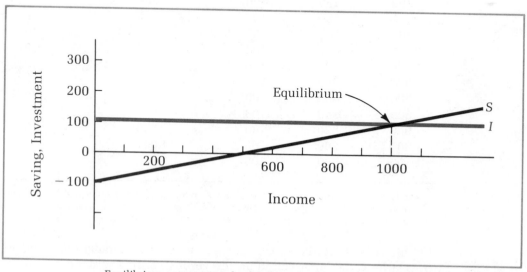

Equilibrium output may also be determined by examining the investment and saving lines. The intersection of these two lines determines equilibrium output. Saving is a *leakage* from the value of factor payments generated from the production of goods and services. The only way for the value of output and aggregate demand to be equal—the condition for equilibrium—is to have a new *injection* of demand to replace the leakage due to saving. The additional injection comes from investment demand. Therefore, when saving is equal to investment, leakages equal injections and the value of output and aggregate demand are the same.

To summarize, we have discovered two approaches to determining the equilibrium level of the economy, the aggregate demand and the leakage and injections approaches. In essence, what happens in both approaches is that equilibrium occurs when the amount of goods and services that firms want to produce just equals the amount of goods and services that individuals and firms want to purchase. Whenever these are not equal, the economy will adjust; the level of output will increase or decrease until equality is obtained.

Adjustment to Equilibrium

If there are forces in the economy that automatically move it toward equilibrium, we say our model is *stable*. Why care whether or not the model is stable? If we know the model is stable, we then know that the economy will always be at an equilibrium or moving toward some equilibrium. We can then solve for the equilibrium level of income and use that level as a reference point, a point at which the economy is presently residing or toward which the economy is presently moving.

Refer once again to the example presented in Table 3-3. Notice that at the $1,100 income level, planned investment is $100 and saving is $120. Obviously, this is not equilibrium since desired or planned investment (I_p) is not equal to saving and, thus, demand is less than production. This can clearly be seen in Figure 3-5. Since demand falls short of production, some goods that were produced have not been purchased. These leftover goods are called *undesired inventories* and are classified as part of investment spending. In effect, we are saying that businesses purchase these inventories from themselves. Therefore, investment, including the undesired inventories, is $120 which is also the level of saving. In sum, actual investment (I_A) is equal to planned investment (I_p) plus undesired investment (I_u), or

$$I_A = I_p + I_u$$

What does the existence of $20 of undesired investment mean? It means that firms were too optimistic in predicting sales and thus overproduced. The overproduction decision resulted in more inventories than the firms wanted and because the inventory accumulation was unintended, firms will react by cutting production and laying off workers while they attempt to sell off the excess inventories. As production is decreased and workers laid off, national income declines (payments to the factors of production decline). This, in turn, means saving will fall. This process will continue as long as there is undesired investment; that is, until desired investment and saving are equal. Thus, *equilibrium income is characterized as being an income level at which there is no unintended investment and thus no unintended inventory changes* ($I_u = 0$).[7]

We have seen that the model is stable when income is above equilibrium income since undesired investment sets forces in motion that move the economy toward equilibrium. But what is the adjustment process when income is below equilibrium? Consider the income level $600. While planned investment is $100, saving is now just $20. Demand is

---

[7] In Chapter 2 it was pointed out that aggregate demand is, by definition, equal to production at any level of demand. But this implies that saving and investment are equal, whatever the level of output. This seems to contradict those statements made in the previous sections where we said that saving and investment are equal only at equilibrium. The apparent contradiction is due to definitional differences. In the national income accounts, variables are measured *ex post* or after the economic events have occurred. For example, the value of investment measured in the national income accounts is called actual or *ex post* investment and consists of planned (desired) investment and unplanned (undesired) investment. On the other hand the investment we refer to in the discussion concerning equilibrium is just the desired investment, investment excluding undesired inventories.

Figure 3-5. Planned Investment, Unplanned Investment, and Equilibrium

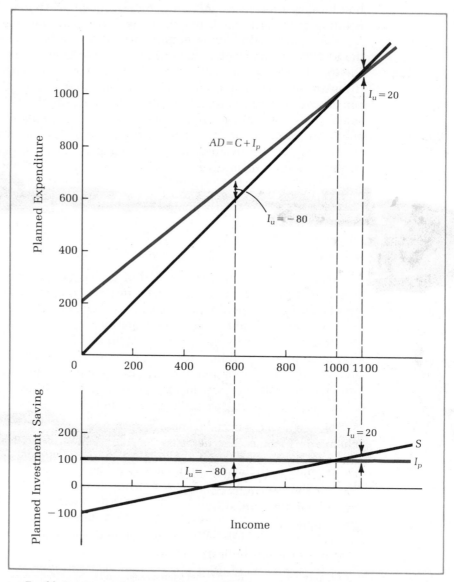

Equilibrium income is determined by setting desired aggregate demand equal to the value of current production or by setting saving equal to desired investment. In this example, equilibrium income is $1,000. At an income level above $1,000, production exceeds desired demand and saving exceeds planned investment. At $1,100 of production, undesired inventories accumulate causing business firms to reduce production and income. Thus, unplanned inventories cause income to fall toward equilibrium. At income levels below $1,000, negative unplanned inventories, or inventory levels below desired level, cause production and income to increase.

larger than the quantity of goods and services produced. As a result, businesses find demand so great that they cannot maintain their desired inventory levels—unintended investment is $-80. The typical entrepreneur will react to falling inventory levels by expanding production and hiring additional workers. The increased production will result in greater income and greater savings levels. This process will continue as long as unintended investment is negative. Thus, the model is also stable when income is below the equilibrium level

The Multiplier

From 1929 to 1933, investment demand dipped by $15.9 billion, driving the economy to a new equilibrium level of income that was $32 billion lower than it had been in 1929. The initial drop in investment seemed to cause a much larger fall in output. The name given to this effect is the *multiplier.*

The clearest explanation of the multiplier effect can be provided with an example. Consider Figure 3-6 where autonomous planned investment is $100 billion and where the initial equilibrium income level is $1,000 billion. Suppose that autonomous investment falls by 50 percent; that is, investment changes by $50 billion ($\Delta I = \$-50$). The lower level of investment means *AD* will fall. More precisely, the *AD* curve shifts down by the change in autonomous spending. This means the *AD* line is now below the 45-degree line at the previous equilibrium income level of $1,000 billion. Since production is greater than desired demand, sales are less than expected, undesired inventories begin accumulating, and businesses begin cutting production and laying off workers. This process continues until the new equilibrium level of $750 billion is reached.

Notice how the initial change in spending led to a larger or multiplied change in income. The decrease in income (ΔY) of $250 billion is five times as large as the initial $50 billion decrease in autonomous spending (ΔI). Will a new equilibrium be reached only after the change in income has been larger (in this case five times larger) than the change in autonomous spending? Recall that equilibrium is obtained when desired investment equals saving. Since investment fell by $50 billion, saving will have to decline by the same amount in order to restore equilibrium. But recall that out of every dollar reduction in income, saving will decline by a fraction (the MPS) of that dollar. In our example, with the MPS equal to 0.2, income must decline by $250 billion in order for saving to decline by $50 billion. This result illustrates a concept known as the *spending multiplier.*

The spending multiplier points out the important role consumption plays in the Keynesian framework—the value of the multiplier is dependent on the MPC. The exact value of the multiplier can be derived quite simply. The change in autonomous investment must equal the change in

Figure 3-6. *The Effects on Output of a $50 Billion Decrease in Autonomous Investment Spending*

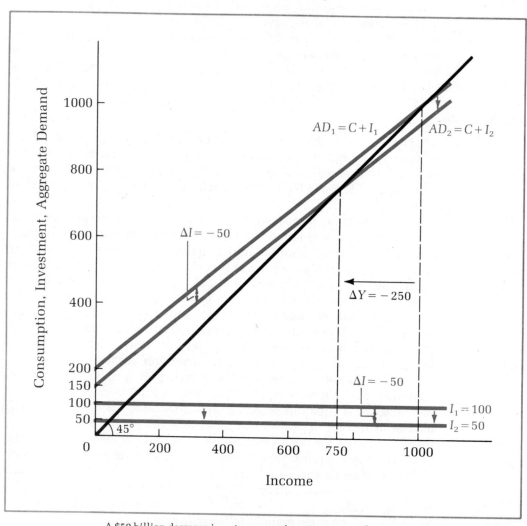

A $50 billion decrease in autonomous investment spending causes the investment curve, and thus the aggregate demand curve, to shift down by $50 billion ($\Delta I = -\$50$). The new equilibrium income is $750 billion which is $250 billion less than the original equilibrium income level. The fact that a $50 billion decrease in investment spending results in a $250 billion decrease in output indicates the multiplier effect.

saving in order for equilibrium to occur. Algebraically, we are stating that

$$(3\text{-}2) \qquad \Delta S = \Delta I$$

An examination of the saving function tells us that the induced change in saving is equal to the MPS times the change in income, or $(1-c_y)\Delta Y$.[8] Using this relationship in Equation 3-2 yields

(3-3) $(1-c_y)\Delta Y = \Delta I_p$

Dividing both sides by $(1-c_y)$ we obtain

(3-4) $\Delta Y = \dfrac{1}{1-c_y}(\Delta I_p)$

This last equation states that the change in income caused by a change in autonomous investment is equal to the reciprocal of the MPS multiplied by the change in investment. The multiplier is therefore 1/MPS or $1/(1-c_y)$. Another approach to deriving the multiplier is to examine the changes in *AD* and income. The total change in income is made up of the autonomous change in investment plus a change in consumption induced by the changing level of income. That is,

(3-5) $\Delta Y = \Delta I_p + \Delta C$

An examination of the consumption function (pages 65-69) tells us that the induced change in consumption is equal to the MPC times the change in income, or $c_y\Delta Y$. Using this relationship in Equation 3-5 yields the following:

(3-6) $\Delta Y = \Delta I_p + \left(c_y \bullet \Delta Y\right)$

Now, when this equation is solved for ΔY, the value of the multiplier is derived.

(3-7) $\Delta Y = \left(\dfrac{1}{1-c_y}\right)\Delta I_p$

Where $1/(1-c_y)$ is the multiplier.

In the example presented in Figure 3-6, the MPC is 0.8. Thus, according to Equations 3-4 and 3-7, the decrease in investment of $50 billion leads to a decline in income of 1 ÷ (1 − 0.8) = 5 times that amount, or $250 billion. If the marginal propensity to consume is 0.9, the same fall in investment means income decreases by 500 since the multiplier is 1 ÷ (1 − 0.9) = 10. Thus, the larger the marginal propensity to consume, or the

---

[8] The induced or endogenous part of saving is $(1 - c_y)$ Y or MPS × Y and the autonomous or fixed part is $(- C_0)$. Thus, a change in saving is the sum of a change of endogenous saving and a change in autonomous saving. In this example, only the endogenous portion is changing, and it changes because income changes. Thus, $\Delta S = (1-c_y) \Delta Y$.

smaller the additional leakage into saving, the greater the multiplier and the subsequent change in income.

The impact on output from the 1927-33 drop in investment was not as dramatic as in the previous example, but nevertheless was very significant. Investment spending measured in terms of 1929 dollars declined from $16.2 billion in 1929 to $0.3 billion in 1933. Hence, $15.9 billion fewer machines, equipment, and new construction were sold. The immediate impact was on those companies supplying the machines and equipment, or constructing the buildings since they received $15.9 billion less income than they had received in 1929. Suppose the MPC was ½. Then in 1933 the suppliers would have consumed $7.95 billion less and saved $7.95 billion less than they did in 1929. Suppose the $7.95 billion would have been used by suppliers to buy goods. The owners of these goods would have received $7.95 billion less in income. This change in income would have induced another $3.97 billion decline in spending. Hence, other producers would have received $3.97 billion less income which, in turn, would have reduced spending by $1.98 billion. This process continues on and on.

We have collected many of the chain effects of income changes in Table 3-4. If the middle column is summed, the total change in income could be calculated. The general form of Table 3-4 is the following equation:

$$\Delta Y = 15.9 + c_y (15.9) + c_y{}^2 (15.9) + c_y{}^3 (15.9) + \ldots$$
$$= 15.9 (1 + c_y + c_y{}^2 + c_y{}^3 + \ldots .)$$

Which, in turn, is equal to

$$15.9 \left(\frac{1}{1 - c_y} \right)$$

With an MPC of 0.5, we obtain

$$15.9 [1 \div (1 - 0.5)] = 31.8$$

This example suggests GNP would have fallen by $31.8 billion between 1929 and 1933, not too far from what actually happened.

Once again, notice what the multiplier concept tells us. If the multiplier is, say 10, and if the economy is at rest at some equilibrium, then a change in autonomous spending (ΔI) will change the equilibrium level of income by ten times the initial change in spending, $\Delta Y = \Delta I (10)$. If the multiplier is 2, then $\Delta Y = \Delta I(2)$, and so on.

The multiplier process is one of the most important concepts in Keynesian economics. It forms the basis of Keynesian or activist policy-making. For example, should the economy be in equilibrium at some level

Table 3-4. The Multiplier Process

INITIAL DECLINE IN INVESTMENT	REDUCTION IN INCOME (Y)	REDUCTION IN INDUCED SPENDING
$15.9	$15.9	$c_y(Y) = \$7.95$
	$ 7.95	$c_y(c_yY) = \$3.97$
	$ 3.97	$c_y(c_y^2Y) = \$1.99$
	$ 1.99	$c_y(c_y^3Y) = \$0.99$
	and so on	

The initial drop in investment caused declines in income and, thus, consumption demand. The multiplier summarizes the chain effects of the investment change.

that is not sufficient to generate full employment, the Keynesian theory suggests that the policymaker use knowledge of the value of the multiplier to change equilibrium to the desired level.

Business Cycles: The 1929-1933 Experience

Our discussion of the adjustment process of the model also forms the basis of a standard description of a business cycle. Using Figure 3-7B and referring to Figure 3-7A notice what occurs as spending decreases from AD_{1929} to AD_{1933}. The economy is initially in equilibrium at Point E_1. Then investment spending declines. The decrease in demand means that firms begin to experience an accumulation of inventories. Once firms realize that this is more than just a temporary phenomenon they decrease production and lay off workers which, in turn, lowers income. As income begins to decline, consumption declines which drives demand down even further. Both production and income continue falling until the excess undesired inventories are sold off, at which time a new equilibrium is reached at Point E_2. Production and demand remain at the new equilibrium level until autonomous demand changes again.

A business cycle, the movement from peak through trough to peak, is a pattern of inventory buildup followed by declining production and inventory, and, eventually, a rise in production. Since 1949 there have been 8 recessions averaging 9 months in length with real GNP falling an average of 4.5 percent. In each case the pattern was similar: demand fell, inventories increased, and production fell. Recovery started once inventories had been reduced.

Compare Figures 3-7A and 3-7B and notice how each provides the same information. The initial drop in autonomous spending is represented by the distance ΔI in both graphs. The buildup of undesired inventories is the difference between the demand and production lines in both

Figure 3-7. The 1929-1933 Business Downturn

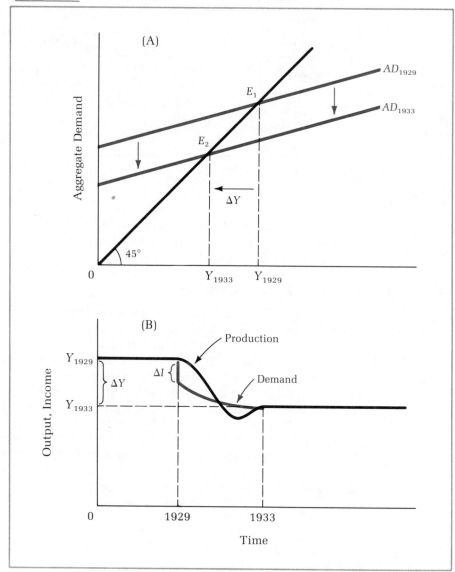

In this figure, the adjustment of production and demand in the United States is presented for the Great Depression. Between 1929 and 1930, investment, measured in 1929 dollars, fell $5.7 billion thus decreasing autonomous spending by the same amount. Firms experienced a buildup of inventories that resulted in production cuts and layoffs. These in turn lowered income and led to further declines in demand, and the process continued. When unwanted inventories were sold off and desired levels reached once again, the new equilibrium (E_2) was achieved. In 1933 that new level was $31.8 billion less than at the original 1929 equilibrium (E_1).

graphs. Finally, notice that the size of the multiplier effect (the distance between the old and the new equilibrium values), is shown on the horizontal axis in Figure 3-7A and on the vertical axis in Figure 3-7B.

In 1929 real gross national product was $104.4 billion and investment was approximately $16.2 billion. In 1930 investment was $10.5 billion, having fallen $5.7 billion. By 1933 production had dropped nearly $30.2 billion, to $74.2 billion. The initial drop in investment drove the economy into a collapse. By 1933 the inventories that had accumulated since 1930 were being sold off. In fact, the change in inventories in 1933 was negative.

The Addition of a Government Sector: The Roosevelt Years

One of the important messages of the Keynesian theory was that the equilibrium level of income need not be the same as the income level that would generate full employment. Keynes's idea was to have government manipulate *AD* so as to drive the economy to its full-employment level. Since consumption decisions are made by households and investment decisions are made by firms, Keynes realized that neither form of demand could be directly controlled by the government. Thus, if policymakers are to directly influence demand, the government must use its spending and taxing powers.[9]

Keynes's idea of using the government to manipulate the *AD* curve was not readily accepted. Despite the presence of a depression, the overwhelming majority of economists, businessmen, and politicians believed in the necessity of balanced budgets. Keynes tried to sell his ideas to President Franklin Roosevelt. The most publicized attempts were on December 31, 1933, when *The New York Times* and a number of other newspapers in the United States carried an open letter from Keynes to President Roosevelt and in June, 1934, when Keynes came to the United States and met with President Roosevelt. Roosevelt was a most reluctant buyer. His views on the role of government spending during the early 1930s were exemplified by his "Forgotten Man" speech on April 7, 1932. He said

> It is the habit of the unthinking to turn in times like this to the illusions of economic magic. People suggest that a huge expenditure of public funds

---

[9] Richard Musgrave in his book, *The Theory of Public Finance,* argues that the government has three roles—to adjust allocation of resources by the market, to modify the income distribution, and to provide stabilization of aggregate demand. Keynes added that last role to this list.

. . . will completely solve the unemployment problem. . . . Let us admit frankly that it would be only a stop-gap.[10]

In this section, we will add government spending and taxation to the model. This will allow us to clearly understand Keynes's idea for solving the Great Depression—the use of fiscal policy.

Determination of Equilibrium

With the addition of a government sector, demand for output produced in the economy consists of three components: consumption demand, investment demand, and government demand. The basic idea behind consumption spending remains unchanged—consumption depends on available income. However, the introduction of government spending affects available income. Taxes are taken out of gross income.[11] The amount remaining is disposable income. And it is on the basis of disposable income that individuals decide to consume or save.

We will represent disposable income by the symbol YD so that $YD = Y - T$. The type of tax (T) we specify can vary considerably. Some taxes are independent of income, such as bicycle licenses or dog licenses. Others are dependent on income, such as income taxes. In addition the manner in which taxes depend on income can vary considerably. The simplest form of tax and the one used in Table 3-5, is the *lump sum tax*, a tax that remains constant no matter the level of income. We have used the material from Table 3-2 along with a tax of $50 and government spending of $60 to complete Table 3-5. At an income level of zero, disposable income is now -50 since, with the lump sum tax, individuals with no income must still pay taxes. Consumption is $100 plus eight-tenths of disposable income so that at an income level of zero, consumption is $60. As in Table 3-2 we assume the MPC is 0.8 so that for each $100 increase in disposable income, consumption increases by $80. An examination of the consumption, income, and disposable income columns in Table 3-5 points out that all of the properties of the consumption function previously discussed continue to hold. For example, the APC declines as income increases and the MPC is a constant. The symbolic representation of the revised consumption function is

---

[10] Franklin D. Roosevelt, *The Public Papers and Addresses of Franklin D. Roosevelt* (New York: Random House, 1938), I:625.

[11] Despite the fact that nominal and real variables are identical in this chapter it is important to realize that government spending is determined in real terms. When the government decides to build a bridge, a bomb, or a park, the decision is made to purchase a real good, not the nominal value of a good. Taxes, on the other hand, are more complicated. The structure of taxes is based on nominal income. For this reason, as inflation drove up nominal income without changing real incomes in the 1970s, individuals were pushed into higher and higher tax brackets—they had to pay more taxes even though their real incomes were unchanged. This situation creates many problems, as we will thoroughly discuss in Chapters 12-14.

Table 3-5. Determination of Equilibrium Income

(1) Y	(2) T	(3) $YD = Y - T$	(4) C		(5) G		(6) I_p		(7) $AD = C + I_p + G$	(8) S	(9) $S + T$	(10) $I_p + G$
0	50	− 50	60	+	60	+	100	=	220	− 110	− 60	160
100	50	50	140	+	60	+	100	=	300	− 90	− 40	160
200	50	150	220	+	60	+	100	=	380	− 70	− 20	160
300	50	250	300	+	60	+	100	=	460	− 50	0	160
400	50	350	380	+	60	+	100	=	540	− 30	20	160
500	50	450	460	+	60	+	100	=	620	− 10	40	160
600	50	550	540	+	60	+	100	=	700	10	60	160
700	50	650	620	+	60	+	100	=	780	30	80	160
800	50	750	700	+	60	+	100	=	860	50	100	160
900	50	850	780	+	60	+	100	=	940	70	120	160
1000	50	950	860	+	60	+	100	=	1020	90	140	160
1100	50	1050	940	+	60	+	100	=	1100	110	160	160
1200	50	1150	1020	+	60	+	100	=	1180	130	180	160

Income determination in a 3-component model with lump sum taxes, autonomous investment, and fixed government spending. Taxes take income away from the consumer thus reducing the amount spent on goods and services. Taxes also take income, which would have been saved, away from individuals. Equilibrium income is determined by equating aggregate demand, $AD = C + I + G$, to income, Y, or by equating injections, $I + G$, to leakages, $S + T$.

$$(3\text{-}8) \qquad C = C_0 + c_y (Y - T)$$

which clearly shows how taxes affect consumption. The rest of Table 3-5 is completed by specifying the other components of demand. We will continue to assume that investment spending is autonomous. Also, since government purchases of goods and services are determined through the legislative process and not induced by income, we assume government spending (G) is also autonomous. (The appropriateness of this assumption is discussed at length in Chapter 12.) Aggregate demand, Column 7, is the sum of $C + I_p + G$, or the sum of Columns 4, 5, and 6. Saving, Column 8, is derived from the definition that saving is what remains of income after consumption and taxes are taken out, $S \equiv Y - C - T$. The appropriate columns from Table 3-5 are plotted in Figure 3-8A, and B.[12]

In the model with only households and businesses, equilibrium income is that income level at which consumption plus investment (aggre-

---

[12] In plotting the aggregate demand and consumption curves, it is important to keep in mind how taxes show up. The lump sum tax affects the intercept of the curves. Consider the consumption equation $C = C_0 + c_y (Y - T_0)$. We wish to plot (C,Y) combinations. Hence, we solve for C in terms of Y. This yields $C = C_0 - c_y T_0 + c_y Y$. The term $(C_0 - c_y T_0)$ is the intercept of the consumption line.

Figure 3-8. Determination of Equilibrium in a
Model with a Government Sector

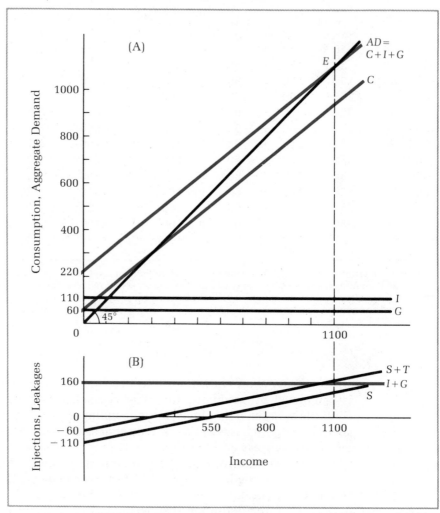

Equilibrium output is determined by the intersection of the aggregate demand curve and the 45-degree line (the upper panel), or the intersection of the total leakages and total injection lines. The aggregate demand curve is derived by vertically adding the consumption, investment, and government spending lines. (Taxes affect the aggregate demand curve via the consumption function.) Aggregate demand intersects the 45-degree line at the output level 1,100. Alternatively, this same output level could be determined by considering leakages and injections. Leakages now consist of savings and taxes while investment and government spending are the injections of demand.

gate demand) is equal to the value of output. With the government sector now added, equilibrium is that income level at which the sum of consumption, investment, and government expenditures (aggregate demand in the 3-component model) is equal to output.[13]

An alternative method for determining equilibrium is to examine the injections into, and leakages out of, the spending stream. For an equilibrium to exist, we know that total leakages from the earned income stream must be offset by an equal amount of injections or alternative forms of demand. The inclusion of the government sector means that an additional leakage and injection occur. Leakages now consist of savings and taxes while the additional injection is government's demand for goods and services.

$$(3-9) \qquad I + G = S + T$$

Table 3-5 and Figure 3-8 indicate that for our example, total leakages and total injections are equal at an income level of $1,100. As should be the case, this is the same equilibrium income found by employing the *AD* approach.

An examination of the leakage-injection Equation 3-9 yields an interesting insight about the government budget. It does not have to be balanced at equilibrium.[14] All that is required for equilibrium is that total leakages and total injections be equal. The state of the government budget is determined by comparing government spending and tax revenues. The budget is in *surplus* when tax revenues are greater than government spending and in *deficit* when government spending is greater than tax revenues. In the example used in this section, the government budget is in deficit at equilibrium.

Multipliers and the Government Sector

By developing the theoretical idea of a multiplier Keynes was able to demonstrate that relatively small spending changes can lead to relatively large changes in income. However, neither the consumer sector nor the business sector could be directed to spend at the appropriate time nor to spend the appropriate amount to drive the economy to its desired level. This, Keynes believed, was up to the government sector. Changes in government spending (as with changes in any autonomous spending) are

---

[13] From this point on we will drop any references to planned or desired. When we speak of investment we will be referring to planned or desired investment. You might have noticed that we have done this throughout with consumption. We will not distinguish between planned and actual consumption.

[14] The straightforward statement that the budget does not have to be balanced at equilibrium is correct only in the simple model presented here. Consider, for example, that the deficit must be paid for and the manner in which it is financed will have an effect on the economy. As long as deficits are run, this effect will occur. We will consider this in detail in later chapters.

reflected as shifts in the *AD* curve. The *AD* curve will shift downwards for decreases in government spending and upwards for increases in government spending. Tax changes also shift the *AD* curve by shifting the consumption function.

Suppose economic policymakers decide that equilibrium income is too low; there are too many people unemployed and too little production is taking place. What options do the policymakers have? According to Keynes, the government should run a deficit by increasing spending and decreasing taxes. But, by how much should spending be increased or taxes decreased? The answer depends on the multiplier.

The total change in income will consist of the autonomous change in government spending and a change in consumption induced by the changing level of income, or

$$(3\text{-}10) \qquad \Delta Y = \Delta C + \Delta G$$

Since only the induced portion of consumption changes as income changes, we find from the consumption equation that $\Delta C = c_y(\Delta Y)$. Substituting the change in consumption into Equation 3-10 we find that

$$(3\text{-}11) \qquad \Delta Y = c_y(\Delta Y) + \Delta G$$

and solving for ΔY we obtain

$$(3\text{-}12) \qquad \Delta Y = \left(\frac{1}{1 - c_y} \right) \Delta G$$

This last term in parentheses is the *government spending multiplier*. Multiplied times the change in autonomous demand, it yields the change in income.

An example may indicate the importance of the government spending multiplier. Suppose the MPC is 0.8 and President Roosevelt's economic advisers in 1933 know that income needs to increase by $100 billion in order to move the economy back to its 1929 level. The advisers need to know how much additional government spending they should recommend. Given the knowledge that the multiplier is $1 \div (1 - 0.8) = 5$, the recommended policy change is $20 billion. This is the only change in government spending that will allow the new equilibrium to be reached. This is illustrated graphically in Figure 3-9.

The economic advisers could recommend tax changes as an alternative method of changing income. In this case, the change in income would be solely due to the change in consumption induced by the change in taxes. The change in consumption is $\Delta C = c_y(\Delta YD)$ so that the change in income is $\Delta Y = \Delta C = c_y (\Delta YD)$. Rewriting disposable income as income

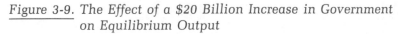

Figure 3-9. The Effect of a $20 Billion Increase in Government on Equilibrium Output

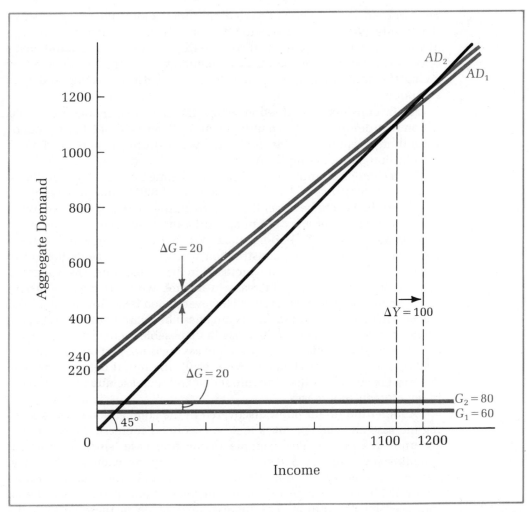

A small change in investment spending can lead to a larger change in income. Similarly, relatively small changes in government spending result in large changes in income. An increase in government spending of $20 billion causes both the government spending and aggregate demand to increase by $20 billion at each income level. As a result of this increase in government spending, excess demand exists at the original equilibrium output level thereby drawing inventories below desired levels and stimulating increased production. The new equilibrium is the output level of $1,250 billion. Hence, a $20 billion increase in government spending increases equilibrium output by a greater amount, illustrating the multiplier principle associated with government spending changes.

less taxes $(Y - T)$ we obtain $\Delta Y = \Delta C = c_y (\Delta YD) = c_y (\Delta Y - \Delta T)$. By solving this expression for ΔY we obtain

$$(3\text{-}13) \qquad \Delta Y \; = \; \left(\frac{-c_y}{1 - c_y} \right) \Delta T$$

The term $-c_y/(1 - c_y)$ is called the *lump sum tax multiplier*. The negative sign points out the inverse relation between changes in taxes and changes in income; if taxes increase, income will decrease. This should make sense since taxes have the effect of reducing consumption demand by giving the individual less income to divide between saving and consumption.

Again consider the situation where income must increase by $100 billion in order to reach full employment. With an MPC of 0.8, a tax cut of $25 billion is required, as can be shown by substituting $c_y = 0.8$ and $\Delta Y \equiv$ $100 billion, and solving for ΔT.

Notice in our example that to increase income by $100 billion, either a tax cut of $25 billion or a spending increase of $20 billion was required. Why must the tax cut be larger than the spending increase? Consider what happens when either a tax cut or spending increase occurs. Suppose the government decides to build a dam. When the government increases spending, the contractors, construction workers, etc., receive the entire amount of the demand as an increase in income. Thus, the spending increase leads to an equal increase in income which is then spent and saved, spent and saved, and so on. However, when taxes are cut, an initial increase in demand equal to the tax cut does not occur. In other words, the decrease in taxes leads to an increase in disposable income which is used to increase saving and consumption. But saving is not part of demand. It is instead a leakage from demand. As a result, the initial demand increase due to a tax cut is less than the initial demand increase due to an increase in government purchases.

Another important point discovered in the comparison of the spending increase and the tax cut is that both policies increase the size of the government's deficit. For example in the first case, since government spending increased by $20 billion without any tax change, the budget deficit increased by $20 billion, while in the second case, since taxes were cut by $25 billion without any change in government spending, the deficit increased by $25 billion. The increase in income in these cases is described as being the result of "deficit spending."

In both of the above examples, expansionary fiscal policy resulted in deficits. However, expansionary fiscal policy can be undertaken without deficits occurring. If government spending could be increased by $100 billion and taxes increased by the same amount, equilibrium income would increase by $100 billion. No deficits would occur as a result of this expansionary policy. This would be described as following a *balanced budget policy.*[15]

---

[15] Since the government spending multiplier is larger than the tax multiplier, an equal

As we have just discovered, the Keynesian model offered policy-makers several alternatives to a depressionary state. Expansionary fiscal policy through increased spending, decreased taxing, or even through a balanced budget increase in spending could lead the economy out of the doldrums of depression. While FDR was a reluctant student of Keynes's, world events eventually forced him to follow the Keynesian prescriptions. Government spending increased dramatically during the Roosevelt years, mainly as a result of World War II. And, as we shall discuss in the next chapter, this spending increase was an unquestionable success in moving the economy upward. The economy rose from the depths of depression just as Keynes had predicted.

The experiences of the Great Depression and the panacea seemingly offered by Keynesian economics revamped economic thinking and policymaking. Keynesian economics brought back the optimism of the 1920s. Roosevelt had said, "we have nothing to fear but fear itself." Keynesian economics said that with active fiscal policy—active governmental participation in the economy—we need not even fear fear.

Keynes attempted to explain the reasons for prolonged departures from full employment, such as what he observed during the 1930s. His explanation stressed the importance of *AD* changes with special attention given to investment spending.[16] He asserted that changes in aggregate demand cause changes in equilibrium output. Moreover, he maintained

---

increase (decrease) in government spending and taxing will lead to a net increase (decrease) in income. In algebraic terms, the change in income is the result of the change in spending and taxes multiplied by their respective multipliers. That is,

$$\Delta Y = \frac{1}{1-c_y} \Delta G + \left(\frac{-c_y}{1-c_y} \right) \Delta T$$

Since $G = T$ under the balanced budget principle, this equation can be rewritten as follows:

$$\Delta Y = \frac{1}{1-c_y} \Delta G + \left(\frac{-c_y}{1-c_y} \right) \Delta G$$

Now simplify

$$\Delta Y = \left(\frac{1}{1-c_y} + \frac{-c_y}{1-c_y} \right) \Delta G = \left(\frac{1-c_y}{1-c_y} \right) \Delta G = 1 \times \Delta G$$

In this particular example, the balanced budget multiplier is unity. Income will still change despite the fact that the stimulatory spending policy is carried out with a contractionary tax policy. The net stimulatory effect is attributable to the larger government spending multiplier. Only if the balanced budget multiplier is zero will the contractionary effects on income offset the expansionary effects of government spending.

[16] On a more theoretical note, Keynes also diverted the focus of the macro model from the supply side to the demand side. In the Keynesian model, supply always adjusts to meet demand. If demand changes, a new equilibrium results due to the adjustments in supply. Before Keynes, the focus was primarily on the supply side and the macro model was ruled by *Say's Law* which stated that demand always adjusted to meet supply. It will become more obvious, particularly in Chapters 13 and 14, how this change in focus has affected our economy.

that there was no reason for the equilibrium level of the economy to necessarily be consistent with full employment. The Keynesian theory provided a straightforward and simple solution to unemployment. Demand could be manipulated through government spending and taxing so as to drive the economy toward a full-employment equilibrium. And because of the multiplier principle, government spending or taxing would only have to be changed a fraction of the desired change in income.

Some of the major findings of this chapter have been:

1. Equilibrium output occurs at the income level at which aggregate demand—planned spending by households on consumption, planned investment by businesses, and government purchases of goods and services—is equal to the value of production, or where total leakages are equal to total injections.
2. The existence of undesired inventories causes the income level to adjust toward equilibrium.
3. A change in aggregate demand will result in a larger change in equilibrium income. This fact indicates that a multiplier is associated with a change in aggregate demand.
4. The equilibrium output level need not generate full employment.
5. Keynes felt government should manipulate the *AD* curve through government spending changes and tax policy changes so as to ensure that equilibrium output would occur at full employment. This type of policy is called *fiscal policy*.
6. Multipliers are associated with changes in both government spending and taxes. The government spending multiplier is larger than the tax multiplier. This result is due to the fact that tax changes affect aggregate demand indirectly by changing disposable income and then consumption.
7. The *government deficit* is defined as the amount that government spending exceeds tax revenues.
8. Expansionary fiscal policy does not require increases in the deficit.

PROBLEMS AND EXERCISES

1. Discuss the relationship, if any, between the government budget deficit (or surplus) and equilibrium income.

2. Consider the following data:

Y	Consumption (C)	Investment (I)
0	180	90
300	360	120
600	540	150
900	720	180
1200	900	210
1500	1080	240

   a. At the Income Level 1,200, what is the average propensity to consume (APC) and save (APS)?

b. What is the value of autonomous consumption? the marginal propensity to consume?

c. Write the equation that represents the consumption schedule, savings schedule, and investment schedule for this economy.

d. What is the value of equilibrium income?

e. Show that the 45° model approach and leakages-injection approach yield the same value for equilibrium income.

3. Explain the concept of *equilibrium* as used in macroeconomics. Is the economy ever in equilibrium? How can the idea of a *business cycle* be interpreted in the context of equilibrium?

4. During 1974-75, the United States economy was in a serious recession. In the last quarter of 1975, most signs indicated the trough of the recession had been in July, 1975. At this time, President Ford proposed to cut taxes and government spending $28 billion each to aid the recovery. The Democrats countered by proposing that only taxes should be cut.

a. Discuss and evaluate these two proposals.

b. During 1980-81 and then 1982-83 the U.S. again fell into recession. During the recession the Democrats suggested raising taxes to balance the budget. President Reagan resisted. Evaluate their positions.

5. Suppose the economy is described by the following equations:

$$Y = C + I + G$$
$$C = 100 + 0.75 \ (Y - T)$$
$$T = 100$$
$$G = 150$$
$$I = 125$$

a. What is the equilibrium level of income?

b. At the equilibrium level of income, is the government running a surplus or a deficit?

c. Assume the full-employment level of income is $1,500. How would you characterize this economy? Suppose you are asked to recommend policies to improve the state of the economy. What is the appropriate change in government expenditure? What will happen to the government's budget position if such a policy is enacted?

d. Instead of a change in government expenditures, a change in taxes could be advocated. What is the appropriate change in taxes, and what will happen to the government budget position?

e. Could the state of the economy be improved without incurring an increase in the government budget deficit? How?

6. Consider the model in which both government spending and taxes are autonomous. If the present income level exceeds the equilibrium income level, will the economy automatically move to the equilibrium level? Explain.

7. In a model with government spending and taxes (exogenous), we defined consumption spending to be a function of disposable income, or

$$C = C_0 + c_y (Y_0)$$

   a. Derive the corresponding saving function.
   b. Throughout this chapter, all of the behavioral relationships have been drawn in diagrams with income (Y) on the horizontal axis. Why?
   c. If the saving function derived in a is to be plotted in a diagram with income (Y) on the horizontal axis, what will the intercept of this function be equal to?

8. In this chapter we discovered that policymakers could employ fiscal policy to manage the economy and maintain a balanced budget. Explain why an equal change in taxes and government spending will result in a change in income.

SUGGESTED READINGS

For a review of economic policy during the Great Depression, see

Cary E. Brown, "Fiscal Policy in the Thirties: A Reappraisal," *American Economic Review* (December, 1956), pp. 857-879.

Karl Brunner, ed., *Contemporary Views of the Great Depression* (Hingham, Mass.: Martinus Nijhoff Pubs., 1980).

Michael Darby, "Three and a Half Million U.S. Employees Have Been Mislaid: Or, an Explanation of Unemployment, 1934-1941," *Journal of Political Economy* (February, 1976).

Milton Friedman and Anna J. Schwartz, *A Monetary History of the United States 1867-1960* (Princeton, N.J.: Princeton University Press, 1963).

Charles Kindleberger, *The World in Depression, 1929-1939* (Berkeley: University of California Press, 1973).

John B. Kirkwood, "The Great Depression: A Structural Analysis," *Journal of Money, Credit and Banking* (November, 1972).

Thomas Mayer, "Money and the Great Depression: A Critique of Professor Temin's Thesis," *Explorations in Economic History* (April, 1978).

Peter Temin, *Did Monetary Forces Cause the Great Depression?* (New York: W. W. Norton & Co., Inc., 1976).

A more popular and accessible treatment is given in

John Kenneth Galbraith, *The Great Crash, Nineteen Twenty-Nine*. (London, England: H. Hamish Hamilton, Ltd., 1955).

Two classic studies of interest to students of the Great Depression are

Robert A. Gordon, *Economic Instability: The American Record* (New York: Harper & Row, Publishers, Inc., 1974), especially Chapter 3.

John Maynard Keynes, *The General Theory of Employment, Interest and Money* (New York: Harcourt, Brace and World, Inc., 1935).

President Roosevelt's views on the Depression are chronicled in

Franklin D. Roosevelt, *The Public Papers and Addresses of Franklin D. Roosevelt* (New York: Random House, Inc., 1938).

_APPENDIX 3A. Two Extensions of the Basic Model_____

In the following chapters we will examine the implication and impacts of the Roosevelt years and of the Keynesian prescriptions for the economy. In this appendix, we introduce two minor modifications to the model.

Induced Investment_____

Investment spending is not just a fixed amount that is independent of developments in the economy. Rather, businesses decide to increase their capital equipment (buildings, machines, etc.) when they expect profits to increase. Profits, in turn, often result from increased sales. Thus, planned investment spending should be specified as being induced by sales or consumption. However, since consumption depends on income, investment will ultimately depend on income as well. In equation form, we can write investment as

$$I = I_0 + I_y Y$$

This investment function states that investment depends on the level of income (Y). As Y goes up, I goes up since I_y is positive. As with the consumption function, the constant term I_0 reflects the influences of variables such as expectations, credit conditions, government regulations, and so on that have a direct impact on the level of investment independently of income. For example, if businesses became very pessimistic about future economic conditions they might reduce investment even though sales or income had not changed. In this case, I_0 would fall.

The primary implication of specifying that investment depends on income is that any time income changes, consumption and investment (rather than just consumption) will also change. This has ramifications for the determination of equilibrium and for the multiplier. In the simpler model, an increase in autonomous spending meant new income which, in turn, induced new consumption. In this more complex model if autonomous spending rises, income will increase which induces more consumption spending. In addition, the increased income means more investment spending as businesses foresee an increased demand for their products. Because the increased spending induces both more consumption and more investment, the resulting change in income will be larger than it would have been in the simpler model. In other words, the size of the multiplier increases as more income dependent spending is introduced into the model.

The implications of the more realistic investment function show up graphically and algebraically. In Table 3 A-1 we have altered the I, AD,

Table 3A-1. Autonomous and Induced Investment

Y	I_{old}	I_{new}	AD_{old}	AD_{new}	$I + G_{old}$	$I + G_{new}$
0	100	100	220	220	160	160
100	100	110	300	310	160	170
200	100	120	380	400	160	180
300	100	130	460	490	160	190
400	100	140	540	580	160	200
500	100	150	620	670	160	210
600	100	160	700	760	160	220
700	100	170	780	850	160	230
800	100	180	860	940	160	240
900	100	190	940	1,030	160	250
1,000	100	200	1,020	1,120	160	260
1,100	100	210	1,100	1,210	160	270
1,200	100	220	1,180	1,300	160	280
1,300	100	230	1,260	1,390	160	290
1,400	100	240	1,340	1,480	160	300

Table 3-5 is altered by using the investment equation $I = 100 + 0.1Y$ rather than $I = 100$. The impact of specifying investment as dependent on income is shown in the comparisons of I_{old}, I_{new}, AD_{old}, AD_{new}, and $I + G_{old}$, $I + G_{new}$.

and $I + G$ columns of Table 3-5 by using the investment specification $I = 100 + 0.1Y$. Notice how the difference between the old and new values gets larger as income gets larger. (Can you explain this?)

Graphically, when investment is just a constant, or is autonomous, the investment line is horizontal. Now with investment induced by income, the investment line has a positive slope. Therefore, as shown in Figure 3A-1, the aggregate demand curve has a slope that equals the sum of the slopes of the consumption and investment lines. Thus the *AD* line is steeper when both investment and consumption depend on income than when just consumption depends on income.

What do these alterations mean for the effect of an autonomous spending change? Since income changes induce changes in both consumption and investment, we should expect a given change in autonomous spending to have a greater impact on the economy than when only consumption depended on income. It is relatively straightforward to demonstrate that this is indeed the case. Graphically, you could draw a new *AD* curve on Figure 3A-1 that intersects the demand axis at a level that is, say, $10 less, and find the income level at which the *AD* curve crosses the 45° line. Or you could complete Table 3A-1 and then create a new column after altering autonomous demand by $10. Algebraically, the differences show up in the size of the multiplier.

Figure 3A-1. Determination of Equilibrium Output in a Model with Induced Investment

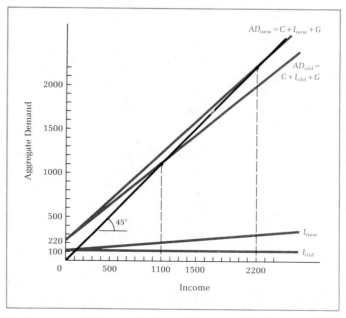

The introduction of induced investment does not affect the way the aggregate demand curve is derived. The various components of demand are still added vertically. Equilibrium output is still determined by the intersection of the aggregate demand and 45° lines. However, making investment vary with income does affect the slope of the investment and aggregate demand lines. With investment dependent on income, the investment line has a positive slope. As a result the aggregate demand line has a steeper slope as compared to the aggregate demand line with an autonomous investment demand.

Taxes that Change as Income Changes

The lump sum tax is a useful representation of taxes in the Keynesian model. It is not, however, a very realistic representation of the United States tax system. The major tax in the U.S. is the personal income tax, a tax that depends on individual incomes. It generates 43 percent of all federal tax revenues.

What is the effect of introducing the income dependent tax? Consider what happens when autonomous spending increases. Suppose demand increases thereby driving up the level of income which, as we have previously observed, induces more consumption and investment. With taxes that depend on income, the increase in income also means more taxes must be paid. And an increase in taxes reduces the disposable income that individuals and businesses have to spend. Thus, the total induced spending that results from an increase in autonomous demand is reduced by the increase in taxes.

The initial change in autonomous spending causes a change in production and income which, in turn, induces a further change in demand (induced consumption and investment). An income tax works in just the opposite direction. As production and income begin to rise, taxes rise, leaving less income to be disposed of and, thus, less induced spending. The result, as presented in Figure 3A-2A, is that the level of production,

Figure 3A-2. Implications of Taxes That Vary with Income

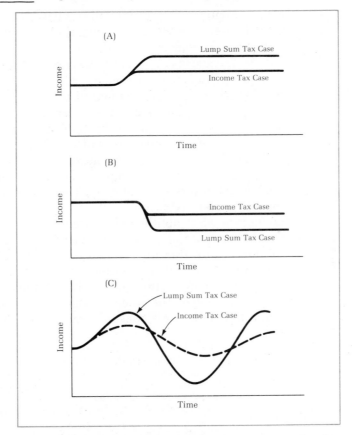

An important characteristic of the United States tax system is that the tax liability increases as income increases. With this type of tax structure changes in autonomous demand have much smaller output effects than when the tax liability does not vary with income. The reason is that the induced increases in consumption and investment that follow an autonomous demand increase are much smaller under a tax system that varies with income due to the increased tax leakages. Panel A illustrates the output effect in the face of an autonomous demand increase. On the other hand, the output effects in the face of a decrease in autonomous demand are less severe. This is shown in Panel B. The fact that output effects are less under a tax system with *endogenous taxes* (taxes dependent on income) means the business cycle is less severe. This is illustrated in Panel C.

income, and demand will not rise as much when taxes depend on income as when they do not. Similarly, as shown in Figure 3A-2B, if production and income should begin to decline, taxes will fall, leaving more income available for spending. The effect of the income tax is to smooth out or stabilize fluctuations in the economy, as represented in Figure 3A-2C.[1]

An Introduction to Nondiscretionary Fiscal Policy

In the previous sections, we discussed how tax and government spending changes could be used to manipulate equilibrium. This type of fiscal policy is known as *discretionary policy*. The introduction of a proportional income tax allows us to discuss another type of fiscal policy, called *nondiscretionary fiscal policy*.

The idea behind nondiscretionary fiscal policy is that any time income changes, tax revenues and the government's budget position will change without any overt action by policymakers. In other words, an automatic fiscal policy change takes place. This characteristic of income taxes is referred to as an *automatic stabilizer*. As we saw in Figure 3A-2, the business cycle is smoothed out or stabilized by the income tax. This stabilizing effect occurs automatically. There are no new laws passed by government to alter taxes.

The income tax is not the only automatic stabilizer. Any instrument that stimulates or decreases spending in a countercyclical manner; that is, in the opposite direction to the change in income, is referred to as an *automatic stabilizer*. Other examples of automatic stabilizers include unemployment compensation and welfare payments. When a worker becomes unemployed, the unemployment compensation he receives allows him to maintain his consumption. This decreases the multiplier

---

[1] Notice that if either taxes or investment depend on income the balanced budget multiplier will not be unity. Suppose we use the model where investment depends on income but taxes are of the lump sum variety. The government spending multiplier is $1/(1 - c_y - I_y)$ and the lump sum tax multiplier is $-c_y/(1 - c_y - I_y)$. Thus the total effect on output due to an equal increase (or decrease) in government spending and taxes is

$$\Delta Y = \frac{1}{1 - c_y - I_y} \Delta G + \left(\frac{-c_y}{1 - c_y - I_y} \right) \Delta T$$

Since $\Delta G = \Delta T$ then

$$\Delta Y = \frac{1}{1 - c_y - I_y} \Delta G + \left(\frac{-c}{1 - c_y - I_y} \right) \Delta G$$

$$= \frac{1 - c_y}{1 - c_y - I_y} \Delta G$$

Thus, the balanced budget multiplier is greater than unity in this case.

effect of a demand decrease because the decline in income does not lead to as large a decline in consumption.

An automatic stabilizer appears to be a good thing when we are discussing its role in reducing the magnitude of economic downturns. However, note that the automatic stabilizer also slows down increases in output. This is shown in Figure 3A-2A. A fiscal policy directed toward stimulating the economy would, if effective, begin increasing output and income. However, as income increases taxes increase, thus reducing the amount of new income that could be spent. This dampening effect is known as *fiscal drag*. Also notice what occurs to the government budget as the economy declines. Keeping government expenditures the same during a recession means that the government runs a deficit as tax revenues decline. This has several implications for the economy and for policymakers, as we shall see in Chapters 12-14.

The U.S. income tax system was instituted in 1913 although tax rates were not of any significant size until the early 1940s. Social Security came into being in 1933 and unemployment compensation was begun in the 1930s. Thus the importance of automatic stabilizers has grown steadily since the 1930s. What has this meant for the economy? We can obtain a fair estimate by examining the size of multipliers before and since the 1930s. We should expect the multiplier to be smaller now due to the automatic stabilizers. Professors Hickman and Coen have derived spending multipliers using a large macro model.[2] They found that the effect on output due to a change in spending in the previous quarter, was 3.23 for the period 1926-40 and 1.88 for the period 1951-65. Thus, for a given change in spending, the level of output or income would have risen more during the 1926-40 period than during 1951-65.

---

[2] B. G. Hickman and R. M. Coen, *An Annual Growth Model of the U. S. Economy* (Amsterdam: North-Holland, 1976), p. 194.

_APPENDIX 3B. Algebraic Presentation of the Simple Keynesian Model_____

Income (Y) can be divided into a consumption component and a saving component. Therefore, if we substitute the consumption function, $C = C_0 + c_yY$, into the income identity, $Y \equiv C+S$, we find

(3B-1) $Y = C_0 + c_yY + S$

If Equation 3B-1 is solved for saving, we find

(3B-2) $S = -C_0 + (1-c_y)Y$

Equation 3B-2 is the algebraic form of the saving function.

The intercept of the saving function, or the autonomous portion of saving, is the negative of the autonomous portion of consumption. This should not be surprising since when income is zero there is still consumption. However, this consumption spending can only be financed by drawing down savings—negative saving.

The slope of the saving function is $1-c_y$, the marginal propensity to save. The slopes of the consumption and saving functions are not necessarily equal. In fact, they are equal only when the marginal propensity to consume (c_y) and the marginal propensity to save $(1-c_y)$ are equal. In addition, if we add the slopes of the consumption and saving functions together, it is clear they sum to unity.

Determination of Equilibrium Income_____

In the simplest model, the equations that constitute the aggregate demand model are

(3B-3) $Y = C + I_p$
(3B-4) $C = C_0 + c_yY$
(3B-5) $I_p = I_0$

Equation 3B-3 is an equilibrium condition that states for equilibrium to exist, the value of output (Y) must be equal to aggregate demand $C + I_p$. The second and third equations are called *behavioral equations*. They describe behavior. Equation 3B-4 represents the consumption function.

Equation 3B-5 represents investment behavior. It says that planned investment spending is constant at level I_0.

In order to solve the model for equilibrium income, Equations 3B-4 and -5 must be substituted into Equation 3B-3. Carrying this out we obtain

$$\text{(3B-6)} \qquad \begin{aligned} Y &= C + I_p \\ &= C_0 + c_y Y + I_0 \end{aligned}$$

Since we are seeking the one value of Y at which the value of output will be equal to total demand, we must solve for Y. The result is the equilibrium level of income.

$$\text{(3B-7)} \qquad Y = \frac{1}{1 - c_y}(C_0 + I_0)$$

An alternative method of determining equilibrium income is to find the income level at which saving and investment are equal. The algebraic form of this model is

$$\text{(3B-8)} \qquad S = I_p$$

$$\text{(3B-9)} \qquad I_p = I_0$$

$$\text{(3B-10)} \qquad S = -C_0 + (1 - c_y)Y$$

The solution of this model requires the substitution of Equations 3B-9 and -10 into Equation 3B-8. That is,

$$\text{(3B-11)} \qquad \begin{aligned} S &= I_0 \\ -C_0 + (1 - c_y)Y &= I_0 \end{aligned}$$

Add C_0 to both sides of Equation 3B-11 in order to isolate Y on one side of the equation.

$$\text{(3B-12)} \qquad (1 - c_y)Y = C_0 + I_0$$

Then, divide both sides of Equation 3B-12 by $1 - c_y$. The result is

$$\text{(3B-13)} \qquad Y = \frac{1}{1 - c_y}(C_0 + I_0)$$

Notice that the solution for equilibrium income is the same in both approaches. Equation 3B-13 is the same as Equation 3B-7.

Determination of Equilibrium Income When a Government Sector Is Included

The principles utilized in the simplest model apply to the model with the government sector as well. The model including the government sector with a lump sum tax is

(3B-14)	$Y = AD$	Equilibrium condition
(3B-15)	$AD \equiv C + I_p + G$	Definition of aggregate demand
(3B-16)	$C = C_0 + c_y(Y - T)$	Consumption as a function of disposable income
(3B-17)	$I_p = I_0$	Investment is autonomous
(3B-18)	$G = G_0$	Government purchases are fixed
(3B-19)	$T = T_0$	Lump sum taxes

Equilibrium is found by substituting Equations 3B-16 through -19 into the equilibrium Equation 3B-14 after Equation 3B-14 and Equation 3B-15 have been combined. The equilibrium equation is

(3B-20) $$Y = C_0 + c_y (Y - T_0) + I_0 + G_0$$

Once again, solving for equilibrium yields

(3B-21) $$Y = \frac{1}{1 - c_y}(C_0 - c_y T_0 + I_0 + G_0)$$

It is also quite easy to solve for equilibrium income via the leakages-injections approach. However, before proceeding, the consumption function must be rewritten as a saving function. With a government sector we know that income can be spent, saved, or paid out in taxes. This is just the following basic accounting definition:

$$Y \equiv C + S + T$$

Or

(3B-22) $$S \equiv Y - C - T$$

Substituting the consumption function into Equation 3B-22 and simplifying yields

(3B-23) $$S = -C_0 + (1 - c_y)(Y - T)$$

Then equilibrium income can be found by substituting Equations 3B-17, -18, -19, and -23 into the equilibrium equation.

$$I + G = S + T$$

Making these substitutions and solving for Y yields the solution for equilibrium. That is,

(3B-24) $$Y = \frac{1}{1-c_y}(C_0 - c_y T_0 + I_0 + G_0)$$

Determination of Equilibrium: Induced Investment

Once we introduce investment as being dependent on income, the model consists of the following equations:

$Y = AD$	Equilibrium
$AD = C + I_p + G$	Definition of aggregate demand
$C = C_0 + c_y(Y-T)$	Consumption function
$I_p = I_0 + I_y Y$	Investment function
$G = G_0$	Government purchases
$T = T_0$	Lump sum taxes

Previously, the government spending multiplier formula was found to be

$$\Delta Y = \frac{1}{1-c_y}\Delta G$$

Now, a change in income can come about from an induced change in consumption and investment as well as from the autonomous change in demand. Algebraically we are saying that $\Delta Y = \Delta C + \Delta I + \Delta G$ and since $\Delta C = c_y(\Delta Y - \Delta T)$ and $\Delta I = I_y(\Delta Y)$ then $\Delta Y = c_y(\Delta Y - \Delta T) + I_y(\Delta Y) + \Delta G$. Since taxes are not changing ($\Delta T = 0$), we find

$$\Delta Y = \frac{1}{1-c_y-I_y}\Delta G$$

Why is the multiplier now $1/(1-c_y-I_y)$ rather than simply $1/(1-c_y)$?

PROBLEMS AND EXERCISES

A-1. Consider an economy described by the following functions (in billions of dollars):

$$Y = C + I + G$$
$$C = 100 + 0.5 \ (YD)$$
$$I = 40 + 0.1Y$$
$$G = 100$$
$$T = -30 + 0.2Y$$
$$YD = Y - T$$

a. Calculate the equilibrium level of income.

b. Calculate the government budget situation at equilibrium income.

c. What is the value of the government expenditure multiplier? How does the fact that both taxes and investment are functions of income affect this multiplier?

d. Show that the change in income generated by decreasing taxes by $10 billion (by decreasing T) is less than that which would be achieved by increasing government expenditures by the same amount. Explain why this is so.

e. If equilibrium income is $100 billion less than the full-employment income level, by how much must government spending be increased in order to obtain the full-employment income level? What happens to the government budget situation?

f. In this model, the effect of a change in government is fully felt immediately. In the real world, this is not likely to occur. Explain briefly.

A-2. What is meant by an automatic stabilizer? Demonstrate whether the proportional or lump sum tax works as an automatic stabilizer. What would you expect to be the case for the progressive income tax?

CHAPTER 4.

The Interaction between Money and Commodity Markets I: The *IS* and *LM* Curves

For my own part I am now somewhat skeptical of the success of a merely monetary policy directed towards influencing the rate of interest. I expect to see the state . . . on the basis of general social advantage, taking an ever greater responsibility for directly organizing investment.

John Maynard Keynes, 1936

In the framework of the previous chapter, money, interest rates, and monetary policy were ignored. In this chapter, a model, known as the IS-LM model, is developed to integrate money and interest rates into the Keynesian framework.

In this chapter we will answer the following questions:

- What does the IS curve represent?

- What causes the IS curve to shift?

- What does the LM curve represent?

- How does a change in the nominal money supply affect the LM curve?

Introduction: A Revival of Money

"Mortgage rates hit an all time high." "The president proposes that banks be allowed to pay higher interest rates on savings." "A survey of businesses indicates that the high interest rates are causing postponements in many investment projects." Statements such as these are found every day in general newspapers, news magazines, and in business newspapers and magazines. The pattern of monetary variables receives as much attention as any topic. The Wall Street Journal, for example, gives prominent coverage to the announcement each Friday of the money supply figures for the previous week. It is obvious from even a cursory glance at economic news that money and interest rates play very important roles in the economy.

This was not always the case. While prior to 1929 monetary factors were thought to be crucial influences on the economy, the Great Contraction of 1929-33 overturned this attitude. Money danced to the tune of business activity, not the other way around as had been believed prior to 1929. In addition, not only was money's influence on the economy considered to be slight, but any influence that did occur took place through a very narrow channel. Changes in the money stock were thought to (perhaps) affect interest rates which might then have an influence on investment.

The role of monetary variables in the Keynesian model was first clearly pointed out by Nobel Laureate John R. Hicks in 1937. Hicks developed a framework called the IS-LM model that integrated money and interest rates into the Keynesian demand model.[1] This model of the economy consists of two markets, the goods market and the money market. In the goods or commodity market, aggregate demand determines equilibrium output and income. In the money market, the demand for money and the supply of money determine the interest rate.

The extension provided by the *IS-LM* model is (1) to allow the stock of money to influence interest rates that, in turn, affect investment spending and (2) to consider the effect of changes in income on the demand for money. The principal outcome of the model is that changes in autonomous spending have smaller effects on equilibrium than was the case in the simple Keynesian model. The reason is as follows: an increase in investment generates an increase in income and spending which requires more money. The increased demand for money drives up interest rates which makes it more costly for business to undertake investment. This limits the increase in business spending and moderates subsequent expansions of income and output.

The purpose of this chapter is to detail the development of the *IS-LM* framework. In the first section of the chapter, the interest rate is introduced as a determinant of aggregate demand and the *IS* curve is developed. Having established the importance of the interest rate in the commodity market, the next order of business is to define factors that influence the level of interest rates. The result is another relationship between interest rates and income levels, but this time the relationship—represented by the *LM* curve—is in the financial markets.

The Commodity Market

Four general markets are traditionally considered in macroeconomics: one for goods and services, one for money, one for other assets, and one for labor. The discussion in Chapter 3 focused on what is termed the *commodity market*, the market for goods and services. In this section, the interest rate is introduced as an important variable in the determination of the demand for output. In the Keynesian framework the interest rate provides a means by which other markets can influence the commodity market. The level of equilibrium income depends on the value of the interest rate. Once the interest rate is introduced, a unique equilibrium income level can no longer be determined by considering the commodity market alone.

---

[1] The abbreviations *IS* and *LM* represent, in turn, goods market equilibrium (investment equals saving) and money market equilibrium (money demand—liquidity preference—equals money supply). These abbreviations and their respective curves were first presented by Sir John Hicks in his "Mr. Keynes and the 'Classics': A Suggested Interpretation," *Econometrica* (April, 1937), pp. 147-159, in an attempt to succinctly summarize the Keynesian model.

The Interest Rate and the Commodity Market

A business decision to purchase a machine or build a new plant depends on that business's expectation of the profitability of that particular investment project. In the first appendix to Chapter 3 we stated that expected profitability depended on expected sales and that sales depended on income. Investment spending was therefore specified to depend solely on the level of income or output. In reality, the profitability of an investment project also depends on the expected opportunity cost of that investment and in this way depends on the rate of interest.

In making an investment decision, a firm must calculate the expected rate of return from its proposed investment project. The *expected rate of return* is calculated by dividing the expected annual dollar earnings less all expenses (except interest payments on borrowed funds) by the cost of the asset. For example, suppose that a firm is contemplating the purchase of a machine expected to increase net earnings by $1,000 each year. Since the machine costs $10,000 the expected rate of return is 10 percent. The expected rate of return is then compared with the expected opportunity cost for the life of the investment. As a first example, suppose a firm has $10,000 sitting in its cash drawer. The firm is contemplating the purchase of a machine that has a rate of return of 10 percent. The firm can make this investment decision by comparing the 10 percent return on investment with the opportunity cost of $10,000. But what is the opportunity cost of $10,000? The firm can put the $10,000 in a savings account and earn perhaps 6 percent. If this is the firm's best alternative to buying the machine, then the opportunity cost of the $10,000 is 6 percent. In this case, the machine should be purchased because the expected return on the investment exceeds the expected return from the savings account.

Now, consider the situation where the firm does not have the required amount of cash on hand for the investment, but instead must borrow the money at, say, a 6 percent interest rate. Obviously, the expected rate of return must exceed the borrowing cost or interest rate if the investment project is to be undertaken. Again, no matter the source of funds, the investment project should be undertaken if the expected rate of return exceeds the opportunity cost.

Suppose our firm is contemplating the purchase of not just one machine for $10,000, but two or more of these machines. The rates of return from various investment alternatives are presented in Table 4-1. As more machines are purchased, the expected rate of return decreases. This is because of the decreasing efficiency as more machines are installed. If the interest rate is 5 percent, the firm can borrow $30,000 and purchase three machines. However, if the interest rate is 9 percent the firm will find it profitable to purchase only one machine. Notice that this simple example points out the important relationship between interest rates and desired investment spending; i.e., higher interest rates lead to less investment. In

Table 4-1. Investment Alternatives

NUMBER OF MACHINES	TOTAL AMOUNT OF INVEST- MENT	EXPECTED RATE OF RETURN ON LAST MACHINE
1	$10,000	10%
2	$20,000	8%
3	$30,000	6%

sum, we specify investment spending (I) to be determined by the real income level (Y) and the interest rate (r). This relationship is captured in the following equation:

(4-1) $I = I(Y, \quad r)$ or $I = I_0 + I_y Y - I_r r$
                    $(+) \ (-)$

where

    I_0 is the autonomous component of investment spending
    I_y measures the sensitivity of investment spending to income
    I_r measures the sensitivity of investment spending to the interest rate
    The plus or minus sign under the variable indicates the direction of the
    relationship between I and Y or r

It might be argued that the interest rate is not only a determinant of investment spending, but is also a determinant of consumption spending. For example, a consumer might undertake more borrowing (consumer installment debt) if interest rates are relatively low. In what follows, we will assume that the interest rate does not influence consumption spending, although this assumption could be changed without invalidating the discussion.[2] In equation form, consumption (C) is specified to depend positively $(+)$ on disposable income (YD).

(4-2) $C = C(YD)$ or $C = C_0 + c_y(YD)$
                    $(+)$

In the previous chapter, equilibrium income was determined by setting aggregate demand equal to the value of output produced, or alternatively, by setting total leakages equal to total injections. These approaches

---

[2] From a technical point of view it can be argued that the change in consumption spending due to an interest rate change is properly captured in the investment function. Consumption should measure current consumption. When a consumer durable is purchased, this good yields a stream of services beyond the current period. Thus, if consumption is to be measured correctly, it should include only the imputed consumption from durables. The remainder of the purchase price of a consumer durable could be considered investment.

will be taken again as equilibrium is derived in a model with investment explained by the interest rate as well as the income level.

As a first step in our attempt to graphically derive equilibrium income, the components of aggregate demand—consumption, investment, and government spending—must be added. Since the consumption demand and government spending curves have not changed from the previous chapter, the curves are not presented in Figure 4-1. The investment function, however, has been changed. Notice that on the vertical axis in Figure 4-1, the components of demand are measured. There is no explicit measurement of the interest rate. Thus, we must take the interest rate into account by including it as part of the intercept. (Any time a variable is not measured on the axis, it will affect the intercept.) Notice from the investment equation $(I = I_0 - I_r r + I_y Y)$ that $I_0 - I_r r$ is the intercept. With the interest rate as part of the intercept, the intercept will change each time the interest rate changes. Thus, to be able to plot just one investment curve we must choose just one interest rate. In Figure 4-1, for example, investment curve $I(r_1)$ is drawn by assuming that the interest rate is r_1. The aggregate demand curve is derived by vertically summing the investment, consumption, and government spending curves. The demand curve AD (r_1) in Figure 4-1 is drawn given that the interest rate is r_1. In order to emphasize that the aggregate demand curve depends on the value of the interest rate, the aggregate demand curve is identified as $C + I(r_1) + G$ where $I(r_1)$ denotes that the investment curve was drawn for a specific interest rate.

The equilibrium income level is determined by the intersection of the aggregate demand curve and the 45-degree line. In terms of figure 4-1, the value Y_1 is the equilibrium income level when the interest rate is r_1. However, since aggregate demand depends on a specific interest rate, so does equilibrium. What happens if the interest rate changes? From 1929 to 1939 interest rates (measured as the 4-6 month commercial paper rate) dropped from 5.85 percent to 0.59 percent. At the much lower interest rate we would have expected more investment to have been undertaken at each level of sales (or output, or income). Graphically, this means the investment function shifts upward by the amount $- I_r$ times the change in the interest rate, Δr, or by $- I_r \Delta r$. The intercept is now $I_0 - I_r r_1 - I_r \Delta r$ which is larger than $I_0 - I_r r_1$.[3] The new investment curve is associated with the lower interest rate r_2. In addition, the aggregate demand curve shifts up by the amount $- I_r \Delta r$. That is, for each income level the quantity demanded will be higher at the lower interest rate than it was at the higher interest rate. The new aggregate demand curve is identified as $AD(r_2) = C + I(r_2) + G$ in Figure 4-1, and the intersection between the new aggregate demand curve and the 45-degree line shows that equilibrium

---

[3] Notice that $\Delta r = r_2 - r_1$ is negative because r_1 is larger than r_2.

Figure 4-1. *The Dependence of Demand on Interest Rates*

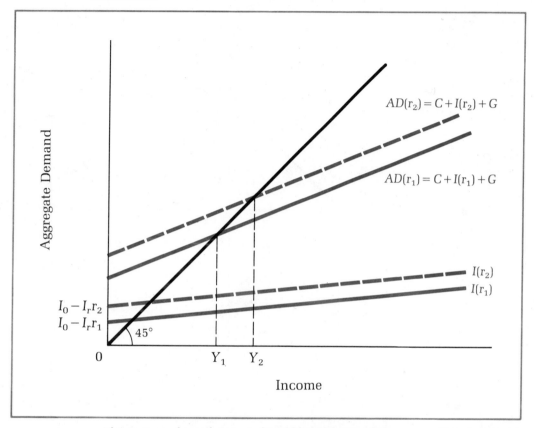

The aggregate demand curve is derived by vertically adding consumption, investment, and government demand. Investment demand, and thus aggregate demand, can be drawn only if a particular interest rate is assumed. If the interest rate is r_1, then the investment demand function is $I(r_1)$ and the aggregate demand curve is $AD(r_1) = C + I(r_1) + G$. For this interest rate, the commodity market will be in equilibrium at the income level Y_1. At the lower interest rate (r_2) equilibrium income is Y_2.

income has increased to Y_2. In sum, a different interest rate results in a different equilibrium income level.

A lower interest rate is typically associated with a higher equilibrium income level. This relationship can be shown graphically by plotting the various combinations of equilibrium income and interest rates with income measured on the horizontal axis and the interest rate measured on the vertical axis. In Figure 4-2B, for example, the combinations of interest rates and equilibrium income levels derived in Figure 4-2A are plotted. The procedure of varying the interest rate, finding the corresponding equilibrium income level, and plotting the income-interest rate combination yields the *IS* or *commodity market equilibrium curve.*

Figure 4-2. Derivation of an IS Curve

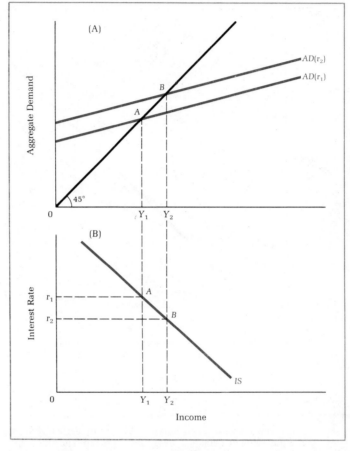

Using the *AD* curves of Panel A the combinations of equilibrium income and interest rates can be traced out. At r_1, the equilibrium income level Y_1 is plotted as Point A in Figure 4-2B. By assuming other interest rates, such as r_2, and then finding the corresponding market clearing income level, a locus of interest rates and income levels that clears the commodity market can be traced out in the lower frame. This locus of points is known as the *IS* curve.

The *IS* curve represents all combinations of interest rates and income levels that clear the commodity market. The curve is negatively sloped reflecting the inverse relationship between the interest rate and equilibrium income which, in turn, is due to the effect of interest rates on investment spending.

Derivation of the *IS* Curve via the Leakages and Injections Diagram

The results derived in this section could just as easily have been derived through the leakages-injections approach. Recall that equilibrium income occurs where total injections are equal to total leakages. The total leakage curve is found by adding the saving and tax functions. Injections in this model are investment and government spending. Since government expenditures are assumed not to be a function of income, this injection can be represented by a horizontal line at the level G_0. As we discussed previously, with investment a function of both the interest rate and income level the investment curve can be drawn only if we assume a particular interest rate. Having done this, total injections are then found by summing investment and government spending.

In Figure 4-3A the injection and leakage functions are plotted under the assumption that the interest rate is r_1. Total leakages and injections are

Figure 4-3. The Leakage-Injection Approach

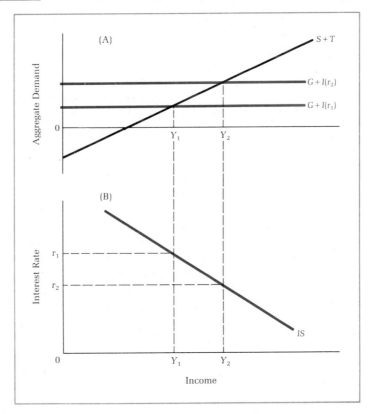

Total leakages, plotted as $S + T$, increase as income increases. Total injections, plotted as $G + I(r)$, do not depend on income and thus are horizontal lines at a level dependent on the interest rate. The greater the interest rate the less the investment and the lower the $G + I$ line. For example, r_2 is less than r_1 which means the $G + I(r_2)$ line is above the $G + I(r_1)$ line. Each intersection between the leakages and injections line determines one point on the IS curve (Panel B). As the interest rate is decreased, $G + I$ increases and the equilibrium level of income is increased to Y_2.

equal at the income level Y_1, and the interest rate-income combination (r_1, Y_1) (representing one point of equilibrium in the commodity market) is plotted in Figure 4-3B. If we choose another interest rate, a different equilibrium income level will be found. Suppose, for example, we lower the interest rate to r_2. As the interest rate is lowered the injections curve shifts upward. This results in a new equilibrium income level (Y_2) as shown in Figure 4-3A. This interest rate-income combination (r_2, Y_2) is also plotted in Figure 4-3B. An IS curve is traced out as more interest rates and the corresponding equilibrium income levels are plotted.

Changes in the Position of the IS Curve: The Roaring Twenties

In deriving the IS curve, the interest rate was varied to see how equilibrium income would change. Then, the interest rate and resulting income levels were plotted. Implicit in this procedure was the assumption that all other variables are held constant. What happens to the IS curve if one of these variables does change?

Let us first consider an example in which one of the autonomous variables C_0, I_0, T_0, or G_0 changes. The decade of the 1920s began somewhat ominously with a bank panic and an economic downturn during 1920-21. But with a rapid recovery an era of optimism set in. Businesses and individuals alike saw only roses on the horizon. The prevailing attitude in 1921 was that a strong economy would last forever. This shift to a more bullish or more optimistic view of the economy's performance can be thought of as an autonomous investment increase—more spending on machinery and buildings to increase capacity in order to meet the public's desire for goods and services.

How can the IS curve be used to represent this increase in autonomous investment? The IS curve in Figure 4-4 is traced out under the assumption that autonomous investment is at its original 1919 level. The aggregate demand curve is denoted with $I(I_0, r_1)$ to indicate that this amount of total expenditure occurs when the autonomous investment level is I_0 and the interest rate is r_1. Similarly, the IS curve is denoted by the autonomous investment level $IS(I_0)$. The interest rate is not included in the parentheses since it is not held constant along the IS curve.

In Chapter 3, when autonomous investment increased, the investment curve shifted up by the amount of the change in investment spending. In this chapter, we have noted that a different investment curve exists for each possible interest rate. Hence, the investment curve associated with each interest rate shifts up by the amount of the change in autonomous investment. For example, at interest rate r_1 the more bullish environment is represented by an upward shift of the investment curve which causes the aggregate demand curve to also shift up by the amount of the change in autonomous investment. Thus, in terms of Figure 4-4, the aggregate

<u>Figure 4-4.</u> *Effect on the IS Curve of an Increase in*
Autonomous Investment

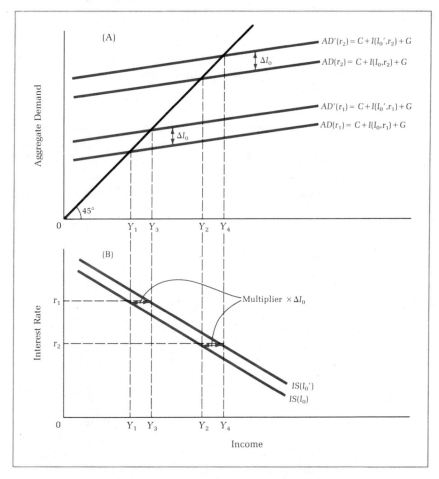

The original IS curve is denoted $IS(I_0)$. An increase in autonomous investment causes the IS curve to shift outward and to the right. The reason for such a shift can be clearly seen by considering the aggregate demand curve for a particular interest rate, r_1. The increase in autonomous investment causes the aggregate demand curve to shift up by ΔI_0. As a result of this change and the existence of a multiplier, equilibrium income increases by ΔI_0 times the multiplier or from Y_1 to Y_3. This interest rate and income level combination is one point on a new IS curve. By considering other interest rates, the new IS curve can be traced out.

demand curve (given interest rate r_1) shifts from the position denoted by $AD = C + I(I_0, r_1) + G$ to the position $AD' = C + I(I_0', r_1) + G$. At the new autonomous investment level (I_0') and the original interest rate (r_1) equilibrium income has risen to Y_3. By plotting this combination (r_1, Y_3) in Figure 4-4B, we obtain a point off the original IS curve.

At a lower interest rate, say r_2, the change in autonomous investment shifts both the investment curve and the aggregate demand curve associated with that interest rate upward. Thus a new equilibrium income for the interest rate r_2 is generated. Again, plotting this new combination (r_2, Y_4), we have a point off the original IS curve. By continuing to vary the interest rate and finding the corresponding equilibrium income levels, a new IS curve (IS') can be traced out.

The Multiplier

One of the important concepts developed in Chapter 3 was the idea of a multiplier. Recall from Chapter 3 that a change in autonomous investment led to a larger change in income. More precisely, the change in income due to a change in autonomous investment is equal to the autonomous investment multiplier times the change in autonomous investment, ΔI_0. Figure 4-4 shows that at the interest rate r_1, income increases from Y_1 to Y_3 due to an increase in autonomous investment. The horizontal distance between $IS(I_0)$ and $IS(I_0')$, which is the change in income at each interest rate, is equal to the multiplier times the change in autonomous investment.

Parameter Changes: The Great Crash Again

In addition to the various autonomous variables, the coefficients on income (c_y and I_y) and the coefficient on the interest rate (I_r) were held constant in the derivation of the IS curve. These coefficients measure the sensitivity or responsiveness of one variable to a change in another variable. Now, let us consider how a change in a parameter affects the IS curve.

The 1929-33 crash not only depressed economic conditions, but it also crushed America's optimism regarding the future. The public questioned whether recovery was even possible. This attitude also permeated the business sector. Hence, it should not be surprising that although interest rates fell dramatically, from 5 percent in 1929 to 0.5 percent in 1933, investment projects did not look profitable.

In the 1920s, the outlook had been substantially different. In response to the overly expansionary policies it had been pursuing during the previous two years, the Federal Reserve put on the brakes in 1920 and subsequently allowed banks to raise their interest rates. The rise, 1.5 percent, was the most rapid since the Federal Reserve System (the Fed) had been established in 1913. The result was a contraction in investment spending and, hence equilibrium income, leading to one of the sharpest declines on record until that point. Output was nearly 6 percent lower in 1921 than it had been in 1920. The 1920-21 contraction was followed by an extremely vigorous expansion as interest rates dropped back to their pre-1920 levels.

The fact that investment spending reacted dramatically to the increase in interest rates in the 1920s, while not reacting to the lower interest rates in the 1930s, led many to claim that the interest sensitivity of investment spending had declined over the decade of the twenties. It appeared that investment was more a function of the ever changing and unpredictable expectations of business than it was of interest rates. The interest sensitivity of investment shows up in the slope of the *IS* curve. A decrease in I_r means any given change in interest rates will cause a smaller change in investment spending and, thus, aggregate demand.[4] Hence, the *IS* curve will be steeper, the less sensitive is investment to interest rate changes. We might then represent the 1920s view as a relatively flat *IS* curve and the 1930's view as a relatively steep *IS* curve.

In summary, any change in the sensitivity of spending to interest or income will cause a rotation of the *IS* curve; that is, it will cause a change in its slope. Any change in the autonomous variables, the *ceteris paribus* variables, will cause a shift of the *IS* curve. These results are summarized in Table 4-2.

Table 4-2. Changes That Shift or Rotate the IS Curve

VARIABLE/PARAMETER	CHANGE	ROTATE	SHIFT
Government spending	Increase		Outward
	Decrease		Inward
Taxes (lump sum)	Increase		Inward
	Decrease		Outward
Autonomous investment	Increase		Outward
	Decrease		Inward
Autonomous consumption	Increase		Outward
	Decrease		Inward
Marginal propensity to consume (c_y)	Increase	Counterclockwise	
	Decrease	Clockwise	
Interest sensitivity coefficient of investment function	Increase	Counterclockwise	
	Decrease	Clockwise	
Income sensitivity coefficient of investment function	Increase	Counterclockwise	
	Decrease	Clockwise	

---

[4] A numerical example may be helpful in explaining this sentence. Suppose $I_0 = 100$ and the initial values of I_r and r are 50 and 0.1 respectively. If the value of I_r doubles, the intercept of the investment function changes by 5 at an interest rate of 0.1. Now, consider an interest rate of 0.2. A doubling of I_r at this interest rate causes the intercept

The Money Market

The *IS* curve represents all possible equilibrium income and interest rate levels in the commodity market. To determine any particular income level, the interest rate must be known. The purpose of this section is to describe how the interest rate is determined.

Individuals have a choice as to the form in which they would like to hold their wealth. This choice is referred to as their *portfolio decision*. At any time, individuals have a given amount of income or wealth that could have been derived from earned income or from the return on previous financial decisions. Individuals must decide how much to spend and how much to save (as given by the average propensity to consume and the average propensity to save) and, then, how best to allocate their savings among various financial assets (the portfolio decision).

In the simplest model, the portfolio decision consists of a choice between the holding of money and the holding of bonds. Which will be chosen? If bonds are used to represent all interest-earning assets and money to represent all noninterest-earning assets, then individuals are likely to hold some of both assets. If their wealth is held entirely in bonds they earn maximum interest, but then have nothing with which to carry out transactions. On the other hand, if no bonds are held no interest earnings are obtained.[5] The aggregate portfolio decision; that is, the economy's portfolio decision, would then simply be the allocation of the economy's real wealth between interest-earning assets (bonds) and non-interest-earning assets (money).

This artificial distinction between bonds and money is no longer clear-cut if it ever was. People can now earn interest on their checking accounts so that money holding is not the holding of a noninterest-earning financial asset. An individual's portfolio decision thus involves the allocation of wealth among a multitude of financial assets, each earning some interest. The interest return on money, however, is less than that on other financial assets. Wealth held in the form of a checking or transaction account is risky for the bank or financial institution in which it is deposited since an individual may draw the funds out of the account at any time. The financial institution would rather the funds were held in non-withdrawable, long-term accounts. On the other hand, if interest earnings were the same, individuals would rather be able to withdraw their funds at any time without penalty. Hence, to induce individuals to place their funds in the long-term accounts a higher interest rate must be paid.

---

of the investment function to decrease by 10. Thus, we find that the shift in the investment function due to an increase in I_r is greater at high interest rates than at low interest rates.

[5] James Tobin showed in a formal manner that both assets will be held. See his "The Interest-Elasticity of Transactions Demand for Cash," *Review of Economics and Statistics*, Vol. 38 (August, 1965).

In this case, why would anyone desire to hold funds in the transactions accounts rather than in the longer-term accounts or in the form of bonds? In other words, why do individuals demand money?

The Demand for Money

We now turn our attention to the factors that determine the real demand for money. Before we do so, ask yourself what is meant by the demand for a good? The demand for tennis balls means that individuals want to purchase tennis balls and are able to do so. The tennis balls are "held" by individuals in the sense that they use these tennis balls. What if an individual, instead of using the tennis balls, offered them in a trade for golf balls? Then that individual is "supplying" tennis balls, not demanding them. Analogously, individuals demand money when they "hold" cash or have a checking account balance. They are demanding other products when they offer the money for another product. Looked at differently, they are supplying money. But the point to be noted here is that the demand for this asset, money, is the holding of the asset, not the use of it to buy goods and services.

For what reasons do individuals hold money? The most obvious reason is because they plan to carry out transactions. And what determines the number and value of transactions that individuals (and firms) plan to carry out? The higher the income, the more transactions will be carried out. Thus, income—real income—is one of the determinants of the demand for money.

What motivations, other than to carry out transactions, do individuals have to hold money balances? One motivation might be to provide insurance against unforeseen contingencies. For example, when individuals go on a vacation they usually carry an extra amount of money to protect themselves against the possibility of an automobile breakdown. Another rationale for holding money might be that, unlike bonds, its value is fixed in nominal terms and therefore money provides a reasonably safe asset in the individual's portfolio. As a result, money balances in excess of those needed to carry out transactions are generally held.

One would expect that as the interest return on nonmoney financial assets relative to the interest on money rises; that is, as the cost of holding money increases, individuals would hold smaller money balances. For example, if the return on bonds is 2 percent more than the interest rate on checking accounts, an individual may decide to hold $100 above balances necessary to carry out transactions. However, when the interest rate differential is 15 percent, the interest earnings foregone by holding money becomes much higher. In this case, the individual is likely to take some of that $100 and use it to purchase bonds or other nonmoney financial assets. Of course, the greater the reward for undertaking a given risk the greater likelihood it will be undertaken. Thus the higher the real interest rate, the more likely individuals will loan their money—purchase bonds, stocks, etc.—rather than hold money balances. As a result we should find an inverse relationship between the demand for money and the interest rate.[6]

The demand-for-real-balances function can be written as

$$(4\text{-}3) \qquad \frac{M^D}{P} = L^D \underset{(+)}{(Y,} \underset{(-)}{r)}$$

or as

$$\frac{M^D}{P} = L_0 + L_y Y - L_r r$$

Where

L^D = the demand for real money balances
M^D = the demand for nominal money balances
P = the price level
L_0 = the autonomous real money demand
L_y = the sensitivity of money demand to changes in income
L_r = the sensitivity of the demand for money to changes in the interest rate

This equation indicates that the quantity of real money demanded (M^D/P) depends inversely on the interest rate and positively on the income level.

The demand for money can be presented graphically as well. Since the demand for money depends on both the interest rate and income level we could plot the combinations of L^D and Y, given an interest rate, to obtain an upward sloping curve with M and Y on the axes. Or we could plot the combinations of L^D and r for a given income level to obtain a downward sloping curve with M and r on the axes. The latter is the most common presentation and the one we show in Figure 4-5A. Notice that the position of the demand for money curve in Figure 4-5A depends on the level of income. Should income increase from Y_1 to Y_2 the quantity of money demanded at each interest rate would increase. Thus, the demand for real balances curve would shift out, from $L^D(Y_1)$ to $L^D(Y_2)$.

---

[6] Keynes and his students separated the demand for money into three components for pedagogical reasons. He described the transactions demand as dependent on income, the precautionary demand dependent on both income and interest rates, while the speculative demand depended on interest rates. While no one believed that individuals put their transaction balances in their left pocket, their speculative balances in their right pocket, and their precautionary balances in their sock, several economists have criticized this separation even at an abstract theoretical level. See, for example, Boris P. Pesek and T. R. Saving, *Money, Wealth and Economic Theory* (New York: Macmillan, Inc., 1967), pp. 323-330.

Figure 4-5. The Money Market Diagram and the LM Curve

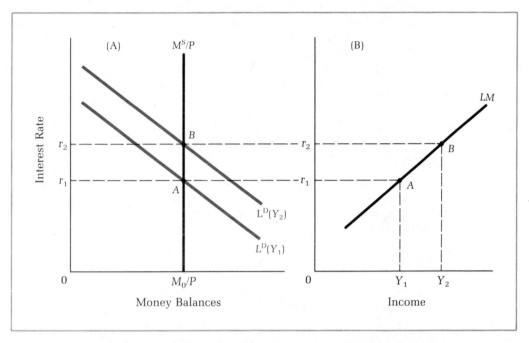

The money market consists of a real money demand function, a real money supply function, and a market clearing equation. The money demand function can be drawn only if a given income level is assumed. An increase in the income level causes the money demand function to shift to the right. The real money supply function is a vertical line at the autonomous money supply. The intersection of the demand and supply curves determines the interest rate that clears the money market. In Panel A at an income level of Y_1, the interest rate r_1 clears the money market while the market clearing interest rate at an income level of Y_2 is r_2. If the interest rate and income level combinations that clear the money market are plotted, as in Panel B, the LM curve is derived.

The Money Market and the Derivation of the *LM* Curve

To complete our introduction to the money market, we must specify the supply side. The nominal supply of money is equal to the sum of the supply of currency and demand deposits (including NOW and ATS account balances). That is, unless otherwise stated, we will use M-1 as the definition of the money supply. The supply of cash is determined by the Fed. The supply of demand deposits is actually determined through a rather complex process of banks lending money to individuals and firms, a process influenced by the rules and regulations of the Fed. We will examine this process and the rules and regulations of the Fed later. For now we will simply assume that the nominal supply of money is determined by the Fed independently of the value of interest rates or income levels. On this basis, the supply of money is autonomous. However, it is important to note that while the Fed has control over the nominal money supply, it does not control the real money supply. The real supply of money is defined as the nominal money supply divided by the price level, M^S/P. While the nominal supply is determined by the Fed, the price level is determined by the interactions of individuals, firms, and the government. For this reason, we have explicitly written M/P even though we have been assuming P is fixed. Therefore, the supply side of the money market can be written as

$$(4\text{-}12) \qquad \frac{M^S}{P} = \frac{M_0}{P}$$

How can the real money supply be represented in terms of a diagram with r and M on the axes? In order to draw the money supply curve we need to know the price level as well as the exogenously given nominal money supply. During the discussion of the IS curve the price level was assumed to be fixed. If we continue with this assumption and, in addition, assume $P = 1$, then the nominal supply of money is equivalent to the real supply of money. In this case, the money supply can be represented as a vertical line at the Fed's chosen value, M_0.

Equilibrium occurs in the money market when the demand for real balances is equal to the real money supply. That is, when

$$(4\text{-}13) \qquad L^D = \frac{M^S}{P}$$

In Figure 4-5A, the money supply and the money demand curves are plotted on the same diagram. The intersection of these curves determines the market clearing interest rate, r_1. However, this is an equilibrium only if the income level remains at Y_1. As we just discussed, when income increases, the demand-for-money curve shifts out. As shown in Figure 4-5A, at the income level Y_2 the demand curve is $L^D(Y_2)$ and the market clearing interest rate is r_2.

Why does the market clearing interest rate rise when the income level increases? If equilibrium in the money market is to occur, the demand for money must equal the supply. But, recall that the money supply is fixed at M_0/P. When income rises, the quantity of money demanded rises. The only way for equilibrium to be reestablished is for the quantity of money demanded to be reduced by an increase in the interest rate.

If the income level is Y_1 in Figure 4-5A, the market clearing interest rate must be r_1 whereas if the income is the higher level Y_2, the market clearing interest rate becomes the higher level r_2. These and all other combinations of interest rates and income levels that clear the money market can be plotted in a diagram with r and Y on the axes. By plotting these points (see Figure 4-5B), a curve known as the *LM curve* is traced out. In sum, the *LM* curve represents all possible combinations of interest rates and income levels at which the quantity of money demanded and the quantity of money supplied are equal.

The *LM* curve in Figure 4-5B is an upward sloping curve. An increase in income leads to an increase in the number of transactions and, thus, an increase in the demand for money in order to carry out these transactions. With an increase in demand and no change in supply, the opportunity cost of holding money must increase. In other words, the interest rate must rise to reestablish equilibrium in the money market.

Changes in the Position of the *LM* Curve: The 1929-33 Contraction of the Money Supply

In deriving the *LM* curve, everything else was held constant so that the effect of changes in income on the money market clearing interest rate could be studied. Exogenous variables such as the money supply or the autonomous demand for money had to remain constant. In addition, the parameters in the money demand function—the income and interest rate sensitivity coefficients—did not change. Let us consider the implications for the *LM* curve of a change in an exogenous variable and then of a change in a parameter value.

The bull market of the late 1920s promoted a desire to restrain stock market speculation. This attitude prevailed among Federal Reserve and Treasury officials even as the stock market crashed in 1929. The result was a policy of decreasing the stock of money. From the cyclical peak in August, 1929, to the trough in March, 1933, the stock of money fell by over one-third. What was the effect of this policy on the economy? A money supply decrease acts as an exogenous or autonomous change in the money market causing the *LM* curve to shift. The nominal money supply value M_{1929} in Figure 4-6 represents the value of the money stock in 1929—$47 billion. The corresponding *LM* curve is denoted as $LM(M_{1929})$. Between 1929 and 1933 the nominal money supply decreased to $30 billion. The new nominal money supply is referred to as M_{1933}. Note in Figure 4-6A that with the original stock of money, the market clearing interest rate is r_1 at income level Y_1. However, at this interest rate and with the lower 1933 money supply, the money market would be characterized by an excess demand of A-B. As a result, the opportunity cost of holding money would rise to r_3. The higher interest rate would induce individuals to hold less money, shown as a move from B to C. When the interest rate-income level combination (r_3, Y_2) is plotted on the *LM* diagram, a point (D) above the original *LM* curve is obtained.

Now consider what happens at the greater income level Y_2. With the larger stock of money available, the interest rate r_2 no longer clears the

Figure 4-6. *The Effect of a Decrease in the Nominal Money Supply on the LM Curve*

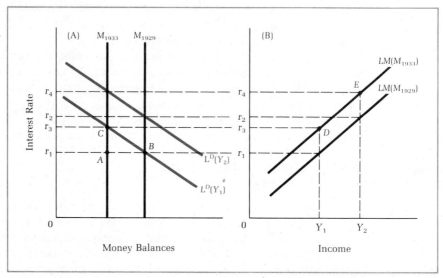

Between 1929 and 1933 the nominal money supply decreased by $17 billion. If the nominal money supply in 1929 is denoted as M_{1929}, the appropriate *LM* curve is $LM(M_{1929})$. In order to see the effect on the *LM* curve of a decrease in the nominal money we focus on the income level Y_1. With the original stock of money, the money market clears at an interest rate of r_1 (Point A). The increase in the nominal money supply creates an excess demand of *A-B* in the money market which causes the interest rate to rise to r_3 (Point C). If this new market clearing interest rate and income level combination is plotted on the *LM* diagram, a point (D) above the original *LM* curve is obtained. If other income levels, such as Y_2, are considered, we find that the new *LM* curve, $LM(M_{1933})$, is above and to the left of the original curve.

money market. Instead, at income level Y_2 a higher interest rate (r_4) is necessary to clear the market. When this interest rate and income combination (r_4, Y_2) is plotted, still another point (E) off the original *LM* curve is discovered. If other equilibrium income and interest rate combinations are plotted, the curve $LM(M_{1933})$ would be traced out. Thus, a decrease in the money supply is represented as an upward, or leftward, shift of the *LM* curve.

This analysis indicates that a change in an autonomous variable will cause the *LM* curve to shift. Now, consider how a change in a parameter, such as the interest rate sensitivity coefficient in the money demand function, affects the *LM* curve.

Changes in the Desire to Hold Money

As the U.S. cut its ties to gold in 1933 and then retied them in a different manner, attitudes toward holding money changed. In February, 1934 gold was fixed by law at a price of $35 an ounce. Individuals were not allowed to hold gold and it no longer circulated as a medium of exchange. Moreover, in December of 1933 the president was given the authority to reduce the gold content of the dollar and to rely more heavily on silver. Finally, the World War II years brought several changes in people's willingness to hold money. In particular, both consumers and business enterprises were prevented from using their funds to purchase some kinds of goods that they regarded as increasing their wealth. Automobiles were no longer available. As a result consumers and business enterprises held larger stocks of money.

Both periods saw changes in the interest sensitivity of the demand for money.[7] In the first case, people shifted their wealth among assets more rapidly—the demand for money was more interest sensitive than had been the case in previous years. In the 1940s the interest sensitivity of money demand decreased. Because of the war, people had a more restricted choice of assets in which they could hold their wealth.

How are these changes shown with the *LM* curve? An increase in the interest sensitivity of money demand means that a given change in the interest rate leads to a greater change in the quantity of money demanded than was previously the case. A greater interest sensitivity of money demand is represented as a flatter demand for money curve as shown in Figure 4-7A where L_r^1 represents the initial value of the coefficient and L_r^2 denotes the new value of the coefficient.

The flatter money demand also translates into a flatter *LM* curve. Consider the effect of a given change in the interest rate for different interest rate sensitivity coefficients. At the initial value of the coefficient L_r^1 a given change in the interest rate will require a change in the income level if money market equilibrium is to be established. Now, consider the identical change in the interest rate with the higher interest rate sensitivity coefficient L_r^2. The decline in the interest rate will lead to a greater rise in the quantity of money demanded. This means that income must fall more than was previously necessary to keep the quantity of money demanded equal to the quantity supplied. In other words the *LM* curve becomes flatter.

Notice in Figure 4-8 what the changing interest rate sensitivity means for money supply changes. A decrease in the nominal money supply would cause interest rates to rise significantly more when money demand is less interest sensitive (the 1940s' case) than when money demand is more interest sensitive as in the 1930s. L_r^2 represents a greater interest rate sensitivity. With this coefficient, interest rates must rise from r_1 to r_2 to clear the money market. The interest rates, however, must rise from r_1 to r_3

---

[7] There has been some debate over whether the proper interpretation of these changes is an interest sensitivity change or an autonomous change. See, for example, R. W. Hafer and Scott E. Hein, "The Shift in Money Demand: What Really Happened?" *Review*, Vol. 64, No. 2 (Federal Reserve of St. Louis, February, 1982), pp. 11-15.

Figure 4-7. The Effect of an Increase in L_r on the LM Curve

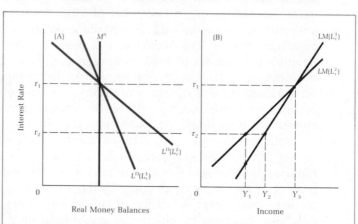

An increase in the interest rate sensitivity of money means that a given change in the interest rate leads to a greater change in the quantity of money demanded than it previously had. For each income level the money demand curve becomes flatter, as can be seen in Panel A where L_r^1 represents the initial value of the coefficient, and L_r^2 denotes the new value of the coefficient. The flatter L^D curve translates into a flatter LM curve. In the LM diagram, a change in the interest rate from r_1 to r_2 would require a smaller change in income (Y_3 to Y_2) to maintain equilibrium (the L^D curve would have to shift further), the smaller the interest sensitivity of money demand.

when the money demand function is less interest rate sensitive. Hence, given everything else the same (which is seldom the case) monetary policy would be more powerful the less the interest rate sensitivity of money demand.

A summary of the effects on the LM curve that come from changes in either the demand for, or supply of, money is presented in Table 4-3.

Table 4-3. Summary Table for Changes in the LM Curve

VARIABLE/PARAMETER	CHANGE	ROTATE	SHIFT
Money supply	Increase		Outward
	Decrease		Inward
Autonomous money	Increase		Inward
demand	Decrease		Outward
Interest sensitivity	Increase	Clockwise	
coefficient of	Decrease	Counterclockwise	
money demand function			
Income sensitivity	Increase	Counterclockwise	
coefficient of	Decrease	Clockwise	
money demand function			

Figure 4-8. *Monetary Policy with Different Interest Rate Sensitivity Coefficients*

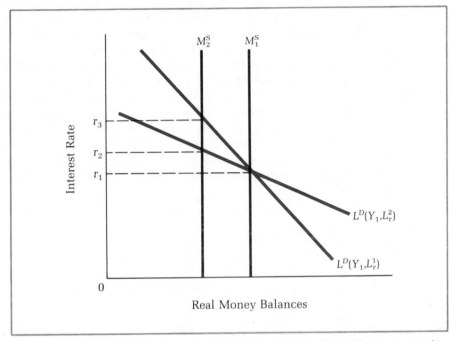

Is monetary policy affected by the interest sensitivity of the demand for money? In this figure two money demand functions are presented with different interest sensitivity coefficients. The coefficient L_r^2 represents greater interest rate sensitivity. A decrease in the nominal money supply from M_1 to M_2 causes the interest rate to rise significantly more when money demand is less interest sensitive (r_1 to r_3) than when money demand is more interest sensitive (r_1 to r_2). This suggests that monetary policy would be more powerful the less the interest rate sensitivity of money demand, given everything else the same.

Conclusions and a Summing-Up:
A Look Ahead

The Great Contraction of 1929-1933 had not only caused a collapse of the economy, but had also fomented a revolution in popular and academic opinion regarding economics. The 1930s were years of search for a new view of economics, a search that culminated in the Keynesian framework. After the analytics offered by Keynes became generally accepted, effort was focused on clarifying, expanding, and refining the framework. The *IS-LM* model was offered in this vein—a way to easily and clearly understand Keynes's model and to compare Keynes's analysis to the pre-Keynesian, or classical, view.

The *IS-LM* framework is a very useful analytical device. At this stage we have only touched the surface of how it can be employed to portray several alternative interpretations of economic events. In the next chapter we will expand on this topic. In particular, we will examine in more detail the contrast between the pre-Keynesian and post-Keynesian views of the economy. The pre-Keynesian view that money was supreme—that business danced to the tune of money—was reversed in the 1930s. The view coming out of the 1930s was of an interest insensitive investment demand (an investment demand determined by the "animal spirits" of business), of an interest sensitive money demand, and of a need for government activity to stabilize the economy. The view in the 1920s had been just the opposite—investment as interest sensitive but stable, and money demand as interest insensitive.

The optimistic outlook of the 1920s seemed gone forever in the 1930s, but rumblings of a revival were stirring in the 1940s. In the next chapter we will consider this revival as we more fully discuss the *IS-LM* model.

PROBLEMS AND EXERCISES

1. Give a clear explanation (using some economic intuition) for the sign of the slope of the following:
    a. The *IS* curve
    b. The *LM* curve

2. Carefully explain why a point to the right of the *IS* curve represents excess supply in the commodity market. Explain why points to the right of the *LM* curve represent excess demand in the money market.

3. Explain why an increase in the coefficient on the interest rate variable in the investment function causes the *IS* function to rotate counter-clockwise.

4. Keynes felt that investor expectations or "animal spirits" had a lot to do with the business cycle. The animal spirits might be represented by the amount of autonomous investment. Assume that at each interest rate and income level investors decide to make large investments.
    a. What variable or parameter has changed?
    b. Identify how this change affects the *IS* curve.

5. Many economists believe saving to be a function of the interest rate. Yet in the commodity market presented in this chapter, saving was only a function of disposable income. How would you modify the commodity market if savings were a function of the interest rate? What would be the implications for the *IS* curve of this modification?

6. Suppose at a given interest rate and income level the money market is characterized by excess demand. Explain why individual actions to

readjust their financial portfolios result in an increase in the interest rate at the given income level.

7. Suppose the money demand coefficient (L_y) increases in value. What does this do to the *LM* curve?

8. During most of the 1970s, the Federal Reserve Board followed an interest rate policy. That is, the Fed reacted to rising interest rates by increasing the money supply and to falling interest rates by decreasing the money supply. By behaving in such a manner it was felt that the interest rate would be stabilized which would, in turn, stabilize investment spending. In terms of our model, such a policy would result in the money supply being a function of the interest rate. Explain how the money market diagram and the *LM* curve would be affected by such a policy.

SUGGESTED READINGS

The original exposition of the IS-LM model was given in a classic paper by Hicks.

John R. Hicks, "Mr. Keynes and the 'Classics': A Suggested Interpretation," *Econometrica* (April, 1937), pp. 147-159.

A constant reading of The Wall Street Journal *will keep you informed of monetary developments, but so much has been written on the demand for money that our best suggestions for reading on the subject are to turn to other macroeconomic textbooks. For example*

Rudiger Dornbusch and Stanley Fischer, *Macroeconomics*, 2d ed. (New York: McGraw-Hill Book Company, 1981), Chapter 7.

David E. Laidler, *The Demand for Money: Theories & Evidence*, 2d ed. (New York: Harper & Row, Publishers, Inc., 1978).

Sherman J. Maisel, *Macroeconomics: Theories and Policies* (New York: W. W. Norton & Co., Inc., 1982), Chapter 7.

For a further discussion of different reasons for holding money see

Brian Motley, "A Note on the Speculative Demand for Money," *Journal of Macroeconomics* (Fall, 1979), pp. 395, 403.

_APPENDIX. Algebraic Presentation of the IS and LM Curves_____

The algebraic derivation of the *IS* curve follows the same procedures that were used to find equilibrium income in Chapter 3.

Algebraic Derivation of the *IS* Curve_____

The commodity market is

$Y = C + I + G$ Equilibrium equation
$C = C_0 + c_y (Y - T)$ Consumption function
$I = I_0 + I_y Y - I_r r$ Investment function
$G = G_0$ Government spending function
$T = T_0$ Lump sum tax function

Where

Y = Income
C = Consumption expenditures
I = Investment expenditures
G = Government expenditures
C_0 = Autonomous consumption spending
c_y = Marginal propensity to consume
I_r = Interest rate sensitivity of investment spending
T = Taxes
I_y = Income sensitivity of investment spending
G_0 = Autonomous level of government spending
T_0 = Autonomous level of taxes

Since we are seeking the income level at which aggregate demand is equal to the value of output (i.e., the equilibrium equation holds), the consumption, investment, tax, and government spending functions must be substituted into the equilibrium equation. Solving the resulting equation for income yields the following:

(4A-1) $$Y = \frac{1}{1 - c_y - I_y} (C_0 + I_0 + G_0 - c_y T_0 - I_r r)$$

And, with some rearrangement we find equilibrium income

(4A-2) $$Y = \frac{C_0 + I_0 + G_0 - c_y T_0}{1 - c_y - I_y} - \frac{I_r}{1 - c_y - I_y} (r)$$

Equation 4A-1 is substantially different from the equilibrium equation of the previous chapter. That equation had only autonomous variables and coefficients on the right side. Equation 4A-2 includes an endogenous variable, the interest rate *(r)*, on the right-hand side as well. An endogenous *variable* is one whose value is determined by the model, whereas the values of the *exogenous* or *autonomous variables* and the coefficients are determined outside of the model. In other words, we choose values for C_0, I_0, T_0, G_0, c_y, I_y and I_r whereas the values of r and Y are determined within the model itself.

The implication of finding an endogenous variable on the right side is that unless we know the value of that variable, r, a unique value of equilibrium income cannot be found. Notice in Equation 4A-3 that for each value of r a different equilibrium income value will be obtained.

Equation 4A-2 is the algebraic version of the IS curve. The slope of the IS curve is given by $\Delta r/\Delta Y$ (the rise over the run) and can be found by taking the first difference of the IS equation and assuming that $1 > c_y + I_y$.

$$\Delta Y = \frac{1}{1 - c_y - I_y}(-I_r\,\Delta r)$$

Dividing both sides of this equation by ΔY and solving for $\Delta r \div \Delta Y$ yields

(4A-3) $$\Delta r/\Delta Y = \frac{1 - c_y - I_y}{-I_r}$$

As was previously pointed out, the slope is negative and depends on the coefficients of the endogenous variables, income and the interest rate.

An example to illustrate the points in the preceding paragraph may be helpful. Assume that $C_0 = 200$, $c_y = 0.5$, $I_0 = 150$, $I_y = 0.25$, $I_r = 1,000$, $G_0 = 100$, and $T_0 = 100$. The IS curve can then be written as

$$Y = \frac{200 + 150 + 100 - 0.5\,(100)}{1 - 0.5 - 0.25} - \frac{1,000}{1 - 0.5 - 0.25}(r)$$

$$Y = 1,600 - 4,000\,r$$

We have already stated that different values of the interest rate generate different equilibrium income levels. For example, an interest rate of 0.05 generates an equilibrium income of 1,400 and an interest rate of 0.20 results in an income level of 800. These results are presented graphically in Figure 4A-1.

Much space was devoted in earlier sections to explaining the factors that can cause the IS curve to change position. Recall that a change in an exogenous (or autonomous) variable shifts the IS curve while a change in the income or interest elasticity is reflected in a rotation of the IS curve. This result is clearly seen in our algebraic derivation. A change in an exogenous variable changes the value of the IS intercept, but not the slope. For example, if autonomous investment increases by 100, the Y intercept increases to 2,000. The r intercept of the IS curve is obtained by

Figure 4A-1. The IS Curve and Shifts in this Curve

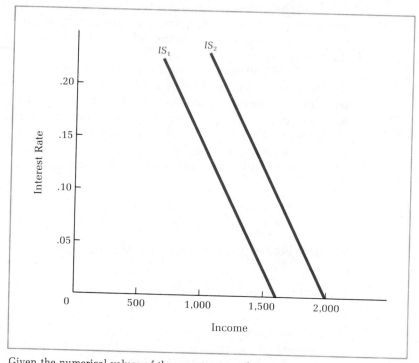

Given the numerical values of the parameters and exogenous variables, the *IS* curve is

$$Y = 1,600 - 4,000 \, r$$

Different values of the interest rate generate different equilibrium income levels. An interest rate of 0.05, for example, generates an equilibrium income of 1,400, and an interest rate of 0.20 results in an income level of 800. Plotting these combinations yields two points on the IS_1 curve. A \$100 billion increase in autonomous investment leads to a new *IS* equation.

$$Y = 2,000 - 4,000r$$

By plotting the various equilibrium income levels generated from various interest rates the curve IS_2 will be traced out.

setting Y equal to zero and solving the *IS* equation for r. In terms of our model, the r intercept is

$$\frac{C_0 + I_0 + G_0 - c_y \, T_0}{I_r} = \frac{200 + 150 + 100 - 0.5\,(100)}{1,000}$$

$$= 0.4$$

An increase in autonomous investment of 100 increases the r intercept from 0.4 to 0.5. Notice that both intercepts changed by the same percentage, 0.25 percent. The Y intercept change by 400, and 400 divided by the original intercept 1,000 gives the percentage change. The r intercept changed by 0.1 which when divided by the original interest rate intercept of 0.4 gives the percentage change. Thus, a parallel shift in the IS curve occurs. This can also be seen by noting that a change in autonomous investment does not affect the slope of the IS curve given by Equation 4A-3.

A change in either I_y, I_r, or c_y results in a change in the slope of the IS curve. In order to see this, assume the exogenous variables and parameters have the values that generated the curve IS_1 in Figure 4A-1. Now, let the marginal propensity to consume increase from 0.5 to 0.65. The new IS equation is

$$Y = \frac{200 + 150 + 100 - 0.65(100)}{1 - 0.65 - 0.25} - \frac{1,000}{1 - 0.65 - 0.25}r$$

$$= 3,850 - 10,000\ r$$

Interest rates of 0.05 and 0.20 generate equilibrium income values of 3,350 and 1,850 respectively. When these points are plotted we obtain a flatter IS curve, IS_2 in Figure 4A-2.

Figure 4A-2. *Parameter Changes and the IS Curve*

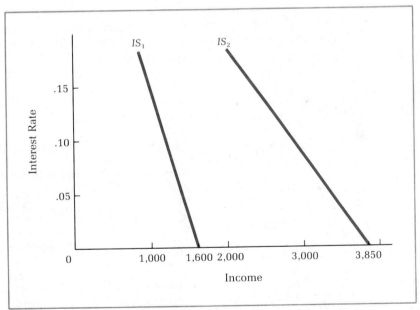

Parameter changes result in a change of the slope of the IS curve. This can be clearly seen algebraically. The equation for IS_1 is

$$Y = 1,600 - 4,000r$$

An increase in the MPC from 0.5 to 0.65 results in a new IS equation which is

$$Y = 3,850 - 10,000r$$

Plotting this equation yields IS_2. Clearly the slope has changed. Of course, this is known by just examining the coefficient on r in the IS equation.

Recall from the text that a less steep *IS* curve reflects a decrease in the income or interest elasticities of spending. In the example just presented, spending became more sensitive to changes in income, and more consumption was induced by any change in income with an MPC of 0.65 than with an MPC of 0.50. Similarly, increasing I_r or I_y would result in a flatter *IS* curve. Looking at the slope of the *IS* curve (Equation 4A-3), we can see that with an MPC of 0.5 the slope is $(1 - 0.5 - 0.25) \div (-1,000) = -0.00025$, whereas with an MPC of 0.65 the slope is $(1 - 0.65 - 0.25) \div (-1,000) = -0.0001$, a smaller (negative) number. Similarly, an increase in I_r from 1,000 to 1,500 would change the slope from -0.00025 to -0.00016.

Multipliers can easily be derived from the *IS* equation. Recall that a multiplier tells us the amount that income will change when a change in an exogenous variable occurs. This implies the intercepts only need to be examined because the slope does not change. Suppose we wish to find the change in income that comes with a change in autonomous investment spending. Then from the *IS* equation we get the following:

$$\Delta Y = \left(\frac{1}{1 - c_y - I_y} \right) (\Delta I_0)$$

The multiplier is identical to the multiplier derived in Chapter 3. The only difference is that with the *IS* model, we must recognize that we get the change in income at each interest rate.

Algebraic Derivation of the *LM* Curve

The equations that constitute the money market are as follows:

$$L^D = \frac{M^D}{P} = L_0 - L_r r + L_y Y \quad \text{Demand for money equation}$$

$$\frac{M^S}{P} = \frac{M_0}{P} \quad \text{Supply of money equation}$$

$$\frac{M^S}{P} = L^D \quad \text{Equilibrium equation}$$

The demand for money equation and the fixed money supply must be substituted into the equilibrium condition if equilibrium is to be found. By making these substitutions and solving for r, we find that

$$(4A\text{-}4) \qquad r = \frac{L_0 - (M_0/P)}{L_r} + \frac{L_y}{L_r} Y$$

This equation clearly reveals our finding that a unique interest rate cannot be derived in the money market unless the income level is known. Since Equation 4A-4 gives us the equilibrium interest rate for each given income level, it is known as the *LM* equation.

A numerical example may be useful to illustrate how the *LM* equation can generate the *LM* curve. Suppose that $L_0 = 200$, $M_0 = 340$, $L_y = 0.2$, $L_r = 1,000$, and $P = 1$. Then the *LM* equation is written as follows:

$$r = \frac{200\text{-}340}{1,000} + \frac{0.2}{1,000}(Y)$$

or

$$r = -0.14 + 0.0002Y$$

Then, if income is 1,200, the market clearing interest rate is 0.10, and at an income level of 2,000 the interest rate that equates money demand and supply is 0.26. If these combinations of income and interest rates are plotted, we obtain two points on an *LM* curve, shown in Figure 4A-3. Of

Figure 4A-3. The LM Curve and Shifts in the LM Curve

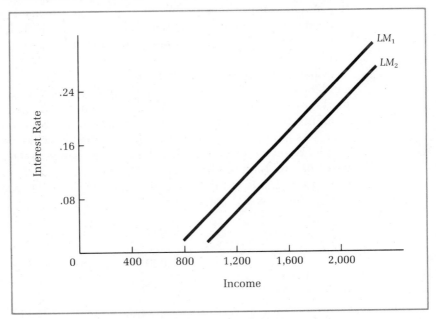

Given the numerical values of L_0, M_0, L_y, and L_r, the *LM* equation is

$$r = -0.14 + 0.0002Y$$

If income is 1,200, the market clearing interest rate is 0.10 and at an income level of 2,000 the interest rate that equates money demand and supply is 0.26. If these combinations of income and interest rates are plotted, we obtain two points of LM_1. If the nominal money supply increases to 380, the *LM* equation is

$$r = -0.18 + 0.0002Y$$

The resulting *LM* curve is LM_2.

course, other points on the LM can be derived by choosing an income level and then calculating the corresponding equilibrium interest rate.

Also in Equation 4A-4 notice that (L_y/L_r) Y is added to the intercept to find the equilibrium interest rate. This suggests that a positive relationship exists between the interest rate and the income level. A more precise approach, however, to illustrating the direct relationship between the interest rate and income level is to find the slope of the LM equation. The slope of the LM equation (the rise over the run, $\Delta r/\Delta Y$) is L_y/L_r which is positive. In terms of our numerical example, the slope of the LM curve is equal to 0.0002.

In order to derive our LM curve, specific values for L_0, L_r, L_y, and M_0 had to be assumed. Earlier we stated that a change in an exogenous or autonomous variable—L_0 or M_0 in the money market—results in the LM curve shifting in a parallel manner. We now want to consider the possible insights that the algebraic approach may offer on this point. Consider the effect of an increase in the money supply to 380 from 340. An increase in the money supply means that at the income levels 1,200 and 2,000, interest rates must decrease to 0.06 and 0.22 respectively from 0.10 to 0.26 if equilibrium in the money market is to occur.

Changes in autonomous variables cause shifts in the LM curve that can be used to represent many economic events as they affect the money market, but not all of them. Legal restrictions on the use of savings accounts as checking accounts, for example, have been relaxed in recent years. As a result, the demand for money may have become less interest elastic. We can represent such a change as a change in the slope of the LM curve or a rotation of the LM curve. Algebraically, an alteration in L_y or L_r changes the slope of the LM curve. For example, if L_y increases from 0.20 to 0.25 the new LM equation is

$$r = \frac{200\text{-}340}{1,000} + \frac{0.25}{1,000} \ (Y)$$

or

$$r = -0.14 + 0.00025 \ (Y)$$

The slope of the LM curve has changed from 0.0002 to 0.00025. Thus, the LM curve has rotated in a counterclockwise direction, as shown in Figure 4A-4.

Figure 4A-4. Parameter Changes and the LM Curve

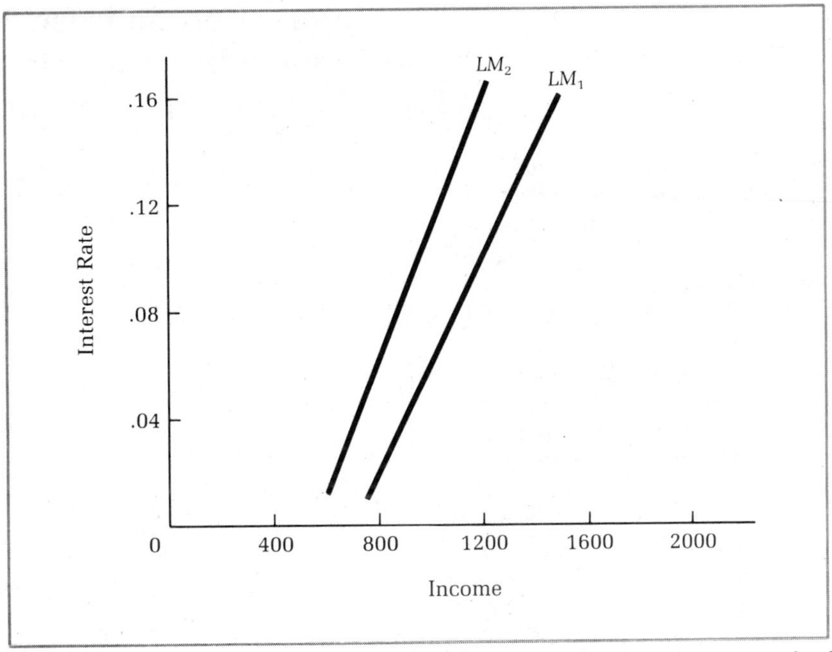

A change in either L_y or L_r will cause the slope of the LM to change. The equation for the LM curve LM_1 is

$$r = 0.14 + 0.0002Y$$

If L_y increases from 0.20 to 0.25, the new LM equation, LM_2, is

$$r = -0.14 + 0.0025Y$$

The slope of the LM curve has changed from 0.0002 to 0.00025 which indicates a counterclockwise rotation.

PROBLEMS AND EXERCISES

A-1. Using the following model solve for equilibrium Y and equilibrium r:

$$Y = C + I + G$$
$$C = C_0 + C_y (Y - T)$$
$$I = I_0 + I_y Y - I_r r$$
$$G = G_0$$

$$T = T_0$$
$$M^D/P = L_0 - L_r r + L_y Y$$
$$M^S/P = M_0/P$$
$$M^S/P = M^D/P$$

A-2. Using the model in Question A-1 find the intercept and slope of the IS curve, and then the LM curve.

A-3. Demonstrate and explain what occurs when
   a. Government spending increases
   b. Taxes decrease
   c. The supply of money increases

CHAPTER 5.

The Interaction between Money and Commodity Markets II: Equilibrium and Applications

In my opinion most, if not all, major booms and slumps can be traced to monetary mismanagement or have been greatly aggravated by monetary factors.
> Gottfried Haberler, 1980

Thus if the animal spirits are dimmed and the spontaneous optimism falters, leaving us to depend on nothing but a mathematical expectation, enterprise will fade and die; . . . though fears of loss may have a basis no more reasonable than hopes of profit had before.
> John Maynard Keynes, 1936

The IS and LM curves were developed in the previous chapter. In this chapter these curves are used to simultaneously determine the equilibrium interest rate and output level. Several economic events that occurred between 1930 and 1935 are then examined from the perspective of the complete IS-LM model. Some of the important questions dealt with in this chapter are

- *How are the equilibrium interest rate and output levels determined?*

- *If an equilibrium is disturbed by an exogenous shock, how does the economy adjust to a new equilibrium?*

- *What caused the Great Depression?*

- *What is the role of monetary and fiscal policy when money demand depends on the income level?*

- *What is a liquidity trap?*

Introduction

The Great Crash of 1929-1933 fomented a revolution in economic thought. The revolution, which became known as Keynesian economics, took hold during the two decades following World War II. Criticism of the Keynesian framework was almost nonexistent during this period. In fact, most of the work in macroeconomics was devoted to expanding and refining the Keynesian model. The IS-LM model is such a refinement providing a framework in which the interaction between money and real variables can be analyzed.

In this chapter, we complete the task of developing and analyzing the IS-LM model begun in the previous chapter. The primary emphasis of this chapter, however, is on the use of the IS-LM framework to discuss economic events. We focus on economic developments of the period from 1930 to 1965 using the perspective provided by the IS-LM model.

Equilibrium in the Commodity and Money Markets

Those combinations of interest rates and income levels that lie on the IS curve satisfy the conditions for commodity market equilibrium. Similarly, those on the *LM* curve satisfy the conditions for money market equilibrium. For both markets to be in equilibrium simultaneously, the same interest rate and income level must clear both the commodity and the money markets. In order to determine this one interest rate and income level combination, the *IS* and *LM* curves are superimposed on one diagram as shown in Figure 5-1. The intersection of these two curves, denoted as Point A, satisfies the condition for simultaneous equilibrium. Therefore, the equilibrium interest rate is r_1 and the equilibrium income level Y_1, given the price level and the other exogenous variables—autonomous consumption, autonomous investment, autonomous money demand, the nominal money supply, and fiscal policy.

Figure 5-1. *Commodity and Money Market Equilibrium*

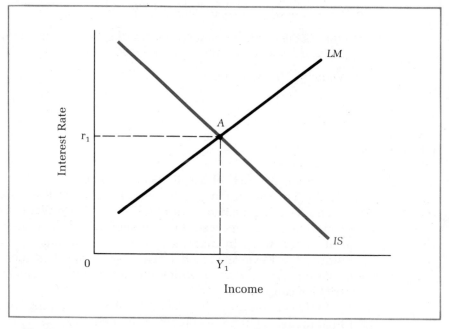

The *IS* curve represents all possible combinations of interest rates and income levels at which the commodity market is in equilibrium while the *LM* curve represents all possible equilibrium combinations of these two variables in the money market. The intersection of these two curves determines the one interest rate and income combination where both markets are simultaneously in equilibrium. This (general) equilibrium interest rate and income level are determined at Point A.

A shift in either the *IS* or *LM* curve will cause the equilibrium interest rate and income level to change. Suppose, for example, the real money supply increases due to an increase in the nominal money supply. This change, which can be thought of as an expansionary monetary policy, is represented by an outward shift of the *LM* curve. In Figure 5-2A, this shift is represented by the movement in the *LM* curve from LM_1 to LM_2. The result is that equilibrium is reestablished at a lower interest rate (r_2) and a higher income level (Y_2). The increase in income should not be surprising. Presumably, the motivation behind an expansionary monetary policy is to expand income and output. The new lower equilibrium interest rate comes about because the public must be induced to hold a larger fraction of its wealth in the form of money.

<u>Figure 5-2.</u> *Monetary and Fiscal Policy in the IS-LM Model*

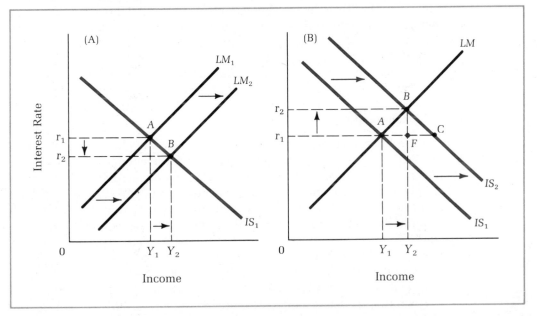

The equilibrium levels of income and interest rate will change when either the *IS* or the *LM* curve shifts. In panel A, an expansionary monetary policy causes the *LM* curve to shift from LM_1 to LM_2. A new equilibrium is established with a lower interest rate and a higher income level. An expansionary fiscal policy shifts the *IS* curve to the right, to IS_2 from IS_1. As indicated in Panel B, both the equilibrium income and interest rate are higher. The increase in the interest rate that accompanies an expansionary fiscal policy results in some crowding out of private investment.

An expansionary fiscal policy is represented by a rightward shift of the *IS* curve, from IS_1 to IS_2 in Figure 5-2B. Just as with the expansionary monetary policy, an expansionary fiscal policy causes the income level to increase. In Figure 5-2B, income increases by the distance *AF* although the horizontal distance between the two *IS* curves is equal to the distance *AC*. The increase in income is smaller because the equilibrium interest rate has been driven upward. A higher interest rate is needed to ensure that the demand for money remains equal to the fixed real money supply, but the effect of the higher interest rate is to reduce private investment spending. As a result, some of the increase in aggregate demand due to the expansionary fiscal policy is offset by the fall in investment spending. When private investment is reduced because of an expansionary fiscal policy, private spending is said to have been *crowded out*.

Adjustments to Equilibrium

Changes in exogenous variables result in shifts in either or both the *IS* and *LM* curves. By comparing the two equilibrium combinations—the one that occurred before the change in the exogenous variable and the new one—the ultimate impact on income and the interest rate can be determined. While this comparative static approach is very useful, it has the disadvantage of concealing the adjustments that must occur in the commodity and money markets for equilibrium to be reestablished.

Adjustments in the Commodity Market

The interest rate-income combination represented by Point *A* in Figure 5-3B is not an equilibrium combination for the commodity market. Is the commodity market characterized by excess demand or excess supply at Point *A*? Will inventories begin accumulating or will they be depleted? At Point *A*, the interest rate is r_1 and income or output is Y_2. For the commodity market to be in equilibrium at the same interest rate (r_1) equilibrium income must be Y_1, a lower level than Y_2. Point *A* then is a point of excess supply since production is greater than demand.

An alternative and more illuminating way of showing that Point *A* represents a state of excess supply is to combine the commodity market diagram (the 45-degree graph) and the *IS* diagram as shown in Figure 5-3. At interest rate r_1, the aggregate demand curve is $C + I(r_1) + G$ which intersects the 45-degree line at income level Y_1. However, at Point *A* the interest r_1 is associated with a greater income level (Y_2). It is obvious in Figure 5-3A that at the income level Y_2 aggregate demand is not sufficient to match production—the demand line lies below the 45-degree line. That is, the commodity market is characterized by excess supply.

Are there forces that will automatically drive the economy back to a point on the *IS* curve? The answer to this question is yes. When production is greater than demand, manufacturers accumulate unintended inventories. The accumulation of inventories induces them to decrease production or output until the excess inventories are reduced to their desired levels. Simply stated, output will contract whenever an excess supply of goods exists. At interest rate r_1 then, economic forces will move income from Y_2 toward Y_1.

Figure 5-3. Disequilibrium in the Commodity Market

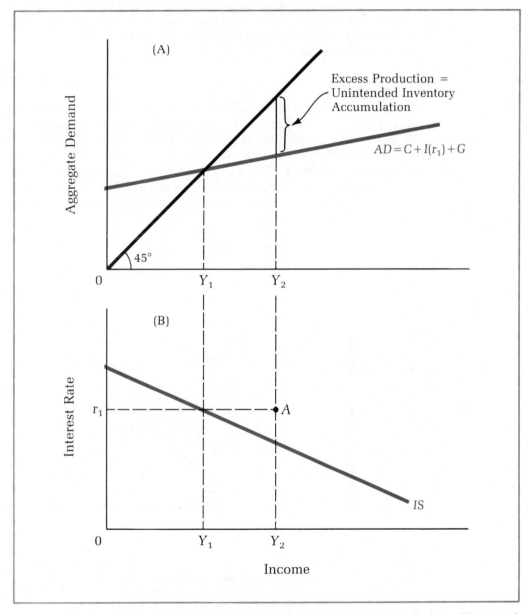

Interest rate and income level combinations off the *IS* curve signify disequilibrium in the commodity market. Consider Point *A* where the interest rate is r_1 and the income level is Y_2. At an interest rate of r_1, the commodity market clears with an income level of Y_1. As can be seen in the upper panel of this figure, the interest rate and income level associated with Point *A* result in excess supply in the commodity market. Thus, points to the right of the *IS* curve represent excess supply, while points to the left of this curve represent excess demand.

A point to the right of the *IS* curve represents a point of excess supply. Similarly, a point to the left of the *IS* curve represents excess demand in the commodity market. Excess demand means inventories are being drawn down below desired levels. Hence, production will increase—a move toward the *IS* curve.

Adjustments in the Money Market

Next, consider points off the *LM* curve. In Figure 5-4B Point *B* is above and to the left of the *LM* curve. Is the money market characterized by excess demand or excess supply at Point *B*? In Figure 5-4B note that interest rate r_2 is greater than interest rate r_1, the rate required to clear the money market at income Y_1. The higher interest rate r_2 means individuals are induced to hold smaller money balances than they would at the lower interest rate r_1. The money market, thus, is in a state of excess supply at the interest rate r_2 and income Y_1.

Figure 5-4. *Disequilibrium in the Money Market*

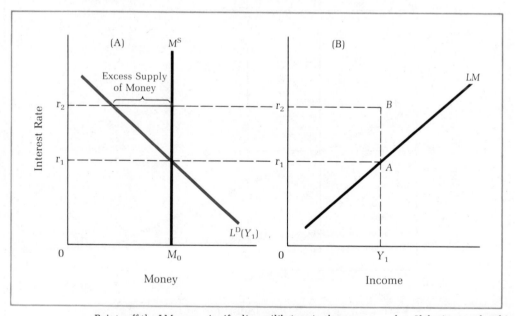

Points off the *LM* curve signify disequilibrium in the money market. If the income level is Y_1, the money market will only be in equilibrium if the interest rate is r_1. At a higher interest rate, such as r_2, the demand for money would be less than the supply of money. In terms of the *LM* diagram, this interest rate and income combination is denoted as Point *B*. Thus points to the left or above the *LM* curve represent excess supply in the money market while points to the right or below signify excess demand.

Another way of determining whether points off the *LM* curve represent excess supply or demand is to use the money market diagram (Figure

5-4A) in conjunction with the *LM* diagram. The income level Y_1 and the interest rate r_1 in the money market diagram result from the intersection of the money demand and money supply curves. Now take the interest rate associated with Point *B* over to the money diagram. The money demand curve at r_2 is crossed prior to intersecting the money supply curve. In other words, Point *B* is associated with a money market characterized by excess supply.

This analysis can be extended to consider any point to the left of or above the *LM* curve thus establishing that points to the left of the *LM* curve correspond to excess supply in the money market. Conversely, any point to the right of the *LM* curve represents excess demand.

What happens in the money market when it is not in equilibrium? Again, consider Figure 5-4 where at income level Y_1 the interest rate r_2 is too high to induce individuals to hold the money supply M_0. Individuals will place their funds into interest-earning assets (or assets earning higher interest rates than the checking type accounts). This has two effects. First, the increased flow of funds drives interest rates down. Second, as the interest rate falls, individuals will be more willing to hold money balances. As the interest rate falls, the opportunity cost of holding money decreases and, thus, the incentive to hold money increases. This process continues until Point *A* on the *LM* curve is reached. In sum, positions of disequilibrium will induce changes that drive interest and income toward their equilibrium values.

Interaction between Markets

Let us now consider the *IS* and *LM* curves simultaneously and examine the adjustments that occur when disequilibrium exists. The intersection of the *IS* and *LM* curves divides the quadrant into four regions as identified in Figure 5-5 and characterized in Table 5-1. Our previous analysis indicates that the money market is in excess supply in Regions I and II while in Regions III and IV this market is excess demand. We know that points to the right of the *IS* curve represent excess supply. Hence, Regions I and IV are associated with excess supply in the commodity

Table 5-1. Regions of Disequilibrium and Adjustments

REGION	GOODS MARKET	ADJUSTMENT IN INCOME	MONEY MARKET	ADJUSTMENT IN INTEREST RATES
I	Excess supply	$Y\downarrow$	Excess supply	$r\downarrow$
II	Excess demand	$Y\uparrow$	Excess supply	$r\downarrow$
III	Excess demand	$Y\uparrow$	Excess demand	$r\uparrow$
IV	Excess supply	$Y\downarrow$	Excess demand	$r\uparrow$

Figure 5-5. Disequilibrium and Adjustments in the IS-LM Model

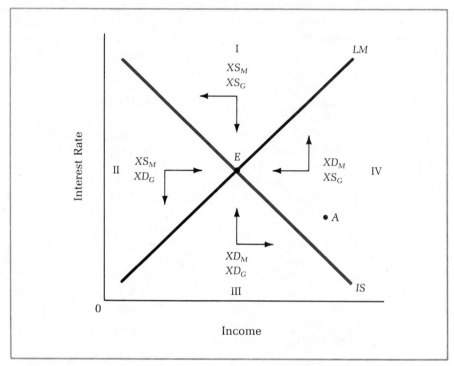

The intersection of the IS and LM curves divides the quadrant into four regions. In Regions I and II the money market is in excess supply (XS_M) while in Regions III and IV this market is in excess demand (XD_M). In terms of the commodity market, Regions I and IV signify excess supply (XS_G), and Regions II and III excess demand (XD_G). Market forces in each region will cause adjustments that result in equilibrium being reestablished. Consider Point A. The unplanned inventory accumulations in the goods market will lead to production cuts and a decrease in income. In the money market, the excess demand for money results in a rise in interest rates. Both changes move the economy toward equilibrium (Point E).

market. In Regions II and III the commodity market is in excess demand.

While the identification of the state of the markets in each quadrant is important, the markets' responses are even more important. These responses determine whether the economy will move toward an interest rate and income level at which both markets clear. Consider Region IV. The excess demand in the money market will cause the interest rate to rise as indicated by the vertical arrow pointing upward. The excess supply in the commodity market, on the other hand, will result in a decrease in output. The horizontal arrow pointing leftward captures this movement. Thus, from Point A in Figure 5-5 interest rates and output would begin moving up and to the left toward equilibrium. Region III is characterized by excess demand in the goods market and excess demand in the money market. The two arrows for this region reflect the fact that both output and the interest rate will increase. The arrows in the other two regions can be interpreted similarly. The major point to notice here is that if the economy is at some interest-income combination that is not at the intersection of the IS and LM curves; that is, if it is not in general equilibrium, economic forces will automatically drive the economy to the equilibrium combination.

Consider the effect of an expansionary fiscal policy in order to see how this adjustment process operates. Suppose the economy is in equilibrium at Point C in Figure 5-6. An increase in government spending from G_1 to G_2 is reflected in a rightward shift of the IS curve, from $IS(G_1)$ to $IS(G_2)$. Point C is no longer an equilibrium point. While the money market remains in equilibrium (still on the LM curve), the commodity market is thrown out of equilibrium. At the interest rate r_1 and production level Y_1, the commodity market is in a state of excess demand since Point C lies to the left of the new IS curve. As a result of the excess demand, inventories are drawn down. This stimulates production and, subsequently, income. However, as income begins to rise, the quantity of money demanded at each interest rate increases. With an increase in the quantity of money demanded and no change in the supply of money, the money market is thrown into a state of excess demand, at a point to the right of the LM curve. As a result, the interest rate begins increasing. The increase in the interest rate affects the commodity market as well as the money market. Investment (and other interest sensitive spending) will decrease as the interest rate rises. This is the crowding out phenomenon that has the effect of slowing down the increase in income. The economy moves from Point C to Point D along some adjustment path.

The actual path the adjustment process follows depends on the relative speeds with which the money and commodity markets adjust. For example, many economists argue that not only does the money market adjust faster than the commodity market, but that the money market adjusts so rapidly as to always be in equilibrium. The reason for this very rapid adjustment is that individuals need only transfer funds among financial assets to reestablish portfolio equilibrium. Adjustment proceeds at a slower rate in the goods market due to the fact that output plans require some time to be adjusted. If the money market adjusts instantaneously, then adjustment toward equilibrium is as illustrated by the movement along LM from Point C to Point D in Figure 5-6. While the exact path taken is an important question, it need not concern us here. We need only note that the adjustment takes place through an interaction between commodity and money markets.[1]

---

[1] If the money market adjusts infinitely fast, the adjustment path is always along the LM curve. On the other hand, if the money market adjusts more rapidly than the commodity market, but not infinitely more rapidly, we would find an adjustment path of interest rate-output combinations that closes in on the equilibrium point. See the first appendix to this chapter for more details.

Figure 5-6. Adjustments following an Expansionary Fiscal Policy

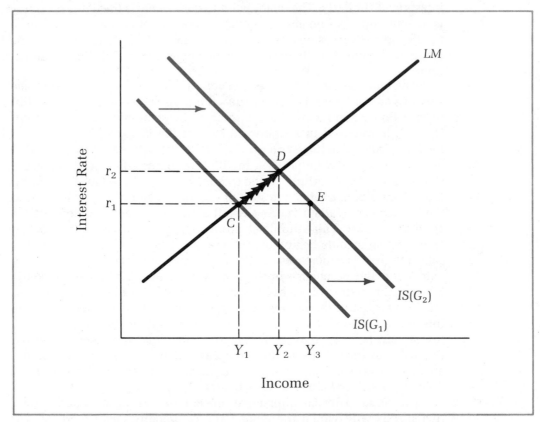

   Point C denotes the initial equilibrium income level and interest rate. An increase in
government spending will cause the IS curve to shift from IS(G$_1$) to IS(G$_2$). The commodity
market at Point C is characterized by excess demand. As a result, inventories are drawn
down stimulating production and, subsequently, income. The rise in income leads to an
increase in the demand for money which disrupts equilibrium in the money market. The
interest rate will increase slowing the increase in income. If the money market adjusts
instantaneously, then adjustment toward equilibrium is illustrated by the movement along
LM from Point C to Point D.

   A similar type of adjustment takes place when the LM curve shifts.
Suppose the money supply is increased, for example. This causes the LM
curve to shift from LM(M$_1$) to LM(M$_2$) in Figure 5-7. Then, at Point A, the
money market is in a state of excess supply although the commodity
market remains in equilibrium (still on the IS curve). Interest rates will
fall to Point B to reestablish money market equilibrium. But then the
commodity market is thrown into a state of excess demand, thereby
stimulating production and income. If the money market clears instantaneously, the output (income) level will increase from Point B to Point C

Figure 5-7. Adjustments following an Expansionary Monetary policy

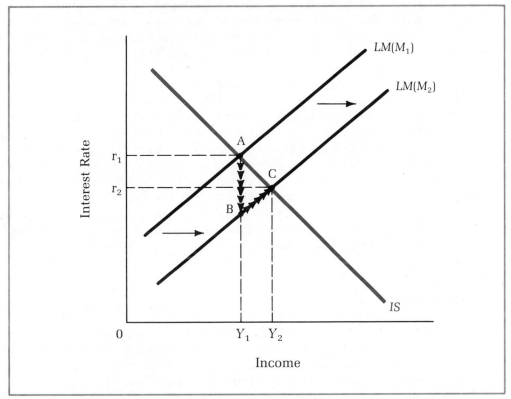

An increase in the money supply causes the LM curve to move from LM(M₁) to LM(M₂) disrupting the equilibrium that occurred at Point A. The increase in the money supply means that at Point A the money market is in a state of excess supply although the commodity market is in equilibrium. Interest rates will fall (Point B) to reestablish money market equilibrium. However, the commodity market is then thrown into a state of excess demand. Production and income are stimulated as a result. If the money market clears instantaneously, output increases from Point B to Point C along the curve LM(M₂).

along the curve $LM(M_2)$. As income rises, the interest rate also rises. This is because increases in income raise the demand for money which can be offset only by higher interest rates. Irrespective of whether the money market clears instantaneously, we again find that the interaction between commodity and money markets shows up in the adjustment from the old to the new equilibrium.

There is a very important lesson in this discussion. As seen in Figure 5-7, an increase in the money supply results in an increase in output. But what is the process by which changes in the money supply get transmitted to changes in output? The increase in the money supply causes individuals to hold a larger quantity of money than they desire. The desire to hold other financial assets and less money causes bond prices to rise and interest rates to fall. Investment spending and aggregate demand increase with lower interest rates. Thus, interest rates transmit monetary policy to the commodity sector. In sum, the Keynesian transmission mechanism for monetary policy can be summarized as follows:

$$\Delta M^S \rightarrow \Delta r \rightarrow \Delta I \rightarrow \Delta AD \rightarrow \Delta Y$$

Compare this transmission mechanism to that specified in the equation of exchange—$MV = PQ$. In the classical model, $\Delta M^S \rightarrow \Delta P$ since Q is fixed at full employment.[2] If we allowed Q to adjust somewhat more slowly, then: $\Delta M^S \rightarrow \Delta(PQ) \rightarrow \Delta P$. In either case, the interest rate does not come into play in the classical transmission mechanism. We will examine these differences in more detail in later chapters.

This completes our discussion of the *IS-LM* apparatus. The remaining portion of this chapter will illustrate how this framework can be used to yield insights into economic events.

Another Look at the Great Depression

The cause of the 1929 downturn in the economy was attributed, at the time, to an adverse shift in investment demand. The fact that private gross investment spending fell 98.2 percent between 1929 and 1933 seemed to verify this explanation. The decrease in investment spending, however, is not the only possible story of what caused the Great Depression. Milton Friedman and Anna Schwartz carefully studied monetary policy over the period 1929-1933 and they attributed the Crash to monetary policy.[3] With the construction of the *IS-LM* apparatus, we can analyze both hypotheses. In addition, we will consider the question, "Could a depression like the

---

[2] An analogy suggested by Professor J. Huston McCulloch of Ohio State University is useful in thinking about why an increase in the money supply should cause prices to rise. Imagine the case of a counterfeiter who prints up a batch of $100 bills. After the printing, the counterfeiter feels wealthier even though the amount of goods and services available in the economy has not changed as a result of his actions. As the counterfeiter begins to spend the bogus bills, various merchants will experience an increased demand for their goods and services. As a consequence, prices in some stores will rise. These merchants also will now feel wealthier and they, in turn, will increase their own purchases. This causes still other sellers to experience increased demand for their products and causes prices to rise still further. There is a ripple effect as the effect of the increased money supply moves through the economy. With more money in circulation, and with the same amount of goods available as before, prices will rise. See J. Huston McCulloch, *Money and Inflation: A Monetarist Approach* (New York: Academic Press, 1975), pp. 18 and 19.

[3] Milton Friedman and Anna Schwartz, *A Monetary History of the United States, 1867-1960* (Princeton, N. J.: Princeton University Press, 1963).

Great Depression happen again?" This is a question that seems to come up everytime a recession occurs. A recent occurrence was in an April, 1982 article in the *Wall Street Journal* titled, "Depression is Unlikely."[4]

What Caused the Great Depression?

The two competing hypotheses about the initial cause of the 1929-1933 downturn in economic activity are the *autonomous spending hypothesis* that attributes the decline to a decrease in investment spending and the *money hypothesis* that claims a contraction in the money supply was the culprit.[5]

The autonomous spending hypothesis can be represented quite simply in terms of the *IS-LM* framework. The massive decrease in gross investment spending that occurred between 1929 and 1933, whether due to pessimistic "animal spirits," as Keynes suggested, or some other factor, is represented as a decrease in autonomous investment and a leftward (downward) shift of the *IS* curve. The decrease in autonomous spending is represented in Figure 5-8A by the *IS* curve for 1933 (IS_{1933}) being to the left of the curve for 1929 (IS_{1929}). As a result, the equilibrium income level in 1933 (Y_{1933}) is less than the income level in 1929 (Y_{1929}).

While Milton Friedman and Anna Schwartz grant that gross investment declined between 1929 and 1933, they argue that this decline was caused by a decline in the nominal money supply rather than by a decline in autonomous investment. Their examination of monetary data indicates that *M*-1 declined 26.5 percent between 1929 and 1933 while *M*-2 declined 33.3 percent over the same period. These patterns are evident in Table 5-2.

According to Friedman and Schwartz, bank failures precipitated this decrease in the nominal money supply and the resulting crisis in the economy. A decrease in the nominal money supply is represented by a leftward shift of the *LM* curve. In Figure 5-8B, the decline in the nominal money supply between 1929 and 1933 is represented by the *LM* curve for 1933 being to the left of the *LM* curve for 1929. Such a shift results in a lower output and a higher interest rate in 1933 as compared with 1929. The higher interest rate, moreover, would cause gross investment spending to be lower in 1933 as compared with 1929.

Yet, this monetary hypothesis that has, for all practical purposes, become the accepted explanation of the Depression, has, itself, recently been challenged. Peter Temin, a professor at M.I.T., claims that the decrease in the money supply could not have been the cause of the business

---

[4] Lindley H. Clark, Jr., and Alfred L. Malabre, Jr., "Depression Is Unlikely, Leading Analysts Say, Despite Painful Slump," *Wall Street Journal* (April 1982).

[5] The names for these two hypotheses were first used in Peter Temin's *Did Monetary Forces Cause the Great Depression* (New York: W. W. Norton and Co., Inc., 1976).

<u>*Table 5-2.*</u> Monetary Policy during the Great Depression

YEAR	M-1	ANNUAL PERCENTAGE GROWTH OF M-1	M-2	ANNUAL PERCENTAGE GROWTH OF M-2
1929	26.4	0.76	46.2	-0.22
1930	25.4	-3.78	45.2	-2.16
1931	23.6	-7.08	41.7	-7.74
1932	20.6	-12.71	34.8	-16.55
1933	19.4	-5.83	30.8	-11.49
1934	21.5	10.82	33.3	8.12
1935	25.5	18.60	38.4	15.32
1936	29.2	14.51	42.9	11.72
1937	30.3	3.76	45.0	4.89
1938	30.3	0.00	44.9	-0.22
1939	33.6	10.89	48.7	8.46

Source: M. Friedman and A. Schwartz, *A Monetary History of the United States, 1867-1960* (Princeton, N.J.: Princeton University Press, 1963), Tables A-1, B-3, pp. 709-16, 801-05.

downturn since interest rates did not rise. If a contractionary policy was the cause, the *IS-LM* model suggests that a rise in short-term interest rates should be visible. Temin notes no such rise in short-term interest rates between 1929 and 1932. In fact, rates declined steadily from the stock market crash to the end of the gold standard in September, 1931. Therefore, Temin asserts, the cause of the Great Depression must lie somewhere in the spending hypothesis. In contrast with earlier explanations that stressed the fall in investment spending, Temin's thesis is that it was a decline in consumption spending that initiated the fall in income and, thus, the fall in investment. Temin argues, moreover, that the decline in the nominal money supply had virtually no impact on the economy. The

Figure 5-8. Explanations of the Great Depression (page 155)

A number of explanations for the Great Depression exist. In Panel A, the *autonomous spending hypothesis* is presented. This explanation argues that the depression was due to a massive decrease in investment spending which could be represented as a decline in autonomous investment spending, and thus a movement in the IS curve to IS_{1933}. An alternative explanation, depicted in Panel B, asserts the fall in income was due to a decline in the nominal money supply. This view is known as the *money hypothesis*. A third explantion has been offered by P. Temin and is presented in Panel C. He argues that the cause of the Great Depression was a decline in autonomous consumption that caused the IS curve to shift to the left. The accompanying bank failures led to a decline in the nominal money supply moving the LM curve to $LM(M_{1933}, P_{1929})$. However, the decline in the price level that occurred caused the real money supply to increase. The LM curve shifted to $LM(M_{1933}, P_{1933})$. In this explanation, output also declined.

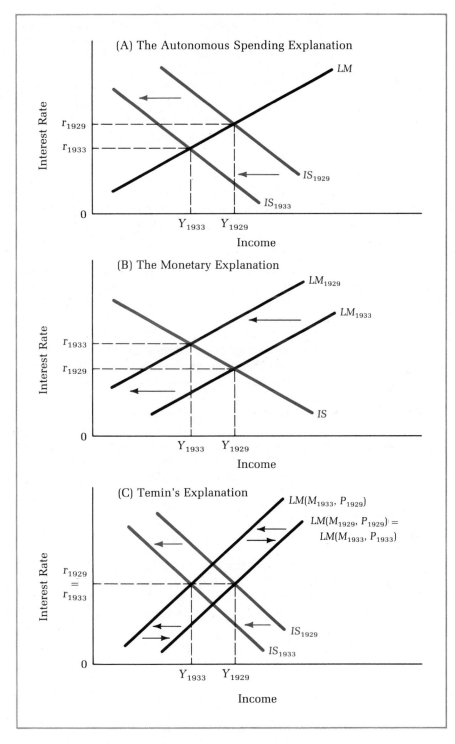

basis for this assertion is that prices fell between 1929 and 1933 due to the decline in spending and it was the fall in prices coupled with declining output and low interest rates that led to bank failures and caused the nominal money supply to fall.

Temin's explanation is not accepted by proponents of the monetary hypothesis but the reasons are beyond us at this point.[6] Let it suffice for now to realize that answers to the question, "What caused the Great Depression?" are not without controversy.

Can the Depression Happen Again?

While economists may disagree over the initial cause of the 1929 downturn in business activity, most tend to agree that such an event is unlikely today, although several began to change their minds in the midst of the 1981-82 recession. From the viewpoint of the Keynesian economists in the forties, fifties, and sixties it was the perverse behavior of policymakers that exacerbated the economic decline of the 1930s. The prevailing economic thought at the time of the Depression was that the government budget should always be balanced. An increase in government spending to offset economic trouble was simply not politically feasible. In fact taxes were often raised during recessions, as they were during the Depression, in an attempt to balance the budget. The Keynesian approach to economic declines is to have the government offset any unexpected changes in private spending irrespective of whether the budget is balanced.

Interestingly, in the midst of the 1981-82 recession Democrats and some Republicans were arguing in support of an increase in taxes to balance the budget. Is this a perverse attitude on the part of the policymakers? Is the Keynesian view inappropriate? We will explore answers to these questions in detail in later chapters.

The Revival of Monetary Policy_____

The 1920s were the heydays of monetary policy. The Federal Reserve System, set up in 1913-14, seemed to have been greatly successful in minimizing downturns and lengthening expansions. The Depression overturned the monetary bandwagon. The collapse of investment spending during 1929-33 and the subsequent growth of the economy due to World War II government spending added to the demise of monetary

---

[6] See Karl Brunner, *Contemporary Views on the Great Depression* (New York: Martinus Nijhoff, 1980); John Kenneth Galbraith, *The Great Crash, 1929* (London: Hamish Hamilton, 1955).

policy. It was not until the 1960s that economists returned to the view that that monetary policy did have a role in the economy. In this section, the *IS-LM* framework is used to examine the evolution of economic thinking about monetary policy.

The Classical View

Prior to the Great Depression, classical economic views dominated. One of the central propositions of this body of thought was the quantity theory of money which, as we have previously noted, expressed a relationship among money, spending, and prices. The relationship is based on the *equation of exchange* ($MV \equiv PQ$) which says that the flow of money purchases—the amount of money *(M)* times its velocity *(V)*—is identical to the nominal value of all goods and services sold—the physical amounts of goods and services *(Q)* multiplied by their prices *(P)*.

This equation can be turned into a theory of price determination or nominal income determination by adding assumptions on the stability of institutional factors and velocity. Alternatively, the equation of exchange can be viewed, with proper assumptions, as a theory of the demand for money.[7] If both sides of the equation of exchange are divided by V, we find that M equals k (the reciprocal of velocity) times P times Q. Assuming that M denotes the demand for money (M^D), then, this formulation says that the demand for money depends only on the level of income and not at all on the interest rate. The only reason for holding money is to use it as a medium of exchange.

How can the *LM* curve be used with such a money demand function? A demand function for money that is totally insensitive to interest rate changes is drawn as a vertical line at a given income level. Such a money demand function translates into a vertical *LM* curve.[8] Very simply, these curves represent the idea that neither demand for, nor supply of, money depends on the interest rate.

An increase in the money supply in the classical world is reflected in a rightward shift of the vertical *LM* curve, from LM_1 to LM_2 in Figure 5-9. The shift of the *LM* curve leads to an increase in income, the magnitude of

---

[7] This alternative view is known as the *Cambridge cash-balance approach* which stresses that spending or price changes can result either from movements in money or from changes in the desire to hold cash balances.

[8] When both the money demand and money supply curves are vertical, it is difficult to derive the *LM* curve graphically. However, we can reason as follows: As long as the price level is fixed, the money market may not be in equilibrium. Yet, all money in existence must be held by someone. People that do not want all the money they hold will try to get rid of the excess. The only way they can do this is by spending it. This drives up income (with the price level fixed) which shifts the vertical money demand curve to the right until it is coincident with the vertical money supply curve. When the two curves coincide, the resulting level of income is compatible with any interest rate. Thus, the *LM* curve will be vertical also.

Figure 5-9. *The Classical LM Curve and Monetary Policy*

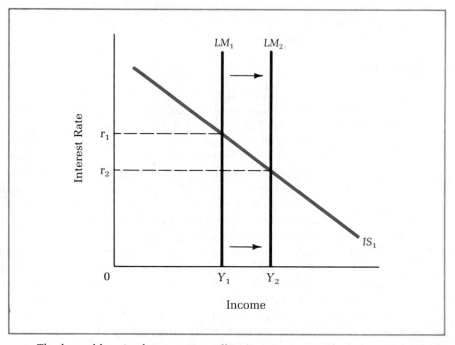

The demand function for money is totally insensitive to interest rate changes in the early classical view. Such a money demand function results in a vertical *LM* curve. An expansionary monetary policy shows up as a movement of the *LM* curve from LM_1 to LM_2. The increase in income, in this case, is determined solely by the increase in the money supply which indicates the potency of monetary policy.

which is determined solely by the amount of the increase in the money supply. In the case where the demand for money is interest sensitive, an increase in the money supply reduces the interest rate which, in turn, increases interest sensitive spending and leads to an increase in income. As income rises, the quantity of money demanded (to carry out transactions) rises. As the interest rate falls, the quantity of money demanded rises even more. The adjustment of these variables stops when the additional money supply is willingly held. In the classical world where the demand for money is interest insensitive, the fall in interest rates does not lead to an increase in the quantity of money demanded. The only way that the quantities of money demanded and supplied will be equalized is if income rises to the extent that individuals are induced to hold the new money. Because the effect on income due to a change in the money supply is greatest when the money demand is interest inelastic, it is easy to see why the classical economists held monetary policy in such high esteem.

It is also interesting to consider the efficacy of fiscal policy when the demand for money is interest insensitive. This case is presented in Figure

5-10. An increase in government spending shifts the IS curve from IS_1 to IS_2 increasing the interest rate, but leaving income unchanged. Fiscal policy cannot influence the income level. Why? An increase in government spending initially results in a greater income level, but this throws the money market into a state of excess demand. If the quantity of money demanded depends on the interest rate, the increase in the interest rate would bring the money market back into equilibrium. Without this channel, income must fall back to the original level for market clearing to occur. What causes the decrease in income? The excess demand in the money market drives up the interest rate which, in turn, induces a reduction in spending and income. Complete crowding out occurs, so that fiscal policy is totally ineffective in stimulating output.

Moreover, with the vertical LM curve, the real (commodity) sector cannot be a source of instability to the economy. Hence, the "animal spirits," which lead to unpredictable shifts in investment, can have no effect on the economy. There would, then, be no need for fiscal policy.

Figure 5-10. *The Classical LM Curve and Fiscal Policy*

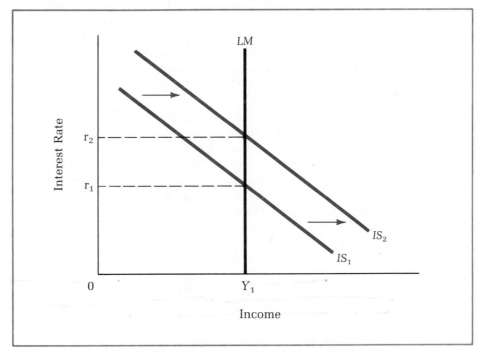

Fiscal policy cannot influence income when the demand for money is interest insensitive. If government expenditures increase—if the IS curve shifts from IS_1 to IS_2—then income will temporarily increase which throws the money market out of equilibrium. But with the demand for money independent of the interest rate, equilibrium can be reestablished only if the interest rate rises enough to drive income back to its original equilibrium level.

The Early Keynesian View

The Great Depression dramatically altered economists' views on monetary policy. The cause of the crash was attributed by many economists to the unexpected fall in investment. And the recovery of the economy after 1933 was not only very slow, but seemed to proceed at its own pace irrespective of monetary policy. Unemployment remained high—even at the peak of the recovery in 1937 unemployment was nearly 6 million, or more than 10 percent. Capital formation through new investment spending was unusually low. In fact, net private investment remained negative until 1936. Recovery waited until the spending associated with the World War II build-up, and the huge government deficits that accompanied this build-up, took place. As a result, the dominant opinion in the United States and elsewhere at the end of the war was that monetary policy was, at most, of minor importance. The Great Contraction and the volatility and apparent unpredictability of investment, the increase in the money supply between 1938 and late 1941 without economic growth, and the growth in the economy as the U.S. entered World War II all contributed to the opinion that monetary policy was impotent. In fact, by the 1940s, monetary policy was virtually ignored by most economists, except perhaps in classroom exercises based on the Hicksian *IS-LM* framework. If accorded any importance, it was because monetary policy supposedly worked in an asymmetrical fashion. It could cause a contraction, but not an expansion and, since the major post-World War II problem was viewed as the prevention of depression, monetary policy lay in complete disrepute.

The prevailing attitude of economists toward monetary policy was reflected in the actual role assigned to the monetary authorities. They had the task of keeping interest rates low so as not to hinder investment. The Federal Reserve System (the Fed) promised to purchase government securities in order to peg interest rates—to keep them at particular levels. This policy continued until 1951 at which time the Treasury and the Fed agreed to loosen up the reins on monetary policy. The agreement, called the *Accord*, enabled the Fed to act independently of the Treasury.

In the 1930s and early 1940s some economists went so far as to say that monetary policy is completely ineffective during severe recessions. The term *liquidity trap* was frequently used. It describes a situation in which the interest rate is so low (and the risk so great) that individuals see no practical alternative to holding money (the opportunity cost is too high). As a result a decrease in interest rates is not necessary to induce individuals to hold more money. The support for this case was the excess liquidity circumstances of 1931-33 wherein an apparently expansionary monetary policy failed to bring immediate results in economic growth.

What are the implications for policy if the economy is in a liquidity trap? Once this liquidity trap, or minimum interest rate, is achieved, individuals will hold any amount of money without the inducement of a lower interest rate. For example, if, at the 1932-33 interest rate level of 0.5 percent, the economy was in a liquidity trap, then a money supply of $10 billion, $30 billion, or any amount would have been held in money form. This statement translates into a horizontal money demand curve and, in turn, implies a horizontal *LM* curve.

The horizontal *LM* curve has some dire implications for monetary policy. An increase in the money supply is automatically absorbed by money holders without the necessity of a drop in the interest rate. This means that the *LM* curve is simply extended horizontally rightwards. In Figure 5-11 we capture this change by noting that $LM(M_1)$ equals $LM(M_2)$. But more important than the change in the *LM* curve is the effect on equilibrium income. The change in the money supply fails to alter either the equilibrium interest rate or income level. Monetary policy is totally ineffective in a liquidity trap.

Figure 5-11. *Monetary Policy and the Liquidity Trap*

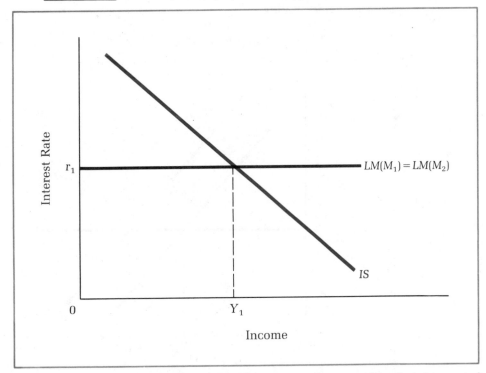

Individuals in a liquidity trap will hold any amount of money without the inducement of a lower interest rate. Therefore, the money demand function is horizontal which, in turn, results in a horizontal *LM* curve. An increase in the money supply simply extends the *LM* curve rightwards. A change in the money supply fails to alter either the equilibrium interest rate or income level.

Fluctuations in investment can lead to fluctuations in the economy. In fact, each change in autonomous spending would be followed by a multiplied change in real output. The horizontal *LM* curve creates an important role for fiscal policy—offsetting the unpredictable changes in investment spending.

Fiscal policy becomes very important in a liquidity trap. Fiscal policy has its maximum impact during this economic situation in fact. Figure 5-12 shows why this is the case. Equilibrium income increases while the interest rate remains constant. In other words, no crowding out occurs. The expansionary fiscal policy leads to an increase in income which, in turn, leads to an increase in transactions demand. In a liquidity trap, however, the additional transactions demand will be met without any increase in the interest rate.

It is no surprise that with an interest rate of just one-half of one percent and with no apparent success of a brief monetary expansion in 1932, coupled with the economic growth resulting from the government expenditures of 1941-45, opinion shifted in support of fiscal policy away from monetary policy.

Figure 5-12. Fiscal Policy and the Liquidity Trap

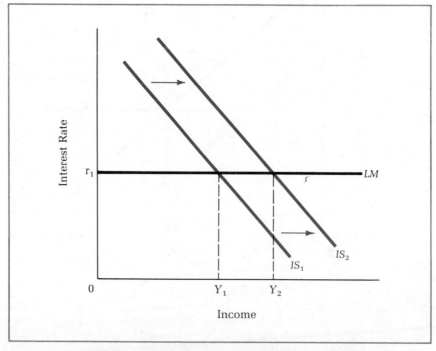

The efficacy of fiscal policy is enhanced in a liquidity trap. As can be seen, an expansionary fiscal policy results in an increase in income without any change in interest rates. In other words, no crowding out occurs.

Keynes's call for active economic policy and a fully participatory government sector did not envision the complete exclusion of the monetary sector. His emphasis on fiscal policy came about because he felt that fiscal policy would be more direct and would operate more quickly than monetary policy. His followers, on the other hand, virtually wrote off monetary policy. Most advocated a passive role whereby monetary authorities would do nothing but support interest rates. And if reference to a liquidity trap was not enough ammunition against monetary policy, the so-called Keynesians believed investment to be unstable, to fluctuate according to the whims of business expectations, and not to depend on interest rates. This instability could be offset only by fiscal action since monetary policy had virtually no effect, certainly no positive effect on investment.

Consider the view that investment is totally insensitive to an interest rate change—that the IS curve is vertical. Initially, in Figure 5-13, the economy is represented by IS_1 and LM_1. An increase in the money supply shifts the LM function to LM_2. The increased money supply lowers the

Figure 5-13. *The Slope of the IS Curve and Fiscal and Monetary Policy*

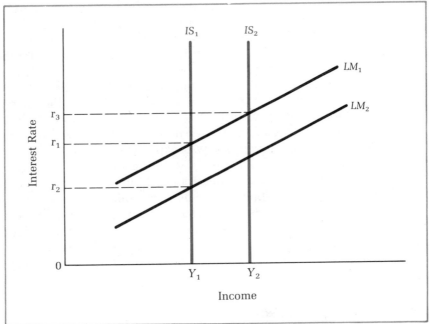

The slope of the IS curve also has implications for the efficacy of fiscal and monetary policy. If investment is totally insensitive to interest rate changes, the IS curve will be vertical. An increase in the money supply which shifts the LM curve from LM_1 to LM_2 only results in lower interest rates. Monetary policy cannot affect output in this case. On the other hand, an expansionary fiscal policy which shifts the IS curve from IS_1 to IS_2 results in a higher equilibrium output level.

interest rate to r_2, but, since investment does not respond to interest rate changes, income is not affected. Fiscal policy, on the other hand, is very effective. An increase in government spending raises income, and although the demand for money increases and so drives the interest rate up to r_3 the rising interest rate has no effect on the commodity market.

The Revival of Monetary Policy, 1950-65

The outbreak of the Korean War in June, 1950, induced consumers and producers expecting shortages like those of World War II, to "buy now while goods are available." Prices began to rise at the unprecedented rates of 6-8 percent per year. Interest rates were driven up (as the *IS* curve shifted out) requiring the Fed to increase the stock of money. The Fed had the responsibility of pegging interest rates which meant that each time rates rose the Fed had to increase the stock of money. But inflation forced the Fed to restrain monetary expansion and to break away from its policy of pegging interest rates. This change in policy was the famous Treasury-Federal Reserve *Accord*.

The higher interest rates that resulted from the *Accord* failed to have any of the disastrous consequences predicted by many economists. As a result, individuals in the Federal Reserve System and elsewhere started debating the proper role of monetary policy. Those who had been advocating that the Fed's proper policy is simply to support the interest rate lost some credibility after the 1951 *Accord*. Support for the use of monetary policy as a countercyclical policy began to slowly emerge. This support grew after the experiences of the 1954 and 1957 recessions. In 1953 monetary authorities concerned about inflationary pressures initiated a series of restrictive actions that led to a decline in the money stock. The economy turned down in 1954 but was revived later that year as the monetary stock was expanded. The July, 1957 contraction was again met with an expansion in the money stock—a rate of 6.5 percent money growth, the largest since 1946—and again the economy revived. But, while support for monetary policy did grow, not all economists attributed the revivals to such policy. There were heated debates about the relative importance of monetary and fiscal policy. Many viewed monetary policy's relation to the economy as analogous to a string on a balloon. The balloon could be pulled down by the string but not pushed up.

The 1965 Kennedy-Johnson Tax Cut

The activist view of fiscal policy reached its zenith in the early 1960s. Walter Heller, Chairman of the Council of Economic Advisors for the

Kennedy and Johnson administrations, stated, "we now take for granted that the government must step in to provide the essential stability at high levels of employment and growth that the market mechanism, left alone, cannot deliver."[9] This view was accepted and, in fact, advocated by most economists in the form of frequent tax cuts. Tax cuts were preferable to changes in government expenditures for stabilization purposes as changes in expenditures interfered with allocative considerations.

When the Kennedy administration came into office in January, 1961, the rate of unemployment was about one percent higher than the 5.3 percent rate of the previous year. One of the reasons given for the sluggish economy was the relative lack of private investment spending. It was asserted that the high rate of taxation on the return from investment deterred businesses from spending. Reduction of such taxes, it was argued, would contribute to both high employment and more rapid growth. Another reason why a tax cut was needed if the economy was to expand was the idea of *fiscal drag*. Walter Heller and others argued that tight fiscal policy had caused the recent business expansion to abort prematurely through the drag of overly high progressive tax rates. The basic idea of fiscal drag is quite simple. If the economy was growing at rates that ensured full employment the progressive income tax system would lead to a growth of output below full employment. In other words, the progressive tax system increases taxes automatically in a growing economy. It was felt that tax cuts were necessary to avoid this drag.

Armed with these reasons and taking an activist fiscal stance, the Kennedy administration proposed a major tax cut in 1962 that was finally enacted in early 1964. The Revenue Act of 1964 reduced the marginal tax rates for individuals, from a range of 20 to 91 percent to a range of 14 to 70 percent. In addition, the corporate income tax rate was reduced from 52 to 48 percent. In dollar terms the personal tax cut was estimated to be worth $10 billion and the corporate tax cut about $3 billion.

This tax cut could be analyzed very simply in terms of the *IS-LM* model by decreasing autonomous taxes (T_0) leading, thereby, to an outward shift of the *IS* curve. Assuming that monetary policy remains constant, the model predicts a higher income level—just what the Kennedy administration desired. This is, in fact, what occurred. The tax cut eventually led to a $36 billion increase in income.[10]

The Kennedy tax cut was just what the doctor ordered—Dr. Keynes, that is. The use of government policies to stimulate the economy and reduce unemployment was an unqualified success. The economy expanded and unemployment fell. Problems were looming on the horizon,

[9] Walter W. Heller, *New Dimensions of Political Economy* (New York: W. W. Norton and Co., Inc., 1966), p. 9.
[10] See Arthur Okun, "Measuring the Impact of the 1964 Tax Reduction," in *Perspectives on Economic Growth*, W. W. Heller, ed. (New York: Random House, Inc., 1968).

however. The Vietnam War, the inflationary 1970s, and OPEC were around the bend. In the following chapters we will discuss these problems and what they meant both for the economy and for economic theory.

Conclusion and Summary

In this chapter, we completed the task of constructing a model that allows monetary and fiscal policy to be studied under the assumption that prices are fixed. The IS curve was developed to summarize equilibrium in the commodity market, and the LM curve was developed to summarize equilibrium in the money market. Simultaneous equilibrium in both markets occurs at the intersection of the IS and LM curves. This point determines the only interest rate and output level combination at which both markets are simultaneously in equilibrium. Once the notion of overall equilibrium was understood, the important issue of how the economy adjusts to changes in exogenous variables was examined. Adjustments to a new equilibrium were accomplished by a series of iterative changes in the commodity and money markets.

With the model constructed, the latter portion of this chapter was devoted to applying the IS-LM framework to economic events and issues that occurred between 1930 and 1965. Various explanations of the Great Depression were examined from the perspective provided by this model. We also discussed the changing views on the efficacy of monetary policy. The classical economists, who felt the demand for cash balances depended only on transaction needs, stressed the potency of monetary policy and the lack of need for any type of stabilization policy, particularly fiscal policy. In contrast to this position, many early Keynesians believed a liquidity trap characterized economies during severe business downturns requiring the use of fiscal policy and rendering monetary policy impotent.

Despite the fixed price assumption, the IS-LM model is an extremely important framework for policy analysis. Throughout the 1960s, most economic problems were analyzed by policymakers and economists either implicitly or explicitly in terms of this framework. The inflation that began in the late 1960s and exploded during the seventies, however, rendered this model obsolete. A framework that allowed prices to be determined along with interest rates and output was needed. In the next few chapters, we modify and expand the IS-LM framework to explain price changes. This new framework is known as the *aggregate demand-aggregate supply model*.

PROBLEMS AND EXERCISES

1. Why does the point of intersection between the IS and LM curves determine the equilibrium income level and interest rate?

2. Show and explain why the multiplier is larger when just the commodity market is considered than when both commodity and money markets are considered.

3. A great deal of press (*Business Week, Wall Street Journal*) has been devoted to the idea of *crowding out*. There it is claimed that increased government spending may not be expansionary. Evaluate this claim.

4. Assume the president of the United States wants to cut taxes. Further, suppose Congress enacts such a tax cut by increasing the standard deduction.
   a. Identify the variable or parameter that changes.
   b. Identify how this change affects either the IS or LM curve.
   c. What are the implications of this change for the following variables:
      (1) The income level
      (2) The interest rate
      (3) The consumption level
      (4) The level of the transaction demand holdings for money

5. Some economists argue that the money demand function is misspecified. It is argued that the demand for money should be a function of disposable income (rather than just income) and the interest rate.
   a. What are the implications for the LM curve of such a money demand function?
   b. Given the revised money demand function, determine the effects of an increase in taxes on the equilibrium values of Y and r.
   c. How do your results in b compare with the corresponding results for the case in which the money demand function does not depend on taxes?

6. During the second half of 1966, the Fed sharply cut back on monetary growth. What does the IS-LM model predict will happen to the economy as a result of this policy? Collect GNP, interest rate, and investment spending data for this period. Is the data consistent with the predictions from the IS-LM model?

7. Why was the phrase "you can't push on a string" associated with the view of early Keynesians about the effectiveness of monetary policy?

8. In the IS-LM framework, where transactions demand for money is a function of the income level, and speculative demand is a function of the interest rate, it has been concluded that fiscal policy and monetary policy may be either totally effective or totally ineffective in the so-called extreme classical and Keynesian ranges of the LM function.

a. For both fiscal and monetary policy, explain why each policy is totally effective or totally ineffective in the extreme ranges. Use either graphs or equations to support your answer to this question, but be certain to explain why the policy is totally effective or ineffective. In either case, state your assumptions very carefully.

b. In this question so far, certain results were obtained for the effectiveness of fiscal policy in the classical range. If there is no speculative demand for money, and transactions demand for money is made a function of the interest rate as well as the income level, the effectiveness of fiscal policy will be different from that already noted. Fully explain the above statement. Include the specific assumptions that yield these results.

9. Explain why the LM curve is horizontal under an interest rate rule.

SUGGESTED READINGS

For the various views of what caused the Depression, read

Karl Brunner, ed., *Contemporary Views of the Great Depression* (Boston: Martinus Nijhoff Publishing Co., 1980).

Charles Kindleberger, *The World in Depression, 1929-1937* (Berkeley: University of California Press, 1973).

Peter Temin, *Did Monetary Forces Cause the Great Depression?* (New York: W. W. Norton & Co., Inc., 1976).

For an overview of the instability of the U. S. economy, read

Robert A. Gordon, *Economic Instability: The American Record* (New York: Harper & Row, Publishers, Inc., 1974), Chapter 3.

It is always a pleasure to read Mark Twain. The following book provides a humorous view of the business cycle:

Mark Twain, *Roughing It* (New York: The New American Library, Inc., 1966).

Current readings on the Depression of the 1980s include

"The Canadian Economy Is in Crisis," *Business Week* (June 28, 1982), p. 80.

"Worry at the World's Banks," *Business Week* (September 6, 1982), p. 80.

"Script for Collapse," *Wall Street Journal* (Wednesday, November 10, 1982), p. 1.

"Up in Smoke?" *Wall Street Journal* (Wednesday, November 17, 1982), p. 1.

For an empirical study of the controversy over Keynesian and classical models see

Daniel L. Thornton and Paul E. Smith, "The Empirical Significance of the Real Balance Effect," *Journal of Macroeconomics* (Summer, 1980), pp. 213-232.

An in-depth discussion of multipliers is given in

Harland W. Whitmore, Jr., "Unbalanced Government Budgets, Private Asset Holdings, and the Traditional Comparative Static Multipliers," *Journal of Macroeconomics* (Spring, 1980), pp. 129-157.

An alternative presentation of the Keynesian system is given in

Robert T. McGee, "A Graphical Exposition of a More Complete Keynesian System," *Journal of Macroeconomics* (Fall, 1981), pp. 559-570.

For a discussion of a model in which taxes enter the demand for money function see

James M. Holmes and David Smyth, "The Specification of the Demand for Money and the Tax Multiplier," *Journal of Political Economy* (January-February, 1972), pp. 179-185.

William J. Boyes, "Built-in Flexibility of Taxation, the Specification of the Demand for Money and Stability in a Dynamic IS-LM Model," *Public Finance* (1975), pp. 268-271.

_APPENDIX 5A. The Adjustment of the Interest Rate and Income to Changes in the IS or LM Curve

If the money market adjusts infinitely fast, the adjustment path is always along the *LM* curve. For example, suppose the initial equilibrium is at Point *A* in Figure 5A-1, and an increase in government spending occurs. The interest rate immediately moves to Point *B* along the *LM* curve. On the other hand, if the money market adjusts more rapidly, but not infinitely more rapidly, than the commodity market, the adjustment path from *A* to *B* might look something like that shown by the dotted line in Figure 5A-2A. This particular path is very interesting when plotted using different axes. Notice that as income initially rises from *A* to *C* to *D* and then falls, that a business cycle path is being traced out as shown in Figure 5A-2B. Other paths and cycles can be obtained by assuming different speeds of adjustment in the two markets.

Figure 5A-1. *Infinitely Fast Money Market Adjustment*

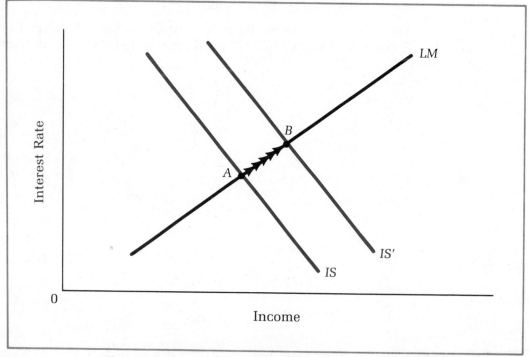

If the money market adjusts infinitely more rapidly than the commodity market, the adjustment path is always along the *LM* curve.

Figure 5A-2. Approximately Equal Speeds of Adjustment
in the Money and Commodity Markets

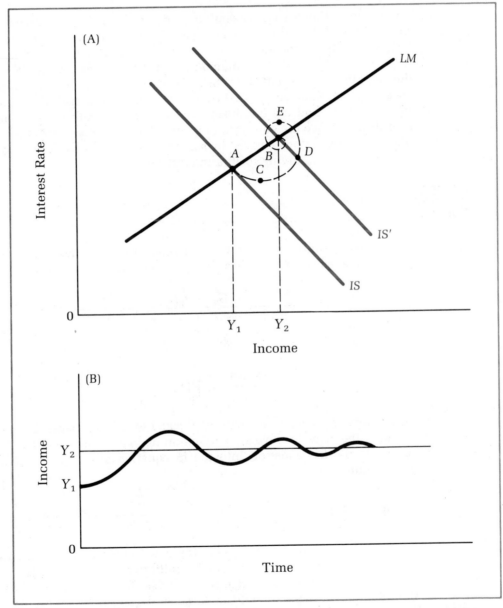

If the two markets adjust at approximately the same speed, the adjustment path is one
that closes in, or spirals in, on the final equilibrium. This is shown in Panel A. The time path
of income in Panel B shows how finite adjustment speeds lead to fluctuations in income—a
business cycle.

_APPENDIX 5B. Algebraic Presentation of the IS-LM Model_____

In this section we again examine the determination of general equilibrium, although this time it is an algebraic examination. The procedure followed to derive the equilibrium interest rate and income level is relatively straightforward. The commodity market is solved for the IS equation, and the money market for the LM equation. Then, the two equations are solved simultaneously. That is, the LM equation is substituted into the IS equation to find the one income level at which both markets are in equilibrium. Once the equilibrium income level is determined, the equilibrium interest rate is derived by substituting this income level into the LM equation and solving for the interest rate.

Algebraic Derivation of Equilibrium_____

In the appendix to the previous chapter, the IS and LM curves were derived in algebraic form. Recall that IS equation is

(5B-1) $$Y = \frac{C_0 + I_0 + G_0 - c_y T_0}{1 - c_y - I_y} - \frac{I_r}{1 - c_y - I_y}(r)$$

and the LM equation is

(5B-2) $$r = \frac{L_0 - (M_0/P)}{L_r} + \frac{L_y}{L_r}(Y)$$

To simplify the algebra, we will set P equal to 1. This makes no fundamental difference since we are still assuming that prices are fixed. Now, substitute the LM equation into the IS equation and find the general equilibrium.

(5B-3) $$Y = \frac{C_0 + I_0 + G_0 - c_y T_0}{1 - c_y - I_y} - \frac{I_r}{1 - c_y - I_y}\left[\frac{L_0 - M_0}{L_r} + \frac{L_y}{L_r}(Y)\right]$$

Solving Equation 5B-3 for Y yields the one income level at which the money and commodity markets are in equilibrium simultaneously. Since the procedure for solving this equation for Y is often not apparent the first time it is attempted, we will go through the algebraic manipulations step-by-step. First, multiply both sides of Equation 5B-3 by $1 - c_y - I_y$. Although this step is not really needed, future algebraic manipulations do become simpler. Conducting this manipulation yields

$$(1 - c_y - I_y) \, Y = C_0 + I_0 + G_0 - c_y T_0$$
$$- I_r \left[\frac{L_0 - M_0}{L_r} + \frac{L_y}{L_r}(Y) \right]$$

Next, the brackets must be removed by multiplying through by the coefficient I_r. That is,

$$(1 - c_y - I_y)Y = C_0 + I_0 + G_0 - c_y T_0 - \frac{I_r}{L_r}(L_0 - M_0)$$
$$- \frac{I_r L_y}{L_r}(Y)$$

If the term $(I_r L_y)/ (L_r)$ times Y is added to both sides of the equation and then the resulting equation simplified, we find

(5B-4) $$\left(1 - c_y - I_y + \frac{I_r L_y}{L_r}\right)Y = C_0 + I_0 + G_0 - c_y T_0 - \frac{I_r}{L_r}(L_0 - M_0)$$

Dividing both sides of this last equation by $1 - c_y - I_y + \frac{I_r L_y}{L_r}$ yields the following expression for equilibrium income:

(5B-5) $$Y = \left[\frac{1}{1 - c_y - I_y + \frac{I_r L_y}{L_r}} \right] \left[C_0 + I_0 + G_0 - c_y T_0 - \frac{I_r}{L_r}(L_0 - M_0) \right]$$

Note, that a *unique equilibrium*, or *general equilibrium*, is found since only exogenous variables and parameters appear on the right-hand side of the equation.

A numerical example may be helpful at this point. Let us use the same numbers we used in the appendix to the previous chapter. We find that Equation 5B-3, then, is written as follows:

$$Y = \frac{1}{1 - 0.50 - 0.25 + \frac{(1,000)\,(0.2)}{1,000}} \times$$

$$\left[200 + 150 + 100 - 0.5(100) - \frac{1,000}{1,000}(200 - 340) \right]$$

or

$$Y = \frac{1}{0.45} \, (540) = 1,200$$

Now, to find the corresponding *general equilibrium interest rate* just substitute $Y = 1,200$ into either the *IS* or *LM* equations. You should find that $r = 0.10$.

In the text, we saw that shifts in either of the *IS* or *LM* curves result in a different market clearing interest rate and income level. For example, let government spending increase by 100. Graphically, the *IS* curve will shift to the right (or upwards). Numerically, the "new" *IS* curve is

$$Y = \frac{200 + 150 + 200 - 0.5(100)}{1 - 0.5 - 0.25} - \frac{1,000}{1 - 0.5 - 0.25}(r)$$

or

$$Y = 2,000 - 4,000\ r$$

The larger intercept (2,000 versus 1,600) tells us that the *IS* curve has shifted to the right. On a graph we would find that this shift causes interest rates to rise along with income. Algebraically, we can obtain this result by solving the *IS* and *LM* equations again. If we do this we will find that $Y = 1,422$ and $r = 0.144$. Thus income has risen by $\Delta Y = 1,422 - 1,200 = 222$, and the interest rate by $\Delta r = 0.144 - 0.10 = 0.044$.

In Appendix 3B a model with induced investment and lump sum taxes was studied. There the government expenditure multiplier was found to be

$$\Delta Y = \frac{1}{1 - c_y - I_y}(\Delta G)$$

In terms of our example, the increase in government expenditure of 100 would result in an increase in income of 400. However, when the money market is incorporated in the analysis, the government spending multiplier (derived from Equation 5B-5) is as follows:

$$\Delta Y = \frac{1}{1 - c_y - I_y + \dfrac{I_r L_y}{L_r}}(\Delta G)$$

The same increase in government spending (100) now increases income by 222. While a multiplier effect still exists when the money market is included, it is much smaller. In fact, in our example, the government spending multiplier falls from 4.00 to 2.22 when a money market is introduced into the model.

The smaller multiplier is due to the fact that the term $I_r L_y/L_r$ is added to the denominator. Of course, mathematically, any time the denominator increases while the numerator remains unchanged, the entire term (in this case the multiplier) becomes smaller. However, what is more important is the explanation or the economics of what is happening here. The term $I_r L_y / L_r$ is made up of the coefficients on the interest rate in the money demand and the investment equations, and the coefficient on income in the money demand equation. These coefficients represent the interaction between the money and commodity markets. When government spending increases, income increases by the multiplier effect discussed in the previous chapter. However, as we have previously discussed, the increase in income causes the demand for money to increase. This is represented by the coefficient L_y. With a given money supply, the interest rate must increase to induce a reduction in money holdings which offsets the income-induced increase in the quantity of money demanded. This is represented by L_r. When the interest rate rises, investment falls, as represented by I_r, which has a dampening effect on income. Thus, some of the expansionary effect of an increase in government spending is offset when the money market is introduced.

Consider the effect of an increase in the money supply. If we consider the money market alone; that is, Equation 5B-2, we find

$$\Delta Y = \frac{1}{L_y} \Delta M_0$$

In other words, an increase in the money supply leads to a proportional $(1/L_y)$ increase in income. If, however, we allow for the interaction of commodity and money markets, we find that an increase in the money supply does not have such a large effect on income. Using Equation 5B-5, we obtain

$$\Delta Y = \frac{1}{\dfrac{1 - c_y - I_y}{(I_r/L_r)} + L_y} \Delta M_0$$

The term $(1 - c_y - I_y)/(I_r/L_r)$ in the denominator makes the multiplier smaller than when only the money market is considered. We leave it as an exercise for the reader to determine what this additional term in the denominator means.

Pure Keynesian and Pure Classical Cases

Suppose that money demand is not responsive to interest rates. How does this alter our model. This case, called the *classical case*, is easily analyzed in terms of algebra. The only change that must be made is that the money demand function be replaced with the following function:

$$M^D = L_y Y$$

The *IS* equation for this case is still

$$Y = \frac{C_0 + G_0 + I_0 - c_y T_0}{1 - c_y - I_y} - \frac{I_r}{1 - c_y - I_y}(r)$$

and the *LM* equation is

$$Y = \frac{1}{L_y} M_0$$

Note that the interest rate does not appear in the *LM* equation. This means that the general equilibrium level of income can be determined solely by solving the *LM* equation. Graphically, the *LM* curve would be vertical. In this case changes in government spending would have no effect on equilibrium income. We saw earlier that the government expenditure multiplier (when the demand for money is interest sensitive) is

$$\Delta Y = \left(\frac{1}{1 - c_y - I_y + \dfrac{I_r L_y}{L_r}} \right) \Delta G$$

In the classical case, L_r equals zero which drives the term $I_r L_y / L_r$ to infinity and thus the entire bracketed term to zero. Thus, the government expenditure multiplier is zero in the classical case.

If we solve for the effect of a change in the money supply on income, on the other hand, we find that ΔY equals $1/L_y$ times ΔM^S. Notice that a change in the money supply leads to a multiplied (by $1/L_y$) change in income. Classical economists developed their demand for money theory from the definitional equation $MV = PY$, known as the *equation of exchange*. *M* is the money supply, *Y* is output, and *P* is the price level. *V* is called the *velocity of money* and is defined as the number of times the money supply must change hands or be turned over to purchase *Y*. In our previous example we set *M* equal to 340, assumed that *P* equaled 1.0, and found that equilibrium *Y* was 1,200. Then the velocity would be approximately 3.5. If we assume that $M^D = M^S$, then we can write

$$M^D = \frac{1}{V} Y$$

which is very similar to our demand for money function, with L_r equal to zero; that is,

$$M^D = L_0 + L_y Y$$

Conversely, what if the demand for money was infinitely interest elastic ($L_r = \infty$)? This case is referred to as the *liquidity trap* or the *pure Keynesian case*. The liquidity trap was hypothesized to occur when the opportunity cost of holding money was so low that individuals could see benefits only from holding money. Thus, any increase in the supply of money would be held. Individuals would not diversify their portfolios.

The algebraic representation of the liquidity trap is somewhat more complicated than the classical case. The money demand function still is of the form

$$M^D = L_0 + L_y (Y) - L_r r$$

However, the difference is that the coefficient L_r is equal to infinity (i.e., $L_r = \infty$) representing an infinite interest elasticity of the demand for money. Thus, the general *IS* and *LM* curves still hold with the qualification that the coefficient L_r takes on a special value.

As with the classical case, the government expenditure multiplier and the money multiplier must be examined to get any insights on policy effectiveness. The government expenditure multiplier is as follows:

$$\Delta Y = \left(\frac{1}{1 - c_y - I_y + \dfrac{I_r L_y}{L_r}} \right) \Delta G$$

If L_r equals ∞, then the term $I_r L_y / L_r$ approaches zero. This means the multiplier reverts back to the situation in Chapter 3, wherein there was no money market and, as a result, no dampening effects on interest elastic spending due to an increase in the interest rate.

The money multiplier in this case is

$$\Delta Y = \left(\frac{I_r L_r}{1 - c_y - I_y + \dfrac{I_r L_y}{L_r}} \right) \Delta M^S$$

If $L_r = \infty$, the term $I_r L_y / L_r$ again approaches zero. In addition the term I_r / L_r approaches zero. Since the numerator goes to zero, this means the multiplier associated with a change in policy is approximated by zero. In other words, monetary policy has no effect on income in a liquidity trap.

Finally consider what occurs when investment is interest inelastic, as represented by $I_r = 0$. Once again the algebraic representation of monetary and fiscal policy can be insightful. The government spending multiplier is

$$\Delta Y = \left(\frac{1}{1 - c_y - I_y + \dfrac{I_r L_y}{L_r}} \right) \Delta G$$

If $I_r = 0$, then the term in brackets reduces to the simple commodity market multiplier, $1/(1 - c_y - I_y)$. There is no crowding out. The money multiplier is

$$\Delta Y = \left(\frac{I_r / L_r}{1 - c_y - I_y + \dfrac{I_r L_y}{L_r}} \right) \Delta M^S$$

With I_r equal to zero, the term in brackets is zero. Thus monetary policy is ineffective.

APPENDIX PROBLEM

Consider the following model of the economy:

$$
\begin{aligned}
C &= 250 + 0.75(YD) \\
I &= 100 + 0.1Y - 30r \\
G &= 200 \\
T &= -20 + 0.2Y \\
YD &= Y - T \\
Y &= C + I + G \\
M^S &= 500 \\
M^D &= 10 + 0.4Y - 50r \\
M^S &= M^D
\end{aligned}
$$

1. Derive the *IS* equation for this model.

2. Derive the *LM* equation for this model.

3. What is the equilibrium level of income and the interest rate?

CHAPTER 6.

The Demise of Keynesian Policymaking: The Friedman-Phelps Alternative

In the 1950s and 1960s the world was easier.

Paul Volcker, 1979
Chairman, Federal Reserve Board

The IS-LM framework captures many of the interactions among economic variables. Yet, it turns out to have serious limitations as a framework used to analyze the economy—it is only a demand-side relation and therefore provides no way to examine the problem of inflation. Therefore, as inflation became more and more of a problem, economists turned to other frameworks in order to gain additional insights. In this chapter we retrace the paths followed by economists in searching for a more complete analytic framework. The following topics and questions are considered in this chapter:

- *The Phillips curve and the Friedman-Phelps alternative*

- *The IS-LM model as a demand-oriented framework*

- *Are inflation and unemployment symmetrical problems? In other words, is there a trade-off between unemployment and inflation?*

- *Is there actually such a thing as unemployment?*

- *Does is matter whether long-term contracts render wages and/or prices inflexible?*

Introduction: The Collapse of the Keynesian System

In the three decades following 1925, the economy experienced several major shocks. The speculative bubble of the middle to late 1920s burst with the 1929 crash and the recession-turned-depression seemed to be never ending. World War II brought production back up, but also led to severe shortages of many consumer goods. Pent up demand, released in the immediate postwar period, drove prices upward at nearly a 15 percent rate. The reaction to this inflationary spurt led to the 1950 recession, but inflation again appeared during the Korean War.

These events were mirrored in economic thought. The Keynesian framework, and the Hicksian IS-LM refinements introduced in the late 1930s, offered economists what seemed to be a clear explanation of the causes of the Depression and a set of prescriptions for offsetting any such economic downturns in the future.

Interestingly, even with the Depression fresh in everyone's mind, the problem of greatest concern in the late 1940s and 1950s was inflation. Perhaps the Keynesian framework had been found so appealing that people believed a depression could not occur again. Or conversely, perhaps the Keynesian theory had not yet permeated the economics profession so that the World War II and Korean War inflationary periods were simply the most recent examples of their lack of understanding of the economy. Whatever the explanation, it was the inflationary problem that most troubled policymakers and economists, and economists strove to use the *IS-LM* model to analyze inflation.

The result was a symmetrical treatment of unemployment and inflation. By arbitrarily specifying some particular level of output as the full-employment level and noting the relative positions of this full-employment level and the level at which the *IS* and *LM* curves intersected, economists could call for more or less demand to solve the unemployment or inflation problem. An intersection of *IS-LM* to the right of full employment was called an *inflationary gap* and an intersection to the left of the full-employment level, a *deflationary gap*. The policy implication was clear. Whenever the *IS-LM* intersection took place at an income level that was not the full-employment level, fiscal policy (and/or monetary policy) could be used to drive the economy to the desired level—to make up for the gap.

The apparent success of the theory and its policy application is visible in Figure 6-1. From the early 1950s through the late 1960s prices and

Figure 6-1. Inflation and Unemployment in the Post-World War II Period

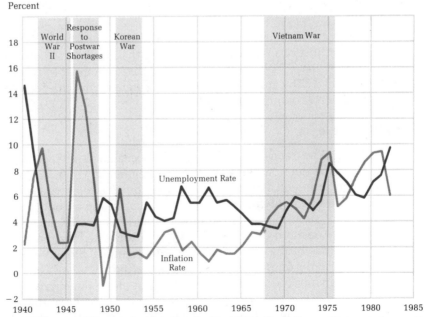

Inflation reared its ugly head during the World War II and Korean War periods as well as in the immediate post-World War II period. Price stability, on the other hand, was the order of the day for the decades of the 1950s and 1960s.

unemployment were remarkably stable. At the same time output grew at a rate near 4 percent. The Keynesian framework seemed to offer a complete, simple explanation of the economy and a readily applicable set of solutions to any problem. It also seemed to offer a straightforward relationship between the two goals of policy, full employment and price stability. As shown in Figure 6-1, until the mid- to late sixties, there was an apparent trade-off between unemployment and inflation. Whenever the inflation rate decreased, the unemployment rate increased and vice versa. But this simple relation, called a Phillips or trade-off curve, was misleading and drew policymakers into a false sense of security. They thought all they had to do was choose the combination of unemployment and inflation they wanted and then use monetary and fiscal policies to drive the economy to that combination.

In the late 1960s, as inflation continued to rise (often accompanied by an increase in unemployment), economists were forced to search for a new paradigm, one that would provide more detail and insight than the IS-LM model. The answer came in the form of the Friedman-Phelps model, a model that reinterpreted the Phillips curve and revolutionized thinking about economic policymaking.

The Trade-off Curve and the Friedman-Phelps Alternative

In this chapter we shall next discuss the Phillips curve and its policy implications. We will then turn to the Friedman-Phelps interpretation of the curve. The objective of these discussions is to introduce Chapters 7 and 8. The material in those chapters forms the foundation of current macroeconomic theory.

The Phillips Curve

The trade-off or Phillips curve became popular during the early 1960s just at the time the Keynesian policymaking approach was taking hold in government. The trade-off curve showed a relationship between inflation and unemployment rates, as depicted in Figure 6-2 (derived from Figure 6-1), such that as inflation declined unemployment rose, and vice versa. The position of the trade-off curve was fixed by the structure and capabilities of the economy—the combinations shown along the curve were the only ones attainable over a period of time. The idea was that the economy could operate at any point along the curve. If the current position of the economy was not to the policymakers' liking, they could use policy to move the economy to any other point along the curve. The only constraint was that if policymakers wanted lower inflation rates they

Figure 6-2. The Phillips Curve

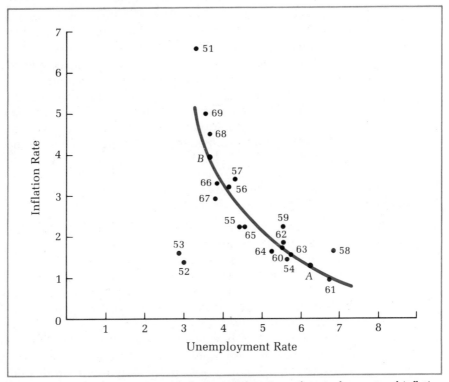

Using the period 1951-1968 and plotting combinations of unemployment and inflation rates, a downward sloping curve is traced out. This curve, known as the *Phillips* or *trade-off* curve, formed the basis of the "fine tuning" policies of the 1960s.

would have to accept higher unemployment rates, and vice versa. If, for example, the policymakers decided Point *A* in Figure 6-2 represented too high of an unemployment rate, expansionary monetary and fiscal policy could be used to drive the economy along the trade-off curve toward Point *B*, generating more inflation, but less unemployment.

The original observation of this curve is attributed to a paper published in 1958 by Professor A. W. Phillips (although his observation was in terms of wage changes rather than price changes).[1] He noticed that years in which the unemployment rate was low were years in which wage increases were high, and years of high-unemployment rates were years in which wage increases were low. Professors Paul Samuelson and Robert Solow popularized that relationship for the U.S. and extended Phillips's

---

[1] A. W. Phillips, "The Relation between Unemployment and the Rate of Change of Money Wage Rates in the United Kingdom, 1861-1957," *Economica* (November, 1958), pp. 283-300.

finding by noticing that an inverse relationship between the inflation rate and the unemployment rate also existed.[2]

According to the Phillips curve of Figure 6-2, price stability, a zero rate of inflation, could be achieved if an unemployment rate in excess of 8 percent was accepted. On the other hand, a lower unemployment rate, such as 3 percent, could only be achieved if the economy was willing to tolerate an inflation rate between 6 and 8 percent.

The discovery of the trade-off curve added another dimension to the Keynesian policy approach. It seemed at the time that the only worries facing the economy were how the curve could be made to shift in—how more favorable unemployment rate-inflation rate combinations could be generated.

The Mid- to Late 1960s: The Kennedy Tax Cut and the 1966 Credit Crunch

It is small wonder that the popularization of the Phillips curve had important policy implications. Policymakers believed any unemployment rate along this curve was attainable if society was willing to accept the corresponding inflation rate. All policymakers had to do was inform economists where on the Phillips curve they wanted to be, and economists would design demand policies to get them there. The Phillips curve analysis both ushered in and reflected a new, more activist view of economic policy. Policymakers throughout the 1960s focused their attention on what the best combination of inflation and unemployment was and used fiscal policy—with the Keynesian multiplier paradigm in mind—to drive the economy toward that chosen inflation-unemployment combination. The idea of using economic policy in this manner has been called *fine tuning*.

When the Democratic Kennedy administration took office in January, 1961, the economy was just recovering from the Eisenhower recession (1959-60). Unemployment was 6.5 percent and inflation only 1.4 percent. Yet, even with this relatively high unemployment rate the Kennedy administration was reluctant to undertake expansionist demand policies. Part of the reason for this hesitancy was the memory of the Korean War and 1956-57 inflations. Another factor was the fear that the balance of payments situation—the trade with other nations—would be made worse if unemployment was attacked.

Kennedy's January, 1962 economic proposal called for a balanced budget even with unemployment still above 6 percent. However, when in late 1962 it appeared that the expected recovery was not taking off, the Council of Economic Advisors (CEA) convinced the president to under-

---

[2] Paul Samuelson and Robert Solow, "Analytical Aspects of Anti-Inflation Policy," *American Economic Review* (May, 1960), pp. 177-194.

take some stimulative fiscal measures. The first such measure was the 1962 investment tax credit and liberalized depreciation guidelines. These measures were intended to make investment more profitable and thereby stimulate capital spending. The second expansionary measure was the Revenue Act of 1964 which decreased tax rates for both households and business firms.

These expansionary measures appeared to be highly successful. The unemployment rate fell from 5.2 percent to 3.8 percent while real GNP grew by 5.3 percent in 1964 and 6.0 percent in 1965 and again in 1966.

John F. Kennedy was not to see the success his program had had. November, 1963, in Dallas, Kennedy was assassinated by Lee Harvey Oswald. Kennedy's vice-president, Lyndon Baines Johnson, took office. Then in the 1964 election, Johnson won in a landslide over Barry Goldwater, the senator from Arizona. The issue of what the United States role in Vietnam should be entered the campaign. A joke making the rounds in the late sixties summarized the campaign and its aftermath: "I was told that if I voted for Goldwater we would be in a war, inflation would be rampant, and unemployment would rise. They were right! I voted for Goldwater, and now we see fighting in Vietnam, inflation is near 6 percent, and unemployment is rising."

By 1966 the monetary authorities were worried about the inflationary surge, a rise from the 1.4 percent rate of 1961-1964 to a rate near 4 percent in 1965. The Federal Reserve System (Fed) reacted by cutting back on monetary growth. The reduction in monetary growth, from an average of 4.5 percent during 1963-64 to a zero growth rate in 1965-66, drove interest rates up by more than 130 basis points (1 percent equals 100 basis points). The Treasury bill rate went from 4 percent to 5.3 percent and the prime commercial paper rate went from 4.4 percent to 6.0 percent. This rise in interest rates ushered in what has become known as a *credit crunch*. Banks, unable to offer the same rate that savers could get by purchasing Treasury bills (government bonds), due to the Federal Reserve's Regulation Q (an interest rate limit on savings accounts), found they could not raise loanable funds. Individuals were unable to get loans for homes which meant that fewer and fewer new houses were built.

The credit crunch was short-lived as monetary expansion accelerated during 1967-69. At the same time government expenditures for defense were exploding as shown in Table 6-1.

The rapidly expanding expenditures and money supply brought still more inflation. President Johnson, with a good deal of hesitancy and only after much debate with his economic advisors, finally asked for a tax increase in 1968. This so-called tax surcharge was to be temporary—a brief action to slow down private spending and reduce the deficit. The surcharge was imposed in 1968 and was intended to expire on June 30, 1969. But by April, 1969, it was obvious the tax had not worked as

Table 6-1. Government Defense Expenditures, 1965-1970

FISCAL YEAR	DEFENSE EXPENDITURES EXCLUDING VIETNAM	EXPENDITURES EXCLUSIVELY FOR VIETNAM
1965	$46.0 billion	$0.1 billion
1966	48.6	6.1
1967	47.5	20.5
1968	50.8	26.8
1969	48.9	29.2
1970	53.1	25.7

planned. President Johnson asked for a one-year extension, again emphasizing the temporary nature of the tax. His request was supported by President-elect Richard M. Nixon who also promised that the tax would be temporary, lasting only until the pressures from Vietnam decreased. The surcharge was extended but inflation continued to grow, from 5.1 percent in 1969 to 5.4 percent in 1970.

The primary economic problem facing the Nixon administration in 1969 was inflation. The decision was made to fight inflation recognizing that unemployment would rise. The policymakers felt they could live with a little increase in the very low 3.5 percent unemployment rate. As a result both monetary and fiscal policies became sharply contractionary in 1969 and 1970. Government spending dropped from 1968 to 1970 while tax revenues rose. The result was a drop in the deficit from $12 billion in 1968 to a $5.4 billion surplus in 1969. The high- or full-employment budget surplus shows this tightening even more dramatically, moving from a $16 billion deficit in 1968 to a $17 billion surplus in 1969. Money growth decreased dramatically as well. Nominal M-1 had grown 8 percent in 1968, but grew only 3 percent in 1969.

What was the impact of the 1969-70 restrictive demand policies? Real GNP fell by 4 percent and the unemployment rate rose to 6 percent as the inflation rate fell from 5 percent in 1969 to 4 percent in the first part of 1971. But something else was occurring, something that threw the Phillips curve and the "fine tuners" for a loop. While the inflation rate had fallen, it had not fallen back to its original level let alone to a zero or negative rate as the Phillips curve had suggested. Instead, inflation and unemployment rate combinations to the right of the Phillips curve of the 1950s-1960s were experienced. The economy no longer operated along the old Phillips curve—no longer faced the trade-offs described by that curve.

These facts are also evident in Figure 6-1. Note there how both inflation and unemployment rates moved upward in the late 1960s. This upward trend was explained in separate path-breaking studies by Professors Milton Friedman and Edmund Phelps.[3] They suggested that policymakers had misread the implications of the trade-off curve and that a permanent trade-off between inflation and unemployment rates simply does not exist. Their thesis was that the only result of attempts to reduce the unemployment rate would be to cause accelerating inflation. The basis of their arguments was that the economy had a natural unemployment rate and output level to which it would return if left alone. Movements along the trade-off curve could only be temporary movements. If driven away from the natural unemployment rate, the economy would automatically find its way back.

The story they presented runs as follows: Suppose the economy is at Point A in Figure 6-3 with an inflation rate of π_A and an unemployment rate (natural) of U_A. The inflation rate that workers expect is the same as the actual rate of inflation, i.e., $\pi^e = \pi_A$. Now suppose policymakers decide that the unemployment rate of U_A is much too high and that they implement expansionary monetary and fiscal policies to move the economy to Point B. Initially, individuals and firms experience an increased demand for their products and services. Increased wages are offered to attract additional workers or to induce workers to put in overtime hours. As a result, production increases and measured unemployment falls. But at the same time, the increased demand for goods means that prices rise. Then, as workers realize that their extra hours of work and pay are not getting them the additional purchasing power they thought they would have, they cut back on their hours. Very simply, if you are paid less to do some task, it is likely that you will have less of an incentive to carry out that task and will probably devote fewer hours to it.

The realization that the rate of inflation has increased causes the Phillips curve to shift to the right, to $PC(\pi^e = \pi_C)$. The end result is that the economy returns to the original unemployment rate of U_A, but now it is saddled with a higher rate of inflation, π_C. The expansionary monetary and fiscal policies had only temporary effects on output and unemployment.

To repeat, Friedman and Phelps maintain that Point B is only a temporary resting place. The increase in output is a direct result of workers' price level expectations remaining constant. The expanded level of aggregate demand forces employers to offer higher nominal wages. At the original level of price expectations, workers perceive an increase in their real wage. Additional labor is supplied which allows output to increase as the economy moves up the short-run Phillips curve, $PC(\pi^e = \pi_A)$ to Point B. Eventually, however, workers will realize that their price

---

[3] Milton Friedman, "The Role of Monetary Policy," *American Economic Review* (March, 1968), pp. 1-17; and Edmund S. Phelps, "Money Wage Dynamics and Labor Market Equilibrium," *Journal of Political Economy* (July/August, 1968), pp. 687-711.

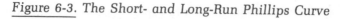

Figure 6-3. The Short- and Long-Run Phillips Curve

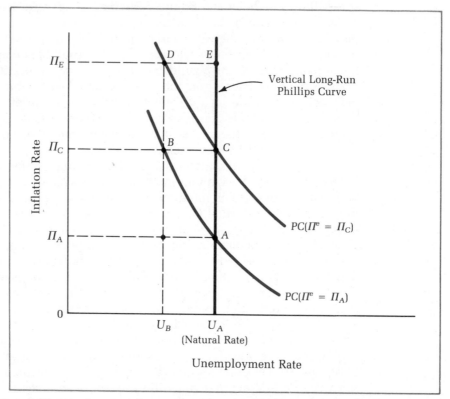

Milton Friedman hypothesized that the Phillips curve was in reality a series of short-run curves that intersected a vertical long-run curve. The vertical curve represented the idea that there was a natural unemployment rate that the economy would seek out if left alone. Attempts to reduce unemployment below this natural rate would at first be successful, but would eventually be met with failure. The economy would move back to the natural rate and operate along a new short-run Phillips curve. The Phillips curve labeled $PC(\pi^e = \pi_A)$ is stable as long as expectations do not change. Should a higher inflation rate be expected, a new, higher Phillips curve would exist, $PC(\pi^e = \pi_C)$. An attempt by policymakers to reduce unemployment, moving the economy from A to B, and thereby driving up inflation, will result in the economy adjusting to the new, higher inflation rate and returning to the same unemployment rate—the move from B to C.

expectations were incorrect. They will bargain for wage increases to cover past price expectation errors as well as the new expected price level. These adjustments are represented by the move from Point B to Point C in Figure 6-3. At Point C the economy is characterized by a higher inflation rate compared with its initial position, but unfortunately, the same unemployment rate. The Friedman-Phelps story is represented by the so-called long-run Phillips curve constructed by connecting all points, such as A and C, where the expected rate of inflation equals the actual rate of inflation. The long-run Phillips curve is vertical at the natural rate of unemployment showing that there is no long-run trade-off between unemployment and inflation.

According to this description, the choice facing policymakers looks grim. If the goal of a lower unemployment rate is given up, the policymakers have left the economy with a higher inflation rate. On the other hand, a sustained commitment to the lower unemployment rate means another increase in inflation. To keep the unemployment rate at U_B after workers' price expectations have adjusted, the government must again increase aggregate demand. The economy will temporarily move up the short-run curve $PC(\pi^e = \pi_c)$ to Point D in Figure 6-3. Unemployment can be kept below the natural rate only by accepting yet another burst of inflation. But again this reduction in unemployment will last only as long as it takes for workers to realize that the inflation rate has risen. If the unemployment rate is to be permanently reduced, the country is doomed to experience higher and higher rates of inflation. Hence, the Friedman-Phelps thesis is also called the *accelerationist hypothesis*.

The conclusion emerging from the accelerationist hypothesis is that the policymaker can attain the lower unemployment rate target, but at the cost of ever increasing inflation. If it always takes workers time to catch on to the new inflation, a higher output level can be realized by continually keeping the actual inflation rate above what workers expect.

Imagine what an impact the Friedman-Phelps alternative had on the profession. Used to thinking about using economic policy to change unemployment and inflation rates, economists were now told that their policies might do more harm than good. The conclusions of Friedman and Phelps were, to put it mildly, controversial. But there is no doubt they have revamped macroeconomics. They have initiated a counterrevolution to that remarkable intellectual event known as the Keynesian Revolution.

To fully appreciate the insights and implications of the Friedman-Phelps model, we must shift to another framework—the aggregate demand-supply (*AD-AS*) model. The trade-off curve obscures the insights of the Friedman-Phelps story. As an example, we will consider the 1973-75 period during which the economy was struck by a series of what are termed *supply shocks*.

The 1973-75 Period: Supply Shocks

The 1969-70 recession ended as monetary and fiscal expansion took place in the latter part of 1970. By 1973, however, inflation had risen to 5.8 percent. Policymakers were worrying a great deal about inflation and began implementing restrictive policies again. At the same time, poor agricultural harvests were experienced in the U.S. and elsewhere. In addition, the Organization of Petroleum Exporting Countries (OPEC) raised prices and, in support of this price rise, imposed an embargo. The prices of food and foodstuffs exploded by nearly 40 percent in 1973. Oil prices also rose dramatically—nearly 30 percent in 1974 alone.

What were policymakers to do? Obviously the economy was being thrown off the Phillips curve, but not by economic policies. Did the Friedman-Phelps analysis apply then? The trade-off curve does not provide enough information to answer these questions. The OPEC embargo and shortfalls in other materials such as food are called *supply shocks.* They are a reduction of the economy's inputs to production. To be able to understand their impacts on the economy and to determine if policy can be used to offset them, a more complete framework for analysis must be used, a framework that has an explicit supply side. Consider, for example, Figure 6-4 wherein the supply shocks are represented as an inward or leftward shift of the aggregate supply curve. Price rises and output falls.

<u>Figure 6-4.</u> *The OPEC Oil Embargo and the AD-AS Model*

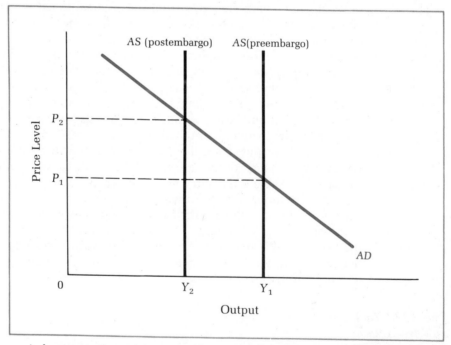

A decrease in the economy's inputs to production leads to a lower capacity to produce—the aggregate supply curve shifts to the left. The result is a decrease in output and a consequent increase in price.

The policy response to the rising price was to implement a restrictive monetary and fiscal policy. Monetary growth dropped from an 8 percent rate in 1973 to a 5 percent rate in 1974. The full-employment budget surplus also rose, reflecting a tighter fiscal policy. Was this the appropriate policy response? Look at the *AD-AS* diagram in Figure 6-4. What would be the impact of a restrictive demand policy? Would it solve the problem of rising prices?

If the leftward shift in the *AD* curve (due to the restrictive policies) was greater than the leftward shift in the *AS* curve (due to the supply shock), the demand policy would help to temper the problem of rising prices, but would not eliminate it altogether. This is, in fact, what policymakers found to be the case in 1975. The economy was thrown into a deep recession in 1974-75, but inflation continued to rise. The unemployment rate jumped to 8.5 percent while inflation exploded to 11 percent. The restrictive demand policies seemed to only make matters worse. It was not until the end of 1975 that inflation began slowing and the unemployment rate began falling.

Professor Alan S. Blinder of Princeton University has studied the 1973-75 period.[4] He estimates that the severe price hikes in food and energy accounted for two-thirds of the 1973-75 recession and a 9.5 percent increase in consumer prices over the three-year period. Given this result, Professor Blinder wondered how things would have differed if a more expansionary stabilization policy had been enacted. He estimates that a demand policy that would have avoided any recession would have raised the price level by 15.6 percent, rather than 9.5 percent, over this period.

While these results supported the accelerationist hypothesis put forth by Friedman and Phelps, they were very distressing to policymakers. It seemed that only certain effects of the oil disruption or any supply shock could be offset with demand policy. The only way to completely offset the effects of this supply-side disturbance would be with a policy that directly affected the supply curve. This might suggest that policy responses should be designed specifically for the disturbance they are to offset. That is, demand policies cannot offset supply-side disturbances. But questions about the appropriateness of activist policy began to arise. For example, might not uncertainty, as to whether a real output change is supply- or demand-side initiated, lead to inappropriate policy responses, responses that serve to make matters worse?

1975-1979: More Questions about Activist Policies

Over 10 million new jobs were created during the 1975-1979 period. Nominal *M*-1, which grew at a rate of only 4.5 percent in 1975, rose to

---

[4] Alan S. Blinder, *Economic Policy and the Great Stagflation* (New York: Academic Press, 1979).

around 7 percent in 1976 and averaged more than 7.5 percent throughout 1977-1979. Inflation fell in 1976 to 5.2 percent but rose each of the following years, reaching 8.6 percent by 1979. The Ford and Carter administrations each were claiming that they had implemented anti-inflationary programs and, in fact, although budget deficits were high, they declined each year. By 1979 the high-employment deficit was near zero. These developments are summarized in Table 6-2.

Table 6.2 *Economic Variables during the 1976-79 Expansion*

	1976	1977	1978	1979
High-Employment surplus (in billions of current dollars)	-22	-25	-14	-3
Growth rate of M-1 (%)	6.7	8.1	8.3	7.1
Three-month Treasury bill rate (%)	5.0	5.3	7.2	10.0
Inflation rate (percentage change of implicit price deflator)	5.2	5.8	7.4	8.6
Unemployment rate (%)	7.7	7.1	6.1	5.8

Sources: *Economic Report of the President* (1982); *U. S. Financial Data* (Federal Reserve Bank of St. Louis, weekly issues 1976 to 1979).

The performance of the economy, especially the inflationary increase over this period, was often attributed to "uncontrollable events." The *Economic Report* of President Carter, submitted to Congress in January of 1980, stated that OPEC oil price rises had continually wreaked havoc on the economy. Policymakers, according to the report, had been remarkably successful in averting recession. The report went on to once again proclaim inflation as the number one economic problem of 1980. What did 1979-80 bring? Inflation rose to 9 percent while the unemployment rate remained near 6 percent. Everyone—the public, economic policymakers, politicians, and economists alike—was frustrated. Economic policies simply did not seem to work. Inflation continued to rise while productivity fell and taxes rose.

Conclusions

The 1969-80 period will best be remembered for its frustrations—the frustration of many people, particularly the young, over the Vietnam War; the frustration of the public over the credibility of politicians; the frustration of economic policymakers in designing and implementing effective policies. These frustrations, nonetheless, led to the emergence of several new ideas in economic thought. Economists were trying to understand why their policies did not work and what was wrong with their theories. The primary development in economic theory during this time was begun by Friedman and Phelps who asserted that while the shocks to the economy were uncontrollable, the attempts to offset the shocks were simply incorrect. According to their thesis, it is not possible to utilize demand policies to fine tune the economy. Once individuals experience price increases and begin to expect further increases, it takes increasingly more rapid rises in aggregate demand to reduce the unemployment rate or even keep it at the current level.

The impact of the Friedman-Phelps hypothesis on the economics profession is probably as large as was the Keynes's. Their assertions spurred the second revolution in macroeconomics (if the first was Keynesianism), one based on the role of expectations in the economy. In the next chapter we fully explore this revolution.

PROBLEMS AND EXERCISES

1. Compare and evaluate the effects of an expansionary monetary policy and an expansionary fiscal policy on interest rates, prices, real income, and unemployment given
   a. A classical aggregate supply curve
   b. A Keynesian aggregate supply curve

2. A popular explanation for inflation during the 1960s and 1970s was the cost-push hypothesis. One aspect of this hypothesis argued that unionized labor used its bargaining power to acquire inflationary wage gains. Examine this hypothesis in terms of the trade-off curve.

3. Suppose tax receipts depend on nominal income. What happens to the government budget situation if the money supply is increased?

4. During the latter part of his administration, President Carter instituted a set of credit control policies attempting to reduce consumer credit card use. Use the trade-off model to predict the result of such a policy.

5. Why did the Vietnam War build-up extract such a heavy toll on the U.S. economy? What would have been the appropriate policy by the Fed?

6. What kind of policy response to supply shocks would you argue for? Defend your position in the context of the 1974-75 recession.

7. What is the Phillips curve? What was the primary policy implication of the curve?

8. What is the difference between a long-run and a short-run Phillips curve?

9. What is the Friedman-Phelps alternative?

10. Using the Friedman-Phelps model, explain the economic events of the late 1960s.

_SUGGESTED READINGS_____

For an overview of Keynesian policymaking, read

Robert Eisner, "What Went Wrong?" *Journal of Political Economy* (May/June, 1971).

R. E. Lucas and T. J. Sargent, "After Keynesian Macroeconomics," in *After the Phillips Curve: Persistence of High Inflation and High Unemployment* (Federal Reserve Bank of Boston, 1978),.

Franco Modigliani, "The Monetarist Controversy, or Should We Forsake Stabilization Policies?" *American Economic Review* (March, 1977).

W. L. Springer "Did the 1968 Surcharge Really Work?" *American Economic Review* (September, 1977).

James Tobin, "Stabilization Policy 10 Years After," *Brookings Papers on Economic Activity*, No. 1 (1980), p. 43.

For more emphasis on monetary policy, read

Phillip Cagan, "Monetary Policy," in Cagan et al., *Economic Policy and Inflation in the Sixties* (Washington, D.C.: American Enterprise Institute, 1972).

————, "Controls and Monetary Policy," in Cagan et al., *A New Look at Inflation* (Washington, D.C.: American Enterprise Institute, 1973).

Milton Friedman, "Irresponsible Monetary Policy," *Newsweek* (January 10, 1972).

You will find the following interesting and informative:

Council of Economic Advisers, *Economic Report of the President* Wash-(ington, D.C.: Government Printing Office, annual issues, 1960-79).

An additional discussion of monetarist models is provided in

Paul McNelis, "Irrepressible Monetarist Conclusions from a non-Monetarist Model," *Journal of Monetary Economics* (January, 1980), pp. 121-127.

For a further development of the role of expectations in the Phillips curve see

Kajal Lahiri and Jung Soo Lee, "Rational Expectations and the Short-Run Phillips Curves," *Journal of Macroeconomics* (Spring, 1979), pp. 167-190.

Some econometric evidence regarding expectations formation is presented in

Stephen Figlewski and Paul Wachtel, "The Formation of Inflationary Expectations," *Review of Economics and Statistics* (February, 1981), pp. 1-10.

Frederic Mishkin, *A Rational Expectations Approach to Macroeconomics: Testing Policy Ineffectiveness and Efficient-Markets Models* (Chicago: University of Chicago Press, 1983).

CHAPTER 7.

From the Trade-off Curve to Demand and Supply: The Analytics of Aggregate Demand and Supply

Very soon the Rabbit noticed Alice as she went hunting about and called out to her in an angry tone, "Why Mary Ann, what are you doing out here? Run home this moment and fetch me a pair of gloves and a fan!" And Alice was so much frightened that she ran off at once in the direction the Rabbit pointed without trying to explain the mistake it had made.

Alice in Wonderland

The aggregate demand-aggregate supply (AD-AS) frame-work provides a much more complete picture of the economy than did the IS-LM model. With the AD-AS model, inflation-ary and unemployment problems can be analyzed and both demand-side and supply-side policies discussed. In this chapter the AD-AS model is derived. Topics to be discussed include the following:

- *The IS-LM model as a model of aggregate demand*

- *The labor market and aggregate supply*

- *The Keynesian assumption of inflexible wages, the neo-classical version of slowly adjusting wages and prices, and the classical model of perfectly flexible wages and prices*

Introduction: "Fine Tuning" the Economy

The 1960s have been described as the halcyon days of Keynesian economics. *Halcyon* means calm, peaceful, affluent, prosperous, and this term does adequately describe the economy and economists' attitudes toward the Keynesian paradigm during the period 1961 to 1967 or so. Prices were reasonably stable, and unemployment, although thought to be too high, remained near 5 percent.

Economists armed with the weapons of Keynesianism believed themselves to be so much in control of the economy that they could fine tune it. In other words, they believed that if policymakers could tell them that a 4 percent unemployment rate coupled with a 2 percent inflation rate was ideal, then they could design policies that would direct the economy toward this point. The clearest example of this attitude was the Kennedy tax cut. Kennedy's advisors convinced him to call for a massive tax cut for individuals and business in order to reduce unemployment without affecting inflation. Although proposed in 1962, the tax cut was not passed by Congress until 1964. And from 1964 to 1966 the economy boomed. Unemployment dropped and inflation rose only slightly. Key-nesian policymaking was obviously successful.

Then came the Vietnam War build-up and the subsequent inflationary surge. Attempting to slow the rate of inflation led to the 1970-71 reces-sion. This was followed by another expansion, then another recession, another expansion, and so on, as the United States economy rode a roller coaster.

The 1970-71 recession was the result of restrictive demand policies aimed at the accelerating inflation of the late 1960s. The 1974-75 recession came about because restrictive demand policies were used in an attempt to offset both the OPEC oil embargo and some poor agricultural harvests. And again in 1979 and 1980, the economic downturn resulted from restrictive demand policies.

These experiences went against the fine tuning attitude of economists and raised several questions for which answers are still being sought today. Were demand policies the appropriate responses to the events of the sixties and seventies? Can the economy be controlled by demand policies? What changed over the decade of the sixties to so undermine the Keynesian Revolution? Also running counter to the fine tuning approach was the theoretical apparatus proposed by Friedman and Phelps *(F-P)*. The *F-P* model raised serious questions about the effectiveness of policy. But the presentation of the *F-P* model in terms of the trade-off curve was less than satisfactory—it obscured several of the implications of the *F-P* thesis. For this reason, as well as to gain insight into several other questions, economists began focusing on the *AD-AS* framework. In this chapter the *AD-AS* model is derived and used to represent a few of the events of the 1969-1980 time period. This chapter is primarily analytical—carrying the reader through a step-by-step derivation of the *AD* and *AS* curves. In the first section the aggregate demand curve is derived from the *IS-LM* model. The aggregate supply curve is then derived from the labor market. The complete *AD-AS* model is put together in the final section.

Aggregate Demand: The *IS-LM* Model in Real Terms

An important point to keep in mind throughout this section and throughout the text is the distinction between real and nominal variables: *real* equals nominal divided by the price level. *Real consumption*, therefore, is nominal consumption deflated by (divided by) the price level; *real investment* is nominal investment deflated by the price level, and so on. Since we have assumed the price level to be constant in the past two chapters, it has made no difference whether the variables in the model were measured in nominal or real terms. However, when prices are allowed to vary, it is important to understand which variables are measured in real terms. Suppose, for example, your income increased by 10 percent, from $20,000 a year to $22,000 a year while at the same time the price level rose by 10 percent, from 1.0 to 1.1. The $22,000 income can buy no more goods and services than the $20,000. The purchasing power of your income, called *real income*, is still $20,000. Will your consumption increase? The nominal value of your consumption will increase but the real value will not. To see this, suppose we live in a world in which there is only one good. If a consumer decides to purchase one unit at a price of $10, nominal consumption is $10 and real consumption is 1.0. Now suppose the price increases to $20. Nominal consumption will increase to $20 while real consumption remains at 1.0. Real consumption depends on real disposable income.

Similarly real investment refers to the acquisition of equipment or a building while nominal investment refers to the dollars spent in obtaining the equipment or building. Surely businesses make their investment decisions in real terms. They decide to purchase a building and do not (typically) purchase only two-thirds of the building when prices rise by 33 percent. The investment function specifies that real investment spending depends on real income and the interest rate.

Government spending is also interpreted in real terms. When the government decides to build a bridge, a bomb, or a park, the decision is made to purchase a real good, not the nominal value of a good.

At this point we will also specify taxes to depend on real income. This is not a totally realistic specification, however. Taxes currently depend on nominal income. In 1985 taxes will be indexed and will depend on real income. However, until 1985, price increases will inflate nominal incomes and push individuals into higher tax brackets even if their real income remains constant. In later chapters we will examine the effects of this form of tax. For now, for the sake of simplification, we will assume that taxes do not vary as prices vary.

The *IS* curve, representing combinations of real income and interest rates that clear the commodity market, is not affected by relaxing the assumption that prices are constant. Should government spending increase in nominal terms but not in real terms the *IS* curve would not change position since no more real output is being purchased at each interest rate, only more nominal output.

The modifications required in the money market to account for a varying price level are similar but slightly more complicated than the modifications required in the commodity market. An individual's demand for money is a demand for real balances since money is held for what it will purchase. Assume that money is held only to purchase food, for example. If the desired quantity of food costs $100, then $100 in money will be held. However, if inflation results in a doubling of the price level, food will cost $200. Nominal balances will have to be doubled in order to purchase the same quantity of food. Real balances will not change. In other words, just as with the commodity market, we assume that a money holder desires to have a command over a certain quantity of goods and services, not a certain value of goods and services.

Now what about the supply of money? Should it be specified in nominal and or real terms? Recall that the Federal Reserve System (Fed) determines the supply of money. It may, and most likely does, attempt to alter the money supply so as to set the real supply of money at desired levels. While the Fed has control over the nominal money supply, however, it does not control the real money supply. The real supply of money is defined as the nominal money supply divided by the price level (M^S/P); and, while the nominal supply is determined by the Fed, the price level is determined by the interaction of individuals, firms, and the government.

Let us now see if these modifications have any effect on the *LM* curve. Consider the money market diagram presented in Figure 7-1A. In order to draw a real money demand curve, a real income level must be assumed. Initially let us assume the income level is Y_1. Then $L^D(Y_1)$ is the relevant (real) money demand curve. Next, the money supply function must be drawn. Here is where the assumption of a varying price level complicates matters. A particular price level must be assumed for the real money supply function to be drawn. If the price level is P_1, then the real money supply is M_0/P_1, and the money market is cleared at the interest rate r_1. One point on the *LM* curve has been derived since the money market is cleared at the interest rate r_1 when real output is Y_1. Other output levels would generate other market-clearing interest rates as previously explained.

Consider the effect of an increase in the price level to P_2. Given the constant nominal money supply, M_0, the higher price level means that the real money supply, M_0/P_2, is smaller. In terms of Figure 7-1A, the real money supply curve shifts to the left. In order to derive the *LM* curve for this price level, assume the real output level is Y_1. When the output level is Y_1 and the price level P_1, the money market clears at the interest r_1. However, at the interest rate r_1 and with the smaller real money supply, the money market is in a state of excess demand. The excess demand condition will be alleviated, as we know, by individuals shifting their portfolios from bonds to money causing the equilibrium interest rate to rise. With output level Y_1, the money market now clears at r_2. When this point is plotted in Figure 7-1B, we find that it is off the curve $LM(P_1)$. If other output levels were examined, the corresponding market-clearing interest rate is determined, and the combinations plotted, a new *LM* curve would be traced out. The *LM* curve for the price level P_2 is presented in Figure 7-1B as $LM(P_2)$. In sum, a different *LM* curve exists for each price level.

Notice that the higher the price level, the farther to the left is the *LM* curve; that is, for each income level, a higher interest rate is required to maintain equilibrium in the money market. An increase in the price level means that the real supply of money has fallen since the nominal money supply is fixed. There is, therefore, a smaller real supply of money to meet the same real demand. To attempt to acquire more money, individuals will try to sell their interest-earning assets. These individuals must offer higher interest rates to attract buyers. And, as the interest rate rises, so too does the opportunity cost of holding money. This continues until the quantity of money demanded is reduced to equal the real quantity available.

Figure 7-1. The LM Curve in Real Terms

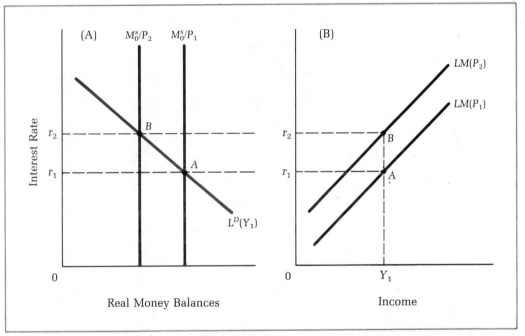

The real money supply changes as prices change. This is true even if the Federal Reserve holds the nominal money supply constant. In Panel A the same nominal supply is drawn for two price levels, P_1 and P_2. Given the income level Y_1, a decrease in the real money supply from M_0^s/P_1 to M_0^s/P_2 increases the market clearing interest rate, from r_1 to r_2. The result is summarized as a leftward or upward shift of the *LM* curve. Each price level results in a new *LM* curve.

When prices were assumed to be constant, the intersection of the *IS* and *LM* curves determined the one interest rate and income level that cleared both markets simultaneously. A unique equilibrium cannot be obtained in our present model where prices are allowed to vary. The intersection between *IS* and *LM* curves still determines an output level and interest rate that clears both markets simultaneously. However, this equilibrium exists only as long as the price level remains constant. A different price level will generate a different *LM* curve and, thus, a different equilibrium income and interest rate, as shown in Figure 7-2A.

Figure 7-2. The Aggregate Demand Curve

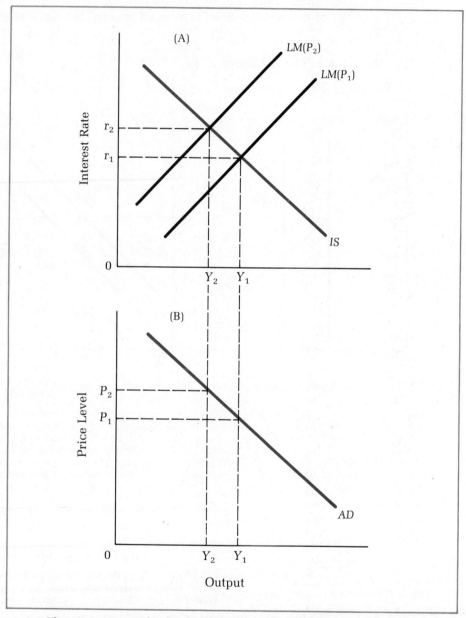

There is one income level and interest rate combination that clears both the money and commodity markets (Y_1, r_1) when the price level is P_1. At a higher price level, P_2, a different LM curve is relevant, $LM(P_2)$, and a new equilibrium income level and interest rate combination is determined (Y_2, r_2). These two points, when translated into the price-real income quadrant, trace out the aggregate demand curve.

The Price-Quantity Aggregate Demand Curve

If we wish to focus our attention on prices and output, a diagram with price on the vertical axis and output on the horizontal axis is more useful than the *IS-LM* diagram. Thus, let us translate the *IS-LM* diagram of Figure 7-2A into the price-output diagram of Figure 7-2B.

As can be seen, at the price level P_1 in Figure 7-2A, the one interest rate and income level that clears the money and commodity markets is r_1 and Y_1. The combination of the price level P_1 and the market-clearing output level Y_1 can be plotted in a diagram with P and Y on the axes. This is done in Figure 7-2B. At the price level P_2, which is greater than P_1, a different *LM* curve is relevant, $LM(P_2)$, which is to the left and above $LM(P_1)$. Recall why this is true. Given the nominal money supply, an increase in the price level means that the real money supply is smaller. Thus, for a given income level, the interest rate must increase to induce individuals to hold a smaller quantity of money. In terms of Figure 7-2A, the equilibrium interest rate-income level combination is r_2 and Y_2 when the price level is P_2. The price level P_2 and the output level Y_2 are plotted in Figure 7-2B.

Other price levels could be assumed and the corresponding interest rate and income levels found. Then, when the various price and output levels are plotted, a locus of price and output points would trace out a downward sloping curve, known as the *aggregate demand (AD) curve*.

The *AD* curve is downward sloping because an increase in the price level lowers the real money supply. This drives up the interest rate, thus inducing a reduction in total expenditures. As a result, real output must decrease as the price level rises if the commodity market is to remain in equilibrium. The *AD* curve summarizes the following sequence of interactions between economic variables:

$$\uparrow P \rightarrow \downarrow (M/P) \rightarrow \uparrow r \rightarrow \downarrow I \rightarrow \downarrow Y$$

Shifts in the Aggregate Demand Curve

Since the *AD* curve is derived from the intersection of the *IS* and *LM* curves, it seems reasonable that a shift in either of these curves (caused by a change in a parameter or in any variable other than price and income) will result in a shift of the aggregate demand. Consider first a shift of the *IS* curve. Assume, as shown in Figure 7-3, that the *IS* curve shifts out due to increased government spending. The additional spending drives up the interest rate and the output level. Hence, as shown in the lower panel of Figure 7-3, the original price level (P_1) is now consistent with a higher output level. This is one point (Point B) on a new demand curve. The increased *IS* curve means that spending will have increased at each price level—in other words, the *AD* curve will have shifted out.

Figure 7-3. Aggregate Demand Shift Caused by a Shift of the IS Curve

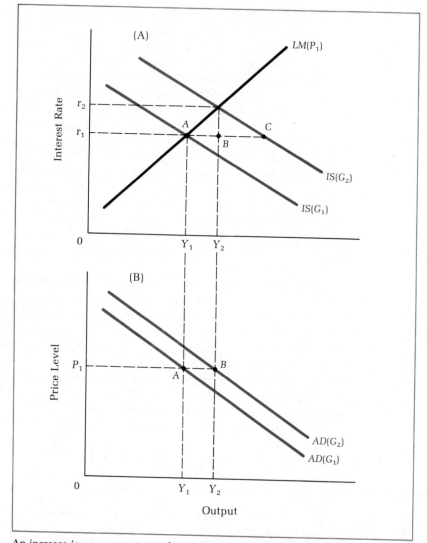

An increase in government spending is represented by an outward or rightward shift of the IS curve. This generates a new level of quantity demanded for each price level. At price level P_1, and given LM curve LM(P_1), an increase in government spending drives income levels and interest rates upward from Y_1, r_1 to Y_2, r_2. In Panel B the higher income level (Y_2) at the same price (P_1) represents one point on the new AD curve.

Varying the price level (shifting the LM curve along the new IS curve) traces out a new AD curve, one we have represented as AD(G_2). The outward shift of the AD curve represents an increase in the quantity of goods and services demanded at each price level.

Since the ultimate effect of a money supply increase is to increase spending, we should expect the AD curve to shift out (to the right) whenever the money stock increases. In Figure 7-4 the nominal money

Figure 7-4. *Aggregate Demand Shift Caused by an Expansion of the Money Supply*

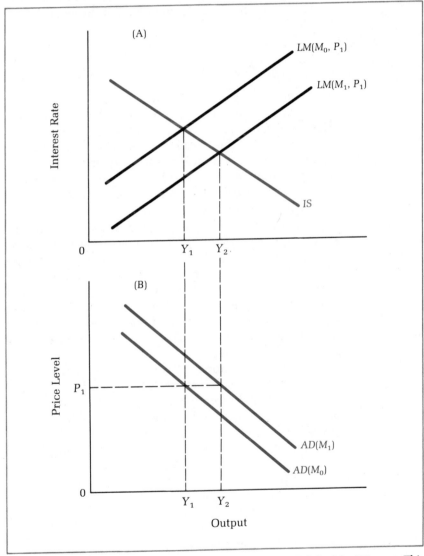

An increase in the money supply is represented by an outward shift of the LM curve. This generates a new level of quantity demanded at each price level. In Panel A the expanded money supply causes output to rise from Y_1 to Y_2. At the initial price level (P_1) the increased output level (Y_2) plots as one point on a new AD curve, $AD(M_1)$.

supply is initially M_0, the price level is P_1, the LM curve is $LM(M_0, P_1)$, and the equilibrium output is Y_1. A larger money stock (M_1) at the same price level (P_1) means the relevant LM curve is $LM(M_1, P_1)$ and the equilibrium output is Y_2. Plotting the combination of price levels and corresponding income levels traces out the demand curve labeled $AD(M_0)$. An increase in the money stock shifts out the LM curve (at each price level), from $LM(M_0, P_1$ to $LM(M_1, P_1)$. This shift results in a new set of price level-output combinations. As a result, the demand curve shifts out, from $AD(M_0)$ to $AD(M_1)$.

Aggregate Supply

It was assumed in previous chapters that producers supply enough output to meet demand without any changes in prices. This procedure enabled us to focus on demand and the determination of output (income). We began with the simplest framework—the Keynesian cross (or 45-degree) model. We then introduced interest rates and the money market into the model with the *IS-LM* framework. Finally, in the first portion of this chapter, prices were incorporated into the *IS-LM* framework to construct the aggregate demand curve.

Once the price level is specified, we are able to determine the values of output, consumption, investment, the quantity of money demanded, and the interest rate. If, however, we are to be successful in studying inflationary problems we must not only be able to describe the impact of price level changes, but we must also be able to identify the factors that determine the price level. The *AD* curve alone does not give us this capability. As with any individual market it takes both supply and demand to determine the price level. We will derive the aggregate supply curve in this section.

The aggregate supply (*AS*) curve is derived in the following manner. A production function relating the quantity of labor employed to the quantity of output produced is presented. At a given price level the equilibrium between labor demand and labor supply determines the quantity of labor employed. Combining this equilibrium quantity of labor with the other factors of production in the production function determines the quantity of outputs produced at that given price level. The price-output combination is one point on the *AS* curve. To trace out the entire curve, the price level is varied and the corresponding output levels are determined. Let us consider this process in more detail.

The Aggregate Production Function

In order to produce a product or output, the firm needs to use a number of inputs such as labor, capital, fuel, land, etc. The manner in which the inputs are combined to produce output is represented in a relationship known as the production function. The production function captures the degree to which inputs can be substituted for each other and illustrates the various combinations of inputs that can be used to generate output.

A simplifying assumption usually employed when the production function is discussed is that one of the inputs is variable in the short run while all others are relatively fixed. This assumption enables investigators to focus on just one input in their analysis. Labor is generally considered to be the variable input while capital represents the fixed inputs.[1]

What happens to output as additional units of labor are employed with a given or fixed quantity of other inputs? Most likely, as the first few units of labor are added to the fixed inputs, the additional output attributable to each additional unit of labor increases. Eventually, as more and more units of labor are added, the additional output produced by each additional unit of labor will decline. This additional output is called the *marginal product (MP)* of labor. In Figure 7-5 we have drawn two such

Figure 7-5. The Total Product Curve

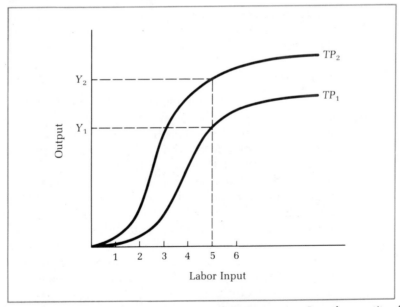

The aggregate production function converts inputs into output. Once the quantity of the variable labor input is determined, the quantity of output can be determined. As the quantity of fixed inputs increases, the quantity of output that can possibly be produced for any quantity of labor will increase. Given five units of labor, output Y_2 can be produced after the quantity of capital (fixed input) is increased whereas only Y_1 could be produced before the fixed input was increased.

---

[1] The gestation period between the decision to invest and the actual use of capital in production is quite long, perhaps as much as eight years according to several studies.

total product (production function) curves. Notice that along the curves each additional unit of labor adds to total output. Yet the amount of additional output produced by each new unit of labor at first increases and then decreases. A production function that displays this pattern is said to exhibit a range of increasing, followed by a range of diminishing, marginal productivity.

What would happen to the total output produced if the fixed inputs were increased? Most likely the additional output that each additional worker could produce would increase. More inputs enable more output to be produced. This is represented by an upward shift or rotation of the total product curve from TP_1 to TP_2 in Figure 7-5. The upward shift of the total product curve represents an increase in productivity, an increase in the quantity of output per worker. For example, in Figure 7-5, notice the increase in output, from Y_1 to Y_2, when five workers are employed and the fixed input increases.

The Labor Market

Once the quantity of variable inputs is combined with the fixed inputs in the aggregate production function, the output of the economy will be determined. We have already assumed that the quantity of the fixed input is known, or at least determined from previous periods. The quantity of the variable labor input employed is determined in the labor market.

The Demand for Labor

A firm's demand for labor is a derived demand; firms demand the services of labor for the output and the resulting profits that these services help to produce. To derive the demand for labor, firms are assumed to operate in a world where they are price takers and act as though they can sell all the output they desire to produce. Then, the quantity of labor demanded depends on the output level at which the firm maximizes profits. More precisely, additional workers are hired until the cost of the next additional worker is just equal to the additional revenue that the worker generates. If the cost of that additional worker would exceed the additional revenue generated, then the worker would add a negative increment to profits and will not be hired. If a prospective employee will cost less than the revenue from the output the employee would produce, the firm will hire that employee.

Let's use the data presented in Table 7-1 to see how this simple notion of hiring results in a labor demand curve. Suppose that a firm is attempting to decide on the number of workers to hire for one day. The firm can sell all the output it wants to produce at a fixed price. (Remember, the firm is a *price taker*; it does not influence price by itself.) The firm has a fixed quantity of capital, perhaps a building and several machines, and

Table 7-1. Data for a Labor Demand Curve

UNITS OF CAPITAL	UNITS OF LABOR	TOTAL OUTPUT	MP	PRICE OF OUTPUT	TOTAL REVENUE	VMP_L	W	$\frac{W}{P}$
1	0	0	0	10	0	0	20	2
1	1	20	20	10	200	200	20	2
1	2	35	15	10	350	150	20	2
1	3	45	10	10	450	100	20	2
1	4	50	5	10	500	50	20	2
1	5	53	3	10	530	30	20	2
1	6	55	2	10	550	20	20	2
1	7	56	1	10	560	10	20	2

must decide how much labor to employ. The manager of the firm knows that as additional units of labor are employed, the MP of labor first increases and then decreases. Does this finding imply that the firm should hire labor until the marginal product begins to decline? The answer is not necessarily. The firm is attempting to maximize profits. Therefore, it is interested in the additional revenue generated by each additional worker, or in the economist's jargon, the *value of the marginal product (VMP) of labor*. The VMP is simply the price of the output (the additional revenue from selling one more unit of output) times the marginal product (the additional output produced by the additional worker); i.e., $P(MP) = VMP$.

We have listed some values in Table 7-1 as a simple example of our discussion. We have assumed that the price of output is $10. In addition, we have fixed the capital stock at one unit. We then added units of labor, one by one, to the fixed input and listed the subsequent output produced. The VMP curve at the $10 price is plotted in Figure 7-6.

To determine the amount of labor to be hired, the cost of each unit of labor must be known. This cost is assumed to be reflected solely in the nominal wage rate. If the nominal wage rate is $20, how many workers will the firm hire? Table 7-1 shows that at least five will be hired since each of the first five workers generates additional revenue in excess of costs. The third worker, for example, costs $20, but brings in $100 in revenue. The sixth worker brings in just enough additional revenue to cover costs. However, the seventh worker would not be hired because only $10 additional revenue is generated for an increase in costs of $20. In our example, profit is maximized by hiring six workers.

The preceding discussion can be formalized by stating that the optimal number of workers is determined at the point where the *nominal wage* (i.e., the marginal cost) is equal to the value of the marginal product of labor; that is, $W = VMP$. In Figure 7-6 this condition is applied

Figure 7-6. The Demand for Labor

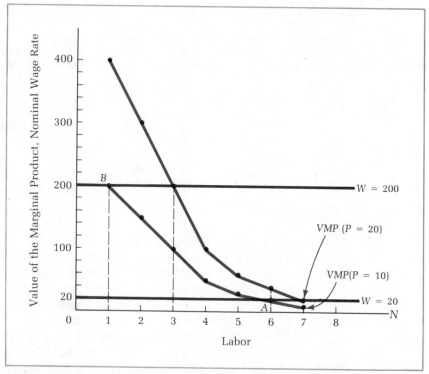

The quantity of labor demanded is determined by equating the value of the marginal product *(VMP)* to the cost of labor *(W)*. As the cost of labor increases, less labor is demanded.

The location of the *VMP* curve is determined by the productivity of labor and by the price of output. As the output price increases, the value of labor's marginal product is increased. This is shown by the upward shift in *VMP* from $VMP(P = 10)$ to $VMP(P = 20)$. After such a shift more labor is demanded at each nominal wage rate.

diagrammatically to determine the optimal number of workers. The *VMP* curve (given a price of $10 per unit of output) intersects the nominal wage curve ($W = 20$) at Point *A*.

In this example we found that when the wage rate is $20 the profit-maximizing firm will hire six workers. This gives us one point on the firm's labor demand curve. Other wage rates would mean that the firm would hire a different number of workers in order to maximize profits. For instance, if the wage rate is $200, only one worker will be hired. This is also shown at Point *B* in Figure 7-6. By varying the wage rate and finding the optimum number of workers at each wage rate, we are able to trace out the firm's labor demand curve. This curve is presented in Figure 7-7. This labor demand curve is denoted as N^D ($P = 10$) so that the assumption that the price level is $10 is easily recognized.

Figure 7-7. *The Demand for Labor and the Output Price*

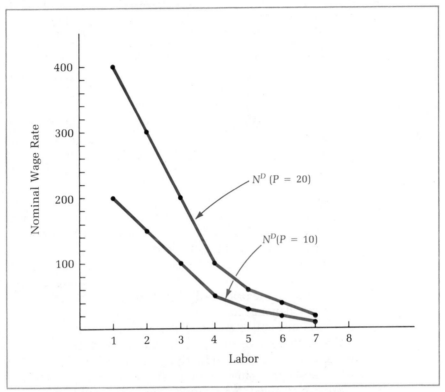

If either the price level or the availability of other inputs changes, the value of the marginal product will change and the labor demand curve will shift. In this graph, the price of output increases from $P = 10$ to $P = 20$. As a result, more labor is demanded at each wage rate—the labor demand curve shifts to the right.

A number of assumptions were made in deriving the labor demand curve. Specifically, the price level and other inputs in the production process were assumed to be fixed. If either the price level or the availability of other inputs changes, the value of the MP will change and, thus, the labor demand curve will shift. Perhaps the easiest way to demonstrate this point is to reconsider our example. Previously, we assumed the price of the firm's product was $10. Now assume that the price increases to $20. This means a new value of the MP curve must be derived. This curve $VMP(P=20)$ is presented in Figure 7-6 and the corresponding values are listed in Table 7-2. An increase in price causes the VMP to shift to the right. If alternative wage rates are compared with the new value of the marginal product, a new labor demand will be derived. As can be seen in Figure 7-7 the demand curve for labor shifts upward and to the right as the price of output increases. For example, at the wage rate of $20 and a price

Table 7-2. Values of the Curve VMP(P = 20)

UNITS OF CAPITAL	UNITS OF LABOR	TOTAL OUTPUT	MP	PRICE	TOTAL REVENUE	VMP_L	W	$\frac{W}{P}$
1	0	0	0	20	0		20	1
1	1	20	20	20	400	400	20	1
1	2	35	15	20	700	300	20	1
1	3	45	10	20	900	200	20	1
1	4	50	5	20	1000	100	20	1
1	5	53	3	20	1060	60	20	1
1	6	55	2	20	1100	40	20	1
1	7	56	1	20	1120	20	20	1

of $10, six workers are hired. At the same wage rate, however, but at the higher price level of $20, seven workers will be hired.

Since each unit of output sold now generates more revenue but costs no more to produce, the firm can increase profits by producing and selling more output. And it requires more inputs to produce more output. Thus, an increase in the price of the firm's product will, *ceteris paribus*, increase the firm's demand for labor. An increase in the quantity of fixed inputs, furthermore, will increase the firm's demand for labor. When the fixed input is increased, the firm is able to produce more output with each worker; that is, the productivity of labor increases. Since each unit of labor costs the same amount, the firm can generate more profits per worker employed. As a result, the firm would be willing to hire more workers at each wage rate.

The quantity of labor demanded by firms, then, depends on the wage rate, the price level (or the real wage—W/P), and the quantity of fixed inputs $(\bar{K})$. The demand curve is represented in general form as

$$N^D = N^D(W, P, \bar{K}) \qquad \text{or} \qquad N^D = N^D(W/P, \bar{K})$$
$$(-)(+)(+) \qquad\qquad\qquad\qquad (-) \ (+)$$

As an aside, notice that it makes no difference whether we write labor demand as $N^D = N^D(W, P, \bar{K})$ or $N^D = N^D(W/P, \bar{K})$. The quantity of labor demanded is determined by $W = VMP$. However, the value of the MP of labor is equal to the MP of labor times the price of output. If both sides of the equilibrium equation $(W = VMP)$ are divided by the price of output, we derive another version of the equation; that is $W/P = MP$. Workers should be hired until the real wage, or the real marginal cost, is equal to the MP of labor. In this case, by varying the real wage and finding the quantity of labor at which the real wage equals the MP of labor, a labor demand curve will be generated. The labor demand curve in Figure 7-7 is drawn in terms of the nominal wage. We could just as easily have measured the real wage on the vertical axis when plotting the labor demand. However, as we will see in Chapter 8, the drawing (as in Figure 7-7) with nominal wage on the axis will be more useful.

The Supply of Labor

For most people the reward for working consists of the goods and services their wage income will buy. This wage income is equal to the nominal wage rate per hour multiplied by the number of hours worked. The *real value* of the wage income, or the *purchasing power* of this income, is defined as the nominal wage rate per hour, divided by the price index, times the number of hours worked.

It is the real wage with which individuals are most concerned. In general it makes no difference whether their income is $500 a month or $1,000 a month if both nominal incomes can buy the same quantity of goods and services. Individuals make their decisions concerning the amount of labor to supply on the basis of the purchasing power they expect their nominal wages to yield. The word *expect* in the previous sentence is important. For most jobs, individuals know what their nominal wage will be, before the job commences. However, they do not receive the wage payment until some of the work is completed, usually after two weeks. The purchasing power of the wage, therefore, must be evaluated at the price expected to exist when the worker will be paid. And most salaried jobs have six-month or one-year contracts so that the nominal wage is fixed for a considerable period of time.

Suppose the wage rate is $5 per hour and the price index for goods and services is 1.00. If this price index is expected to exist when the worker is paid, then the expected real wage is $5. On the other hand, an expected price level of 2.00 would mean the wage is worth $2.50. At the expected real wage of $2.50, will workers supply the same, more, or less labor than they would have at an expected real wage of $5? In response to the lower income level, workers may attempt to maintain the same consumption by supplying more labor. On the other hand, because the rewards for working have decreased, workers may be discouraged and simply reduce their hours of work (which is the same thing as saying they purchase more leisure). Thus, two conflicting effects may occur. Which effect dominates is still a question of some controversy. We will assume that, for the economy as a whole, lower real wages will reduce the amount of labor supplied. A direct relationship thus exists between the expected real wage and the supply of labor, as represented by

$$N^S = N^S(W, \quad P^e) = N^S (W/P^e)$$
$$\quad (+) \ (-) \quad\quad (+)$$

The labor supply curve must be drawn in terms of a particular expected price.[2] In Figure 7-8 we use the notation $N^S(P^e = 1.0)$ to indicate that the labor supply curve depends on the expected price level. The upward sloping labor supply curve comes about because the expected real wage increases and, therefore, the quantity of labor supplied increases as the nominal wage rises. If the expected price level changes, the labor supply curve shifts. For example, should workers expect the price level to increase to $P^e = 2.0$, they expect the same nominal wage to be worth less in real terms. The quantity of labor supplied at each nominal wage should also fall. Therefore, an increase in the expected price level shifts the labor supply curve upward (or to the left). The new labor supply curve in Figure 7-8 is denoted as $N^S(P^e = 2.0)$. At each price level, the quantity of labor supplied will be the same, since the nominal wage will rise so that the real

Figure 7-8. The Labor Supply Curve

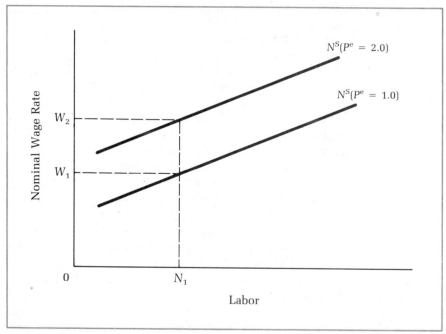

The labor supply curve is upward sloping because more labor is offered as real wages increase. Should the price level that workers expect to prevail increase, the real wage they expect to earn decreases. Hence, they offer to work fewer hours, or conversely, they demand higher nominal wages to work the same number of hours. This is represented by an upward shift of the N^S curve.

---

[2] It should be stressed that in order to draw the labor supply curve, the *ceteris paribus* assumption is invoked. Laborers' preferences to work, for example, are assumed constant. If these preferences change, such as would be the case when labor force participation rates change, the labor supply curve would shift.

wage (W/P) remains the same. For example, at the expected price level $P^e = 1.0$, the nominal wage W_1 means a quantity of labor supplied of N_1 in Figure 7-8. At the expected price level of $P^e = 2.0$, the nominal wage W_2 will keep the real wage the same and, therefore, the quantity of labor supplied will remain the same. Only if the real wage changes will the quantity of labor supplied change.

Derivation of the Aggregate Supply Curve:
Flexible Wages and Perfect Information

In the last section, the quantity of labor demanded was postulated to depend on the real wage and the quantity of labor supplied was specified to depend on the expected real wage. Classical economists assumed that individuals have complete (perfect) information in the same manner that complete information exists under perfect competition. Complete information, in our use of the expression, means that the expected price level is, in fact, the actual price level ($P^e = P$). With complete information and with perfectly flexible wages and prices, equilibrium will occur at the real wage at which firms are willing to hire all the people willing and able to work. In Figure 7-9 (if the price level is P_1) equilibrium employment is N_1, and the equilibrium nominal wage is W_1.

If the nominal wage is W_2 (see Figure 7-9), the labor market is characterized by excess demand. At the price level P_1, the nominal wage W_2 means that the real wage is lower than when the nominal wage was W_1. Employers respond to the lower real wage by demanding more labor while workers respond by supplying less labor. Since firms are not able to hire all the workers they desire, they will offer a higher nominal wage. This process will continue until the nominal wage (and, thus, the real wage) rises to clear the labor market.

In order to derive the aggregate supply curve, the labor market and the aggregate production function must be combined. In Figures 7-9 and 7-10, with price level P_1, equilibrium occurs at the nominal wage rate W_1 and employment level N_1. The total product curve in Figure 7-10B shows that an output level of Y_1 will be produced with labor N_1. Thus, if the price level is P_1, the output level will be Y_1. This combination (P_1, Y_1) is one point on the AS curve, as shown in Figure 7-10D. What if the price level increases, say to P_2? In this case, the demand curve for labor shifts to the right as the price level rises, as shown in Figure 7-10A. The reason for the shift is that, for a given nominal wage, the higher price level means a lower real wage and, thus, a greater quantity of labor demanded. The labor supply curve shifts to the left due to the higher price level. Workers are willing to supply less labor at each nominal wage because, at each nominal wage, the real wage has decreased.

After the curves shift, the new equilibrium nominal wage is W_2, but employment remains at N_1. The nominal wage rate is bid up just enough

Figure 7-9. Labor Market Equilibrium

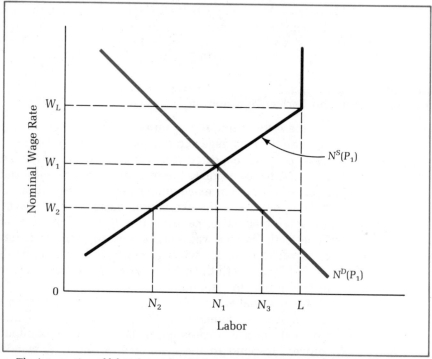

The intersection of labor demand and labor supply curves determines the nominal wage and the number of workers employed. At a nominal wage lower than the equilibrium wage, say W_2, the quantity of labor demanded will exceed the quantity supplied and the wage will be driven up. If L *is defined as the total labor force, then at any nominal wage below* W_L *the total labor force will not be employed.*

so that the real wage remains unchanged. Why does this occur? Suppose the labor supply curve did not shift as far as the labor demand curve. Then we would be saying that workers are willing to accept a lower real wage to produce even more output. Does this seem reasonable? On the other hand, if the labor supply curve shifts more than the labor demand, we will be saying that workers are requiring a higher real wage to produce even lower output. But, under our *ceteris paribus* assumption, this change in tastes cannot occur. Thus, after the price rise, the labor demand and supply curves must intersect at the same quantity of labor as before the price rise.

The employment quantity is N_1 at the price level P_2. Combining N_1 with the fixed inputs again generates output level Y_1. Thus, the quantity of output supplied is the same at either price level. In fact, if other prices are considered, the quantity of output produced will continue to be Y_1. This is shown in Figure 7-10D as a vertical AS curve. Why is the aggregate

Figure 7-10. The Aggregate Supply Curve When Wages and Prices Are Flexible

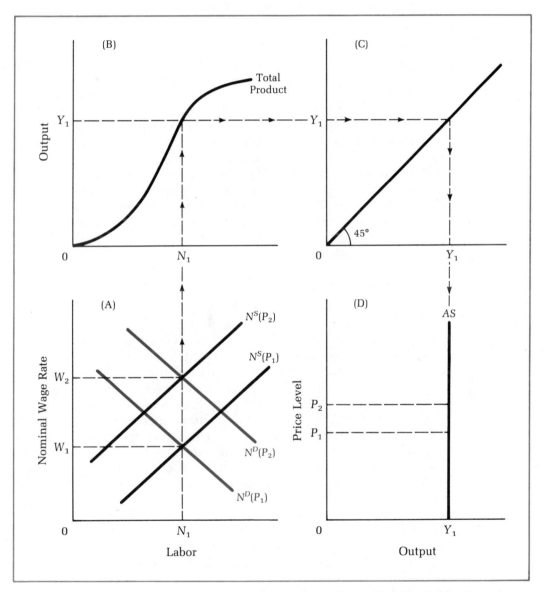

The labor market is represented in Panel A. At the price level P_1, the labor demand curve $N^D(P_1)$ and the labor supply curve $N^S(P_1)$ determine the nominal wage (W_1) and the quantity of labor employed (N_1). Combining N_1 with the fixed inputs in Panel B indicates the quantity of output that can be produced at price P_1. Combining this output level Y_1 and price P_1 yields one point on the AS curve in Panel D. Panel C is simply a geometric construction that enables the output level determined in the total product curve to be translated into the AS curve.

supply curve a vertical line? The reason stems from the flexibility of prices and wages and complete information. This flexibility ensures that all those willing and able to work at the market wage will have jobs.

Unemployment

Determining whether unemployment exists is not as simple as one might think. Consider Figure 7-9 and ask yourself whether unemployment exists at the wage rate W_1. One response might be yes, since employment (N_1) is less than the available labor force (L). Another response might be no, the logic being that everyone who wants a job at W_1 has one. Which response is correct depends on which definition of unemployment one uses. If an individual wants a job but cannot find one, *involuntary unemployment* exists.[3] At the nominal wage rate W_1 in Figure 7-9 involuntary unemployment does not exist since everyone who desires a job has a job. Notice that at W_1 employment is less than the available labor force. Therefore, some unemployment does exist. This unemployment is described as *voluntary unemployment* since workers have decided at their own discretion not to seek a job.

Aggregate Supply in the Keynesian Framework

As long as wages are perfectly flexible, and individuals have complete information, wages will adjust to equate quantities supplied and demanded. Whenever there are members of the labor force willing and able to work who do not have jobs, wages will fall. Whenever firms want to hire workers but none are available, wages will rise.

Viewing the world in the 1930s, a time period during which the unemployment rate reached extremely high levels, Keynes could not accept this classical conclusion. How could he alter the model in order to explain an equilibrium that was not at full employment? Keynes had noted that workers did not respond immediately to wage and price changes. They did not have perfect information and did not, therefore, always know what their alternatives were. He also observed that most wage contracts were made in nominal or money terms rather than in real terms. Workers may have thought in real terms, but the overwhelming majority of contracts were not, in those times, written that way. Thus, if workers had a contract to work for $8 an hour when the price index was 1.00, and then the price index rose to 2.00, workers supplied the same

---

[3] Because we are assuming that all laborers are identical to the firm and each worker faces the same wage rate, this definition is unambiguous. In reality, though, how do you classify someone who has certain job and pay aspirations and will not consider offers that are lower than these aspirations? Suppose that I decide to become a professor of economics and find upon completing graduate school that there are no positions available for me at the institutions I want and at the wage I want. If I will not accept other offers and refuse to change careers, am I voluntarily or involuntarily unemployed?

amount of labor even though they were working at a lower real wage. At least they did so until the next contract was signed. As a result of the nominal wage contracts and the less-than-perfect information that workers had, wages may not have instantaneously changed so as to equate demand and supply. Keynes further observed that nominal wages tended to be downwardly rigid. The rationale for this rigidity arose from workers' concern about their wage status relative to other workers as well as from their lack of perfect information. Keynes believed that workers were more likely to resist a reduction in nominal wages with prices constant than a real wage decline caused by rising prices but with nominal wages constant. When the nominal wage fell, the worker did not know whether all other alternatives were also paying less. The worker, therefore, had an incentive to quit and search for another job when the nominal wage fell. A price rise, however, affected everyone, and, consequently, the worker did not expect to be able to find another position at a higher wage. This tendency for workers to quit and search for alternatives kept the nominal wage from declining.

What does Keynes's view that the nominal wage is downwardly rigid mean for the labor market? In Figure 7-11 the money wage has been set at the level W_1. The labor market is characterized at this wage level by excess supply since the quantity of labor demanded is N^D and the quantity of labor supplied is N^S. With the market in disequilibrium, the *short side* (that is, whichever is smaller, demand or supply) will determine the number of workers employed. Therefore, the labor demand curve dictates that N^D workers will be employed. Since not everyone desiring a job at that wage rate is able to find one, involuntary unemployment equal to the horizontal distance between the labor demand and supply curves ($N^S - N^D$ in Figure 7-11) exists. The distance $L - N^S$ measures the amount of voluntary unemployment.

The *AS* curve, for the case of downwardly rigid nominal wages, can be derived following the same procedures that were used to develop the flexible wage *AS* curve. Consider Figure 7-12 and, initially, assume the price level to be P_1 and the nominal wage W_1.[4] Since the labor demand curve determines the number of workers hired, employment is N_1. Combining this employment level with the fixed inputs, the aggregate production function generates an output level of Y_1. The price level P_1 is consistent with the output level Y_1. One point on the *AS* curve has been derived.

If the price level is increased to P_2, the demand for labor curve shifts out (at the same nominal wage rate the firm will demand more labor as the real wage rate falls), and the supply of labor shifts inward (at the same

---

[4] One can think of the wage W_1 evolving in one of two ways. One would be for a new labor contract to set the wage at W_1. Another approach would be to state that the wage was set at the market-clearing wage W_1 when prices were at some higher level.

Figure 7-11. The Keynesian Labor Market

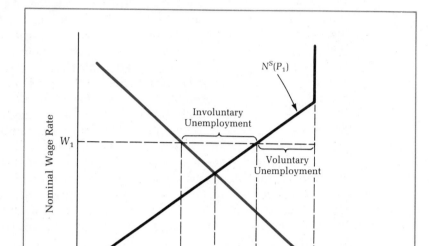

If the nominal wage is rigid downward at a level greater than the equilibrium nominal wage, the quantity of labor supplied would be greater than the quantity of labor demanded. The difference, $N^S - N^D$, is referred to as *involuntary unemployment*. The distance $L - N^S$ (the difference between the total labor force and the quantity of workers willing and able to work at a given nominal wage) is termed *voluntary unemployment*.

nominal wage rate the supply of labor will decrease as the real wage decreases). At the price level P_2, the quantity of labor hired is N_2 and output is Y_2. Another point on the *AS* curve is derived. This process—an increase in the price level leading to an increased quantity of output—continues until the demand curve for labor and the supply curve of labor intersect at the downwardly rigid nominal wage W_1. Further price increases will not result in increases in output from that point on. The result is an *AS* curve that is upward sloping until the price level has been increased to the point at which the downwardly rigid nominal wage is no longer an effective source of disequilibrium. At this point the Keynesian aggregate supply curve becomes identical to the classical vertical supply curve. In the extreme, the Keynesian *AS* curve is a backward *L* where output will increase without a rise in price until full employment is reached. (See Figure 7-13A.) In the less extreme case, the Keynesian *AS* curve is upward sloping until the full-employment level of output is reached as shown in Figure 7-13B.

Figure 7-12. The Aggregate Supply Curve When Wages Are Not Flexible

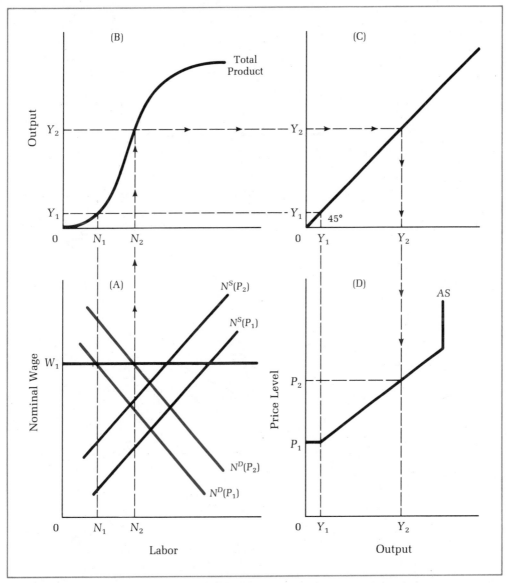

The AS curve slopes up when wages are not perfectly flexible since the nominal wage does not instantaneously and completely adjust to changes in the price level. In Panel A the fixed nominal wage W_1 and the price level P_1 determine the quantities of labor demanded and supplied. When the quantity supplied is greater than the quantity demanded, a surplus exists, and the quantity of labor employed (N_1) is determined by the short side of the market. As the price level is increased, the quantity demanded rises and more labor is employed. As more labor is employed, more output is produced. This is reflected in Panel B. The combinations of price and output are plotted in Panel D tracing out the AS curve.

Figure 7-13. Two Possible AS Curves

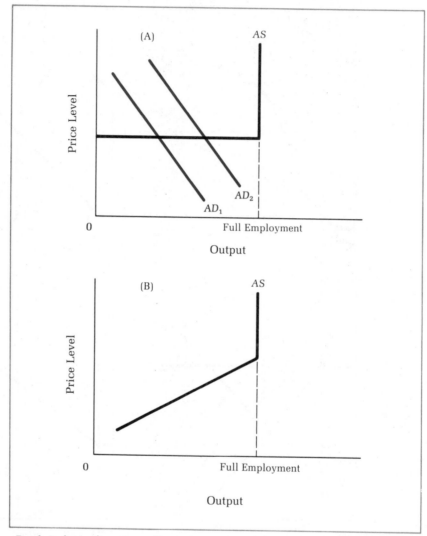

Panel A shows the extreme Keynesian version of the AS curve. When AD increases, output rises with no change in the price level until full employment is reached.

Panel B shows the AS curve for the case of flexible prices but rigid wages. Below full employment, the curve has a positive slope. Consequently, increases in AD will result in increases in both output and the price level.

The Neoclassical Synthesis: The Friedman-Phelps Labor Supply Curve

The rigid nominal wage drawn on the labor market diagram is a simplified illustration not only of Keynes's view, but also that of present-day economists who argue that wages and prices are not perfectly flexible. Hardly anyone will disagree with the premise that if wages and prices are perfectly and instantaneously flexible there can be no involuntary unemployment. At the equilibrium real wage, all those wanting jobs will have jobs. The current controversy is over the degree of flexibility of wages and prices. Keynes asserted, as do many economists today, that wages will not adjust immediately to imbalances. Contracts between employer and employee that are set only once a year or once every other year restrict the flexibility of wages. It is argued that wages will not be able to respond immediately to demand changes and that not all people wanting jobs will be able to obtain them. Whenever such a situation occurs, the *AS* curve is upward sloping instead of being vertical.

The fixed price-fixed nominal wage model has (at best) limited usefulness in a world that experiences continual price rises. A glance back at Figure 1-1 points out that, beginning in the mid-1950s, prices have risen year after year. At the same time there were periods in which real output declined and unemployment rose. During the 1950s and 1960s a series of scholars (in particular, Friedman and Phelps) introduced variations to the Keynesian model that attempted to make it more realistic, more in tune with the events of the time. These alterations have become known as the *neoclassical synthesis.*

Friedman and Phelps argued that slowly adjusting wages and prices might be explained by a lack of information rather than by contracts or some other rigidity. If workers misinterpret increases in the demand for their services as being real increases rather than economy-wide nominal increases, they may work more hours. Also, some workers previously not seeking work may take a full- or part-time job. For example, in Figure 7-14, an increase in the demand for a product shifts the labor demand curve out. But if the demand increase was due simply to an increase in the supply of money (an economy-wide increase, not a relative demand increase), then the price level will rise. Since workers base their work decision on the expected real wage and their expectation is for price to remain at P_1 the labor supply curve does not shift immediately. Once they discover their real wage has not increased, they will return to their former position. This means the labor supply curve shifts upward. The result of this type of behavior in the labor market is an *AS* curve that slopes upward during the short run, but becomes vertical in the long run.

While we devote considerable attention to the neoclassical synthesis, and particularly the Friedman-Phelps model in the next chapter, we should note here that the neoclassical synthesis incorporates both the Keynesian aggregate demand theory and a theory of aggregate supply in which wage and price adjustments take place gradually over time. The result is an upward sloping *AS* curve for a period of time called the *short run.* Once the short run has elapsed, the vertical *AS* curve of the classical model reappears. It is called the *long-run aggregate supply curve.*

Figure 7-14. The Friedman-Phelps Labor Supply Curve

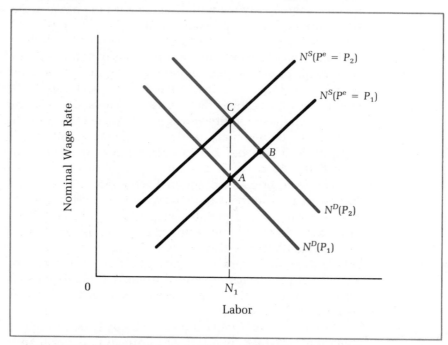

An increase in the demand for output increases the demand for *labor*, as shown by the outward shifting labor demand curve. Prices rise, but if this is not perceived by workers, they will believe their real wage has increased. More labor is supplied as shown by the move from A to B. But as workers learn of the price rise, they adjust their expectations and demand higher nominal wages. The result is an upward shift of the labor supply curve. Equilibrium returns at the original employment level (Point C).

Conclusions

Whether the aggregate supply curve is vertical, upward sloping, or a combination of the two, is crucially important for determining the effects of monetary and fiscal policy on the economy. Consider Figure 7-15 wherein a vertical *AS* curve is drawn in Panel A and an upward sloping curve in Panel B. An expansionary monetary or fiscal policy is represented by an outward or rightward shift of the *AD* curve. The results of the policy are totally different, depending on the shape of the *AS* curve. In the vertical case—the flexible wage case—only prices rise. Output does not expand. Output, in contrast, expands along with an increase in prices in the less flexible wage case (shown in Panel B).

In the next chapter we will examine the neoclassical synthesis and further develop the macroeconomic framework discussed in this chapter. Moreover, we will discuss how well the various theories explain the economic events of the sixties and seventies.

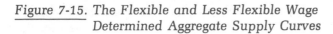

Figure 7-15. The Flexible and Less Flexible Wage
Determined Aggregate Supply Curves

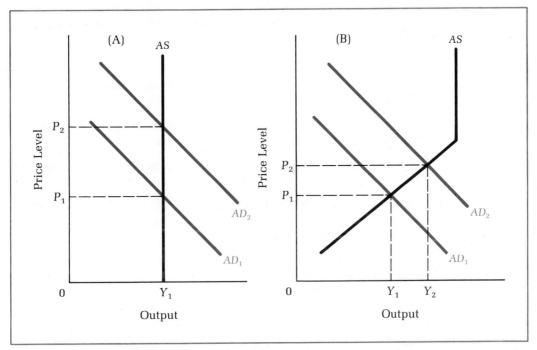

In Panel A the AS curve is drawn under the assumption that wages and prices are perfectly flexible. The less flexible wage assumption is used to draw the supply curve in Panel B. As demand increases, prices rise in both cases. Only prices rise, however, in the flexible case. Output does not change. Both output and prices rise when wages are less than perfectly flexible.

PROBLEMS AND EXERCISES

1. Explain why the AD curve is downward sloping when price is on the vertical axis and quantity is measured on the horizontal axis.

2. What is the effect of a tax cut?

3. Prior to Keynes's work the demand for money was postulated to depend only on the income level. Assuming a money demand function that depends only on income, derive the AD curve.

4. Saving was postulated to depend on disposable income in this chapter. Suppose saving is now postulated to depend on the interest rate in addition to disposable income. What are the implications of such a modification for the AD curve?

5. In this chapter real taxes have been specified to be a function of real income. A more realistic specification, at least for the United States, would postulate real taxes to be a function of nominal income. What are the implications of such a specification for the *IS* curve and the *AD* curve?

6. Why is the Keynesian *AS* curve upward sloping?

7. What is the difference between the Keynesian labor market and the Friedman-Phelps labor market?

8. Comment on the following assertion: We really did not have any unemployment during the Great Depression.

9. Explain why a change in the price level causes the labor demand and labor supply curves to shift by the same horizontal distance.

10. Suppose workers decide to take more leisure at each wage. What are the implications for the *AS* curve if the labor market clears? if the labor market does not clear?

11. If the labor demand and labor supply curves intersect above the negotiated wage $\overline{W}$, what are the implications for the *AS* curve?

SUGGESTED READINGS

For an analysis of the Keynesian model

Robert Clower and Axel Leijonhufvud, "The Coordination of Economic Activities: A Keynesian Perspective," *American Economic Review* (May, 1975).

Axel Leijonhufvud, *On Keynesian Economics and the Economics of Keynes* (New York: Oxford University Press, 1968).

For an overview of inflation theories

Robert J. Gordon, "Recent Developments in the Theory of Inflation and Unemployment," *Journal of Monetary Economics*, 2 (1976), pp. 185-219.

Walter W. Heller, "Monetary Policy at the Cross Roads," *The Wall Street Journal* (October 14, 1977), p. 18.

Gardiner Means, "Industrial Prices and their Relative Inflexibility," *A Report to the Secretary of Agriculture. Senate Document No. 13* (74th Congress, 1935).

For a flavor of the inflationary fears prevailing in the 1950s

Paul A. Samuelson and Robert Solow, "The Problem of Achieving and Maintaining a Stable Price Level: Analytical Aspects of Anti-Inflation Policy," *American Economic Review* (May, 1960), pp. 177-194.

Charles Schultze, "Recent Inflation in the United States," *Joint Economic Committee Study of Employment, Growth, and Price Levels* (86th Congress, September, 1959).

The critical role played by expectations is emphasized in

Kajal Lahiri, "A Joint Study of Expectations Formation and the Shifting Phillips Curve," *Journal of Monetary Economics*, 3 (1977), pp. 347-357.

Richard Bookstaber, "The Effect of Inflation Uncertainty on 'Crowding Out'," *Journal of Macroeconomics* (Winter, 1980), pp. 85-95.

_APPENDIX. The Complete *AD-AS* Model_____

While we focused on and utilized the aggregate demand-aggregate supply model in Chapter 7 and will continue to do so in most of the subsequent chapters, it is important to recognize that these curves represent the interaction and movements of other curves and economic variables—the *IS*, *LM*, total product, labor demand, and labor supply curves, for example. To emphasize that the *AD-AS* framework captures all the other components of the model, we have collected all the diagrams in one place, in Figure 7A-1. The supply-side graphs are drawn as Panels A and B. The demand-side graph *(IS-LM)* is drawn as Panel E. The *AD-AS* graph is drawn in Panel D. This organizational scheme provides a convenient way to organize thoughts and check logic when just the *AD-AS* model is used to discuss particular economic events.

The complete *AD-AS* model can be used to examine demand or supply shocks. Simply for the exercise, let us use this perfectly flexible wage and price model to examine the 1974 supply shocks. The policy reaction to the 1974 supply shocks was a restrictive demand policy. Was this the appropriate response?

A decrease in the quantity of inputs can be represented as a downward rotation of the total product curve, as shown in Figure 7A-2B. Recall that the total product curve is drawn with the assumption of a constant supply of fixed inputs—capital, oil, foodstuffs, whatever is required. If, then, the quantity of these inputs is altered, the total product curve will shift or rotate since the quantity of output that can be produced with each quantity of labor will have changed. With fewer resources, labor will be less productive—each unit of labor will be able to produce less output. In other words, after the supply shock, the same amount of labor input would generate a smaller output, as shown in Figure 7A-2B. In addition, the labor demand curve shifts to the left. A decrease in labor productivity means less labor will be demanded by firms.

Prior to the decrease in the raw materials, the relevant labor demand and labor supply functions are $N^D_{1974}(P_1)$ and $N^S_{1974}(P_1)$ respectively. Equilibrium employment is therefore N_{1974}. With the 1974 supplies of raw

---

Figure 7A-1. The Complete Model (page 229)

At price level P_1 the quantity of labor employed is N_1. In Panel B, labor input N_1 generates output Y_1 which, when traced to Panel D, plots as Point A. When the price level rises, the quantity of labor employed increases unless the price rise is known (completely expected) by workers. If workers do not know about the price increase they will work more, more output will be produced, and the upward sloping *AS* curve in Panel D will be traced out. If workers do know about (or learn about) the price rise, the vertical *AS* curve in Panel D will be traced out. The *IS-LM* curves in Panel E trace out the *AD* curve as prices change.

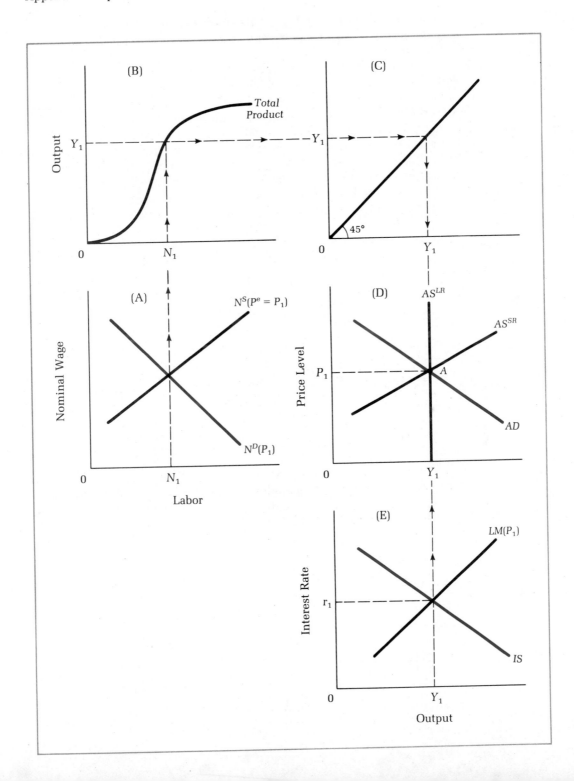

materials, total output is Y_{1974}. This output level is the position of the vertical aggregate supply (we are using the flexible wage model) in the AD-AS diagram.

The decrease in raw materials is represented by the downward rotation of the total product curve. The decline in the total product curve causes the aggregate supply curve to shift inward (leftward) to AS_{1975}. After the shift in the AS curve to AS_{1975} the economy is in a state of excess demand at the price level P_1. As soon as the price level begins rising, the labor market is affected. The labor demand curve shifts from $N^D_{1975}(P_1)$ to $N^D_{1975}(P_2)$, and the labor supply curve moves to $N^S(P_2)$, from $N^S(P_1)$, assuming workers know of and expect the price rise. The labor market clears at a lower nominal wage rate (W_2) and a lower level of employment (N_{1975}). Table 7A-1 summarizes the effects of the supply shocks.

Table 7A-1. *Response of Variables to a Decrease in Fixed Raw Material Inputs (the Classical Case)*

VARIABLE	RESULT
Y	Decrease
C	Decrease
I	Decrease
r	Increase
P	Increase
N	Decrease
W/P	Decrease

While, as stated in the text, neither the fixed wage-price nor the perfectly flexible wage-price model satisfactorily describes the economic events of the sixties and seventies, it is useful to run through several experiments similar to those performed in this appendix with the complete model.

Figure 7A-2. *Supply Shocks of 1974: The Flexible Wage Case* (page 231)

The OPEC oil embargo and/or the shortfall in foodstuffs is represented as a downward rotation of the total product curve in Panel B. As a result, with the same employment level, N_{1974}, less output can be produced. As the AS curve shifts in, the price level is driven up, from P_1 to P_2. A higher price level means a lower quantity of real money—the LM curve shifts up, driving the interest rate up and the quantity of output demanded down (see Panel E). At the same time the labor demand and supply curves shift up reflecting the fallen real wage. Employment drops to N_{1975} and output declines.

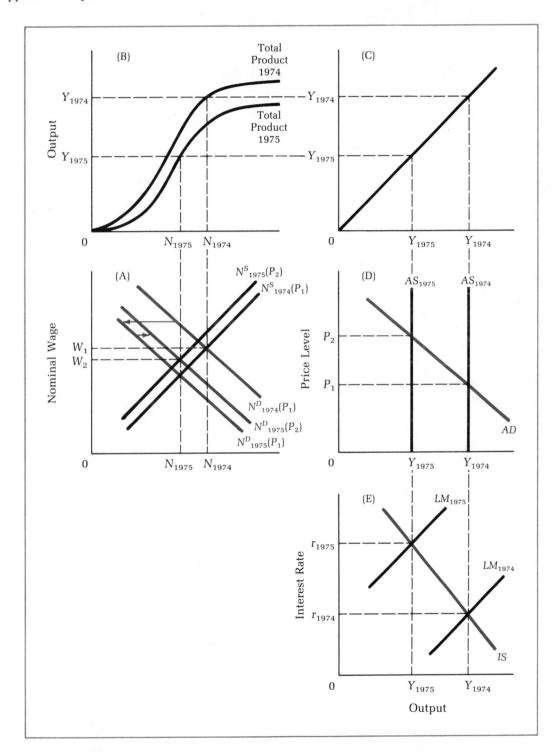

CHAPTER 8.

Expectations: Macroeconomics in the Eighties

You can fool all of the people some of the time and some of the people all of the time, but you cannot fool all of the people all of the time.
                                    Abraham Lincoln

> The frustrations felt by policymakers in the mid- and late 1970s led to a reexamination of Keynesian economics. What had been accepted as effective and necessary policy now began to be questioned. The basis for the erosion of Keynesianism was the question of how economic agents form and use expectations. In this chapter two hypotheses about the formation of expectations are examined. Some questions to be dealt with include the following:
>
> - Is there a trade-off, even in the short run, between inflation and unemployment?
>
> - Is demand management (fiscal/monetary) policy effective?
>
> - What are rational expectations?
>
> - What is the accelerationist hypothesis?

Introduction

Figure 8-1 makes it obvious why economists today doubt the existence of a permanent trade-off between inflation and unemployment. Notice the apparent shifts of the curve (the red lines) from the 1950s and 60s to the 1970s and 80s. Also notice the spiral or loops in the solid line connecting the year-to-year combinations of unemployment and inflation rates. When the unemployment rate fell, as from 1971 to 1973, inflation picked up steam. Then both unemployment and inflation rose (1973-74), and the cycle began again. But as the next cycle or loop began it did so at an even higher rate of inflation. Milton Friedman and Edmund Phelps, in separate studies, concluded that these cycles result because individuals learn to expect inflation and adjust their contracts and their purchases to offset the costs due to inflation. Each time policymakers attempt to reduce unemployment, as was the case in 1972-73 and 1975-78, they create some inflation. Economic agents (firms and individuals) learn that the attempt to reduce unemployment creates inflation. They react to this knowledge by adjusting their contracts, their purchases, and their hours of work. This results in more inflation and a return to the original unemployment rate. The next time policymakers wish to reduce unemployment, then, they must live with an even higher rate of inflation. The Friedman-Phelps viewpoint is called the *accelerationist hypothesis* or, sometimes, the *natural rate hypothesis*. The first name derives from having to accept accelerating inflation in order to stimulate employment.

Figure 8-1. The Inflation-Unemployment Trade-off

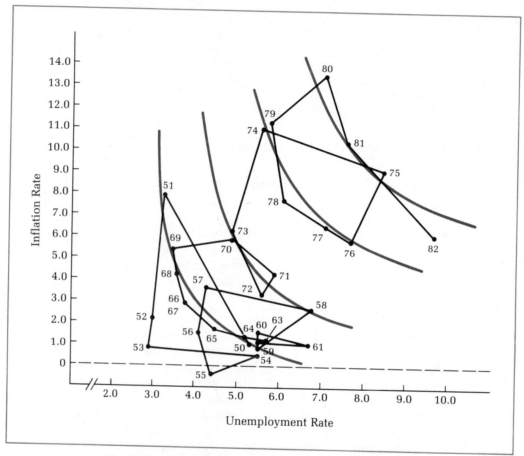

The Phillips curve, stable during the 1950s and 1960s, shifted out in the 1970s. Each attempt to fine tune the economy led to a higher inflation rate and a worse trade-off.

The second name derives from the idea that there is a rate of unemployment consistent with real conditions in the labor market—a level below which the economy can be driven only by accelerating inflation.

In terms of the aggregate demand-aggregate supply (AD-AS) framework, Friedman asserted that the AS curve is vertical in the long run and is upward sloping only in the short run. As a result, activist demand policies cannot work—cannot permanently reduce unemployment (or increase real output). Other economists concluded that Friedman's positive sloping short-run curve left room, even if only temporarily, for demand policies to influence employment and output. It was this conclusion that led to an extension of Friedman's analysis called the *rational expectations hypothesis (REH)*. The *REH* rejected the upward sloping *AS* curve even in the short run. According to the *REH* there simply is no room—long- or short-run—for active demand policies.

The difference between the *REH* and the accelerationist hypothesis depends primarily on how individuals form expectations. In this chapter we focus on expectations formation, the accelerationist hypothesis and the *REH*, and what they imply for demand management policies.

The Aggregate Supply Curve and Expectations

On the evening of December 19, 1973, Johnny Carson began his *Tonight* show with a typical monologue. Just prior to the show one of Carson's writers had informed him of a pending shortage of toilet paper so Johnny decided to tip his viewers off about this shortage during the monologue. However the next night, December 20, Carson had to apologize for this tip. He explained that his writer had not informed him about all the facts. What the writer left out was that the paper shortage was going to occur only in government buildings. Since the government was not getting many supply bids from paper firms for its purchases of low-grade toilet paper for government employee use, there might be a shortage of toilet paper in government buildings. However, by the time Johnny Carson made his apology, it was too late. During the day of December 20, people had rushed out to stockpile toilet paper. An actual shortage had been created on the basis of an expected shortage.

During the summer of 1978 rumors that McDonald's Corporation used earthworms to fill out their hamburgers abounded in the southeastern United States.[1] As a result demand for McDonald's products fell drastically leading to layoffs and cutbacks. McDonalds finally enlisted an agricultural official and an extensive advertising campaign to help put an end to the rumors.

During the summer of 1979 gasoline shortages led to long lines at gas stations in California. The news media daily carried stories of the California situation to the rest of the U.S. This in turn panicked buyers in other states to begin "topping off" their tanks and attempting to stockpile gasoline creating long lines at gas stations in these other states.

These and many other examples point out how important expectations are in influencing individual behavior. Whether a business believes a demand change to be temporary or long-lived will determine whether that business will hire additional workers, increase production, accumulate inventories, raise prices, or, perhaps, do nothing. Similarly, a worker's belief that inflation will increase (or decrease) temporarily or for a

---

[1] "Wormburger Scare," *Newsweek* (November 27, 1978).

long period of time will influence that employee's wage demands and the hours that the employee is willing to work.

In previous chapters it was assumed that businesses and workers had complete knowledge of the marketplace. The difference between the classical and Keynesian approaches was in the degree of wage flexibility, not in the amount of information each person had. However, the assumption that businesses and individuals have complete information is unrealistic. It is costly for them to gather information and, as a result, it is unlikely they would have perfect information. Economic agents, therefore, must forecast or form expectations of the values of variables and events about which they have, at best, only limited information. Workers forecast prices, business firms forecast the demands for their products and the costs of their inputs, the Federal Reserve System (Fed) forecasts the demand for money, and so on.

In this chapter the assumption that economic agents have complete information, or that information is costless to gather, is relaxed. Alternative assumptions about how economic agents form expectations and the implications of these assumptions for the economy are considered.

The Labor Supply Curve with Expected Prices

Individuals decide to supply labor on the basis of their expected real wage. This assumption implies that if workers have perfect information they will know the purchasing power of their nominal wage before they begin to work. We relax this assumption in this section and examine the implications of this action for the labor supply curve and, hence, the AS curve.

The quantity of labor supplied is specified to be directly or positively related to the expected real wage. Recall that the expected real wage, rather than the actual real wage, is the correct decision variable. Individuals make their decisions concerning the amount of labor they wish to supply knowing the nominal wage, but not the purchasing power that this wage will command when payment is actually made. In previous chapters the labor supply curve has been drawn with nominal wages on the vertical axis so that for each price level there was a different labor supply curve. At any given nominal wage, as we vary the price level upward, the real wage is being decreased. Hence, individuals are not willing to supply as much labor at each nominal wage as they would have at the lower price level. Similarly, individuals will not be willing to supply as much labor at a given nominal wage if they expect prices to rise. There is a different labor supply curve for each expected price level.

Suppose the expected price level is $P^e = 1.0$ in Figure 8-2. The labor supply curve corresponding to this expected price level is denoted as $N^S(P^e = 1.0)$. Now, suppose workers expect the price level to increase to $P^e = 2.0$. This means a nominal wage, such as W_1, will be worth less in real

Figure 8-2. Labor Supply When Actual and Expected Prices May Differ

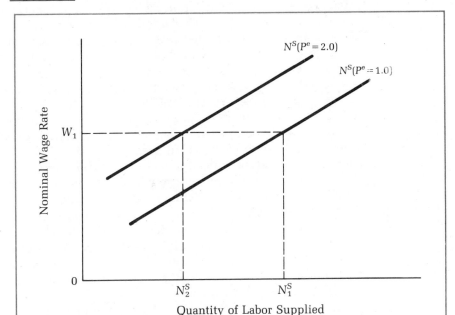

Workers offer their labor services on the basis of the real wage they expect to earn. For each expected price level, the larger the nominal wage, the greater the quantity of labor services supplied. Conversely, for each nominal wage, W_1 for example, the greater the expected price level the less the quantity supplied.

terms and, therefore, the quantity of labor individuals will be willing to supply will be smaller. An increase in the expected price level is, therefore, reflected as a leftward or upward shift of the labor supply curve. The new labor supply curve in Figure 8-2 is denoted as $N^S(P^e = 2.0)$.

Aggregate Supply

How does this reaction by individuals to an expected decline in real wages affect the total amount of output the economy produces? In other words, what is the effect of changing price expectations on the aggregate supply curve?

Let us review the procedure we previously employed to derive the AS curve. The demand and supply curves, assuming market clearing and a specific price level, determine the quantity of labor employed. Combining the quantity of labor employed with the quantity of fixed inputs in the aggregate production function determines the quantity of output produced. If other price levels are specified and the corresponding output levels derived, the AS curve can be traced out.

Only one modification to this proce⁻lure is necessary when expected prices are allowed to vary from actual prices. An expected price level must be introduced. This is accomplished most simply by assuming that individuals react to expected real wages while businesses focus on the actual real wage. As a result, neither the total product curve nor the labor demand relationship is affected by allowing expected prices to differ from actual prices. The demand for labor depends on the actual real wage and not the expected real wage. Firms do not have to predict what the price will be since the relevant price to the firm is simply the price of its product; one single price in a market it knows well. Individuals, on the other hand, have to worry about the entire cost of living—a much more complex information collecting task. It is this discrepancy that accounts for businesses determining how much labor to demand on the basis of the actual price level while individuals decide how much labor to supply on the basis of the price level they expect to prevail.

In order to see the implication of incomplete information (expected prices differing from actual prices) for the AS curve, let us assume initially that both the expected price level and the actual price level have values of unity ($P^e = P = 1.0$). As shown in Figure 8-3A the equilibrium nominal wage is W_1 and the equilibrium quantity of labor is N_1. This labor input, combined with the fixed inputs in the total product curve, Figure 8-3B, produces the output level Y_1. By plotting the price-output combinations ($P = 1.0$ and Y_1), we have one point on the AS curve, Point A in Figure 8-3D. Now, what happens as we vary the price level to derive the rest of the AS curve? Suppose for some as yet unspecified reason, the price level rises to $P = 2.0$. The labor demand curve will shift to the right since, with the higher price level, the real wage is lower at each nominal wage. Firms will want to hire more labor at each nominal wage (at the higher price level). Notice, however, that if the expected price level does not rise, the labor supply curve will not shift. And, in many circumstances, it is very likely that a price will have risen before individuals begin expecting the higher level.[2] With the new labor demand curve and the same labor supply curve, a higher nominal wage (W_2) and a larger quantity of labor employed (N_2) will result. As shown in Figure 8-3 the labor input N_2 combined with the fixed inputs generates the output level Y_2. This output level and the price level P_2 are plotted as Point B in Figure 8-3D. When Points A and B are connected, the AS curve is derived. This curve is denoted as $AS(P^e = 1.0)$.

As can be seen in Figure 8-3D, allowing expected prices to deviate from actual prices results in an upward sloping AS curve. This means that

---

[2] Of course, in the economic environment of the U. S. since the early 1970s inflation has been occurring for so long that individuals began anticipating a more rapid inflation rate than actually occurred. But again, notice that in this case there also is a discrepancy between the actual and the expected inflation rate.

Figure 8-3. The Short-run Aggregate Supply Curve

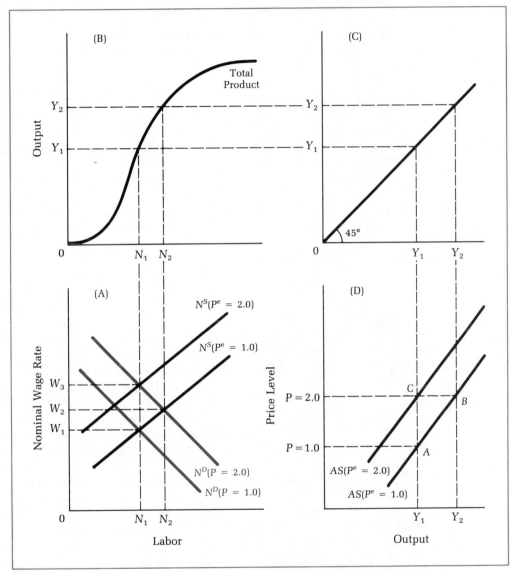

If the expected price level may differ from the actual price level, the AS curve will slope upward. In Panel A the price level varies from $P = 1.0$ to $P = 2.0$. This change is realized by firms, as represented by the outward (upward) shift of the labor demand curve, $N^D(P = 1.0)$ to $N^D(P = 2.0)$. The price change is not immediately recognized by workers however. Hence, the number of workers initially employed at $P = 2.0$ is more than that at $P = 1.0$, N_2 instead of N_1. More labor means more output. Hence, in Panel D more output is produced at the higher price level; the economy moves from Point A to B. As workers adjust to the higher price level they offer to work less as reflected by an upward shift of the labor supply curve $N^S(P^e = 2.0)$. Output produced then declines to Y_1 and the economy moves to Point C. Further price rises will trace out new AS curves.

even though wages are not assumed to be fixed or rigid downward, a price level increase leads to a greater output level. This is a very important result.

Remember that workers supply labor on the basis of their expected real wage. When the price level is increased, more labor is demanded and the nominal wage is bid up. The higher nominal wage, along with workers' expectations that the price will be 1.0 rather than 2.0, brings forth a larger labor supply. In other words, workers think their real wage has increased. In a sense, workers are fooled into supplying more labor by the unanticipated price increase.

Now, let us consider the implications of a change in workers' price expectation for the AS curve. Suppose workers believe the price level will double by the time they get paid ($P^e = 2.0$). The labor supply curve will shift upward, as shown in Figure 8-3A by $N^S(P^e = 2.0)$. If the price level actually is $P = 2.0$, N_1 workers will be employed in the labor market, and an output level of Y_1 will be produced. This price-output level combination is not on the AS curve $AS(P^e = 1.0)$. Instead, it lies above the $AS(P^e = 1.0)$ schedule at Point C in Panel D. If other price levels are specified and the corresponding output levels derived, a new AS schedule representing the higher expected price level will be traced out. This AS curve, $AS(P^e = 2.0)$ lies above the original AS curve. Thus, a change in the expected price level is reflected in a shift of the AS curve.

Before proceeding, let us examine Figure 8-3D in a little more detail. Points A and C are quite different from the other points, B and D. Point A is the one point on the $AS(P^e = 1.0)$ curve where expected prices are equal to actual prices. Similarly, Point C represents the only point where the expected price level ($P^e = 2.0$) is the same as the actual price level. If all the points where the expected price level is the same as the actual price level are connected, a vertical AS curve is traced out. This schedule represents those combinations of output and price levels resulting after workers have "learned" what prices and wages have done, in other words, after expectations have fully adjusted. For this reason, we will refer to this locus of points as the long-run AS curve. The output level associated with this curve is known as the *natural employment level of output*, or just the *natural output level*, and corresponds to the natural unemployment rate.

Let us summarize the discussion to this point. First, for a specific expected price level, the AS curve slopes upward from left to right. The existence of such a schedule is the result of workers incorrectly anticipating changes in the price level. Second, a vertical AS curve exists when workers have adjusted their expectations so as to be consistent with the actual price level. An important issue that has yet to be raised in our discussion is how individuals react to an incorrect price level forecast. The answer to this question is also the answer to the more general question, How do individuals form their price level expectations? These questions, which have important policy implications, will be discussed in the next two sections.

The Formation of Price Expectations: The Adaptive Expectations Hypothesis

Prior to the mid-1970s, the dominant theory explaining how price expectations formed was the *adaptive hypothesis*. According to this theory, the price level expected to prevail is based on the behavior of past prices. More precisely, if the price level individuals expect this period is not equal to the actual price level, individuals will use this forecasting error to revise their forecast or expectation of next period's price. Mathematically, this expectation process is usually written as

$$(8\text{-}1) \qquad P^e_t - P^e_{t-1} = \lambda(P_{t-1} - P^e_{t-1})$$

Where the term $P^e_t - P^e_{t-1}$ measures the change in expected price this period as compared with last period, and $P_{t-1} - P^e_{t-1}$ represents the amount that last period's actual price differed from the expected price in that period. The parameter λ represents the fraction of the forecasting error people use to alter or adapt their forecast of the price level. This parameter is generally assumed to range in size from zero to one. The idea behind this *partial adjustment coefficient* is that individuals may be reluctant to fully adjust expectations to a one period increase in the price level because they are not sure that the increase will be permanent. They feel it is too risky to completely adjust to price changes.[3]

In order to understand the adaptive expectations scheme, let us consider some examples that illustrate a few of its properties. These examples will be more easily understood if Equation 8-1 is rewritten as follows:

$$(8\text{-}2) \qquad P^e_t = P^e_{t-1} + \lambda(P_{t-1} - P^e_{t-1})$$

Suppose the actual and expected price levels for Period $t-1$ are 1.0 and that the adjustment coefficient is 0.5. Suppose also, that the actual price level increases to a new and permanent level of 2.0 in Period t. In Figure 8-3A, the solid line represents the behavior of actual price levels. As a result of this price level change, individuals will discover that their forecast for Period t was incorrect, and, thus, their forecast of the Period $t+1$ price level will be revised upwards. With λ equal to 0.5, the expected

---

[3] λ indicates how important the more recent past is relative to the more distant past. The larger λ is, the more important is the recent past. (See Appendix 8A for more details.)

price level will be raised to the level 1.5 in Period $t+1$, which is the original price expectation revised upward by one-half of the difference between actual and expected prices in Period t. With the actual level in Period $t+1$ being 2.0, a forecasting error still occurs, though smaller than before. Once again, individuals will appropriately adjust their expectation of the price level for the next period—Period $t+2$. This adjustment process will continue and expected prices will gradually approach the actual price level. The behavior of the expected price level over time due to this adjustment pattern is represented by the dashed line in Figure 8-4A. The speed at which expected prices adjust to actual price changes is

Figure 8-4. *Adaptive Price Expectations*

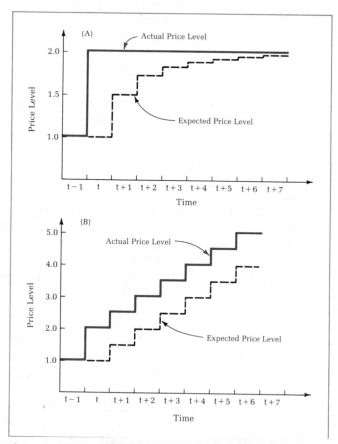

Panel A shows the adaptive adjustment of price expectations to a one-time increase in the actual price level. With expectations adjusting in this manner, it takes several time periods before the expected price level and the actual price level are the same.

Panel B shows the adjustment of adaptive price expectations to a continuous increase in the actual price level. When the actual price level continues to change, expectations will never completely adjust. For example, if actual prices are increasing, individuals who form their price expectations adaptively will consistently underpredict the actual price level.

determined by λ. The larger (smaller) is this value, the shorter (longer) time it would take these expectations to adjust. At one extreme, a λ of one means the adjustment period lasts one period; Equation 8-2 reduces to $P_t^e = P_{t-1}$. At the other extreme (λ equal to zero) price expectations do not change ($P_t^e = P_{t-1}^e$).

How do individuals forming expectations adaptively respond to an environment of repeated price increases? Again assume that the actual and expected price level for Period $t-1$ is 1.0 and that the adjustment coefficient is 0.5. In contrast to the previous example, suppose the price level doubles in Period t and from then on increases by 0.5 each period. The resulting pattern of the actual price level is presented in Figure 8-4B. In this environment individuals will continue to adjust their price forecasts according to the gap between the actual and the expected price. For example, individuals will forecast a price level of 1.0 in Period t. Upon realizing that the actual price level is 2.0, the expected price level for Period $t+1$ will be revised to 1.5 for the following period. In this environment of rising price levels, the expected price level will be repeatedly adjusted upwards as presented in Figure 8-4B. However, as long as the price level is rising, an adaptively formed price expectation will consistently underpredict the price level. Only if the actual price level stops increasing will the expected price level adjust so as to be consistent with the actual price level.

Adaptive Price Expectations and Demand Policy

The adaptive expectations model has some very interesting implications for demand management policies. In particular, the gradual adjustment of expected to actual prices enables fiscal or monetary authorities to affect the levels of output and employment.

Since actual and expected prices may differ, there are two types of equilibrium—one where expected and actual prices are the same and one where they differ. Suppose the economy is at Point A in Figure 8-5. This point represents long-run equilibrium since the *AD* curve, the short-run *AS* curve, and the long-run *AS* curve all intersect there. Not only is the aggregate demand for goods equal to the value of goods being produced at full employment, but individuals' forecasts of the price level are identical to the actual price level. In contrast a short-run equilibrium price and output level occurs at a point, such as B, where the *AD* and short-run *AS* curves intersect. But notice that Point B is not on the long-run *AS* curve. The expected and actual price levels differ at this equilibrium.

Suppose the economy is in long-run equilibrium at Point A in Figure 8-5 where Y_1 is the output level associated with a 6 percent unemployment rate—a rate policymakers find unacceptable. As a result monetary or fiscal policy is employed to reduce the unemployment rate. This policy

Figure 8-5. Expansionary Demand Policy and Adaptive Expectations

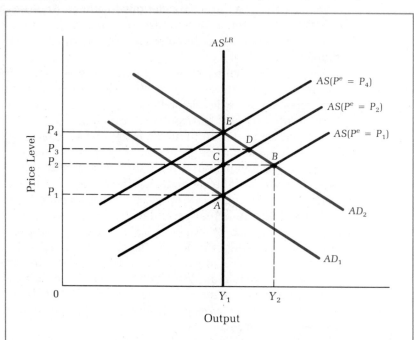

If the economy is at rest at Point A and policymakers decide to stimulate the economy through demand policy, the *AD* curve will shift outward (upward) driving prices up. Since individuals form price expectations adaptively, they will underpredict the actual price increase. The result is an upward shift of the short-run *AS* curve, but a shift that does not move all the way to Point E. In other words, the expansionary demand policy will increase both output and prices. Once workers learn that they have made an error, they will again adjust their price expectations, eventually moving the short-run *AS* curve upward until it intersects the long-run curve at Point E.

action is reflected in a rightward shift of the *AD* curve to AD_2 in Figure 8-5. The increase in aggregate demand drives the price level up to P_2 causing the labor demand curve to shift and, hence, the nominal wage to increase. Since, under the adaptive price expectations hypothesis, workers have no reason to expect the price level to increase to P_2 they believe their real wage has risen and consequently, offer to supply more labor. It is this increase in labor supply that allows output to increase to Y_2 at Point B. Thus, an expansionary demand policy does bring the unemployment rate down. However, since real wages and expected real wages differ, workers will eventually realize their forecasting errors and correct them.

Suppose the adjustment coefficient is equal to unity so that $P^e_t = P_{t-1}$. With this particular expectations process, the discrepancy between actual and expected real prices will not last long. Workers will revise their price expectations for the next period so as to be in agreement with the actual price level, P_2. As a result of this revision in their price forecast, individuals decrease the quantity of labor they are willing to supply at each nominal wage, the labor supply curve shifts to the left, and the short-run AS curve shifts up, intersecting AS^{LR} at Point C. The process does not stop here, for at Point C the quantity of output demanded is greater than the quantity supplied—the price level is driven up to P_3 at Point D. Once again, as expectations adjust to actual prices the short-run AS curve shifts up. This process continues until expected and actual prices are equal and the corresponding long- and short-run AS curves intersect the AD curve, $AS^{LR} = AS^{SR} = AD$ (Point E). In the long run, that is, after expectations have completely adjusted, the expansionary policy has had no effect on real output. Only higher prices have resulted.

Should policymakers attempt to reduce unemployment (increase real output) again, they can do so temporarily, but at the cost of further price level increases. If policymakers attempt to permanently reduce the unemployment rate (increase real output), what will result? To keep real output at the level Y_2 in Figure 8-5, AD would have to be continually shifted out further and further, thus driving up prices more and more rapidly—the accelerationist hypothesis.

Adaptive Expectations and Partial Adjustment

The length of time that output can be held above the natural level (AS^{LR}) by demand policies depends on how rapidly expectations adjust to actual changes. Up to this point, we have made the assumption that expected prices are fully adjusted to the past period's price. Now consider the policy implications of an adaptive expectations scheme where prices do not completely adjust to the past price level. In other words, assume that the adjustment coefficient (λ) lies between zero and one.

Suppose the economy is in long-run equilibrium and policymakers enact an expansionary monetary policy with hopes of reducing unemployment. The AD increase initially results in an increase in both the price and output levels. As workers realize their forecasting error, they will adjust their forecast of future price levels. When the adjustment coefficient is less than one, however, the revised expected price level will be less than the new actual price level that results from the expansionary monetary policy. The revised price level forecast is reflected in a leftward shift of the labor supply curve, but a shift that is smaller than the one that occurred when λ was equal to one. Consequently, the short-run AS curve also does not shift as far to the left as it would if the adjustment coefficient was one. With the short-run AS curve shifting back more slowly, long-run equilibrium is reestablished more slowly. Of course, this also means the temporary output effect lasts longer. More precisely, output will remain above the natural output level until the expected and actual price levels are once again the same.

Anti-Inflationary Policies under
Adaptive Expectations

So far we have discussed the implications of adaptively formed price expectations for expansionary demand policies. But what if policymakers desire to reduce the price level? Suppose that the economy is at Point A in Panel D of Figure 8-6 where the price level is higher than the level desired

Figure 8-6. Anti-Inflationary Policy and Adaptive Expectations

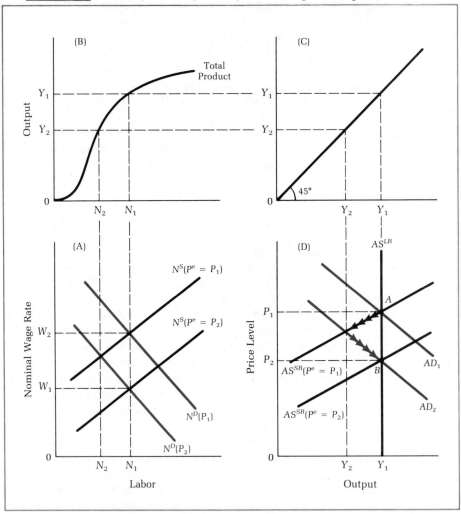

An attempt to reduce prices from the current level of Point A in Panel D will lead to an output reduction; that is, a recession. As AD shifts down, prices begin to fall and labor demand falls (the real wage increases). Until workers adjust their price expectations to the actual decline in prices output will decline. Eventually, as workers' expectations catch up with reality, the economy will move to Point B.

by policymakers. Can they lower the price level? If the supply of money or the government's deficit is decreased, the AD curve will shift down to AD_2 causing prices to fall and labor demand to decrease. Initially labor supply will not change because workers will not expect prices to fall. As a result, fewer workers will be employed and real output will decline. In other words a recession will have been created. When workers realize that their real wage has risen (the price level has fallen), the labor supply curve will shift out to $N^S(P^e = P_2)$ as shown in Figure 8-6. The quantity of labor employed will return to N_1 and the quantity of output produced will return to Y_1, but at a lower price level (Point B rather than Point A).

When expectations adjust adaptively, the only way to reduce the price level through demand management policies is to create a recession. How deep or how long a recession is necessary? The answer depends on how rapidly expectations adapt or adjust.

The Formation of Price Expectations: The Rational Expectations Hypothesis

The adaptive expectations story described in the previous paragraphs was the essence of Milton Friedman's 1968 message to the economics profession. He warned that we should not expect too much from monetary policy—it could not permanently influence the levels of real output and unemployment. It could, in the short run, influence these variables and, in the long run, affect the rate of inflation. But to expect more would be pure folly. The force of Friedman's argument was given impetus by the events of the late 1960s and 1970s—the rapidly accelerating inflation without concurrent declines in the unemployment rate. By the mid-1970s, however, a number of economists were criticizing the adaptive expectations view saying that it is not a good representation of how people actually behave. An individual who forms expectations adaptively uses only past values of the price level to forecast the price level. It is argued that such an approach ignores potentially useful information. For instance, if a person knows that increases in the money supply lead to price increases, then this is important information that should be included in the formation of the price expectation. An individual operating in his or her self-interest, would not ignore this information.

Probably, the most important criticism is that under an adaptively formed price expectation individuals can make systematic errors; they can repeat the same error over and over again. We saw an example of this when we examined how an adaptively formed price expectation will consistently underpredict the actual price level (see Figure 8-4B). Opponents of adaptive expectations argue that individuals operating in their self-interest would not behave in such a manner.

Because of these and other criticisms, an alternative hypothesis concerning the formation of price expectations evolved. Recall that this hypothesis, which essentially assumes individuals or workers use all available information efficiently and avoid making systematic mistakes in their forecasts, is known as the *rational expectations hypothesis (REH).*[4] In this section we will examine the essential ideas behind this hypothesis. In addition we consider the policy implications of the *REH.* In many ways the controversiality of this hypothesis (and it is controversial) is a result of these implications.

The Essential Ideas of the *REH*

Unlike the adaptive expectations hypothesis, a simple equation cannot be easily written to specify the rational expectations hypothesis. Instead we will discuss two examples that point out the essential notions behind the hypothesis.

Suppose we want to forecast the price of oranges next period. How would we do this? If we used the adaptive specification, only past orange prices would be used. However, since the price of oranges today is determined by today's demand for and supply of oranges, shouldn't we be able to make a better forecast of tomorrow's price by forecasting what the demand for, and the supply of, oranges will be next period instead of simply using all past prices? Hence, given today's demand and supply curves we can form rational expectations of the price by considering all the information relevant to changes in these curves. A change in the price of complementary or substitute goods, a change in income, or a change in tastes will cause a shift in position of the demand curve. A change in variables such as costs, technology, or weather conditions will result in the supply curve of oranges shifting position. All we need is information about whether any or all of these *ceteris paribus* variables change. A rational expectations' forecast will be formed by considering the major determinants of the positions of the demand and supply curves.

Another example that illustrates the notion of the rational expectations hypothesis can be found in the stock market. This is a market with many traders, and one in which current information is readily available. Suppose it is well-known that a stock price follows the pattern shown in Figure 8-7. Furthermore, suppose the stock price is currently at Point *A* in Period $t+1$. If people form expectations adaptively, the stock price they would expect for Period $t+2$ would be below Point *B*. Does it make sense that individuals will ignore the information they have about the stock

---

[4] The original notion of a rational expectation was developed by John Muth in 1961. He defined *rational expectations* as "informed predictions of future events," and said that they are "essentially the same as the predictions of the relevant economic theory." See John Muth, "Rational Expectations and the Theory of Price Movements," *Econometrica* (July, 1961).

Figure 8-7. *Stock Prices: Adaptive and Rational Expectations Compared*

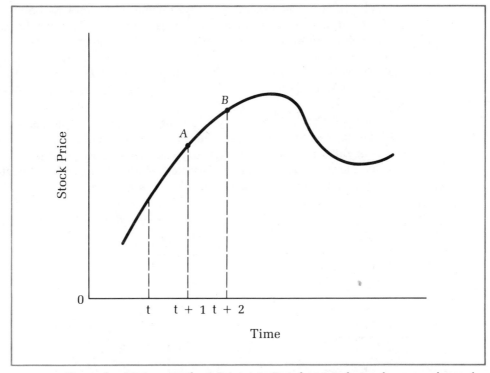

If a stock price is currently at Point A in Period $t+1$ (today) and everyone knows for certain that the price will rise to Point B tomorrow, what will happen if everyone forms expectations adaptively? Everyone will expect the price to rise, but not all the way to B since their forecasts would be based only on past prices. This assumption, that expectations depend only on past values, is much too restrictive. The rational expectations school argues that everyone will take their knowledge into account and buy now at any price below the peak of the hill. This will be done irrespective of what prices did yesterday (Period t) or the day before.

price and form expectations on past prices only? We assume individuals are rational in every other aspect of economics, why not in forming expectations? A rational individual will utilize all available information in forming price expectations, not just past prices. How does this approach differ from adaptive expectations? Suppose individuals know the path of the stock price as pictured in Figure 8-7 and use this knowledge to form their expectations of future stock prices. What will they do? At Point A they expect the price to rise and will, therefore, buy the stock expecting to sell it at the peak. As everyone does this, the price rises immediately, not waiting until Period $t+2$. Under the adaptive scheme the price would not rise immediately and, thus, people would be ignoring profit-making opportunities.

The Policy Implications of the *REH*

The *REH* has generated a heated debate because of its policy implications. In this subsection we will discuss these implications. Let us start by considering an extreme form of rational expectations known as the *perfect foresight assumption* that assumes individuals always predict the future price level correctly. The perfect foresight assumption, in effect, returns us to the world of perfect information. Forecasting errors are not possible.

Suppose an expansionary monetary policy is implemented in an attempt to lower the unemployment rate. Such a policy change is reflected as an outward shift of the *AD* curve from AD_1 to AD_2 in Figure 8-8. The initial long-run equilibrium is disrupted. Under the adaptive expectations hypothesis the economy goes from Point *A* to Point *B* to Point *C*. With

Figure 8-8. *The Short- and Long-run Aggregate Supply*
Curves under Rational Expectations

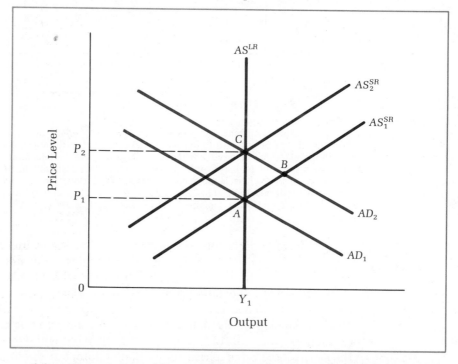

If the economy is in equilibrium at Point *A* and an expansionary monetary policy is implemented, what will happen? Under rational expectations, if individuals correctly forecast what the Fed will do or if individuals know what is happening to the money supply, they will expect prices to rise. They will expect this immediately, not after some time has elapsed. Hence, rather than moving from Point *A* to *B* to *C* as occurred under adaptive expectations, the economy will adjust immediately from Point *A* to *C*. In this case, the expansionary policy has no effect on output. It only drives prices up.

perfect foresight expectations, however, individuals forecast the change in the money supply. Since these same individuals know that an upward shift in the *AD* curve causes prices to increase, they will expect the price level to rise. Thus, rather than being fooled into supplying more labor, individuals will expect their real wage to fall. As a result, they will demand higher nominal wages to work the same number of hours. This leads to an upward shift in the labor supply curve, and, as shown in Figure 8-8, an upward shift of the short-run *AS* curve from AS_1^{SR} to AS_2^{SR}. Since under the perfect foresight assumption workers will correctly forecast the price effects from the expansionary monetary policy, the short-run *AS* curve will intersect the *AD* curve and long-run *AS* curve at Point *C*, and will do so immediately, not after a period of time. In this case the economy does not experience even temporary increases in output due to the change in the money supply. The only effect from the monetary policy change is an increase in the price level. In sum, under perfect foresight expectations systematic monetary and fiscal policy cannot affect real output and employment.

Costly Information

Information is neither perfectly available nor costless in the real world. For the manager of a department store to know the price of each item charged by a competitor, he would have to survey the competitor or spend time reading ads. Similarly, for that manager to know whether an increase in the number of customers in his store is an increase in the demand for his merchandise alone or an increase in the demand for all such merchandise stores, he would have to spend time visiting the other stores or pay someone to obtain that information. Therefore, it is not rational for individuals to gather every bit of information; they will gather information up to the point where the marginal cost of search equals the marginal benefit. It is logical then that individuals will have different amounts of information about various markets. They will know the price of their product (their labor or other products), but perhaps not know the prices of other products as well. Thus, an increase in all prices may be temporarily interpreted by an individual as an increase in the price of his product relative to other prices. He may, therefore, supply more of his product—until he realizes the mistake.

Demand Management Policy with the *REH*

What is the implication for stabilization policy in a world of costly information and rationally formed expectations? In a world with uncertainty, a rationally formed expectation can still be incorrect even though individuals take into account all relevant information in forming their expectations; that is, all information that they gather in their search process. If the money supply increased by an amount greater than that expected, the expected price level will understate the actual price level increase. In terms of Figure 8-8 if individuals forecast that a policymaker's desire to reduce the unemployment rate will result in an expansionary demand policy they will also forecast higher prices. The short-run *AS* curve will shift by an amount corresponding to the increase in the price expectations. However, the *AS* curve need not shift back to Point *C*. The price expectation may be incorrect. If so, the short-run *AS* curve will intersect the *AD* curve somewhere between Points *B* and *C*. This means monetary policy can have a temporary output effect in addition to its effects on the price level. The temporary output effect is due to unanticipated changes in aggregate demand. Individuals will learn of these errors and make appropriate corrections in their expectations for the next period.

The stock market example discussed previously can provide some insights into the difference between anticipated and unanticipated events and their effects on the economy. Under the reasonable assumption that people do not ignore profit-making opportunities, the current price of the stock reflects all available information. There is not some inside information that one person can use to always make more profit than others. Such profits would induce others to gain this inside information or copy the behavior of the person with the information. Eventually, the information would become "public." In this sense, the current price of the stock is the result of individuals acting on essentially the same information. Markets in which this occurs are called *efficient markets*.

You may have heard someone say that stock prices follow a *random walk,* or you may have read a popular book by Professor Burton Malkiel called *A Random Walk Down Wall Street.*[5] A random walk means that the current price was not predictable from the past price. Just because the stock price increased last period does not mean it will increase next period. Saying that stock prices follow a random walk is just another way of stating that current prices reflect or incorporate all available information. However, if individuals act on the basis of anticipated price movements so that current prices reflect those anticipations, what can cause a movement in stock prices? Only unanticipated developments (surprises) or new information will lead to price changes and these price changes will occur immediately once the unanticipated development takes place or the new information is available. Is it likely that an individual could consistently learn about these developments or gain this information before other individuals and as a result systematically make a profit? While an individual may occasionally have inside information, it does not seem likely that anyone could always have such information. Other

---

[5] Burton Malkiel, *A Random Walk Down Wall Street,* student ed. (New York: W. W. Norton & Co., Inc., 1981).

individuals, seeing the profit the first person was making, will attempt to gain this information. Profits would tend to return to normal levels with more and more people using this information.

Similarly, unanticipated demand changes can affect real output and employment. Systematic changes can not. Hence, if the money supply is expanded each time the economy turns down, people will learn to anticipate the monetary expansion. Hence, they will not be surprised or fooled. Instead, they will predict price rises and will demand wage increases to match, thereby offsetting any possible effects on output and employment.

Rational or Adaptive Expectations?

While either thesis—the rational or adaptive—could be used to explain the pattern of inflation-unemployment combinations observed in Figure 8-1, the logic of the "costly information" form of the *REH* seems more compelling. In fact, very few economists who support the accelerationist hypothesis or adaptive expectations approach would object to the nonperfect foresight form of the *REH*. It is the perfect foresight assumption, and the policy implications that flow from it, to which many economists object.

The argument is often made that while it may be illogical to assume people form expectations by only looking backward, it is just as illogical to assume people have perfect information or even as much information as the monetary authorities. Hence, there must be a trade-off curve in the short run and one that the Fed can exploit or use to direct the economy. The crux of the debate surrounding the *REH* is whether this trade-off can be systematically exploited—that is, can policy do the same thing time after time and be successful?

The major points of controversy or confusion and the unresolved issues surrounding the *REH* are summarized in the following five paragraphs. These points will be considered in detail in later chapters.

The rational expectations postulate that private economic agents (individuals and businesses) gather and use information efficiently is simply that the marginal costs of gathering and using information are equated to their marginal benefits. Yet, economic theorists often assert that individual agents use all available information. This creates confusion and unnecessary disagreements. Virtually no one would argue that all agents have all information.

Government policy will increase the level of real income only if it is able to fool people into confusing nominal changes with real ones. This assertion also generates a great deal of controversy. Clearly, governmental policies affect real output and employment. For example, rules on immigration, taxes, minimum wages, and so on, affect employment. The *REH* interpretation of the first sentence of this paragraph is the following: Systematic or repetitive governmental policies cannot cause deviations from the natural output level. Only random governmental actions can. However, the natural output level can be altered by certain governmental policies such as immigration laws, taxes, etc. Hence, the *REH* totally discounts the value of demand management or so-called stabilization policies.

If expectations are rational then the level of output (or unemployment) should fluctuate randomly about the natural output level. Yet it is common knowledge that output and unemployment are each serially correlated. Indeed, look at Figure 2-4 to observe this relationship. *Serial correlation* means that if output is above the natural output level in one period, it is more likely to be above it than below it the next period. In fact, serial correlation is merely another term for a business cycle. This persistence creates a thorny problem for the *REH*, one that has stimulated a literature known as the *Equilibrium Business Cycle*.[6]

The following two sentences point out another criticism leveled at the *REH*: Assume that all information is freely available. Even in this unrealistic case the *REH* requires the very strict assumption that everybody knows the true structure of the economy. This criticism is not valid. All that is necessary is that one individual take advantage of a profit opportunity. If all but one person is ill-informed, then the one "rational" individual could make a profit on his investment or could sell his information to others. This will inevitably produce the rational expectations result. John Maynard Keynes noted this in his *Treatise on Money*, "actions based on inaccurate anticipations will not long survive. . . ."[7]

A final point of controversy surrounds the objectives of government. If the government's objective is to stabilize the economy, it will inform the public of any new policy approach and will do exactly as it says. Then there will be no random deviations. Suppose, however, that the government's objective is not to stabilize the economy, but, instead, to stay in power. Then it might best serve its objective by fooling the public, creating what is termed a *political business cycle*. If that is the case the public cannot be expected to believe the government's announcements and, thus, the process degenerates into a big guessing game.

In Chapters 12-15 we will more fully develop the controversies over the effectiveness of activist demand policies. We will examine some extensions or alterations of the *REH* known as *long-term contracting* and the *credibility effect*. In the next three chapters the role of expectations in the demand side of the economy is discussed.

---

[6]This literature is discussed in Chapter 15.

[7] John Maynard Keynes, *Treatise on Money* (New York: Harcourt Brace & Company, 1930), p. 160.

Conclusions

Frank E. Morris, the president of the Boston Federal Reserve, opened a conference in June, 1978, with a paragraph that captured the frustration of economic policymakers during the 1970s.

> It is probably fair to say that economic policy is now being made in at least a partial vacuum of economic theory. Unlike earlier periods, no one body of theory seems to have a very broad acceptance. If Keynesianism is not bankrupt, . . . it is at least in disarray. Certainly, the confidence that I felt as a member of the Kennedy Treasury in our ability to use the Keynesian system to generate outcomes for the economy which were highly predictable has been shaken, and I believe a great many other people have also lost that confidence. I look back with nostalgia on those years in the early sixties. . . .

This paragraph also captures the unease that even the staunchest of the fine-tuners now have regarding the Phillips curve. Milton Friedman was primarily responsible for this unease, undermining the idea that there is a trade-off between unemployment and inflation that the government can exploit by influencing aggregate demand. His accelerationist thesis laid the Phillips curve to rest. It also formed the basis for the final nail in the Phillips curve coffin, the *REH*. Yet, not all economists accept the implications of the *REH*, nor are all controversies surrounding the *REH* resolved.

_QUESTIONS AND EXERCISES

1. Derive and explain how a decrease in the expected price level affects the short-run *AS* curve.

2. Consider the following model of the supply side of the economy:
   (1) $Y = 20 + 5 N$
   (2) $N^D = 100 - 10 W + 10 P$
   (3) $N^S = 90 + 10 W - 10 P^e$
   (4) $N^D = N^S = N$
   a. Explain each of these equations.
   b. Graphically derive the labor supply curve in this model. How does a change in P^e affect the curve?
   c. Derive, either graphically or algebraically, the short-run *AS* curve.
   d. What is the value of the natural rate of output?

3. Suppose expectations are formed adaptively. Individuals believe the price level in the next period to be 1.0. The actual price level is 1.0. Assume in the next period the actual price is 2.0, and the price level remains at this level for the next five periods. Calculate the expected price level for the next five periods under the assumption that $\lambda = 0.8$. Under the assumption that $\lambda = 0.3$.

4. Consider the following statement: If price expectations are important, very restrictive aggregate demand policies may not restore reasonable price stability in the next 5 years. Comment.

5. If you were a classical economist, would adaptive expectations or rational expectations be more consistent with your beliefs? Explain.

6. Explain why individuals who use information efficiently will not make systematic mistakes in their expectations.

7. Discuss the similarity between the adaptive scheme of formulating price level expectations and the manner in which estimates of permanent income are calculated. (See Chapter 10.)

8. Suppose a policymaker desires to attain a lower price level by enacting a contractionary demand policy. Discuss the implications of both the adaptively formed and rationally formed price expectations for the length and severity of the resulting recession.

9. Explain why rational expectations theorists relate real income effects of monetary policy to the innovations (real changes) in the money supply and not to predicted changes. What happens to the predicted or expected changes?

_SUGGESTED READINGS

Two excellent surveys of the issues surrounding rational and adaptive expectations are

Robert J. Gordon, "Output Fluctuations and Gradual Price Adjustment," *Journal of Economic Literature*, Vol. 19 (June, 1981), pp. 493-530.
Rooney Maddock and Michael Carter, "A Child's Guide to Rational Expectations," *Journal of Economic Literature*, Vol. 20 (March, 1982), pp. 39-51.

The references to these two articles should provide the reader with sufficient material. Yet, on the still lighter side, the following might be examined:

Federal Reserve Bank of Minneapolis *Report on Rational Expectations* (1980).

W. Guzzardi, Jr., "The New Down-to-Earth Economics," *Fortune Magazine* (December, 31, 1978), pp, 72-79.

The important distinction between real and nominal interest rates is explored in

William W. Brown, "Unreal Estimates of the Real Rate of Interest," *Review,* Federal Reserve Bank of St. Louis, Vol. 63, No. 1 (1981).

James M. Boughton and James S. Fackler, "The Nominal Rate of Interest, the Rate of Return on Money, and Inflationary Expectations," *Journal of Macroeconomics* (Fall, 1981), pp. 531-545.

For a further discussion of monetary policy and the REH, see

Douglas G. Waldo, "Rational Expectations and the Role of Countercyclical Monetary Policy," *Journal of Monetary Economics* (1982), pp. 101-109.

_APPENDIX 8A. The Algebra of Rational and Adaptive Expectations_____

The following is a typical algebraic presentation of the expectations type of macro model:

(8A-1)   Supply: $Y_t - \overline{Y} = a(P_t - P_t^e) + U_t$
(8A–2)   Demand: $Y_t = -bP_t + cX_t$

Where

Y = real output or income
$\overline{Y}$ = natural output level
P = price
P^e = expected price
X_t = government policy variable, e.g., spending or money supply
U_t = random term having an average value of zero $(U_t^e = 0)$

The expectations term P_t^e is the crucial variable. Recall that if we assume adaptive expectations, then

$$P_t^e = \lambda P_{t-1} + \lambda(1-\lambda)P_{t-2} + \lambda(1-\lambda)^2 P_{t-3} + \ldots \text{ etc.}$$

Under rational expectations, P_t^e is the expected price level for Period t given *all* information in Period $t-1$, not just past prices. Setting demand equal to supply yields

(8A-3) $$P_t = \frac{1}{a+b}(aP_t^e + cX_t - \overline{Y} - U_t)$$

The rational expectations forecast (assuming the demand and supply equations, i.e., the structure of the economy, are known) will be the solution given by Equation 8A-3 where X_t and U_t must be forecast since only X_{t-1} and U_{t-1} are known. Hence,

$$P_t^e = \frac{1}{a+b}(aP_t^e + cX_t^e - \overline{Y} - U_t^e)$$

But $U_t^e = 0$ so that

(8A-4) $$P_t^e = \frac{1}{a+b}(aP_t^e + cX_t^e - \overline{Y})$$

Subtracting Equation 8A-4 from Equation 8A-3 yields

(8A-5) $\qquad P_t - P_t^e = \dfrac{1}{a+b}[c(X_t - X_t^e) - U_t]$

and substituting Equation 8A-5 into Equation 8A-1 yields

(8A-6) $\qquad Y_t - \overline{Y_t} = \dfrac{ac}{a+b}(X_t - X_t^e) + \dfrac{b}{a+b}U_t$

Equation 8A-6 says that the deviation of output (Y) from the natural level ($\overline{Y}$) depends only on the surprises or nonsystematic part of government policy ($X_t - X_t^e$). If $X_t^e = X_t$, then government policy has no effect.

In the text we stated that an adaptively formed price expectation only uses past values of prices to forecast the future price. This can be easily proven if we rewrite the adaptive scheme $P_t^e = P_{t-1}^e + \lambda(P_{t-1} - P_{t-1}^e)$ for Period $t-1$ rather than Period t as: $P_{t-1}^e = P_{t-2}^e + \lambda(P_{t-2} - P_{t-2}^e)$. Substituting this expression for P_{t-1}^e we obtain

$$P_t^e = \lambda P_{t-1} + (1-\lambda)[P_{t-2}^e + \lambda(P_{t-2} - P_{t-2}^e)]$$

Now, writing the adaptive form for P_{t-2}^e, then P_{t-3}^e, P_{t-4}^e, and so on, and substituting, we obtain an expression which states that the expected price level today depends only on past prices.

$$P_t^e = \lambda P_{t-1} + \lambda(1-\lambda)P_{t-2} + \lambda(1-\lambda)^2 P_{t-3} + \ldots \text{ etc.}$$

In other words, the adaptive scheme requires that expectations of prices are formed on the basis of past values of prices only. In this specification the value of λ indicates how important the more recent past is relative to the more distant past. Suppose λ is three-fourths. Then the price expected for Period t consists of ¾ of last period's price plus $^3/_{16}$ of two period ago's price plus a diminishing portion of previous periods' past prices. (This type of expectations scheme is also referred to as *autoregressive*; which means that the forecast value, P^e, is determined by past values of P.)

_APPENDIX 8B. Inflation: Statics and Dynamics_____

The static aggregate demand-aggregate supply model lends itself to analyses of price changes. While we can, and have, extrapolated from these static or one-time price rises to the rate of inflation in our discussions, it is not strictly theoretically correct to do so. In this appendix, however, it is shown that our reliance on the static framework to describe dynamic relations is really quite reasonable. The static framework is very useful for guiding discussions involving inflation, inflationary expectations, and monetary growth; that is, the dynamics of the macro model, if a little imagination is used and some slight theoretical laxity is permitted.

Inflation and the
AD-AS Model_____

The *AD-AS* model developed in the preceding chapters enables the determination of income and price levels for the economy at one point in time. For this reason, the model is often referred to as a *static model*. Yet, inflation is a *dynamic* event; it refers to price level changes from one period to the next. Does this mean we must discard our static model and construct a new model in order to discuss the inflation rate? The answer is, not necessarily. The static *AD-AS* model can provide insights into the problems of inflation.

An examination of the behavior of economic variables over time points out an apparent relationship between money growth and inflation as shown in Figure 8B-1. Our previous treatment of the equation of exchange ($MV = PY$) or of the money market equilibrium condition ($M^S = M^D$) should help show this relationship. Equilibrium in the money market can be represented as follows:

$$M/P = L(r,Y) \qquad \text{or} \qquad M = P \cdot L(r,Y)$$

In long-run equilibrium where all adjustments have taken place, expectations and reality are the same, and the interest rate and the output level are constant. In such an equilibrium situation the demand for money does not change. Thus, if the stock of money (M) grows, the only way equilibrium can be maintained is for the price level to grow—at the same rate the money stock grows.

(8B-1) $\Delta M = \Delta P \cdot L(r,Y)$

or from the equation of exchange

(8B-2) $\Delta M(V) = \Delta P(Y) \text{ or } \Delta M = \Delta P(kY)$

Figure 8B-1. The Relationship between the Growth
Rates of Money and Inflation

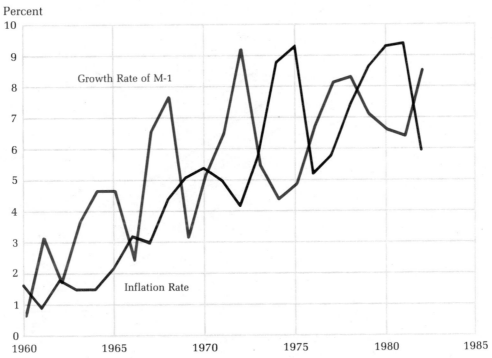

Source: *Economic Report of the President* (1982).
In the long run the inflation rate is determined by the growth rate of the money stock.
Notice how movements in the growth rate of M-1 are followed by similar movements in the
inflation rate.

Where k = 1/V. For instance, if the money supply is growing at 5% a year,
prices will also have to be rising at 5%. In symbols this will be $\pi = m$.
Where π = the inflation rate and $m = \Delta M/M$ = the rate of growth of
money.

This long-run relationship can be represented with the static AD-AS
model. Suppose the money supply has been increasing at about a 5% rate
each period. This means that the AD curve is shifting out each period by
about 5%. In Figure 8B-2 such a shift for one year is characterized by the
movement in the AD curve from $AD(M_{1983})$ to $AD(M_{1984})$. The short-run AS
curve is also shifting upward each period. Why? Because individuals
realize that increases in the money stock result in higher prices. Thus, the
expected price level will increase by the same percentage that the money
supply is expected to increase. The consequence of these shifts is a price
level (P_{1984}) that is 5% greater than it was in 1983. As long as the money
stock continues to increase at the same rate and price expectations in-

Figure 8B-2. The Static Diagram and Inflation

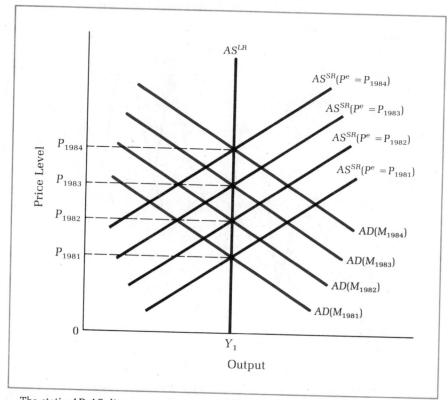

The static *AD-AS* diagram can be used to represent inflation. The *AD* and AS^{SR} curves must shift upward each period.

crease correspondingly the price level will increase. This is what is meant by a steady, continual inflation. To represent this steady increase, the *AD* and the short-run *AS* curves will have to continually shift up by 5%, as shown in Figure 8B-2.

Output (potential or natural) does not remain fixed in the long run as assumed in Equations 8B-1 and 8B-2. Natural output increases by the rate of growth of productivity; that is, the rate of growth of output per member of the labor force. Recall that in the *AD-AS* model productivity increases are represented as outward shifts of the short- and long-run *AS* curves. What is the implication of a productivity increase for inflation? Assume, as before, that the money stock has been growing at 5%. In addition, assume productivity has been increasing at an annual rate of 2%. This productivity change causes the long-run *AS* curve to shift to the right by 2% each year. Without the productivity change, the short-run *AS* curve and the *AD* curve would each shift so as to intersect at Point *B* in Figure 8B-3. The productivity increase has the effect of reducing the size of the

Figure 8B-3. Productivity Growth and Monetary Expansion

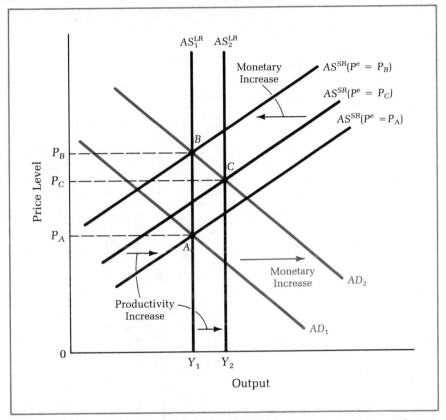

The AD-AS diagram can be used to demonstrate the relationship between productivity growth and monetary growth. Productivity growth is represented by outward shifts of the short- and long-run AS curves. Money growth is represented by an outward shift of the AD curve, and any increase in price level expectations is represented by an inward shift of the short-run AS curve. In Figure 8B-3, monetary growth of 5% is represented by an outward shift of the AD curve of 5% and an inward shift of the short-run AS curve (as price level expectations rise) of 5%. Productivity growth of 2% is represented by an outward shift of both short- and long-run AS curves of 2%. The net change is a price level increase of 3% (Point C).

price increase. This is shown by an outward shift of the long-run AS curve and an outward shift of the short-run AS curve. In sum, then, the short-run AS curve shifts out by 2% due to the productivity increase and it shifts in by 5% due to the money increase for a net inward shift of 3%. The intersection between the three curves takes place at Point C in Figure 8B-3.

The price level in the second period is greater than the price level in the first period by 3%. If productivity and the money stock continued to increase at the stated percentages (2% and 5% respectively), the curves will shift each period and the price level will increase by 3% each period. Again a steady inflation will result, although at a rate less than the 5% money growth (actually 3%, which is monetary growth minus productivity growth). This is shown in Figure 8B-4.

Figure 8B-4. *Steady Inflation*

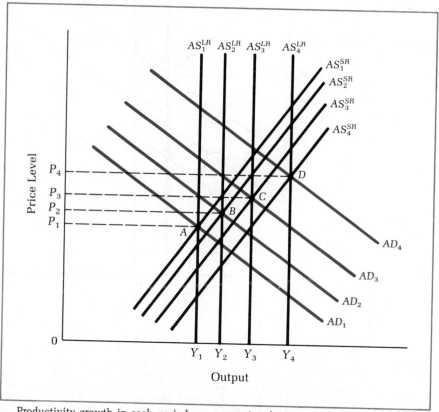

Productivity growth in each period means continual outward shifts of the short- and long-run *AS* curves. Monetary expansion in excess of productivity increases is shown by continual inward shifts of the short-run *AS* curve (as price expectations rise) and outward shifts of the *AD* curve. Monetary expansion in excess of productivity growth, causes increases in the price level as shown by the movement from Points *A* to *B* to *C* to *D*.

The inflation we have just described is a special type of inflation. In each period we found that (1) *AD* is equal to *AS*, (2) output is at the natural level, and (3) actual and expected inflation are equal. When these conditions hold, we have *steady inflation*.

Suppose both the money supply and productivity have been increasing at a 2% rate while the other exogenous variables have remained unchanged. The economy is not experiencing price rises: Productivity increases offset money growth increases. This situation is characterized in Figure 8B-5 by the shift in the relevant curves from AD_1, AS^{SR}_1, and AS^{LR}_1 to AD_2, AS^{SR}_2, and AS^{LR}_2, and, then, to AD_3, AS^{SR}_3, and AS^{LR}_3 . Individuals expect the price level to remain the same in this dynamic situation.

Figure 8B-5. *A Case of Zero Inflation*

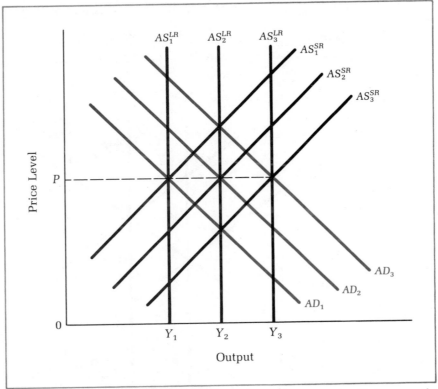

Productivity increases and monetary expansion at the same rate offset one another leading to a zero rate of inflation.

A One-Period Change:
Perfect Foresight
Expectations

Suppose monetary expansion has been a constant 2% and productivity has been increasing at the same rate. Then, the monetary authority increases the money supply by 4% for one period only. After one period the growth rate returns to 2%. Also assume individuals have formed their price level expectations rationally and with complete knowledge of the monetary change so that, in effect, they are not fooled by the policy change. The *AD* curve shifts to the right by 4%, from AD_1 to AD_2 (shown in Figure 8B-6), as a result of the money supply increase. The long-run *AS* curve shifts to the right by 2% due to the normal productivity increase from AS_1^{LR} to AS_2^{LR} while the short-run supply curve, in effect, does not change. It shifts out by 2% due to the productivity increase and back by 2% due to the increase in price expectations. If, in the next period, money growth returns to the 2% rate, the steady zero inflation rate will return and the price level will remain constant at P_2.

<u>Figure 8B-6.</u> *A One-Period Policy Change: Perfect Foresight*

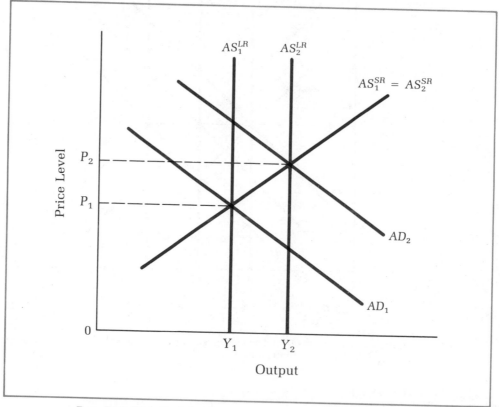

From Period 1 to Period 2 the rate of monetary growth is 4% which is reflected in an outward shift of the *AD* curve. Productivity growth is 2% as shown by outward shifts in both the long-run and short-run *AS* curves. Since the *AD* shift is greater than the *AS* shifts, the price level rises. The expectation of these rising prices is shown as an inward shift of the short-run *AS* curve. The net effect of these changes is a 4% outward shift in the *AD* curve and a 2% outward shift in the long-run *AS* curve. The short-run *AS* curve shifts out by 2% (due to the productivity gain) and then back by the same amount (due to the expected price rise). Thus, the short-run *AS* curve shows no net movement ($AS_1^{SR} = AS_2^{SR}$).

If productivity change and monetary growth take place at the same rate after Period 2, there will be a zero rate of inflation thereafter. This was the pattern shown in Figure 8B-5.

A One-Period Change:
Imperfect Foresight

Suppose the one-period increase in money growth had not been expected. What would have occurred? Since people are fooled by the money policy change, the short-run supply curve would shift out and AD_2 and AS_1^{SR} would intersect at an output level larger than the natural output level. This is shown in Figure 8B-7—ignoring the productivity change. As individuals learn of their forecasting errors they will adjust their price expectations and the short-run AS curve will shift back or up. The increase in output (from Point A to B) will have been only temporary. If monetary growth returns to the rate of growth of productivity, the inflation rate will return to zero and the price level will remain constant at P_2.

Figure 8B-7. A One-Period Policy Change: Imperfect Foresight

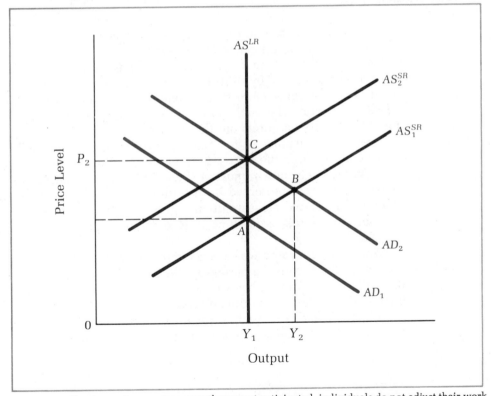

If a change in monetary growth was not anticipated, individuals do not adjust their work hours. Output increases temporarily only to return to the natural output level. The monetary growth is represented by the outward shift in AD. Output increases from Point A to Point B and prices begin to rise. As workers realize their purchasing power loss, they adjust their hours and the short-run AS curve shifts up. Long-run equilibrium occurs at Point C.

A Supply Shock

Suppose the economy is hit with a one-time supply shock, such as the 1974 OPEC oil embargo, which reduces the growth of potential or natural output from, say, 2% to 0%, for one year. What is the impact? If monetary expansion continues at 2% that year, then, without the productivity increase, prices will rise by 2%. If the supply shock is even larger, causing potential output to decrease, say, by 3%, then not only will prices rise but output will fall. This will occur until the steady state is reattained. This event can also be pictured using the *AD-AS* framework. The AS^{LR} curve shifts to the left, while the AS^{SR} curve and the *AD* curve shift as discussed previously depending on whether the monetary expansion is anticipated or not.

From the Static to the Dynamic Model

Several important points arise from the previous discussions. In particular, (1) steady inflation requires a steady increase in the money supply that exceeds the growth in productivity, and (2) a one-shot burst of inflation can be caused by shifts in aggregate demand or aggregate supply, but it cannot become more than a temporary phenomenon without an increase in the rate of growth of the money supply. On a more mechanical note, the discussion points out that it is, at best, messy to appropriately represent the dynamics of the economy with the static *AD-AS* curves. Continually shifting the curves is troublesome. But is this really necessary? As we have shown, most of the points made in our discussion of dynamics can be represented in the simple static *AD-AS* framework. In other words, if we are careful in interpreting the movements in the economy we can use a one-time shift to demonstrate a move away from the steady state.

This is the approach we have taken throughout this book. While some theoretical laxity must be permitted, the approach appears much clearer than alternative approaches.[1] However, in addition to recognizing the distinction between a one-time money stock increase or a one-time price level increase and continual movements in these variables, we must also be careful to distinguish between nominal and real interest rates.

---

[1] For comparison to other approaches you might look at Rudiger Dornbusch and S. Fischer, *Macroeconomics*, 2d ed. (New York: McGraw-Hill Book Company, 1981), Chapter 13; and Robert J. Gordon, *Macroeconomics*, 2d ed. (Boston: Little, Brown & Co., 1981), Chapter 8.

The Real Interest Rate and
the Fisher Effect_____

By definition, the nominal interest rate (r) is the sum of the real interest rate (r*) and the expected rate of inflation (π^e). Thus, $r = r* + \pi^e$. According to this definition the real and nominal interest rates are the same only when inflationary expectations are zero ($\pi^e = 0$). This occurs (1) if the price level does not change, such as was assumed in Chapters 3-5; and (2) if the economy is in steady growth with zero inflation. But notice that the nominal interest rate will exceed the real interest rate whenever positive inflation is expected. For example, if the economy is in a steady state with, say, a 3% inflation rate, then nominal rates exceed real rates by 3%. It is at this point that we must be careful in using our *IS-LM* and *AD-AS* frameworks to examine economic problems. There is no straightforward way to represent nominal and real interest rates in the static *AD-AS* diagram. Yet, this is not to say that the logic derived from the *AD-AS* framework will be incorrect. Quite the contrary. The only problem is that it is difficult to separate the nominal and real rates explicitly on the diagram.

For example, consider what happens during a move away from a steady state. Suppose monetary expansion has been a constant 5% per year for several years and that inflation has been a constant 2.5% so that nominal interest rates have exceeded real rates by 2.5%. Then, suppose the monetary authorities decide to increase the rate of monetary growth by an additional 5%. What occurs? Once again, the exact paths which economic variables take depend on how expectations are formed. Under the perfect foresight form of rational expectations, everyone knows that the additional monetary expansion will result in an additional 5% inflation. The expectation of a 7.5% inflation rate is immediately translated into a nominal interest rate increase of 5% but with no change in the real rate. Suppose, however, a period of time must elapse before people realize that the monetary expansion has taken place. Then, as we have previously discussed, output temporarily rises as people form their new inflationary expectations. The monetary expansion results initially in a fall in nominal interest rates and a decline in real rates. As people learn the errors of their ways, however, their inflationary expectations rise, nominal interest rates rise, and output falls back to the natural level.

There are at least two important points brought out in the previous paragraph. (1) If the perfect foresight form of the *REH* is assumed, nominal rates will adjust immediately to incorporate changes in inflation rates; and (2) if the perfect foresight assumption is not made, an increase in the rate of growth of money will initially cause the nominal interest rate to fall (called the *liquidity effect*), but will eventually lead to increased inflation and higher nominal rates (called the *Fisher effect*). Again, with some imagination even this point can be made with the static diagrams. In the *IS-LM* diagram an increase in the money stock initially increases the *LM* curve and decreases interest rates. As expectations adjust to the increase in money, the *LM* curve shifts up, driving interest rates up. Increased money growth will (either immediately or eventually) lead to rising interest rates, not falling rates. The historical relationship between monetary growth and nominal interest rates is shown in Figure 2-6 on page 46.

Finally, just so we are not always talking about increases in the rate of expansion of money and of inflation rates, let us very briefly take a look at the events of the 1980-1982 period and the nominal and real interest rate behavior.

The 1980-1982 Period: Record High Real Interest Rates

From 1975 to 1978 the rate of growth of *M*-1 had averaged nearly 8%, but in 1980 the Fed began putting on the brakes. *M*-1 expanded only 7% in 1980 and less than 5% in 1981. The result was that while inflation fell from a high of 16% to less than 5%, long-term interest rates fell by less than 6%, from 18% to 12%. In other words, real interest rates (measured as the difference between nominal interest rates and actual inflation rates) increased from less than 2% to more than 7%. The result was a rapid decline in real economic activity—investment and consumption fell dramatically.

How does this pattern square with our previous discussion? In the mid-1970s the U. S. economy was in a steady state in which inflationary expectations were high and even increasing. During this period the Fed continued to announce anti-inflationary policies but continued to run proinflationary policies. Hence, in 1980 when the Fed did as it said it was doing, the Fed's credibility was in low esteem. People continued to expect continued high inflation. This kept nominal interest rates high, and (as actual inflation fell) real interest rates rose. The transition to a new steady state with lower inflation rates has meant declines in real output and rises in unemployment.

Many of the points made in this appendix are developed in more detail in Chapter 13. You may wish to read that chapter before turning to Chapters 9-12 to reinforce many of the ideas raised here.

PART THREE. Extensions of the Basic Model: A Counterrevolution in Economic Thought

Chapters 9 - 12

According as circumstances are favorable, one should modify one's plans.
Sun Tzu Wu, On the Art of War,
2400 B.C.

Towards the end of his life, Keynes was certainly not happy about the direction of the efforts of his closest associates. I can well believe his saying that, just as Marx was never a Marxist, so he was never a Keynesian.
Friedrich von Hayek, 1983

The policy implications of the Keynesian model did not sit well with a few economists. They mounted a counterrevolution by challenging the basics of Keynesian theory. In particular, the private sector was shown not to be as unstable as the Keynesians had claimed. In fact, it was claimed that the primary cause of fluctuations in economic activity was not the behavior of private individuals and firms, but, instead, the government's behavior; that is, economic policy. Attempts to use monetary and fiscal policy to "fine tune" the economy and the freedom from having to maintain balanced budgets set in motion forces that created the roller coaster of recessions and booms experienced during the 1970s and early 1980s.

The purpose of Chapters 9-12 is to discuss this counterrevolution in economic thought and to examine the implications for theory and policy arising from the counterrevolution. In Chapter 9 the consumption and saving behavior of individuals is analyzed. The two modern theories of consumption behavior, the *permanent income hypothesis* and the *life cycle theory*, are used to demonstrate that it is the events expected to be long-term in nature rather than short-term events that influence the way individuals allocate their income between consumption and saving. The effects of governmental policy on saving are discussed in the context of these theories.

In Chapter 10 the analysis is extended to investment spending. The modern theories of investment are discussed, again with one principal implication being that businesses tend to look at events expected to be long lasting. Hence, although investment does fluctuate a great deal relative to consumption spending, the fluctuations are not simply due to the unstable, unpredictable whims of business. In the balance of the chapter, governmental policies directed toward investment are discussed and the implications of recent tax policies for investment spending are examined.

Chapter 11 is devoted to monetary policy. The policy process is discussed, and the difficulties and problems confronting the Federal Reserve (Fed) are examined. The controversies and criticisms directed toward the Fed since the early 1970s have led to changes in the way monetary policy is carried out. In addition, the counterrevolution has led to a recognition that money plays a pivotal role in determining the path that the economy follows. Recent controversies over the Fed's control of the money supply are discussed along with some of the recent proposals to alter the Fed's role in the U. S. economy.

Finally, Chapter 12 is devoted to the budget and fiscal policy. The primary practical point of this chapter is that the budget and resulting fiscal policies are more political than economic instruments. The principal theoretical point is that the deficits that have resulted since the early 1960s have effects on the economy primarily through their implications for monetary policy. The so-called government budget constraint that states that government spending must be paid for either by issuing more debt, increasing the money supply, or raising taxes means that there is no free lunch—the economy will bear the effect sooner or later.

CHAPTER 9.

Consumption and Saving: From the Keynesian Perspective to Supply-Side Economics

As 1979 proved, economists can be dead wrong about consumer spending habits. Among other mistakes, they clearly underestimated the extent to which inflation would prompt people to hedge-buy, even at the risk of taking on a lot more debt and skimping on savings.

The Wall Street Journal, *1980*

The most important thing to consider in a tax-cut strategy is that all important economic decisions are based on expectations. What matters for current actions—investment, saving, the choice of jobs—is not the current tax rates but the rates that are expected.

Martin Feldstein, *1980*

The message that came from the Keynesian model was one of private sector instability (investment and consumption) and the need for activist governmental policies to offset this instability. This message went against the grain of a few economists' instincts. Milton Friedman, particularly, believed that individuals and businesses tend to react less to temporary or short-run phenomena than was implied by the Keynesian model. Friedman's belief was manifest in his new theory of consumption presented in the late 1950s. The result of Friedman's and others' work is a theory of consumption that relies heavily on expectations, one that attributes changes in consumption to events that are expected to be long-lived. The new view of consumption not only altered economists' perception of the effects of policy on consumption but also changed the way economists regarded saving. With the decline of personal saving since the mid-1970s and the consequent fears of a stagnating economy, one without the funds to finance expansion, several proposals to stimulate saving based on the new theory of consumption have been put forth. These issues and the following questions are to be discussed in this chapter:

- *Tax cuts in the early 1960s stimulated the economy, but failed to do so in the late 1960s. Why?*

- *Why is the so-called supply-side economics based on a long-run view of the consumption, saving, and work decisions?*

- *Can saving be stimulated rapidly?*

Introduction

Although inflation in the 1945-52 period seems almost miniscule according to the standards set in the middle to late 1970s, the 7 percent rate experienced in 1948 and again in 1951 made inflation public enemy number one throughout the rest of the 1950s. The Eisenhower administration met this enemy with what was considered to be a non-Keynesian approach (balanced budgets and limited government spending), and this anti-inflationary policy was successful. Annual inflation averaged only 1.45 percent during 1952-1960. On the other hand, unemployment began to rise during the Eisenhower years, and this fact accelerated the growth in popularity of Keynesian economics—employment did seem to respond to the rate of growth of government spending as Keynes had predicted. Consequently, the 1960s ushered in a full-blown commitment to Keynesian policies. By 1970, even President Richard Nixon had proclaimed, "I am now a Keynesian."

Nixon's statement characterized the prevailing attitude that not only could demand management policies effectively direct the economy toward prosperity and full employment, but they could also be used to fine tune the economy so that the rate of growth of output could be altered with little or no ill effects for either inflation or employment. These beliefs were manifest in the economic policies of John F. Kennedy's administration.

Kennedy's economic advisors convinced him that the high-unemployment rates in 1961 and 1962 (6.7 percent and 5.5 percent respectively) could be decreased (by the use of discretionary demand management policies) without driving the inflation rate much higher. A tax credit for investment was enacted in October, 1962, along with more liberal depreciation write-offs for business. In January, 1963, a tax cut for individuals and businesses was proposed and in February, 1964, finally enacted. What were the effects of these policies? Most economists interpreted the tax policy as having successfully stimulated the economy: Real GNP spurted upward and, as shown in Table 9-1, unemployment rates fell.

Table 9-1. Unemployment and Inflation in the 1960s

	YEAR									
	1960	1961	1962	1963	1964	1965	1966	1967	1968	1969
CPI (% change)	1.6	1.0	1.1	1.2	1.3	1.7	2.9	2.8	4.2	5.4
Unemployment rate	5.5	6.7	5.5	5.7	5.2	4.5	3.8	3.8	3.6	3.5

Source: *Economic Report of the President* (1980).

The halcyon days of Keynesian policies were not to last beyond the late 1960s however. Even with the inflation rate rising in the late 1960s, President Johnson resisted calling for a tax increase to cool down the overheated economy because of his fear that the public and Congress would force him to reduce expenditures on the Vietnam War or on his Great Society programs. As a result of the attempt by Johnson to have both guns and butter, large government deficits and subsequent increases in the inflation rate occurred. By 1968 inflation had risen to over 4 percent. Johnson was finally convinced by his advisors to implement a 10 percent tax surcharge. However, again concerned with the upcoming elections and the effect on his Great Society programs, he announced that the tax was to last for only one year. Johnson's advisors predicted that the temporary tax increase would bring a slowdown in inflation along with a slight increase in the unemployment rate. But unlike the 1964 tax cut, the 1968 tax increase did not work as predicted. Instead of decreasing consumption spending, the tax increase reduced saving. Since aggregate demand was not reduced, inflation did not slow. In fact the 3 percent rate of increase in the consumer price index (CPI) in 1967 was followed by a 4.2 percent rate in 1968 and a 5.4 percent rate in 1969.

What went wrong?[1] Why were the Keynesian forecasts not as accurate in 1968 as they had been in 1963? Most economists now maintain that the failure of the tax increase was primarily due to the Federal Reserve's expansionary monetary policy over this period. In addition, many believe a problem with the 1968 tax was that it was to be only a temporary tax. Since consumers did not expect to have a permanent reduction in their incomes, they did not reduce their consumption. Why change your living style if your income reduction is to be only a temporary one? However, because the simple Keynesian consumption function does not make a distinction between the effects on consumption of a temporary and a long-lived change in income, policymakers, forecasting on the basis of that simple model of consumption, were unable to predict that the temporary tax would not reduce aggregate demand. It suddenly became very obvious that economists did not understand the economy as well as they had thought. They were forced to reconsider and carefully scrutinize the entire Keynesian apparatus.

In seeking an explanation of consumption behavior in the late 1960s, economists turned to two theories that had actually been developed in the late 1950s. The two theories, known as the *permanent income hypothesis (PIH)* and the *life cycle theory (LCT)*, had originally been developed to reconcile the theory of consumption behavior with observed facts, something the simple Keynesian theory had been unable to do. But it was not until the events of the late 1960s-early 1970s forced economists to reexamine consumption that these alternative explanations were generally accepted.

In the following section we will observe how the Keynesian consumption function fails to correspond to reality. The next section is devoted to the modern theories of consumption, the *PIH* and the *LCT*. We will discover how these theories do account for observed facts. In the final portion of the chapter the implications of the modern consumption theories for economic policy are discussed.

---

[1] Robert Eisner directed an article to this question."What Went Wrong?" *Journal of Political Economy* (May-June, 1971), pp. 629-641.

The Keynesian
Consumption Function and
Empirical Facts

As we have mentioned many times, Keynes's objective in 1936 was to change the belief that full employment will come about automatically. Once this belief was modified, the case could be made for the use of an active demand management policy to ensure full employment. A pivotal point in Keynes's thesis was the consumption function since, as we have seen, it is this relationship that leads to the important concept of a multiplier.

Recall that in its simplest form the Keynesian consumption function can be written as

$$C = C_0 + c_y YD$$

This form makes explicit several implications of the Keynesian consumption theory. First, the marginal propensity to consume (c_y) is "fairly stable" (in this case it is constant) and less than one. Second, the average propensity to consume (APC) is larger than the marginal propensity to consume (MPC). In order to clearly see this important point divide both sides of the consumption function by disposable income (YD). The result is

$$\frac{C}{YD} = \text{APC} = \frac{C_0}{YD} + c_y$$

This shows that for a given level of disposable income the term C_0/YD must be added to the MPC in order to equal the APC. Thus, the average propensity to consume exceeds the marginal propensity to consume. Third, the APC declines and approaches the MPC as disposable income increases.[2]

Notice what this third implication means for the saving-to-income ratio. Since the APC and the average propensity to save (APS) sum to one, the APS rises as the APC declines. Consequently, we should observe that the saving-to-income ratio (the APS) varies directly with income over the business cycle. In other words, the saving-to-income ratio should rise during an expansionary period and fall during a recessionary period.

In sum, the Keynesian consumption theory states that (1) the MPC is stable and less than one, (2) the APC is larger than the MPC, and (3) the APS rises during expansions and falls during recessions (as income rises

---

[2] This clearly shows up in the algebra. Note that C_0/YD declines as YD increases.

so does the APS). Are these implications consistent with actual consumption behavior? This question could be, and was, answered by two different types of studies, one called a *cross section* and the other a *time series*. To carry out a cross-sectional study, one would have to find out how much disposable income each household earned during a particular time period, usually a year, and how much of that income each household consumed. One could then plot the income-consumption combination of each household to determine whether or not the graph looked like the Keynesian consumption function. This type of study is called a *cross-sectional study* because the view of consumption behavior provided by the survey is one that cuts across all households at one particular point in time. Another approach that could be taken is to utilize the *Economic Report of the President* where personal disposable income and consumption for the U. S. economy, as a whole, are reported on a yearly or quarterly basis for several years and plot the income-consumption combination for each year. This type of approach is termed a *time series study* because the observations are taken over several time periods.

Beginning in the late 1940s several cross-sectional and several time series studies were carried out utilizing different years or sample groups. In general, both types of studies supported the view that the MPC is less than one. In addition, cross-sectional studies found that higher income individuals tended to save proportionately more than lower income persons, implying that the APC declined (APS rose) and approached the MPC as income increased. However, when the various cross-sectional studies were compared, something appeared that did not seem to conform to the Keynesian theory. When the studies were carried out using cross sections at different periods of time, the consumption function derived for one year differed from that derived for another year; the consumption function seemed to shift upward over time. With the use of a simple example we can see what was happening in these cross-sectional studies. Suppose a cross-sectional or, as it is sometimes called, a *budget study*, is conducted using income and consumption levels of families for the year 1978. Furthermore, suppose the economy is composed of only five families and that their consumption and income levels are as follows:

Family	Income	Consumption
A	10,000	13,000
B	20,000	18,000
C	30,000	23,000
D	40,000	28,000
E	50,000	33,000

If the income-consumption combinations from the cross-sectional sample are plotted, the 1978 consumption function will be that shown in Figure 9-1 as C_{1978}. (In algebraic form, the cross-sectional data are represented by the equation $C = 8,000 + 0.5Y$.)

Figure 9-1. The Shifting Cross-Sectional Consumption Function

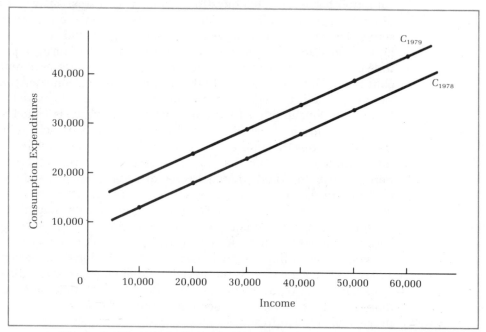

The result of (hypothetical) cross-sectional studies in the years 1978 and 1979 are shown here. The upward shifting cross-sectional or short-run consumption curve presented economists with an unexplained puzzle. What caused the shift?

Now, suppose that another budget study is conducted on these same five families in 1979 and their income and consumption levels are found to be as shown below. This cross-sectional sample is plotted as C_{1979} in Figure 9-1.

Family	Income	Consumption
A	20,000	24,000
B	30,000	29,000
C	40,000	34,000
D	50,000	39,000
E	60,000	44,000

(The algebraic form for this cross-sectional data is $C = 14{,}000 + 0.5Y$.) As can be seen in Figure 9-1, the 1979 consumption function lies above the 1978 consumption function. Algebraically, while the MPC is the same in both equations, the constant or autonomous part of consumption increased from 1978 to 1979.

The time series studies presented even more problems for the simple Keynesian consumption function. When data obtained over just a few years were used to calculate the Keynesian consumption function, it appeared that the APC exceeded the MPC. However, when an extended period of time was considered, the MPC and APC appeared to be identical. For example, in 1946 Professor Simon Kuznets derived a consumption function for the long time period of 1869-1938 wherein he discovered consumption was proportional to income (APC = MPC).[3]

Utilizing Figure 9-2, we can discover the problems of the time series results. Consumption-income combinations are plotted for the years 1960-1980. If the line is extended to the axes it will intersect very near zero. Hence, the consumption equation has no constant term. The MPC equals the APC.

Figure 9-2. *The Time Series Consumption-Income Relationship Plotted Using Actual Data*

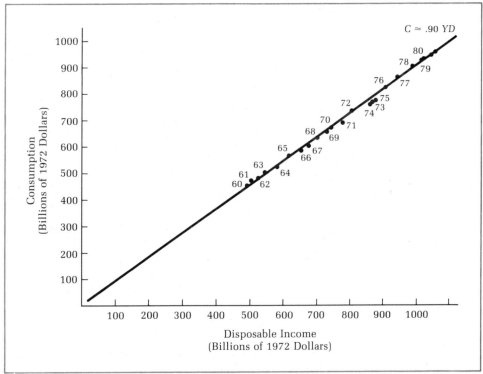

Source: *Economic Report of the President*, (1983), Tables B-2, and B-23.

The time series, or long-run, consumption curve intersects the origin. Algebraically, the consumption equation does not have a constant term.

---

[3] The difference between cross-sectional and time series studies was first pointed out by Simon S. Kuznets, in *National Product since 1869* (New York: National Bureau of Economic Research, 1946) when, using data for 1924-1938, he obtained an MPC of 0.9 and a constant APC of about 0.9. Raymond W. Goldsmith, *A Study of Saving in the United States*, Vol. 1 (Princeton: Princeton University Press, 1955) followed Kuznets' study and also obtained an APC that was roughly constant at 0.9 rather than declining.

The Modern Theories
of Consumption_____

By the early 1950s economists had been left with two results from the consumption studies that did not conform with the simple Keynesian theory. First, the upward shifting cross-sectional (short-run) consumption function. Second, the proportional time series (long-run) consumption function. As a result, economists began looking for an alternative explanation of consumption behavior, one that could account for the various findings. While several very insightful alternatives were put forth, two have become more widely accepted than the others. We will focus our attention on these two.[4]

The Permanent Income Hypothesis

The first modern theory of consumption we will consider is Milton Friedman's permanent income hypothesis.[5] Friedman asserts that individuals consume a constant proportion of their permanent income. But what does the term *permanent income* mean? Very simply, permanent income is what an individual estimates or expects to earn over a long period of time. Friedman defines permanent income as the amount an individual can consume while maintaining his or her wealth unchanged. What does this mean? Perhaps the following example will help to clarify this concept of permanent income.

Suppose that a real estate salesman has averaged a $10,000 income each year for the few years he has been in the business although his actual income has varied from a low of $2,000 to a maximum of $35,000. Also, suppose that he expects his average income to increase substantially, perhaps to $50,000 or $60,000 in the next ten years. On which figure do you expect this individual to base his consumption decision? It would be most unlikely for him to consume on the basis of $10,000 since he expects his average income to increase substantially. Most likely the salesman will consume according to a higher income level, perhaps in the range of $40,000 to $50,000. Whatever figure the salesman bases his decision on is his estimate of his permanent income. Suppose the salesman's estimate of his permanent income is $45,000. If out of his $45,000 he spends $40,500 and saves $4,500, his APC based on permanent income is 0.9.

Now suppose instead, that the salesman's current income has, on average, been at the same level as his permanent income level ($45,000)

---

[4] See James S. Duesenberry, *Income, Saving, and the Theory of Consumer Behavior* (Cambridge: Harvard University Press, 1944) and James Tobin, "Relative Income, Absolute Income, and Saving," in *Money, Trade and Economic Growth: Essays in Honor of John Williams* (New York: Macmillan Publishing Co. Inc., 1951), pp. 135-156 for some alternatives to the theories discussed in this chapter.

[5] Milton Friedman, *A Theory of the Consumption Function* (Princeton: Princeton University Press, 1957).

for several years. What will he do if in one year his income drops to $25,000? Most likely he will not cut back spending to the extent that he would be spending only 0.9 of $25,000 and saving the rest, $2,500. Instead, we expect him to maintain his lifestyle and to consume somewhere near the $40,500 he had been spending in previous years by borrowing or drawing down savings. If he spends $38,000 by drawing down savings by $13,000, his APC is 1.52 (i.e., $38,000 ÷ $25,000).

Conversely, suppose his income rises one year to $80,000. Will he spend $72,000 and save only $8,000? Most likely the salesman will attempt to keep his consumption in line with his permanent income of $45,000, perhaps spending $44,000 and saving $36,000. In this case his APC is 0.55 (i.e., $44,000 ÷ $80,000). In this example, when the real estate salesman's current income is below his permanent income, he saves a disproportionately small percentage of his current income and conversely, when his current income is greater than his permanent income, he saves a disproportionately large percentage of his current income. As a result, his APC declines as his income rises, from 1.52 to 0.55.

The real estate salesman's behavior can be represented using Figure 9-3. For several years he has been earning, on average, his estimate of his permanent income, $45,000, shown as income level *OJ*. Then when his current income falls, say to income level *OA*, he does not cut back his consumption to the extent he would if he expected the reduced income level *(OA)* to be his permanent level. Instead, he attempts to maintain consumption by drawing down his savings, consuming amount *AD* rather than the amount *AB*. Conversely, at income levels above his permanent level, such as at income level *OH*, the salesman does not increase his consumption to the level that would be commensurate with his belief that *OH* was to be permanent *(HG)*. Instead, only *HF* is consumed.

Suppose the salesman's income, on average, rises to *OH* so that he alters his estimate of his permanent income from *OJ* to *OH*. With *OH* expected to be a permanent level of income, the salesman consumes a corresponding amount *(HG)*. Should current income fall below or rise above *OH*, the salesman will continue to consume commensurate with his permanent income level *OH* rather than with what the salesman believes to be a temporary decline or rise in his income. This behavior traces out a new short-run consumption curve, one that is above the short-run curve shown in Figure 9-3 and intersects Point G.

Suppose that instead of observing just one individual, the real estate salesman, we observe the current income-consumption combinations of several different people. In other words, suppose that we gather a cross-sectional sample of individuals. What will we find? We are likely to discover several people who are currently earning below their permanent incomes, people such as a general contractor experiencing a housing slump or a carpenter out of a job. On the other hand, we are also likely to find several people who are having a very good year, currently earning

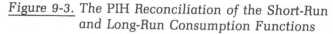

Figure 9-3. The PIH Reconciliation of the Short-Run
            and Long-Run Consumption Functions

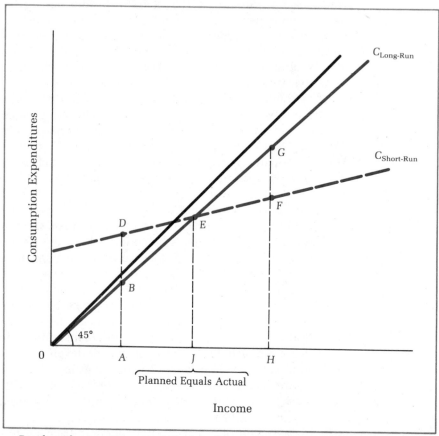

People with current incomes to the left of Point E are earning less than their permanent income, and those with current incomes to the right of Point E are earning more than their permanent incomes. Yet all consume according to their permanent income OJ. Hence those earning current income OA will consume more than AB since their permanent income is OJ, not OA. Similarly, those earning OH will consume less than HG since their permanent income is OJ, not OH. The result is that the observed relationship between current consumption and current income is traced out by curve $C_{Short-Run}$.

more than their permanent incomes, people such as the farmer who had a bumper crop while other farmers were having mediocre crops. Notice that if we plot the current consumption-income combinations of each of these people we will trace out a short-run consumption function as shown in Figure 9-3.

Let us now interpret the horizontal axis of Figure 9-3 as all possible income levels that the individuals in our cross-sectional sample might have earned last year. If, then, income level OJ is, on average, the permanent income level of our cross section, the contractor and the carpenter will be represented as earning income level *OA* and consuming level *AD*, a level commensurate with the permanent income level *OJ* rather than their current income level *OA*, while the farmer will be represented as earning income level *OH* and consuming *HF*.

If the individuals in this cross section raise their estimates of permanent income to *OH*, consumption commensurate with this new higher permanent income level will take place. This would be represented by a new short-run consumption line that lies above the previous line and intersects Point *G*.

With regard to explaining the time series observation that the nation-wide saving to income ratio is relatively constant over time, we can reinterpret Figure 9-3 once again. This time consider the horizontal axis as the nation's average income. During a temporary expansionary period, average income may rise from *OJ* to *OH*. Since this expansionary period is considered to be temporary, the nation's APC falls. Conversely, during a temporary slump, the APC rises. This behavior is shown by the short-run consumption line. However, if the average income rises to *OH* and remains at that level, the nation as a whole adjusts so as to consider the new, higher level as a permanent level. Over an extended period of time, as average income rises and estimates of permanent income are revised upward, the long-run consumption line is traced out.

The *PIH* is able to reconcile the time series and cross-sectional observations of consumption behavior by characterizing consumption in terms of permanent income rather than current income. But how do we know a person is consuming according to her permanent income? How does an individual know what her permanent income is?

Obviously, explaining how a person goes about determining permanent income; that is, what information an individual uses in forming expectations regarding the future income stream, is a crucial element in the *PIH*. If you are asked to identify the most important determinant of an individual's expectation of future income, how will you respond? If your answer is that an individual's current and recent past income levels are the most important determinants in the forecast of future income you would, for most people, be right on target.[6] Furthermore, you may respond that current and recent past incomes will be more important in the formation of a person's estimate of permanent income than will more distant past incomes. For example, suppose our real estate salesman found his income to be averaging more than he had expected? Will he keep his view of permanent income at $45,000? Most likely not. He will adapt to the new levels of current income and revise his view of permanent income upward. However, you would not expect this individual to

---

[6] Expectation formation was considered at some length in Chapter 8.

revise his view of permanent income each time and by the same amount that current income changes. For most individuals, and especially for a person with an income stream that fluctuates a great deal, permanent income will not change as much as will current income. An individual with a steady income stream will probably place much more emphasis on current income in determining permanent income than will the real estate salesman. Yet, it is very unlikely that individuals' estimates of permanent income will change each time and by exactly as much as current income changes, even for individuals with steady income streams. In other words, we expect permanent income not to fluctuate as much as current income.

Algebraic Discussion of the PIH. Algebraically, we might characterize permanent income (Y^P) as a weighted average. For example,

(9-1) $Y^P_t = 0.8Y_t + 0.16Y_{t-1} + 0.032Y_{t-2}$

Current income Y_t and recent past income Y_{t-1} are more important than the more distant past incomes such as Y_{t-2}. The coefficient 0.8, called the *partial adjustment* or *revision coefficient*, tells us how important current income is in the calculation of permanent income. Notice how the weights or coefficients decrease as we move further back in time. This suggests that incomes earned in previous periods have less impact on the forecast of permanent income than do incomes earned more recently. In Equation 9-1, all past incomes account for only two-tenths of the determination of the individual's estimate of permanent income.

Equations of the form of 9-1, written somewhat differently, are often used in economics because they appear to describe the adjustment of many different economic variables over time. Let us digress for just a moment to see how this equation can be rewritten in its more commonly seen form. Equation 9-1 expressed permanent income in Period t. What would that individual's estimate of permanent income have been last period, Period $t-1$? It would have been described by Equation 9-2, which is just Equation 9-1 lagged one period.

(9-2) $Y^P_{t-1} = 0.8Y_{t-1} + 0.16Y_{t-2} + 0.032Y_{t-3}$

Thus, the individual has revised his or her estimate of permanent income from that described by Equation 9-2 to that described by Equation 9-1 because of the additional information obtained during the time period from $t-1$ to t. Notice that the new information is just the value of current income, Y_t. Also, notice from Equations 9-1 and 9-2 that the current income carries a weight of eight-tenths in the calculation of permanent income. The remainder consists of all past incomes, or simply, the previous permanent income. Thus, this period's permanent income (shown in Equation 9-1) is approximately equal to the sum of the newly obtained current income and last period's permanent income, weighted by 0.8 and 0.2 respectively. Since $0.2Y^P_t$ is approximately equal to $0.16Y_{t-1} + 0.032Y_{t-2}$, then

(9-3) $\qquad Y^P_t \approx 0.8Y_t + 0.2Y^P_{t-1}$

Equation 9-3 can be rewritten in a more intuitively appealing form by noting that $0.2Y^P_{t-1}$ is $(1-0.8)Y^P_{t-1}$ which is simply, $Y^P_{t-1} - 0.8Y^P_{t-1}$. Now, we can rewrite Equation 9-3 as Equation 9-4.

(9-4) $\qquad Y^P_t = Y^P_{t-1} + 0.8(Y_t - Y^P_{t-1})$

Equation 9-4 is referred to as an *adaptive process*. It states that estimates of expected or permanent income this year (Y^P_t) differ from those made last year (Y^P_{t-1}) by a proportion of the difference between current income and last year's estimate of permanent income $(Y_t - Y^P_{t-1})$. If current income (Y_t) and last year's estimate of permanent income (Y^P_{t-1}) are the same, then the estimate of permanent income is not revised. Should actual income and the estimate of permanent income differ, however, the estimate of permanent income will be revised. The size of the revision depends upon the size of the adjustment coefficient. Rather than 0.8, suppose the revision or adjustment coefficient is small, say 0.1. Also suppose last year's estimate of permanent income (Y^P_{t-1}) was $20,000, and this year's actual income (Y_t) is $30,000. Since actual income is substantially larger than the estimate of permanent income, the estimate of permanent income in the next period will be revised upward, but only by $1,000, rather than the $10,000 actual income increase. Algebraically, this is expressed as follows:

$$Y^P_t = \$20,000 + 0.1(\$30,000 - \$20,000)$$
$$= \$21,000$$

On the other hand, if the revision coefficient is large, such as the 0.8 we have been using, then the revision of the estimate of permanent income will be larger. If, as in the previous example, $Y^P_{t-1} = \$20,000$ and $Y_t = \$30,000$, then, since actual income is substantially larger than last period's estimate of permanent income, this period's estimate will be revised upward, from $20,000 to $28,000. Algebraically,

$$Y^P_t = \$20,000 + 0.8(\$30,000 - \$20,000)$$
$$= \$28,000$$

Notice that in both of these examples permanent income does not change by as much as does actual income. In other words, permanent income does not fully reflect the variations in actual income. Consequently, since permanent income, from which consumption is determined, does not fully reflect the variations in current income, neither will consumption; consumption is smoothed out over a fairly long time period.

The PIH and Expectations. In summary, we have noted that a person's income profile (past incomes) determines how the estimate of permanent income will be formed. However, specifying permanent income to depend only on past and current income levels is quite restrictive. They are not the only factors that influence a person's expectations about future income. As we emphasized in the previous chapter, it is logical and rational for individuals to take into account all the information they have in forming their expectations. People's beliefs or expectations about the future prospects of their industry or occupation will influence their permanent income, as will their expectations regarding monetary and fiscal policy. All of these circumstances or developments will influence permanent income even though none of them are specified as part of the weighted average of current and past incomes. Hence, individuals' expectations will play a very important role in determining consumption. Those developments that affect individuals' estimates of their permanent incomes also affect their consumption. Those events that do not affect permanent income estimates do not have an impact on consumption.

As a summary of our discussion of the *PIH*, we list the following points:

1. The *PIH* reconciles the findings regarding the long-run and short-run consumption functions by distinguishing how individual and aggregate consumption behavior vary according to whether income changes are believed to be long-lived or only temporary.
2. Consumption depends on permanent income, not current income. As a result, consumption fluctuates much less than was implied by the simple Keynesian consumption theory.
3. Expectations play an important role in the *PIH*. Individuals base their estimates of permanent income on their previous experiences, such as past incomes, but also on their anticipation of economic events that will affect them.

The Life Cycle Theory

Like Friedman's *PIH*, the life cycle theory, formulated by Franco Modigliani and Richard Brumberg and updated and extended by Albert Ando and Modigliani, significantly altered the prevailing view of consumption behavior.[7] Both theories focused attention on the long run and

---

[7] Franco Modigliani and R. B. Brumberg, "Utility Analysis and the Consumption Function" in *Post Keynesian Economics*, K. K. Kurihara, ed. (New Brunswick, N. J.: Rutgers University Press, 1954), pp. 388-436; Albert Ando and F. Modigliani, "The 'Life Cycle' Hypothesis of Saving: Aggregate Implications and Tests," *American Economic Review* (March, 1963), pp. 55-84.

on individuals' reactions to events that are expected to be long-lived. The approach taken by the *LCT* differs from that of the *PIH*, however. As the name suggests, the emphasis of the *LCT* is on the relationship between an individual's age and consumption behavior.

Individuals typically undergo three distinct income-earning periods in their lifetimes. They earn very little income during the early years of their lives as they mature, attend school, and begin their working careers. The middle years of life mark the greatest income-earning years as individuals work their way up the ladder and mature in their professions. Finally, during the later or retirement years people earn little income. If people consumed according to what their current income was, they would consume the least during their early and later years and would consume the most during their middle years. People do not, however, generally behave in this manner. Instead, they tend to smooth out their consumption, using the wealth they accumulate during the middle years to pay for consumption in the retirement years and the negative saving or debt of the early years.

The pattern between consumption and income over a typical individual's life cycle is shown in Figure 9-4. We can use this figure to demonstrate how the *LCT* reconciles the short-run and long-run consumption functions. Suppose we again look at the cross section of individuals discussed in our consideration of the *PIH*. This cross section includes some people currently earning less than their permanent incomes and others currently earning more than their permanent incomes. What else can we discover in this cross-sectional sample? We find people of all ages and thus people represented by each of the income-consumption combinations shown in Figure 9-4. A disproportionate share of the middle-aged group is in the upper income brackets while the lower income brackets are made up of disproportionately large shares of people in the early and late years of their life cycle.

Notice in Figure 9-4 that people in their middle years are earning their greatest income, but are also consuming a smaller proportion of their income than when they are very young or are in their retirement years. This means that a plot of the income-consumption combinations of our cross-sectional sample traces out the short-run consumption function shown in Figure 9-5. Why? Because as income is increased fewer of the older and younger people and more of the middle-aged people are included in the sample. Thus, the consumption to income ratio (APC) decreases.

How does the life cycle theory account for the long-run consumption function? Assume that the proportion of total population in each age bracket of Figure 9-4 remains about the same from one year to the next. Then, the ratio of average consumption to average income will remain relatively constant over time. In other words, the average APC will remain constant as the short-run consumption function shifts up. But what makes

Figure 9-4. The Life Cycle Theory of Consumption

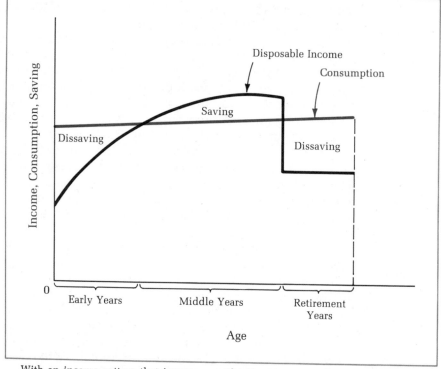

With an income pattern that increases until retirement, a person will save during the middle years to pay for debt in the early and later years. Consumption, on the other hand, will tend to be based on the average of this income profile.

the short-run curve shift up over time? The answer to this question is one of the major contributions to our understanding of consumption behavior provided by the life cycle theory.

An individual born into wealth or one who receives a large inheritance will have a different life-style or life stream of consumption than someone who does not have such wealth. If two people have identical income streams over their life cycle, but one has more wealth than the other, their consumption patterns will not, in all likelihood, be the same. The person with wealth does not have to accumulate as many assets or save as much during the middle portion of life in order to finance the retirement years as does the person without this wealth. As a result, we can expect the more wealthy individual to consume a higher proportion of any given income level than the less wealthy individual. Two such consumption-income patterns are shown in Figure 9-6.

If, instead of comparing two individuals, we look at the nation as a whole, what would we predict will occur to consumption as the nation's

Figure 9-5. The LCT Explanation of the Short-Run Consumption Curve

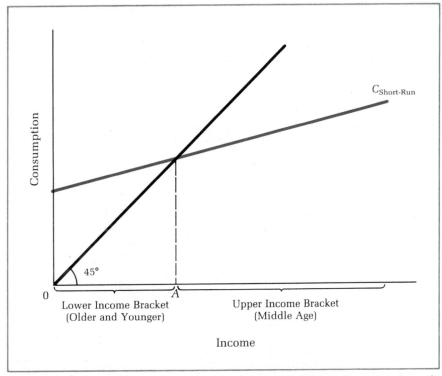

The lower income brackets will consist of younger and older members of society, who *dissave*—consume more than their current incomes. Saving is done by those in income brackets to the right of *OA*, consisting primarily of middle-aged individuals.

stock of wealth increases? We would expect that each individual in our cross section will consume a higher proportion of current income after the wealth increase than before.[8] Graphically, this translates into an upward shift of the short-run consumption function.

In summary, the *LCT* reconciles the long- and short-run consumption functions by characterizing consumption behavior as depending on an individual's lifetime income profile and the individual's wealth. Changes in income or changes in wealth expected to be long-lived will induce individuals to change their consumption. On the other hand, changes in income or wealth expected to be only temporary interruptions in an individual's life cycle income pattern will have very little effect on consumption.

---

[8] Modigliani found that events that raise the value of assets $1 will raise current consumption by about 6 cents.

Figure 9-6. *The Effect of Wealth on Consumption*

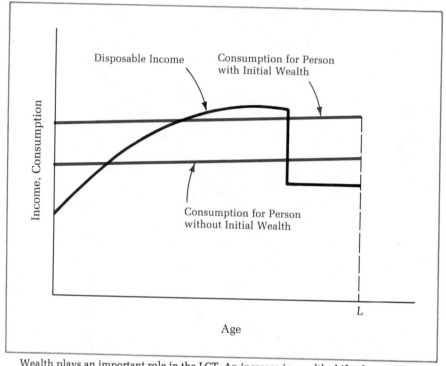

Wealth plays an important role in the *LCT*. An increase in wealth shifts the consumption stream upward. More is consumed at each earned income level over an individual's lifetime.

As a summary of our discussion of the *LCT* we list the following points:

1. The *LCT* reconciles the findings regarding the short-run and the long-run consumption functions by characterizing how individuals consume varying proportions of their current income level at each stage of their life cycle.

2. Like the *PIH*, the life cycle theory implies that increases or decreases in income expected to be temporary will not affect consumption. For example, suppose someone who expects thirty more years of life receives a temporary or onetime increase in income of $3,000. Rather than spending three-fourths of $3,000 (if the current value MPC is ¾), the individual will smooth that $3,000 over the thirty years of her life, spending only something on the order of ¾ of $3,000 ÷ 30 years (i.e., $75) this period.[9]

3. The *LCT* emphasizes the importance of wealth for an individual's consumption decision. Household wealth consists of (a) short-term financial assets such as cash holdings, checking and savings accounts,

---

[9] We are, of course, abstracting from present values and simply assuming that equal expenditures are made in each period.

and some types of bonds such as Treasury bills; (b) long-term financial assets such as stocks, long-term bonds, and insurance policies; (c) real assets such as the real market value of consumer durables (refrigerators, automobiles, etc.,) net of the debt on these durables, and houses and other real estate net of mortgage debt. An increase in any of these is an increase in wealth. For example, an increase in the quantity of bonds held by the public, *ceteris paribus*, is an example of a wealth increase. On the other hand if the increase in wealth is expected to be followed with an increase in the price level, individuals will not have experienced a long-lived wealth increase and will not, therefore, alter their consumption.

Summary of the Permanent Income and Life Cycle Theories

Although the emphasis of the *PIH* is on the formation of income expectations and that of the *LCT* is on the roles of wealth and individuals' ages in determining consumption, the two theories are quite similar in their approaches to consumption behavior. It is the long-run view of income and wealth that determines consumption, not the current or short-run view. Thus, both the *PIH* and the *LCT* imply that income fluctuations which are considered to be only temporary will have little effect on consumption. In other words, both theories assert that the short-run MPC is less than the long-run MPC.

What do these modern theories of consumption imply for monetary and fiscal policy? Since consumption depends on wealth as well as on income, if policy changes affect wealth, these changes will affect consumption. Furthermore, if policy changes are expected to be temporary, they will have little or no effect on consumption. Let us consider these points in more detail.

Consumption, Wealth Effects, and Expectations

What is the effect of specifying that consumption depends upon wealth? Real wealth consists of the real value of financial assets, real cash balances, and the real value of physical assets. Hence changes in any of the types of real wealth may induce changes in consumption. For example, changes in the money supply could, theoretically, affect consumption. Changes in the interest rate can also affect consumption by altering the value of financial assets.

The emergence and acceptance of the *PIH* and *LCT* explanations of consumption occurred at the same time that the monetarist school reached full prominence. The frustrations of economic policymakers in the late 1960s led economists to look for new, more complete explanations of economic events. More and more they accepted money as an important variable in the economy, and more and more they questioned the Keynesian explanations of the behavior of economic agents (individuals and business), in particular, the unpredictable "animal spirits" of business. It is not surprising, given that Milton Friedman was instrumental in both the consumption theories and monetarism, that the new theories of consumption support many of the monetarists' propositions. The consumption theories argue against the early Keynesian view that the private sector is very unstable. Moreover, the theories attribute an important role in determining consumption behavior to interest rates, wealth and, thus, monetary policy.

Temporary Changes: The Temporary Tax Increase of 1968-70

Perhaps the most important impact that the *PIH* and the *LCT* have had on the economic profession and on economic policy is the recognition that temporary economic policy changes have very little effect. For example, in discussing the Johnson temporary tax surcharge, Professor Robert Eisner concluded,

> The basic economic error of those who saw in the 10 percent income tax surcharge an adequate measure against inflation may be charged to failure to take into account the implications of the permanent income hypothesis.[10]

During the recessions of 1980-81 and 1981-83, the debates over policy seldom suggested temporary measures. The tax cuts of the Reagan Administration were to be permanent cuts just as was the tax increase embodied in the 1982 Revenue Enhancement Act. However, as recovery emerged in 1983, Martin Feldstein, the chairman of the Council of Economic Advisers (CEA), called for a standby tax surcharge as an approach to reducing the large budget deficits of 1983 and 1984. He argued that this temporary tax would slow consumption and stimulate saving, a curious conclusion given the *PIH* and the *LCT*.

The modern theories of consumption recognize that consumption spending is more stable than had been previously realized. Consumer spending simply does not respond very much to income changes that are perceived to be short-lived. It should be noted, however, that these results do not mean that the short-run MPC is necessarily stable nor that the long-run adjustment period is predictable. As we mentioned previously, several factors other than current and past incomes influence consumption. Individuals' expectations regarding their jobs, the economy, monetary and fiscal policy, or other events will also play an important role in their consumption decisions.

---

[10] Eisner, "Fiscal and Monetary Policy Reconsidered," *American Economic Review* (December, 1969), p. 898.

Some Applications of the
PIH and the *LCT*

The revised theories of consumption can be used to shed light on a variety of policy issues. In this section, we will examine some of the implications of these theories.

Saving and Investment

Total national saving comes from three primary sources. (1) Individuals save out of their personal income; (2) businesses retain, and thereby save, some of their profits; and (3) governments save when they run a budget surplus. The ratio of gross saving to GNP has declined only very slightly over the past thirty years. However, the personal saving rate (the ratio of net personal saving to disposable personal income) has dropped sharply over the last several years. As a result, the flow of private funds to the credit market has dropped sharply as well. The ratio of household saving to investment has followed the patterns of private saving.

The reliance of the business sector on household saving as a source of funds has heightened concerns about the recent behavior of the personal saving rate. The fear is that with the household providing fewer funds for investment (capital accumulation) and with the government sector taking away more funds, the U. S. economy will be unable to maintain a rate of growth even close to the growth it has experienced over the past thirty years.

Why has personal saving declined? Are there policies that can be undertaken to stimulate personal saving? While we will leave several of the answers to these questions to the next chapter where we discuss investment, there are two issues we wish to examine here. The first point of discussion is the recent decline in the personal saving rate. The second point we will consider concerns several recent policy attempts to stimulate saving.

According to the life cycle model, individuals maximize their welfare by maintaining a steady stream of consumption over their lifetimes. During their working years, they do not consume all their income but set aside savings which they later use up during retirement. In this setting, a worker who received $1 of compensation in promised pension benefits rather than current wages would be expected to reduce saving in other forms in order to maintain his initial consumption path.[11] The growth of

---

[11] While the life cycle theory has been widely accepted, the idea that investors might reduce their saving in anticipation of pension benefits is relatively new. See, for example, Joseph A. Pechman, Henry J. Aaron, and Michael R. Taussy, *Social Security: Perspectives for Reform* (Washington, D. C.: The Brookings Institution, 1968).

pension funds and of social security has meant a decline in private saving.

The net impact on national saving of the increase in pension funds and social security depends on whether the reduction in private saving is offset by the accumulation of pension fund assets. In the case of private pensions, the funding provisions serve to offset most of the reduction in individual saving. In contrast, social security is financed on a pay-as-you-go basis and contributions are immediately paid out in benefits rather than accumulated in a fund. Therefore, a shift in pension saving from private funds to social security implies a reduction in total saving and fewer funds available for capital accumulation. Similarly, other large government pensions, such as the military, civil service, and state and local government retirement systems, that are financed on a pay-as-you-go or partially funded basis will also reduce national saving.[12]

The greatest impact on saving is due to inflation and income taxes. The accelerating inflation rate during the last half of the 1970s induced individuals to seek out inflation hedges with their saving. They purchased physical assets, such as houses and art, instead of leaving their cash in a savings account, as shown in Figure 9-7. This behavior is reinforced by the effect of inflation on income taxes. The income tax reduces the after-tax rate of return from saving and, thus, drives a wedge between the reward for postponing consumption and the market rate of interest. As a result present consumption becomes relatively more attractive than future consumption, and saving is discouraged.

The inflationary period of the 1970s seemed to induce several behavioral changes. Policymakers were bemoaning the increased consumption and decreased saving. It was suggested that inflation drove people to buy immediately on the basis that prices would only be higher in the future. This drove prices up even faster. Moreover, spending right away means less saving which, in turn, causes all kinds of problems for the economy. And, as we have mentioned, the saving rate did decrease during the 1970s.

The *PIH* tells us what the effect of a long-term period of inflation will be on consumption and saving. Individuals will purchase durable goods. Obviously, nondurables, such as doughnuts, and services, such as golf lessons, will not be as likely to be stocked up on as would durables because of the perishability of the nondurables and services. But how many refrigerators does a family need?

---

[12] See Alicia H. Munnell, *The Effect of Social Security on Personal Saving* (Cambridge, Mass.: Ballinger Publishing Co., 1974); Martin Feldstein, "Social Security, Induced Retirement, and Aggregate Capital Accumulation," *Journal of Political Economy*, Vol. 82 (September/October, 1974), pp. 905-926.

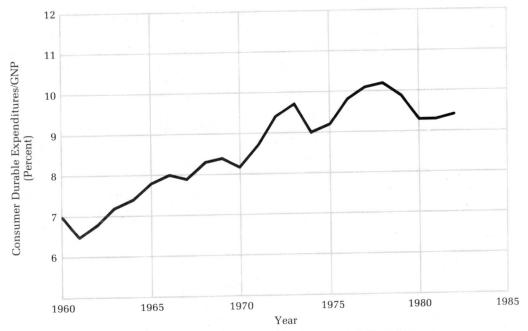

Figure 9-7. Consumer Expenditures on Durables as a Percentage of GNP

Source: *Economic Report of the President* (1982), Table B-2.

The purchase of consumer durables has replaced other, more traditional forms of saving since the mid-1970s as households searched for hedges against inflation.

Approaches to Stimulate Saving: Supply-Side Economics

A policy intended to increase the rate of capital formation by increasing the supply of saving is subject to the objection that the reduction in demand for final products might push the economy into an extended period of low resource utilization causing individuals to lower their projections of permanent income. As a result, in addition to provoking unemployment, the sluggish economy resulting from this type of policy might generate even less saving and investment than it did before. Therefore, proposals to stimulate saving must be formulated with the PIH and LCT in mind. In other words, if proposed as short-run or stopgap solutions, they will inevitably fail. Several of these stopgap proposals and a few long-term type proposals to stimulate saving have been made.

To offset the negative effect of pay-as-you-go pension funds, a proposal was put forth a few years ago to move the social security system to a funded basis by doubling the associated payment taxes.[13] The objections

---

[13] See Martin Feldstein, "The Optimal Financing of Social Security." *Discussion Paper 338* (Harvard University, 1974).

to this proposal centered on the depressing effects of the tax on the economy and thereby on private saving.

Most proposals put forth to stimulate saving focus on the negative impacts of the combination of inflation and nonindexed taxes. As prices rise, individuals are pushed into higher and higher tax brackets even though their real income does not increase. Hence, their incentives to work and to save are reduced. Moreover, any interest earned from saving is taxed at higher and higher rates. The result, as stated before, is to reduce the reward for saving.

Proposals to liberalize the tax on capital gains or to adjust the tax for inflation have been made several times.[14] Moreover, several proposals have been put forth regarding new types of taxes—value-added and expenditure or consumption taxes, especially.[15] It is contended that these taxes will have smaller distortionary effects on consumption versus saving. Because durables provide more than a very short-run service to the consumer (as compared to a doughnut, for example), individuals have a tendency to keep the consumption of the services of durables plus purchases of nondurables and services in a constant proportion to permanent income. They will not have six refrigerators, four stoves, etc., just because the prices of these goods are expected to increase. Only a certain stock of durables can be used. For this reason, although expectations of inflation may induce people to purchase a durable good now rather than next year, consumption over the long run will not be altered unless perceptions of permanent income are changed.

Consumer expenditures did increase quite rapidly during 1976-1979. There are two principal reasons for the increased consumer spending during this period. First, during 1976-1978 real incomes rose. Second, inflation in this period induced a decrease in the real cost of borrowing. For example, suppose lenders expect to receive a 3 percent increase in the real value of their money. Then, if the inflation rate is 7 percent, the nominal interest rate will have to be 10 percent. If inflation rises to 13 percent, then a 16 percent nominal interest rate still will mean only a 3 percent real return. However, if a taxpayer is in a 30 percent tax bracket, then at the 10 percent nominal interest rate, 3 percent can be written off to taxes while at the 16 percent rate, 4.8 percent can be written off. The real cost to the borrower is zero when interest is 10 percent (and inflation 7 percent), and the cost is -1.8 percent when the interest rate is 16 percent (and inflation is 13 percent). In other words, as the inflation rate rose to 13 percent, the tax system was paying the individual to borrow funds. Indeed, consumer installment credit rose to record levels during 1976-1978.

---

[14] See, for example, Martin Feldstein and Joel Slemrod, "Inflation and the Excess Taxation of Capital Gains on Corporate Stock," *National Tax Journal*, Vol. 31 (June, 1978), pp. 107-118.

[15] See James S. Fratick, "Tax Incentives and Private Saving: Some Policy Options," in *Public Policy and Capital Formation* (a study by the Federal Reserve System), pp. 143-159.

The ratio of consumer installment credit to personal income rose 13.8 percent from 1976 to 1978, a slightly higher rate than occurred during the period 1971-1976 and three times higher than the rate of increase from 1960 to 1971. As "measured" consumer spending increased, "measured" saving decreased. However, if these durables purchases are considered saving, as the *PIH* suggests, the saving rate did not decrease. Saving simply took forms not conventionally called *saving*.

The Reagan administration was elected partly on the premise that it would stimulate saving, productivity, and economic growth. The first approach the administration took centered around what is referred to as *supply-side economics* and focused on the negative impacts of taxes and inflation on saving. The 1981 Economic Recovery Act, therefore, made three changes in the federal personal income tax. First, marginal tax rates on given levels of nominal income were reduced, in three stages, summing to 23 percent by 1984. Beginning in 1985 the personal income tax structure will be indexed to inflation. In addition, the maximum rate on income from capital was reduced from 70 percent to 50 percent.[16] Relying on the permanent income and life cycle theories, the Reagan administration believed it necessary to implement changes that would endure and would reduce uncertainty regarding future policies.

Another important change in the personal income tax introduced by the 1981 tax legislation was the extension of the opportunity to use Individual Retirement Accounts (IRAs) to all working households. IRAs provide two tax advantages to contributors. First, contributions are deductible from taxable income. Second, returns on IRA investments accumulate tax-exempt as long as the funds are not withdrawn from the account.

At the time of this writing, although the economy was recovering from the monetary policy induced recession of 1980-82, the full impact of Reagan's economic program is not evident. We will have to wait a few more years to determine whether the policies were successful. In the next several chapters we will continue to examine many of the recent proposals to stimulate the economy through saving and investment, although we will focus attention on the investment side in the next chapter.

SUMMARY

The revised theories of consumption behavior have enriched our understanding of household behavior. The major points covered in this chapter have been:

---

[16] See *Economic Report of the President* (1982), p. 119-122.

1. Studies carried out in the 1940s and 1950s could not verify all of the implications of the Keynesian consumption theory. In particular, these studies found that
   a. The MPC is relatively stable.
   b. The APC is larger than the MPC in the short run, but not in the long run.
   c. The APC falls during expansions and rises during recessions.
2. The modern theories of consumption reconcile theory with the evidence generated by the consumption studies.
3. The PIH and the LCT take different approaches to explaining consumption behavior, but generate essentially similar implications. These implications are
   a. Consumption depends on an individual's expectations.
   b. Consumption depends on real wealth.
   c. Events expected to have only short-lived effects will not affect consumption.
4. Current fears about the personal saving rate have generated several policy prescriptions, based on the PIH and the LCT. These proposals focus on the negative impact of taxes and inflation on saving.

PROBLEMS AND EXERCISES

1. Outline a cross-sectional study of the effects of inflation. How will it differ from a time series study?

2. Explain the controversy that existed concerning cross-sectional and time series studies of the consumption function.

3. Describe what is meant by the concept of *permanent income*. Briefly describe how the PIH reconciles the cross-sectional and time series evidence on consumption.

4. Describe why permanent income is not expected to fluctuate as much as current or measured income.

5. Briefly describe how the LCT reconciles the cross-sectional and time series evidence on consumption.

6. According to the LCT, what is the effect of a reduction in the average retirement age?

7. Using an IS-LM model explain the effect of an increase in the nominal money supply when consumption is described by the PIH or the LCT and depends on real wealth.

8. Why might policy changes take several years before their effects are fully felt?

9. Using the *PIH* or the *LCT* of consumption, develop a story that might explain why in 1980-81 President Reagan was so adamant on a 3-year tax cut; why he would not compromise and accept a 1-year tax cut.

10. How might the expectations of increasing inflation affect individuals' consumption behavior? Will the *LCT* differ from the *PIH* in explaining why people might "buy now before prices rise"?

_SUGGESTED READINGS

A good, though somewhat dated, survey of the literature on consumption is given in

Robert Ferber, "Consumer Economics: A Survey," *Journal of Economic Literature*, Vol. 11 (1973), pp. 1303-1342.

The failure of the temporary tax surcharge is analyzed in

Robert Eisner, "What Went Wrong?" *Journal of Political Economy*, (May/June, 1971).
Arthur M. Okun, "The Personal Tax Surcharge and Consumer Demand," *Brookings Papers on Economic Activity*, Vol. 1 (1971).

An interesting and nontechnical discussion of social security and saving is provided in

Martin Feldstein, "Seven Principles of Social Insurance," *Challenge* (November-December, 1976).

For a discussion of the 1981 and 1982 tax law changes, read

Tax Equity and Fiscal Responsibility Act of 1981, Touche Ross & Co. This and similar manuals are available from Touche Ross and other public accounting firms.

A recent test of the Permanent Income Hypothesis is

Robert G. James, "A Restatement of the 'Narrowing Cells Test' of the Permanent Income Hypothesis," *Journal of Macroeconomics* (Summer, 1980), pp. 233-238.

CHAPTER 10.

Investment and the Capital Cost Recovery Act of 1981

We must recognize that only experience can show how far the common will, embodied in the policy of the state, ought to be directed to increasing and supplementing the inducement to invest.
      John Maynard Keynes, 1935

Government tax policy has stifled investment leading to a long-term deterioration in the nation's ability to produce. We must alter the investment climate in this country as soon as possible to get ourselves straightened out.
Martin Feldstein, Chairman of the
                    CEA, 1980

While gross private domestic investment has remained a relatively constant proportion of GNP, the amounts devoted to various components of investment spending have changed quite dramatically. Investment in short-lived equipment has risen while the proportion devoted to long-term investment has fallen. Business has found the shorter-lived capital a better investment than the longer-lived capital. In this chapter we will examine several possible explanations of this phenomenon. In addition, we will focus on the following questions:

- *What are the implications for the economy of the shift from long- to short-lived capital?*

- *What is the impact of Reaganomics on the availability of funds for investment and on the ability to increase the proportion of spending devoted to long-lived capital?*

- *Is investment the unstable villain portrayed by the Keynesians?*

Introduction: A Capital Crisis?

Instability of the private sector was one of the primary justifications for activist demand management policies in the Keynesian system. The horizontal *LM* curve coupled with unpredictable fluctuations in investment induced wide fluctuations in output. According to Keynes, businesses undertook investment when the expected rates of return on the new capital exceeded the expected costs. While this statement sounds very much like the modern theories of investment developed in this chapter, the interpretation of expectations in the Keynesian model and in the modern theories is significantly and importantly different. As we have seen in the last three chapters, the modern view of expectations is one which stresses stability, focusing on long-lived influences instead of short-term events. Keynesians, on the other hand, essentially threw up their hands in desperation when it came to businesses' expectations.

> The basis for such expectations is precarious. Being based on shifting and unreliable evidence, they are subject to sudden and violent changes.[1]

---

[1] John Maynard Keynes, *The General Theory of Employment, Interest, and Money* (New York: Harcourt, Brace and World, Inc., 1935), p. 315.

While debate continues over the need for stabilization policy, another controversy over investment has emerged. Since the early 1970s a growing concern has developed about the adequacy of capital formation (that is, of investment) in the United States. This concern has been expressed in popular magazines as a "capital crisis"[2] and in the economics literature as the primary cause of declining labor productivity[3] and of the relative decline in stock market values.[4] It has also been reflected in the calls for tax changes, either in the mold of President Reagan's 1981 Capital Cost Recovery Act (CCRA) or of some alternative having the same basic objective as Reagan's proposals.[5]

These concerns appear to be well founded. While labor productivity grew about 3 percent each year for the twenty-year period ending in 1968, it slowed to about 1.5 percent per year from 1968 to 1976, and from 1977 to 1982 it grew less than 1 percent per year. The stock market has followed just about the same pattern, rising during the fifties and sixties, peaking about 1968, and then declining until August, 1982. At the same time the ratio of gross investment to GNP has remained relatively constant while the ratio of net investment to GNP has decreased steadily.

What is the connection between capital accumulation, productivity, growth, and stock market values? What are the causes of their declines since the late 1960s? We will pursue answers to these questions in this chapter.

Let's begin with a brief discussion of recent investment behavior and of policy related to investment. We will then turn to two modern theories of business fixed investment, the *neoclassical* and the *q* theories. After outlining the factors involved in the firm's investment decision, we will examine the impact of policy on investment. In the final two sections we will examine the other two components of gross private domestic investment, residential and inventory investment.

The Recent Behavior of Gross Private Domestic Investment

Investment has not been an economic variable whose behavior can be easily described. Forecasts of GNP have gone astray more because of

---

[2] See *Business Week* (December 11, 1978).

[3] A compendium published by the Federal Reserve Board has several interesting studies. See *Public Policy and Capital Formation* (Board of Governors of the Federal Reserve System, April, 1981).

[4] Alan J. Auerbach, "Inflation and the Choice of Asset Life," *Journal of Political Economy* (June, 1979), pp. 621-638.

[5] Dale W. Jorgenson and Martin A. Sullivan, "Reforming Capital Recovery under the Corporate Income Tax," mimeographed (Harvard Institute for Economic Research, 1981).

erroneous predictions of investment spending than because of errors in forecasting any other economic variable. Although gross private domestic investment (GPDI) averages about 15 percent of GNP, it has ranged from near zero in 1933 to almost 19 percent in 1950.

Investment is actually business spending on the following three different types of products: (1) on plant—structures—and equipment, known as *fixed investment*; (2) on inventories, called *inventory investment*; and (3) on the construction of apartments and houses, termed *residential investment*. The reasons for investing vary according to the type of investment to be undertaken. Moreover, the costs, the rates of return, and the impacts of fiscal and monetary policy vary among the types of investment.

The structure of investment spending since 1960 is traced out in Figure 10-1. The most striking observations in this chart are the growth in equipment purchases relative to structures, the fluctuations in residential investment, the spurts in investment spending following tax changes in 1962 and 1971, and the fact that gross investment as a proportion of GNP has remained relatively stable over the past twenty years. Two other points regarding investment, not traced out in Figure 10-1, should be mentioned. First, depreciation (capital consumption allowance) as a percent of GPDI has risen since 1960 from about 60 percent to about 66 percent. This is related to the shift in investment from structures to the shorter-lived equipment. Equipment has higher depreciation rates because of its shorter service life. Second, inventory investment is a very volatile component of investment.[6]

The pattern of investment spending on structures and equipment is particularly worrisome to economists. Many fear that a continued downward trend of long-term capital accumulation will spell further productivity declines, inflationary problems, and unemployment.

The reason for this concern is that, in the past, long-term capital has been the foundation upon which production has taken place—the buildings and the factories in which labor has been able to create increasingly more output. Short-term capital, on the other hand, has been associated with the peripheral aspects of production—the autos, typewriters, filing cabinets, and such—that have not generated the output gains associated with long-term capital.[7]

---

[6] The behavior of inventory investment is traced out in Figure 10-5.

[7] It is possible that this trend will not continue in the near future. The short-term capital in the form of personal computers, word processors, and other information processing systems is likely to expand the productivity of the service sector, a sector that has made very few productivity gains in the past. To gain a perspective on these trends see John Naisbitt's *Megatrends: Ten New Directions Transforming Our Lives* (New York: Warner Books, Inc., 1982).

Figure 10-1. The Pattern of Investment Spending (1960-1982)

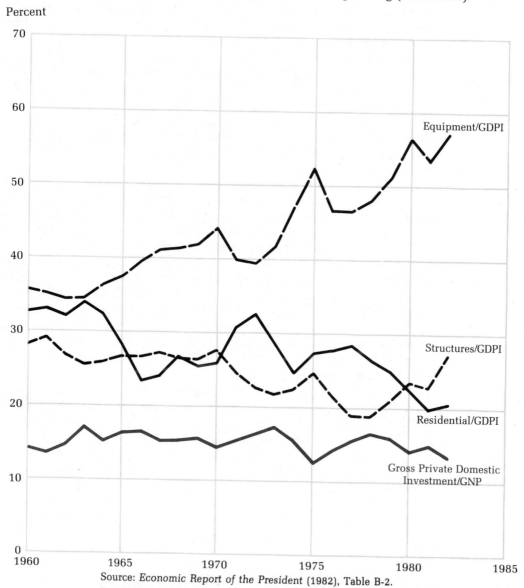

Source: *Economic Report of the President* (1982), Table B-2.

Equipment purchases have grown relative to other investment categories. Gross investment as a percentage of GNP has been relatively constant while residential investment has fluctuated widely.

Capital accumulation has both demand-side and supply-side effects on the economy. On the demand side, investment is, simply, business spending and one of the components of aggregate demand. On the supply side, however, investment adds to the capital stock and thereby increases the productive capacity of the economy. It is on this supply side that the type of investment undertaken is so important. The purchase of equipment is business spending just as is the purchase of structures. One million dollars spent on either is one million dollars of demand. On the other hand, one million dollars spent on one type of capital may increase the productive capacity of the economy substantially more than will one million dollars spent on some other type of capital. Hence, it is the supply side of the economy that economists worry about when they see a trend toward investment in short-lived capital away from investment in long-lived capital. It was also the supply side that was foremost in mind when the CCRA was passed. As we will discuss later, the intent of this act was to stimulate investment and, more importantly, to stimulate investment in long-term capital.

Why has business purchased equipment at the expense of structures? Why has net investment as a percentage of GNP fallen? We will answer these questions in the following section as we analyze why a firm decides to expand its capital stock; i.e., why it decides to invest.

Before delving into theory it is important to note that *gross investment* involves both the replacement of worn-out or obsolete capital and the accumulation of new capital. The former is called *depreciation* and the latter is *net investment*. Only net investment increases the stock of capital. Hence, theories of investment focus on net investment.

Business Fixed Investment

To lay some groundwork for answering the question of what induces a firm to undertake investment expenditures, let us assume that units of capital can be easily acquired or discarded, much like individuals can rent lawn and household equipment from local rental stores. Furthermore, suppose a firm has determined the size of its labor stock, say two workers, for the day. Then, the firm will rent an additional unit of capital only as long as that additional unit costs less than the revenue it produces. However, with the usual assumption of a diminishing marginal product, there will be some point at which the cost of an additional unit will be greater than the revenue that unit brings in. The firm will not rent additional units of capital beyond that point. Under these circumstances, more capital will be rented the lower the rental cost is. This is illustrated graphically in Figure 10-2. The return to each additional unit of capital, which in a price searcher's market is called the *marginal revenue product* (MRP), is shown by the downward sloping line. The desired stock of capital (K^D_1) is determined by the intersection of the rental cost line (RC_1) and the MRP curve. As the rental cost decreases, the desired quantity of

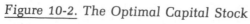

Figure 10-2. The Optimal Capital Stock

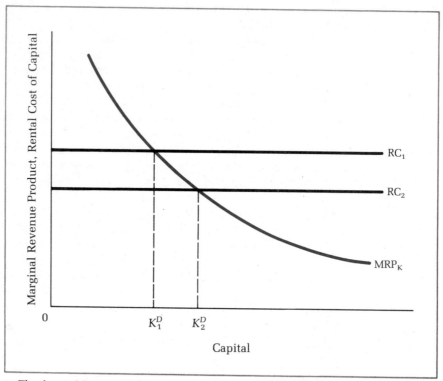

The demand for capital, MRP, is equated to the rental cost of capital to determine the optimal or desired capital stock.

capital increases, as shown by the intersection of the MRP curve and the lower rental cost line (RC_2).

The User Cost of Capital

The practice of accumulating capital is more complicated than simply renting it on a daily basis. When a capital good is general in its use (computers, bulldozers, etc.) rental markets often develop. Figure 10-2 provides a good representation of the investment decision in such a case. However, most capital is not generally suitable for daily rental markets because it is often tailored to an individual company's needs. Most often, firms can vary the quantity of labor they use much more easily than they can vary the quantity of capital.

The typical process a firm goes through in deciding how much capital to acquire can be characterized as follows. A firm decides how much output to produce over the next year or so. It then acquires the necessary capital and labor (the mix of which depends on expected factor prices), perhaps by signing labor contracts and attempting to increase or decrease its capital stock. Once it has acquired a particular capital stock, the firm is pretty well committed to produce its planned output. However, as demand varies and the firm realizes that the output it is producing is temporarily insufficient to meet the new demand, it will use existing inventories and/or vary the number of man-hours of labor it uses, combining more or less of those with the fixed quantity of capital. However, should the firm believe the demand shift it has experienced will be long-lived, it will then go about the process of altering its capital stock. Thus, rather than acquiring or discarding capital until the MRP equals the current rental cost, it is the firm's long-run expected profitability that determines whether additional capital should be acquired or not. Much like consumption, it is the long-run view that is important for investment. Temporary changes will have only a minor effect on the firm's investment decision. Thus, for a firm to increase its capital stock it must believe that the long-run variable analogous to the rental cost of capital is no greater than the present value or long-run return (MRP) on the new capital.

What is the appropriate measure of rental costs? Firms do not often acquire capital for short time periods only and then return the capital. Once acquired, capital yields a flow of services for at least 3 to 5 years. Thus, the price of capital services to the firm is not the acquisition price of the capital equipment but, instead, the cost per unit of service, called the *user cost of capital*. The user cost of capital is the opportunity cost a firm faces when its money is tied up in capital. The firm foregoes interest it could earn with the money it used to purchase the capital. The firm also ties up its money in capital that becomes obsolete or worn out. Thus, the opportunity cost per year (u) is the sum of the interest rate (r) and the rate at which capital wears out or becomes obsolete (the rate of depreciation, d).

Once we recognize that firms pay taxes, the question of whether or not certain costs of acquiring capital can be written off against taxes will influence the user cost of capital to the firm. Suppose that for each dollar spent on capital the firm can reduce its annual tax liability by some specific amount. Then, the user cost is reduced by that amount. In particular, tax laws allow firms to write off a certain proportion of their depreciation (δ) as well as a proportion of their interest charges (γ). These tax laws serve to reduce the user cost of capital. Algebraically, the user cost is, therefore, $u = r + d - \delta d - \gamma r$. In addition, firms are allowed to deduct from taxes a certain fraction of their investment expenditures, called an *investment tax credit* (τ). This tax credit reduces the user cost of capital by τ. The user cost of capital can be symbolized as follows:

$$u = (1-\tau)(r + d - \gamma r - \delta d)$$
$$= (1-\tau)[(1-\gamma)r + (1-\delta)d]$$

This equation indicates that the user cost of capital is increased by increases in the interest rate and in the rate of depreciation and is decreased by increases in the investment tax credit and in the rate at which investment expenditures can be written off against taxes.

Equating the user cost of capital and the expected rate of return on capital in deciding whether or not to purchase another unit of capital is referred to as the *neoclassical theory of investment*. This theory says, simply, that the firm will purchase capital until the last unit costs exactly as much as the additional revenue expected to be generated by that unit of capital. Hence, should the user cost decrease, *ceteris paribus*, the firm would purchase more capital.

The neoclassical theory provides a very convenient way to examine the impact of economic policy on investment. For example, over the last two decades, the United States tax system has treated structures and equipment differently. The investment tax credit (ITC) first introduced in 1962 applied only to equipment until 1981. The ITC was repealed in 1969 only to be adopted again in 1971, liberalized in 1975, in 1976, and once again in 1981. The tax credit had the effect of reducing the user cost of short-lived capital equipment relative to that of longer-lived equipment and structures. In fact, a study carried out for the Congressional Budget Office calculated that the *effective tax rate* (the rate actually paid after deductions and other adjustments) for equipment has, for the last 15 years, been lowest for equipment having asset lives from 6 to 10 years— about half as much as the rate for equipment having lives of 20 to 35 years. Another study found the effective tax rate for equipment to be about one-third of that for structures.[8] It is no wonder that in the last decade firms have invested in short-lived assets rather than in long-lived ones.

The 10-5-3 Plan

In 1981, the Capital Cost Recovery Act was passed. This legislation was intended to decrease the bias against long-lived equipment and structures and to stimulate investment in general. Federal income tax law has long required the cost of most machinery and other assets employed by businesses in the production of goods and services to be depreciated over a period of years, representing the anticipated useful life of the assets as recognized by the Internal Revenue Service. *Depreciation* is the process by which the cost of an asset is allocated to the years of its anticipated useful life. By increasing the rate at which capital can be depreciated (the accounting rate of depreciation) the user cost is decreased. The 1981 act, referred to as *10-5-3*, increased the rate of depreciation on all capital and

---

[8] See notes 3 and 5. See also Jane G. Gravelle, *The Capital Cost Recovery System and the Corporate Income Tax* (Congressional Research Service, September 21, 1979).

attempted to increase relatively more the depreciation rate on long-term equipment and structures. Long-term assets are depreciated over a period of ten years and are allowed a 10 percent ITC. Equipment is depreciated over five years and is allowed the same 10 percent ITC, while autos, taxis, and light-duty trucks are depreciated over three years and have a 6 percent ITC.[9] If long-term capital has an actual service life of, say 50 years, and shorter-term capital an actual life of 20 years, the 10-5 depreciation differential treats the long-term capital more favorably than the shorter-term. The long-term capital's 50 year value can be written off against taxes in just one-fifth of the time, 10 years, while the shorter-term capital's 20 year value can be written off in one-fourth of the time, 5 years. If this example appropriately represents reality, then the user cost of long-term capital should decrease relative to the shorter-term capital due to the 10-5-3 plan.

When proposed, the 10-5-3 plan drew criticism from Professors Dale Jorgenson and Alan Auerbach among others. Their disagreement with the bill stemmed not from the objectives of the plan but from the actual impacts as they saw them. Jorgenson and Auerbach maintained that the bias in favor of short-term equipment would be exacerbated rather than diminished by the 10-5-3 depreciation plan leading to an even more rapid accumulation of short-lived equipment at the expense of long-lived assets. They asserted that the 10-5-3 plan would result in widely divergent tax rates on various kinds of investment shifting investments away from their most productive uses and into less productive tax favored areas. For investments in new equipment, the effective tax rates would actually be negative. In other words, instead of taxing the income from such investments, the government would subsidize it. This would happen because the proposed equipment write-offs, in conjunction with the investment tax credit, would produce tax savings worth more than the immediate expensing of the entire cost of an asset. The lowest tax rates—that is, the largest tax subsidies—would be granted to short-lived equipment, exacerbating the bias already present in current law.

Jorgenson and Auerbach maintained that a better, more neutral, way to reorganize the tax system would be to allow the acquisition cost of an asset to be immediately written off against taxes. This proposal, the First Year Recovery Proposal, would reduce and perhaps eliminate the differences in user costs of different types of capital due to varying depreciation methods. It would induce investment in the most productive type of capital rather than the most tax favored type of capital.[10]

---

[9] Under the 1981 Capital Cost Recovery Act these tax credits could be sold to third parties if the principal did not have the income to use them. This was called *safe harbor leasing*. The Tax Equity and Fiscal Responsibility Act of 1982 (Revenue Enhancement Act) reduced the benefits of safe harbor leasing and rescinded leasing starting in 1984.

[10] As an example of the problems with which Jorgenson and Auerbach were concerned consider the following. Suppose you are going to purchase a personal computer,

The CCRA and the Stock Market

The evaluation of the supply-side effects of the CCRA must wait a few years; the plan is being phased in over a period of three years beginning in 1982. On the demand side, the act was supposed to spur investment and stimulate the economy. However, during the summer and fall of 1981 many believed the plan would fail on both the demand and the supply sides. According to the stock market, as interpreted by the news media, the act definitely failed on the demand side. The stock market turned down after the passage of the act and this, according to several analysts, was a signal of businesses' displeasure with the CCRA. Any surprise at the stock market's downturn was quite uncalled-for since if the act had been carefully examined, a downturn would have been predicted. One of the primary effects of the CCRA was to make existing or old capital worth less relative to new capital. The provisions of the CCRA applied only to new capital, and, hence, the user cost of old capital was increased relative to new capital. The stock market downturn was merely a reflection of the change in user costs. Firms with old capital became worth less after the CCRA was passed; the market value of a representative corporation dropped below the replacement value of its capital stock. Moreover, as economists have long recognized, capital and technology are closely related. Changes in technology are diffused through the economy by means of new plant and equipment that incorporate technological advances. Hence, increased obsolescence diminishes the growth rate of productivity, and this decrease in the effectiveness of capital should be reflected in the market value of capital; that is, in the value of stocks held against capital. Should the user cost of new capital (that incorporating new technology) be reduced, firms would have an incentive to purchase new capital and sell existing capital. This should reduce the price of old capital, as was the case after the CCRA was passed.

Tobin's q

In recent years the ratio of the market value of existing capital to the replacement cost of that capital, called the q ratio, has been carefully scrutinized as an indicator of investment spending. In a 1968 study, Professors James Tobin and William Brainard pointed out that q contains important information about investment incentives that cannot be ade-

---

costing $6,000, for use in your business. An ITC of 10 percent would take $600 directly off your taxable income or, conversely, in a 50 percent tax bracket, would make the $600 ITC worth $1,200 in depreciation. You would be subject to taxes on $600 less income. You then could depreciate the $6,000 over five years ($5,400 beginning in 1983). In the 50 percent marginal tax bracket, the machine would then actually cost about $2,400; i.e., $6,000 − $600 − ½(6,000). Taxes make this type of investment very attractive. Notice that $6,000 depreciated over 3 years would be even more attractive, making the 3-year project relatively better than the 5-year project.

quately conveyed by traditional variables such as interest rates. They asserted that market valuations matter because "investment is stimulated when capital is valued more highly in the market than it costs to produce it."[11] If the replacement value is higher than the existing capital; that is, if q is less than one, the quantity of existing capital demanded should rise—for example, through increased merger activity as firms bid for other firms—thus driving q toward unity. Conversely, if q is larger than 1.0, the quantity of replacement (new) capital demanded should rise, driving up the price of replacement capital and driving q back toward unity.

The Tobin-Brainard discussion has become known as the q *theory of investment*. The q theory has been compared and contrasted with the neoclassical theory and depending on which study one reads, one may conclude that the q theory is superior, inferior, or identical to the neoclassical theory.

The value of q increased from 1956 until 1968 and has declined since then. For the past 13 years it has been below unity. As we have previously mentioned, the ratio of GPDI to GNP remained relatively constant over this period while the ratio of net investment to GNP declined. However, the user cost of capital has also risen steadily since the late 1960s, as inflation increased the firm's tax burden.[12] Hence, it would seem that both the neoclassical and the q theories of investment could be consistent with recent investment behavior. In fact, Professor Robert Hall has maintained that the two theories are essentially the same.[13] According to Tobin, however, an advantage of q is that it registers expectations and balances them against capital costs even though the way in which expectations are related to events may change from time to time.[14]

While critics of both theories abound, the profession appears to believe that the neoclassical theory forms a better foundation for understanding the investment decision than the q theory does. Critics of the q theory assert that because q depends in some unspecified way on investor expectations there is no way the theory can be used to predict the impact of policy changes. While it is, perhaps, useful information to the firm in deciding how to allocate its internal funds or in the market allocation of resources among firms, critics maintain that an aggregate or average q

---

[11] James Tobin and William Brainard, "Asset Markets and the Cost of Capital," *Economic Progress, Private Values, and Public Policy, Essays in Honor of William Fellner*, Bela Belassa and Richard Nelson, eds. (Amsterdam: North-Holland, 1977), pp. 235-262; and "Pitfalls in Financial Model Building," *American Economic Review* (May, 1968), p. 104.

[12] See Martha S. Scanton, "Postwar Trends in Corporate Rates of Return," *Public Policy and Capital Formation* (Board of Governors of the Federal Reserve System, 1981), pp. 75-89.

[13] Robert E. Hall, "Investment, Interest Rates, and the Effects of Stabilization Policies," *Brookings Papers on Economic Activity* (1: 1977), pp. 61-122.

[14] James Tobin, "Comments," *Brookings Papers on Economic Activity* (2: 1977), p. 404.

cannot be useful as a theory of investment.[15] Moreover, the profession is bothered by the fact that q has been below unity for more than a decade. Critics have asserted that this cannot happen in Tobin and Brainard's theory unless it relies on frictions or rigidities in the economy, a reliance many economists feel is unsatisfactory. Professor Tobin even expresses some uncertainty regarding the use of q as a theory of investment.

> The notion that q does not matter in the aggregate has some credibility because the downward trend in q since the mid-1960s has not been accompanied by a complete downward trend in capital investment. I too find this a puzzle.[16]

The primary value of the q theory is in empirical testing. The variables necessary to calculate q are readily observable; the necessity of calculating the expected rate of profit and the expected or required rates of return on capital (variables used in the Keynesian theory) does not exist with the q formulation.

Summary of Investment Theory

Although questions remain about the relative importance of alternative economic variables in the investment decision, economists do believe that they have isolated the main variables involved. Both the neoclassical and the q theories maintain that interest rates, depreciation rates, and tax policies have major impacts on investment. In addition, both provide a role for expectations although the roles may not be identical. For example, in the neoclassical theory, it is the expectations of revenue or sales and of economic policy that matter. Businesses also must forecast the rate of depreciation they will be allowed to write off against taxes, the tax credit available on capital expenditures, the proportion of interest expenses that may be claimed against taxes and, of course, interest rates and monetary policy. In the q theory, expectations must be formed regarding the total market value of capital and not of individual items such as tax credits and so on. Nevertheless, in both theories, the expectations are not the animal spirits or whims and fancies of business managers, but rather the best informed judgements that can be made with the information (economically) available.

The importance attached to expectations places additional emphasis on the long-run nature of the investment decision, as it did with consumption. It is generally agreed that expectations have the effect of lengthening the horizon involved in the investment decision and, as was

---

[15] George M. von Furstenberg, "Corporate Investment: Does Market Valuation Matter in the Aggregate?" *Brookings Papers on Economic Activity* (2: 1977), pp. 347-397.

[16] Tobin, loc. cit.

the case for the consumption theories, of placing an emphasis on events expected to be long-lived.

In the past three decades the government has attempted to directly influence investment expenditures through the use of tax policies. The use of accelerated depreciation (initiated in 1954, extended in 1971, and rewritten in 1981 to be more liberal) and of the ITC (enacted in 1962, suspended in 1966-67, repealed in 1969, reinstated in 1971, raised in 1975, raised again and made permanent in 1976, and extended to structures in 1981) have been the most common approaches taken by government to influence investment. Studies have shown that these approaches have dramatic effects on investment (as shown in Figure 10-1) and, also, that these effects take place over several years. This latter result led two experts on the ITC to conclude that the ITC cannot be used as a short-run stabilization measure because the time lags involved are too long.[17]

The neoclassical theory places interest rates in a primary and explicit position in the user cost expression, while the q theory imbeds interest rates into the q ratio only in an implicit manner. Yet, no matter which theory is supported, economists tend to attach a good deal of importance to interest rates as a determinant of investment. An example of the importance attached to interest rates is the often expressed worry about the impact of government deficits on investment. Economists fear that increasing deficits will drive up interest rates and crowd out investment. The federal deficit was $23.3 billion in 1972, jumped to $76 billion in 1975, was $66.5 billion in 1976, $55 billion in 1977, $60 billion in 1978, fell to $30 billion in 1979, rose again in 1980 to $60 billion, in 1981 to more than $80 billion, and to more than $100 billion in 1982. In other words, from 1975 to 1982 the credit markets had to provide more than $500 billion in funds just to finance federal government spending. Without substantial increases in the money supply or in saving, interest rates were sure to rise. During 1976-1979 the Federal Reserve (Fed) did finance much of the debt. However, in 1980-81 the Fed pursued tighter money policies and the combination of deficits, inflation, and tight money policies drove interest rates up. And, *ceteris paribus*, rising interest rates mean falling investment.

The large deficits created problems for the Reagan supply-siders who had fought for the CCRA as a stimulus for investment. The high interest rate (particularly the high real rate of interest) in 1982 more than offset the lower taxes thereby inhibiting investment spending. Moreover, the expectations of low to no profits over 1982-83 combined with low capacity utilization rates kept investment spending down throughout 1982 and part of 1983.

---

[17] For a general discussion see G. F. Break and J. A. Pechman, "Investment Spending: Accelerated Depreciation and Tax Credits," *Taxation: Myths and Realities*, G. Break, ed. (Reading, Mass.: Addison-Wesley Publishing Co., Inc., 1978).

Residential Investment

The most interest sensitive component of investment is residential investment. The 1979-81 period provides a very good example of this interest sensitivity. As mortgage rates rose from 9 to 18 percent, residential investment fell to its lowest level in over twenty years. The interest sensitivity comes about primarily because of the institutional features of the United States economy's mortgage market. These features have caused funds to flow away from the housing sector whenever interest rates rose. This, in turn, has caused the quantity of new housing constructed to drop significantly. In Figure 10-3 we have traced out the patterns of residential

Figure 10-3. *Residential Investment and Interest Rates (1960-1982)*

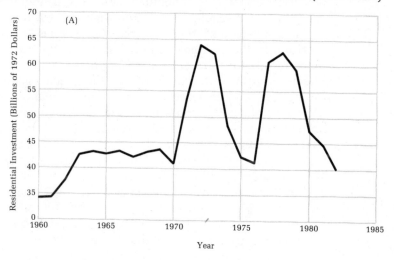

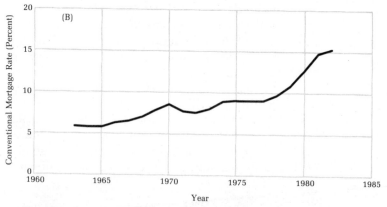

Source: *Economic Report of the President* (1982), Tables B-2 and B-67.

As interest rates rise (indicated by the conventional mortgage rate), residential investment falls.

investment and the conventional mortgage rate from 1960 to 1982. The relationship between housing construction and interest rates is readily apparent.

Residential investment measures the construction of single family and multifamily dwellings and is the addition to the existing stock of housing. Theoretically, the main difference between residential and fixed investment is the source of demand. The demand for fixed capital is a demand originating in the business sector whereas the demand for residential capital (housing) arises from the consumer sector. This theoretical difference combined with the institutional features of the mortgage market makes the residential component of investment entirely distinct from the other components. To analyze residential investment, let us first describe the theory of residential investment and then link that to the institutional features of the mortgage market.

Theory of Residential Investment

The pattern of residential investment as a percentage of GPDI is drawn in Figure 10-1. As is readily apparent there, residential investment has tended to lead the movement of structures and equipment investment, rising and falling before structures and equipment. Residential investment is isolated in Figure 10-3. It is obvious there that substantial declines in residential investments took place in 1965, 1969, 1973, and 1980. What are the reasons for these patterns? To answer this question we must understand why residential investment is undertaken.

Like the additions to the stock of plant and equipment, the additions to the stock of residential capital can be explained in several ways, the most prominent of which are the neoclassical and the q theories. While the neoclassical theory maintains that new housing will be constructed until the expected return on that housing equals its user cost, the q theory compares the value of the existing stock of housing with the replacement cost of housing. If replacement cost is less than the value of existing housing, investment will take place. The principal determinants of residential investment can perhaps best be described by examining which factors determine the value of the stock of housing and then by describing the determinants of the addition to this stock.

Housing is a long-term asset that may be held by individuals in their portfolio of assets. Hence, the demand for housing depends on wealth; the greater the wealth, the greater the demand for housing. In addition, the quantity of housing demanded depends on the expected return on, and the opportunity or user cost of, housing. Hence, the lower the expected return on other assets or, conversely, the greater the expected net return on housing, *ceteris paribus*, the greater the quantity of housing demanded.

The net return on housing consists of the rent, if the house is rented out, or the implicit return the owner receives from living in the house plus capital gains expected to be earned less the costs of the home. The costs consist of the interest cost plus taxes and depreciation less the write-off of interest against taxes. A decrease in the return to housing, *ceteris paribus*, such as would be due to an increase in the mortgage rate, makes housing a relatively less attractive form in which to hold wealth. Hence, the demand for housing decreases as the mortgage rate rises.

The price of housing is determined by the intersection between the demand for, and supply of, housing curves, as shown in Figure 10-4A. The supply of housing consists of the existing stock of houses. Should the demand for housing rise, say to D_1 in Figure 10-4A, a shortage (of $Q_1 - Q_0$) will exist at price P_0. This shortage will drive up housing prices. If housing contractors believe the higher price will yield them a positive economic profit they will begin constructing new houses. This new con-

Figure 10-4. *The Determination of Residential Investment*

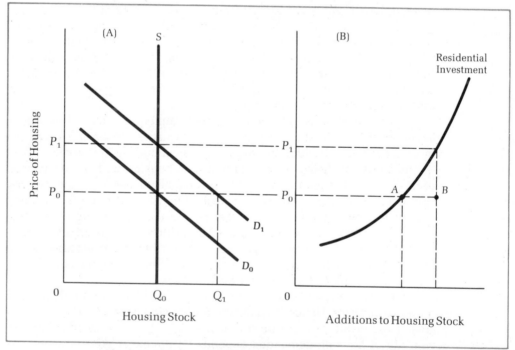

The demand for housing (D_0) and the existing stock of housing (Q_0) determine the current price of housing (P_0). Should demand increase to D_1, the existing housing stock will be insufficient to meet demand, and housing prices will begin to rise. This is shown in Panel A.

The quantity of new housing offered is dependent on the price of housing. If the price of housing rises, say to P_1, the new housing or residential investment of AB (in addition to the new housing planned at price P_0) takes place. This is shown in Panel B.

struction is residential investment. Hence, residential investment depends positively on the price of houses. In Figure 10-4B we have drawn the residential investment curve as the upward sloping supply curve of new housing.[18]

Should interest rates rise, *ceteris paribus*, the expected return on housing will decline. As a result the demand for housing will drop, driving the price of housing down and leading to a decline in residential investment. Conversely, should the expected return on housing increase, the demand will rise, driving up the asset price and stimulating residential investment. Residential investment, then, depends on the demand for housing and is influenced by the same factors that influence this demand—the interest rate, other costs, and the expected return.

According to the q theory, whenever the market value of existing capital (the price of existing houses) is more than the replacement cost, investment will take place. As before, the major difference between the two theories appears to be the explicit role of interest rates in the neoclassical theory and their hidden or implicit role in the q theory.

Institutional Features of the Mortgage Market

In both the neoclassical and q theories the mortgage interest rate is an important determinant of residential investment. The mortgage rate is, in turn, influenced by several institutional features of the U.S. economy. For example, most mortgage lending is undertaken by savings and loan associations (S&Ls). In 1979, 46 percent of mortgage debt outstanding on one to four family nonfarm properties was held by S&Ls. Obviously, residential housing demand is very sensitive to developments pertaining to the S&Ls.

The commitment of S&Ls to mortgage credit has been encouraged over the years by federal tax incentives and by state law. Under federal tax laws instituted in 1962 and 1967, S&Ls had to maintain at least 82 percent of their assets in specified items including housing related loans, to be eligible for favorable tax treatment. This commitment placed S&Ls in a precarious position each time interest rates rose. Since their assets were primarily long-term (mortgages have a contract life of 25-30 years), their rates of return on these assets fluctuated very little and only very slowly. Their liabilities, primarily savings deposits, were almost entirely short-term, however, and prior to 1966 when interest rate ceilings were imposed, the cost of these liabilities fluctuated a great deal, varying as market conditions varied. What this meant was that during tight money periods the cost of liabilities rose while the return on assets did not. The

---

[18] Residential investment is a typically very small proportion of the existing housing stock. Hence, we need not worry about the shift of the existing housing stock curve and its effect on price over a short-run period.

S&Ls were then faced with a two-edged sword. They could raise new mortgage rates sufficiently to recoup current losses in the near future, or they could refuse to pay higher rates of interest on deposits. In the first case, the quantity of housing and mortgages demanded would fall. In the second case, depositors would withdraw their deposits seeking to buy higher yielding assets, a process called *disintermediation*. This, in turn, would mean fewer funds available for mortgages. This latter case became the standard after 1966 when a ceiling was placed on the interest rates financial institutions could pay on savings deposits. This ceiling, called Regulation Q, was supposed to protect the S&Ls.[19] It did not do so. The process of disintermediation occurred in 1966, 1969, and 1973, precipitating recessions.

The first comprehensive financial institutions reform bill in over four decades was signed into law on March 31, 1980. The Depository Institutions Deregulation and Monetary Control Act of 1980 made over 100 changes in existing law. This act is an attempt to deregulate the financial industry, and some of its intention is to allow the free market to do what regulations and restrictions have been unable to do—ameliorate the wide swings in housing construction activity.

Most of the changes made by this act are being phased in over six years. A change of major importance, implemented before this act, was to allow S&Ls to issue money market certificates on which interest rates above Regulation Q ceilings could be paid. As a result, there was little of the credit crunch (disintermediation) of previous recessions during the 1979-81 high interest rate period. As interest rates rose, the S&Ls continued to attract funds by offering to pay higher rates on the money market certificates. What this meant, however, was that the increased competition for funds drove interest rates to record high levels, and this, in turn, reduced the quantity of loans demanded, thereby driving down housing construction.

Tax Benefits of Home Ownership

Since 1965, the price of the median-priced house in the United States has more than tripled.[20] From 1965 to 1980 prices of consumption goods doubled. This means that housing prices rose significantly more rapidly than the price of other goods. A primary reason for this was the favorable tax treatment of home ownership.

An individual is allowed to deduct mortgage interest expenses from taxable income in determining his or her income tax. Hence, as inflation

---

[19] The interest ceiling on S&Ls was set by the Federal Home Loan Bank Board (FHLBB) and that on banks by the Fed. There was coordination between the two agencies, however.
[20] See Scott E. Hein and James C. Lamb, Jr., "Why the Median-Priced Home Costs So Much," *Review* (Federal Reserve Bank of St. Louis, June-July, 1981), pp. 11-19.

pushed people into higher tax brackets and drove up mortgage interest payments, borrowers could deduct larger interest expenses even if the real cost of borrowing was unchanged. In other words, the higher the antici-pated future inflation, the cheaper it was to borrow, given the current U.S. tax system. Moreover, as inflation pushed individuals into higher brack-ets (bracket creep) borrowing became even less costly. For example, bracket creep increased the marginal tax rate for the median income family from 17 percent in 1965 to 24 percent in 1980. Thus, interest expenses became 7 percent less costly due simply to bracket creep.

As is evident in Figure 10-3, residential investment grew rapidly from 1975-1978, primarily in response to the financial benefits of home own-ership during an inflationary period. However, the very high interest rates of 1980 overcame these benefits and forced residential investment into a nose dive. Housing starts hit and stayed near record low levels throughout 1981 and 1982.[21]

Inventory Investment

The reasons for fluctuations in residential investment are well known. We cannot say this for inventory investment, however. Inventory invest-ment, the change in inventories, fluctuates more than any other compo-nent of demand. (The wide fluctuations of inventory investment since 1964 are shown in Figure 10-5). Indeed, fluctuations in inventory accu-mulation accounted for over 70 percent of the decline in real GNP experi-enced in the five recessions between 1948 and 1961. Yet, a single unified theoretical explanation of inventory investment has been difficult to find.

Firms hold inventories to serve as a buffer. They can meet short-run or temporary fluctuations in demand, without having to alter their long-run contracts with suppliers, by allowing inventories to accumulate or decu-mulate. Some inventories are held because firms find it too costly to purchase inputs instantaneously. Inventories are also held when firms expect difficulties in obtaining inputs in the future or when the prices of the inputs are expected to rise. Finally, inventories of finished products are held when sales are less than what they were expected to be. These we called unanticipated or unintended inventory accumulation in earlier chapters.

What causes the fluctuations in inventory holdings? Since there are a number of reasons for holding inventories, a number of economic vari-ables have been suggested as being the primary determinant of inventory investment. For example, because a firm must tie up its money when it

---

[21] Economic Report of the President (1982), p. 126. The CEA forecast that residential investment will not grow at the rate it experienced during the 1970s because of the changes in tax laws.

Figure 10-5. Inventory Investment

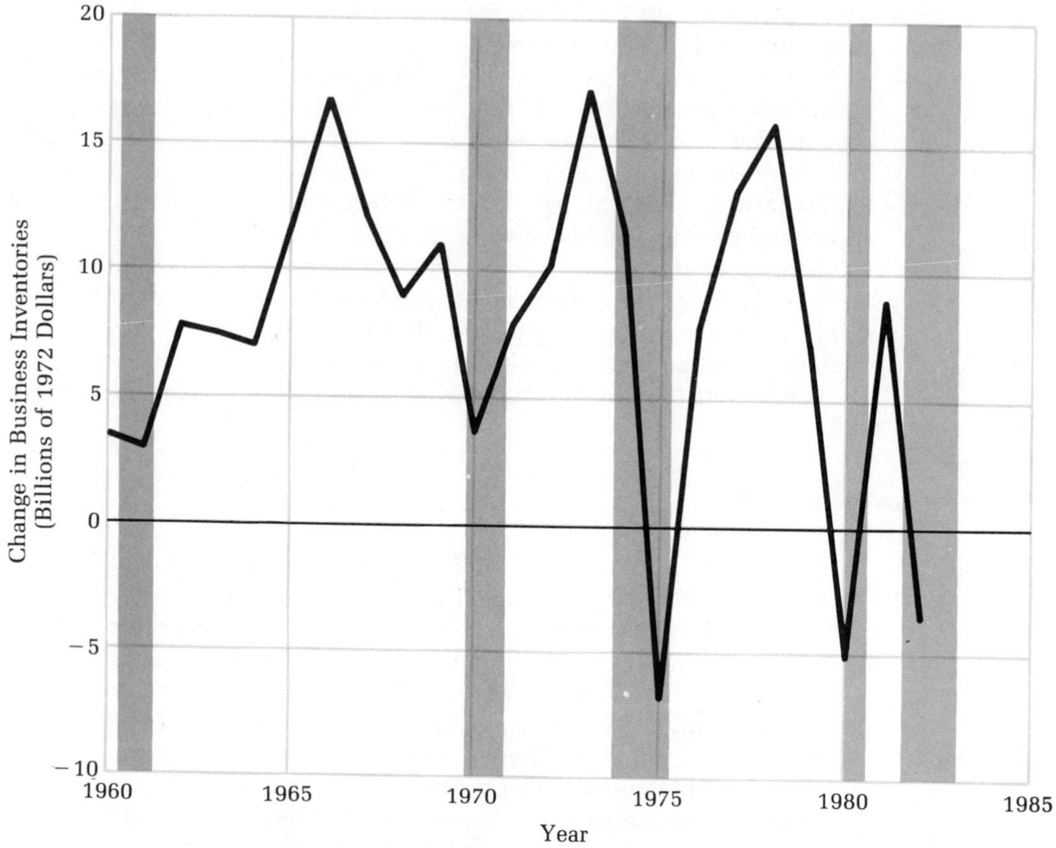

Source: *Economic Report of the President* (1982), Table B-2.

Changes in business inventories (shown here in billions of 1972 dollars) signal movements in the economy. A buildup of inventories typically signals a downturn in the economy.

holds inventories, the opportunity cost of this money should be important. As the opportunity cost rises, inventory investment should fall. Increased uncertainty, either about the demand for the firm's products or about the supply of inputs, should also induce a rise in inventory holding. But these ideas have not been strongly documented by empirical evidence.

What has been well documented is the behavior of inventory investment during a recession. Consider the 1974-75, 1979-80, and 1981-82 business downturns. As demand, or final sales, begins to decline, production is still increasing. As firms learn that the decline in demand is more than just temporary, they trim their staffs and cut production. However, it takes some time before firms have cut back production to meet demand.

Because they have accumulated inventories they must cut production below sales for a period of time in order to sell off excess inventories. Eventually, as inventories decline to the firm's desired level, production will be increased to meet sales. Output, income, and employment all start increasing again. Changes in inventories indicate where the economy is headed. An unintended accumulation of inventories signals a decline in output; that is, a business downturn, and a decline in inventories signals a business upturn. Notice also that inventory investment is quite parallel to the business cycle; inventory investment is negative during a recession and positive during an expansion.

In the recessions of the 1960s and 1970s the following pattern has been fairly typical. A period of tight money leads to a rise in interest rates which stimulates disintermediation and a subsequent decline in residential investment. Inventory investment increases as production outpaces sales. Production is decreased and the recession begins. As demand picks up relative to production, inventories are reduced to the firm's desired level. At this point production begins to increase bringing with it increases in employment and income.

SUMMARY

In this chapter we have discussed the three major components of investment—plant and equipment, residential, and inventory—and have examined the primary determinants of each. We discovered that interest rates, income, wealth, tax policies, and expectations were the major determinants of investment. The exact role each of these variables plays depends on which theory one believes best explains the investment process. We discussed the two theories that are generally accepted as the best current explanations of the investment decision, the neoclassical and the q theories.

Before leaving the topic of investment we need to make a couple clarifying points. The first involves expectations. In both the q and the neoclassical theories whether events such as monetary and fiscal policy changes are expected to be temporary or long-lived will determine whether they influence investment. Events expected to be short-lived will not affect existing or replacement values in the q theory, nor will those events affect the expected returns or user costs in the neoclassical theory.

The second point that should be mentioned concerns the lags involved in the accumulation of capital. New capital cannot be added to the existing stock instantaneously. Depending on the type of capital, the adjustment from the existing stock to the desired stock can take three to four years or even longer. The lags involved in the adjustment of the capital stock emphasize the long-term nature of investment. Hence, even ignoring the effect of expectations, the lags alone would suggest that short-run policy directed toward investment is probably misguided. Moreover, supply-side policies must necessarily be long-term. The productive capacity of the economy cannot increase at a rate beyond the rate of accumulation of capital.

_PROBLEMS AND EXERCISES_____

1. Explain the user cost of capital and compare the user cost to q.

2. In 1981 a debate over appropriate ways to stimulate investment was in full swing. Why, in a period of double digit inflation, would anyone want to stimulate investment?

3. The debate mentioned in Question 2 centered on accelerated depreciation. What would be the effect of increasing the rate at which capital could be depreciated? Explain this using the neoclassical theory and then relate the answer to the q theory.

4. Keynes believed that investment was very unstable, that it was the result of the uncontrollable psychology of the business world. Describe how modern theorists believing in the neoclassical theory would argue against Keynes's view. In which theory would Keynes's view be most strongly supported, the neoclassical or the q theory? Why?

5. Why is it important whether or not investment (or the private sector in general) is uncontrollably volatile or unstable?

6. What is the primary cause of fluctuations in housing construction? Can you describe a policy to minimize these fluctuations?

7. What does disintermediation mean? What is the primary cause of disintermediation?

8. What is meant by an inventory cycle? What economic events could lead to an inventory cycle?

9. What is meant by the statement that the U.S. tax system biases investment in favor of less productive tax-favored areas?

10. In December, 1981, inventories were at very high levels. What did this portend for the economy during the first few months of 1982? How long did it take business to reduce inventories to a desired level?

_SUGGESTED READINGS

An overview of investment theory is presented in

Dale Jorgenson, "Econometric Studies of Investment Behavior: A Survey," *Journal of Economic Literature* (December, 1971), pp. 1111-1147.

An interesting study that compares various theories of investment behavior is

Peter K. Clark, "Investment in the 1970s: Theory, Performance and Prediction," *Brookings Papers on Economic Activity* (1:1979), pp. 73-124.

An excellent survey of governmental influences on saving and capital formation is

George von Furstenberg and Burton Malkiel, "The Government and Capital Formation: A Survey of Recent Issues," *Journal of Economic Literature* (September, 1977), pp. 835-878.

Analyses of recent legislation affecting investment spending include

The Capital Cost Recovery Act Proposal (Washington, D.C.: American Enterprise Institute, 1980).
Tax Equity and Fiscal Responsibility Act of 1982 (New York: Touche Ross & Co., 1982).

CHAPTER 11.

The Money Market: The Money Supply Process, Federal Reserve Policy and Credibility, and the Demand for Money

The gyrations in monetary growth have been pronounced during the past several years. Rapid growth prior to September 1978 spurred the boom then under way and fueled the ongoing inflation. The resultant flight from the dollar frightened Washington and led the Fed, as so often, to overreact, cutting monetary growth sharply. In May 1979, the Fed again shifted course.

Milton Friedman, 1980

To return to the question of the predictability of our control over some target variable selected from among monetary aggregates, I seriously doubt that we could ever attain complete control, but I think it's quite true that we could come significantly closer to such control than we do now—if we wished to make that variable our exclusive target. But the wisdom of such an exclusive orientation for monetary policy is, of course, the basic question.

William McChesney Martin, Jr., former Federal Reserve Chairman, 1969

The events of the late 1960s and 1970s drove economists back to their chalkboards. Unable to solve or explain many of the problems of the period (particularly the simultaneous growth of inflation and unemployment) with existing theories, economists focused attention on expectations. Both consumption and investment were shown to depend on economic developments expected to be long-lived and not to fluctuate wildly in response to sudden short-lived changes. This reexamination of macroeconomic theories also altered the perception of monetary policy. By the middle 1970s the Monetarist contention concerning the importance of money had been generally accepted, as were many of the Monetarist suggestions about how monetary policy should be carried out. Moreover, the emergence of the rational expectations hypothesis led to a renewed emphasis on implementing monetary policy as a set of predictable rules. In this chapter these developments are examined and the following questions are treated:

- How is monetary policy implemented?

- Can the Federal Reserve actually control the money supply?

- How do financial markets react to Federal Reserve policy?

Introduction

In late 1979 the Federal Reserve (Fed) switched from carrying out monetary policy based on an interest rate target to one based on a monetary aggregate (money supply) target. Simultaneously it expanded the number of definitions of the money supply. It has watched M-1 fall below target levels at the same time that M-2 rose above target levels;[1] and, it has watched interest rates soar to record high levels. These facts placed the Fed under increasingly severe criticism. Several commentators argued that the Fed should return to an interest rate strategy; others that the financial markets change too rapidly for the Fed to attempt to control the economy by focusing only on M-1 or M-2. Some have argued for a return

---

[1] M-1 is the sum of currency, demand deposits, traveler's checks, and other checkable deposits. M-2 is M-1 plus overnight repurchases and Eurodollars, money market mutual fund shares, and savings and small time deposits. M-3 is M-2 plus large time deposits and term repurchase agreements. L is M-3 plus other liquid assets.

to the gold standard; and still others have begun debating whether the independence of the Fed is beneficial for the economy.[2]

To understand these arguments and the changes in Fed policy we must reexamine the money market. The discussion in Chapter 5 assumed a money market totally and easily controlled by the Fed. The purpose of this chapter is to extend the analysis of Chapter 5 in order to point out what the Fed can and cannot do. We will initially examine the money supply process—how the money supply is created and how the Fed attempts to control it. We then will turn to the demand for money and analyze its impact on Fed policy.

Finally, we will discuss some current problems and issues in monetary policy.

The Money Supply Process

It is within a complex system of financial institutions and regulations and restrictions that the supply of money is determined. In the past, it was common for textbooks to focus on commercial banks in their examinations of the money supply process because at that time only commercial banks created money through demand deposits. This approach is outdated now for in recent years other financial institutions have been allowed to move onto the turf of the banks through negotiable order of withdrawal (NOW) and automatic transfer system (ATS) accounts, which are essentially interest earning checking accounts. Past treatments of the money supply process have also typically assumed that the Fed had complete control of commercial banks and, thus, the money supply. If it ever did have such control, it has not existed in recent years. According to Fed chairman Paul Volcker, at least, the Fed's control over commercial banks had been seriously eroding in recent years as commercial banks left the Federal Reserve System. For this reason Volcker supported the Depository Institutions Deregulation and Monetary Control Act of 1980.

> The manner in which reserves are applied is the source of our present problem. Members of the Federal Reserve System are currently subject to a special burden—from their point of view, the equivalent of a special tax—because they must maintain substantial levels of reserves in non-interest bearing balances at the Federal Reserve Banks. Nonmember commercial banks . . . have no comparable requirement. . . . In these circumstances, members leave the System, narrowing our base of control.[3]

---

[2] See *Business Week* (May 14, 1982), p. 148 and (June 14, 1982) p. 127. Under consideration as of January, 1983, in Congress, are several proposals designed to curb the Fed's "independence" in the interests of achieving a better coordination of monetary and fiscal policies. These proposals are listed in the appendix to this chapter.

[3] *Federal Reserve Bulletin* (1979), p. 823.

The Fed and Its Critics

The 1980 act is the first major monetary act since the Fed was set up in 1913 and reorganized in 1935. This act changes the reporting requirements of depository institutions, alters reserve requirements, and gives the Fed control over NOW and ATS accounts. These changes are substantial. First, all institutions, members and nonmembers, are subject to the reserve requirements. Second, rather than the previous system where there were five different reserve requirements on demand deposits (ranging from 7 to 16.25 percent depending on the amount of deposits) and two different reserve requirements on savings deposits (depending on the amount of deposit), there is now a uniform reserve requirement.[4] The reserve requirement is the percentage of total deposits that must be held as deposits at the Fed or in the vaults of financial institutions.

Even with these changes, critics point out that the Fed has failed and will continue to fail in its attempt to appropriately control the money supply. Let us examine the behavior of a few financial variables to see if we can discover why the critics continue to hound the Fed.

In Figure 11-1 we have plotted the monthly rates of growth of M-1 and M-2, and in Figure 11-2 we have traced out the 3-month Treasury bill rate and the federal funds rate for the four-year period 1979-1982. There are several things to note about these figures. First, the variability from month to month in each of the monetary aggregates is extremely high. Second, the rates of growth of the various money supply measures are incredibly different. In one period M-1 declined by 25 percent while M-2 grew by 10 percent. Third, the 3-month Treasury bill rate has been very high, rising throughout the latter part of 1980, falling slightly in 1981 but remaining at high levels throughout 1982. Each of these observations is used as ammunition against the Fed. For example, the fluctuations in all the money supply measures indicate the Fed's inconsistency. The different rates of growth of M-1 and M-2 point out the Fed's inability to control the money supply.

Critics also argue that the primary result of the Fed's inconsistencies was the 1981-82 disaster associated with rising interest rates. Rising interest rates discourage investment, particularly housing construction and consumer borrowing. With an inflation rate declining to near 10 percent in 1981 and near 4 percent in 1982 (while nominal interest rates rose to around 16 percent), the real interest rate (calculated using actual rather than expected inflation rates) was rising to a very high 6 percent. It is no wonder that housing construction declined to its lowest level in thirty years and that auto sales plunged again.

---

[4] For a thorough review of the 1980 act, see Thomas Cargill and Gillian Garcia, *Financial Deregulation and Monetary Control* (Stanford, Calif.: Hoover Institution Press, 1982).

Figure 11-1. Month to Month Percentage Changes in M-1 and M-2

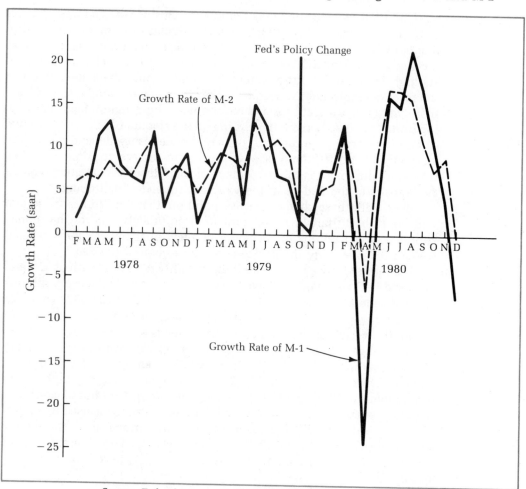

Source: *Federal Reserve Bulletin* (various issues).

Wide fluctuations persist even though the Fed became a money watcher in October, 1979. Furthermore, M-1 and M-2 do not always move together. Since M-2 includes M-1, it is the overnight repurchases, Eurodollars, money market mutual fund shares, and savings and small time deposits that do not move totally in conjunction with M-1.

Are the Fed's critics correct? Is the Fed unable or unwilling to carry out a reasonable monetary policy? To put these criticisms into perspective let us briefly consider the money supply process—the determination of the money supply. This discussion will point out the technical difficulties the Fed faces in its attempt to carry out monetary policy. Once completed, we can join these technical difficulties with other, even more complex problems faced by the Fed.

Figure 11-2. Interest Rate Behavior

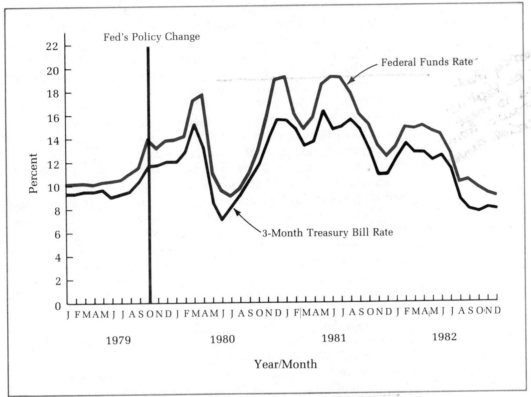

Source: *Federal Reserve Bulletin* (various issues).

Interest rates appear to have fluctuated more since the October, 1979 policy change than they did before, suggesting that the Fed did relax its strategy of controlling interest rates.

The Mechanics of the Money Supply Process

The money supply measured as M-1 was near $480 billion in 1983. In 1933, comparably measured, it was $32 billion. How could the money supply increase by $450 billion in 50 years? A simple example may demonstrate how money is created and distributed.

Suppose we have a very simple economy in which there is a central bank, called the Fed, a system of commercial banks, a government, and the general public. The government issues bonds (IOUs) to the Fed in exchange for paper money which the government may then spend. The commercial banking system provides a place to deposit funds. Initially, let's assume that a commercial bank may only issue deposits, dollar for dollar, in exchange for paper money and that all reserves must be held in the form of deposits at the Fed. Suppose the government has run deficits of $1,000, so that $1,000 of money has been issued to the public. The money supply, therefore, is $1,000. If the public deposits $600 in commercial banks, the banks must place the $600 in a Fed deposit. The money supply now consists of $400 in currency and $600 in deposits.

Now suppose banks are allowed to loan some of their deposits out, but must keep some on deposit at the Fed to meet withdrawals. This is called a *fractional reserve banking system*. If the Fed sets the fraction, the *reserve requirement*, at say 20 percent, banks can loan out 80 percent of deposits. The $600 of deposits now consists of $120 in required reserves and $480 in *free* or *excess reserves*, reserves that can be loaned out.

If the banks loan out all they can, they loan out $480. That $480 is spent by the persons taking out the loans and may be redeposited by those receiving the $480 of expenditures. If all $480 is deposited, the banks will have an additional $480 in deposits, of which 20 percent must be kept on hand and 80 percent can be loaned out. The money supply at this stage consists of $400 in currency, another $600 in deposits, the initial amount deposited and still on the books as a liability, and another $480 in deposits for a total of $1,480. Of the new deposits of $480, eighty percent can be loaned out. If loaned out and spent and then redeposited, the money supply will increase once again. This process can continue on and on with a smaller amount being loaned and redeposited each time and the money supply expanding with each new deposit.

One of the more interesting aspects of this example is that the money supply process looks like a spiral or funnel cloud with a very wide top and a small base. Notice that on the basis of the $400 currency and the initial $600 on deposit at the Fed, the money supply multiplied several times. The sum of currency and Fed deposits or reserves is known as the *monetary base* or *high-powered money*. As we have seen, once the loan to deposit process is completed, the money supply is many times larger than the monetary base. In other words, the ultimate money supply that can be created from a given base is some multiple of that base. The value of that multiple is known as the *money multiplier*.

While the Fed may have control over part or all of the monetary base, its control of the size of the money multiplier is much more tenuous. Let us examine the money multiplier and of what it consists. Let the money supply *(M)* be defined as M-1 so that *M* equals currency plus demand deposits, or, in symbols, $M = X + D$. The monetary base or high-powered money stock is *H* which is currency plus Federal Reserve deposits, or, in symbols, $H = X + R$. The money multiplier *(m)* is then defined as the ratio of the money supply to the stock of high-powered money. Symbolically, this is represented as follows:

$$m = \frac{M}{H} = \frac{X + D}{X + R}$$

[handwritten margin note: money that must be kept at the Fed to meet withdrawals from commercial banks]

Now multiply both numerator and denominator by $1/D$ to find the money multiplier

$$m = \frac{X/D + 1}{X/D + R/D}$$

Since

$$M = mH = \left(\frac{X/D + 1}{X/D + R/D} \right) H$$

it should be clear that decisions of the public also affect the money supply. Had the public deposited more than the $600 in the bank, in our example, the money supply could have been even larger. The public chose a currency to deposit ratio of 400 to 600 or $2/3$. If instead it had deposited $900 and kept $100 in currency, the money supply could have been much larger. Suppose that X/D is $2/3$ and R/D is 120/600. The money multiplier would be 1.93; i.e., 1.66/(0.66 + 0.20). However, if X/D is 1/9 and R/D is 1/5, then the money multiplier would be 3.58; i.e., 1.11/(0.11 + 0.2).

Why in this example was the reserve to deposit ratio (R/D) assumed to be 0.20? We made the assumption that the bank would loan out all it could. This means that total reserves (R) are just required reserves. Therefore, the ratio of required reserves to deposits is determined by the Fed. In our example that ratio is 0.20.

If the commercial banks had not been allowed to loan any of their deposits, the money supply would have remained at $1,000. Similarly, if the banks had found that the paper work and risk of default cost more than some of the loans were worth, the banks might not have loaned out all that they were allowed to. In such a case the ratio of reserves to deposits would have been larger, and the money multiplier smaller. Suppose R/D is 0.40 and X/D is 0.66. Then the money multiplier would be 1.56; i.e., 1.66/(0.66 + 0.4) which is smaller than 1.93, calculated with X/D equal to 0.66 and R/D equal to 0.2. Additionally, if instead of depositing and redepositing the money into the commercial banks, individuals had chosen to deposit their funds in saving accounts at saving and loan associations or credit unions, what would have happened to the money supply? If the money supply is defined as M-1, then nondemand deposits would not have been part of the money supply. As a result, deposits would have been smaller. Suppose demand deposits are $500 rather than $600. The ratio of currency to deposits would be 4/5 rather than 4/6, the ratio of reserves to deposits would be 120/500, and the money multiplier would be 1.73 rather than 1.93.

Even though the Fed does not have direct control over all of the components of the money supply, if the money multiplier was constant over time, the Fed would know by how much it must increase the monetary base (H) to get a particular increase in the money supply. The money multiplier is far from constant, however. Moreover, the multipliers that correspond to each definition of the money supply differ considerably from each other. Why? Perhaps we can get an idea of the causes of changes in the money multiplier by examining its components, the currency-deposit ratio and the reserve-deposit ratio.

The Currency to Deposit Ratio (X/D)

The currency to demand deposit ratio has increased since 1970. Currency has increased at nearly a 10 percent rate while demand deposits in commercial banks have grown just over 6 percent. The rise in interest rates, the increased use of credit cards, and the development of NOW and ATS accounts have led to a decline in demand deposits. Since individuals can earn interest on their checking accounts via NOW and ATS accounts, many of them reason that noninterest earning demand deposits make little sense. And since, with the use of credit cards, individuals can synchronize their expenditures more closely to the receipt of their paychecks, many depositors feel that they need not keep as large a balance in their checking accounts.

The ratio of currency to deposits when deposits include ATS and NOW accounts and credit union share draft balances or when deposits include these accounts and saving and time deposits has not decreased as rapidly as the ratio of currency to demand deposits. Why? The primary reason is that individuals have switched from demand deposits to other types of deposits.[5]

The Reserve to Deposit Ratio (R/D)

The other component of the money multiplier is the ratio of reserves to deposits. Recall that reserves consist of required and excess reserves. Thus, since the Fed controls required reserves but not excess reserves, the reserve to deposit ratio is not completely determined by the Fed. The excess reserves to deposit ratio depends on the desires of financial institutions.[6] Institutions lose potential revenues by holding excess reserves

---

[5] Some economists suspect that the increased currency-deposit ratio also reflects the growth of crime and of the underground economy. Criminals and individuals seeking to avoid income taxation have an incentive to use cash only. In this way, there are no records of illegal or underground transactions.

[6] The Monetary Control Act of 1980 gives authority to set reserves on all ATS and NOW accounts to the Fed. As a result, the excess reserve to deposit ratio now depends on the behavior of all of the deposit institutions.

but, on the other hand, avoid the costs of having insufficient reserves. Since reserves earn no interest, holding excess reserves means a loss of potential revenue. Yet, a bank that is fully loaned up or has no excess reserves may have some problems if it faces withdrawals or loan demands. A shortage of reserves often has led to banking panics in the past. A rumor that a bank had even a temporary shortage might have touched off a panic wherein all customers hurried to the bank to withdraw their funds. The panic often spread to other banks, and then bank failures or collapses began. Such a panic in 1907 induced legislators to organize the Federal Reserve System. Interestingly, the Fed did not prevent a panic and collapse in 1930. The 1930 collapse led to the creation of the Federal Deposit Insurance Corporation (FDIC) which insures bank deposits so that the depositors will not lose their money even if their bank fails. This insurance insulates banks and, thus, the public against bank runs. Before the FDIC was set up, banks kept substantially more excess reserves than they have since.[7]

Another cost to the bank of having a shortfall in reserves is that money to make up the shortfall must be raised. One way banks can raise this money is by borrowing from the Fed and paying interest at a rate, called the *discount rate*, which is determined by the Fed. Another way to raise funds in a short time and for short-term use is for banks to borrow the excess reserves of other banks or to borrow the excess deposits of non-financial corporations. These are referred to as *federal funds* and *repurchase agreements (RPs)*, and the interest rate on these funds is the *federal funds rate*. The use of federal funds has increased dramatically in recent years. Federal funds and RP borrowings from nonbank sources since 1970 are plotted in Figure 11-3 on page 336. Obviously, this type of fund raising activity has grown rapidly. As a result, banks have reduced their holdings of excess reserves.

Federal Funds

The federal funds market has become such an important aspect of recent monetary theory that we need to consider it further.[8] In 1963 the

---

[7] The FDIC once again points up how important expectations are in the economy. While the FDIC does not have nearly enough funds to cover a large scale banking panic, such as those that occurred during the early 1900s, just the idea or expectation that somehow a depositor will not lose her deposits induces her not to attempt to withdraw all her deposits. This precludes a run on banks.

[8] The name *federal funds* comes from the required use of a Federal Reserve wire to carry out transactions. In other words, the federal funds transactions are carried out on a Federal Reserve communication line. For more information about the operation of the federal funds market see D. DePamphilis, *A Micro Economic Econometric Analysis of the Short-Term Commercial Bank Adjustment Process* (Federal Reserve Bank of Boston, Research Report No. 55, 1974) and R. E. Lombra and H. M. Kaufman, "Commercial Banks and the Federal Funds Market: Recent Developments and Implications," *Economic Inquiry* (October, 1978), pp. 549-561.

Figure 11-3. Federal Funds and RP Borrowings from Nonbank Sources

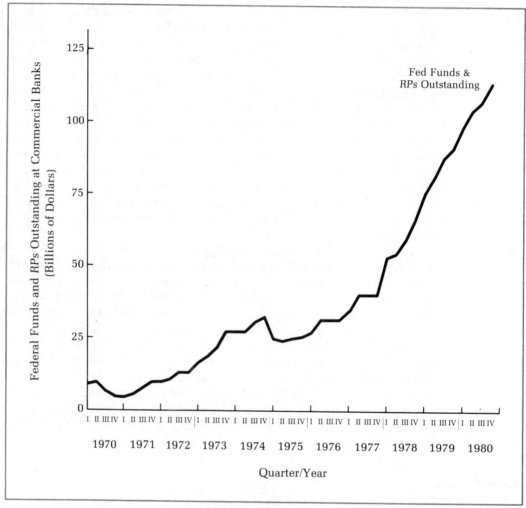

Source: Thomas B. Simpson, "The Market for Federal Funds and Repurchase Agreements," *Staff Study* (Federal Reserve Board, July, 1979).

The rise of nonbank borrowing (federal funds and RPs) has grown substantially since the early 1970s. These funds were not subject to reserve requirements and, hence, provided a less expensive source of funds. As a result, institutions have held fewer excess reserves.

Comptroller of the Currency ruled that unsecured federal funds transactions were not subject to a reserve requirement. That ruling stimulated the growth of the federal funds market. Since federal funds could be obtained without the requirement of holding a portion in reserves and since other deposit sources required reserves, the relative cost of federal funds was decreased.

Federal funds transactions involve the borrowing (or lending) of *immediately available funds; funds* that often can be used immediately. Usually one bank borrows the excess reserves of another bank, thus effectively reducing the R-D ratio and increasing the money multiplier. However, short-term transactions often take the form of RPs. For example, a corporation having $25 million in its checking account may purchase a Treasury bill from a commercial bank with the bank agreeing to buy it back a day or two later. This transaction provides funds for the bank while allowing the corporation to earn interest on its deposits. In addition, because the transaction involves a transfer of funds from demand deposits which require reserves to be held against them to RPs on which reserves do not have to be held, the expansion of the money supply on a given base may be larger than if RPs did not exist.

In summary, the Fed has direct control over only a portion of the money multiplier. The other components depend on the public and commercial banks' behavior and response to Fed actions. In addition, financial institutions have an incentive to develop new sources of funds that are not subject to tight Fed control, such as RPs and Fed funds, for these provide loanable funds without the necessity of reserve requirements. Each new source of funds creates difficulties for the Fed in its attempt to control the money supply. Moreover, there are incentives for the financial community to outguess and outmaneuver the Fed, and these activities further weaken the Fed's ability to control the money supply.

The Fed views the federal funds rate as a very good indicator of day-to-day conditions in the money market. The rate increases as the demand for short-term funds increases relative to the supply of excess reserves. If the Fed does not want money to be tight; that is, if the Fed does not want interest rates to rise, it supplies more funds so as to increase reserves. In the following section we will describe exactly how the federal funds market fits into monetary policy decisions.

The Money Supply Process and the Implementation of Monetary Policy

The purpose of this section is to describe the framework within which monetary policy decisions are made.[9] The Federal Reserve Open Market Committee (FOMC) is the policy making arm of the Fed. The FOMC consists of the seven members of the Board of Governors and five of the twelve regional Federal Reserve Bank presidents. The chairperson of the Board of Governors also chairs the FOMC. The FOMC meets approximately once each month at which time

---

[9] For further discussion see W. Poole, "The Making of Monetary Policy: Description and Analysis," *Economic Inquiry* (June, 1975), pp. 253-265.

1. The Federal Reserve Board staff presents alternative economic forecasts with each alternative dependent on alternative rates of growth of
   the money supply.
2. The FOMC selects a near term target for the rate of growth of the
   money supply.
3. The Federal Reserve Board staff presents short-run (two to six months)
   forecasts under alternative federal funds rates.
4. The FOMC selects both a target range for the federal funds rate and a
   guideline as to how the manager of the Open Market Account should
   adjust the funds rate within the target range.

Thus, the Fed has two *instruments* with which to work. One, the money
stock, is used to try to meet the Fed's two long-range goals—the reduction
of unemployment and inflation. The other, the federal funds rate, is
treated as the instrument with which the Fed attempts to meet its short-
range target—the rate of growth of the money stock.

At each meeting forecasts are presented, issues surrounding the forecasts are debated and the FOMC's monetary stance is determined. The
FOMC *Policy Record* is published approximately one month after each
FOMC meeting. In addition, beginning in 1975, the Fed has published its
twelve-month target rates of growth for the money stock.

Procedures before October, 1979

Prior to October of 1979, the Fed's short-run policy implementation
procedure involved the use of the federal funds rate to keep the level of
the money stock in a neighborhood of the long-run growth path selected at
the monthly FOMC meeting. The Fed did not attempt to control the
federal funds rate exactly. It could have done so, had it wished, by
offering to borrow or lend unlimited amounts of federal funds at a particular rate. Instead, the Open Market Desk (often referred to as the *Desk*)
talked with the federal funds brokers several times each day and supplied
(absorbed) reserves if the fund rate was higher (lower) than desired.[10] The
reserves were supplied or absorbed either through standard open market
operations (the buying or selling of government bonds) or by repurchase
agreements with government securities dealers.

Notice in Figure 11-4 that while the federal funds rate was within the
Fed's desired ranges virtually 100 percent of the time during 1979, the
rate of growth of M-1 was outside of the FOMC's desired ranges most of
the time. Why did the Fed have such trouble meeting its money supply
target while being so successful in meeting its interest rate target? The
primary reason is that the financial community (firms and individuals
operating in the financial market) complicated matters by using the federal funds market as an indicator of future Fed actions. For example, during

---

[10] The *Open Market Desk*, or the *Desk*, is the colloquial term for the manager and traders of
the Open Market Account located at the New York Federal Reserve Bank.

Figure 11-4. FOMC Short-Run Ranges for 1979 M-1 and FOMC
Ranges for the 1979 Federal Funds Rate

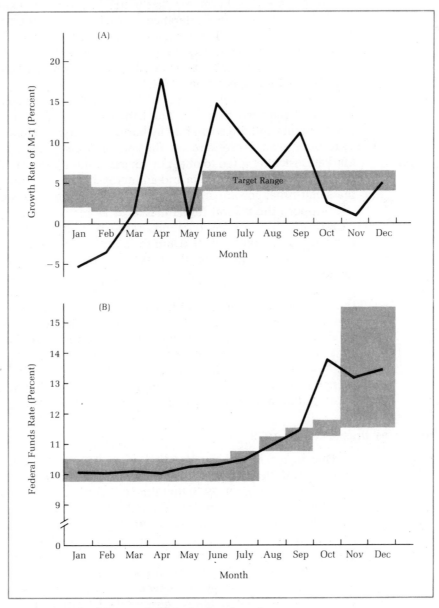

Source: *Federal Reserve Bulletin* (various issues).

The announced Fed target ranges for M-1 proved elusive in 1979. Panel A shows that the actual growth rate of M-1 was virtually never in the ranges announced by the Fed.

The announced Fed target ranges for interest rates were met nearly 100 percent of the time in 1979, although actual rates were always near the top of the target range. In October, 1979, the Fed widened its interest rate target range.

this time period the financial community knew the Open Market Desk would supply and absorb reserves to hold the federal funds rate within a tolerance range. Furthermore, the financial community expected that the FOMC would move this tolerance range in light of the behavior of the monetary aggregates. The financial community was able, therefore, to guess which way the funds rate would move over the near term. If money growth had been high, it was generally expected that the funds rate would rise. Given the expectation of higher rates, firms attempted to borrow more, leading to an expansion of bank credit and deposits and, thus, additional required reserves. The banks, then, had to meet the reserve requirements and did so mainly by borrowing in the federal funds market. This put upward pressure on the federal funds rate which the Open Market Desk attempted to offset by injecting more reserves. As a result, an increasing federal funds rate and an increasing money supply occurred at the same time, accompanied by an increase in (net) federal funds.

Suppose the federal funds market is as pictured in Figure 11-5. The current equilibrium federal funds rate (r^e) is at the intersection of the demand for federal funds (F_0^D) and the supply of federal funds (F_0^S) curves. The tolerance range set by the FOMC is from r^l to r^h. Now suppose the money supply has been rising rapidly. The financial community believes the Fed will reduce the supply of federal funds by absorbing reserves and thus raise the current federal funds rate. Because they expect the rate to rise they attempt to borrow more now. As a result, the demand for federal funds rises (to F_1^D), and the federal funds rate does rise. To bring the rate back down into the tolerance range, the Fed increases reserves so as to increase the supply of federal funds. This has the effect of increasing the money supply when, in fact, the reason for policy action in the first place was that the money supply had been growing more rapidly than desired.

Procedures since October, 1979

Due to the record the Fed had compiled in controlling the money supply, Paul Volcker, the chairman of the Federal Reserve Board, announced on October 6, 1979 that the Fed would begin focusing solely on monetary aggregates. Interest rates, including the federal funds rate would be allowed to go where demand and supply forced them. In addition, federal funds and RPs would have an 8 percent reserve requirement. These moves were intended to tighten up the Fed's control of the money stock. The moves were met by applause from those who had been arguing for an aggregates strategy. However, not everyone was pleased by this apparent policy switch. Many economists disagree with having an isolated focus on monetary aggregates. Some feel that it takes too long to obtain information on the movements of the monetary aggregates since most of the aggregates are reported weekly whereas interest rates can be watched daily. Hence, the debate over the proper way to carry out monetary policy continues.

Figure 11-5. The Federal Funds Market and an Interest Rate Strategy

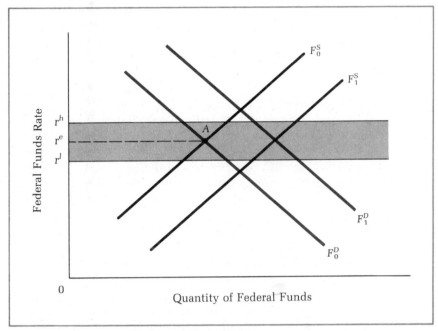

The federal funds market is in equilibrium at Point A. Given the demand for federal funds (F^D_0) and the supply of funds (F^S_0), the equilibrium interest rate is r^e. If the federal funds rate has been falling below the target range because the money supply has been growing too fast, as shown by F^S_1, the financial community will expect the Fed to reduce the supply of funds to bring the rate back into the tolerance range between r^h and r^l. Because they expect the rate to rise, they borrow now at the lower rate. This has the effect of raising the federal funds rate. The Fed must then increase the rate of growth of the money supply to lower the rate rather than decrease money growth. The expectations of the financial community offset the actions of the Fed.

In their review of operating procedures in monetary policy, Federal Reserve Board governor Henry Wallich and Fed economist Peter Keir report that some members of the FOMC were questioning the committee's emphasis on money market conditions and interest rates as early as the late 1950s.[11] The debate over whether to use interest rates or monetary aggregates is, therefore, nothing new. Yet, despite the debate, it seems the FOMC has never really moved away from a preoccupation with money market conditions—that is, interest rates.

In the 1950s, after the Fed-Treasury accord liberated the Fed from its obligation to peg prices of Treasury securities, the monetary authorities usually "leaned gently against the wind." From meeting to meeting the

---

[11] "The Role of Operating Guides in U. S. Monetary Policy: A Historical Review," *Federal Reserve Bulletin* (September, 1979).

FOMC instructed the manager of the Open Market Account to hold free reserves, or net borrowed reserves, at a level thought to provide the desired degree of restraint over the growth of bank credit and money supply.

In the 1960s, with the swing to generally expansive fiscal policies under Presidents Kennedy and Johnson, interest rates began to rise. The Fed attempted to dampen the rise which led to expansive money growth. Concern over the consequences of the Fed's rate cushioning policies led the Fed chairman, Arthur Burns, to include monetary targets as well as interest rate targets in the policy directives of the 1970s. Under Burns's directives the Fed's staff developed a procedure by which they could combine the old practice of stabilizing federal funds rates and the new practice of pursuing money growth targets. It was their belief that they could peg federal funds at a level that would induce the public to demand, and the banks to supply, the quantity of money the FOMC thought appropriate. Unfortunately, the relationship between federal funds rates and the money stock proved difficult to pin down. As we have previously discussed, although the Desk managed to hold federal funds rates within a very narrow range, money growth rates fluctuated widely.

By producing larger changes in the money supply than the FOMC wanted, the monetary control procedures of the 1970s made the Fed a major source of instability in the economy. Economic swings were wider than had been the case in the 1950s and 1960s when money growth rates were merely incidental objectives of Fed policy (see Figure 1-3, page 11).

The strong surge of money growth, the rise of inflation, and the increasing inflation expectations during the second and third quarters of 1979 called for a change of direction in monetary policy. Fed chairman Volcker's October 6, 1979 announcement included both a declaration of intent to curb expansion of money and bank credit and a change in procedures. The crucial change in the procedures was the requirement that the manager of the Open Market Account supply or withdraw specific quantities of bank reserves. The quantities were to be estimated by starting from the desired change in money supply specified by the FOMC and calculating the quantity of reserves required to obtain this monetary growth. These quantities had to be adjusted for reserves not directly controlled by the Fed. At the end of the calculation the manager would purportedly have a good estimate of the amount of securities to be bought or sold.

Under interest rate targeting, the manager bought or sold whatever quantities of securities were necessary to hold federal funds within some desired range. The shift from having the market determine the quantities of reserves provided and the Fed determining the price to having the Fed determine the quantities and the market determine the price was the objective of the October, 1979 announcement.

The Results of the October Change

The year 1980 saw extraordinarily wide fluctuations in both monetary aggregates and interest rates. Why? One explanation is that the Fed did not really abandon its old practice of stabilizing federal funds rates from day to day. Fed watchers claimed that open market operations appeared to be directed at holding the federal funds rate within a narrow band even though the stated target was a wide band.

> Commenting on the Oct. 6 statement, I noted that, "those of us who have long favored such a change have repeatedly licked our wounds when we mistakenly interpreted earlier Fed statements as portending a change in operating procedures. I hope that this time will be different—but remain skeptical until performance matches pronouncements." Unfortunately, subsequent performance confirms the doubts rather than the hopes. Instead of steadier monetary growth, we have had wild swings: first slow growth, then rapid growth, and then actual decline.[12]

The counterargument claims that the Desk is not concerned with the rate level *per se*, but is instead using movements in funds to check projections of the supply of nonborrowed reserves.[13] A fall in the funds rate might be interpreted as evidence that the actual supply of reserves exceeded the staff's projections and in this case reserves would be absorbed. A rise in the funds rate might be interpreted as evidence that reserve supply projections were too low and reserves would be injected. The official explanation, then, is that the federal funds rate triggers open market operations.

The problem is that it is difficult to see how the Desk can distinguish between a change in the funds rate resulting from an error in the forecast of the supply of reserves and a change resulting from an unanticipated change in credit demands or supplies.[14] If the latter is accommodated accidently there is no difference between the pre- and post-October procedures.

Lagged Reserve Accounting

The most serious mechanical problem handicapping the Fed today is the procedure of allowing a two-week lag in determining required reserves. Lagged reserve accounting *(LRA)* was established in 1968 as a public relations measure to keep small member banks from leaving the Federal Reserve System. Under *LRA*, the reserve requirements the banks

---

[12] Milton Friedman, *Newsweek* (July 4, 1980).

[13] Peter Sternlight, "Monetary Policy and Open Market Operations in 1979," *Quarterly Review* (Federal Reserve Bank of New York, Summer, 1980).

[14] For more details on this discussion see A. James Meigs, "The Fed and Financial Markets: Is It Killing Them with Kindness?" *Financial Analysts Journal* (January-February, 1981), pp. 18-26.

must meet each week are based on deposits they held two weeks earlier. If banks decide to make a large volume of loans or to buy securities in a particular week they do not immediately have to acquire reserves to meet a higher requirement that week. A bulge in deposits and the money supply can therefore occur at the initiative of the banks. Two weeks later as banks try to borrow the reserves to meet the increased requirement, federal funds rates rise. Under the pre-October, 1979 interest rate targeting, such a rise was a signal to the manager of the Open Market Account to supply more reserves. Under the post-October, 1979 approach, the Fed still had to accommodate the rise. The Fed could not allow the banking system to be short of reserves—it had to supply sufficient reserves to enable the banking system to meet its reserve requirements. If the Desk held down the supply of nonborrowed reserves, the banks could meet the rest of their requirements through borrowing from the regional Federal Reserve Banks.

The story would be different under contemporaneous reserve accounting (CRA). (CRA would require financial institutions to keep reserves based on contemporaneous deposits, whereas LRA requires reserves based on the deposits of two weeks prior.) Banks making loans or investments according to CRA would start seeking reserves in the federal funds market or by bidding for certificates of deposit (CDs). That would put upward pressure on the funds rate, inducing banks elsewhere in the system to sell federal funds rather than make loans on investments. Unless the Desk intervenes to keep the funds rate from rising, the existing stock of total reserves will be redistributed leaving the money supply unchanged. Beginning February 2, 1984, the Fed is switching to CRA.

The Demand for Money

The financial community attempts to outmaneuver the Fed, and individuals alter their behavior in response to Fed policy and economic conditions by holding more or less cash or demand deposits in order to minimize interest rate or purchasing power losses. This rational behavior on the part of the public regarding its demand for money complicates policy making by the Fed.

The implementation of monetary policy would be relatively straightforward if the demand for money was completely stable and predictable—if the financial community did not try to forecast and outmaneuver the Fed. Suppose the income elasticity of demand for money, for example, is one-half. (Income elasticity is the percentage change in money demand that comes from a one percent change in income.) Furthermore, suppose the goal for the annual growth in real GNP is five percent. To accommodate that growth in real GNP without raising interest rates (i.e., keeping M^D equal to M^S) the Fed would have to increase the stock of M-1 by 2.5

percent (i.e., 5 percent times ½). If the target for nominal GNP was 8 percent, 5 percent real and 3 percent inflation, the Fed would have to increase M-1 by 5.5 percent to avoid driving interest rates up. Why? A 3 percent increase in the price level lowers the real stock of money (M/P) by approximately 3 percent or, conversely, raises the demand for nominal balances by 3 percent. In addition, the 5 percent rise in real income means M-1 must rise by 2.5 percent. Overall, then, the Fed would have to increase the stock of M-1 by 5.5 percent.

The world, however, is just not that simple. Money demand is not a totally predictable element in the economy. The best that we and the Fed can do is to try to understand the demand for money—why individuals and businesses hold a greater or lesser quantity of M-1 or M-2 in various circumstances. And understanding the demand for money means understanding velocity—the speed with which a given stock of money changes hands.

Velocity

Suppose individuals have decided to hold less money, *ceteris paribus*. What does it mean to say that less money is held? How does one go about holding less money? The answer to the first question partially depends on how money is defined. If it is M-1, then to hold less money means individuals have less currency and smaller demand, NOW, or ATS deposit account balances. How can individuals reduce the balances in their accounts if the money supply has not changed? Individuals attempt to reduce their money holdings by purchasing goods and services. Thus, the existing money supply changes hands or is passed from one individual to another more rapidly than was the case previously. This is referred to as an *increase in the velocity of M-1*. Thus, an attempt by the public to hold less money increases the velocity of money.

The *velocity of money* is defined as the ratio of nominal income to the quantity of money balances demanded ($V = PY/M^D$). It is evident in Figure 11-6 that the velocity of money corresponding to the narrow definition of the money supply (M-1) has increased since 1960 while velocities for the broader definitions (M-2 and M-3) have remained nearly constant. This means that the quantity of money demanded, when money is defined as M-1, has fallen relative to GNP. In other words, it has taken less money (M-1) to purchase goods and services. Why? What can account for these developments? To answer these questions we need to look more carefully at what motivates people to hold money balances.

Most people are paid either weekly, biweekly, or monthly. Yet these people must carry out transactions between pay periods. Suppose you are paid $400 every two weeks and have decided to spend $380 and save $20. You do not spend the $380 only when you receive your check. Instead, you spend some of it when you receive your paycheck and keep the rest as

Figure 11-6. Velocities for M-1, M-2, and M-3

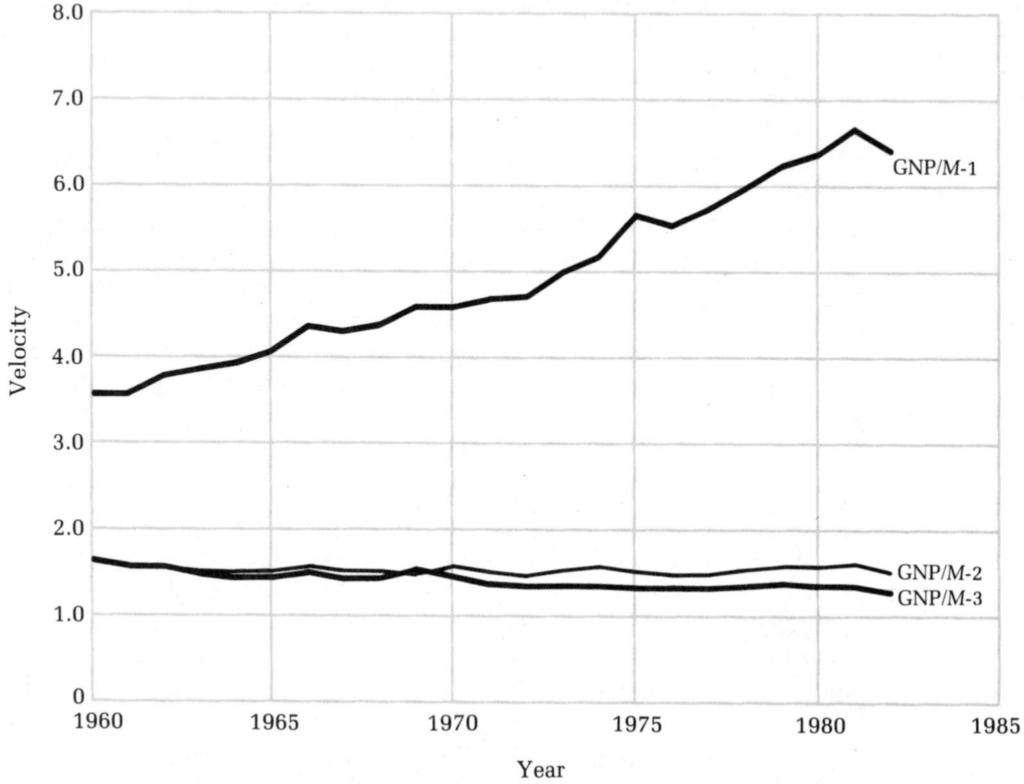

Source: *Economic Report of the President* (1983), Tables B-1 and B-61.

While the velocity for *M*-1 has risen dramatically in the past two decades, that for *M*-2 has risen only slightly and that for *M*-3 has actually declined. The implication of this pattern is that individuals have reduced their relative holdings of transactions balances, attempting to minimize their foregone interest and purchasing power losses.

cash or as a balance in your checking account to make payments throughout the two weeks. You will draw down your stock of money as you make your expenditures throughout the weeks. In other words, the stock of money is serving the role of a stock of inventories. You could have immediately purchased most of the goods you were going to purchase throughout the two weeks and held the stock of goods, but, instead, you held a stock of money. Why? Because the storage and other costs of holding money were less than they would be for holding goods. Similarly, firms will hold money as inventories instead of goods in many cases.

What costs are involved in holding cash or demand deposits? Obviously, the opportunity cost of foregone interest is a major cost. As interest rates rise relative to the rates earned on demand deposits (NOW,

ATS) the opportunity cost of holding cash and demand deposits rises. Hence, we would expect individuals to hold less cash and smaller demand deposit balances as market rates rise. In other words, the demand for money (M-1) depends inversely on the interest rate.

We should also recognize that if transactions were perfectly synchronized with receipts of income (paychecks), the need for cash, demand deposits, ATS, and/or NOW deposits would decrease. Credit cards have enabled individuals to synchronize more closely their receipts and outlays of funds.[15] The emergence of credit card use and the development of the ATS and NOW accounts are important elements in the explanation of the rise in the velocity of M-1. Again note in Figure 11-6 that M-1 velocity has risen much more rapidly than M-2 velocity.

Individuals do not hold money solely to be able to carry out transactions. Money is often considered a relatively safe haven in which an individual may hold assets. An individual with wealth has a choice of many assets in which to hold this wealth. Confronted with a choice of many assets, which will the individual choose? We might be tempted to conclude that that asset with the highest yield would be chosen. But, by choosing only this one asset, the risk of loss or of a small return may be high. Most individuals will diversify their portfolios so as to include some risky, some less risky, and some safe assets. In fact, economic theory can be used to demonstrate that an individual can combine assets with different risks so as to obtain a given return with smaller risk than by choosing just one asset. The desire to obtain the greatest return at the smallest risk comes about because most individuals are risk averse. They need to be paid a premium to take a risk. As a result, they have a demand for safe (nonrisky) assets. They will, therefore, put some of their wealth in the form of the safest asset with the highest return. In many cases this asset is money.[16]

What factors influence the portfolio choice or the asset demand for money? An increase in the return on other assets without a change in their risk will reduce the demand for money. Because the interest that banks and thrift institutions can pay on savings accounts has been limited by the Fed, it has often been the case that the interest rate on other assets rises while that on savings accounts does not.[17] In such cases, money flows from thrift institutions to other assets, a process of disintermediation. Also important to the asset demand for money is wealth. An increase in

---

[15] See Kenneth J. White, "The Effect of Bank Credit Cards on the Household Transactions Demand for Money," *The Journal of Money, Credit and Banking* (February, 1976), pp. 61-62.

[16] For a more detailed explanation, see James Tobin, "Liquidity Preference as Behavior Towards Risk," *Review of Economic Studies* (February, 1958).

[17] This restriction is called Regulation Q. The 1980 Monetary Control Act is phasing out Regulation Q over a period of several years.

an individual's total wealth means that more of every type of asset will be held, including money. Thus, the greater the level of wealth, the greater will be the demand for money. In summary, we would expect the quantity of real money balances demanded to increase as wealth and income increase and to decrease as interest rates increase.

What does this imply for the velocity of money? Suppose we write the demand for money as dependent on the interest rate (r), real wealth (A/P), and real income (Y).

$$M^D = P \cdot L(r, A/P, Y)$$
$$(-)(+)(+)$$

Then velocity is $V = PY/M^D = Y/L^D(r, A/P, R)$. An increase in the interest rate reduces the quantity of real money balances demanded and thus increases velocity, *ceteris paribus*. As the opportunity cost of holding money increases, less is held, but this smaller amount is required to do as much work. An increase in real assets, on the other hand, tends to increase the demand for money and reduce velocity.

Finally, since real income appears in both numerator and denominator of the velocity ratio, what happens to velocity when real income changes? If the income elasticity of the demand for money is less than one, a 1 percent increase in income will raise the quantity of money demanded by less than 1 percent. This means the numerator rises by more than the denominator of the velocity ratio, and, thus, velocity rises. Empirical evidence has found the income elasticity of the demand for money to be near, but generally less than, one.[18] During the period 1979-82 M-1 velocity varied considerably.

In 1979-80, as interest rates rose to very high levels, a new form of savings account was created. This new account, called the *All-Savers account*, provided a tax free rate of interest so that individuals in high tax brackets could earn after tax rates of return on their deposits which would match the opportunities available outside of financial institutions. The result was a fairly large shift of funds from NOW, ATS, and demand deposits to the All-Savers accounts. The demand for M-1 dropped considerably. Conversely, in the FOMC's October, 1982 meeting it was decided that the maturing of the All-Savers certificates would mean an inflow of funds to the M-1 accounts. Hence, the FOMC decided to suspend its scrutiny of M-1 because of the "inevitable distortion" due to the maturing

---

[18] See William Baumol, "The Transactions Demand for Cash: An Inventory Theoretic Approach," *Quarterly Journal of Economics* (November, 1952); James Tobin, "The Interest Elasticity of Transactions Demand for Cash," *Review of Economics and Statistics* (August, 1956); and M. Miller and D. Orr, "A Model of the Demand for Money by Firms," *Quarterly Journal of Economics* (August, 1966), pp. 513-535.

of the All-Savers certificates and the introduction of new money market accounts.

Switching funds from those measured as M-1 to those counted as part of M-2 or M-3 has at least one major implication for monetary policy. Economists who assert that the Fed should return to an interest rate strategy, ask, Which aggregate should the Fed watch? what if the demand for M-1 falls while the demand for M-2 rises? should the Fed watch one of these and, if so, which one? The FOMC is, itself, uncertain of the answers to these questions, and this uncertainty fuels the flames of debate over monetary policy.[19] We will return to this debate in later chapters.

Inflation, Expectations, and the Demand for Money

With an expected inflation rate near 10 percent and savings accounts restricted by Regulation Q to yield no more than 5.5 percent, any money left in saving accounts will lose value. Thus, anticipation of inflation increases velocity as people more carefully manage their cash balances. The higher opportunity cost of money makes it relatively more worthwhile to spend time planning how much and in what form wealth should be held.[20]

The anticipation of inflation will induce individuals to reduce their real money balances and will be reflected in increased nominal interest rates. What are the implications for the economy as a whole? Suppose the economy is characterized by rational expectations but information is not costlessly available. Hence, the short-run aggregate supply curve is upward sloping. If the Fed increases the money supply, the economy may experience a temporary increase in real income but will eventually find that prices have risen in the same proportion by which the money stock rose. Recall from Chapter 8 that the length of the temporary real output effect depends on the way in which expectations are formed.

The price rise leads individuals to attempt to reduce their quantity of real money balances demanded. But for this to occur, the quantity of the real money supply must decrease. Since the quantity of nominal money is

---

[19] *Wall Street Journal* (November 22, 1982), p. 18. The FOMC's uncertainty was emphasized at the Federal Reserve Bank of San Francisco Academic Conference, October, 1982.

[20] Phillip Cagan studied the German hyperinflation of 1921-1923. See his "The Monetary Dynamics of Inflation," in *Studies in the Quantity Theory of Money*, Milton Friedman, ed. (Chicago: University of Chicago Press, 1956). Cagan found that money demand decreased rapidly during the period and that velocity increased rapidly. See also Andrew Abel et al., "Money Demand during Hyperinflation," *Journal of Monetary Economics* (5, 1979), pp. 97-104. They found that during the period 1921-1923, in Germany, individuals looked not only at other assets but also at other countries' currencies as places in which to put their wealth. This could explain why countries experiencing high inflation have tended to restrict the amount of money individuals may take out of the country.

increasing, however, the only way the quantity of real money can decrease is for prices to increase more rapidly than the nominal money
supply. Thus, the typical pattern observed in response to a money supply
increase is a temporary output change, a period in which prices rise more
rapidly than the money supply increases and, finally, a period in which
prices rise at the same rate at which the money supply increases. Notice
also that as prices rise, the nominal interest rate rises, and, as a result, we
observe both a rising money supply and rising interest rates.

1979-1982: The Credibility Effect

We might consider the situation where information is freely available—people know what the Fed does, when the Fed does it, and what
effect the Fed's actions will have—and where expectations are rational. In
this case the short-run aggregate supply curve would be vertical, and
policy actions would have no temporary output effects. For example, if
the Fed increases the money supply, individuals will try to divest themselves of money because they anticipate a price rise; that is, they reduce
the quantity of real money balances demanded. As velocity rises, *ceteris
paribus*, prices must rise. Immediately, not after some period of time
during which real income has risen, prices rise. The only effect of the
money supply increase in this case has been to drive up prices.

In the case just outlined we could say that policy is totally *credible*.
Whatever action the Fed undertakes, its policies will be known and,
therefore, will be believable or credible. Whatever announcements the
Fed makes regarding policy will be known to be true or false.

On the other hand, when information is not costlessly available it is
possible for Fed actions to go generally unnoticed until the effects are felt.
Moreover, it is likely that Fed announcements of its goals or objectives
will be believed when they should not be or not believed when they
should be. In these cases, Fed policy is *not credible*.

In October, 1979, the Fed announced a change in its operating procedure as an attempt to better control the money supply and fight inflation.
Irrespective of the often stated objective of fighting inflation, the Fed
continued to expand the money supply leading to more inflation. This
occurred throughout the period 1978-1981 leading to a great deal of
skepticism on the part of the public regarding Fed intentions. As a consequence of the Fed's lack of credibility, when inflation did begin to
decline rapidly in 1982, the public kept anticipating a weakening of
resolve by the Fed, an expansionary monetary policy, and a return to high
inflation. The result was the record high interest rates of January-July,
1982. The fears that government deficits would force the Fed to monetize
(purchase) the debt kept nominal interest rates high, and as inflation

dropped, the resulting high interest rates forced business to cut back on capital spending all of which drove the economy into a severe recession. In other words, the Fed's lack of credibility forced it to undertake a much larger, and probably more severe, contractionary policy than would have been necessary had policy been credible.

As we shall discuss in a great deal of detail in the following chapters, several economic schools of thought have proposed solutions to the Fed's credibility problem. Monetarists and rational expectationists have argued for a policy rule whereby the money supply would grow by some fixed percentage year after year. Others, such as the supply-siders, have asserted that a return to the gold standard is the only possible solution.

Other economists have called for a congressional override of Fed policy, while still others have argued for a much more powerful and independent Fed, one which would have the power to fine-tune the economy. In the following chapters we will examine these proposals and their implications.

Summary

In this chapter we discovered that the determination of the money supply involves the interaction of the public, the depository institutions, and the Federal Reserve System. We noted that the Fed has only limited control over the money multiplier since the value of the money multiplier depends on the behavior of the public and financial institutions. We found that the money multiplier tended to rise as interest rates rose. In other words, rather than being exogenous, the quantity of money supplied depends on the interest rate.[21] Additionally, we found that the use of the federal funds rate to implement monetary policy has tended to result in a positive relationship between interest rates and the quantity of money supplied. On the demand side of the money market, we discovered that the velocity of money or, conversely, the quantity of money demanded, depends on interest rates, real wealth, and real income and that the velocity of M-1 has steadily risen since 1960. Regarding the implementation of monetary policy we observed that until October, 1979, the Fed had focused on controlling interest rates (the federal funds rate) rather than the monetary aggregates. This approach resulted in the actual money supply being consistently outside of the Fed's target ranges. Beginning October 6, 1979, the Fed purportedly gave up the interest rate approach and began a monetary aggregates approach to implementing monetary policy. A 3.2 percent growth rate of M-1 in October and November, 1979,

---

[21] With the supply of money depending on the interest rate, the derivation of the LM curve is altered slightly. Its slope now depends on how sensitive both the demand for and supply of money are to the interest rate.

was taken as evidence that the Fed was living up to its October 6 announcement. However, when monetary growth accelerated to 7.5 percent during the period from November, 1979, to February, 1980, the financial community suspected that the Fed had reverted to its old habits. Coupled with President Carter's January, 1980 budget, the accelerated monetary growth stimulated expectations of more double digit inflation. The Fed then reacted by slamming the brakes on money growth. M-1 declined by 5 percent from February to May, 1980, a rate substantially below the FOMC's target ranges. Then in the latter months of 1982, the Fed began allowing monetary growth substantially above target ranges.

Does this mean the Fed has abandoned the October 6 promise or that it is simply unable to forecast the value of the money multiplier sufficiently well to be able to keep monetary growth in the FOMC's target ranges? What does this recent history mean for the economy? Do the wide swings in monetary growth imply that monetary policy is being implemented incorrectly? Is there a better approach? We will attempt to answer these questions in the following chapters.

Summary of Aggregate Demand Extensions

In the past three chapters, we have extended the demand side of our model. Let us recap the main features of our discussion of demand.

1. Consumption and investment decisions are made by households and businesses looking at economic developments expected to be long-lived. Temporary or short-lived economic events have only very little, if any, effect.
2. Consumption depends on the level of real income and real wealth. As a result, alterations in the stock of money and changes in interest rates affect consumption. In other words, monetary changes will affect the *IS* curve as well as the *LM* curve.
3. Investment depends on financial and real variables; that is, on interest rates as well as on expected or permanent real sales or real income. In addition, fiscal policy variables such as tax credits and depreciation guidelines influence investment.
4. While we have discovered that consumption and investment are more stable than we had previously thought, we noted that the length of time it takes consumption and investment to completely respond to economic events is uncertain and the actual size of the response is not perfectly predictable.
5. The quantity of money demanded depends on interest rates, real wealth, and real income. Several recent developments have influenced the demand for money. These include the emergence of ATS and NOW accounts.
6. The control of the supply of money is much less certain than we had previously thought. The actual stock of money depends not only on the Fed, but also on the profit maximizing behavior of banks and other

financial institutions in determining the amount of excess reserves to hold and the choice by individuals as to how much cash to hold. These decisions influence the size of the money multiplier. In addition, the variation in the relative amounts of excess reserves and cash held causes variations in the money multiplier which, in turn, causes more difficulty for the Fed in controlling the money supply.

7. The extensive use of federal funds and RPs (and other sources of funds such as Eurodollars) has created even more difficulty for the Fed in its attempt to control the money supply. Coupled with these sources of funds, the Fed has been losing membership. The Monetary Control Act of 1980 was, partly, an attempt to give the Fed more control over the money supply, however defined.

8. Finally, we have noted throughout these last several chapters the important role that expectations play in the demand side of the economy. For economic developments to influence demand they must be expected to be long-lived. Inflationary expectations will influence the holdings of cash balances and, thus, the expenditures for consumption and investment. Expectations of policy changes will influence an individual's desire to hold cash balances and, thus, to make expenditures.

PROBLEMS AND EXERCISES

1. Suppose the Fed announces that next month it will increase the money supply at a much more rapid rate than it has done in the past. If everyone believes the Fed, what will occur today? If the Fed does not follow through on its promise, what occurs?

2. Why are there so many definitions of the money supply?

3. If the elasticity of the demand for money is 0.8, what rate of money supply growth should the Fed strive for, given that the capacity of the economy grows 4 percent per year?

4. Explain why the Fed is concerned with the value of the money multiplier.

5. Suppose some financial innovation takes place that induces individuals to drastically reduce the amount of currency they hold. What is the short-run effect? The long-run effect?

6. What does an increase in the federal funds rate mean?

7. Compare the money multiplier when reserve requirements are required on federal funds and when they are not. Hint: high-powered money (i.e., H) = $R + D$. Where $R = FF + O$, FF = federal funds, and O = other items. Thus, $H = FF + O + D$.

8. Visit a library and find a current issue of the *Federal Reserve Bulletin*. Look at the report of the FOMC meeting and find the short- and long-term targets.

9. In this chapter, a discussion was presented about how the Fed can be manipulated by expectations of the public into expanding the money supply when a decrease was deemed the correct stance. If the Fed was carrying out a monetary aggregates' strategy (controlling the money supply), would it be as susceptible to the public's expectations as when it carries out an interest rate strategy?

10. The strict classical quantity theory of money asserted that velocity was constant over, at least, the short-run. The modern quantity theory, on the other hand, allowed velocity to vary. Which version seems more appropriate? Why? What variables does velocity depend on?

11. What if any, is the relationship between the money multiplier and the velocity of money? Why does the Fed worry about the values of these two variables?

SUGGESTED READINGS

For an overview of Fed decisionmaking, see

"The Fed's Plan for Economic Recovery," *Business Week* (December 13, 1982), pp. 90-97.

"A Fed Watcher's Guide," *Money* (December, 1981), pp. 77.

Raymond Lombra and Michael Moran, "Policy Advice and Policymaking at the Federal Reserve," *Journal of Monetary Economics* (Autumn, 1980), pp. 9-68.

Various issues relating to the money supply process and the Fed's operating procedures are discussed in

Daniel Thornton, "The Simple Analytics of the Money Supply Process and Money Control," *Review* (Federal Reserve Bank of St. Louis, October, 1982), pp. 22-39.

"The Role of Operating Guides in U.S. Monetary Policy: A Historical Review," *Federal Reserve Bulletin* (September, 1979).

James Meigs, "The Fed and Financial Markets: Is It Killing Them with Kindness?" *Financial Analysts Journal* (January-February, 1981), pp. 18-26.

James Boughton, "Money and Its Substitutes," *Journal of Monetary Economics* (November, 1981), pp. 375-386.

The voluminous literature on the demand for money is ably reviewed in

David Laidler, *The Demand for Money: Theories and Evidence*, 2d ed. (New York: Harper & Row, 1977).

J. Judd and J. Scadding, "The Search for a Stable Money Demand Function: A Survey of the Post-1973 Literature," *Journal of Economic Literature* (September, 1982), pp. 993-1023.

The Fed's credibility problem is discussed in

"What the Fed Says Is Not What It Does," *Business Week* (June 7, 1982), p. 29.

"The Fed's New Credibility is a Mixed Blessing," *Business Week* (February 15, 1982), p. 41.

Virtually any issue of the Wall Street Journal, Business Week, Fortune or Forbes contains accounts of the effects of financial innovations in response to deregulation of the financial services industry. For example,

"Cash Management Accounts Proliferating as Banks, Brokers Vie for People's Money," *Wall Street Journal* (November 15, 1982), p. 27

A very complete overview of the Depository Institutions Deregulation and Monetary Control Act of 1980 is provided in

Thomas Cargill and Gillian Garcia, *Financial Deregulation and Monetary Control* (Stanford, Calif.: Hoover Institution Press, 1982).

For a review of bank procedures and Fed policy, see

Martin Mayer, *The Bankers* (New York: Ballentine Books, Inc., 1980).
Richard Friedman and William Roberts, "The Carry Forward Provision and the Management of Bank Reserves," *Journal of Finance* (June, 1983).

Interest rates, expectations, and Fed policy are discussed in

Giorgio Camello and Neil Garston, "Money, Expectations and Interest Rates," *Journal of Macroeconomics* (Fall, 1981), pp. 517-530.
Douglas Mitchell, "The Relation between Alternative Choices of Monetary Tool and Information Variable," *Journal of Macroeconomics* (Summer, 1980), pp. 247-256.

_APPENDIX. Proposals to Reduce Federal Reserve System Independence————————————————————

As of early 1983, there were at least eight proposals under consideration in Congress to reduce the independence of the Federal Reserve System from congressional authority. The following are brief summaries of these proposals:

1. There are resolutions that are attached to the House and Senate budget resolution. These call for the FOMC to reassess its targets for 1982 in view of the Congress's steps "to restore fiscal responsibility and reduce prospective deficits in a substantial and permanent way."
2. S 2807, the Balanced Monetary Policy Act of 1982 was submitted by Senator Robert Byrd (D-W. Va.) and cosponsored by thirty Senate Democrats, including Cranston (Calif.), Inouye and Matsunaga (Hawaii), DeConcini (Ariz.), Cannon (Nev.), and Jackson (Wash.). S 2807 would amend Section 2A of the Federal Reserve Act to require the Fed to establish "yearly targets for positive real short-term interest rates consistent with historic levels . . . and sustained economic growth and stable prices," as well as set annual targets for the monetary and credit aggregates consistent with the interest rate targets. A similarly named HR 6967 was authored by House Banking Committee chairman St. Germain (D-R. I.) and cosponsored by sixty House Democrats. It would require the Board and the FOMC to establish targets for long-term interest rates as well as for the monetary and credit aggregates, and would also require the president to state the administration's position on every vote of the FOMC. Both bills also would require the Board to report semiannually on the relationship of its targets to the goals stipulated by the president in his *Economic Report* and "to any short-term goals approved by the Congress."
3. S 2726, the Interest Rate Reduction Act (Sasser, D-Tenn.), would mandate the Fed to raise the growth range of M-1 to 9 to 10 percent for 1982 (from 2½ to 5½ percent), and to 6 to 8 percent for 1983.
4. Various bills and resolutions call for Chairman Volcker's resignation and/or impeachment; for example, HR 226 (Gonzales, D-Tex.).
5. HR 733, the Federal Reserve Modernization Act (Reuss, D-Wis.), and HR 4024 (Mottl, D-Ohio) would amend the Federal Reserve Act to eliminate the FOMC and vest its powers in the Board of Governors.
6. S 1609 (Pressler, R-S. Dak.) would amend the Federal Reserve Act to reduce the term of the Board of Governors from 14 to 7 years, make two members of Congress ex *officio* Board members, and require that one governor represent agriculture and another small business.
7. S 1691, the Federal Reserve Amendments Act (Hawkins, R-Fla.), proposes that the term of Board members be reduced to 5 years, that the terms of the chairman and vice-chairman be made coterminous with that of the president, and that the Fed be subject to the appropriations process. S 2147, The Federal Reserve System Reform Act (Cranston, D-Calif.), and HR 6639, the Monetary Policy Reform Act (Patterson, D-Calif.), would both provide for coterminous terms of the chairman and vice-chairman with that of the president, shorten other governors' terms to 7 years, place the Treasury Secretary back on the Board, and

subject the Fed to the appropriations process. Senator Cranston states that his bill is explicitly intended to give the Congress and the executive greater responsibility over the actions of the Federal Reserve by "abolishing the Fed as an independent agency and making it part of the Treasury Department."

8. HR 2322 was introduced by Congressman Ron Paul (R-Tex.) last year and was recently endorsed by Congressman Norman Shumway (R-Calif.). The bill would "authorize and direct the General Accounting office to audit the Federal Reserve Board, the Federal Advisory Council, the Federal Open Market Committee and Federal Reserve banks and their branches." In his recent endorsement of the bill, Congressman Shumway incorrectly asserted that "the Fed is the only government entity exempted from GAO audit."

CHAPTER 12.

Fiscal Policy Issues: Politics, the Budget Process, and the Burden of the Debt

What is prudence in the conduct of every private family can scarce be folly in that of a great kingdom.
    Adam Smith, The Wealth
    of Nations, 1776

WHAT TO EXPECT

Economic policy is not a recipe made up of equal parts of economic analysis and politics. Politics has the greater share. The most politically conceived economic policy instrument is the federal government budget. In it, the allocation of spending is spelled out and the resulting budget deficit or surplus created. In this chapter the process of creating a budget statement is discussed. In addition, the effects of budgetary deficits and the cumulative debt are examined. Topics to be discussed are

- *The delays in implementing the fiscal policy*

- *The sources and uses of funds collected by the federal government*

- *The uncontrollable nature of government spending*

- *The crowding out effect*

Introduction: The Politics of Economic Policymaking

Economic policy is not formulated or carried out free of political influence, even in a democracy. It emerges from a political process, a process in which politicians look at alternative policies more for what they mean for their constituents and thereby their own chances of election (or reelection) than for the actual impact on the economy. Yet textbooks typically present the policymaker as being like a plumber who is able to turn this or that valve to adjust water pressure.

One of the basic tenets of economics is that individuals act in their own self-interest. A congressman wants to get reelected; a president wants to be reelected or to see his party remain in power; an economic adviser wants to see the people he or she advises continue holding office. Economic policies will be implemented because politicians believe these policies are what their constituents desire. This means that economic policies are seldom implemented in the forms they were originally proposed or in the manner that textbook economics say is best.

In this chapter we will discuss the process by which the budget of the United States government evolves into its final form.[1] This discussion includes an institutional description of economic policymaking, a review

---

[1]It is important to realize that the government sector in macroeconomic models consists of federal, state, and local governments. Throughout this chapter, we will be discussing only the federal government, its budget, and its budget deficits. This is because only

of the facts about the resulting budget, and an examination of the question of whether the national debt that results from repeated deficits is actually a burden on society.

The Budgetary Process in the United States

Over the past three and a half decades, the cornerstone of economic policymaking in the United States has been the Employment Act of 1946. This act established the Council of Economic Advisers (CEA) to advise the president on economic matters, required the president to submit an annual report to Congress, and required Congress, through the Joint Economic Committee, to review the president's report. The act stated that

> It is the continuing policy and responsibility of the Federal Government to use all practical means consistent with its needs and obligations and other essential considerations of national policy—to coordinate and utilize all its plans, functions, and resources for the purpose of creating and maintaining, in a manner calculated to foster and promote free competitive enterprise and the general conditions under which there will be afforded useful employment opportunities, including self-employment for those able, willing, and seeking to work, and to promote maximum employment, production and purchasing power.

The Employment Act of 1946 was amended by the Congressional Budget and Impoundment Control Act of 1974. This act requires Congress to begin its role in the budget process by setting expenditure goals for each major category along with recommendations for necessary tax changes by May 15 of each year.

Significant changes in the economic policymaking process were made when the Full Employment and Balanced Growth Act of 1978 was passed. This act, also known as the Humphrey–Hawkins Bill, requires that economic policy be designed to achieve specific, flexible, short- and long-term numerical goals for economic performance.[2] In addition, a framework for policy formulation involving the president, the Congress, and the Federal Reserve Board was set up. Furthermore, an economic policy time schedule was included in the act. This schedule is presented in Table 12-1.[3]

---

the federal government's budget can be used as a tool for economic stabilization. Most state and local governments are forbidden by law from running budget deficits. In 1982, for example, state and local governments ran a budget surplus of $31.9 billion at the same time that the federal government was running a deficit of $147.9 billion.

[2]The statutory numerical goals were (1) 3 percent or less unemployment among adults by 1983, (2) 4 percent or less unemployment overall by 1983, and (3) 3 percent or less rate of inflation by 1983.

[3]A description of changes in policymaking under the Humphrey-Hawkins Bill can be found in Steven M. Roberts, "Economic Policymaking in the United States," *Journal of Economic Dynamics and Control* (August, 1979).

Table 12-1.   Economic Policy Timetable

JANUARY	The *President* issues his Economic Report containing numerical goals for employment, unemployment, production, real income, productivity and prices during each of the next five years. Report due within the first 20 days of the new Congressional session.
FEBRUARY	The *Joint Economic Committee* holds hearings on the President's Economic Report including review of the short-term and medium-term numerical goals.
	The *Federal Reserve Board* issues a report by the 20th to the Banking Committees of the Congress on its monetary policy plans for the calendar year and their relationship to the short-term goals of the President.
	The *Banking Committees* hold hearings on the Federal Reserve's monetary policy report.
MARCH	The *Joint Economic Committee* issues its report on the President's Economic Report, including its views and recommendations with respect to the short- and medium-term numerical goals, to the Budget Committees by the 15th of the month.
	The *Banking Committees* issue a report to their respective bodies on the Federal Reserve's intended monetary policies, including their views and recommendations.
APRIL	The *Budget Committees* report out the first concurrent resolution on the Budget for the fiscal year beginning on October 1. The resolution may include short- and medium-term economic goals.
MAY	The *House* and *Senate* debate the first budget resolution, limited to four hours on economic goals, policies and possible changes in the short- and medium-term goals. Action to be completed by the 15th.
JULY	The *Federal Reserve Board* issues a report by the 20th to the Banking Committees on its monetary policy plans for the remainder of the year and for the next year, and their relationship to the numerical economic goals of the President.
AUGUST	The *Banking Committees* issue a report on the monetary policy plan of the Federal Reserve, including views and recommendations.
SEPTEMBER	By the 1st the *Budget Committees* report out the second concurrent resolution on the budget.
	By the 15th the *House* and *Senate* complete action on the budget resolution.
OCTOBER	Fiscal year begins.

Source: Steven M. Roberts, "Economic Policymaking in the United States," *Journal of Economic Dynamics and Control* (August, 1979).

The budget is the result of a process that includes the executive and legislative branches of government. The process begins each January when the president sends his budget recommendations for the following fiscal year, which runs from October 1 through September 30, to Congress.

The budget proposal normally runs over 1,000 pages and is the result of many months of preparatory work. The Treasury, the CEA, and the Office of Management and Budget (OMB) contribute to the development of this document.

After Congress receives the budget document, subcommittees of the House of Representatives' Appropriations Committee hold hearings on various components. As a result, recommendations with revisions are sent to the full Appropriations Committee, and eventually to the House of Representatives for action. Once the House passes a version of the budget, the Senate considers it. As with the House, the Senate sends the bill first to subcommittees, then to full committees, and finally the entire Senate. If the Senate passes a budget identical to that passed by the House, the bill is sent to the president. If the Senate passes a budget that differs from the House's version, the bill must go to a joint conference committee. When both the Senate and the House of Representatives agree on a budget, the bill is sent to the president. The president can either sign the bill, veto the bill, or allow it to become law without approval.

Once a budget bill becomes law, appropriation warrants are issued to the various government agencies. These warrants represent the approved appropriations that the agencies must follow. The U.S. Treasury issues the checks for the appropriations.[4]

Tax policy is formulated in much the same manner and is, in fact, an integral part of the budget process. Tax changes must originate in the House, go through committees, the Senate, and finally, to the president.

The state of the budget, whether it is in surplus or deficit, depends on the actions taken by the president, the House, and the Senate, as well as on the state of the economy. For example, when the economy dips into recession, tax revenues decline and expenditures automatically increase to cover unemployment and welfare programs, and conversely for expansionary periods.

Deficits and Surpluses

Before the 1960s, deficits occurred only in wartime—the 1940-1945 and the 1952-1954 periods. Since the late 1950s, as Figure 12-1 shows, the budget has been in deficit virtually every year. Moreover, these deficits have increased dramatically since the 1960s.

Professors James Buchanan and Richard Wagner have explained this trend as a consequence of the interaction of macroeconomics and poli-

---

[4] A very interesting discussion of the budgetary process is presented in George Schultz and Kenneth Dam, *Economic Policy beyond the Headlines* (New York: W. W. Norton & Co., Inc., 1977).

Figure 12-1. The High-Employment Surplus and Federal Budget Deficits

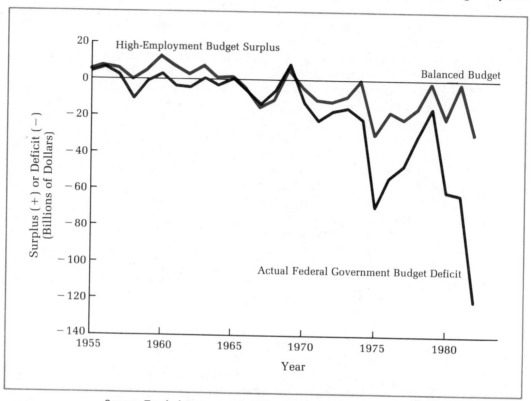

Source: Frank deLeeuw et al., "The High-Employment Budget: Revised Estimates and Automatic Inflation Effects," *Survey of Current Business* (April, 1982), pp. 21-33.

Before the 1960s deficits rarely occurred except in wartime years. Since the late 1960s deficits have been a common occurrence, and the size of the deficits has almost consistently been growing.

tics.[5] They claim that it was the acceptance of Keynesian theories by policymakers and politicians that stimulated the growth of deficits. Prior to the acceptance of Keynesian ideas, a clear set of rules guided fiscal choice. These rules were based on the principle that public finance and private finance are analogous. This meant that government expenditures should be limited by tax revenue just as households' expenditures should be limited by their income. Households cannot run deficits year after year. C. F. Bastable, one of the leading public finance scholars of the late nineteenth and early twentieth centuries, succinctly summarized this view on the relationship between government expenditures and revenues by stating that

---

[5]James M. Buchanan and Richard E. Wagner, *Democracy in Deficit: The Political Legacy of Lord Keynes* (New York: Academic Press, Inc., 1977).

there ought to be a balance between these two sides of financial activity. Outlay should not exceed income . . . tax revenue should be kept up to the amount required to defray expenses.[6]

Keynes criticized the idea that the government budget must be balanced, arguing for deficits during recession and surpluses during expansions. Once accepted, this Keynesian prescription became abused. Deficit spending, no matter the state of the economy, became acceptable. According to Buchanan and Wagner, the reason for this change is quite obvious. In general, expenditure programs result in additional political support while taxes reduce political support. Predictably, politicians responded by generating budget deficits as a normal course of events.

Why would politicians continue to create deficits, and why do voters support politicians who behave irresponsibly in a fiscal sense? In a democracy, political competition is not unlike market competition. Politicians compete among themselves for the support of the electorate, and they do so by offering policies and programs that they feel will get them elected or reelected. A politician in a democratic society can be viewed as proposing and attempting to enact a combination of expenditure programs and financing schemes that secures her or him the support of a majority of the electorate. A candidate gets elected by forming enough coalitions out of different interest groups to gain a plurality.

The candidate therefore offers a series of programs, one for this group of constituents, another for that group, and so on, rather than offering one general philosophy. Environmentalists support a particular candidate because of the candidate's plan to control auto emissions while the teamsters support him for his stand against hauling in both directions. This, even though environmentalists may disagree with the trucking stand, and truckers may disagree with the enviromentalist stand. Even after he is elected, the congressman gets his programs passed into law by trading votes, agreeing to support some other legislator's pet projects in return for support for his. All of this is done with very little consideration for the effects of these programs on the economy.

Why was it not until the mid-1960s that large deficits occurred year after year? After all, political institutions, the appeal to constituent groups, and vote trading have existed in the United States since 1776. The answer given to this question is that the acceptance of Keynesian ideas by politicians and the general voting public is often dated from the onset of the 1960s. But the fault does not lie with Keynes himself. Keynes was operating under the supposition that economic policy was made and should be made by a benevolent dictator, or policymaker, or a group of

---

[6]C. F. Bastable, *Public Finance*, 3d ed. (New York: The Macmillian Co., 1903), p. 611.

enlightened men. Keynes did not think about the application of his policy in what we would call a democratic setting. Instead his benevolent dictator would tend to act in accordance with the public interest, even when this might run counter to political pressures.

In the combined economic and political environment Keynes envisioned, there could be little or no question raised about the application of the Keynesian policy instruments. In order to secure a stable, prosperous economy, expenditures would be expanded and contracted symmetrically. Budget deficits would be created during periods of sluggish economic activity and surpluses would be created as the pace of economic activity accelerated. There would be no political pressures operating to avoid surpluses and lead to deficits that would be disproportionately large or ill timed.

Futhermore, the underlying model of the national economy in Keynes's analysis is one that must deal with depression. It is an economy in which policy induced shifts in aggregate demand can increase real output and employment without any effects on price levels. In addition, the economy might be characterized by an excess of monetary liquidity—the liquidity trap. Therefore, economic policy that aims at increasing liquidity through increases in the supply of money alone is ineffective. The policy implication is clear and simple. Demand may be increased only by increased spending, and this can be accomplished only if government increases its rate of outlays relative to its rate of revenue withdrawal from the economy. Deficit creation by government offers the only available means of increasing output and employment. The budget deficit may be financed either by money creation or by the issue of public debt instruments. Ideally, money creation is preferable, because of the absence of interest payments. However, the means of financing the deficit are unimportant; the critical element is the creation of the deficit and the enhanced rate of total spending in the economy that it facilitates. As a result, Buchanan and Wagner claim, the lifting of the necessity of balanced budgets by Keynesian theory freed legislators from the shackles of not being able to offer their constituents new programs.

Whatever the validity of the Buchanan–Wagner thesis, it is true that deficits have increased over the past two decades. Prior to 1968, major deficits occurred only over the period of 1940 to 1946 and 1952 to 1954—times of world conflict. If our sample was extended significantly back in time, we would find that the primary cause of major sustained deficits has been war. Certainly, deficits occurred in nonwar years, but most of these deficits were the result of business downturns. When the economy improved, surpluses tended to occur. In other words, prior to the late 1960s the federal budget *appeared* to be balanced over the business cycle. Since the late 1960s the federal budget has been in deficit nearly every year, and the size of the deficits has grown.

Budgetary Facts_____

The major sources of budget receipts in the United States (listed in Table 12-2) are individual income taxes, corporate income taxes, and social insurance taxes (i.e., the payroll tax). As a percentage of GNP, tax receipts have increased moderately since 1965. Since corporate profit taxes have fallen as a fraction of GNP, and the ratio of income taxes to GNP has been practically constant, the increase in tax revenues as a percentage of GNP has to be due to the growth of the social insurance tax. Revenue from this tax has increased approximately fourfold over the past decade.

Table 12-2. *Sources of Budget Receipts (Billions of Dollars)*

YEAR	TOTAL RECEIPTS		INDIVIDUAL INCOME TAX	
	RECEIPTS	% GNP	RECEIPTS	% GNP
1965	116.8	16.9	48.7	7.0
1970	193.7	19.5	90.4	9.1
1975	291.0	18.8	122.4	7.9
1980	517.1	19.6	244.1	9.3
1982	617.8	20.2	297.7	9.7

YEAR	CORPORATE INCOME TAX		SOCIAL INSURANCE TAX	
	RECEIPTS	% GNP	RECEIPTS	% GNP
1965	25.5	3.6	17.3	2.5
1970	32.8	3.3	45.3	4.6
1975	40.6	2.6	86.4	5.6
1980	64.6	2.5	157.8	6.0
1982	49.2	1.6	201.5	6.6

Source: *Economic Report of the President* (1983), Table B-72.

In Table 12-3, the major sources of expenditures are presented. As a fraction of GNP, budget outlays have increased from 17 in 1965 to 24 percent in 1982. There is one overriding reason for this increase. It is the tremendous increase in domestic transfer payments. For the purposes at hand, domestic transfer payments are the sum of health, income security, veterans' benefits, and education, training, and Social Security expenditures. In 1965, national defense expenditures accounted for 41.9 percent of expenditures, while domestic transfer payments accounted for 29.9 percent. By 1982, transfer payments were 52.1 percent of expenditures.

Table 12-3. *Sources of Budget Outlays (Billions of Dollars)*

YEAR	TOTAL OUTLAYS		NATIONAL DEFENSE	
	EXPENDITURE	% GNP	EXPENDITURE	% GNP
1965	118.4	17.1	49.6	7.2
1970	196.6	19.8	79.3	8.0
1975	324.6	21.0	85.6	5.6
1980	576.7	29.9	135.9	5.2
1982	728.4	23.8	187.4	6.1

YEAR	DOMESTIC TRANSFER PAYMENTS		INTEREST	
	EXPENDITURE	% GNP	EXPENDITURE	% GNP
1965	35.4	5.1	10.3	1.5
1970	65.7	6.6	18.3	1.8
1975	172.5	11.1	31.0	2.0
1980	310.3	11.8	52.5	2.0
1982	379.8	12.4	84.7	2.8

Source: *Economic Report of the President* (1983), Table B-72.

For the same year national defense had decreased to 25.7 percent of total expenditures.

The Uncontrollable Budget

During Jimmy Carter's 1976 presidential campaign, he promised to produce a balanced budget by the end of his term. Yet, Carter's budget aimed for a $27.5 billion deficit in the fiscal year ending September 30, 1982. Comparing his budget and his campaign promises Carter lamented that "we have reached a point where uncontrollable spending threatens the effectiveness of the budget as an instrument of discretionary national economic policy."[7] According to President Carter, 75 percent of the budget proposed for fiscal 1982 was uncontrollable. In Figure 12-2 the growth pattern for the uncontrollable portion of the budget since 1974 is presented.

What constitutes *uncontrollable expenditures*? The Carter administration defined the following categories as uncontrollable expenditures: interest on the national debt, funds obligated under contract, social security payments, railroad retirement, federal employees retirement, unemployment compensation, medicare, medicaid, food stamps, and other

---

[7]*Economic Report of the President* (1980).

Figure 12-2. The Uncontrollable Budget

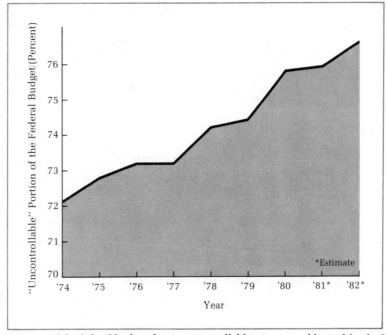

The portion of the federal budget that is uncontrollable—interest, obligated funds, Social Security, retirement, and other entitlement programs—has been growing rapidly throughout the 1980s.

programs that entitle qualified individuals to government payments. The interest on the debt has moved into third place in total outlays. Defense is first, Social Security second, and other transfer payments, health, and interest run a close race for third. These outlays are uncontrollable for a variety of reasons, but perhaps the primary one is that most of these programs are indexed—payment increases automatically as inflation rises. As an indication of the cost involved due to indexation, the Carter administration estimated that should the inflation rate be one percentage point higher than projected, outlays would automatically increase by $6 billion.

Why was the budget allowed to become uncontrollable? The reason is really quite obvious. If you are a representative, senator, or even president and want to make sure a program your constituents greatly desire is not trimmed back or cut out entirely, you will try to get the program funded without having to be reviewed each year. You will set up the program so that if anyone meets the qualifications then payment is automatic. This is called an *entitlement program*. For example, if someone is 65 or if someone under 18 years of age is the survivor of a Social Security recipient, then that person receives payment automatically. In fact, while over 70 percent of the budget is uncontrollable, over 40 percent becomes effective without any congressional review.

Social Security is an extremely good example of uncontrollable spending. The constituents opposed to cuts in Social Security are vocal and form a powerful voting group. Hence, even during the early Reagan years when David Stockman, Reagan's Budget Director, was scurrying around looking for ways to cut spending, Social Security was considered untouchable.

Off Budget

An even more drastic way to insulate a program is to take it out of the budget entirely. For example, the U. S. Railway Association, the Pension Guaranty Corporation, the Federal Financing Bank, the Post Office, and others are off budget institutions. Total outlays for off budget programs have grown tremendously—they reached over $17 billion in fiscal 1982, as shown in Table 12-4. Off budget federal programs are federally owned

Table 12-4. *Outlays for the Budget, Off Budget Federal Entities, and Government Sponsored Enterprises (Billions of Dollars)*

| | FEDERAL GOVERNMENT | | | GOVERNMENT SPONSORED ENTERPRISES[b] |
| | BUDGET | OFF BUDGET FEDERAL ENTITIES[b] | TOTAL | |
FISCAL YEAR[a]				
1969	184.5	. . .	184.5	4.3
1970	196.6	. . .	196.6	9.6
1971	211.4	. . .	211.4	c
1972	232.0	. . .	232.0	4.4
1973	247.1	0.1	247.1	11.4
1974	269.6	1.4	271.1	14.5
1975	326.2	8.1	334.2	7.0
1976	366.4	7.3	373.7	4.6
1977	402.7	8.7	411.4	10.2
1978	450.8	10.3	461.2	12.7
1979	491.0	12.5	503.5	12.3
1980	576.7	14.2	590.9	19.3
1981	576.7	21.0	597.7	21.4
1982	728.4	17.3	745.7	22.3

Source: *The Budget of the United States Government, Fiscal Year 1984*, p. 313.

[a]Ending June 30 for 1969–76 and September 30 for 1977–79.

[b]The off budget federal entities and the privately owned, government sponsored enterprises primarily carry out loan programs. To prevent double counting, outlays of government sponsored enterprises exclude loans to other government sponsored enterprises and loans to or from federal agencies and off budget federal entities.

[c]$50 million or less.

in whole or in part. Their transactions belong in the budget under current budget accounting concepts but have been excluded from the budget totals under provision of law. Their expenditures are part of total federal spending but are not reflected in budget totals although Treasury borrowing to finance the outlays does add to the federal debt.

Loan Guarantees

Government guarantees of credit have also grown tremendously in recent years. The provision of guaranteed credit has a history dating back to the Great Depression and the establishment of agencies such as the Federal Housing Administration (FHA). The loan guarantee was originally designed to aid home buyers. The programs were placed on an actuarially sound basis which meant that the present value of revenues met or exceeded the present value of outlays. In the 1960s, however, these guarantees were extended through subsidies to borrowers such as students and low income families. In addition guarantees have been directed at relatively large projects like Lockheed, New York City, and Chrysler. The federal budget lists thirty-one programs and, after adjustment to avoid double counting (for example the guarantee of one program by another program), total guarantees were $240 billion in 1980 and growing rapidly—approaching $300 billion in the early to middle 1980s.

Federal credit provided through guarantees has particular appeal in the political process. Guarantees are regarded by many as virtually costless since subsidy and large venture guarantees show up in the federal budget only if the guarantee is exercised; i.e., only if the borrower defaults. For actuarially sound programs such as FHA insurance, risk of default is covered by insurance premiums. Defaults are never expected to show up in the budget, therefore. Thus, Congress can provide benefits to constituent groups with the appearance of no cost to the government. However, as we shall discuss in the next section, the costlessness of the guarantee programs may be an illusion. The guarantee of private borrowing distorts the market decision on credit allocation.[8]

Deficits and the Economy:
The Burden of the Debt_____

Much like an individual, the federal government spends on goods and services and gains income (in the form of tax revenue). If expenditures exceed tax revenues, the excess spending has to be paid for with borrowed funds. In the United States, the Treasury receives most of the

---

[8]For analysis of this program, see Herbert M. Kaufman, "Loan Guarantees and Crowding Out," CBO Conference on the Economics of Federal Credit (September, 1981).

taxes and makes payments for the government. How does the Treasury borrow funds? By selling securities—notes, bonds, and bills. The securities are purchased by the central bank (the Federal Reserve System—Fed), the public, or by foreigners.

When the Fed purchases the securities, it pays for them by writing a check on itself. Such an action—an *open market operation*—creates additional high–powered money. For this reason, Treasury sales of bonds to the Fed are known as *monetizing the debt.* In financing the deficit through the sale of securities to the public, the amount of high–powered money in the hands of the public does not change. The public simply holds additional Treasury securities. Since the public could purchase the bonds needed to finance the deficit, there is no necessary relationship between the size of the deficit and the change in the money stock. Only if the central bank monetizes the deficit will the stock of high–powered money, and thus the money supply, increase.

Deficit Financing and the Aggregate Demand–Aggregate Supply (*AD-AS*) Model

The impact on the economy of deficit financing is readily apparent once the *AD-AS* model is modified to incorporate government securities. Government securities, like corporate securities, are ingredients of most portfolios. Hence, like private securities, we might introduce government bonds into the model through wealth. Then, changes in the value of government securities are changes in real wealth that cause real consumption spending to change. This implies that, like an increase in the money supply, an increase in the supply of bonds is represented by a rightward shift of the *AD* curve.

With these modifications to the *AD-AS* model, we are ready to examine the effects of alternative methods of financing a government deficit. A complete analysis of this question not only distinguishes between money financing and bond financing, but also between the effects of a temporary deficit and a permanent deficit.

A One-Period Deficit: Monetized

Let us start by considering the case where a temporary (one–year) deficit is financed by borrowing from the central bank. We will also assume throughout the discussion of the relationship between deficits and monetary policy that expectations are adjusted fully to actual price changes by the time the period under consideration has passed. This assumption means that the short-run *AS* curve will shift as expectations adjust and will come to rest at the long-run equilibrium by the time the period under consideration has expired.

Prior to the increase in government spending, the economy is at Point A in Figure 12-3. The increase in government spending to the level G_2 causes the AD curve to shift to the right. The new AD curve is denoted as AD(G_2, M_1). As a result of the shift, both the price and output levels increase. However, the resulting deficit must be financed. If financed through the Fed, the accompanying increase in the money supply gives rise to a further shift in the AD curve. With this demand curve, AD (G_2, M_2), the price and output levels increase even more.

Figure 12-3. A One-Period Monetized Debt

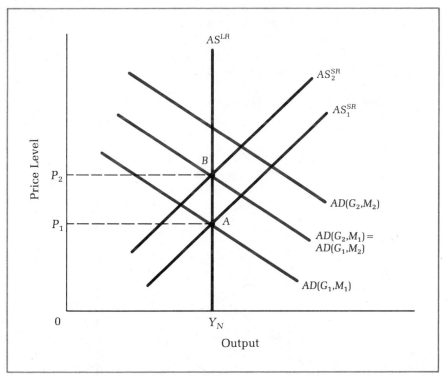

The economy is intially at Point A. An increase in government spending increases AD, as represented by a shift to AD (G_2, M_1). The Fed finances the resulting deficit which increases the money supply to M_2 and the AD curve shifts out to AD (G_2, M_2). Since the spending increase was one period only, G decreases to G_1, and the AD curve shifts back to AD(G_1, M_2). The short-run AS curve shifts up as expectations of price increases change. Once the one-period change is over, the economy comes to rest at Point B.

After one period, the government spending reverts back to its original level while the nominal money supply remains at M_2. The AD curve shifts back to AD (G_1, M_2). When long-run equilibrium is reestablished (Point B), we find that a transitory increase in government spending that is money financed will cause the price level to increase but leave output unaffected.

In other words, a one-time money financed deficit results in a one-time increase in the price level. Notice that if the financing of the deficit had been ignored, we would have concluded that the AD curve would return to its initial position, AD (G_1, M_1). Other than for possible short-run price and output effects, we would conclude that a temporary increase in government spending did nothing to the economy. This example clearly indicates the importance of including the financing issue in any policy analysis.

A Multiperiod Deficit: Monetized

Now, let us consider a permanent increase in government spending that is financed via the central bank. The increase in government expenditures and the accompanying increase in the money supply cause the AD curve to shift from its initial position denoted as AD (G_1, M_1) to AD (G_2, M_2) in the first period. This shift is presented in Figure 12-4. If, as we

Figure 12-4. A Multiperiod Deficit: Monetized

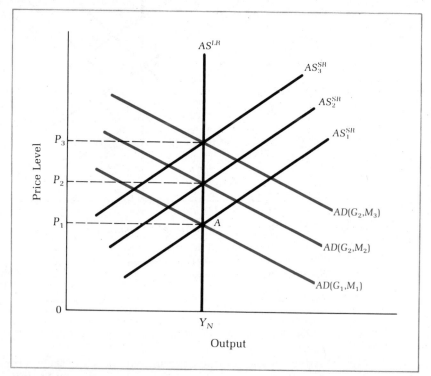

A one-period increase in government spending financed by creating additional money is represented as a shift to AD (G_2, M_2). If the spending takes place each period, additional money must be created each period. The result is a continuous increase in the price level, as shown by the move to AD (G_2, M_2) and then to AD (G_2, M_3). The AD curve will continue to shift out.

assumed in the one-period case, expectations are fully adjusted over this period, then by the end of the period the short-run AS curve will have shifted to AS_2 and any temporary output increase will have disappeared. Of course, prices will have risen to P_2. During the next period, the money supply will be increased once again to finance the deficit that arises from the higher level of government expenditures. As a result, the AD curve shifts to AD (G_2, M_3). With the accompanying shift in the AS curve over this period, we find that at the end of the period the price level will be P_3. Since the money supply will have to increase each period to finance the deficit, the result will be continuous increases in the price level. In this case, a government budget deficit results in inflation.

A One-Period Deficit: Nonmonetized

What are the effects of the deficit when that deficit is not financed by the central bank? Let us start by considering a temporary budget deficit. The combined effect of the increase in government expenditures and the increase in the supply of bonds, which increases wealth, causes the AD curve to shift from $AD(G_1, B_1)$ to $AD(G_2, B_2)$ in Figure 12-5.[9] Given the short-run AS curve AS_1, both prices and output will increase. However, this is a short-run effect. Expectations will adjust. In addition, the increase in government spending will revert to its initial level, G_1. The AD curve shifts back—towards but not all the way—to its initial level, because of the higher stock of bonds in existence. Let this demand curve be denoted as $AD(G_1, B_2)$. When long-run equilibrium is reestablished, the price level will be a higher level (P_2), and the output level will be unchanged. The increase in the stock of bonds means the amount of future interest payments will be increased. If tax revenues are constant, a small budget deficit will occur in future periods. Since these deficits will have to be financed, there will be some minor increases in the AD curve in the future, and thus some future price increases.

If we ignore the interest payments associated with bond financing, can we draw any conclusions concerning the difference between debt and money financing? Both financing methods result in one-time increases in the price level, but the increase in the price level is greater under money financing. The reason is that an increase in the money supply increases aggregate demand both through the wealth effect and by lowering interest rates, whereas the increase in aggregate demand when bond financing is employed is due solely to the wealth effect. Furthermore, the increased supply of bonds (or demand for credit) without a corresponding increase in the money supply drives up the interest rate which crowds out private interest sensitive spending.

---

[9]This result is contingent on the *IS* curve shifting more than the *LM* curve. The *IS* curve shifts due to the increased government spending and increased bond supply while the *LM* curve shifts due to increased bond supply.

Figure 12-5. A One-Period Deficit: Nonmonetized

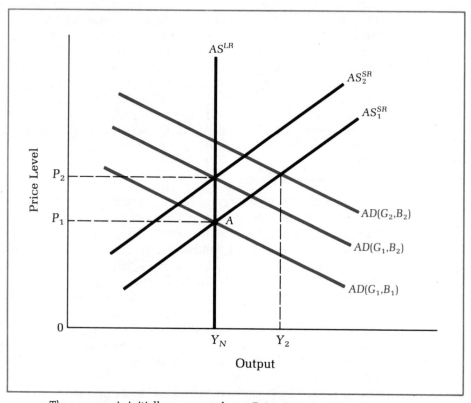

The economy is initially represented as at Point A. An increase in government expenditures is financed by sales of Treasury bonds. This is represented as an outward shift of AD to $AD(G_2, B_2)$. The one-period spending increase means G returns to G_1, but the stock of bonds has been permanently enlarged. As a result, AD shifts back toward its original level. Whether or not it reaches the level depends on whether government bonds are wealth. If people anticipate that their taxes will increase to pay off the new debt, they will not consider Treasury bonds as wealth, and AD will shift to $AD(G_1, B_1)$.

Some economists question whether there is any wealth effect associated with bond financing.[10] It is argued that bonds are nothing more than debt that must be paid off eventually with higher tax payments. If everyone believes government debt will be retired, then individuals will realize that their permanent income will be lower in the future because their tax payments will be higher by the amount that the stock of bonds has increased. As a result, the present value of wealth does not increase and all that government spending does is crowd out private spending.

[10]Robert J. Barro, "Are Government Bonds Net Wealth?" *Journal of Political Economy* (December, 1974).

A Multiperiod Deficit: Nonmonetized

Suppose the economy is at Point A (in Figure 12-6) prior to the permanent change in government spending. Again, recall that we are assuming that price and price expectation changes occur during the period under consideration. In the case of a multiperiod debt, we will assume that the price effects of each period are fully incorporated into the price expectations of that period. This is the same assumption we have been using throughout this discussion. In the first period, the combined increase in government expenditures and the stock of bonds cause the AD curve to shift to AD (G_2, B_2). A new equilibrium is established with a price level of P_2. In contrast to a temporary change in government expenditures,

Figure 12-6. A Multiperiod Deficit: Nonmonetized

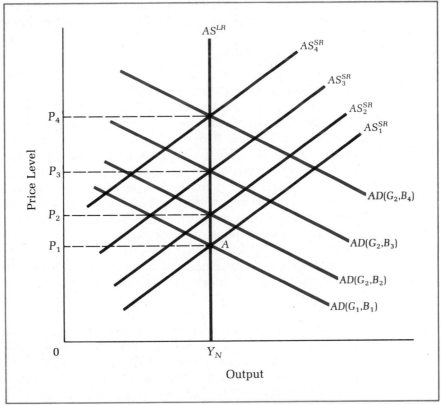

In the first period the combined increase in government expenditures and the stock of bonds is represented by the AD curve shifting to AD (G_2, B_2). In the second, third, and so on periods, the AD curve will continue to shift out. The outward shift will occur only if government bonds are considered wealth. If not, the government spending will drive up interest rates which will actually reduce the real value of assets and shift the AD curve back to its original level.

the stock of bonds must increase each period to finance the permanent increase. In fact, the additional increase in bonds needed to finance the resulting deficit progressively increases due to the increasing interest payments on the government bonds. As can be seen in Figure 12-6 the *AD* curve shifts each period by progressively larger amounts, and the equilibrium price level increases by larger amounts. But this result must be tempered by the realization that interest rates rise unless the deficit is monetized. The permanent deficit drives up the nominal supply of bonds but also drives up the real interest rate. As a result, although the *AD* curve may initially shift to the right, it then shifts (or more correctly shifts and rotates) back to the left as interest rates rise and real wealth decreases. Furthermore, if people have perfect foresight and if they fully discount future tax payments, the permanent deficit, not financed by money supply increases, leads neither to increases in real output nor to inflation. This, of course, would be the view of the monetarists who assert that inflation is everywhere and always a monetary phenomenon.

The 1980-82 Struggle over Deficits

Consider another implication or interpretation of the multiperiod deficit. Let us assume the deficit will occur for a very long time, virtually forever, and everyone knows this. The deficit will then either have to be monetized eventually or else the present value of bonds will be zero and they cannot be sold. If the deficit will not be monetized and everyone knows this, the deficit will grow each period by the interest on the outstanding bonds. Since the number of bonds outstanding will have to be increased each period to pay for the debt, the expectation is that the number of bonds outstanding will become infinite and so their value will be zero. The Treasury will then be unable to sell bonds.

Conversely, suppose the deficit is eventually to be monetized, and everyone knows this. In this case, the longer the monetization is postponed, the greater the amount of money that will have to be printed when the deficit finally is monetized. The result will be an immediate spurt of inflation since individuals will anticipate a large increase in monetary growth.

These results have some implications for the way fiscal and monetary policy were carried out during the 1980-82 period. In 1980 a 3-year series of tax cuts was implemented. At the same time government spending continued to increase and monetary growth was slowed. Very large deficits occurred. In fact the outcome was deficits of over $100 billion a year for several years. Assuming that everyone expected the deficits to occur for several years but to be eventually monetized, inflationary expectations would have been high. This may have been the cause of the very high interest rates even as inflation dropped rapidly in 1981; people expected inflation to reappear, and with a vengeance.

If the story described above is valid, then how should policy have been carried out during 1980-82 in order to slow inflation without a considerable drop in real output? Rather than a tight monetary policy and a loose fiscal policy, a tight fiscal policy and a loose monetary policy would have been the answer. If everyone had expected the Treasury to return to a balanced budget or even a surplus, expectations of extensive monetizing would not have existed, thereby driving inflationary expectations and real interest rates down.

Government Guarantees

The amount of crowding out is not solely a function of the size of the deficit and the amount of monetization. The off budget and guaranteed programs, not part of the deficit, affect the credit markets as well. Guaranteed borowers, in the absence of guarantees, would have to pay a higher cost for funds or would not be able to borrow at all. Thus, the pecking order in the market is altered in favor of guaranteed lending and away from nonguaranteed lending. Further, the additional demand for funds by those guaranteed borrowers (who in the absence of guarantees would not otherwise have been able to obtain credit at all) puts upward pressure on interest rates, implying that at a minimum, nonguaranteed borrowers are in some sense paying for the guarantees through higher interest rates on their borrowing. In fact, to the extent that interest rates rise because of these credit demands, the Treasury itself is paying more for its borrowings—a direct budget cost.

Monetary or Fiscal Policy?

Whenever the government spends more than it takes in, it must borrow by selling securities. If the Fed purchases these securities, the monetary base increases. Is this a monetary or fiscal action? If the Treasury sells securities without Fed monetization, interest rates are driven up. If the Fed is using an interest rate strategy and the federal funds rate begins to rise out of its range, the Fed will purchase securities and drive interest rates down. Is this a monetary or fiscal action? If the Fed is employing a monetary aggregates strategy, the Treasury sells securities and interest rates rise, what occurs? As rates rise, the portions of the money supply not directly controllable by the Fed begin to rise. First, a higher federal funds rate relative to the discount rate induces banks to borrow more from the Fed. Second, the high interest rates attract foreign investors and governments that provide gold and other currencies to buy U. S. securities. This increases bank deposits. Under lagged reserve accounting, banks will have to come up with reserves two weeks later, which puts pressure on the Fed to provide those reserves. Is this a monetary or fiscal action?

The economics profession has not reached a consensus on the answers to these questions. Several economists argue that if the initiator of an action is the Treasury, it is a fiscal action. Others assert that any time monetization occurs it is a monetary action.

The Burden of the Debt

It is often claimed that the debt is a burden on the economy. The counterargument to this claim is that while the deficits have been reaching record levels, until recently they have actually been a declining portion of gross national product, as shown in Figure 12-7. Similarly, while the national debt has been rising over the post-World War II period, it has not risen as rapidly as GNP. Thus, as alarming as the growth of deficits and the national debt might appear, the growth has not been as rapid as the growth of the economy. Which view is correct? Is the debt a burden?

Figure 12-7. Ratios of Federal Government Deficits to GNP

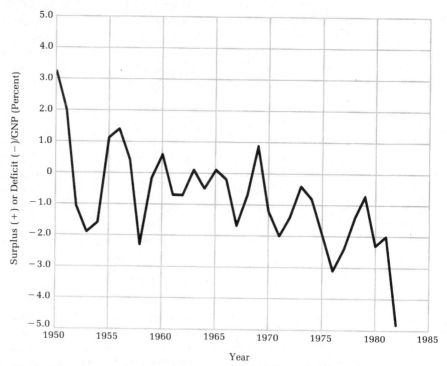

Source: *Economic Report of the President* (1983), Tables B–1 and B–75.

If federal government deficits are a burden on the economy, it is not evident when ratios of deficits to GNP are calculated. According to those ratios, the burden of federal government deficits has increased only slightly since 1960.

There are several effects of a deficit, some of which we have previously discussed. A deficit financed by increases in high-powered money leads to inflation and reduces the flexibility or credibility the Fed has in carrying out anti-inflation policies. If the deficit is not financed by monetary base increases, interest rates are driven up, thus crowding out private investment and consumption and reducing the value of individuals' wealth. A large national debt may mean a lower capital stock and less potential for producing output than without the national debt. In addition, if the public realizes that debt must eventually be paid for with higher taxes, then increased government spending will be exactly balanced by a decrease in the public's spending. Moreover, if the prospect of higher taxes reduces the incentive to work and produce, the national debt may be said to cause a decrease in productivity and growth of the economy. But these are subjective judgments and open to criticism.

Effects on Financial Markets

In terms of the financial markets, the burden of the debt is to draw investable funds away from private uses into public uses. Hence, perhaps an appropriate measure of the burden of the deficits should be based on a *flow-of-funds approach*. In this approach the proportion of total loanable funds diverted to Treasury securities is a measure of governmental influence.

A picture of the flow-of-funds approach for the period 1973-1981 is shown in Figure 12-8. At first glance, Treasury financing appears to have had little effect. Interest rates did not rise during 1974-77 even as the Treasury absorbed an increasing amount of loanable funds. Yet, given the knowledge of Fed strategies over the 1973-81 period and the fact that 1974-75 was a recessionary period, the pattern shown in Figure 12-8 provides another interpretation. Before October, 1979, the Fed accommodated Treasury borrowing. With the Fed's interest rate strategy, as the pressure on interest rates increased, the Fed pumped up the money supply to keep rates down. Moreover, private borrowing decreased during the 1974-75 recession. As private borrowing picked up in 1977, the pressure on interest rates increased. Then, in 1979, the Fed's new policy approach meant that Treasury borrowing was not accommodated—interest rates were driven up. In sum, without monetary accommodation, the deficits do draw significant funds away from the private sector. In this sense, the debt is a burden on the economy.

The Fed ownership of Treasury debt is shown in Table 12-5. While the Fed's portion of total Treasury debt has been declining, the rate of growth of Treasury debt accelerated in the late 1970s and has grown rapidly since. As a result, the Fed ownership of Treasury securities grew rapidly in the late 1970s. As the Fed tightened the monetary growth in 1979, 1980, and 1981, its ownership of Treasury debt grew more slowly.

Table 12-5. Fed Ownership of Public Debt (Billions of Dollars)

FISCAL YEAR	TOTAL	YEAR TO YEAR % CHANGE	HELD BY FEDERAL RESERVE BANKS		
			TOTAL	YEAR TO YEAR % CHANGE	AS A RATIO OF TOTAL DEBT
1967	322.9	—	46.7	—	0.145
1968	345.4	7.0	52.2	11.8	0.151
1969	352.9	2.2	54.1	3.6	0.153
1970	370.1	4.9	57.7	6.7	0.156
1971	397.3	7.3	65.5	13.5	0.165
1972	426.4	7.3	71.4	9.0	0.167
1973	457.3	7.2	75.0	5.0	0.164
1974	474.2	3.7	80.5	7.3	0.169
1975	533.2	12.4	84.7	5.2	0.159
1976	620.4	16.4	94.4	11.5	0.152
1977	698.8	12.6	104.7	10.9	0.150
1978	771.5	10.4	115.3	10.1	0.149
1979	826.5	7.1	115.5	1.7	0.140
1980	907.7	9.8	120.7	4.5	0.133
1981	997.9	9.9	124.3	3.0	0.124
1982	1,142.0	14.4	134.4	8.1	0.118

Source: Economic Report of the President (1983), Table B-80.

Figure 12-8. *The Flow of Funds and Federal Deficits*

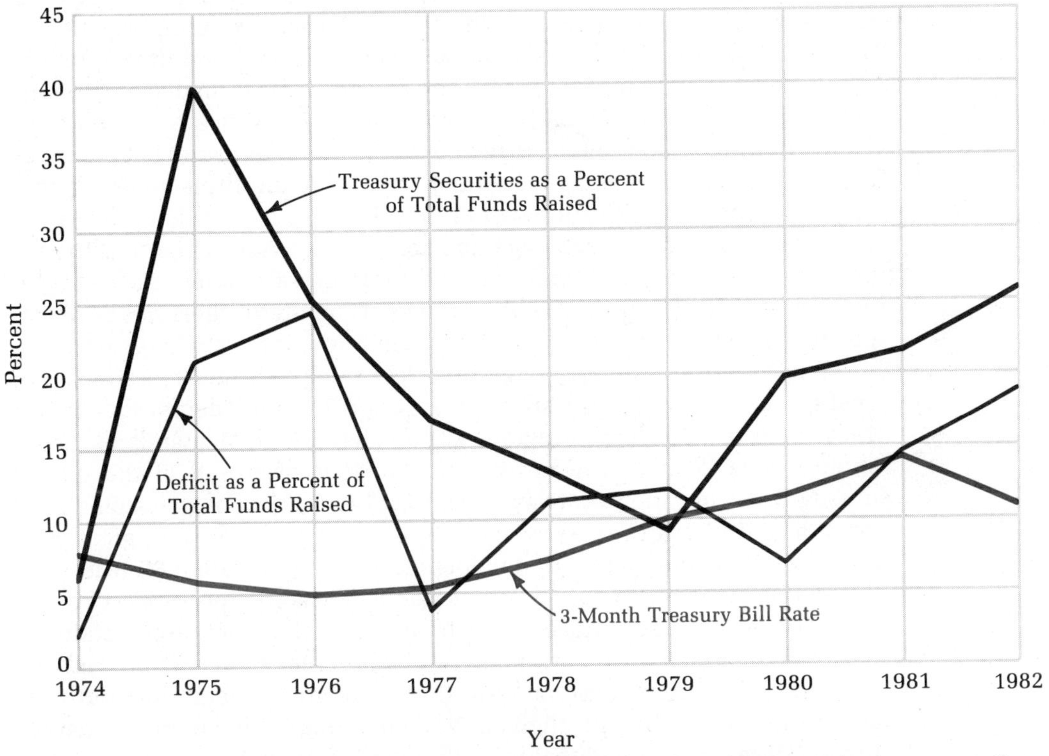

Sources: *Economic Report of the President* (1983), Table B-1; *Federal Reserve Bulletin* (February, 1983), Table 1.58; *Economic Indicators* (April, 1983).

During the middle 1970s and again in the early 1980s the Treasury captured an increasing proportion of total loanable funds. The result during the latter period was a rising interest rate, whereas the Treasury bill (T-bill) rate actually fell during the former period.

The Maturity Structure of Government Debt

The concern over the effect of deficits on the economy stems primarily from the crowding out effect. Increased government debt causes interest rates to rise and drives out interest sensitive private spending. This was a topic of considerable interest during 1974-76 as Treasury debt took a larger and larger portion of loanable funds. However, when interest rates failed to rise, the volume of the debate was turned down. The concern seemed misplaced. With the deficits of the eighties, however, the topic has surfaced again.

An additional aspect of this concern is the potential perversion of the structure of the financial market by the deficits. Many people—stockbrokers, investment managers, and so on— are saying that not only does the Treasury force itself upon the market but that by selling primarily long- or short-term securities the Treasury interferes with the maturity structure of the financial markets.[11] If the Treasury, for example, sells primarily long-term securities it drives up long-term interest rates forcing private borrowers to shift to the short-term market. The effect of this shift is to reduce investments in long-term projects. The reason stems from one of the rules of thumb of financial management—to match long-term assets with long-term liabilities. Hence, being driven out of the long-term end of the market forces firms to forego long-term investments. While firms could finance long-term projects with short-term liabilities, it is argued that the costs of continuous offerings (brokerage and regulatory costs) make that too expensive. Moreover, the long-term debt provides a modicum of security. An investment that is profitable at current long-term rates might not be profitable should financing be short-term and short-term rates rise.

The maturity structure of public debt is shown in Table 12–6. The average length increased slightly during 1981 and decreased during 1982.[12] According to the previous arguments, private demands for credit should have been driven away from the long-term end of the market during 1981 and, hence, away from long-lived types of investments.

While firms did focus on short–term security issues and greatly diminished their long-term capital spending during the 1980-82 recession, it is certainly not clear that this was due to Treasury "perversion" of the maturity structure. Many economists maintain that such a perversion is not possible since assets are highly substitutable. Hence, if the risk adjusted rates of return on long-term assets are greater than on short-term assets, investors will shift their funds to the long-term end of the market. In this sense it is asserted that this efficiency of financial markets will rule out any potential crowding out due to debt management policy.[13]

Which side of the argument is correct? Is there a portfolio type of crowding out? During the summer of 1982, Wall Street and the economics profession were worried about the effect of Treasury credit demands on the expected late 1982 recovery. The fears stemmed more from the size of the Treasury's needs than they did from whether the Treasury went long or short term. The prevailing belief seems to have been on the side of those arguing against a portfolio type of crowding out.

---

[11]See "A Scramble for Long-Term Loans," *Business Week* (February 16, 1981), p. 20.

[12]The Treasury's intention was to increase the length, but Congress refused to allow the Treasury to offer long-term bonds at more than the 4.5 percent interest rate in the second quarter of 1982. The effect of this refusal was to force the Treasury to "deep discount" bonds to such an extent that it went to more intermediate term bonds.

[13]There are three alternative views or theories regarding the maturity structure of debt (the term structure of interest rates). They are (1) the expectations theory, (2) the risk premium theory, and (3) the institutional, or preferred habitat, theory. For a good explanation, see Burton Malkiel, *The Term Structure of Interest Rates* (Morristown, N. J.: General Learning Press, 1970).

Table 12-6. *Maturity Distribution and Average Length of Marketable Interest-Bearing Public Debt Securities Held by Private Investors, 1967-81*

END OF YEAR OR MONTH	AMOUNT OUT-STANDING, PRIVATELY HELD	MATURITY CLASS					AVERAGE LENGTH	
		WITHIN 1 YEAR	1 TO 5 YEARS	5 TO 10 YEARS	10 TO 20 YEARS	20 YEARS AND OVER	YEARS	MONTHS
	MILLIONS OF DOLLARS							
FISCAL YEAR:								
1967..........	150,321	56,561	53,584	21,057	6,153	12,968	5	1
1968..........	159,671	66,746	52,295	21,850	6,110	12,670	4	5
1969..........	156,008	69,311	50,182	18,078	6,097	12,337	4	2
1970..........	157,910	76,443	57,035	8,286	7,876	8,272	3	8
1971..........	161,863	74,803	58,557	14,503	6,357	7,645	3	6
1972..........	165,978	79,509	57,157	16,033	6,358	6,922	3	3
1973..........	167,869	84,041	54,139	16,385	8,741	4,564	3	1
1974..........	164,862	87,150	50,103	14,197	9,930	3,481	2	11
1975..........	210,382	115,677	65,852	15,385	8,857	4,611	2	8
1976..........	279,782	151,723	89,151	24,169	8,087	6,652	2	7
1977..........	326,674	161,329	113,319	33,067	8,428	10,531	2	11
1978..........	356,501	163,819	132,993	33,500	11,383	14,805	3	3
1979..........	380,530	181,883	127,574	32,279	18,489	20,304	3	7
1980..........	463,717	220,084	156,244	38,809	25,901	22,679	3	9
1981..........	549,863	256,187	182,237	48,743	32,569	30,127	4	3
1982..........	682,043	314,436	221,783	75,749	33,017	37,058	3	11

Source: *Economic Report of the President* (1980), Table B-81.

Lags in Fiscal Policy_____

The final fiscal policy issue to be discussed here stems from the first section of this chapter. It should have become readily apparent after reading the first section that fiscal policy cannot be implemented rapidly.

The time delay in implementing policy has been referred to as a policy lag. Economists have described this policy lag as consisting of the following three parts: (1) a recognition lag, (2) an administrative lag, and (3) an operational lag. *Recognition lag* represents the time it takes for policymakers to realize a problem is present. *Administrative lag* summarizes the length of time for the political process to work. These two lags are often called the *inside lags*. The final lag, *operational* or *outside lag*, captures the length of time it takes for the policy to be effective once implemented.

Given the description of the annual budgetary process and the lags that exist, an obvious question is, Can discretionary fiscal policy be effectively used? This question initiated the Congressional Budget and Impoundment Control Act of 1974 that allowed the formulation of tax and government spending policy for business cycle purposes to be separated from the general budgetary process. While this shortened the administrative lag, it did not remove it. In 1975, a tax rebate bill was passed in what was described as record time. Still, it took three and a half months to pass. In 1967, the Johnson administration requested a 10 percent surcharge on income taxes. It took Congress a year and a half to enact what was supposed to be an early anti-inflation policy. President Reagan's 1981 and 1982 tax and expenditure packages are good examples of the difficulty with which spending and taxing changes are made. They are also exemplary of the length of time it takes to implement spending and taxing changes. Reagan's 1981 proposal was made in January, but not passed until August, and this was near record speed time.

One would think that the recognition lag would have had to have been reduced over the years as the technology for data collecting and processing improved. And if events occur in the same way, or if disturbances have the same impacts time after time, the recognition lag should have been shortened. However, as the 1980-82 recession makes so clear, economists and policymakers were not so fortunate. During the mid-1970s an apparently new phenomenon occurred—inflation and unemployment rose simultaneously. Then, during the 1980-82 downturn inflation rates dropped significantly while interest rates remained at record high levels. Again, a new phenomenon. In these types of cases, policymakers know and recognize that something is amiss, but they are not sure just what.

Whether this type of uncertainty is part of recognition lag or part of operational lag is open to question. Perhaps more important, is whether such uncertainty (and the fact that the economy does not always respond in the same way) renders the study of lags unimportant. In other words, is it possible for policymakers to reduce the length of fiscal policy lag? If not, devoting time and effort to classifying lags is nothing but a mental exercise. If so, then we must return to the question of how expectations are formed and ask whether the reduction of a particular fiscal policy lag would make any difference for the effectiveness of fiscal policy. Since these questions are currently being debated, we cannot provide a definitive answer. We leave them for the reader to struggle with.

Summary and a Look Ahead

Many statements made every day in newspapers, magazines, and on radio and television point out the interaction between fiscal policy and the rest of the economy. For example,

> Corporations eager to raise long-term debt are being shoved aside as a borrower with more clout—the federal government—satisfies its voracious need for money first.[14]

> Sky-high interest rates, off-budget financing, and rising outlays are bloating federal borrowing.[15]

> The deficit is definitely inflationary only if it is financed by creating new money. But the deficit need not be so financed. If it is, that is a failure of monetary policy, not of fiscal policy.[16]

In this chapter we have attempted to highlight the main issues of fiscal policy while recognizing the complicated nature of the process by which fiscal policy is formulated and implemented. The statement of fiscal policy—the federal budget—is more a statement of political processes in the United States than it is an economic policy statement. The growth of particular government expenditure programs without annual congressional or presidential review has set off a major portion of the budget as uncontrollable. Hence, unless revenues are increasing to match the growing expenditures, deficits will occur. And since taxes are politically unpopular, deficits have become commonplace. We also discussed the impact these deficits and the resultant government debt can have on the economy. Finally, we discussed the relationship between fiscal and monetary policy; that is, the Fed's monetization of the government's debt. In the following two chapters, we will be examining these fiscal and monetary policy issues in the context of the events of the 1970s and early 1980s.

---

[14]*Business Week* (February 16, 1981), p. 21.
[15]*Business Week* (February 16, 1981), p. 20.
[16]*Newsweek* (July 27, 1981), p. 60.

PROBLEMS AND EXERCISES

1. In 1776, Adam Smith stated that "what is prudence in the conduct of every private family can scarce be folly in that of a great kingdom." Does this quote apply to the United States? Discuss.

2. The Fed is not required by law to monetize the deficit. If the Fed buys outstanding debt rather than newly issued debt of the Treasury, is the debt still monetized?

3. Comment on the statement, All deficits are not alike, even when they are the same size because it makes a big difference how each deficit is financed.

4. In an article in the *Wall Street Journal* dated July 21, 1981, David Meiselman stated

   The conventional wisdom holds that budget deficits are a major cause of inflation. . . . Contrary to these widely and deeply held beliefs, the evidence is that there is little, if any, direct historical connection between deficit and inflation, or between deficits and money growth that causes inflation.

   Can Meiselman's claim be explained in terms of the aggregate demand-aggregate supply model?

5. Between 1941 and 1951 there was a more or less automatic association between the Federal Reserve System open market purchases and Treasury borrowing. The agreement between the Fed and the Treasury was made so that the interest rate on government bonds would remain constant. Analyze the macroeconomic implication of this agreement for the economy. What would be the effect of implementing this agreement today?

6. Is the government debt a burden?

7. In Part Two of the book, the issue of whether fiscal policy crowded out private investment was discussed. We found, in a world of fixed prices, the slope of the *LM* curve to be an important factor in determining the efficacy of fiscal policy. However, this discussion failed to include the fact that deficits from an increase in government spending (or a decrease in taxes) must be financed. Reanalyze the crowding out issue in light of the fact that deficits must be financed.

8. In the previous question, the crowding out issue was analyzed under the fixed price assumption. How do your conclusions change if this assumption is dropped? (Hint: Use the *IS-LM* model in conjunction with the *AD-AS* model).

9. Interest on the debt and Social Security are referred to as *uncontrollable*. What does this mean?

10. If there are such long lags in the implementation of fiscal policy then how did the Reagan administration time its large deficits to occur during the 1980-1982 recession?

SUGGESTED READINGS

There are two annual publications which are practically indispensible to students of government fiscal and budget policy. These are the Economic Report of the President, *which appears in February of each year, and the Brookings Institution volume entitled* Setting National Priorities.

The growth of government and government budget deficits are analyzed in

Allan Meltzer, "Why Government Grows (and Grows) in a Democracy," *The Public Interest* (Summer,1978), pp. 111-18.

Michael Boskin, "Federal Government Deficits: Some Myths and Realities," *American Economic Review: Papers and Proceedings* (May, 1982), pp. 296-303.

"The Built-In Deficit: Special Report," *Business Week* (August 16, 1982), pp. 84-93.

"Making Room for the Deficit," *Fortune* (February 22, 1982), pp. 41-42.

On selective credit allocation, read

Edward Kane, "Good Intentions and Unintended Evil: The Case Against Selective Credit Allocation," *Journal of Money, Credit and Banking* (February, 1977), pp. 55-69.

For differing views on the subject of crowding out of private spending, see

J. K. Dew, "The Capital Market Crowding Out Problem in Perspective," *Economic Review* (Federal Reserve Bank of San Francisco, December, 1975).

Benjamin Friedman, "Crowding Out or Crowding in? The Economic Consequences of Financing Government Deficits," *Brookings Papers on Economic Activity* (3:1978), pp. 593-654.

For a discussion of the interaction between fiscal and monetary policy, see

Mark Toma, "Inflationary Bias of the Federal Reserve System: A Bureaucratic Perspective," *Journal of Monetary Economics* (September, 1982), pp. 163-190.

W. Douglas McMillin and Thomas R. Beard, "Deficits, Money and Inflation: Comment," *Journal of Monetary Economics* (September, 1982), pp. 273-277.

How could I have been so mistaken as to have trusted the experts?
John F. Kennedy, referring to the Bay of Pigs fiasco

Things are seldom what they seem, skim milk masquerades as cream.
Gilbert and Sullivan, H. M. S. Pinafore

The counterrevolution in economic thought generated as many questions as answers. The economic events of the 1970s and the early 1980s did not make things easier. Together, these two developments led to a reemphasis in economic policy. Whereas the policy perspectives of Keynesianism had been intervention and fine tuning, the counterrevolution, coupled with the roller coaster economy of the seventies and eighties, argued against government intervention. In fact, a growing number of economists were asserting that government was the problem, not the solution.

In the remaining chapters we will examine the events of the 1970s and the 1980s and the impact of these events on the counterrevolution in economic thought. In Chapter 13, we focus on the Great Stagflation, the period from 1973 to 1976. In the early 1970s the U. S. economy experienced rates of inflation and unemployment that were nearly double the rates of the previous decade. In addition, the economy was struck by the effects of a series of events occurring in other parts of the world. These events elicited responses from U. S. policymakers that seemed to be ineffective at best and that, at worst, intensified the problem.

The period of the Great Stagflation provided many lessons in economic theory and policy. But as we shall see in Chapter 14, many of these lessons had to be relearned in the late 1970s. Chapter 15 is devoted to the late 1970s and the first three years of the eighties. The failure of policies in the seventies and the acceleration of inflation led to an emphasis on the distortionary effects of taxes and other governmental policies. In the first year of the Reagan presidency the so-called supply-side economists were able to implement policies meant to offset these distortions. As we shall see, these policies were thrown overboard when the Reagan ship appeared to be sinking. The economy was thrown into a deep recession, governmental deficits accelerated, and real interest rates rose to record levels. These difficulties exacerbated several other problems. The Social Security System was nearly bankrupt and was becoming a serious drain on the budget. Productivity was declining, many thought, because of the disincentive effects of taxes. However, because of the politically sensitive nature of the issues many of the proposals for solving the problem were severely compromised.

The discussion of the events of the seventies and early eighties points out several issues in economic theory and economic policy. Economists began questioning whether economic policy could affect real output and employment and whether fluctuations in economic activity could be minimized by economic policy. In Chapter 15 we examine the theoretical debates over these subjects.

Finally, Chapter 16 is devoted to an overview of the open economy. The U.S. can no longer ignore the influence of the rest of the world on its economy. In this chapter the transmission process of events occurring in other parts of the world to the U.S. economy is examined. In addition, some of the current theory and policy issues in international trade and finance, or what is called *open economy macroeconomics*, are discussed.

CHAPTER 13.

The Great Stagflation: Economic Policy throughout the 1970s

*Sure Money Talks! It
Says Inflation.*
  Billboard near an expressway

*It sounded an excellent
plan, no doubt, and very neatly
and simply arranged:
the only difficulty was
that she had not the
smallest idea how to
set about it.*
          Alice in Wonderland

The message that came from the first half of the 1960s was one of policy activism and fine tuning. The message of the late sixties and seventies was inflation and policy confusion. The inflation and unemployment rates of the decade from the mid-1950s to the mid-1960s were virtually doubled during the next decade, and policymakers were confused as to what should be done. Moreover, the economy was struck by a series of events in other parts of the world that forced policymakers to seek different solutions to these problems and economists to reconsider their theories and policy suggestions.

In this chapter we examine the decade of the 1970s. The following are the questions of major concern in this examination:

- *What are the causes of stagflation?*

- *What are the effects of supply shocks?*

- *Are there policies that should be directed toward supply shocks and stagflation?*

- *What are incomes policies and are they effective?*

- *Is inflation a monetary phenomenon?*

Introduction: The Great Stagflation

During the ten years from 1954 to 1964 inflation averaged less than 1.9 percent annually while unemployment averaged slightly more than 5 percent. In the 1965-69 period the inflation rate doubled to an average near 4 percent while unemployment only inched downward to 3.6 percent. This, however, was merely a prelude to more serious problems. Lyndon Johnson's attempt during 1965-68 to finance both his Great Society program and the Vietnam War led the U.S. economy into a new world of economic problems that has become known as the *Great Stagflation*.[1] Stagflation, a term meant to connote the simultaneous occurrence of stagnation and relatively high rates of inflation, had been experienced previously in the U. S., but the rates experienced in the 1970s were

---

[1] For a detailed investigation of the Great Stagflation see Alan S. Blinder, *Economic Policy and the Great Stagflation* (New York: Academic Press, Inc., 1979).

unprecedented. From 1969 to 1977 inflation averaged 6.4 percent while unemployment averaged 6.3 percent.

It has been widely claimed by journalists, politicians, and some economists that the phenomenon of stagflation once again demonstrated the failure of economic theory and made policy advice useless, if not dangerous.[2] The following excerpt from *Time Magazine* provides an example of this criticism:

> The relentless daily providing of dismal news drives deeper the public's conviction that the economy is in a profound and morose crisis. Feverish inflation, previously a rare malady limited primarily to wartime, has become chronic. Price spurts once associated with profligate banana republics are now common to North America and Western Europe and threaten the foundations of democratic societies. . . .
> The litany of U. S. economic woes at times seems endless. Week after week, interest rates crack new records; homeowners face 17% mortgages, and companies confront 20% business loans.
> Amid all this, the Administration has appeared paralyzed and unable to cope with problems that it does not fully understand.[3]

The purpose of this chapter is to chronicle the Great Stagflation: to examine the policies that led to the stagflation and to examine those implemented in an attempt to resolve the problem. As we shall see in this chapter, although criticisms of economic policies were valid, the policy failures could not be ascribed to the inability of economic theory to describe the Great Stagflation.

The Setting: Events Leading to the Great Stagflation

In Table 13-1 the behavior of the major economic variables during the Great Stagflation are noted. In particular, note (1) the 1974-75 recession (the drop in real GNP, and the rising unemployment), (2) inflation in 1974 (the burst of price increases in food items during 1973 and 1974 and in energy items in 1974 and 1975), and (3) the growth rate of monetary aggregates over the period.

A recession had been induced in 1970 to cool the overheated economy of the late 1960s. Yet while inflation inched downward from 6.1 percent during 1969 to 5.5 percent during 1970 the unemployment rate steadily increased. By January, 1971, unemployment had climbed to 6 percent from a low in February, 1969, of 3.3 percent.

President Nixon, unhappy with the progress of demand management policies, during the summer of 1971 sought what he termed, a new game

[2] Arthur M. Okun, "The Great Stagflation Swamp," *Challenge* (November-December, 1977).
[3] "Capitalism: Is It Working?" *Time* (April 21, 1980). p. 40.

plan. He found one. On August 15, 1971, he imposed a 90-day freeze on prices and wages using the authority Congress had given him a year earlier. His price controls eventually went through four phases and were finally dismantled in early 1974. Another part of Nixon's game plan, but one we do not discuss until Chapter 16, was the breakdown of the Bretton Woods system of fixed exchange rates. President Nixon announced that the U.S. would no longer sell gold for dollars.

Table 13-1. *Economic Variables during the Great Stagflation*

| Year | Percentage Change | | Percentage Change in CPI | | | Percentage Change | |
	Real GNP	Unemployment	All Items	Food	Energy	M-1	M-2
1971	3.4	5.9	4.3	3.0	3.9	6.5	13.5
1972	5.7	5.6	3.3	4.3	2.8	9.3	13.0
1973	5.8	4.9	6.2	14.5	2.8	5.5	7.0
1974	−0.6	5.6	11.0	14.4	29.3	4.4	5.6
1975	−1.1	8.5	9.1	8.5	10.6	5.0	12.8
1976	5.4	7.7	5.8	6.3	7.2	6.6	14.2

Source: *Economic Report of The President* (1982), Table B-55.

Under the wage-price control program, fiscal and monetary policy became quite stimulative. The high-employment surplus declined from a moderate positive number to a deficit of nearly $12 billion from 1970 to 1972. Growth rates in M-1 averaged 6.5 percent during 1970-71 and 9.3 percent during 1972. That year, 1972, was a year of economic expansion. It also saw the beginning of a series of supply shocks that profoundly affected the economy. In 1973 poor agricultural harvests worldwide combined with a disease that virtually wiped out the world's greatest protein source—the anchovy population—to decrease the supply of foodstuffs and drive prices upward. In addition, the Organization of Petroleum Exporting Countries (OPEC) imposed an oil embargo to support its price rises and to penalize those nations supporting Israel during the Arab-Israeli War. After rising at a rate of 3.4 percent during 1971-72 (the inital stages of the incomes policies), the consumer price index jumped by 6.2 percent during 1973 and 11.0 percent in 1974. The poor harvests of the preceding year began to affect the retail price level in early 1973: Food prices soared at an annual rate near 15 percent. The OPEC policy led to skyrocketing prices of oil and other energy sources. The retail price of gasoline, for example, rose 200 percent in just two years. The final factor striking the economy was the termination of wage and price controls. Phase IV was lifted in the spring of 1974 leading to a period of catch up inflation.

As inflation rose, real economic activity fell. Real GNP in 1974 fell 0.6 percent from its 1973 level, and the unemployment rate rose to 7.2 percent by the end of 1974. The U.S. had entered the Great Stagflation. Why? What caused it, and what could be done about it? Recovery from this stagflation did not take place until 1976. Why was the stagflationary problem so prolonged?

In the following section we are going to consider a number of possible answers to these questions. More specifically, we will discuss several possible explanations for the Great Stagflation—not all of which are satisfactory.

Understanding Stagflation: Demand Side or Supply Side?

Until at least the 1970s, inflation had been dichotomized into demand-side and supply-side descriptions. Any event that could be represented as an outward shift of the aggregate demand (AD) curve was classified as demand-pull inflation, while any event that could be represented as an inward shift of the aggregate supply (AS) curve was classified as cost-push inflation. Could this dichotomy also be used to describe stagflation?

Let us first consider how an increase in the growth of aggregate demand might account for stagflation. Suppose the economy is in long-run equilibrium at price level P_1 and output level Y_N as shown in Figure 13-1. Then suppose the monetary authorities increase the money supply. The AD curve shifts to AD_2 as a result of this policy change. If the policy change was unanticipated, the expected price level remains at P_1, and the short-run AS curve does not change. Real output increases while the price level rises only very slowly. However, the increase in demand will eventually create shortages and higher prices. This adjustment process is reflected in the movement from Point B to Point C in Figure 13-1. At Point B, the economy is only in short-run equilibrium. Individuals will revise their price level expectations as they realize their previous expectations were incorrect. And the expectation of higher price levels means that the short-run AS curve shifts to the left. Eventually, price level expectations will be consistent with the actual price level, such as at Point C.

As a result of the one-time demand shift, the price level increased while output rose temporarily and returned to its natural level. The stagflationary phase of this adjustment is from Point B to C. Prices rose as output (and employment) fell. The theoretical reason for the stagflation was a combination of unanticipated demand changes and sluggish adjustments in wages and prices.

Figure 13-1. Aggregate Demand and Stagflation

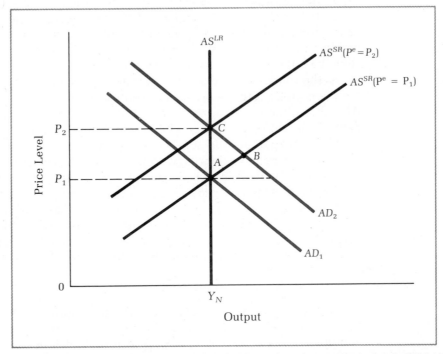

An expansionary monetary policy leads, if it is unexpected, to an outward shift of the *AD* curve and, consequently, to a rising price level and a rising real output level. As individuals and firms learn of the monetary expansion, however, they adjust their expectations and behavior accordingly. The economy then adjusts from Point A to Point B and, finally, to Point C. The adjustment from Point B to C is one of rising prices and falling real output—stagflation.

Can the stagflation that occurred during the period 1971-76 in the U.S. be satisfactorily explained by this approach? While the inflationary recession of 1969-70 followed a boom, the Great Stagflation did not follow such a pattern. Moreover, the stagflation of 1971-76 lasted much too long to be explained simply by an adjustment process.

Some economists argue that this stagflation was a direct result of stop-and-go macroeconomic policies.[4] Even though this explanation for stagflation is nothing more than a variant of the aggregate demand interpretation, its logic is worth consideration. Perhaps the easiest way to explain what is meant by stop-and-go policy is through an example. Suppose the president is faced with what his administration considers to

---

[4] Milton Friedman, *An Economist's Protest* (New York: Thomas Horton and Daughters, 1972), and his *Newsweek* columns between 1977-1980.

be an excessively high unemployment rate. The administration reacts by expanding aggregate demand. As depicted in Figure 13-1, the economy moves to Point *B*. However, at Point *B* the price level is higher than it was before the aggregate demand increase. Public opinion turns against the administration—inflation is too high. As a result, policies are enacted to slow the inflation. Usually this means a contraction in aggregate demand. Yet as the contractionary policy takes place individuals are still adjusting their expectations to the price rises resulting from the initial expansion in *AD*. Hence, the short-run *AS* curve shifts up at the same time aggregate demand is shifting inward. The result is a higher price level and a decreased output level. In sum, the stop-and-go policy has led to a period of inflation and recession. Now suppose that, faced with inflation and unemployment, politicians decide to sacrifice the inflation target and fight unemployment. Accordingly, aggregate demand is increased once again driving prices up further. This policy continues until inflation once again becomes a target. While this stop-and-go explanation may be an adequate description of the way policy is actually applied, it is difficult to account for the length of the Great Stagflation solely from this perspective.

Supply-Side Explanations for a Stagflation

At least since the Great Depression, some economists have attributed inflation to supply-side causes. Perhaps the most well known is the administered price explanation proposed by Professor Gardiner Means.[5] He suggested that U.S. industry is becoming more concentrated (fewer firms in each industry) and that this monopoly-like power enables firms to administer or set prices independently of demand. So, when demand falls and employment declines, prices might even increase. The implications Means drew are very controversial and his study has been the subject of much criticism. For example, Professors G. Warren Nutter and Henry Einhorn disagreed with Means's results.[6] Their studies showed that the finding that industry is becoming more concentrated depends on the time period over which a study is carried out and on industry definitions and other data differences. The microeconomic models of monopoly and perfect competition show that if a perfectly competitive market becomes monopolized, prices will rise and output will fall. But such a price increase is simply a one-shot price rise, not a continual inflation. And,

---

[5] Gardiner Means, National Resources Committee, *The Structure of the American Economy* (Washington, D.C.: U. S. Government Printing Office, 1939); and *Industrial Prices and their Relative Inflexibility* (Senate Document 13, 74th Congress, 1st Session, January 17, 1935).

[6] G. Warren Nutter and Henry A. Einhorn, *Enterprise Monopoly in the United States: 1899-1958* (New York: Columbia University Press, 1969). For a counterview to Nutter and Einhorn see Joan Robinson, "Solving the Stagflation Puzzle," *Challenge* (November-December, 1979), pp. 40-46.

monopolists cannot continually raise prices—eventually no one would buy the product, and substitute products would emerge. Moreover, the monopolist operates to maximize profits by producing where marginal costs and marginal revenue are equal. This does not occur at the highest possible price. In recent years the debate has continued with a slightly different focus. The more recent version of this argument focuses more on the lack of flexibility of wages and prices than on just the costs of monopoly power.

Wage-Push Inflation

The wage-push version of cost-push inflation asserts that unionized labor has some degree of monopoly power over the supply of labor. As a result, unionized labor can use this power, perhaps via the threat of strikes, to force wages up. Then relying on the administered price or so-called markup-price thesis, it is argued that firms react to the increase in costs by raising prices.

Let us examine this contention a little more carefully. Suppose a labor union is successful in raising wages above the level that would have prevailed in the absence of the union. Without an increase in demand for the product produced by that unionized industry, the firm will produce less output and hire less labor. If the output price is raised to cover the input costs, the quantity of output demanded will decline. If the firm equates marginal revenue to marginal cost and prices accordingly, price will rise since marginal cost has risen. Less output will be produced and since less output means less labor is required, some workers (who had jobs before the union's success) will lose their jobs. What will these workers do? They may collect unemployment for awhile, or they may seek work in another industry. This means the supply of labor will be increased in the other industry which, in turn, puts downward pressure on wages in that industry. What is the net effect of union monopoly? After the period of time it takes the market mechanism to adjust, the union wage increase can hardly be inflationary since, while prices in one industry rose, in another they fell.

How then can a wage increase cause permanent inflation? By itself it cannot. Suppose, however, that American workers thrown out of jobs in a particular industry organize and put political pressure on the government to keep them working in that industry. The government does this by increasing the demand for the product produced by that industry. How? It could purchase that industry's goods and services. Alternatively, it could restrict competition from foreign producers, or it could require that foreign producers utilize U.S. labor and products to produce their competing product. But here again, the question arises, Can these policies cause permanent inflation? Each event is only a one-time price rise. To turn into inflation, these events must occur one on top of the other and then must be accommodated with money supply increases. We will return to that point later.

As interesting as they are to study, it was not these wage-push factors that received the major portion of the blame for the Great Stagflation. The supply shocks of the OPEC oil embargo and worldwide agricultural failures were the alleged culprits. What was the basis for asserting that a bad crop led to stagflation? In terms of the *AD-AS* framework, the short-run and long-run *AS* curves shift to the left when a shortfall in agricultural production occurs. There are fewer inputs (agricultural products) available. The price level increases and the output level decreases. In Figure 13-2 this is depicted by the movement from Point A to Point B.

However, an agricultural shortfall in production is unlikely, by itself, to generate a stagflation like the one that existed in the 1970s in the U.S. Poor harvests in one year, or even in two consecutive years, are likely to be followed by normal or good harvests in succeeding years. When the

Figure 13-2. *Aggregate Supply and Stagflation*

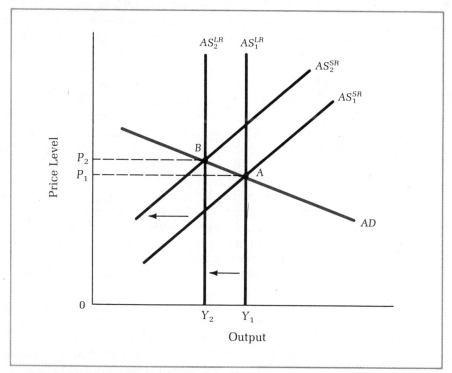

A supply shock (such as a poor harvest or the OPEC oil embargo) initially reduces the quantity of inputs as represented by the leftward shift of the long- and short-run *AS* curves. The economy adjusts from Point A to Point B. This is an adjustment consisting of a rising price level and a falling real output—a stagflation.

normal harvests return, the *AS* curves will shift back to the right. The stagflation from a temporary crop failure will itself be only temporary.

Furthermore, if prices rise in one sector of the economy, people will have less to spend in other sectors. Hence, although agricultural prices rise, we should expect other prices to fall. Yet, this might not be reflected in the CPI because of the way it is constructed. If the falling price items are relatively smaller portions of the basket of goods in the base year than the rising price items, the CPI will rise much more than the true rate of price increase.

If the stagflation that occurred in the U.S. during the 1970s is to be explained by supply-side factors, we must look to shocks that are more permanent in nature than the agricultural shortfalls. One possibility is the supply shock that originated from OPEC. The cartel's validation of its price increases by appropriate production decisions resulted in a leftward shift of the *AS* curves. Again, in Figure 13-2, we find that the price level increases, to P_2 from P_1, and output falls. In contrast to the agricultural shortfall, this supply shock will not likely be reversed. Can the OPEC oil supply decrease be the culprit of the long-term stagflation? As the price of oil rises, either less oil is purchased or a smaller quantity of other goods must be purchased. Since the demand for oil is considered to be relatively inelastic (insensitive to price changes) over a short period of time, the price rise does not lead to a substantial decrease in the quantity purchased. This leaves less income to be spent on other goods and services. Prices should fall in these other industries, should they not? It is argued, however, that petroleum is used in all kinds of products—records, clothes, tires, paper, and many other commodities—so the costs of these products will rise also, resulting in a general inflation. As pictured in Figure 13-2, the leftward shift of the *AS* curves drives up prices, but also reduces output throwing machines and people out of work. Shouldn't these displaced inputs drive the wage and capital costs to industries down, thus offsetting somewhat the increased petroleum prices? Yes, the story goes, but only if the inputs, labor and capital, are substitutable for petroleum, so that industry can use more of the cheaper labor and less of the more expensive petroleum. Furthermore, some economists argue, even if the inputs are substitutable, the length of time it takes to gear up for the changing inputs is several years, and stagflation will occur during these years.

Striving to Achieve One Goal

Since we have come this far, it would be good to review the explanations for the Great Stagflation we have covered so far. The following are the different explanations that have been briefly discussed:

1. The adjustment process following a demand shift
2. The stop-and-go nature of demand management policies
3. The administered price thesis or what is also termed the *markup price strategy* of U.S. industry
4. The wage-push (which subsequently turns into the price push) inflation
5. The agricultural shortfall
6. The OPEC oil embargo

Whichever explanations are valid descriptions of the event that initiated the stagflation, the important question, once the economy is in a stagflation, is, How to get out of it?

Some economists feel that in the short run the twin goals of low inflation and low unemployment may not be simultaneously obtainable once the economy is in a stagflation. But which goal should be pursued and which abandoned? We will examine possible answers to that question by discussing the costs of ignoring one of the goals.

The Costs of Inflation

The costs of inflation depend on whether the rate of inflation was anticipated or not. If the inflation was anticipated, individuals will have made decisions that take into account the effects of inflation. When inflation is unanticipated, however, people are surprised or fooled. They did not plan for its effects.

The Costs of Anticipated Inflation. If the economy could be fully indexed, there would be no unanticipated inflation. All contracts, agreements, and the like would be written in such a way that price changes would be entirely accounted for. As an example, suppose that a wage contract in which a nominal wage of $4.00 an hour is agreed upon for the next year. The price level is 1.0 at the time the contract is negotiated, and 10 percent inflation is expected to occur. If the inflation rate had not been taken into account, the real wage would have fallen by the end of the contract to $3.64; i.e., $4.00 ÷ 1.1. However, if the contract states that the nominal wage will be increased by the same percentage or at the same rate as the inflation rate, the real wage at the end of the period will be the same as the real wage originally bargained for. In this situation, a ten percent inflation rate would mean a nominal wage of $4.40 at the end of the contract which would leave the real wage at $4.00. This is what is meant by an *indexed contract.*

Even though unanticipated inflation would have no effects in a fully indexed economy, it is possible that anticipated inflation would have an impact. Since inflation reduces the value of money and increases the opportunity cost of holding it, individuals will attempt to economize on their holdings of money. This means that individuals will make extra trips to the bank, carry less cash, and more carefully manage their monies such as by using charge cards. The costs associated with more careful cash management have become known as the *shoe leather costs* of inflation.

These shoe leather costs can be represented on the demand-for-money diagram. Suppose that no inflation exists and the interest rate is 10 percent. Given that the opportunity cost of holding money is 10 percent, individuals will demand M_1 dollars (see Figure 13-3). If the inflation rate is expected to increase to 10 percent, the nominal interest rate will increase to 20 percent with indexed financial agreements. The opportunity cost of holding money increases and, as a result, the quantity of money demanded will fall to M_2. The area M_2M_1AB represents the costs of the 10 percent inflation in terms of the reduced money demand.[7]

Figure 13-3. *The Shoe Leather Costs of Anticipated Inflation*

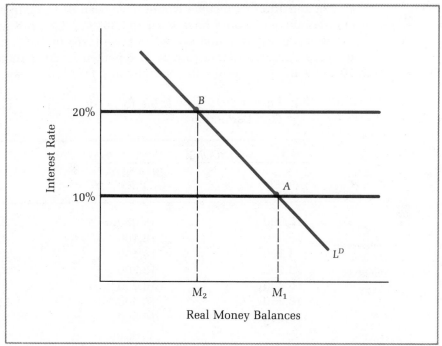

With no expected inflation and with the nominal and real interest rates at 10 percent, the quantity of money demanded is represented by A or M_1. As expected inflation rises to 10 percent, the nominal interest rate rises to 20 percent, and the quantity of money demanded falls to B or M_2. The decline in money demand is an implicit measure of the shoe leather costs of inflation.

---

[7] In order to get some idea of the costs involved, assume that the stock of money is $100 billion and that the interest elasticity of the demand for money is one-half. Under these assumptions, a one percent increase in the inflation rate would mean a $0.5 billion cost.

The costs of anticipated inflation are not restricted to just the shoe leather costs. Price changes mean that things like price lists, menus, and Sears' catalogues have to be reprinted which requires the use of real resources. Thus, anticipated inflation does involve real costs.

Let us now drop the assumption of a fully indexed economy and assume, as is the case in the U.S. economy, that the tax system is not indexed. Tax brackets are stated in nominal terms which means that as nominal income rises, the proportion of income that is taken by personal taxes rises. In Table 13-2 a portion of the 1979 Tax Table A for single individuals with one deduction is presented. An individual who earned $18,000 paid $3,213 in taxes. After-tax income, thus, was $14,787. If inflation had been 10 percent for the year, the indexation of wages and salaries would have driven the individual's income to $19,800. At this level, taxes (based on brackets that are not indexed) would have been $3,778 and after-tax income would have been $16,022. In real terms, the after-tax income would have been $14,565.46. Even in this partially indexed economy, inflation served to raise taxes by $565, a 17.6 percent increase. And while taxes rose by 17.6 percent, income increased by only 10 percent. As a result, the individual's take-home pay decreased by

Table 13-2. Partial 1979 Tax Table for a Single Individual with One Deduction

| INCOME | | |
OVER	BUT NOT OVER	TAX
18,000	18,050	3,213
18,050	18,100	3,228
18,100	18,150	3,243
18,150	18,200	3,258
18,200	18,250	3,273
18,250	18,300	3,228
18,300	18,350	3,303
—	—	—
—	—	—
—	—	—
19,700	19,750	3,744
19,750	19,800	3,761
19,800	19,850	3,778
19,850	19,900	3,795
19,900	19,950	3,812
19,950	20,000	3,829

$221.54—in real terms. Obviously, there is a cost to anticipated inflation when taxes are not indexed. In a recent study, Professors Sunley and Pechman argue that a one percent increase in the price level in 1977 would have increased taxes by about three-quarters of a billion dollars.[8]

The tax system, based as it is on nominal values, has implications for corporations and asset holders as well. Since there are numerous tax effects, some quite complicated, we will discuss only a few simple examples. Depreciation is typically charged off against taxes on the basis of the historical, or the original, cost of the capital. Therefore, after a few periods of price increases, the actual replacement cost of capital will exceed the depreciation write-off. As a result, the firm faces a higher user cost of capital. The effects on investment are obvious. A second example concerns the valuation of inventories. Suppose a firm places a value on inventories using the first-in, first-out (FIFO) inventory method. This means that firms measure the cost of goods sold at their original costs. As a result, profits will be overstated in an inflationary period since the inventories have increased in value while just sitting on the shelves. With a nominal tax system the higher profits mean that taxes increase and real after-tax income decreases.

The net real rate of return on assets is also reduced by inflation and a nominal tax system. To see this, assume that an individual's marginal tax rate is 50 percent, and that the individual is earning a 5 percent nominal return on a bond. With no inflation, the after-tax real return is 2.5 percent. If inflation goes to 5 percent, however, the nominal return on bonds will increase to 10 percent and the nominal after-tax return to 5 percent. But in real terms, the investor will fail to earn even a positive return (5 percent nominal less 5 percent inflation).

The Costs of Unanticipated Inflation. The primary costs of unanticipated inflation result from changes in income distribution—some individuals gain from unanticipated inflation at the expense of others.[9] It is almost common knowledge now that inflation hurts the creditor and helps the debtor. But, why is this the case? Suppose you lend an individual $1,000 for a one year period with a 10 percent interest charge. At the end of the one year period you are repaid $1,100. If no inflation occurred, you can now purchase an extra $100 worth of goods, the reward for sacrificing spending last year. However, if an inflation rate of 11.3 percent occurred, as was the case in 1979, the $1,100 you are repaid is worth only $988.30. In other words, you are repaid with dollars that command fewer resources. Wealth has been transferred from the creditor to the debtor.

---

[8] E. M. Sunley and J. A. Pechman, "Inflation Adjustment for the Individual Income Tax," *Inflation and the Income Tax*, H. Aaron, ed. (Washington, D.C.: The Brookings Institution, Studies in Government Finance, Series 2, 1976).

[9] Joseph J. Minarik, "Who Wins, Who Loses from Inflation?" and Leslie Ellen Nulty, "How Inflation Hits the Majority," *Challenge* (January-February, 1979), pp. 26-38.

In the United States, the household sector has been a net creditor during the postwar years. Professors Bach and Stephenson claim that between the end of the Second World War and 1971, approximately $500 billion was redistributed away from households.[10] They claim that for every percentage point in unanticipated inflation, the household sector loses about $40 billion. According to Bach and Stephenson the sectors of the economy that gain from unanticipated inflation are the corporations (because of their debt financed capital structure) and the federal government (because of its debt financed spending).

Whatever the segmentation—by economic sector, by age, by income source—we find that unanticipated inflation causes a distortion. Some gain and some lose. As a result, one of the major costs of unanticipated inflation may be a general attitude of uncertainty and unease. Individuals who have borne some costs, due to their past forecasting errors, will be cautious in committing their resources or their firm's to *inflexible uses*—uses that will not account for either more or less inflation. This uncertainty, or increased risk, may induce businesses to delay investment or to require higher expected rates of return to undertake an investment. It may also lead to a shortening of contract lengths either explicitly so that contracts are negotiated more often, or implicitly through automatic clauses such as cost of living adjustments (COLAs). In addition, patterns of asset accumulation may change. Individuals may shift out of traditional nominal assets since the safety of these assets is reduced. In their place, individuals will look toward real assets as both a hedge against inflation and an investment. By *real assets*, we mean items such as gold, land, paintings, or even baseball cards. While purchasing these items may be a wise move for an individual, it does represent a distortion from what would have occurred without the experience of unanticipated inflation and it may lead to a slower rate of economic growth.

Should We Index the Economy?

Do these costs suggest that the economy should be indexed? Recall that *indexation* is the linking of nominal contracts to changes in the price level. Proponents of indexation argue that (1) the opportunity cost of attaining low inflation rates—high unemployment—is simply too high, (2) under indexation this cost need not be incurred, and (3) the costs of the redistribution of income and wealth due to unanticipated inflation would be minimized.

Milton Friedman has offered a different type of argument in favor of indexation.[11] He asserts that without indexation governments have a

---

[10] G. L. Bach and J. B. Stephenson, "Inflation and the Redistribution of Wealth," Review of Economics and Statistics, 63 (February, 1974), pp. 1-13.

[11] Milton Friedman, *Monetary Correction* (London: The Institute of Economic Affairs, 1974), and his *Newsweek* columns.

built-in incentive to inflate. The U.S. tax system is currently organized in nominal terms—inflation increases nominal income which results in taxpayers being driven into higher tax brackets. Tax payments, therefore, increase more than in proportion to the increase in nominal income. Real tax revenue increases as inflation continues. For the politician, this is a very attractive position since government spending can be increased without explicit tax increases. Friedman argues that by indexing the tax system, inflation will not automatically increase tax revenues. The incentives to increase government spending and, thus, aggregate demand will be reduced.

The opponents of indexation argue that the inflation problem would become more, not less, severe if the economy was indexed. In an economy without indexation, inflation imposes explicit costs on society which, in turn, result in a desire on the part of politicians and policymakers to control inflation. If indexation is instituted, the costs of inflation are reduced to the point that society no longer demands that its politicians moderate inflation. A second argument against indexation is more theoretical in nature. It is that indexation reinforces the inflationary effects of aggregate supply changes. Suppose, for example, that OPEC reduces the supply of oil coming into the U.S. An increase in prices and a decrease in output result. Under indexation (since the nominal wage would increase as the price level increases) the real wage would not decrease as quickly as it would without indexation. In other words the adjustment process would be lengthened and, obviously, the costs of the supply-side shock increased.

The proponents of indexation appear to have won a portion of the battle. As of this writing, the tax system is scheduled to become indexed January 1, 1985.

The Costs of Unemployment

Unemployment rates higher than the natural rate of unemployment mean that output or production is less than the level the economy could potentially generate. Arthur Okun, chairman of the Council of Economic Advisers during the Johnson administration, discovered a short-run empirical relationship between unemployment rates and output that can be used to provide a rough measure of these output losses due to unemployment. Okun examined the relationship between the GNP gap and the difference between the actual unemployment rate (U) and the natural unemployment rate (U_N). As the following formula illustrates, the *GNP gap* is defined as the percentage shortfall of actual from full-employment output:

$$GNP_{gap} = (Y_N - Y)/Y_N$$

This relationship can be expressed as Okun's *law*:

$$\text{GNP}_{\text{gap}} = B(U - U_N)$$

Okun found that B was constant and approximately equal to 3.0 which means that an additional percentage point increase in the unemployment rate over the natural rate results in a three percent decrease in real output.[12]

We can use Okun's law to derive an estimate of the cost of unemployment to society. In 1979, for example, the unemployment rate was 5.8 percent. Assuming a natural unemployment rate of 6.0 percent (remember that the natural unemployment rate is a somewhat arbitrary number), the economy was 0.2 percent above the natural unemployment rate. In other words, since actual real GNP was $1,483.0 billion (in 1972 dollars), unemployment cost the economy $8.9 billion (i.e., $1,483 billion × 0.002 × 3) in lost output. Perhaps a more dramatic example would be helpful. In 1983, the unemployment rate was over 10 percent. This is more than 4 percent above the natural unemployment rate. Since GNP was $1,530 billion in 1972 dollars, unemployment cost the economy $183 billion in lost output in 1982.

Another cost of unemployment is the personal, or individual, loss suffered by those who are unemployed. To note these losses, we need to consider the distribution of unemployment across the population. By knowing what groups or sectors suffer from increased unemployment, a politician can better decide if the benefits of lower inflation are worthwhile. If a major voting block would bear the costs of unemployment, the politician would not have the incentive to support a policy that would increase unemployment.

Table 13-3 presents unemployment rates by various demographic categories for the 1970s. During the recession year 1975, the unemployment rate for the civilian labor force was 8.5 percent. Notice the distribution of unemployment by color. The unemployment rate for whites was 7.8 percent while the rate for nonwhites was 13.9 percent. Also notice the distribution of unemployment by sex. White females had a slightly higher unemployment rate than white males (notice that the unemployment rate for white males, 7.2 percent, was below the total unemployment rate). However, for nonwhites, the female unemployment rate was 14.0 percent and the nonwhite male rate was 13.7 percent.

The last category to be considered is age. For whites, the unemployment rate for youths, as defined by the 16-19 age bracket, was more than double the total unemployment rate. On the other hand, for the white over

---

[12] Since $(Y_N - Y)/Y_N = 3(U - U_N)$, then if U increases by 1 percent, $(Y_N - Y)/Y_N$ must increase by 3 percent. Since Y_N is constant, actual output (Y) must fall by 3 percent.

Table 13-3. Unemployment Rates in the 1970s by Demographic Characteristics

| | | WHITE | | | | | |
| | | MALE | | | FEMALE | | |
YEAR	TOTAL	TOTAL	16-19 YEARS	OVER 20 YEARS	TOTAL	16-19 YEARS	OVER 20 YEARS
1970	4.9	4.0	13.7	3.2	5.4	13.4	4.4
1971	5.9	4.9	15.1	4.0	6.3	15.1	5.3
1972	5.6	4.5	14.2	3.6	5.9	14.2	4.9
1973	4.9	3.7	12.3	2.9	5.3	13.0	4.3
1974	5.6	4.3	13.5	3.5	6.1	14.5	5.0
1975	8.5	7.2	18.3	6.2	8.6	17.4	7.5
1976	7.7	6.4	17.3	5.4	7.9	16.4	6.8
1977	7.0	5.5	15.0	4.6	7.3	15.9	6.2
1978	6.0	4.5	13.5	3.7	6.2	14.4	5.2
1979	5.8	4.4	13.9	3.6	5.9	13.9	5.0

| | | NONWHITE | | | | | |
| | | MALE | | | FEMALE | | |
YEAR	TOTAL	TOTAL	16-19 YEARS	OVER 20 YEARS	TOTAL	16-19 YEARS	OVER 20 YEARS
1970	8.2	7.3	25.0	5.6	9.3	34.4	6.9
1971	9.9	9.1	28.9	7.2	10.8	35.4	8.7
1972	10.0	8.9	29.7	6.8	11.3	38.5	8.8
1973	8.9	7.6	26.9	5.7	10.5	34.5	8.2
1974	9.9	9.1	31.6	6.8	10.7	34.6	8.4
1975	13.9	13.7	35.4	11.7	14.0	38.5	11.5
1976	13.1	12.7	35.4	10.6	13.6	39.0	11.3
1977	13.1	12.4	37.0	10.0	14.0	39.9	11.7
1978	11.9	10.9	34.4	8.6	13.1	38.4	10.6
1979	11.3	10.3	31.5	8.4	12.3	35.7	10.1

Source: *Economic Report of the President* (1980).

20 age group the unemployment rate was less than the total rate. The unemployment rate for nonwhite youths was 35.4 percent for males and 38.5 percent for females. The nonwhite youth unemployment rate was four times as large as the total unemployment rate. The unemployment rate for nonwhites over 20 years of age was approximately one and one-half times as large as their white counterparts'.

From 1973, a boom year, to 1975 the overall unemployment rate rose from 4.9 to 8.5. This is an increase of 3.6 percentage points—a whopping 73 percent increase. The rate for whites rose from 4.3 to 7.8 percent, an increase of 3.5 percentage points—an incredible 81 percent increase—while the rate for nonwhites rose 5 percentage points from 8.9 to 13.9 percent—an increase of 56 percent. In other words, while the nonwhite sector of society bears the greatest burden of unemployment regardless of whether the economy is experiencing a boom or a bust, the white sector bears the greatest amount of adjustment as the economy goes from boom to bust and vice versa.

What conclusions can be gleaned from these statistics? First, nearly every constituency—males, females, whites, nonwhites, adults, and youths—will be hurt by increased unemployment. Second, whether in bad or good times, three groups in society bear a disproportionate share of the costs of unemployment—youth, females, and nonwhites.

Incomes Policies

The Reagan administration and Paul Volcker seem to have pursued one goal at the expense of the other goal during 1980-82. But because the risk of having the public believe "the rascals should be thrown out of office" and because the costs of ignoring one goal have typically been too high, policymakers have searched for policies that would solve both problems simultaneously. One of the most common fallback positions is for policymakers to undertake some type of *incomes policy*, or *wage and price control program* as it is more commonly called in the United States. By imposing an incomes policy the policymaker hopes to solve the inflation problem without exacerbating the unemployment problem.

The Case for and against Incomes Policies

The case for an incomes policy boils down to essentially one argument: Incomes policies will take the *expectations effect* out of the inflationary process. Proponents argue that as inflation becomes more severe, it becomes embedded in individuals' expectations, which results in higher wage demands and, subsequently, still higher prices. Moreover, if inflationary expectations exceed actual inflation (as shown in Figure 13-4 in the move from A to B) real output will decrease. A decrease in price expectations will reverse this process. Hence, advocates of incomes policies claim that by controlling prices, incomes policies will modify price expectations in an appropriate manner. The proponents also note that incomes policies allow policymakers time to use demand management policies to solve the inflationary problems without the costs of very high unemployment rates.

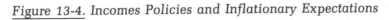

Figure 13-4. Incomes Policies and Inflationary Expectations

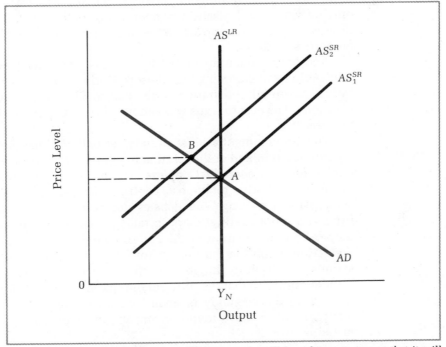

If the economy has been in an inflation, people will have begun to expect that it will continue. Then expectations can precede reality. In this case the short-run *AS* curve will shift up faster than the other curves shift. The result, as shown in the move from Point *A* to *B*, is a rising price level and a declining real output level. Proponents of incomes policies argue that if this process can be reversed; that is, if expectations followed rather than led, then real output could be increased and price forced to drop rather than increase. The objective of an incomes policy would be to get the economy to move from *B* to *A* as the short-run *AS* curve shifts out.

The most frequent criticism of incomes policies is that they interfere with the operation of the market and lead to a misallocation of resources. In this respect an incomes policy works just like any type of price control—controls on the rent of apartments, controls on interest rates, controls on the price of gasoline, and so on. If effective, the price is below that which would equate demand and supply, and there is, therefore, an excess demand. Faced with an excess demand, sellers must figure out ways to allocate their output. They can choose first come, first serve; they can take bribes; they can rent or sell only to those individuals they like; or they can choose a million other ways to allocate the products. In addition, an incomes policy (like any price control program) creates increasingly more distortions the longer the controls are in place.

A second argument against controls concerns the manner in which incomes policies are implemented. It is claimed that incomes policies are always imposed so that some sector of society bears an unfair proportion of the burden of the program. For example, an incomes policy imposed only on wages will disadvantage workers; controls on prices alone will disadvantage firms; controls on the price of food items will disadvantage farmers; and so on.[13]

Another problem attributed to incomes programs is the cost of administering and enforcing the controls. During the program implemented by the Nixon administration, firms had to file reports on their pricing decisions. The cost to firms was estimated to be nearly one billion dollars per year.[14]

The last argument against an incomes policy is that prices explode at the introduction and at the termination of the program. This is called the *bubble effect.* Generally Congress will have to pass a law giving the president authority to impose controls. To pass such a law requires congressional hearings and debates during which time groups such as firms and unions will attempt to raise prices as rapidly and as often as they can in anticipation of the controls programs. In addition, the suppressed inflation that builds up from the use of a controls program is a serious drawback to the goals of the controls program. Professor Alan Blinder estimated that the lifting of the Nixon administration controls was a shock to the economy of about two-thirds the size of the OPEC oil embargo. Others have found an impact, but one smaller than that estimated by Blinder.[15]

Nixon's Attempt at Wage and Price Controls

President Nixon's controls over wages and prices in 1971 was the first peacetime use of mandatory controls.[16] The controls program began with a freeze. Wage and price increases were, for a period of 90 days, simply illegal. The second phase of Nixon's program began in mid-November, 1971, and lasted until December, 1972. Under this phase, wages could not be raised more than 5.5 percent per year while price increases could be only those justified by input cost increases. The third phase which began in January, 1973, was supposed to be the first step toward decontrol. The general standard for permissible wage and price increases was stressed, but rigid adherence was not emphasized. But as inflation accelerated to a

---

[13] Robert L. Schuettinger, "Wage-Price Controls: Forty Centuries of Solid Failure," *Nation's Business* (May, 1980); "A Step toward Controls," *Newsweek* (September, 25, 1978), p. 76.

[14] Marvin H. Kosters, *Controls and Inflation: The Economic Stabilization Program in Retrospect* (Washington, D.C.: American Enterprise Institute for Public Policy Research, 1975).

[15] Blinder, op. cit., p. 131.

[16] Controls had been imposed during World War II and during the Korean War. Voluntary guidelines were used during the Kennedy-Johnson years.

9.1 percent rate, another freeze was imposed. This second freeze in June, 1973, lasted until August, 1973, when the fourth phase was implemented.

What was the impact of this incomes policy? Indications point to a failure, not only along the lines indicated by the opponents of controls programs but also in terms of obscuring the effects of the supply shocks that hit the economy in 1973 and 1974. Professor Blinder studied the impact of the controls program in great detail and his conclusion was "that the program was clearly a mistake—and probably a very serious one."[17]

The controls program also played a major role in the deployment of a series of confused monetary and fiscal policies. Note how this could come about. Suppose, for example, that the economy has been experiencing a fairly rapid inflation rate when a price freeze is imposed. In Figure 13-5 the freeze is denoted as the horizontal line at price P^*. Since inflation has

Figure 13-5. *A Price Freeze and Demand Management Policies*

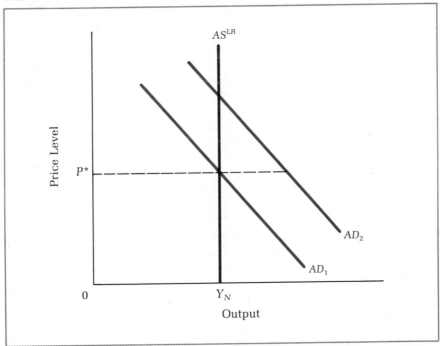

A price freeze imposed at price P^* means that inflation cannot legally occur. Notice, however, that the frozen price means there is no signal of the impacts of demand management policies. An expansionary policy, such as shown here in the shift of the *AD* curve, does not show up in higher prices—only in shortages or in other more subtle economic signals.

---

[17] Blinder, op. cit., p. 132.

been terminated by the freeze—prices cannot legally rise and, thus, the impacts of demand policies are not immediately evident. As *AD* shifts out, price rises do not result, but shortages build up. As people learn of the shortages, their expectations will be for large price rises in the future.

The Confused Policies of 1971-76

Highly expansionary fiscal policies took the lead in 1971 and 1972. The high-employment budget, nearly balanced in 1970, moved to a $10 billion deficit in 1971 and a $12 billion deficit in 1972. Moreover, Social Security benefits were raised significantly in 1971, the investment tax credit was reimplemented, and personal income tax exemptions were increased. A major switch in fiscal policy took place after the 1972 elections. The $12 billion high-employment budget deficit in 1972 slipped to $8 billion in 1973 and turned into a surplus of $3 billion in 1974. When inflation hit its peak in 1974, and the economy was falling into a deep recession, however, President Nixon and Congress were devoting virtually full time to the Watergate crisis. Gerald Ford took over the presidency in August, 1974, facing severe economic problems—inflation was soaring at double-digit rates, and the economy had just experienced two consecutive quarters of negative real growth in GNP (the formal definition of recession).

President Ford decided to launch an attack on the inflation problem. He asked Congress to place a tight ceiling on federal spending and to enact a 5 percent temporary income tax surcharge. By January, 1975, the economy was in a serious recession, and President Ford's priorities changed accordingly. Instead of the income tax increase, he asked Congress for a large tax reduction and an increase in the investment tax credit. His request was enacted in the Tax Reduction Act of 1975. In total, the fiscal package moved the high-employment budget from approximate balance at the beginning of 1975 to a deficit of $29 billion by November of 1975.

Analysis shows that other than the tax cut in 1975, fiscal policy was totally misdirected during the Great Stagflation. In 1972, fiscal policy was stimulative at the time the economy was expanding. In 1973, fiscal policy was contractionary when the economy was nose-diving into a major recession. In 1975, the work of the Tax Reduction Act was vitiated by its temporary nature, something that has been shown both theoretically (according to the Permanent Income Hypothesis) and practically (by the tax surcharge of 1968).

Monetary policy during the 1971-76 period is subject to many of the same criticisms that have been leveled at fiscal policy. The Federal Reserve (Fed) undertook an extremely expansionary policy in 1972, switched to an extremely contractionary policy in 1973, and failed to ease toward expansion as much of the economy sank lower in 1974.

The Fed's policy directives (target ranges mandatorily made explicit since 1974 and only discussed in general terms before then) indicated expansion during 1971-72 and a backing away from the expansion during the first half of 1973. The general statement provided by the Federal Open Market Committee (FOMC) in early 1973 was for slower growth in monetary aggregates. By late 1973 the attitude of the FOMC was changing toward a somewhat faster rate of monetary expansion although several members were concerned about such a policy while inflation rates were still high. In fact, up until December, 1974, the FOMC's primary concern was with inflation. Their instructions to the Open Market Desk were to maintain only moderate growth. The minutes of the FOMC meetings in 1975 indicate that the Fed wanted to speed up growth in the monetary aggregates but was unable, for some reason, to succeed.[18] The growth rates of the money aggregates M-1 and M-2 are shown on a quarterly basis in Table 13-4 and on an annual basis in Table 13-1 (see page 397).

Table 13-4. Monetary Growth Rates during the 1975-76 Recovery

Money Category	1975:2	1975:3	1975:4	1976:1	1976:2	1976:3
M-1	5.9	7.5	3.0	4.7	6.5	4.2
M-2	9.9	10.4	7.0	11.0	10.3	9.1

Source: Alan Blinder, *Economic Policy and the Great Stagflation* (New York: Academic Press, Inc., 1979), p. 196.

The record of economic policymakers during the 1971-76 period is dismal. One explanation is that the incomes policies obscured the real effects of the supply shocks and fooled the fiscal and monetary authorities into thinking that the impacts of their policies were smaller than they imagined and into taking actions that were inappropriate. What would have happened without the incomes policies? While the exact answer cannot be known, it is very likely that both fiscal and monetary policy would have been more responsive to the behavior of the economy. As demonstrated in the appendix to Chapter 8 and in Chapter 12, there is a fundamental distinction between sustained inflation and one-time adjustments of the price level. The supply shocks of 1972-74 were primarily

---

[18] Nancy Jianakoplos, "The FOMC in 1975: Announcing Monetary Targets," *Review*, 58, 3 (Federal Reserve Bank of St. Louis, March, 1976), pp. 8-22; and Jerry L. Jordan, "FOMC Policy Actions in 1972," *Review*, 55, 3 (Federal Reserve Bank of St. Louis, March, 1973), pp. 10-24.

of the latter category. A policy designed with this in mind would have minimized the length of the recession and the effects of these supply shocks.

The growth of money during 1971 and 1972 was excessive. An average annual rate of growth of M-2 of over 13 percent was more than that necessary to keep up with productivity growth. Without the imposition of the price freeze, the true rate of inflation during the latter half of 1971 and during 1972 would have indicated what the impact of the expansionary monetary policy was.[19] Moreover, in 1974 when the controls were dismantled and the combination of OPEC price increases and the suppressed inflation of the controls period burst forth, the Fed acted precipitously by putting the brakes to monetary growth. The decline in 1973-74 of M-2 growth to a rate that was less than one-half the 1972 rate was much too contractionary. At the same time, the economy was reeling under the supply shock imposed by OPEC. These events meant that both *AD* and *AS* curves shifted inward (the short-run *AS* curve shifted even further inward than the others due to the large jump in price expectations).

What were the lessons of the Great Stagflation? They were primarily three. One, there is a fundamental difference between events that lead to one-time price changes and events that lead to permanent inflation. Two, wage and price controls, while perhaps defensible from a theoretical standpoint, are difficult to defend from a practicable sense. And three, monetary and fiscal authorites may have some control over the demand side of the macroeconomic paradigm but have virtually no control over the supply side, at least in the short run. Perhaps the most fundamental questions brought to the surface by the experiences of the 1971-76 period are (1) Is inflation solely a monetary phenomenon? and (2) Should policymakers pursue discretionary policy?

Money and Inflation

A sign adjacent to an expressway in a major city in the U.S. reads, "Sure Money Talks! It says Inflation." In a similar but more direct vein, Milton Friedman claims that "inflation is always and everywhere a monetary phenomenon."[20] In Figure 13-6 the rate of inflation and the rate of growth of the money supply is presented for four countries for the period 1965-1980—the U.S., the United Kingdom, France, and West Germany.

---

[19] For a debate on these issues see Arthur F. Burns, "A Letter to his Critics: Money Supply in the Conduct of Monetary Policy," testimony to the Joint Economic Committee (September, 1973); and Milton Friedman "A Response to Burns," a letter to the Joint Economic Committee in Martin N. Baily and Arthur M. Okun's *The Battle against Unemployment and Inflation* (New York: W. W. Norton & Co., Inc., 1982).

[20] Friedman, "A Theoretical Framework for Monetary Analysis," *Journal of Political Economy* (March-April, 1970), p. 217.

To smooth the data series so as to bring out the long-run trend, the rate of increase of the money supply and inflation are calculated by averaging the rates for the current and past three years. It is evident that the growth rates of money and inflation do move together, although the movements are not exactly the same. Why are they not identical?

From the money market equilibrium condition we know that

$$M = P \cdot L(r, Y)$$

so that if the equilibrium values of the real interest rate (r) and real income (Y) do not change over time, then P must increase each period as M changes. If, however, income is growing, then the real demand for money is also increasing. An increase in real money demand as a result of an increase in real income depends on the income elasticity of money demand (the sensitivity of money demand to income changes). Assume that this income elasticity is 0.8. Then an income growth rate of 3.5 percent will cause the demand for money to increase by the income growth times the income elasticity, or 2.8 percent. If the money supply increases at the same rate that the real demand for money (2.8 percent in our example), the price level will not change. However, if the money supply increases faster than the real demand for money, inflation results. In fact the rate of inflation is equal to the growth rate of the money supply less the growth rate of the demand for real balances.

$$\pi = \Delta M/M - \Delta L(r, Y)/L(r, Y)$$

Thus, there is no reason to expect the rate of growth of prices to equal exactly the rate of growth of the money supply. This is illustrated in Figure 13-6. West Germany's rate of growth of output exceeded the corresponding rates for the U.S. and the United Kingdom. This is reflected by the West German money supply line being significantly higher than the inflation line relative to the other countries.

While inflation is a monetary phenomenon from a long-run viewpoint, we must still reconcile Friedman's statement with what is sometimes called *supply-side inflation*. The key to the reconciliation is the distinction between a steady inflation and a one-time price increase. A supply shock, whether it be an increase in oil prices, an increase in wages, or an agricultural shortfall, results in an increase in the price level. But as long as the demand curve remains unchanged, the inflation will be only a one-time price increase. Only if the supply shock is validated by repeated increases in the money stock can a sustained inflation result.

Some might argue that the monetary explanation, while definitionally accurate, ignores some important realities. Supply shocks (whether due to extreme wage increases, OPEC embargoes, or agricultural shortfalls) cause increased unemployment. If the government is not willing to tolerate the increase in the unemployment rate, the money supply will be increased to offset the decreased employment. But is the resulting inflation then always a monetary phenomenon?

Percent Change

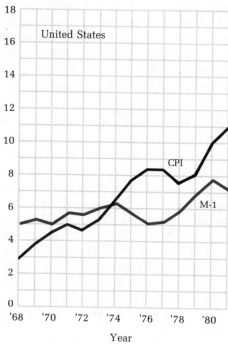

Percent Change

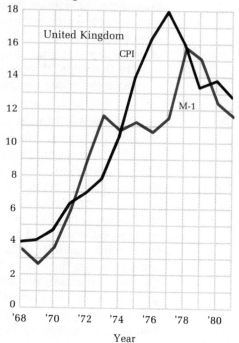

Percent Change

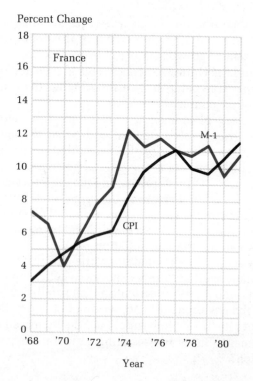

Percent Change

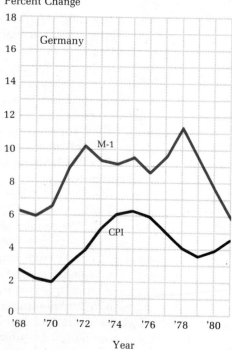

Figure 13-6. Money Growth and Inflation in Four Developed Countries

(page 420)

Source: *International Financial Statistics* (IMF: annual issue, 1982), data are four-year moving averages of annual figures.

The long-run relationship between monetary growth and inflation is fairly obvious in these graphs. Yet, the two lines, the monetary growth line and the price level growth line, do not lie directly on top of each other. Why? First, the difference between the long-run growth rate of the money supply and the inflation rate is productivity, and productivity varies between countries. Second, in the short run, a change in monetary growth need not necessarily be met immediately with a change in inflation.

The second question that is raised by the events of 1971-76 is whether discretionary policy is the most effective type of policy. What would have happened if monetary and fiscal authorities had been unable to alter the rate of growth of the money supply? For example, if monetary policy consisted not of the Fed but, instead, of a machine that cranked out a new supply of currency each period at a rate of growth of X percent, would the events of 1971-76 have occurred with fewer economic difficulties? We will leave the reader to ponder that question until Chapter 15.

PROBLEMS AND EXERCISES

1. Describe the following possible explanations of a stagflation:
   a. Wage-push inflation
   b. Administered price
   c. Demand policies
   d. Demand or supply shocks (such as the OPEC oil embargo)

2. Is it possible for the explanations listed in Question 1 to lead to stagflation? If so, explain how. If not, explain what role they might have in a stagflation.

3. Is the idea of giving up one goal—low inflation or low unemployment—to escape stagflation a reasonable approach? Why or why not?

4. What is meant by stop-and-go policies? Why would such policies occur? What would you propose to solve them?

5. What is an incomes policy? Why might an incomes policy delude the monetary authorities into forgetting about inflationary problems? Explain, using the *AD-AS* model.

6. Explain the difference between a steady inflation and a one-time price increase.
7. Would you support indexing the economy? Why or why not?
8. What is the difference between anticipated and unanticipated inflation? What impact does each have on the economy?

SUGGESTED READINGS

A variety of perspectives on the Great Stagflation are provided in

Alan S. Blinder, *Economic Policy and the Great Stagflation* (New York: Academic Press Inc., 1979).

Robert J. Gordon, "The Response of Wages and Prices to the First Two Years of Controls," *Brookings Papers on Economic Activity* (1:1973), pp. 765-778.

Abba P. Lerner, "Stagflation—Its Cause and Cure," *Challenge* (September-October, 1977), pp. 14-19.

Arthur M. Okun, "The Great Stagflation Swamp," *Challenge* (November-December, 1977), pp. 6-13.

Three discussions of the wage and price controls program, in increasing order of technical complexity, are

Robert L. Schuettinger, "Wage-Price Controls: Forty Centuries of Solid Failure," *Nation's Business* (May, 1980), pp. 36-38.

Marvin H. Kosters, *Controls and Inflation: The Economic Stabilization Program in Retrospect* (Washington, D.C.: American Enterprise Institute for Public Policy Research, May, 1980).

The Economics of Price and Wage Controls, K. Brunner and A. Meltzer, eds. (Amsterdam: North-Holland, 1976).

For a review of Fed policy during the period, examine issues of the Federal Reserve Bank of St. Louis Review.

For discussions of effective and anticipated tax rates, see

William Dunkelberg and Richard Peterson, "Consumer Anticipation of Federal Income Tax Changes," *Journal of Macroeconomics* (Spring, 1979), pp. 191-208.

John Seater, "Marginal Federal Personal and Corporate Income Tax Rates in the U.S., 1909-1975," *Journal of Monetary Economics* (November, 1982), pp. 361-381.

For more on the supply side, consult

Robert Rasche and John Tatom, "Energy Price Shocks, Aggregate Supply and Monetary Policy: The Theory and the International Evidence," *Journal of Monetary Economics* (Spring, 1981), pp. 9-93.

CHAPTER 14.

Lessons in Economic Policy following the Great Stagflation: An Emphasis on the Supply Side

"But then," thought Alice, "shall I never get any older than I am now? That'll be a comfort, one way— never to be an old woman—but then—always to have lessons to learn! Oh, I shouldn't like that!"

Alice in Wonderland

The 1980 campaign for the presidency of the U.S. took place in the midst of rising inflation and the seemingly endless accumulation of governmental deficits. Perhaps even more important was the fact that it took place in the aftermath of California's Proposition 13 that put a limit on government spending there. Politicians were forced to endorse the reduction of government spending whether they wanted to or not. Ronald Reagan wanted to. His campaign centered on this issue and was based on the arguments of a chorus of economists and policymakers who were known as *supply-siders*. Whether the actual policies implemented by the Reagan administration followed their campaign promises is a topic of debate. But the results of the first few years of the administration's economic policies, referred to as *Reaganomics*, are now history. In this chapter we take a look at the policies of the supply-siders and discuss the results of their policies. Questions dealt with include the following:

- *What is the Laffer curve?*

- *Does taxation have an effect on the incentives to work, consume, and save?*

- *What do Reaganomics and supply-side economics have to offer?*

- *What is the Social Security muddle?*

- *What is the flat rate tax proposal?*

Introduction: The Carter Legacy and Reaganomics

A number of lessons were offered by the wrenching experience of the Great Stagflation. Yet these economic problems elicited the same old policies: inflation was attributed to a series of one-time supply shocks; tax changes, temporary in nature, were proposed; unrealistic combinations of inflation and unemployment rates were used as targets; and wage and price controls were imposed. Moreover, virtually no attention was paid to the implications of either Friedman's accelerationist hypothesis or the rational expectations hypothesis. Yet this happened during an administration that was supposed to be a breath of fresh air, composed of outsiders not encumbered by the traditions of Washington.

Jimmy Carter took office as the economy was recovering from the Great Stagflation. In 1976 the inflation rate had dropped to less than six percent and the unemployment rate had fallen to 7.7 percent. As the expansion continued during 1977 and 1978 the rate of inflation moved upward to 6.5 percent in 1977, to 7.7 percent in 1978, and then exploded to over 11 percent during 1979. The Carter administration initially reacted to the economy's slow growth during 1976 by proposing a temporary tax rebate but withdrew the proposal as the robustness of the economy became evident. As the administration became concerned with inflation, it focused on the supply shocks of the period. For example, the lead paragraph in the 1980 *Economic Report of the President* stated, "Last year world oil prices more than doubled. . . . Higher oil prices were the major reason for the worldwide speedup in inflation." And a few pages later Mr. Carter noted that, "Recent history has driven home the lesson that events outside our country—such as worldwide crop shortages or sudden increases in OPEC oil prices—can have major inflationary impacts on the domestic economy."[1]

The Carter administration's anti-inflation policy began with a so-called voluntary incomes policy.[2] The Federal Reserve (Fed) embarked on a very tight monetary policy in November, 1978, and Mr. Carter's January, 1979, budget address proposed a very restrictive fiscal policy. In sum then, the 1977-1979 acceleration of inflation elicited tight money, a tight budget, and something akin to price controls. The result was a recession, rising unemployment, and a new president.

Ronald Reagan was elected on November 4, 1980, on a promise reiterated in the opening paragraph of his January, 1982, budget message.

> In the year just ended, the first decisive steps were taken toward a fundamental reorientation of the role of the Federal Government in our economy—a reorientation that will mean more jobs, more opportunity, and more freedom for all Americans.[3]

The economic policies proposed and implemented by the Reagan administration have become collectively known as *Reaganomics* although pieces of the package have been called *supply-side* and even *voodoo economics*.[4] In this chapter we will examine the issues and the policies of

---

[1] *Economic Report of the President* (1980), p. 3.

[2] For a discussion of the Carter program see "The Politics of Price Controls," *Wall Street Journal* (October 31, 1978), p. 6; "The Carter Program: Can It Work?" *Wall Street Journal* (November 7, 1978), p. 15; "A Step Toward Controls?" *Newsweek* (September 25, 1978), p. 76; "Here Are More Answers to Questions on Carter's Wage-Price Guidelines," *Wall Street Journal* (November 14, 1978), p. 18

[3] *Economic Report of the President* (1982), p. 1.

[4] The term *voodoo economics* was first applied to the supply-side proposals by George Bush while he was a candidate for the Republican nomination for president. After Reagan won the nomination and chose Bush as his vice-presidential running mate, the Democrats adopted the term.

Reaganomics. In the process we shall discuss the Laffer curve, the application of monetarism, and the impacts of the combination of tight monetary policy and supply-side fiscal policy on the economy. We will also discuss two of the controversial issues of the period 1980-84—Social Security and various proposals for fundamental tax reform.

The First Year Proposal: Supply-Side Economics and Monetarism

The Carter legacy was a series of lessons that had to be relearned. It was the beginning of a trend toward more conservative economic policies. In February of 1979, the Joint Economic Committee of the Congress of the U.S. completed its thirty-third annual report as required by the Full Employment Act of 1946. The report was unanimously endorsed by both the Republican minority and the Democratic majority (for the first time in over two decades). It denounced wage and price controls, excessive regulation, and government inefficiency. It pointed to inflation as the number one economic problem and looked to monetary restraint, tax restraint, and spending restraint as the solutions. Then in the summer of 1979 a major component of the Carter legacy was put in place. Paul Volcker was appointed chairman of the Board of Governors of the Fed. Volcker began implementing the Joint Economic Committee's recommendation immediately although his greatest impact came on October 6, 1979, when he committed the U.S. central bank to one component of the doctrine of monetarism—watching monetary aggregates rather than interest rates.

With the Carter legacy in place, the primary focus of Reaganomics during the presidential campaign of 1980 and the first year budget was supply-side economics. The primary instigators of this focus were two economists, Arthur Laffer of the University of Southern California and Robert Mundell of Columbia University who first argued that tax rates, beyond a certain point, were depressing both industrial growth and tax collections. Their ideas were publicized by Irving Kristol, editor of *The Public Interest*, by Jude Wanniski and Paul Craig Roberts, editorial writers for the *Wall Street Journal*, and were given impetus by Congressman Jack Kemp, the Office of Management and Budget director David Stockman, and former Nelson Rockefeller aide George Gilder. The ideas contained in their papers, books, and speeches were put into practice with the Kemp-Roth bill of 1980.[5]

---

[5] See Thomas J. Hailstones, *A Guide to Supply-Side Economics* (Richmond, Va: Robert F. Dame, Inc., 1982), for an overview of the writings of Laffer, Gilder, Kristol, Wanniski, and other supply-siders.

While it has long been widely acknowledged that taxes cause considerable distortions in economic and social behavior, the supply-siders presented the knowledge in a policy package. Their policy package was based on the following arguments. Taxes induce people to do many things that they would not do in an untaxed environment—such as buy forests, drill holes in the ground, farm jojoba beans, and buy sports franchises. One of the primary causes of such distortions is the tax on the amount of time and effort that people devote to acquiring income. As the marginal income tax rates increase, the incentive to undertake additional work is reduced. It is not the average rate of tax, but the marginal rate that matters. So, what can be said about the effects of increased marginal rates of tax on effort, hours, and income? Increased marginal tax rates make the incentive to work less attractive so that there is bound to be a reduction in income. However, if a person wants income badly enough, then the higher tax rates (as long as they are not 100 percent) mean that person may work harder and longer in order to obtain a required level of income. But, except in the very short run, this is likely to be an unusual reaction to increases in taxes. One expects the individual, after a while, to reduce effort and increase leisure. For example, consider a worker who is paid piece rate for at least eight hours a day. Because of special skills this worker is able to produce two to three units of output per hour more than the average worker. At the end of an eight-hour day, the worker must decide whether to work an additional hour. Since the additional hour means a higher wage income but also higher tax payments under a progressive income tax system, the worker may feel that the additional after-tax income does not compensate for the hour of foregone leisure. Because of his or her higher marginal tax bracket, the worker's take-home pay for that last hour of work could be less than the hour of pay for the average worker. In this sense, the economy suffers from a decrease in labor supply and a decrease in productivity.

Tax Rates and Tax Revenues: The Laffer Curve

Can we use this argument to conclude that the reduction of tax rates always adds to incentives and thus always increases incomes? Always, no, but often, yes. And with this answer comes the appropriate policy for stimulating growth and a prosperous economy—reduce marginal tax rates.

Martin Feldstein, chairman of the Council of Economic Advisers during the Reagan administration, has argued that the lack of a significant gap between after-tax take-home pay and untaxed unemployment benefits has made leisure a free good for one million workers, thus shrinking GNP and the tax base by the value of their lost production.[6]

---

[6] Martin Feldstein, "The Economics of the New Unemployment," *Public Interest* (Fall,

Arthur Laffer and other supply-siders take the analysis several steps
further. They argue that, because of taxation's effect on the work-leisure
choice, an interesting and policy-oriented relationship exists between tax
rates and tax revenue. This relationship, called the *Laffer curve*, is presented in Figure 14-1. Note that the curve intersects the vertical axis
twice, at a zero tax rate and a 100 percent tax rate. At a zero tax rate, zero
revenue will be raised. But why at a tax rate of 100 percent will tax
revenue be zero? The reason is that at a 100 percent tax rate, no one will
work (assuming that the government does not distribute the money back
to the taxpayer in any relation to the amount contributed). All income is

Figure 14-1. *The Laffer Curve*

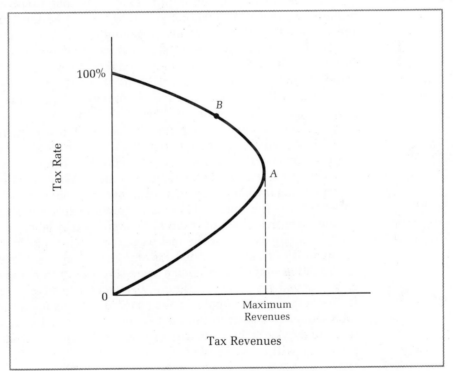

As the tax rate is increased from zero, tax revenues collected increase only up to the point
that the incentives to work, earn income, and report income fail to offset the disincentives
caused by paying increased marginal taxes. This point is denoted by Point A. Note that this
point need not, and probably would not, be a 50 percent marginal tax rate. The policy of
Laffer and other supply-siders proposed during the Reagan presidency was based on the
economy being at Point B. According to the Laffer curve, a decrease in marginal tax rates will
lead to more, not fewer, tax revenues.

1973), pp. 3-42, and "The Private and Social Costs of Unemployment," *American
Economic Review* (May, 1978), pp. 155-158.

taxed away, and on the basis that work itself yields no utility the worker will not supply any labor (at least labor on which taxes are paid). Between these two extremes (zero to 100 percent) a positive tax revenue will be raised. As the tax rate is raised from zero, tax revenues will increase until beyond some tax rate (not necessarily 50 percent), shown as Point *A* in Figure 14-1, an increase in the tax rate results in less tax revenue. This result is derived from the fact that an increase in revenue from a higher tax rate is more than offset by the loss in revenue from a decrease in labor supply and productivity. On the other hand, if the economy is operating on the upper portion of the Laffer curve, such as Point *B*, a tax increase will result in decreased tax revenues, or, conversely, a tax cut will actually result in an increase in tax revenue.

Another aspect of the supply-side argument involves the underground economy. As taxation becomes an increasing burden, it pays individuals to find ways to avoid paying taxes. One of the most direct forms of avoiding taxes is to earn income that is not reported to the Internal Revenue Service—to trade products or services for other services rather than for dollars. All activities that take place without being measured in the national income accounts are part of the *underground economy*. Supply-siders argue that if the rewards to operating in the underground economy are reduced; that is, if taxes are reduced, then individuals will bring their underground activities above ground, measured income will increase, and, therefore, tax revenues will increase.

What is the validity of the Laffer argument? We can outline its logic by incorporating the Laffer curve into our macro model. Since the basis of the Laffer curve is the effect of taxes on the work-leisure decision, we account for the incentive effect of taxation by arguing that labor supply depends on the tax rate as well as the real wage. The higher the tax rate the lower the quantity of labor supplied for any given real wage level.

Taxation may also influence aggregate supply in a less obvious way. As was stated previously, taxation can affect the level of productivity; that is, the output per manhour in the economy. A change in productivity is represented as a shift in the total product curve and a shift in the labor demand curve. At the same real wage and with a lower productivity level, less labor will be demanded.

Taxation and Aggregate Supply

We are now ready to see how a tax cut affects the aggregate supply curve. For simplicity, let us initially ignore the role of expectations. Then the tax cut from T_0 to T_1 in Figure 14-2 may cause the labor supply curve to shift to the right because workers are willing to work more hours for the increased after-tax income. In addition to the increased supply of labor, the tax cut may lead to an increase in work effort that raises productivity, reflected in an upward rotation of the total product curve and an outward

Figure 14-2. The Laffer Curve and the Macro Model

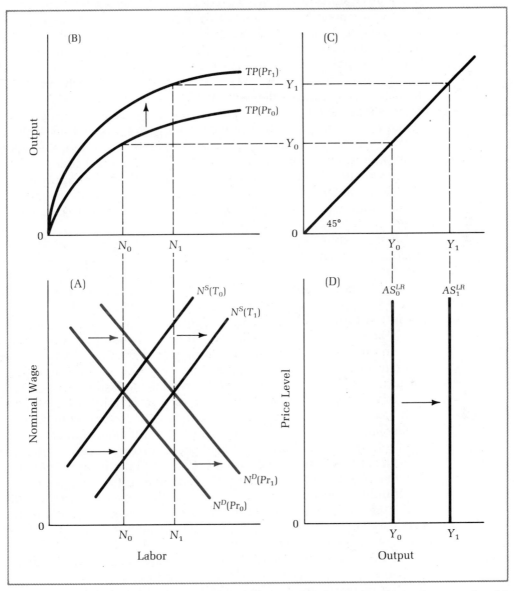

A decrease in the tax rate from T_0 to T_1 will lead to increased incentives to work and to increased productivity as denoted by the outward shift of the labor supply and demand curves and the upward shift of the total product curve. The result is an outward shift of the aggregate supply curve, shown in Panel D.

shift of the labor demand curve. The result is that the level of output will increase—the aggregate supply curve will shift out.

What are the policy implications of a tax cut? The answer depends on the relative shifts of the aggregate demand and aggregate supply curves. Before incorporating the supply-side arguments, a tax cut affected only the aggregate demand curve. As a result, the price level and the level of output would increase for a given nominal wage, at least in the short-run. Once the supply-side arguments are included, the supply curve also shifts to the right. The net result: output increases. Whether the price level increases or decreases depends on the magnitude of the shift of the aggregate demand *(AD)* curve relative to the aggregate supply *(AS)* curve. When the *AS* curve shifts relatively more prices fall, and when the *AD* curve shifts relatively more prices rise. But these results are, at best, only suggestive since the model abstracts so much from real life.

Let us introduce more realism by allowing the labor supply curve to depend on individuals' expectations and assuming that expectations are formed rationally. Then what happens as a large tax cut is passed into law?

If the public believes the tax cuts will stimulate production and remove significant activity from the underground economy so that tax revenues will actually increase, then at a given level of government expenditures the public will expect lower deficits, slower money growth, and reduced rates of inflation. This series of events would be illustrated by outward shifts in the *AD* and *AS* curves, such as shown in Figure 14-3.

If, however, the public believes the tax cuts will not stimulate production and income tax revenues for several years, then it expects increased deficits in the intervening years if government expenditures do not change. The increased deficits will be expected to lead to increased rates of growth of the money stock and increased rates of inflation. Moreover, with tax brackets not indexed, individuals will also expect to move into higher tax brackets. This will induce them to shift more of their activity to the underground economy and avoid paying taxes. In this case the short-run *AS* curve will shift up due to the increased inflationary expectations, and the long-run *AS* curve may shift in either direction, or not shift at all.

If individuals have no confidence that the decreased marginal taxes will stimulate production and increase tax revenues, they will then expect very large deficits and eventual monetization of these deficits. The increased rates of growth of the money supply will necessarily imply increased rates of inflation. This will be reflected as an inward shift of the short-run *AS* curve without any offsetting effects of future expected production increases and tax revenue increases.

The results suggest that the net effect of a tax cut depends on individuals' expectations of both the speed of the supply-side effects and the size of the supply-side effects. One way to help ensure the positive effects would be to limit the growth of the deficit. If the tax cuts are accompanied with spending cuts of approximately the same size (so that the possibility of an increased deficit is lessened), then the supply-side effects may have more of an opportunity to gain favor with the public and be incorporated into their expectations and behavior.

Figure 14-3. *Supply-Side Tax Cuts and the AD-AS Model*

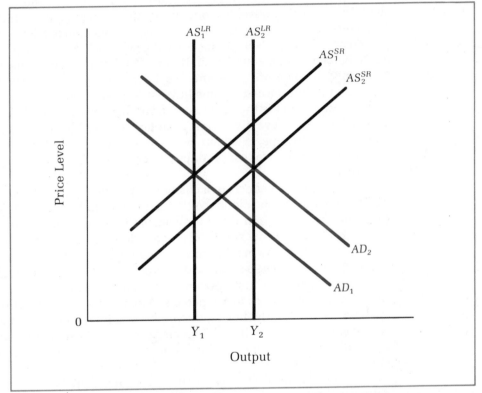

A tax cut that stimulates production and increases income could generate increased tax revenues and, therefore, reduce expectations of monetary growth and inflation. The *AD* curve will shift out, followed by outward shifts of the *AS* curves. On the other hand, if the expectations are of reduced production and tax revenues, and, therefore, of increased deficits, monetization of these deficits, and increased inflation, then the *AD* curve will shift out. This, however, would not be followed by outward shifts of the *AS* curves.

Supply-siders maintain that the effects of a tax cut are immediate, that there are no increased deficits and, therefore, no offsetting inflationary expectations on the part of the public. Others assert that the supply-side effects would have little, if any, effect; others argue that the tax cuts would be dangerous rather than productive; and still others maintain that the supply-side effects would take too long, that their benefits would be swamped by the difficulties of the intervening time period. What evidence is used to support the supply-side arguments?

Supply-Side Evidence

It is difficult to compile evidence of the effects of marginal income taxes on effort and incentives. As with so much in economics, the effects of tax changes are often confounded with other events and it is difficult to separate their consequences. One approach is to compare countries that have a high marginal tax rate with those that have a low one.[7] It appears that Sweden, on average, has one of the highest marginal tax rates. Most taxpayers have marginal rates of tax on earned income of between 60 and 70 percent. To put this in perspective, the average U.S. marginal tax rate is 18-20 percent. Other countries in Europe that have high marginal tax rates on earned income are Italy and the United Kingdom. In contrast, the marginal rates on earned income in West Germany and France are considerably lower. What is the conclusion from this comparison? Italy and the United Kingdom have higher marginal tax rates and have had the sickest economies in Europe.[8] Sweden seems an exception, but this appearance could be illusory. Swedish productivity deteriorated rapidly in the 1960s and 1970s.

Evidence on the effects of a change in marginal tax rates is even more difficult to assess. The evidence that is thought to be most persuasive is the boom in production that followed the Kennedy-Johnson tax cuts of 1964-65.[9] There was a substantial reduction in the marginal personal income tax rates—the maximum fell from a value of 91 percent in 1950-63, to 77 percent in 1964, and to 70 percent in 1965. But the evidence is not as clear cut as it first appears. Productivity growth fell during this period from 2.4 percent to 1.5 percent. Moreover, the money supply was expanded significantly. In fact, the production increases of the mid-1960s can be explained as the initial impacts of the increased rates of expansion of money—an expansion not immediately incorporated into inflationary expectations.

Another piece of evidence comes from the British experience with substantial tax cuts during 1971. The response of the economy was apparently speedy and dramatic. The level of output increased by about 8 percent and industrial production rose by about 10 percent. But again, what appears clear at first glance becomes confused upon closer scrutiny. During this period the growth of the money supply (which had been increasing at something less than 9 percent per year) accelerated to a rate of more than 20 percent per year, and productivity fell.

---

[7] For a more detailed discussion of the points made in this section read Carl Christ and A. A. Walters, "The Mythology of Tax Cuts," *Policy Review* (Spring, 1981), pp. 73-86. Reagan's view on these points is expressed in an "Interview with Ronald Reagan: Sharp Contrast with Carter's Economics," *Business Week* (March 31, 1980), pp. 94-95.

[8] The rates of growth of real GNP during the 1960s and the 1970s in these countries were as follows: Italy—5.2 percent (1960-73), 2.1 percent (1974-81); the United Kingdom—3.1 percent (1960-73), 0.9 percent (1974-81).

[9] See Arthur Laffer, "Two Views of the Kemp-Roth Bill," *The AEI Economist* (July, 1978).

Hence, the two greatest tax cuts in the history of the U.S. and the United Kingdom were associated with monetary expansion. What then is the conclusion of this brief search into historical support for the supply-side case? It is that when tax cuts are advocated they need to be supported by spending cuts of approximately the same size; otherwise, the increased deficits will inexorably lead to increased rates of growth of money that must imply increased rates of inflation. With this lesson in mind let us investigate the effects of the Reagan experiment with supply-side tax cuts.

The Reagan Program

During his first few weeks in office, President Reagan ordered (1) a freeze on the hiring of federal employees, (2) a reduction of government travel, (3) the elimination of the Council on Wage and Price Stability (the council set up by President Carter to run the wage-price controls program), and (4) a cutback on other federal programs. But this was not the major portion of the policies Reagan wanted to institute. In his State of the Union Message on February 18, 1981, Reagan asked Congress to adopt his Economic Recovery Program which included

1. An across-the-board Kemp-Roth style 10 percent annual personal income tax reduction for three years beginning in July, 1981
2. A reduction, over a 3-year period, in the maximum marginal tax rate on investment income (unearned income) from 70 percent to 50 percent to make it equal to the maximum rate on wage and salary income
3. An increase in the income level at which the maximum tax rates take effect
4. Accelerated depreciation via a version of the Capital Cost Recovery Act (discussed in Chapter 10)
5. A continuation and increase in the use of tax credits for new investment
6. A reduction of $5.5 billion in the current 1981 budget
7. A $49.9 billion cut in federal expenditures for fiscal 1982, $79.7 billion in 1983, and $126.8 billion by 1986[10]

The president asked for cutbacks in many programs. The only program exempt from such cutbacks was defense. Reagan also recommended that the Fed keep the growth of the money supply at a more stable rate and reduce the rate of growth by more than one-half.

On the basis of the president's economic recovery program, administration officials were forecasting a 1.1 percent rise in real GNP for 1981, 4.2 percent for 1982, 5.0 percent for 1983, and a real growth rate of 4.5 percent for 1984. At the same time they projected a drop in the inflation rate from 11.1 in 1981, to 8.3 percent in 1982, and to 5.5 percent by 1984.

---

[10] "A Program for Economic Recovery." Summary fact sheet (The White House, February 18, 1981); David I. Fand, "The Reagan Economic Program," *Financial Analysts Journal* (July-August, 1981), pp. 28-34.

During that period unemployment was forecast to fall from 7.8 percent in 1981 to 6.4 percent by 1984. Finally, a balanced budget was predicted for 1984.

The administration's forecasts were not greeted with enthusiasm. Alice Rivlin, then director of the Congressional Budget Office (CBO), argued that the date of 1984 for a balanced budget was unrealistic.[11] In addition, most major forecasting services maintained that President Reagan's economic recovery plan was inflationary and would result in less real GNP growth, a smaller reduction in interest rates, and slower progress than the administration was forecasting.[12] While both President Reagan and OMB director David Stockman were publicly critical of the forecasters' adverse comments, Stockman provided a glimpse of his private views in an interview with the *Atlantic* in which he voiced serious reservations about the expected success of the program.[13]

What have been the early results? The behavior of major economic variables during 1979-82 is presented in Table 14-1. The data indicate that the administration placed too much emphasis on the positive effects of the supply-side program as implemented in the actual bills passed by Congress.[14] Inflation began to slow, but interest rates did not follow inflation downward. Expectations of inflation continued to be high. Consequently, real interest rates rose and consumption and investment fell. Real GNP slowed considerably. As the economy failed to perform according to the administration's script, scapegoats (or actual causes) were

Table 14-1. *Economic Variables 1979 to 1982*

YEAR	% CHANGE		DEFICIT (BILLIONS)	INFLATION RATE	UNEMPLOYMENT RATE
	M-1	M-2			
1979	7.1	8.2	27.7	11.3	5.8
1980	6.6	9.0	59.6	13.5	7.1
1981	6.4	10.1	57.9	10.4	7.6
1982	8.5	9.7	110.6	6.1	9.7

Source: *Economic Report of the President* (1983).

---

[11] See Hailstones, *A Guide to Supply-Side Economics*, p. 140.

[12] See *Blue Chip Indicators* (published by R. Eggert of Sedona, Arizona).

[13] William Greider, "The Education of David Stockman," *Atlantic* (December, 1981), pp. 27-40.

[14] Many, if not most, of the supply-siders claimed that this implementation of their arguments was not a valid experiment of supply-side economics. For example, they argued that the 3-year tax cut should have been a 1-year cut, that social security taxes should not have been increased, and, furthermore, that the indexation of tax brackets should have taken place immediately, not in 1985.

sought. The Fed was the administration's first choice. Paul Volcker was blamed for the record high interest rates and, consequently, for the sluggish economy.[15]

Monetary Policy during the First Year Plan

On October 6, 1979, Paul Volcker publicly embraced monetarism, or at least the monetarists' suggestion that monetary aggregates, rather than interest rates, should be the primary target for monetary policy. The Fed clamped down on the money supply during the first half of 1980 and loosened up on it considerably during the second half. It then slammed on the brakes during 1981. Many Fed watchers accused the Fed of still attempting to control interest rates (hence the large volatility in the aggregates).[16] The behavior of the money aggregates and two short-term interest rates are shown in Table 14-2 on a quarterly basis for the period 1980 to the first quarter of 1982. The month-to-month and even quarter-to-quarter variation in growth rates was very large. Yet interest rates were allowed to fluctuate much more than they had in the previous two decades. They rose to record levels, and the economy plummeted.

Many blamed the high interest rates on the large (and projected to be even larger) deficits rather than purely on monetary policy. Deficits, in

Table 14-2. Annual Percentage Changes in M-1 and M-2 and Short-Term Quarterly Interest Rates, 1980:1-1982:2

	80:1	80:2	80:3	80:4	81:1	81:2	81:3	81:4	82:1	82:2
M-1	5.8	−2.6	14.6	10.8	4.9	9.2	.3	5.7	10.4	3.3
M-2	7.3	5.6	16.0	9.1	8.3	12.0	8.3	8.9	9.8	9.5
Federal Funds Rate	15.05	12.69	9.83	15.85	16.6	17.78	17.78	13.59	14.23	14.5
Three-Month T-bill Rate	13.35	9.65	9.15	13.61	14.39	14.91	15.05	11.75	12.81	12.4

Source: *Federal Reserve Bulletin* (December, 1982).

---

[15] See, for example, "A Treasury-Fed Spat As Interest Rates Slip," *Business Week* (October 19, 1981), p. 45.

[16] See the discussion in Chapter 11 on monetary policy after October, 1979.

1980 and 1981, had doubled from 1979. Supply-siders were on the defensive and the administration returned to the drawing boards for the second year program.[17]

The Tax Equity and Fiscal Responsibility Act: To Tax, or Not to Tax?

The apparent lack of success of the first year program, particularly the large deficit and the even larger deficits projected for subsequent years, led the administration to revise its policies the second year. Deficits near $200 billion were being forecast for fiscal years 1983 and 1984. Projections of these large deficits were affecting expectations of inflation and keeping interest rates high even as actual inflation fell. In addition, the Fed seemed to gain control of the money supply during 1982—the growth rate of the aggregates declined considerably. Many in Congress were calling for increased taxes and for the president to give up his demands for massive increases in defense spending. Social Security was increasingly running in the red, and it and other entitlement programs came to the forefront of issues that had to be dealt with. The 1982 budget that President Reagan presented to Congress called for increases in defense spending, very small increases in social spending, and increased taxes—called *revenue enhancements.*

The Reagan tax program, as presented in his 1982 budget, represented a major switch from the previous year's efforts to spur economic activity through tax cuts. The second year proposal was an attempt to enhance revenues by improving tax collections and closing loopholes.

In 1981, the president's budget, as passed by Congress, enacted the largest tax cuts in U.S. history—reducing federal revenues by $750 billion over the five years following passage. In 1982, the budget as enacted by Congress included the Tax Equity and Fiscal Responsibility Act. Of the $750 billion given up by the government in 1981-86, the 1982 act will take back approximately $215 billion in the five years after enactment.[18]

The economy continued to slide in 1982. Unemployment rose to near 11 percent, although inflation dropped precipitously, to less than 5 percent. Interest rates, particularly short-term rates, dropped fairly dramatically. But deficits continued to increase, and the outlook for the 1983 and 1984 budgets was for record high deficits, reaching and exceeding $200 billion. The experiment with supply-side economics was apparently over.

---

[17] For an example of this defensiveness early in 1981, see "Putting Reaganomics to the Test," *Newsweek* (June 15, 1981), p. 28.

[18] *Tax Equity and Fiscal Responsibility Act of 1982* (New York: Touche-Ross, Inc., 1982).

Although the president was calling for staying the course, the course was no longer the one proposed by supply-side economics and the Laffer curve.

Monetary Policy during the Second Year

What went wrong? Why was the economy continuing to flounder in a recession? Look for answers to the Fed and monetary policy. The monetary aggregate M-1, although somewhat volatile, was definitely allowed to grow very little. From June, 1982, to August, 1982, it grew at only a 2.6 percent annual rate, and over the year from August, 1981, to August, 1982, at a 5.5 percent rate. The relatively tight monetary conditions combined with the large (and expected to be even larger) federal government deficits to keep interest rates high. During the end of 1981 and the first 6-8 months of 1982 this situation created difficulties for firms' balance sheets.

Forecasting that interest rates would fall during the 1980 slowdown, firms shortened their debt maturity; that is, they borrowed short-term rather than long-term and waited for the time to jump into the long-term end of the market. They did not want to find themselves burdened with long-term debt at very high interest rates in 1981 and beyond. Yet as rates remained high, firms were placed in precarious positions. They had to continue to turn over their short-term debt and to borrow from commercial banks at ever higher rates.[19] This can be compared to the interest on the federal government debt that continually grows and must be financed in each year's budget. Firms had to borrow to finance their increasing interest payments. The result of an increasingly poor cash flow situation led more and more firms into bankruptcy. As a result of the combination of the 1978 Bankruptcy Act and the poor economy, the number of bankruptcies each month during 1982 ran at levels paralleling those of the Great Depression.[20]

Many firms in the financial industry were also finding themselves in difficult situations, but many of their problems were in adjusting to the provisions of the Financial Deregulation and Monetary Control Act of 1980. The act liberalized what the various financial institutions were permitted to do. Savings and loan associations (S&Ls) were allowed to

---

[19] See "Debt's New Dangers," *Business Week* (July 26, 1982), pp. 44-50.

[20] The Bankruptcy Reform Act of 1978 is described as *a debtor's act*. Its provisions reduce the penalties of bankruptcy, enabling individuals to retain more of their assets after bankruptcy than had been the previous case. It has been estimated that some 5 to 10 percent of all bankruptcies during 1979-82 were the result of the new act. See W. J. Boyes and Roger Faith, "Economics and the Bankruptcy Reform Act of 1978," *Law and Economics Working Paper Series* (Arizona State University, 1983).

move onto the turf of commercial banks, and other traditionally nonfinancial institutions were allowed to compete with the financial institutions. For example, many brokerage houses began offering money market accounts that took money away from the financial depository institutions. Several firms, such as Prudential Insurance, American Express, Sears, and Bank of America acquired brokerage firms.[21] These developments combined to place the financial industry in a potentially precarious situation. Since many of the regulations, such as Regulation Q (which restricts the activities of S&Ls and commercial banks), were not to be altered for several years; i.e., phased in over five years, the deregulation placed financial institutions in competitively adverse positions. Many feared that the setting was appropriate for a major collapse of the financial industry much like in the Great Depression. One possible scenario envisioned one firm collapsing into bankruptcy, thus forcing its creditors to write off the firm's liabilities at a loss. The creditors, specifically the financial institutions, would lose much of their base for providing loans. The combination of runs on the banks and the loss of assets could force many other financial institutions into bankruptcy as well. Each bankruptcy would reduce the supply of credit or money and thereby lead to the rapid decline of the economy. In addition to the parallels with the Great Depression, the 1980 period had an additional unfavorable factor—the poor financial position of many of the less developed countries and the Eastern European countries. Banks in the United States, other Western countries, and Japan had large loans to countries having severe liquidity problems.[22] The collapse did not occur. One difference between the 1930s and the 1980s was that the Fed actively worked to avoid such collapses in the latter period. The Fed undertook a policy of forcing mergers among financial institutions and of providing short-term funds to help financially distressed institutions over temporary cash flow problems.

This specific approach by the Fed created a relative easing in monetary policy during the last quarter of 1982. Interest rates fell precipitously in August and September of 1982. The monetary aggregates provided little indication of what was happening in monetary policy because of the deregulation movement however. The myriad of new accounts being offered confused the definitions of M-1 and M-2. The Federal Open Market Committee (FOMC) acknowledged in its October 1982 meeting that it was going to ignore M-1 because of the possible confusion of the M-1

---

[21] Prudential acquired the Bache Group; American Express acquired Shearson, Loeb, and Rhodes; Sears acquired Dean, Witter Reynolds; and Bank of America acquired Schwab.

[22] See "A Case for Default?" *The Banker* (April, 1982), pp. 7-22, for a discussion of the international problems.

definition over the next several months. Irrespective of the confusion of definitions, however, all measures pointed to significant easing on the part of the Fed. M-1 grew 15 percent and M-2 grew 9.3 percent at annual rates during August, September, and October of 1982. From October through the rest of 1982, interest rates remained nearly constant even as money growth continued to be relatively rapid. The federal funds rate, for example, remained near 9 percent throughout November and December after having been near 13 percent in August. Long-term rates remained relatively high, as indicated by the 20-year Treasury bond, the rate of which remained near 10.5 percent. With the annual rate of inflation running about 4 percent during this period, the real interest rate was a relatively high 6 percent. Either expectations of a revival in inflation were keeping rates high, or monetary policy was tighter than indicated by monetary aggregates. Most analysts believed the former explanation correct. Virtually all indications were that the Fed had eased considerably.

It was the budget situation that most concerned Wall Street, Congress, and the public. And it was the budget that the Reagan administration was focusing on as it entered its third year.

The Productivity Puzzle

As indicated in the discussion of supply-side economics, one of the major concerns of the period was the distortions and inefficiencies caused by taxes and government in general.[23] These were usually considered to be one of the causes of an important and perplexing problem facing the U.S. economy in recent years—the dramatic decrease in productivity growth in the past decade. The trend rate of growth of productivity, defined as output per hour, in the U.S. since the end of World War II has been declining. During the first 20 years after that war, productivity in the private nonfarm business sector rose at an average annual rate of just under 2.5 percent. For the period 1965 to 1973, the annual increase in productivity slowed to 1.6 percent. Since 1973 the annual growth of productivity has been less than 1 percent.

This pattern of declining growth in productivity has serious implications for the economy.[24] In particular it signals a potential decline in the real standard of living. For example, from 1948 to 1965, hourly nominal compensation in the nonfarm business sector increased at an annual rate

---

[23] Much of this section is from work carried out by Art Blakemore, an economist with the Council on Wage and Price Stability. See, in particular, the release of Tuesday, July 24, 1979, entitled *Productivity: A Report Submitted to the Congress by the Council on Wage and Price Stability* (July 23, 1979).

[24] For a brief overview see Martin Neil Baily, "The Productivity Growth Slowdown," *The Battle against Unemployment and Inflation*, Martin N. Baily and Arthur M. Okun, eds. (New York: W. W. Norton & Co., Inc., 1982).

of 4.6 percent. With an annual productivity growth rate of almost 2.6 percent and inflation of 2.0 percent, real hourly compensation on average grew 2.9 percent annually. From 1965 to 1973 the growth rate of hourly compensation accelerated to 6.6 percent annually, inflation to 4.5 percent, but productivity growth declined to an annual rate of 2.0 percent. As a result, real hourly compensation increased at a somewhat slower annual rate of 2.1 percent. Since 1973, there has been almost no productivity increase, and the deceleration of real compensation gains has continued, despite a further acceleration in the growth of nominal hourly compensation to 8.1 percent. The annual rate of productivity growth over the period has been only 0.8 percent while inflation has been 10 percent, and, consequently, real hourly compensation has increased by only 0.9 percent per year. Of course, the slow-down in productivity is only one factor in the acceleration of unit labor costs and consumer prices. Inflation could have been held to the low rates of the 1948-65 period even with the present rate of growth of productivity if monetary growth and nominal hourly compensation had grown at a lesser rate.

Comparison of international economic data is always suspect because the conceptual foundations and reliability of the data differ widely between countries. With this in mind, available data indicate that the U.S. productivity performance has lagged behind that of all other major developed countries. Table 14-3 illustrates this point. The reasons for this relatively inefficient American performance are not fully understood. However, the most common explanation for the higher rates of productivity growth of our foreign competitors are their relatively higher rates of investment and savings. What accounts for this differential? Several studies have pointed to the government as the major cause. Government regulations have increased business' costs, forcing them to forego research and development and forcing them to utilize nonproductive capital. Also, the U.S. tax system causes a great deal of investment and saving to take place in areas where there would be no such investment or saving without taxes. These distortions lead to the use of less productive capital or even involvement in projects that yield only tax savings. Social Security taxes, the progressive income tax, the effect of bracket creep, and the double taxation of business profits when distributed to equity holders create distortions.

The impetus for Reaganomics and supply-side economics was an attempt to stem this tide of declining productivity. The tax system was indexed to inflation beginning in 1985, marginal tax rates were cut, investment tax credits were increased and extended, and an attempt was made to reduce the regulatory burden on business. Several other policies have been and are being examined but have not yet been implemented. In the remainder of this chapter we will discuss two of the more topical or controversial subjects related to governmental impacts on saving and investment—the Social Security problem and fundamental tax reform.

Table 14-3. *Productivity in Six Major Developed Countries*
(Average Annual Percentage Change)

COUNTRY	MANUFACTURING		
	1950-73	*1973-81*	*1950-81*
United States	2.8	1.8	2.6
United Kingdom	3.6	2.3	3.4
Canada	4.2	1.4	3.9
West Germany	5.9	4.6	5.6
France	5.2	4.7	5.3
Japan	9.5	6.8	9.2

Source: *Productivity and the Economy: A Chartbook* (Bulletin 2172, U. S. Department of Labor, Bureau of Labor Statistics, June, 1983), pp.25-27.

The Social Security Muddle

The package that goes under the name *Social Security* consists of the following three programs: (1) old age and survivors insurance (OASI); (2) disability insurance (DI); and (3) hospital insurance, which is also known as Medicare. The OASI and the DI are not welfare systems: No need must be established in order to obtain benefits. The benefits are received as a matter of right, based on the wages earned and taxes paid. To obtain the funds from which benefits are paid, a tax of 13.3 percent is levied on individual earnings, half paid by the employee and the other half by the employer. In 1983, the tax rate was applied to the first $34,700 of each individual's earnings; in 1976, the tax rate had been applied to the first $15,300 of each individual's earnings.

As originally conceived in the mid-1930s, Social Security was an insurance scheme financed by compulsory employer and employee contributions to a trust fund that would provide wage related pensions to workers as a matter of right. It was not intended to provide the bulk of retirement income to average wage earners or disability and medical care, but merely, as the Social Security Act of 1935 reads, a "floor of protection" that would be supplemented by savings and private pensions.

For several decades the system fared well. Indeed only a decade ago Social Security seemed so robust that the 1971 Social Security Advisory Council suggested that the system was so overfinanced that it should begin dispensing more or reducing collections.[25] Congress passed a 20

---

[25] The Social Security Act requires the appointment every four years of an advisory council

percent benefit increase and actually cut future tax rates. Since Social Security benefits were tied to the consumer price index and wages as inflation began accelerating, recipients were benefitting from double indexing. These developments set the stage for the current problems. The economic projections on which Congress relied proved wildly optimistic. Within a year after the landmark 1972 legislation was passed, the economy plunged into recession and the economy headed for double-digit inflation. Because benefits were tied to the consumer price index (CPI) as well as wages, expenditures soared faster than the wage base, while unemployment also cut into tax revenues.

In May 1982, the Reagan administration suggested some changes in Social Security rules to solve the system's problems.[26] These included reducing early retirement (before 65) benefits, moving the effective date of the 1982 cost of living adjustment from July to October, changing the way benefits are computed, and making it more difficult for individuals to qualify for "disproportionately high" pensions with a minimum of payments into the system. A storm of protest greeted the proposals. Even congressional Republicans failed to back the administration. The Senate voted 96 to zero for a resolution against "precipitously and unfairly" reducing benefits for early retirees or "reductions in benefits which exceed those necessary."

Social Security is not only a political problem but also an economic one. In the Social Security program the worker-retiree ratio is crucially important because today's Social Security recipients are paid from the tax on today's workers and employers and not from the return on an invested principal. As a pay-as-you-go system, Social Security results in less saving in the private sector and less investment than if true trust funds or annuities (where the return on invested principal helps pay the bills) carried more of the financing load. Furthermore, the availability of Social Security benefits may reduce the incentive for individual workers and employers to set up retirement trusts. Thus less money is saved, and less is available for private investment.[27] Another complaint is that a tax like Social Security discourages employment. It makes hiring an employee more costly for the employer who has to pay the going wage plus half the tax, and it reduces the number of people willing to work for the going wage less the Social Security taxes.

---

consisting of thirteen members representing labor, business, and the public who are charged with examining the Social Security System.

[26] Barry Crickmer, "Social Security: Is a Patch Up Enough?" *Nation's Business* (October, 1981).

[27] See Martin Feldstein, "Social Security, Induced Retirement, and Aggregate Capital Accumulation," *Journal of Political Economy* (September-October, 1974), pp. 905-926; and Alice Munnell, *The Effect of Social Security on Personal Saving* (Cambridge, Mass.: Ballinger Publishing Company, 1974).

In addition to the distortions caused by Social Security, there are several specific problems associated with the system itself. First, because it is an entitlement program, it is an uncontrollable item in the budget. Second, the Social Security system faces an immediate crisis: The financial viability of the OASI program is in question.[28] In fiscal 1982, the OASI trust fund paid out $15 billion more than it took in. Its accumulated surplus was completely wiped out, and it was forced to borrow some $600 million from the disability trust fund. Third, the system faces a long-run problem: The decline in birth and death rates will lead to a very serious financial problem around the year 2010 when the baby boom generation begins to retire. Moreover, it has been belatedly realized that the drop in the birth rate since the baby boom foreshadows a huge deficit in the next century. By 2030, only two workers may be paying into the fund for every retiree drawing from it. When the system began, the ratio was 16 to 1; it is now 3 to 1.

Possible Solutions to the Social Security Muddle

President Reagan set up the National Commission on Social Security Reform to examine the problems of the system and to devise solutions to these problems. The commission projected a $150 to $200 billion deficit through 1989 and proposed a number of possible solutions.

1. Advancing to 1984 the payroll tax increases scheduled to go into effect between 1985 and 1990 (This would raise rates from 13.4 percent to 15.3 percent.)
2. Including newly hired government employees into the program (They are now exempt.)
3. Changing the cost-of-living adjustment by indexing pension benefits to wages adjusted for productivity increases instead of the CPI
4. Financing part of Social Security with general revenues, that is, revenues financed by all other federal taxes

For the short-term problem, any of these solutions, or a combination of them, can patch up Social Security. The mandatory coverage of government (both federal and state) employees not now in the program trades off a short-run fix for a long-run problem. By including more employees in the program, current revenues will increase. However, the number of potential recipients in future years will also increase, and the problem beginning in 2010 will be exacerbated.

The increase in taxes runs counter to the Reagan philosophy and is contradictory to the supply-side policies the administration initially em-

---

[28] See "The Political Posturing on Social Security Must End," *Wall Street Journal* (November 11, 1982), p. 27.

braced. Social Security tax increases imposed in 1977 were the largest tax increases in U.S. history. An attempt to speed up the payroll taxes would nearly equal the 1977 increase, and an attempt to increase taxes during difficult economic times is not typically a politically viable option.

The macroeconomic problem of the pay-as-you-go nature of the Social Security System is unlikely to be altered. Therefore, whatever ill effects the system has on national saving and, consequently, on national investment and productivity will probably not be diminished. A few suggestions along these lines have been made, however. One is to slowly turn the system into a private pension fund by increasing the retirement age and reducing benefits, taxing the portion of benefits that is financed by employer contributions, and using these taxes to build up a pension fund. Because of the politically sensitive nature of such a measure, it is unlikely to be enacted in the near future.

The use of general revenues is the easiest political route, but rather than helping the budget problems, this approach most likely will make them worse since there then will be no constraint on Social Security spending. There would be no outstanding record of its own deficits.

The solution offered by the commission and accepted by the president and Congress primarily focused on the short-run problems but did attempt to address the long-run difficulties of the system. It extended coverage to all employees of private nonprofit institutions and all new federal employees, and it prohibited further withdrawals of state and local government employees from the system. Very few benefits were cut. Instead, tax increases were scheduled in order to make up most of the projected deficit.

The solution offered by the commission was expected to save $169 billion between 1983 and 1989 leaving an expected deficit of $30 billion.[29] The solution does little in terms of reducing the impact of Social Security on the budget. About one-third of the $169 billion to be added to the trust fund will come from other government accounts.

The Flat Rate Income Tax

There are three criteria by which tax systems are normally judged. First, the system should be fair. It should impose an equitable burden on all individual taxpayers. The second criterion is economic efficiency. The tax system should not produce incentives that distort individual decisions or cause undesirable movement of resources between alternative uses. In this sense the tax system should be as neutral as possible across all uses of time and resources. Finally, the tax code should be easily

---

[29] See *Business Week* (January 21, 1983), pp. 20 and 21.

administered. The current tax structure of the U.S. appears to be failing all these criteria.

The federal income tax is widely perceived to be complicated and unfair.[30] Although many of the provisions in the current law were enacted to promote social and economic goals, one result has been that individuals or families of equal means may pay quite different amounts of tax, depending on how they earn or use their incomes. Also, taxpayers in very unequal economic circumstances may pay the same amount of tax because of loopholes and exemptions. This complex and uneven tax system has led to excessive planning and rearranging of personal finances and business affairs.

The income tax has also been a serious impediment to private capital formation and to individual efforts to work and save. Throughout the 1970s, high inflation caused the systematic overstatement of investment income and pushed more and more taxpayers into high marginal tax brackets. The result was to reduce households' reward for saving and to raise the cost of business investment.

Some of the more prevalent distortions are illustrated by the following examples in which income is treated in different ways for tax purposes.

1. Compensation is fully taxed if it is in the form of cash wages but left untaxed if it is in the form of fringe benefits such as employer contributions to health plans or the personal consumption elements of employee business expenses. The exclusion of many fringe benefits from taxation encourages workers to choose more fringe benefits than they would if all forms of compensation were taxed equally.
2. Capital income may be taxed at high rates if it is in the form of dividends from corporate stock because both the corporation income tax and the individual income tax apply. It may be taxed at a zero rate if it is in the form of tax-exempt bond interest, or it may even be taxed at negative rates on certain sheltered investments. The tax may apply only to a fraction of the real income from capital gains or, when inflation is greater than the gain, a tax will be assessed on what is really a loss.
3. Income spent on most goods and services is taxed while income spent on selected goods and services, such as home energy saving devices, owner-occupied housing, and some medical expenses, is sheltered from tax.
4. Preferential tax treatment among industries distorts investment decisions. For example, the capital gains treatment for livestock or the expensing of mining costs allows those industries to attract investors in projects that yield lower pretax returns than those in other industries.

---

[30] Much of this discussion of the flat rate tax comes from the "Statement of the Honorable John E. Chapoton, Assistant Secretary of the Treasury for Tax Policy, before the Senate Finance Committee" (September 28, 1982); Robert E. Hall and Alvin Rabushka, *Low Tax, Simple Tax, Flat Tax* (Stanford, Calif.: Hoover Institution Press, 1982); and the *White House Conference on Productivity: Fundamental Tax Reform,* Arthur E. Blakemore and William J. Boyes, eds. (Washington, D. C.: USGPO, 1983).

5. The separate corporate income tax distorts economic decisions. By imposing a double tax on dividends, the corporate income tax encourages firms to issue debt rather than equity, and to retain earnings rather than to pay out dividends. It also favors the unincorporated business over the corporation.

6. Accelerated cost recovery and the investment tax credit have reduced the tax burden on investment in equipment and machines, but the income tax continues to fall heavily on investments in structures and inventories. This differential distorts choices of production methods and raises the relative tax burden on activities and industries that naturally require more of the heavily taxed capital.

The outstanding disadvantage of the income tax is its built-in bias against saving. The income tax discourages saving by reducing the rate of return to the saver below the market return derived from investing in capital. A taxpayer who would be willing to postpone consumption to obtain a 10 percent return, thereby making resources available for capital formation, may not be willing to make the same sacrifice for an after-tax 6 percent return. This is not a double tax on savings as some have asserted; it is a single tax on capital income. But this single tax has the inevitable consequence of reducing the reward for deferring consumption, and by making less saving available for investment it impairs the future growth and productivity of the economy.

High marginal tax rates amplify these initial price distortions, both those inherent even in uniform taxes, like the disincentive to work, and those resulting from lack of uniformity in the tax treatment of similar activities. The higher the rates, the greater the penalty on fully taxed activities and the greater the value of tax preferences. In addition, legal tax avoidance and illegal tax evasion are more rewarding with high than with low tax rates.

Sharply graduated rates introduce further distortions by encouraging individuals to change the timing of transactions from year to year or to arrange for taxable income and deductions to be traded between higher and lower taxed individuals. The cost to the economy comes, again, from exaggerating the relative worth of certain activities that the taxpayer would otherwise find unprofitable.

Scholarly research, along with Internal Revenue Service reports, reveals widespread evidence of tax evasion on interest, dividend, and other forms of household or professional income. Also, tax shelters are now a commonplace feature of the financial landscape. In fact, estimates of the underground economy range from several tens of billions to several hundred billion dollars. The tax structure has also generated several "nonproductive" cottage industries, such as one that simply fills out tax forms and another that lobbies Congress and the executive branch for special interest tax favors.

The failure of the present tax code to achieve any of the three criteria by which tax systems are judged, combined with the growing opinion that the tax system is beyond repair on an item-by-item basis, has led many tax experts to advocate sweeping reforms of the system. Prior to the twentieth century, federal revenues, collected largely from the custom duties, comprised about 3 percent of GNP. Since the adoption of the Sixteenth Amendment in 1913 and the payroll tax in the 1930s, federal revenues have grown to consume nearly 24 percent of GNP. The problems with the tax system became particularly evident during the 1970s when growing numbers of taxpayers were taxed at increasingly higher brackets as their nominal incomes grew due to inflation. The increased tax rates imply a decreased return to income included in the tax base and, therefore, an increased return to income not included in the base. This also means an increased return to activities that remove income from the tax base and tax-avoiding activities. Although the tax structure generated *misallocations* of resources (allocations based on after tax rather than pretax returns) before the 1970s, the inflationary decade exacerbated its difficulties. The consumption bias of the present system and the differential treatment of alternative investment and saving decisions also became more evident during this decade.

In addition, the tax structure, while still progressive, has become less progressive in the past decade. The tax base has eroded continuously so that the personal income tax is far from a comprehensive income tax. The least costly tax to collect has been payroll taxes so that wage and salary earners have been subject to the most rapidly accelerating marginal tax rates.

All these effects have induced a search for a tax structure that is more equitable, neutral, and administrable. Several proposals have been aired, but the three most common evocations are for a flat rate tax in the form of either a consumption tax or a comprehensive income tax and a value added tax (VAT).

The flat rate tax would broaden the tax base and apply a single uniform rate to this broadened base.[31] Any tax system distorts some market signals and thereby distorts decisions on how much to work, when and what to consume, when and how to save, how much to invest, and in what types of capital to invest. Even a completely uniform income tax will affect individual choices between work and leisure, and between consuming now or saving for future consumption. Yet, while a distortion of the choice between work and leisure is inherent in virtually any tax, distortions that result from differential taxation among goods or particular activities need not exist. A lack of uniformity of the tax burden among alternative uses of capital, such as we have in our current system, distorts

---

[31] By broadening the tax base it is meant that exemptions, such as for dependents and homeownership, would be disallowed.

the allocation of resources to the extent that it can make financial successes out of projects that are less productive, and losers out of undertakings that would otherwise be winners. Choices among investment projects, financial arrangements, and production methods are biased toward those that are tax favored.

Proposals on flat rate taxes vary as to whether they would allow any progressiveness by altering the exemptions that would be permitted. Some proposals envision a pure flat rate tax that has a broad uniform tax base and a single tax rate, but permits no exemptions for the taxpayer or dependents. In the absence of personal exemptions, the single rate for a uniform income tax could be lowered to about 13 percent on the uniform income tax base without altering the amount currently collected. However, any broad based option with a single rate would involve a significant redistribution of income.

If a flat rate tax is designed to raise the same revenue as present law, every dollar of tax reduction for one taxpayer must mean a dollar of increase for some other taxpayers. A single rate income tax with no exemptions would result in a tax reduction of about $40 billion for taxpayers above the $50,000 income level matched by a similar tax increase for those below the $30,000 income level. Even though the total tax revenue would be about the same, about 77 percent of taxpayers would experience a tax increase under this type of flat tax. Base broadening, however, does not dictate the answer to the separate and distinct question of how taxes might be allowed to vary by income class. If the tax base were broadened, marginal rates could be lowered in every bracket without affecting the overall distribution of the tax burden by income class. The net result would be a lower rate schedule without affecting the existing progressiveness of the tax system.

An alternative possibility is to apply a uniform tax on consumed rather than earned income. The uniform tax on consumed income would differ from the uniform income tax by excluding net saving from the tax base. Under the consumed income tax, the taxpayer would include in his tax base all forms of current monetary compensation, the current consumption value of all fringe benefits supplied by employers, and the proceeds of all borrowing, in excess of loan repayments. The taxpayer would be allowed to deduct from the tax base all net purchases of income earning assets and all net deposits in interest bearing accounts. Accrued interest, earnings from ownership of corporate shares, increases in the value of pension and life insurance reserves, and other increases in the value of asset holdings would not be subject to tax until withdrawn and paid out for consumption.

As a simple example, consider a family with $20,000 in wages out of which $4,000 is saved. It would be taxed on $16,000, not on $20,000 as under a uniform income tax. On the other hand, if the family spent more than it earned, say $25,000, by borrowing or dipping into its savings account for the extra $5,000, it would be taxed on the $25,000 of consumption. Note that since total consumption in the economy is less than income, tax rates would need to be higher to generate the same amount of revenue.

Stipulating that only individuals consume, there would be no separate corporate tax nor any need to integrate personal and corporate earnings. Taxable income of an individual would include distributions from corporations and individuals' sales of corporate shares. In effect, corporate income would be taxed when it found its way into individual consumption. Retained earnings would receive no tax advantage over dividends, so attributing retentions to stockholders would be unnecessary. A tax on consumed income would, however, encourage corporations, particularly closely held corporations, to buy consumption for their employees, permitting the workers to evade taxes unless fringe benefit rules were tightly drawn and applied.

One version of a flat tax that approximates a uniform tax on consumed income is S 2147, introduced by Senator Dennis DeConcini. It is based on the flat tax proposal developed by Robert Hall and Alvin Rabushka of the Hoover Institution. Under S 2147 there would be a single rate tax on employee compensation and on business cash flow. Corporations and noncorporate business entities would be taxed on total revenues less purchases of assets, wages, and purchases of goods and services from other firms. Dividends and interest payments would not be deductible in computing the business tax, nor would they be included in the income of the recipient.

Several people have wanted to copy the European tax system which is a VAT. A VAT is basically a sales tax but on a federal level. As under a sales tax, various types of consumption can be eliminated from the tax base, but the manner in which this is accomplished can cause distortions in the allocation of resources. First, there are some exclusions necessary for administrative reasons, such as housing, domestic services, food consumed on farms, and services provided free. Other exclusions may be selected to narrow the tax base for equity reasons (items such as food consumed at home, medical expenses, and other necessities).

Most of the advantages of a VAT concern its neutrality and administrability. With respect to neutrality, there seems to be very little difference between a flat rate tax on personal consumption and a VAT free from most exclusions. Both in theory appear to be more neutral than an income tax. Once exclusions are added to the VAT, it becomes less efficient than an idealized consumption tax. Some observers believe political considerations would probably make any consumption tax actually adopted much less neutral. Like the existing personal income tax, a personal consumption tax would probably contain a variety of tax preferences that would change its neutrality. It is then an open question whether a VAT in its most likely final form would be more or less neutral than either a personal consumption tax or the existing personal income tax.

A VAT would increase the federal tax base, thus permitting additions to revenue and the reduction of large budget deficits. Of course, whether this is an advantage or a disadvantage depends on one's opinion on the need for large public expenditures. A VAT may also be easier to implement than a broad based income tax reform or the adoption of a consumption tax. There is some evidence that the sales tax as now imposed by states (or the possibility of a VAT) is more popular among the American public than the present system.

Its major disadvantage involves equity considerations. A comprehensive sales tax levied on all consumption is clearly regressive when compared with income. In this regard, it might not be very different from a payroll tax, in the aggregate, but it impinges more heavily on the aged. By comparison, a personal consumption tax can be levied at graduated rates. The personal consumption tax then can be less regressive than a VAT, and it can even be progressive. If the VAT is used as a replacement for the present personal and corporate income tax system, it would substantially reduce the progressiveness of the tax system.

The regressiveness of the VAT could be reduced through the use of exemptions or zero rating for goods and services deemed to be necessities and differential rates on luxuries. But European experience indicates that these modifications make the administration and enforcement of the tax much more difficult.

Whether or not some type of fundamental tax reform takes place, it is clear that economists are concerned with the distortions caused by taxes. Tax policy is not just a tool of stabilization policy. It also creates incentives and disincentives to undertake particular activities. This concern was manifest in the supply-side programs and in the proposals for first year expensing of capital expenditures that we discussed in Chapter 10 as well as here. Such distortions were at one time considered only the province of microeconomics. Clearly they are also a macroeconomic issue. Productivity changes, inflation, and other macroeconomic topics depend on the impacts of different tax policies.

Conclusions: Issues in Stabilization Policy

The experiences of the 1970s and the 1980s provided a great many lessons not only for economic policymakers, but for economic theorists as well. Perhaps *lessons* is not the correct word to use—*questions* would be more appropriate. As we have seen in the past two chapters, as many questions as answers were provided by the application of policies during the decade and a half since 1970. Perhaps the most central question is, Should activist stabilization policy be used?

This, to some extent, is a normative (value judgement based) question, and the answers given are derived from a blend of normative and positive (nonvalue based) analyses. In the following chapter we will examine the controversies of stabilization policy—the answers proposed to this question. We will also discuss several closely related questions, such as, (1) Should monetary policy be governed by rules or discretion? and (2) What do the lags in fiscal policy mean for stabilization policy?

PROBLEMS AND EXERCISES

1. Why could Carter's anti-inflation policy have been expected to fail? What policies would you have proposed?

2. Is it fair to call Volcker's October 6, 1979 statement a commitment to monetarism? Why or why not?

3. Using the *AD-AS* model demonstrate the effect of a tax cut if the economy is operating on the upper portion of the Laffer curve. On the lower portion of the curve. Explain the difference.

4. In Table 14-1 there are four observations of inflation rate-unemployment rate combinations. Plot these on a graph with the inflation rate on the vertical axis and the unemployment rate on the horizontal axis. What is the curve you have plotted? How do you rationalize the shape of the curve?

5. Explain why Social Security is in trouble. What solutions would you offer? Why?

6. What is the theory behind the flat rate income tax proposals? Would you expect these proposals to be passed by Congress? Why or why not?

SUGGESTED READINGS

For an overview of supply-side economics, see

Thomas J. Hailstones, *A Guide to Supply-Side Economics* (Richmond, Va.: Robert F. Dame, Inc., 1982).

An early evaluation of Reaganomics is presented in

William Craig Stubblebine and Thomas Willett, eds., *Reaganomics: A Mid-Term Report* (San Francisco: Institute for Contemporary Studies, 1983).

Analyses of Social Security issues are provided in

Robert Ball, *Social Security Today and Tomorrow* (New York: Columbia University Press, 1978).

Alicia Munnell, *The Future of Social Security* (Washington, D.C.: The Brookings Institution, 1977).

Social Security Financing and Benefits, Report of the 1979 Advisory Council (Washington, D.C.: U.S. Government Printing Office, 1980).

Declining productivity growth is analyzed in

John Kendrick, "Productivity Trends and the Recent Slowdown: Historical Perspectives, Causal Factors and Policy Options," pp. 17-77 in *Contemporary Economic Problems,* W. Fellner, ed. (Washington, D.C.: American Enterprise Institute for Public Policy Research, 1979).

J. R. Norsworthy, Michael Harper, and Kent Kunze, "The Slowdown in Productivity Growth: Analysis of Some Contributing Factors," *Brookings Papers on Economic Activity* (2:1979), pp. 387-421.

For an analysis of the S 2171 flat rate tax proposal, see

Robert Hall and Alvin Rabushka, *Low Tax, Simple Tax, Flat Tax* (Stanford, Calif.: Hoover Institution Press, 1982).

CHAPTER 15.

Issues in Stabilization Policy

Is fiscal policy being oversold? Is monetary policy being oversold? . . . My answer is yes to both of those questions.
            Milton Friedman, 1968

If to do were as easy as to know what to do, chapels had been churches, and poor men's cottages princes' palaces.
            Shakespeare, The Merchant of
                                Venice

Does it make any sense to use monetary and/or fiscal policy to attempt to control the economy? Are matters made worse or better by the use of discretionary policies? These were fundamental questions faced by economists after the Great Stagflation and are still points of contention among economists today. In this chapter we will discuss the various answers provided to these questions. As might be expected there is no consensus, although it has become clear that the answer one gives depends primarily on whether one believes prices generally are free to adjust so as to equate demands and supplies or whether one believes that some type of rigidity keeps demands and supplies from equating. In this chapter we will discuss these different views in detail and will consider the following questions:

- *What is the effect of uncertainty about whether events are temporary or permanent?*

- *How should policy be run, by rules or with discretion?*

- *What is the role of politics in economic policymaking?*

- *Can lags in the application of policy be reduced?*

Introduction

In the 1960s many economists began to talk about the death of the business cycle. It was believed that the Keynesian framework had produced an easily applied, readily acceptable set of relationships between governmental policy and economic activity so that the economy never again needed to weather the vicissitudes of recessions and inflations. The 1970s altered that view and revived the debate over whether the economy can and should be controlled through fiscal and monetary policies—the so-called stabilization policies. Moreover, the framework in which stabilization policy is judged has changed. Theories designed to explain the linkage between aggregate demand policy and real economic variables have been revised, the effects of expectations on stabilization policy have been incorporated, supply considerations have been recognized, the micro effects of macro policy are now points of concern, and theories underlying the choice between rules and discretionary policy have been altered and refined. The debate over whether policy *should* be carried out in an active, discretionary manner or by a set of consistent rules that take out the human judgment aspect of policy has been further developed.

Our discussions of the policies and events that shaped the 1960s, 1970s, and early 1980s pointed out several of the most important aspects of the recent concern over economic policy. In analyzing the issues, the following questions have been raised:

1. Does economic policy affect real output and employment?
2. What accounts for the fluctuations in economic activity we observed throughout the 1970s and early 1980s?
3. Can fluctuations in economic activity be minimized by economic policy?
4. How should economic policy be carried out?

In this chapter we will examine the issues of stabilization policy and provide answers to these questions. The chapter is presented in two major sections. The first is concerned with the relationship between economic policy and real economic activity, and the second with the debate over how policy should be carried out. In this chapter we will tie together many of the theoretical issues raised in Chapters 11-14 and complete our discussion of the domestic (closed) economy. In the next and final chapter we will look at many of the issues of concern in the open, or international economy.

The Effects of Policy on Real Output

In the early days of Keynesian policymaking, the primary debate among economists centered on the relative effectiveness of monetary versus fiscal policy. Recent developments have altered that debate. The primary question now is whether policy is effective at all; that is, whether real variables, such as output and unemployment, can be altered by either monetary or fiscal policy.

The debate centers on the structure of the economy. In the idealized world of complete markets with perfect information, changes in aggregate demand generated by changes in the money supply or some other factor do not affect real economic variables such as real GNP and employment. Aggregate demand fluctuations are translated point-for-point into price fluctuations. Money is neutral. The question that naturally arises after a review of the behavior of the economy during the seventies is why this theoretical result is not observed in the real world. Many of the theoretical developments in macroeconomics in the 1970s and early 1980s have been concerned with answering this question. Each theory has relaxed one or more of the assumptions associated with the perfectly competitive model.

As we have noted in previous chapters there are basically two classes of theories that explain the observed relationship between aggregate demand and real variables—the information based theories, and the rigidities, or contract, based theories.[1] Except for the strictest form of the REH models, the information based theories typically relax the assumption of perfect information and substitute some type of imperfect knowledge or uncertainty. One class of information based theories studies the effects of uncertainty concerning whether an observed economic change is local or economy wide. Another class of theories concerns uncertainty about whether aggregate demand changes are temporary or permanent. The contract theories introduce some type of rigidity in prices so that the competitive markets cannot always clear—quantities demanded cannot always equal quantities supplied. Among the contract based theories we can distinguish between those in which relative price shifts occur because of asymmetrical rigidities (prices are rigid downward but not upward, for example) and those that assume a general persistence or sluggishness of all prices.

If you think this discussion sounds familar, you are correct. Read Chapter 1 again and you will notice much of the same flavor in the criticism John Maynard Keynes levied against the classical model. The new classical models (the information based models) argue that the profession was premature in abandoning the classical theory. This work is referred to as *equilibrium business cycle theory* or *classical business cycle theory.* The contract based theories, on the other hand, fall more along Keynesian lines. The difference is that the rigidites these models introduce are not *ad hoc* impositions, but instead, the results of microeconomic decisions.

Uncertainty Explanations: Local versus Economy-Wide Uncertainty

In the microeconomic world of perfect competition the assumption is made that perfect certainty holds: that all participants are knowledgeable of the opportunities available. The implication of this assumption is that equilibrium must obtain in each and every market and, as long as prices are flexible, that equilibrium must occur instantaneously. Introducing uncertainty alters this conclusion and generates many real world implications. For example, individuals may react in different ways after observing some economic change, such as an increase in the number of people in line at the grocery store, depending on how they interpret the change. The longer lines may be interpreted as evidence of an economy-wide increase in demand, an increase in demand for groceries only, or an increase in demand for the groceries of only this particular store.

---

[1] This terminology is widespread as can be seen in the surveys by John Taylor, "Recent Developments in the Theory of Stabilization Policy," unpublished manuscript; and Robert J. Gordon, "Output Fluctuations and Gradual Price Adjustment," *Journal of Economic Literature* (June, 1981), pp. 493-530.

Suppose the demand change is actually an aggregate demand increase due to a higher rate of money growth, but this is generally unknown. Then individual firms, upon experiencing an increased demand for their products, will respond by increasing their production (and perhaps running down their inventories). But much or all of this higher real production may be due to the misperception on the part of each firm that the increased demand is a relative shift toward the product it sells. If each firm knew that the increase in demand was common to all firms in the economy and was due to the purely nominal increase in the money supply, then the production response would be much smaller or perhaps nonexistent. As long as prices and wages are generally flexible, firms would know that prices and wages would quickly rise to offset the increase in the money supply and, therefore, that an increase in output was not warranted.

In the limiting case of perfectly flexible prices, good information about what is going on elsewhere in the economy enables firms to respond just as they would be predicted to do in the money-neutral world of perfect competition. This is the case discussed in previous chapters where there is, in effect, no short-run aggregate supply curve (the short- and long-run curves are the same vertical line). But imperfect information creates a nonneutrality in which firms respond to the aggregate demand stimulus by increasing real output even with perfectly flexible prices. The link between aggregrate demand and real variables, according to this theory, depends in no essential way on price or wage rigidities. As long as there is imperfect information about the source of aggregate demand shifts, the relationship (correlation) between aggregate demand and real output would exist.

This class of macromodels has been termed the *island parable* because of the framework in which the theory is developed.[2] An economy consisting of a series of islands, each informationally isolated from the others for some period of time, is assumed. By this it is meant that one island does not learn what occurs on the other islands for a period of time. The inhabitants of the islands must make decisions on the basis of the best information they have available (which is what has just occurred locally on their island in the present period and what occurred last period for the economy as a whole). After their decisions are made and the markets on each island cleared, the flow of demands (goods and services) and information takes place from island to island. In this framework rational decisions can be incorrect and can induce the wrong responses. Real output changes as demand changes because of the mistakes or misperceptions on the part of the inhabitants.

---

[2] Robert Lucas, "An Equilibrium Model of the Business Cycle," *Journal of Political Economy* (December, 1975), pp. 1113-1144.

In this uncertainty theory, aggregate demand can affect real output and therefore the implications of the theory correspond with reality. However, the persistence of unemployment and the duration of recessions are more difficult to explain. Unemployment actually lasts much longer than what seems to be implied by the uncertainty theory. Does it take 1 to 3 years (or months or quarters) for information to flow from one island to another?

A number of modifications have been suggested that would enable the theory to account for this persistence. One suggestion is that unanticipated shocks might have the additional effect of causing firms' capital stock to get out of line, to diverge from the levels firms would ideally choose to maintain. Then as the firms adjust their capital stock in later periods, production would be affected. Another suggestion is that firms are hesitant to lay off workers but, once done, they are also hesitant to reinstate workers or hire new ones. As a result, the unemployment effects last longer than the island model indicates. Finally, it is possible that the process of inventory reduction or accumulation might prolong the output effects since inventory adjustments in later periods will require production changes. Although one or all of these additions to the model may turn out to explain the persistence of unemployment, many economists have not been satisfied; the persistence effects continue to bother them. For that reason, another type of uncertainty has been introduced.[3]

Uncertainty about Temporary versus Permanent Changes

Another source of uncertainty, discussed several times throughout the text but used in a slightly different manner here, is whether an economic change is temporary or permanent. The general point is that a change in nominal aggregate demand that is expected to be permanent will have a much smaller effect on real output and a correspondingly larger effect on prices than a shift that is expected to be temporary. Suppose, for example, that in an attempt to reduce the rate of inflation the Federal Reserve (Fed) reduces the growth rate of the money supply. If individuals and firms expect the Fed to give up on its resolve to lower the growth rate of the money supply they will behave differently than if they expect the Fed to confirm the anti-inflation policy.

We referred to this uncertainty as the *credibility effect* in Chapter 11 and pointed out there that lack of credibility may be cured only by the public observing the results of a new policy for some period of time. Thus there will be a more persistent recession or decline in real output and employment than would be necessary without this uncertainty. During

---

[3] See Edmund Phelps, ed., *Microeconomic Foundations of Employment and Inflation Theory* (New York: W. W. Norton & Co., Inc., 1970).

the transition period, as people learn whether the shift of policy is temporary or permanent, the policy can have real effects even if prices are perfectly flexible. The less credibility there is about a new policy, the larger the resulting effect on real output.[4] Like the other uncertainty theory, this one is theoretically appealing although not all economists agree that it alone can explain real world observations.

Many economists maintain that prices are not perfectly flexible, not because of some *ad hoc* rigidity imposed on the model, but because it is optimal for both customer and firm not to have perfectly flexible prices in all circumstances. The uncertainty created by fluctuating prices may in some cases offset the benefits of immediate adjustment to demand and supply changes. A restaurant, for example, does not double its prices on a busy night because that would then induce customers to carry out a search before dinner (something the customer would rather not do) rather than simply going to a chosen spot.

Rigidities and Contracts Explanations: Relative Price Rigidities

Temporary rigidities in prices or wages could link some of the changes in nominal demand to changes in real production. For example, as we saw in Chapter 13, a supply shock could shift the demand curve for labor (marginal product curve) downward, requiring a reduction in the real wage if equilibrium is to result. With sticky nominal wages, this reduction would be difficult. However, if the monetary authorities increase the money supply they will drive the price level to a position (P_2 in Figure 15-1) such that the real wage is equal to the level workers would have aimed for had they known about the shock when they signed their contracts. In this case, aggregate demand and real output are related. Notice how the economy moves from Point A to B and then, as aggregate demand increases, to Point C in Figure 15-1.

Evidence does not seem to lend much support to the idea that output and employment are affected by policy simply because the nominal wage is fixed for some reason. In recent years, the real wage, which is the ratio of the nominal wage to the general price level, has been more stable than either the nominal wage or the general price level. Changes in both nominal wages and prices are more highly correlated with business cycle fluctuations than are changes in the real wage. Hence, one might suspect that this rigidity-of-nominal-wages explanation of employment and output changes might be omitting some important factors.[5] An attempt to

---

[4] See William Fellner, *Towards a Reconstruction of Macroeconomics: Problems of Theory and Policy* (Washington, D.C.: American Enterprise Institute for Public Policy Research, 1976).

[5] See, for example, Guillermo Calvo, "Tax Financed Government Spending in a Neoclassical

Figure 15-1. Rigidities in the Nominal Wage

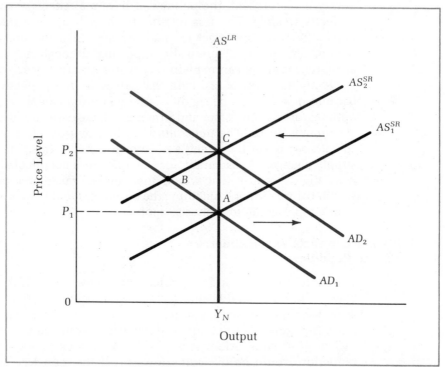

A supply shock forces the short-run aggregate supply (AS) curve to shift in. The immediate impact is a reduction in output and employment as shown in the move from Point A to B. Since the wage level is slow to move, a large real output decline is experienced. The monetary authorities could increase the money supply in order to drive up prices. This would cause real wages to decline and help to minimize the real output decline. The result is the move from Point B to C.

account for these observations is made by another class of models that emphasize staggered contracts.

Rigidities in General Prices. Not all prices and wages are set in unison across the economy. Instead, they are generally staggered—approximately one-third of all contracts are set each year for the following three years. Consequently, nominal wages and the general price level are slow to adjust and are characterized by abrupt transitions.[6]

Model with Sticky Wages and Rational Expectations," *Journal of Economic Dynamics and Control* (February, 1980), pp. 61-78; and Stanley Fischer, "Long-Term Contracts, Rational Expectations, and the Optimal Policy Rule," *Journal of Political Economy* (February, 1977), pp. 191-206.

[6] Robert E. Hall, "The Role of Prevailing Prices and Wages in the Efficient Organization of Markets," unpublished manuscript (Stanford University, 1979), and "The Rigidity of

According to this theory, since the nominal wage is fixed by contracts, and if firms are assumed to simply mark up prices to cover wages so that profit margins are not altered, the price level is also fixed. In this setting, an increase in the money supply increases real balances. Since people now hold larger money stocks than they desire, they will increase the demand for goods. This results in an increase in production and an increase in employment. As contracts are renegotiated, wages will rise because the favorable demand conditions give firms the incentive to pay the increased wage demands. Then, to maintain profit margins, firms will raise prices. Hence, real money balances are reduced. Eventually a new equilibrium is reached at a higher price level but with the same level of production as before. *Money is neutral in the long run. Yet since convergence to the new equilibrium takes time, the persistence effects described previously are accounted for.*

Comparison of the Policy Implications of the Alternative Theories. **What differentiates the contract models from the information based models is, of course, the use of sticky prices and the corresponding neglect of the market clearing assumptions.** In the contract models, prices adjust to clear markets only after a time period equal to the length of the average contract has passed. In the information models, on the other hand, prices instantaneously adjust to clear markets given whatever information people have at the time. Which approach is better or more realistic?

Many economists support the contract models because they believe these models correspond more closely with the market mechanisms in the real world. At the same time, many like the theoretical elegance of the information based models and assert that the rigidities assumed by the contract models could not continue period after period. Knowing that they might lose money, workers would arrange for different terms in their contracts and firms would alter their profit margins. In sum, a consensus as to the appropriate description of adjustments in the economy eludes the economics profession. As a consequence, the profession disagrees about policy as well. In the market clearing setting (information based models) only unanticipated changes in aggregate demand policy matter, so announced policies do not affect output. In contract models, aggregate demand policy has an effect whether it is anticipated or not.

Suppose the rate of inflation has become too high for policymakers, either because of past policy mistakes or unavoidable money velocity shifts, and that the monetary authorities want to reduce the rate of growth of money. The important question is whether the monetary restraint necessary to achieve the goal of lower inflation will cause a recession and,

---

Wages and the Persistence of Unemployment," *Brookings Papers on Economic Activity* (2:1975), pp. 301-35.

if so, how great a recession. The answer to that question will obviously influence the policymakers' choice of how much restraint to apply, but the answer depends on which description of the economy is correct.

If we take literally the information based and the rational expectations hypothesis *(REH)* models that emphasize the uncertainty between aggregate and local shocks, then we must conclude that an announced policy of restraint will have no effect on real output. There will be no recession since reduced inflation will match the reduction in monetary growth point-for-point. On the other hand, if there is some uncertainty about whether the changes in policy are permanent or temporary, then real effects of policy will ensue, and a recession would be expected. The size and duration of the recession would depend on the speed at which people begin to believe that the central bank is firm in its resolve to restrain money growth; that is, the amount of time it takes the Fed to gain credibility. If the Fed's credibility is high or increases quickly, then the recession could be very mild. (Many financial writers argued that the 1980-82 recession was prolonged by the lack of Fed credibility and that the 1983 recovery was based on credibility and on Paul Volcker's reappointment as Fed chairman.)

The contract based models yield somewhat different conclusions. These models, which emphasize real wage shifts because of *asymmetric rigidities*, do not suggest any reason for a recession to last longer than the length of the average contract. For example, if contracts last one period, the inflation rate could be put on its new target path in the first period; in the second period wages would adjust. However, if contracts last for several periods and only a portion of all contracts are negotiated each period, then the recession will last the average length of the contracts.

Perhaps a combination of the two approaches (information and contracts) would be more accurate than either one alone—people are rational, imperfect information does exist, and there are rigidities in the movements of prices and wages. Yet agreement even on this compromise eludes the profession, perhaps because each of the models reviewed has implications about the appropriate approach for policymakers and these implications are almost diametrically opposed.

The implications of the information based model are fairly obvious. Policy should be run in such a way that uncertainty is minimized. Combined with the *REH* implication that anticipated policy has no effects on real economic activity, this class of models implies that policy should be run in the simplest, most straightforward, and most evident manner possible, perhaps by a fixed set of rules. For example, monetary policy could be run by doing away with the Fed and setting up a computer to crank out currency, or any particular monetary aggregate, at a specific rate of X percent per year. People would know the rule and be able to make decisions *with certainty* about economic policy. There would be no more stop-and-go type policy actions and resulting economic fluctuations. Another type of rule often suggested is to place the dollar on a gold or commodity standard or to have policy carried out according to the real bills doctrine.[7]

Each of these proposals is an attempt to restrict the production of money and to do so in a consistent, widely known manner. Very briefly and simply, the gold standard requires that each dollar of currency be tied to the existing stock of gold. A commodity standard is analogous to the gold standard but the commodity suggested as the foundation is not gold. Instead, it is a basket of commodities such as silver, gold, other ores, and other limited commodities. The *real bills doctrine* is, in essence, a commodity standard. It requires that currency be based on the supply of *real bills*—those securities issued when commodities are exchanged. Each of these approaches minimizes the discretionary powers of the monetary authority and makes monetary policy as predictable as possible.

Not surprisingly, these suggestions are opposed by most supporters of contract based descriptions of the economy. The essence of their argument is (1) that the economy is slow to adjust to supply shocks or shifts in demand on the part of the private sector and (2) that policy can and should be used to speed up the adjustment process and thereby offset these shocks or shifts. In sum, those economists supporting the view of the economy captured by the information models—rational expectationists and monetarists are among the most prominent—argue for rules and a nondiscretionary approach to policy. Those supporting the contracts, or rigidities, view of the economy argue for some type of discretionary policy. In the following section, we will discuss several aspects of the rules versus activism debate.

Rules versus Discretion

The debate between those favoring a rules policy and those favoring discretionary policy has not diminished but has taken on a different form in recent years. In the earliest stages of the debate, the idea of rules meant a fixed and predetermined policy that would not change as economic conditions changed. For example, in 1960 Milton Friedman argued that the Fed should be abolished and replaced by a computer programmed to print money at a fixed X percent per year. Currently, however, the so-called feedback rules, according to which economic variables are set to economic developments, are thought to be as strict as Friedman's constant

---

[7] Thomas J. Sargent and Neil Wallace, "The Real-Bills Doctrine versus the Quantity Theory: A Reconsideration," *Journal of Political Economy* (December, 1982), pp. 1212-1236. The *Economic Report of the President* (1982), pp. 62-77 contains a discussion of the gold standard and discusses money versus credit.

money growth standard.[8] An example of a monetary feedback rule would be something like increasing the rate of growth of M-1 by 1 percent each time the rate of growth of real GNP fell 2 percent below its trend rate of growth. Similarly a fiscal rule would be something like specifying that the high-employment budget always be balanced. Another fiscal rule, proposed by President Reagan in 1983, called for an automatic tax increase each time the budget reached a deficit of $100 billion. (His so-called standby tax was never formally proposed to Congress.) This is a feedback rule since its implementation depends on the behavior or feedback of the economy. A more explicit fiscal feedback rule would be to link tax increases or tax cuts to percentage changes in real GNP or inflation. *In general, as long as the same thing is done each time a given event occurs, policy is said to be applied as a rule.*

As we have seen, the differences between those supporting rules and those supporting activism are not just whimsical or even political. They rest primarily on differing views of the behavior of the economy. However, there are several other practical and theoretical aspects of the debate. Those arguing for either fixed rules or some type of feedback rules often refer to the stop-and-go nature in which discretionary policy was handled in the past. We noted in Chapters 13 and 14 that this occurred in the 1970s and early 1980s. It is argued that the greatest instability in the economy comes from these policy actions and not from the private sector of the economy.

Another argument offered in support of the rules approach to policy is that such rules would end the instability caused by politicians attempting to provide benefits to their constitutents in order to increase the probability of reelection. This argument is called the *political business cycle.*

The Political Business Cycle

In the typical approach to macroeconomic theory and policy, the policymakers—the president, Congress, the Fed, and others—are assumed to be acting in the best interests of society. The motives of the politicians, board members, and others are not considered. A literature referred to as *Public Choice* has questioned that premise.[9] This literature asserts that

---

[8] Bennett McCallum and J. K. Whitaker, "The Effectiveness of Fiscal Feedback Rules and Automatic Stabilizers under Rational Expectations," *Journal of Monetary Economics* (April, 1979), pp. 171-186; Finn Kydland and Edward Prescott, "Rules Rather Than Discretion: The Inconsistency of Optimal Plans," *Journal of Political Economy* (June, 1977), pp. 473-492.

[9] Edward Tufte, *Political Control of the Economy* (Princeton, N.J.: Princeton University Press, 1978); Ryan C. Amacher, William J. Boyes, and Robert Tollison, "The Political Business Cycle: A Review of Theoretical and Empirical Evidence," *ACES Bulletin*

politicians will use whatever means they can to influence the economy in the direction that will promote their own political interests. For example, many observers have noted that most presidential elections since the advent of Keynesianism have taken place during growth phases of business cycles. The implication drawn from this observation is that the economy is manipulated by politicians to enhance reelection chances and that events nearest the election are most remembered by the electorate. In Figure 15-2, we have traced out the rate of growth of real GNP and have emphasized the presidential election years. Do you observe any evidence in support of a political business cycle?

Figure 15-2. The Political Business Cycle

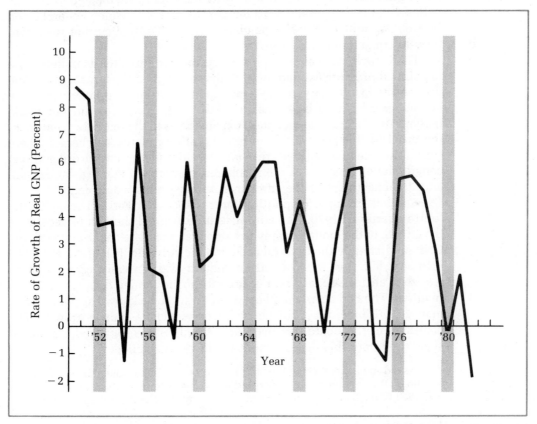

The rate of growth of real GNP is traced out here for the years since 1950. Presidential election years are shaded. Is there evidence of a political business cycle?

(Spring, 1979), pp. 1-42. One of the original works that applies economic analysis to political behavior is Anthony Downs, *An Economic Theory of Democracy* (New York: Harper & Row, Publishers, Inc., 1957).

If there is a politically created business cycle, how is it that politicians control the economy? In particular, how can politicians affect the determination of the rate of growth of the money supply? The Fed is one of the most independent central banks in the Western world. However, because its officials wish to maintain that independence, they may try to cooperate with elected officials at times. By choosing to follow policies which Congress and the president desire, the Fed can defuse attempts to reduce its independence. Since 1978, the Federal Reserve chairperson has had to appear before Congress once every six months to explain Fed policy. This gives Congress an opportunity to lobby the Fed. For example, in July of 1981, Chairman Paul Volcker was threatened with impeachment by Congressman Henry Gonzalez of Texas if Volcker did not force the Fed to ease up on interest rates. While this pressure may not cause the Fed to alter its policies, at the very least it must temper the zeal with which Federal Open Market Committee (FOMC) members support Fed policy that runs contrary to congressional desires.

There are historical examples where the Fed did alter its policies due to political pressure exerted on it. When the income tax surcharge of 1968 was enacted, monetary policy was eased in order to prevent what the FOMC feared would be "fiscal overkill." The surcharge did not work, perhaps due as much to monetary expansion as to the temporary nature of the tax. Did the Fed want to offset the effects of the surcharge? There could have been a political reason: The administration, in order to get congressional support for the surcharge, guaranteed key legislators that, after the enactment of the surcharge, interest rates would fall.[10]

Another example of political pressure on the Fed occurred in the fourth quarter of 1970. The administration wanted the Fed to accelerate the growth of the money supply to a rate that would be consistent with the GNP predicted by the Council of Economic Advisers (CEA). Most FOMC members felt that the council prediction was unrealistic and that to realize it an inflationary rate of growth of the money supply would be required. The Fed board members do not want to be known as poor money managers. Hence, they did not want to accelerate money growth. The chairman of the Board of Governors, Arthur Burns, outlined a scenario suggesting how this disagreement might be reconciled.

> I asked some members of the Staff who attended FOMC meetings whether the FOMC members are concerned about the Administration's predicted 1971 GNP. They replied, "The room is full of it." I asked if it entered into

---

[10] See Sherman Maisel, *Managing the Dollar* (New York: W. W. Norton & Co., Inc., 1973); Edward Tufte, *Political Control of the Economy* (Princeton, N. J.: Princeton University Press, 1978); the surveys by Bruno Frey, "Politico-Economic Models and Cycles," *Journal of Public Economics* (April, 1978) and Ryan Amacher, William Boyes, and Robert Tollison, "The Political Business Cycle: A Review of Theoretical and Empirical Evidence," *ACES Bulletin* (Spring, 1979).

their discussion or affected their decisions. They replied, "Not at all." I asked what would happen if President Nixon were to phone the Governors to ask them to 'go along' with him by permitting a faster rate of growth of the money supply. They replied, "Though there would be a small minority which would vote against it, the FOMC would go along."[11]

The theory behind the political business cycle is represented in Figure 15-3. Suppose that the economy faces a Phillips curve that is vertical in the long run but negatively sloped in the short run. In addition, suppose that voters evaluate both inflation and unemployment negatively. It is then possible to develop a locus of unemployment and inflation rates, like an indifference curve in microeconomics, that represents the likelihood or odds of voters supporting an incumbent party. In Figure 15-3, three such voter preference curves are presented. As compared to the curve i_1u_1, the curve i_2u_2 represents a lower probability that voters will support the incumbent party since higher unemployment rates are associated with each inflation rate.

Now suppose an election is approaching and the economy is at Point A in Figure 15-3. If the incumbent policymakers believe the odds of reelection (along i_2u_2) are too low (given present economic conditions), an expansionary demand policy may be enacted. With such a policy, the unemployment rate will fall if workers misforecast the accompanying price increase. The policymakers' goal would be to reach the lowest voter preference curve possible since the lower the curve, the higher the odds of reelection. However, they are constrained to move along the short-run Phillips curve PC_1. Thus, they must choose the inflation-unemployment combination along PC_1 that will put them on the lowest voter preference curve. This is shown at Point B where the short-run Phillips curve PC_1 is just tangent to the voter preference curve i_1u_1. If the policymakers can move to this point just prior to the election, their chances of reelection will be improved.

The inflation and unemployment rate combination represented by Point B is not sustainable. Workers will eventually realize that prices are rising and the short-run Phillips curve will shift to PC_2 as the economy moves to Point C. Notice that Point C lies on voter preference curve i_3u_3 which is inferior to the trade-off existing before the stimulative policy was instituted. This adjustment will likely occur after the election. However, it may not. Recall that the short-run curve PC_1 is relevant only so long as it takes workers to realize that their price forecasts were incorrect. If policymakers stimulate demand (and move the economy from Point A to Point B) only to have workers' price expectations adjust quickly, they may

---

[11] Arthur Burns, testimony before the Joint Economic Committee of Congress, February 19, 1971.

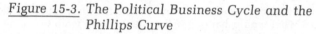

Figure 15-3. *The Political Business Cycle and the*
                Phillips Curve

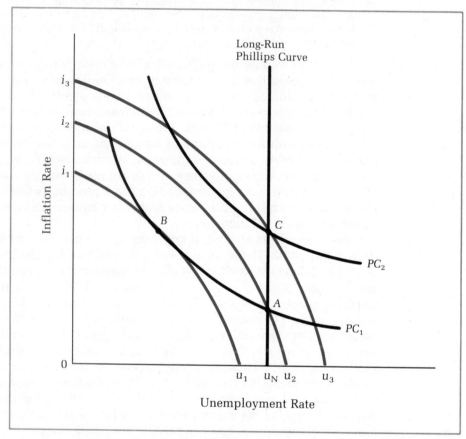

The structure of the economy is represented by the short-run and long-run Phillips curves. The voters have definite feelings about the combinations of inflation and unemployment. The higher the combination, the less likely they will vote for the incumbent party. These voter attitudes are repesented by the voter indiffence curves *(iu)*. The farther from the origin, the fewer votes cast for the incumbents. Now suppose the economy is at rest at Point A. With an election approaching, the incumbent is worried that the election may be lost. An expansionary monetary or fiscal policy is undertaken that, as long as it is not fully realized by the public, shifts the economy to Point B. This reduction in unemployment increases the votes received by the incumbents. Once the election is over the rising price level will drive the economy to Point C. At Point C the political business cycle would occur once again when the next election approaches.

end up with a lower likelihood of reelection (at Point C) than if they had done nothing. So, for the incumbents, timing is everything. Their policy change must be initiated early enough to lower the unemployment rate but late enough so that inflationary expectations have no time to adjust. A miscalculation may cost them the election.

If the political business cycle theory is correct, we should find that the unemployment and inflation rates behave in a certain manner over time. As the election period approaches, the unemployment rate should decrease. After the election is over, it should increase again. If the theory is correct, the stop-and-go policies experienced throughout the sixties, seventies, and early eighties could have been the result of political manuvering.

The Political Business Cycle and the *REH*

How can a political business cycle be created unless people are fooled period after period? The result requires shortsightedness or myopia on the part of the voter-workers. After one or two experiences, according to the *REH*, voters would correctly perceive what the politicians want to do and account for it in their expectations. Under these circumstances the demand expansion would convert point-for-point immediately into price changes. Several suggestions have been put forth to reconcile the political business cycle theory with the *REH*. First, the manner in which a political business cycle is created may differ from election to election. For example, transfer payments such as Social Security might provide a way of distributing funds without the immediate, necessary expansion of money. Some research has shown that Social Security benefits have increased much more rapidly in election years than nonelection years. Social Security, Medicare, and other transfer payments typically peak in December. However, during election years that peak is speeded up to October and November so that the checks arrive immediately before, or at nearly the same time as, the election. Hence, transfer payments could be used one time, and deficits the next time. A second suggestion stems from work carried out by Nobel Prize winner Friedrich von Hayek.[12] This work suggests that although the legislators' intent is not to create such a cycle, the way in which they dole out benefits to their constituents creates the political business cycle. A single legislator has the incentive of obtaining as many benefits as possible for his or her constituents since the payment for these benefits will come from general revenues or from monetary expansion and inflation. Either financing alternative means that the entire populace pays for the benefits whereas only a relatively few constituents receive the benefits. Those legislators able to obtain the benefits increase the likelihood of reelection while the others perhaps increase the probability of defeat. And of course, the nearer the election, the greater the attempt to obtain the benefits that create an expansion of demand during the election period. The result is a political business cycle.

---

[12] Friedrich von Hayek, *Monetary Theory and the Trade Cycle* (New York: Harcourt, Brace, 1932); James Buchanan and Richard Wagner, *Democracy in Deficit: The Political Legacy of Lord Keynes* (New York: Academic Press, Inc., 1977).

Lags in Policy

One of the oldest arguments in the policy debate is that there are lags in the implementation and effects of monetary and fiscal policy. The effects of a monetary or fiscal action are typically spread out over a long period so that an action to stimulate or slow the economy taken at one time may be totally inappropriate by the time the effect is felt. We saw this in our discussion of the 1970s in particular. Proposals to raise taxes and slow the growth of the economy became outdated when the economy slowed before the tax was imposed. Similarly, proposals to stimulate the economy were not implemented until the economy had already started to expand at a very rapid rate. In both cases policy disturbed the economy instead of stabilizing it.

Economists have studied lags in policymaking both to attempt to shorten the lags and also to gather ammunition for their arguments for or against monetary and/or fiscal policy. They have divided lags into two types, the inside lag and the outside lag. The *inside lag* refers to the time it takes for a policy action to be taken; the *outside (or impact) lag* refers to the time it takes for the policy action to have an effect once such an action has been taken. While in the past a great deal of research has been done on these various lags, the issue has taken a backseat, or perhaps been pushed out of the car entirely, by recent policy debates. If one supports the REH view, then one need not even consider policy lags. Nevertheless, the fact that there are inevitable delays in the recognition of an economic problem and in gaining the political agreement necessary to implement a policy action creates difficulties for the activist position.

The Evaluation of Stabilization Policies

A more serious issue than the lags in policy implementation for the policy debate has been raised in recent years by Professor Robert Lucas of the University of Chicago.[13] He has argued that the typical approach to policymaking is outdated if not totally incorrect.

The policymaking process has changed very little since the 1950s. As we noted in Chapters 11 and 12, the formulation of monetary and fiscal policy involves a process of asking what-if questions or carrying out what are called policy simulations and forecasts. The first steps in the actual process of policymaking are to choose a model of the economy and to obtain estimates of the parameters of the model. The estimated model is then used to simulate or forecast the effects of various policy options. For example, the first order of business at the FOMC meetings typically is for the staff economists of the Fed to present the results of computer experi-

---

[13] Robert Lucas, "Econometric Policy Evaluation: A Critique," in his *Studies in Business Cycle Theory* (Cambridge, Mass.: The MIT Press, 1981), pp. 104-130.

ments in which they have asked what will occur if money growth is 4 percent, 6 percent, or 10 percent; or what will occur if the federal funds rate is allowed to go to 7 percent, 9 percent, or 15 percent. The answers they obtain from the models into which they plug these hypothetical money growth or federal funds rates provides the basis for the FOMC's decisions. Similarly, the staff of the Congressional Budget Office presents Congress with the results of their forecasts of what happens if a 10 percent tax cut scheduled for next year is reduced to 5 percent or increased to 15 percent, or if the expenditures scheduled for next year are cut by 10 percent or increased by 20 percent. These results provide Congress with a framework in which to make their policy decisions. Similarly, the Office of Management and Budget (OMB), the CEA, and virtually every policy-making agency performs many series of such experiments, or simulations, as the basis for policymaking decisions. Once the economists have presented their forecasts and simulations to their policymaking agency and the actual policy decisions have been implemented, the process of comparing goals with actual economic performance is continually carried out.

According to Lucas, this policymaking process is old-fashioned if not actually inaccurate in the sense that the estimated models typically do not take into account the degree that the policy will be anticipated, or whether the Fed's announcements are considered credible, or to what extent behavior will actually change on account of the policy. Lucas has argued that the models cannot be assumed to remain the same for each policy alternative. Individuals will alter their behavior depending on the particular policy implemented. Rational economic agents forecast the future effects of policy and modify their behavior in a way not described by the computer models. Recall the analogy with a football game pointed out in an earlier chapter. Suppose that one team, say the San Diego Chargers, was playing the L. A. Raiders, and quarterback Dan Fouts noticed that the L. A. defense always put two linebackers on the left and one on the right. Would he be correct in assuming that the L.A. defense would not change if San Diego places all its receivers on the right side? The policymaking process described above makes such an assumption.

Referring to an economic example, suppose the economy is currently represented by the structure shown in Figure 15-4. Suppose that the government decides to levy a three-part tax on income. The tax will be increased at a rate of 5 percent this year, 10 percent next year, and 20 percent the third year. Based on its model of the economy, the government expects the aggregate demand curve to shift down and the price level (the rate of inflation) to slow. What might happen, however, is that the public, seeing a steady increase in taxes for the next several years, shifts as much as possible of its spending and income earning to the current year (through borrowing and drawing down of tax shelters) away from future years. The result could be a rapid increase, rather than a

Figure 15-4. Old-Fashioned Policymaking

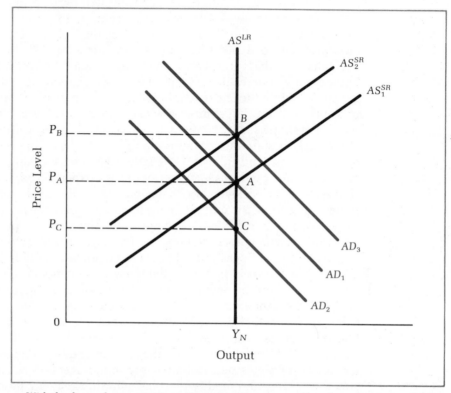

With the demand curve at AD_1, policymakers impose a graduated tax increase to slow the economy: 5 percent this year, 10 percent the following year, and a further 20 percent the third year. Policymakers assume that behavior will not change and, therefore, assume that the demand curve will drop to AD_2 and, hence, that the price level wll decline to P_C. Behavior does change, however. People spend now because they expect to have less discretionary income in the future years. The demand curve shifts out to AD_3 and prices rise to P_B.

slowdown, in spending. The point is that individuals' reactions to policy can and do influence the actual impact of policy and these reactions or expectations must be taken into account in formulating policy.

The case for discretionary policy rests primarily on the belief that economists should be able to design policies that will enable them to control economic fluctuations. In this belief it is asserted that the Fed knows best what is good monetary policy for the country and should be allowed to alter policy as it sees fit. The Fed, obviously, is most up-to-date with respect to developments in the economy and has, therefore, a great deal more information than either the general public or individuals involved with the financial markets. This informational advantage allows the Fed to exploit a trade-off or short-run aggregate supply curve. The argument is made that there would be a loss to society if the Fed and fiscal authorities simply did nothing and waited for all adjustments to take place.

Professor Stanley Fischer of M.I.T. has suggested a compromise resolution to the rules versus discretion debate.[14] He asserts that rules should be used in normal times, but in the case of an unanticipated disaster discretion should come into play. Given our discussion of the political business cycle we must consider the political implications of this compromise. First, who would define what is normal and what is abnormal? It is likely that if abnormality allows legislators to provide increased benefits to constitutents, then abnormality will become the standard case with respect to fiscal policies as much as deficits have become a continuing part of our political-economic system.

No doubt the debate over the appropriate way to implement policy will continue. There are too many philosophical differences among economists for it not to.

A Summation and a Look Ahead

We have now completed the primary portion of our study of macroeconomics. Now you are familiar with the major controversies of macroeconomic theory and policy and have an understanding of why policies and theories emerged when they did.

Albert Einstein once said that everything should be made as simple as possible, but not too much so. With this rule in mind, the study of macroeconomics should be carried out in much the same manner that it, the field, has evolved. How can we understand the policies of Reaganomics without understanding what went before and on what theoretical basis the policy decisions were formulated? Similarly, how can we understand the Great Stagflation without understanding how the connection between balanced budgets and political success was broken? The overriding objective of this book has been to point out the interaction between economic policy, economic events, and economic theory. Economic theory is not developed in an ivory tower isolated from events in the real world. Nor are economic events unrelated to economic theory. Who is to say what would have happened had Keynes not written his *General Theory* or had Milton Friedman not studied the ramifications of monetary policy on the economy. As the title to this book suggests, theory and policy can best be

---

[14] Stanley Fischer, "Long-Term Contracts, Rational Expectations, and the Optimal Money Supply Rule," *Journal of Political Economy* (February, 1977), pp. 191-206, and "On Activist Monetary Policy with Rational Expectations," *Rational Expectations and Economic Policy*, Stanley Fischer, ed. (Chicago: University of Chicago Press, 1982).

described in a dynamic context—as one changes, it affects the other, and that one, in turn, affects the first. Perhaps Keynes said it best,

> The ideas of economists, both when they are right and when they are wrong, are more powerful than is commonly understood. . . . Practical men, who believe themselves to be quite exempt from any intellectual influences, are usually the slaves of some defunct economist.

We have traversed a great deal of territory in this book. We began with the Great Depression, the world in which Keynesian economics was born, and tracked economic theory and policy through the stagnant 1950s and the Camelot period of the 1960s into the turbulent period of the late 1960s-early 1970s. Since then, the economy has been wracked with one catastrophe after another—the recession of the early seventies, the Great Stagflation, and the Great Inflation. As a result, economists began sifting through the ashes of the Keynesian Revolution to determine what was worth saving and what should be discarded. The answer is not yet apparent. Several of the controversial issues that emerged following the publication of Keynes's *General Theory* still command the attention of the profession today, albeit in a more sophisticated theoretical setting. But the dynamic interaction of theory and policy continues.

The interaction of countries and their policies also continues and, in fact, continues to grow. In the following and final chapter we will discuss several of the current issues in what is termed the *open economy*.

PROBLEMS AND EXERCISES

1. As an indication of the result of a constant money supply rule, Professor Franco Modigliani of M.I.T. suggests we examine the period from 1971 to 1974, or from 1972 to 1975, if a one year lag in monetary policy is allowed. He argues that while this was a period of relatively stable money growth, it was one of the most unstable periods in the United States in terms of fluctuations in output and prices. Comment on Professor Modigliani's argument.

2. An example of an automatic stabilizer is a progressive income tax system. Is a constant money supply rule an *automatic stabilizer*?

3. Suppose the economy is hit by another oil embargo and that the money supply is fixed, growing at a 5% rate of growth. What will be the impact of this shock on the economy if the information based models correctly represent the economy? if the contracts based models more adequately represent the economy?

4. The June, 1981 issue of *Journal of Economic Literature* contains two articles that support the idea that there is a positive correlation between output and price fluctuations. (1) Robert J. Gordon, an economist at Northwestern University at Evanston, Illinois, states that "business cycles in real variables rest upon the incomplete and gradual extent of price adjustment." (2) James Tobin, Yale University economist and Nobel Laureate, suggests that policy is effective in the short run and it is the short run with which we should be concerned. Your assignment is to describe how the modern Keynesians and the modern classical economists explain the positive correlation.
5. The media are often remarking how economists never seem to agree. How would you explain to a journalist what the fundamental disagreement in macroeconomics is today?

SUGGESTED READINGS

The literature on stabilization policy is vast. Representative selections include

Martin N. Baily and Arthur Okun, eds., *The Battle Against Unemployment and Inflation* (New York: W. W. Norton & Co., Inc., 1982).
Robert Gordon, "What Can Stabilization Policy Achieve?" *American Economic Review* (May, 1978), pp. 335-341.
Franco Modigliani, "The Monetarist Controversy, or Should We Forsake Stabilization Policy?" *American Economic Review* (March, 1977), pp. 1-19.

A variety of points of view on unemployment and inflation are presented in

Robert Gordon, "Recent Developments in the Theory of Inflation and Unemployment," *Journal of Monetary Economics* (April, 1976), pp. 185-219.
Robert Hall, "Is Unemployment a Macroeconomic Problem?" *American Economic Review* (May, 1983), pp. 219-222.

For fairly nontechnical discussions of rational expectations and Robert Lucas's critique of conventional policy evaluation, see

Donald Mullineaux, "On Active and Passive Monetary Policies: What Have We Learned from the Rational Expectations Debate?" *Business Review* (Federal Reserve Bank of Philadelphia, November-December, 1977), pp. 11-19.

Thomas Turner and Charles Whiteman, "Econometric Policy Evaluation under Rational Expectations," *Quarterly Review* (Federal Reserve Bank of Minneapolis, Spring-Summer, 1981), pp. 6-15.

Political Influences on the policymaking process are discussed in

S. F. Borins, "The Political Economy of the Fed," *Public Policy* (Spring, 1972), pp. 175-198.

James Buchanan and Richard Wagner, *Democracy in Deficit: The Political Legacy of Lord Keynes* (New York: Academic Press, Inc., 1977).

Ray Fair, "The Effect of Economic Events on Votes for President," *Review of Economics and Statistics* (May, 1978), pp. 159-173.

Ryan Amacher and William J. Boyes, "Unemployment Rates and Political Outcomes: An Incentive for Manufacturing a Political Business Cycle," *Public Choice* (1982), pp. 197-203.

For more on the contract based models, see

Gary Fethke and Andrew Policano, "Labor Contracts, Informational Discrepancies, and the Role of Monetary Policy," *Journal of Macroeconomics* (Winter, 1979), pp. 1-18.

Additional discussion of policy lags is available in

J. Ernest Tanner, "Are the Lags in the Effects of Monetary Policy Variable?" *Journal of Monetary Economics* (January, 1979), pp. 105-121.

CHAPTER 16.

Policy in an Open Economy Setting

Under a system of a perfectly free commerce, each country naturally devotes its capital and labor to such employments as are most beneficial to each. This pursuit of individual advantage is admirably connected with the universal good of the whole.

David Ricardo, 1877

I am writing this chapter partly for the satisfaction of abusing that accomplished knave Billfinger, and partly to show whosoever shall read this how Americans fare at the hands of the Paris guides and what sort of people Paris guides are. It need not be supposed that we were a stupider or an easier prey than our countrymen generally are, for we were not. The guides deceive and defraud every American who goes to Paris for the first time and sees its sights alone or in company with others as little experienced as himself. I shall visit Paris again someday, and then let the guides beware! I shall go in my war paint—I shall carry my tomahawk along.

Mark Twain,
Innocents Abroad

The U.S. is criticized by European nations for its domestic policy; the Japanese are hounded by nations attempting to break into Japanese markets; gold rises on the international exchange markets, pounds fall, and the dollar rises; the staggering debt owed by the Third World to Western banks places them both in precarious positions; and worldwide recovery depends on U.S. recovery. In short, the world is becoming smaller and smaller—events in one part of the world impact on the rest of the world, dictating that the study of macroeconomics include the interaction among economies. In this chapter we provide an overview of the issues of open economy macroeconomics; i.e., macroeconomics in an international setting. Some of the topics we discuss are

- *The relative merits of flexible and fixed exchange rate regimes*

- *The transmission process of events occurring in one part of the world to other parts of the world*

- *The law of one price and the purchasing power parity theory*

- *The balance of payments*

- *The world money supply and worldwide inflation*

- *Third World debt and its implications for the developed countries*

Introduction: Current Issues in International Economics

Perhaps in the 1950s and 1960s the study of macroeconomics could ignore the effects of the rest of the world on the domestic economy. But if possible then, it certainly is possible no longer. The interaction among nations has been steadily increasing since the end of World War II and has accelerated with the OPEC oil production and price policies of the 1970s.

One measure of the economic interrelationship between countries is the ratio of real imports (the purchases of foreign products by the residents of the domestic country) to real GNP. In Table 16-1, this ratio is presented for a few countries. While all the ratios have increased it should be noted that they understate the actual degree of openness since the government sector has grown in every country and most government goods are nontraded goods (not counted as part of imports).

Table 16-1. The Ratio of Imports to GNP for Six Countries

COUNTRY	1960	1965	1970	1975	1980
Japan	.07	.09	.11	.12	.13
Canada	.20	.21	.23	.26	.28
West Germany	.13	.17	.20	.24	.28
Italy	.11	.14	.17	.20	.25
United Kingdom	.25	.25	.29	.31	.35
United States	.04	.05	.06	.06	.07

Source: *International Financial Statistics* (IMF Yearbook, 1982).

Compared with the other developed Western countries and Japan, the U.S. is relatively self-sufficient. Yet, this self-sufficiency is decreasing as indicated in Table 16-1 and as indicated by the fact that U.S. holdings of financial assets no longer completely dominate the international capital market. Foreigners held 2 percent of outstanding U.S. government debt in 1951, 6 percent in 1965, and 19 percent at the end of of 1979. Indeed, for several years during the 1970s, foreign monetary authorities absorbed most new net debt issued by the U.S. Treasury.[1].

International trade policy has received greater and greater attention in the U.S. in recent years. The Japanese are under pressure from the U.S. administration to open up their country to foreign trade; domestic content legislation that would restrict sales of foreign goods to the U.S. to those assembled using at least 70 percent American made components was introduced in the 98th Congress; the latest economic summit of the Western economies focused on other nations' displeasure with U.S. domestic monetary policies and with the flexible exchange rate system; U.S. tomato growers complain about "dumping" from Mexico while steel producers complain about Japanese "dumping;" flexible exchange rates are blamed for speculation and the collapse of several financial institutions and for the depth of the 1980-82 recession; and the loans several less developed countries (LDCs) and Eastern European countries seem unable to repay are being blamed for a potential worldwide reinflation.[2]

---

[1] Ronald I. McKinnon, "The Exchange Rate and Macroeconomic Policy: Changing Postwar Perceptions," *Journal of Economic Literature* (June, 1981), p. 533.

[2] See for example, "The Third World Threat to the West's Recovery," *Business Week* (February 7, 1983), pp. 54-57.

The increasingly important role the world economy plays domestically requires that some portion of a study of macroeconomics be devoted to international issues. Yet at the same time, the increasingly complex world economy requires a great deal more study than is possible in a chapter or two. A course in international finance or open economy economics is a must for students of macroeconomics.[3] It is not possible here to examine every issue nor to analyze each in the detail that would appear in a text designed for such a course, so the aim of this chapter is to acquaint the reader with several of the more important issues of open economy macroeconomics. In the next section we provide an overview of open economy macroeconomics and discuss the processes by which events occurring in one country affect the economies of other countries. The following section of the chapter is devoted to the traditional manner in which the macroeconomics of open economies has been studied. In the final section some implications and conclusions are drawn, and some current unresolved issues are discussed.

General Information: The International Payments Mechanism

If trade is to be carried out between two countries, whose money is to be used? Should the transactions take place in yen or dollars or lira or francs, pounds, pesos, or what? Since most countries employ different currencies, one currency must be convertible into another in order for exchange to take place between most nations. The rate at which one currency can be converted into another is called the *exchange rate*. How are dollars converted into yen, pounds, lira, pesos, or other currencies? An American importer buys West German automobiles and sells them to customers in the U.S. The importer receives dollars in return for the cars. But the American importer must pay the West German exporter in West German currency, Deutsche marks, not U.S. dollars. How is the U.S. importer, who has dollars, going to pay the West German exporter who wants marks?

The answer is that there are individuals in these countries who are making opposite transactions—an American exporter who receives Deutsche marks from West German importers but needs dollars to pay American firms, or a West German importer who receives Deutsche marks from West German consumers but needs dollars to pay the American exporter. There is no need for the traders to search out each other. International

---

[3] See for example, Rudiger Dornbusch, *Open Economy Macroeconomics* (New York: Basic Books, Inc., Publishers, 1980); and George Feiger and Bertrand Jacquillar, *International Finance* (Boston: Allyn & Bacon, Inc., 1982).

clearinghouses exist to service these international transactions. The main dealers in foreign exchange, as these clearinghouses are called, are large private banks. These banks keep checking accounts in various currencies so that an importer or exporter can purchase or sell foreign currency. Should one of these banks find it has more customers wanting to purchase a foreign currency, such as yen, than those wanting to sell it, then the bank's checking account balance in Tokyo will decline. The bank can replenish the account by purchasing yen somewhere, such as from another bank or from the Federal Reserve (since the Fed also maintains supplies of currencies).

What causes currencies to be in short supply or to accumulate? It is the relative demand for goods and services of the various countries and the relative prices of the currencies. For example, if the Japanese demand for U.S. goods is greater than the U.S. demand for Japanese goods, then either the exchange rate will change so as to equate the two demands (dollars will become more expensive in terms of yen) or dollars will flow to Japan. Which occurs depends on the international exchange system; namely, whether it consists primarily of *flexible exchange rates* or *fixed exchange rates*. We will discuss each of these systems below. Before doing so we need to examine one of the most important aspects of the link between countries; i.e., the relationship between a country's money supply and its stock of foreign exchange reserves.

A glance at the Fed's, or any central bank's, balance sheet points out the international impact on the domestic money supply. On the asset side of the balance sheet are gold, foreign exchange, and government securities. The gold represents actual gold in the vaults of the central bank. The foreign exchange is either bank accounts that the Fed maintains with the central banks of other countries or foreign currency denominated securities. The domestic government securities held by the Fed are those purchased during open market operations. The liabilities of the Fed are just the monetary base, the stock of notes and coins that have been issued and are held either by the general public or in the drawers of commercial banks. Since assets must equal liabilities in a balance sheet, we know that the monetary base (MB) must equal the sum of foreign exchange and gold (F) and domestic securities (DS).

$$MB = F + DS$$

Since the money supply depends on the size of the monetary base, in the open economy the money supply depends on the amount of foreign exchange held by the central bank. Thus, changes in the monetary base can occur as a result of changes in either the foreign component or the domestic component. Representing that fact in a simple equation we have the following:

$$\Delta MB = \Delta F + \Delta DS$$

Where ΔMB represents the change in the monetary base, ΔF the change in foreign exchange and/or gold, and ΔDS the change in the Fed's holdings of domestic securities. ΔF is called the *official reserve transactions balance* which, as we shall see, plays a crucial role under fixed exchange rates.

Fixed Rates: The Bretton Woods System

Before 1914 the major trading countries maintained fixed exchange rates with each other and used gold as the main form of international reserves and medium of exchange (the world was on a *gold standard*). However, after World War I there was considerable confusion in the international monetary system. Most countries imposed severe restrictions on foreign trade and took themselves off the gold standard. By the end of World War II, a period of international cooperation was at hand. At a conference held at Bretton Woods, New Hampshire in 1944, the International Monetary Fund (IMF) was set up, and the international exchange system that was to operate until 1971 was instituted.[4] Under this system each member pledged to maintain a *fixed exchange rate* for its currency in terms of gold and hence in terms of the other currencies. This system was referred to as an *adjustable peg system* because small exchange rate changes were allowed. While gold was still important, it no longer played the prime role it had before 1914. Gold no longer circulated internally as currency, and it formed a shrinking percentage of international reserves. In effect, the dollar took over the role of gold. It was convertible into gold and was the major currency used for foreign transactions. For this reason the international financial system was called a *gold exchange standard*.

By the late 1960s, the continual purchases of foreign goods in excess of sales to foreigners by the U.S. placed the Bretton Woods system in jeopardy. Since most currencies were pegged to the U.S. dollar, the U.S. was unable to change the situation. It could not, in effect, alter the exchange rate to remedy the problem. The essence of the difficulty was that during the sixties and early seventies some countries, primarily the U.S., pursued expansionary policies while other countries, particularly West Germany, wanted lower inflation rates than the world economy was experiencing and followed less expansionary policies. With fixed exchange rates, the lower rate of inflation in West Germany meant that West German goods were becoming progressively cheaper relative to American goods. As a result, West Germany ran increasingly large balance of payments surpluses (bought less than it sold) while the U.S. and Britain had large deficits. Under such circumstances, countries with large surpluses

---

[4] See Victor Argy, *The Postwar International Money Crisis* (London: George Allen & Unwin Ltd., 1981) for more details.

accumulate other currencies (particularly dollars) or gold while the deficit countries lose currencies or gold. These flows create problems for the domestic economy since the domestic money supply becomes difficult, if not impossible, to control. For those countries attempting to run slower or contractionary policies, the money supply expansion forces them to import the other countries' inflation.

The only solution is to *devalue* or *revalue the currency*; that is, to change the rate at which one currency can be converted into another. A devaluation of the dollar, for example, would lower the price of dollars in terms of other currencies, and conversely for a revaluation of the dollar. However, a fixed exchange rate system with free capital flows between countries is poorly equipped to deal with revaluations or devaluations that are widely anticipated. For instance, in West Germany in 1973, there were recurrent rumors that the Deutsche mark would be revalued. The rumors arose because the exchange rate adjustment of 1971 had not appreciably reduced the U. S. balance of payments deficit relative to West Germany. The belief in an imminent Deutsche mark revaluation led to large capital outflows from the U.S. and inflows to West Germany.

As a result of the expected revaluation, the West German Bundesbank (central bank) had to buy about $10 billion in foreign currency over a five week period to meet foreign demands for marks at the existing exchange rate. In essence, the Bundesbank supported the exchange rate by supplying marks. Since that $10 billion was about 20 percent of the West German money supply at the time, the Bundesbank was forced to expand the West German money supply—to import inflation from the United States.

A country that is expected to devalue also faces an intractable problem under fixed exchange rates. The expected devaluation produces an outflow of capital from the country. An example was provided by Mexico during 1976-1982. The Mexican peso was fixed relative to the U.S. dollar. Yet the rapid inflation in Mexico relative to the U.S. was increasing the speculation that Mexico would devalue its peso. Capital flowed from Mexico to the U.S. at such a rate that Mexico finally imposed a legal restriction—no money could leave Mexico.

The general point is that a fixed exchange rate system is not viable if countries pursue policies that lead to different rates of inflation and if there is free mobility of capital. The very act of pegging the foreign exchange rate means that the central bank must always be willing to buy and sell foreign exchange at that rate. In other words, the central bank must always be willing to raise or lower its own stock of foreign exchange in order to preserve the fixed value of its own currency in terms of foreign currencies. Thus, although the central bank can decide how many domestic assets to buy and hold, it has no control over the gold and foreign exchange reserves that it holds. It follows then that it cannot fully control its domestic money supply.

Flexible Exchange Rates

Since 1973 a new system has emerged. The new system is essentially a flexible exchange rate system although not every country has followed a purely market determined exchange rate. We have already mentioned Mexico's attachment to the U.S. dollar. In addition, the nations of the European Economic Community (EEC) joined together in a currency area venture called the *snake*.[5] The snake was an arrangement whereby exchange rates between member countries could fluctuate only within narrow limits while the overall exchange rate would fluctuate with respect to the U.S. dollar according to demands and supplies.

The flexible exchange rate system that has emerged since 1973 has not been a pure (or clean) system.[6] Governments have intervened in foreign exchange markets; that is, they have bought or sold their currency to attempt to control their exchange rates. This is referred to as a *dirty float system*. The fact that rates have varied is shown in Figure 16-1 by the movement of the exchange rate of U.S. dollars to an index of other countries' currencies for the period 1974 to 1983.

The basis for the move to a floating exchange rate system was the belief that such a system would allow countries to pursue their domestic policies independently of what other countries were doing. The importation or exportation of inflation (the lack of control of the money supply) under fixed exchange rates would be avoided. In general the following differences between the two systems exist.

Under fixed exchange rates, central banks stand ready to meet all demands for foreign currencies arising from balance of payments deficits or surpluses at a fixed price in terms of the domestic currency. They have to finance the excess demands for, or supplies of, foreign currency at the pegged (fixed) exchange rate by running down or adding to their reserves of foreign currency. The flows of currency alter the domestic country's money supply and, subsequently, the inflation rate.

Under flexible exchange rates, the demands for, and the supplies of, foreign currency can be made equal through movements in exchange rates. Under clean floating, there is no central bank intervention. If one country is running an expansionary domestic policy and another a contractionary one, and if inflation rises in the first relative to the second, the demand for goods in the first will fall relative to the second. In such a case the exchange rate will adjust so that foreign reserves need not flow between countries and affect either country's money supply.

---

[5] France seems to have attempted to break away from the snake in its intervention policies. See Dean Taylor, "The Mismanaged Float," *The International Monetary System*, Dreyer, Haberler, and Willett, eds. (Washington, D. C.: American Enterprise Institute for Public Policy Research, 1982).

[6] See Argy, op. cit., Chapter 26; and Ronald I. McKinnon, *Money in International Exchange* (New York: Oxford University Press, Inc., 1979), Chapter 2.

Figure 16-1. A Multilateral Trade Weighted Exchange Rate Index: The U.S. to the Rest of the World

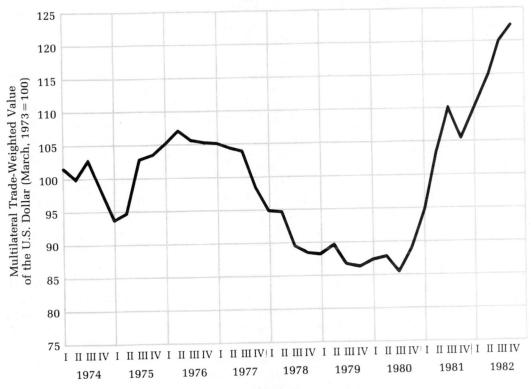

Year/Quarter

Sources: *Economic Report of the President* (1981), Table B-98; *Economic Report of the President* (1982), Table B-100.

Since the collapse of the Bretton Woods system of fixed exchange rates the exchange rate has been floating. The value of the dollar fell during the middle to late seventies but has risen very rapidly since.

The Law of One Price

What determines the flow of currencies in the fixed rate regime or the exchange rate in the flexible exchange rate system? The answer, known as the *law of one price*, is a simple, very basic proposition stating that whenever profit opportunities exist people will take advantage of them. Suppose, for example, that identical commodities could be purchased in the U.S. and the U.K. In each country the domestic currency price of the good is P = 1.0, and the exchange rate between the two countries is 1 dollar to 2 pounds. This means that the item is half as expensive in the U.K. as it is in the U.S. In the U.S. the item costs 1 dollar while in the U.K.

it costs 1 pound which is worth a half dollar. As long as people know this and can transfer their funds without costs, people will buy the good in the U.K. and sell it in the U.S. This will continue until the exchange adjusted prices are the same. Either the exchange rate will change to one-to-one (under the flexible rate system), or the price of the good in the U.K. will rise until it is double the price in the U.S. (under the fixed exchange rate system). The law of one price says that this arbitrage process will compete away all price differences between identical commodities. Whenever there are transport costs between the two locations, government restrictions on the flow of goods and services or capital, or whenever there are costs of acquiring information, the arbitrage process will drive prices to the point that there are no profits to be made in merely buying and simultaneously selling the commodity.

A theory known as *purchasing power parity* (PPP) extends the law of one price to a multigood setting. It states that the rate at which two currencies can be exchanged (the exchange rate) should reflect the relative purchasing powers of the two currencies since the prices of all traded goods should be the same throughout the world after allowances have been made for transportation costs and trade barriers.

Suppose the world consists of two countries, all goods are traded, and there are no transportation costs or trade barriers. Market forces should equalize the purchasing power of the currency in each country. However, if a market basket of goods is selling for 1 dollar in the U.S. and 1.5 pounds in Britain, and if 1 dollar is worth 2 pounds, then the price of the goods is cheaper in Britain than in the U.S. (the purchasing power of the pound is greater). As a result, individuals will attempt to purchase the goods in Britain, causing the British price to rise. In equilibrium we should find that prices in the U.S. equal prices in Britain once the British pound price has been converted to U.S. dollars. In equation form, this can be expressed as follows:

$$P = (1/e)P^f$$

Where P^f represents the foreign (British) currency price, P the domestic price, and e the exchange rate of foreign to domestic (U.S.) currencies. This equation is known as the *absolute version* of the PPP doctrine.

An alternative form is known as the *relative version*. It states that the percentage change of the exchange rate will be equal to the difference between the percentage changes of the foreign and home price levels. The percentage change of the exchange rate (defined as dollars per unit of foreign currency) and the percentage changes in the consumer price indices for Canada, Japan, the U.K., and West Germany, relative to the U.S. are presented in Figure 16-2. As can be seen there, a tendency exists for the exchange rate to appreciate in terms of the foreign currency when the inflation rate of the U.S. exceeds the foreign inflation rate. In contrast

Figure 16-2. Purchasing Power Parity

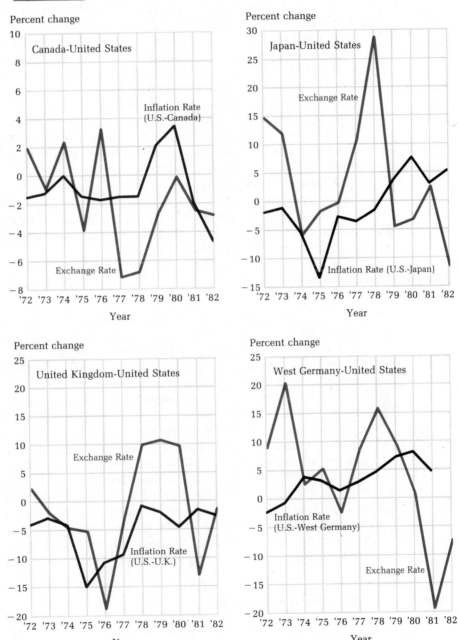

In each chart the U.S. rate of inflation is compared to the rate in one of the other countries, either Canada, Japan, the U.K., or West Germany. If the relative version of purchasing power parity holds, the differences between the inflation rates should equal the percentage change of the exchange rate.

to the relative version of the PPP theory, the percentage change in the exchange rate is not exactly equal to the difference in the percentage change in the price levels of the two countries.

A number of explanations have been offered to deal with the divergence between the percentage change in the exchange rate and the differences in inflation rates. One is that not all goods are traded. The existence of nontraded goods means competitive forces may not equilibrate prices between countries over the long run. Since nontraded goods are included in the price indices used in calculating inflation rates, this could account for the divergence from the PPP theory. Another explanation points to the intervention by governments which do not allow the exchange rates to adjust to relative inflation differences.[7]

Although the PPP theory may not hold at each and every moment, it does describe the relationship between price levels and exchange rates in most countries. If exchange rates are not free to vary, the price levels will change. If the exchange rates are free to vary, prices need not change in order to drive adjusted prices to equality.

Summary: Stable Exchange Rates versus Stable Prices

The main point of the discussion so far is that a country cannot choose both its inflation rate and the behavior of its exchange rate simultaneously. A country may choose to achieve stable prices, thereby allowing its exchange rate to adjust from time to time to reflect the difference between domestic and foreign inflation. Alternatively, it may decide to achieve a fixed exchange rate with the rest of the world, in which case it will have to allow the foreign inflation rate to be fully reflected in the domestic inflation rate. A country gives up control over its money supply with a fixed exchange rate. The automatic flows of foreign exchange reserves ensure that the growth rate of the money supply is adjusted to equal the growth rate of the demand for money. In the case of flexible exchange rates, the domestic monetary authority controls the stock of foreign exchange reserves and the domestic money supply thereby forcing adjustments onto the exchange rate itself. It is movements in the exchange rate that ensure that the stock of money that has been determined by the central bank will be willingly held by the public.

Fixed or Flexible Rates: Was the Move to a Flexible System a Good One?

Professor Robert Mundell of Columbia University argues that the floating exchange rate system, wherein there is no mechanism for international control over the quantity of international reserves, has led to a

---

[7] See Dornbusch, op. cit., for more details.

decade of monetary accommodation and debt creation.[8] In the 1960s it was widely believed that the movement to a system of flexible exchange rates would eliminate balance of payments problems, the need for foreign exchange reserves, and intervention in foreign exchange markets. According to Mundell, all these notions about the way a world of floating national currencies would behave should have been dispelled by now. Since 1973, money creation has been constrained only by the fear of depreciation and the fear of inflation, and these fears have surfaced only recently. The problem is that the floating rate system did not provide discipline or monetary restraint. On the contrary it provided inflation, unrepayable debt, and the de facto bankruptcy of many countries. When all currencies float and each country controls its own money supply, there is no anchor of stability.

Before 1981, most of the nations in the Bretton Woods arrangements kept their currencies stable, directly or through another currency, in terms of the dollar while the U.S. kept its currency stable in terms of gold. Once this anchor was gone, monetary discipline also went and world inflation was the order of the day. In previous chapters, and particularly in Chapter 13, we discussed the political pressures to expand the U.S. money supply in response to the Great Stagflation. This same type of pressure was created in virtually every industrialized country. To offset this pressure, Professor Mundell argues for a return to a fixed set of exchange rates and a return to convertibility to gold. Only then, he argues, would authorities be disciplined or restricted from yielding to political pressure.

Professor Ronald McKinnon of Stanford University, although agreeing in general with Mundell's approach, nevertheless takes a different tack.[9] He argues that the Fed, believing it was insulated from the rest of the world, made a serious policy error during 1979-82 because it failed to recognize what the exchange rate was saying. According to McKinnon, the move to the post Bretton Woods system of domestic autonomy should not have meant that world events could be ignored. McKinnon claims that the Fed slowed money growth in the U.S. after October, 1979, without reference to the foreign exchange or monetary conditions in other industrial countries. For example, in the summer of 1980, the following events in other countries led to an increase in the demand for dollars: (1) Arab sheiks, multinational companies, and foreign central banks were investing in the U.S., (2) the election of a socialist government in France and the crisis in Poland led to an outflow of capital from these counties, and (3) the Japanese government intervened (bought dollars) to keep the yen from

---

[8] Robert Mundell, "The Debt Crisis: Causes and Solutions," *Wall Street Journal* (January 31, 1983), p. 24.

[9] Ronald I. McKinnon, "How a Strong Dollar Threw the Fed," *New York Times* (January 23, 1983), and "How to Coordinate Central Bank Policies," *New York Times* (January 30, 1983).

rising relative to other currencies. These events increased the demand for dollars in the U.S. while at the same time the Fed was running its tight money policy. These two developments drove internationally sensitive and interest sensitive industries in the U.S. into, or near, bankruptcy.

Between 1980 and December, 1982, the dollar had risen about 20 percent against the yen and 25 percent against the mark. Yet, West Germany and Japan had had much lower rates of domestic inflation over the same period. Those American industries most exposed to foreign trade suddenly lost international competitiveness. As the dollar rose people began to anticipate that it would soon depreciate to its "appropriate" level. The law of one price dictated a drop in the value of the dollar. This expectation meant that speculators would hold other currencies—dollars would flow out of the U.S. To attract funds, U.S. financial institutions had to offer higher interest rates on dollar assets than on yen or mark assets and this adversely affected the interest sensitive industries in the U.S.

According to McKinnon, the Fed should abandon its attempt to control any of the monetary aggregates or domestic interest rates and aim instead for an internationalist monetary policy of stabilizing the exchange rate. Then, when American monetary policy was too tight, upward pressure on the dollar in the foreign exchange markets would clearly signal so.

While the approaches offered by Professors McKinnon and Mundell have little similarity, they do both argue for a global view of economics and economic policies rather than a domestic insular approach. This is a significant change from the way open economy macroeconomics has been studied in the past. As with macroeconomics of the closed economy, the basis for the study of open economy macroeconomics was formed by the Keynesian revolution. During the 1920s and 1930s, great shocks were transmitted from one economy to another. Yet Keynes's *General Theory* analyzed the fiscal or monetary means for stimulating aggregate demand domestically without attempting to get a handle on difficult questions of currency convertibility, the exchange rate system, tariff restrictions, and the macro policies of other countries. He was probably very astute in taking this approach since the controversies his domestic approach raised were sufficient for any one publication. Later, Keynes's followers continued to minimize the importance of international developments. Only when problems arose as the U.S. recovered after the end of World War II much more rapidly than other countries did a branch of macroeconomic theory devoted to the open economy emerge. Even then the basis for this field of study was the autonomous or insulated nation. Moreover, the policy aim of this field of study was to further protect the nation by insulating it from potentially disruptive shocks coming through the balance of payments.

To understand the policies that emerged from this field of study and policies that continue to be examined and referred to today, we must understand how, according to this branch of study, international events affected the U.S. economy. We turn to this approach now.

Short-Run Adjustments and the Balance of Payments

In earlier chapters we discussed Milton Friedman's famous statement that inflation is always and everywhere a monetary phenomenon. We noted that it is common for the price effects of money supply growth to take place over time, and during this adjustment time, for real variables to change as the money supply changes. The same type of arguments apply to the open economy. In the long run, the law of one price holds, and the relative rates of growth of money supplies determine either exchange rates or rates of inflation. But it is common for some period of time to elapse before all monetary growth changes are reflected in rates of inflation and/or exchange rates. Monetary growth changes might have real effects during this period of time. In this portion of the chapter we present the traditional approach to examining the interdependence among countries and the international impacts on the domestic economy. The traditional approach emphasizes the short run, or adjustment period.

The Balance of Payments

The record of economic transactions between residents of the U.S. and residents of the rest of the world is known as the balance of payments. The balance of payments can be divided into two major sections and a balancing account. The first section is called the *current account* and the second is called the *capital account*. Adding the balances on the two accounts yields the *official reserve transactions balance* which indicates the magnitude of official balancing transactions. If the official reserve transactions balance is positive, then the country in question has increased its holdings of gold and foreign exchange reserves; i.e., $\Delta F > 0$.

The Current Account. This is the account in which the values of the flows of goods and services (and other current receipts and payments) between residents of the U.S. and residents of the rest of the world are recorded. The current receipts and payments include exports, imports, and transfer payments. Exports measure the value of goods and services sold to residents of the rest of the world while imports measure the value of goods and services sold to residents of the U.S. by the rest of the world. Transfer payments refer to the transfer of funds without the subsequent provision of goods and services, such as is the case with foreign aid.

The Capital Account. The second major account, called the *capital account*, records the flow of financial assets. Included in this account are capital inflows such as the deposit of funds in à U. S. bank by a resident of another country; the purchase of shares of stock in U. S. firms by residents of other countries; and capital outflows such as U. S. government loans to other countries, purchases of plants and facilities abroad by U. S. businesses, and the purchase of foreign government securities by private residents of the U. S.

The Official Reserves Transactions Balance. The balance of payments is based on double-entry bookkeeping and, therefore, must always be balanced. Should the private transactions on current and capital accounts not balance, offsetting official transactions are required to assure a zero balance of payments. If, for example, the sum of the current and capital accounts were negative, official reserves, such as gold or foreign exchange, would have to be sold. These official sales of reserves are called *official settlement transactions.* They are equal in value to, but have the opposite sign of, the sum of the current and capital accounts balances. The U. S. balance of payments statistics prior to 1976 listed the official reserve transactions balance indicating the net change in the country's foreign reserve position. This is expressed in the following formula:

$$\Delta F = CA + KA$$

Where ΔF is the official reserves transactions balance
                CA is the current account
                KA is the capital account

Table 16-2 shows the U.S. balance of payments statistics for selected years of the 1960-80 period. In interpreting the official settlement item in Table 16-2, it should be pointed out that it refers to increases in U. S. liabilities to foreign official agencies and declines in U. S. reserve assets. These official settlement transactions are equal in magnitude, but opposite in sign, to the official reserve transactions balance; i.e., $OS = -\Delta F$, where OS is the official settlement transactions.

Table 16-2. The Balance of Payments Accounts
            (in Billions of Dollars)

YEAR	CA	KA	STATISTICAL DISCREPANCY	OS
1960	2.8	−5.4	−1.0	3.6
1965	5.4	−6.3	−0.5	1.4
1970	2.3	−12.4	−0.2	9.4
1975	18.3	−30.2	5.9	5.9
1980	0.1	−42.5	35.8	6.6

Source: *Economic Report of the President* (1983).

In 1980 the current account was nearly in balance, experiencing a $100 million surplus, the capital account showed a $42.5 billion deficit, and the official reserve transactions balance was in deficit for about $7 billion (the two accounts plus the statistical discrepancy). The deficit meant that positive official settlement transactions of almost $7 billion were required, implying that dollars went abroad or that the U.S. experienced a net outflow of gold, special drawing rights (SDRs), or other settling currency. Note that although the two accounts showed a net deficit, the balance of payments was in balance.

As stated, double-entry bookkeeping requires that the balance of payments always be zero. For economic policy purposes, however, the balance of payments is the sum of the current and capital accounts, or the official reserve transactions account, that is of importance. Finally, it should be mentioned that the bottom line of the current account is often referred to as the balance of payments by the media, although that is in fact the trade balance.

The Balance of Payments Curve. In this section we will be placing the international sector into the *IS-LM* framework, using the Keynesian assumption of fixed price levels. The most important change from the domestic, or closed, *IS-LM* model is that domestic spending on domestic goods does not fully determine domestic output. Spending by domestic residents falls in part on domestic goods and in part on foreign goods while sales of domestic goods are made to both domestic and foreign residents. Hence, we must add foreign spending on domestic goods and subtract domestic spending on foreign goods to obtain the total demand for domestic goods.

$$D = (C + I + G) + (X - M)$$

Where

> D is total demand for domestic goods
> C is total domestic consumer spending
> I is total domestic investment spending
> G is total domestic government spending
> X is foreign spending on domestic goods
> M is domestic spending on foreign goods

Net foreign spending consists of the difference between the amount foreigners spend on U. S. goods (exports) and the amount U. S. residents spend on foreign goods (imports) and is denoted by *NX* (exports minus imports). The definition of total spending on domestic goods by domestic residents is the combination of total consumer domestic spending plus total domestic investment spending plus total domestic government spending. We continue to assume that domestic spending depends on the domestic interest rate and income levels. We will also assume that foreign demand for domestic goods is fixed at X^*, while the domestic demand for foreign goods depends only on the domestic level of income. As income rises domestic residents spend more on both domestic and foreign goods.

The trade balance then is NX = exports (X) − imports (M), and total demand (after adjusting for the exchange rate so that everything is measured in dollars) is equal to

$$C + I + G + NX(Y, X^*)$$

The goods market will be in equilibrium when the amount of output produced domestically (Y) is equal to the demand for that output. If prices are held constant, the *IS* equation for the open economy is as follows:

$$Y = C + I + G + NX(Y, X^*)$$

The *LM* curve is assumed to be exactly the same as the *LM* curve for the closed economy.

Some useful insights into the interaction among economies can be obtained by focusing solely on the balance of trade; that is, by ignoring capital flows. In Figure 16-3, the *IS* and *LM* curves are drawn along with a vertical line representing the trade balance position. Points to the left of $NX = 0$ are trade balance surpluses, while points to the right represent trade balance deficits. The reason for this is that the lower the domestic income level, *ceteris paribus*, the lower is the domestic demand for foreign goods relative to the foreign demand for domestic goods. Using Figure 16-3, suppose that income and interest rates are at Y_A and r_A respectively. At Point *A*, with a large surplus in the trade balance, the U.S. government increases its spending. The *IS* curve shifts out to *IS'* driving interest rates and income up to Point *B*. The increased income leads to increases in spending on both domestic and foreign goods. This increased spending increases imports and, with a given export level (X^*), reduces the surplus in the trade balance as we move to Point *B*. This is said to have worsened the trade position.

This exercise should point out the following lesson: Domestic expansion results in a worsening of the trade balance. In addition, since the *IS* curve depends on net exports, domestic expansion is smaller (the *IS* curve shifts out less) in the open than in the closed economy. To the extent that increased spending results in more imports, it "leaks out" and does not contribute to an increase in expenditures on domestic goods.

Now consider what occurs if one country expands from a recession more rapidly than other countries. The U. S. recovered more rapidly than Europe from the 1980-82 recession, for example. The result was a worsening of the trade balance; accordingly, the U. S. ran increasingly large trade deficits. This meant that U. S. spending on foreign goods increased the

Figure 16-3. The IS-LM Framework under the Open Economy with No Capital Flows

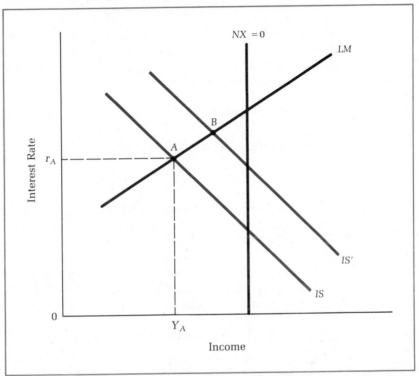

Points to the left of the NX = 0 line represent trade balance surpluses, while points to the right are trade balance deficits. Should government spending in the U. S. increase, the IS curve will shift out to IS' driving interest rates and income to Point B. Increased income means increased imports which, with a constant level of exports, drives the trade balance closer toward the deficit position.

demand for goods in those countries thereby stimulating their recoveries, while at the same time the U. S. recovery was slowed as spending leaked out.

The Balance of Payments and Capital Flows. Let us now turn to the effects of capital flows.[10] There are many interesting aspects of international finance and capital flows that we are unable to study in detail here. Instead, we only briefly survey the high points. We begin by noting two important facts.

1. If domestic interest rates are higher than foreign interest rates, capital will flow into the domestic country and away from the foreign country. This will drive the interest rates toward equality.

---

[10] See Feiger and Jacquillar, op. cit., for a summary of the issues.

2. If capital is perfectly mobile; i.e., domestic and foreign assets are
    perfect substitutes and can move from one country to another rapidly
    and without cost, interest rates throughout the world will equalize.
    (This is a version of the law of one price.)

With these two points in mind we can specify that capital flows depend
on the ratio of the U. S. interest rate (r) to the world interest rate (r*). The
higher the U. S. interest rate the greater the capital inflow. The balance of
payments equation then becomes

$$\text{Balance of payments} = NX(Y, X^*) + KA(r/r^*) - \Delta F$$

Since the balance of payments is always in balance, then

$$\Delta F = NX(Y, X^*) + KA(r/r^*)$$

The official reserve transactions balance will equal the sum of the net
outflows of goods and services and capital. If the trade balance is, say, a
negative $(NX < 0)$ \$6 billion and the capital account is a positive $(KA > 0)$
\$2 billion, then foreign reserve outflows of \$4 billion must take place.

Notice that there are combinations of Y and r at which ΔF would equal
zero. Plotting all those combinations gives us the balance of payments
curve, as shown in Figure 16-4. Hence, we now have an additional curve

Figure 16-4. The Balance of Payments Curve

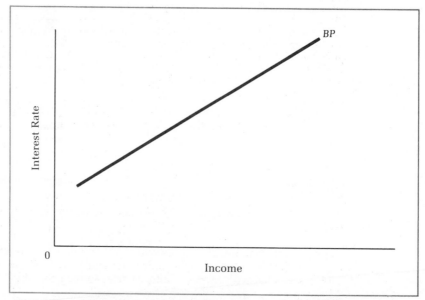

The balance of payments curve (BP) shows all combinations of domestic interest rates
and domestic income at which the official reserve transactions balance equals zero ($\Delta F = 0$).

in the *IS-LM* diagram, the balance of payments curve, that shows all combinations of domestic interest rates and income levels at which the official reserve transactions balance is zero; that is, $\Delta F = 0$. The balance of payments curve is typically shown to be upward sloping since increases in domestic income increase imports, while increases in domestic interest rates increase capital inflows. The two flows must offset one another so that $\Delta F = 0$. If perfect capital mobility held, so that interest rate differentials between countries were immediately offset by flows of capital, and if all interest rates were the same, the domestic interest rate would be constant at the world level and the balance of payments curve would be a horizontal line at that level.

Equilibrium, the Balance of Trade, and Disturbances

Let's begin with the fixed exchange rate regime and examine the impact of monetary or fiscal policy shocks on the economy. Is the short-run equilibrium at the intersection of the *IS* and *LM* schedules, or at the intersection of one of those schedules with the balance of payments schedule, or do all schedules have to intersect (see Figure 16-5)? The

Figure 16-5. Equilibrium in the Open Economy

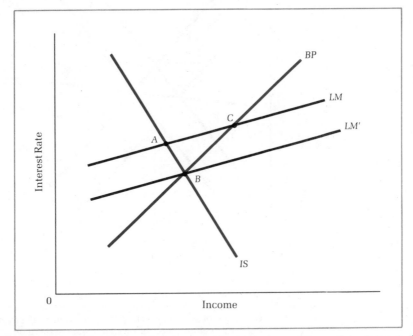

Intersections at Points *A* and *C* can only be temporary resting points. Point *A*, for example, is a point of trade surplus. Foreign exchange will flow in, thereby driving the money supply up. This means that the *LM* curve will shift down toward Point *B*.

answer is that all the schedules must intersect. If, for example, the IS and LM schedules intersect at a point above the balance of payments curve, say at Point A, the economy will be experiencing a balance of payments surplus and the LM curve will have to shift to the right as the inflow of foreign reserves drives up the money supply. Recall that the domestic money supply is composed of domestic and foreign components. In other words, $\Delta MB = \Delta F + \Delta DS$. The foreign component increases if the official reserve transactions balance is positive ($\Delta F > 0$). Foreign exchange or gold flowing into or out of the country causes the quantity of money to change. The LM curve will shift out until a three way intersection takes place at Point B.

How do disturbances affect the economy in this open system? Suppose first that an increase in domestic spending takes place—perhaps an increase in government spending, from G_0 to G_1 in Figure 16-6. Starting

Figure 16-6. *An Increase in Government Spending under Fixed Exchange Rates*

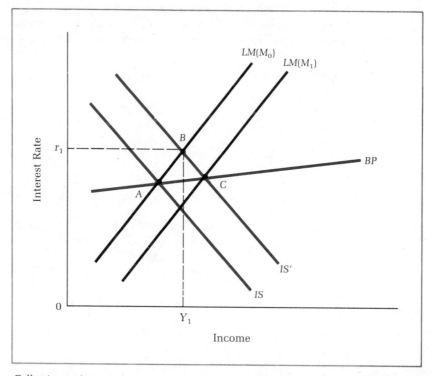

Following an increase in government spending, the IS curve shifts out driving domestic income and interest rates up. However, since the intersection between IS and LM curves occurs above the balance of payments curve (BP), a balance of payments surplus is run (thereby increasing net foreign reserve inflows and causing the money supply to increase). The LM curve shifts outward until all three curves intersect at Point C.

from an initial equilibrium at Point A, the IS curve shifts up or out leading to an increase in domestic income and an increase in the interest rate. The new intersection between IS and LM curves is above the balance of payments curve at Point B. This means that a balance of payments surplus is occurring (income is too low at the interest rate r_1 for imports to offset exports), and the surplus means that the official reserve transactions balance is positive. A net foreign reserves inflow occurs, and this causes the money supply to increase from M_0 to M_1. The LM curve shifts outward and continues shifting until the intersection of all three curves occurs at Point C.[11] Note that the domestic authorities lack total control over the money supply. The increased demand simply sets off forces that automatically drive the domestic money supply up. This is a very important point and lies at the center of the controversy over whether fixed or flexible exchange rates is the better system.

Suppose that instead of an increase in government spending, the domestic policymakers decided to use monetary policy to drive output and employment up. In Figure 16-7 we begin at Point A, which is a point of equilibrium but one that lies below the natural output level (Y_N). Policymakers decide to undertake an open market operation to expand the money supply. The LM curve shifts out, driving interest rates lower and income higher. The intersection between IS and LM′ curves occurs at Point B below the balance of payments curve (a balance of payments deficit occurs). The deficit means that foreign exchange or gold will flow out of the U.S. and that the domestic money supply will decrease. The LM curve will shift back to its original position. Monetary policy is powerless—the domestic authorities have no control over the money supply.

Suppose the exchange rate regime is flexible rather than fixed. Are the relative effects of fiscal and monetary policy different? Before answering this question we must be sure that we understand the differences between the fixed and the flexible exchange rate regimes. In the fixed exchange rate system, central banks will supply or purchase the domestic currency in order to maintain the pegged exchange rate. Hence, if the U. S. runs a large trade balance deficit and a very small capital account surplus with, say, West Germany, then in order to keep the U. S. dollar equal to its pegged price vis-a-vis the West German mark, the U. S. would have to purchase dollars (too many dollars are flowing to West Germany to maintain the price of dollars). Under the flexible exchange rate regime, the value of the dollar will fall relative to the mark. The U. S. would not have to give up its gold or foreign reserves to purchase dollars.

What is the impact of an exchange rate change? First, note the following definitions:

---

[11] If the balance of payments curve was steeper than the LM curve, the result would have been a capital outflow and a money supply decrease. You might demonstrate this to yourself.

Figure 16-7. An Expansionary Monetary Policy under Fixed Exchange
Rates

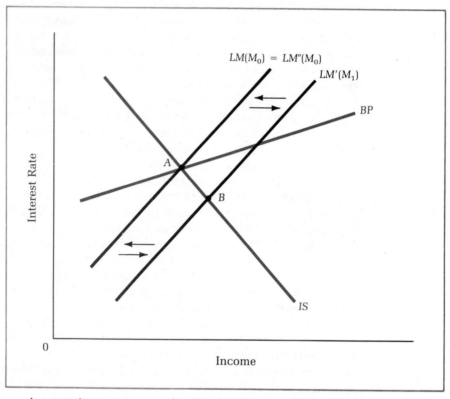

An expansionary monetary policy drives interest rates down and income up as the *LM*
curve shifts out. However, since the domestic equilibrium, between the *IS* and *LM* curves, is
a point below the balance of payments curve (*BP*), a balance of payments deficit occurs. This
leads to a foreign reserves outflow and a decrease in the money supply.

1. *Appreciation of the dollar* means that the price of the dollar rises
   relative to other currencies. (It takes three marks to buy one dollar
   instead of two marks, for example.)
2. *Depreciation of the dollar* means that the price of the dollar falls
   relative to other currencies.
3. *Devaluation of the dollar* means that the fixed exchange rate is raised
   so that the price of the dollar falls relative to other currencies.
4. *Revaluation of the dollar* means that the fixed exchange rate is
   lowered so that the price of the dollar rises relative to other currencies.

Under the flexible exchange rate system the dollar appreciates or depreci-
ates as dictated by demand and supply. Under the fixed rate regime the
authorities simply redefine the price of the dollar thereby devaluing or
revaluing.

If the dollar becomes more expensive because of revaluation or appreciation, then U. S. goods become more expensive to foreigners and foreign goods become less expensive to U. S. residents. As a result, *ceteris paribus*, foreigners spend less on U. S. goods, and U. S. residents spend more on foreign goods. The trade balance worsens. In terms of the *IS-LM*-balance of payments diagram, the *IS* curve shifts in (at each interest rate there is less spending on domestic goods), and the balance of payments curve shifts in (at each interest rate the trade account is more in deficit which means a lower domestic income is necessary to maintain the official reserve transactions balance at zero).

If government spending increases, the *IS* curve shifts out to *IS'* and income and the interest rate rise (from Point *A* to Point *B* in Figure 16-8). Recall that under flexible exchange rates the domestic money supply is not affected by balance of payments deficits or surpluses. The exchange rate adjusts so that the official reserve transactions balance is maintained at zero. Since the *LM* curve does not change, we know that the final equilibrium must be a point on the *LM* curve and must intersect the *IS* curve.[12] But since the changing exchange rate affects the *IS* and the balance of payments curves, both these curves must shift. Why would the exchange rate change affect these two curves? Recall that both depend on exports and imports and that an exchange rate change alters the relative prices of goods in the various countries. If the dollar appreciates, U. S. goods become relatively more expensive (imports increase and exports decrease). The result is a lower demand for U. S. goods: an inward shift of the *IS* curve from *IS'* to *IS''*. Moreover, under the flexible exchange rate system the official reserve transactions balance must always be zero. Hence, if imports increase and exports decrease, there is a new combination of interest rates and income at which the official reserve transactions balance equals zero: The interest rate must be higher for each income level than was previously the case. What happens is that the exchange rate has to change in order to shift the *IS* and the balance of payments curves back. The new equilibrium at Point *C* will be closer to the original equilibrium than Point *B* is.

Begin again with equilibrium, as shown in Figure 16-9, at Point *A* and suppose that an expansionary monetary policy is implemented. The *LM* curve shifts out driving income up and the interest rate down. The new equilibrium has to occur somewhere on the new *LM* curve since the money supply is fixed at the new, higher level after the domestic policy change. With a higher level of income U. S. residents will demand more foreign goods driving imports up relative to exports. The excess supply of

---

[12] Strictly speaking, the *LM* curve will also shift as the exchange rate changes. For example, a depreciation results in a decline in real money balances implying that the *LM* curve shifts to the left. For convenience sake, these shifts are ignored in the diagrams.

Figure 16-8. Expansionary Fiscal Policy under Flexible Exchange
Rates

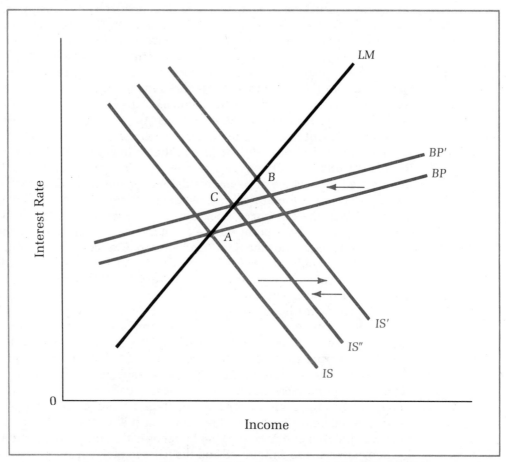

An expansionary fiscal policy shifts the IS curve to IS' under flexible exchange rates. The domestic money supply is not affected by balance of payments deficits or surpluses. Since the LM curve does not change we know that the final equilibrium must be a point on the original LM curve. We also know that both the balance of payments curve (BP) and the IS curve are affected by changing exchange rates since the relative prices of domestic and foreign goods are changed. The changing exchange rate drives both curves to the left since U. S. goods have become more expensive (imports have increased and exports decreased).

dollars to the foreign exchange market (U. S. residents supply dollars to purchase the foreign goods) means that the value of the dollar will decrease, and, thus, the exchange rate rises. Foreign goods then become more expensive, and U. S. goods less expensive. The increase in net exports shifts the IS and the balance of payments curves out until all three schedules intersect (at Point B).

Figure 16-9. An Expansionary Monetary Policy under Flexible Exchange Rates

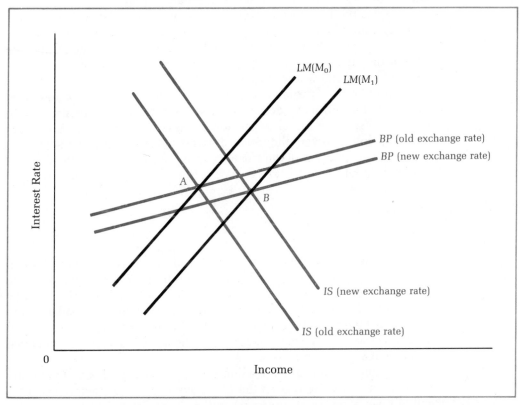

The *LM* curve shifts out as the money supply is increased. This drives the interest rate down and income up. With a higher level of income U. S. residents will demand more foreign goods. This increases imports and decreases the value of the dollar relative to other currencies. The exchange rate changes, and the *IS* curve and the balance of payments curve *(BP)* both shift.

Summary: Determination of Output, Interest Rates, and Balance of Payments in a Fixed Exchange Rate Regime

The income and interest rate levels are determined at the intersection of the *IS* and the *LM* curves. If that intersection is off the balance of payments curve, capital flows will cause the *LM* curve to shift until a three way intersection occurs. Expansionary fiscal policy raises output and interest rates and leads to a temporary balance of payments surplus. Foreign reserve inflows then automatically cause an increase in the domestic money supply. On the other hand, expansionary monetary policy has only temporary effects since capital inflows or outflows will automatically alter the money supply (offset the initial monetary expansion). Shocks from the rest of the world would be transmitted through the balance of payments to the domestic money supply.

Whereas the *LM* curve was at the mercy of the balance of payments situation under fixed exchange rates, the position of the *LM* curve is determined domestically under flexible exchange rates. The *IS* and the balance of payments curves will shift as the exchange rate adjusts to maintain an official reserve transactions balance of zero. An expansionary fiscal policy raises income and the rate of interest and causes an appreciation of the currency (domestic goods become more expensive) that partially offsets the initial expansionary fiscal policy. An expansionary monetary policy lowers the rate of interest, raises the income level, and leads to a depreciation of the currency (domestic goods become relatively less expensive).

Prices, Expectations, and the Open Economy

The view of the open economy presented in the last section is limited. It assumes constant prices and ignores the influence of expectations. The approach is simple and very insular, focusing on the domestic economy and on those domestic policies that have the objective of insulating the economy from events in the rest of the world. In this final section we will summarize some of the extensions to this theory of the open economy that have emerged in recent years.

First consider the effect of a domestic price change. Recall that under a fixed exchange rate regime the *LM* curve is a passive actor. Suppose, without worrying about the source of the change, that the domestic price level declines. This has three effects. First, the lower price makes domestic goods cheaper and foreign goods more expensive. The trade balance moves toward more of a surplus. This is represented by an outward shift of the *IS* curve. Second, the lower price level increases real money balances as represented by an outward shift of the *LM* curve. Third, the surplus in the trade balance causes foreign exchange to flow in (the *LM* curve shifts out further).

Under a flexible exchange rate regime, it is the *IS* curve that is passive. The lower domestic price leads immediately to an exchange rate change (the dollar appreciates). The effects of the price change are (1) real money balances increase as represented by an outward shift of the *LM* curve, and (2) the exchange rate changes, making dollars more expensive. This is represented by an outward shift of the *IS* curve.

In Figure 16-10 the aggregate demand (*AD*) curve is sketched out assuming a fixed exchange rate regime and perfect capital mobility. As was the case with the closed economy, the demand curve is derived by

Figure 16-10. *Derivation of the Open Economy Aggregate Demand Curve*

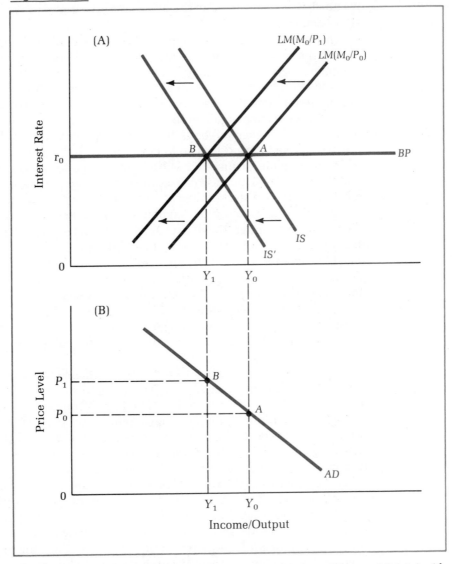

In Panel A, and assuming price level P_0, the economy is in equilibrium at Point A with income Y_0. Should the price level increase to P_1, the real money supply will fall. Consequently, the LM curve will shift to the left until equilibrium is reestablished with lower income level Y_1 at Point B in Panel A. This new equilibrium price-income combination is plotted as Point B in Panel B. Points A and B in the lower panel represent two points on the open economy aggregate demand curve.

carrying out the experiment of varying the domestic price level and finding the combinations of price level and real output at which the commodity and money markets are in equilibrium. In the open economy we must also make sure that the official reserve transactions account has a zero balance.

In Panel A of Figure 16-10 the *IS*, *LM*, and balance of payments curves (under the conditions of perfect capital mobility so that the balance of payments curve is horizontal) are drawn. The intersection, Point A, provides the initial domestic price level and real output level combination plotted in Panel B. Assume that the domestic price level is increased to P_1. With the exchange rate fixed, as U. S. prices rise relative to the rest of the world, domestic goods become more expensive and exports decrease relative to imports. The *IS* curve shifts to the left, and the worsening trade situation causes an outflow of foreign exchange. This outflow and the price level increase causes the real money supply to decrease. The result is a leftward shift of the *LM* curve. The new intersection, Point B, is one more point (price-output combination) on the *AD* curve. Notice that the *AD* curve under fixed exchange rates depends on the *LM* curve shifting until it intersects both the *IS* and the balance of payments curves. The *LM* curve responds to any changes in the other curves. The position of the *AD* curve, therefore, depends only upon those events that influence the position of the *IS* and the balance of payments curves; i.e., the rest of the world's price level, domestic income, the world's (equal to the domestic) rate of interest, domestic government spending and taxes, and the exchange rate. The *LM* curve will adjust to changes in any of these variables.

As you might imagine, in the flexible exchange rate world it is the *IS* curve that takes the passive role. The *LM* and the balance of payments curves essentially determine the *AD* curve. The graphical derivation of the *AD* curve under flexible exchange rates does not look much different from that used for the fixed exchange rate. Hence, we will refer to Figure 16-10 again. An increase in the domestic price level causes real money balances to fall and makes domestic goods more expensive relative to the output of the rest of the world. The exchange rate must adjust to force the law of one price to hold—to equate the prices of goods across countries. The rising price level thus leads to an inward shift of the *LM* curve followed by a passive shift of the *IS* curve. The new intersection at Point B determines an additional point on the *AD* curve. Once the price level has reduced real balances, the *LM* curve does not shift as foreign exchange flows in or out, as was the case in the fixed exchange rate system.

The difference between the two *AD* curves is in the set of independent variables upon which each depends. Under the fixed exchange rate regime the position of the curve depends upon those variables that determine the positions of the *IS* and the balance of payments curves—the foreign price level, the foreign interest rate, domestic income, government spending and taxes, and the exchange rate. Under flexible exchange rates, the AD curve depends on those variables that determine the position of the LM and the balance of payments curves—the domestic money supply and the foreign interest rate.

The difference between the open and the closed AD-AS model is that the AD curve is affected by world events rather than only by domestic events. In addition, if these events affect domestic prices they affect the short-run AS curve as individuals determine their wage demands and form their expectations of prices.

Suppose that the U.S. decides to run a contractionary monetary policy. Beginning from the initial equilibrium, the contractionary monetary policy will be represented by an inward shift of the AD curve. If fully anticipated, the contractionary policy would lead immediately to lower prices (the short-run AS curve would immediately shift down). At the same time, the lower U.S. price level relative to the rest of the world would cause an increase in U.S. exports and an appreciation of the dollar (a fall of the exchange rate).

While this sounds like the picture of a closed economy's reaction to a contractionary monetary policy, there are differences. Consider Figure 16-11. First, without the balance of payments curve and the worldwide pressure on interest rates, the LM curve would shift in and intersect the IS curve at Point C. The IS curve would not shift in as far (the impact of the rest of the world is to reduce the quantity demanded at price level P_0). The effect on the economy is shown in Panel B. If expectations do not adjust immediately, the recession in the closed economy (from Point A to E to F) will be smaller than in the open economy (from Point A to D to G). Under perfect information and rational expectations the adjustment is from Point A to F rather from Point A to G.

This difference between the closed and open economy adjustments is representative of the arguments Professor McKinnon has made for a recognition of the open economy when policy is made. Policymakers operating only on the basis of a recession such as shown from Point A to E to F will miss the additional output effects illustrated by the space from Point E to D.

Perhaps the most important difference is in how the exchange rate signals information about aggregate demand and relative prices. This is very important for those models we have discussed that account for expectations. With flexible exchange rates, shocks from the rest of the world do not affect the position of the AD curve as they would under fixed exchange rates. However, they do affect the exchange rate and, in so doing, lead individuals to make inferences about the position of the AD curve. It is possible for foreign shocks to be confused with domestic demand shocks. To the extent that they are so misperceived, they will lead to a shift in the short-run AS curve and, therefore, to a change in the level of output and prices. For example, a foreign shock that causes

Figure 16-11. The AD Curve and Monetary Policy in the Open Economy

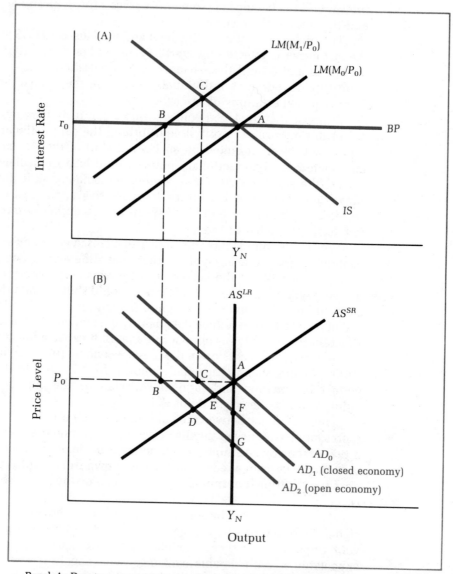

Panel A: Due to a monetary correction, the AD curve in the open economy shifts in further than it would in the closed economy. Beginning from Point A, a reduction in M leads to an inward shift of the LM curve. In the closed economy the new equilibrium is at Point C. In the open economy it is at Point B.

Panel B: The greater shift of the AD curve in the open economy (as compared with its shift in the closed economy) means that there will be a larger price change (from Point A to G as compared with Point A to F in the closed economy) if expectations are rational and information is complete. If expectations are adaptive or formed with a lag, then the recession will be more severe in the open economy (from Point A to D rather than from Point A to E).

individuals to expect a price rise will, other things being equal, produce a stagflation type of result comparable to that which we discussed in Chapter 13.[13]

Suppose that West German authorities decide to impose a very severe contractionary monetary policy. The purpose of this is to increase the dollar-mark exchange rate (to make dollars more expensive). If this change is a surprise to U. S. residents and monetary authorities, they might suspect that domestic monetary policies have changed—that they have become more expansionary. Hence, while the West German policy has no effect on the U. S. *AD* curve, individuals suspect that the *AD* curve has shifted. As a result, they expect more U. S. inflation, and these expectations will lead to an upward shift of the short-run *AS* curve. The effect is a recession until the error in expectations is corrected.

The flexible exchange rate does offer insulation from the effects of fully anticipated foreign shocks since any such shocks will be reflected entirely in the exchange rate and leave the domestic price level and output level undisturbed. It is the unanticipated shocks that can affect the domestic economy through mistaken forecasts.

Under the fixed exchange rate system, the exchange rates obviously do not signal relative developments in foreign economies nor do they insulate the domestic economy. Foreign shocks will affect the domestic economy through the flows of foreign exchange. For this reason, several economists have made the case that the Fed will have an informational advantage (it has continuous information about foreign developments through its foreign exchange reserves account) and this informational advantage means that the Fed can (and should) run an activist policy.[14]

Hence, the role of expectations enters the debate over fixed versus flexible exchange rates. Those economists supporting activist monetary policy use the fixed regime as one more plank in their platform. Conversely, those economists calling for less activism want the flexible regime. Of course reality complicates this dichotomy. Under the flexible regime of 1973-present, countries have pursued generally expansionary monetary policies and have not allowed the exchange rates to float. This intervention has merged the flexible and fixed types of regimes.

Summary: Unresolved Issues

The discussion of expectations seems to lend support to the flexible exchange regime. Yet floating rates have not been overly successful since

---

[13] The short-run *AS* curve would shift up (thus intersecting the *AD* curve to the left of the natural output level) until the error is recognized.

[14] See Arthur B. Laffer and Marc A. Miles, *International Economics in an Integrated World* (Glenview, Ill.: Scott, Foresman & Company, 1982), Chapter 20, for a review of some of

1973, at least according to several economists. What has been the problem? Do policies in the major countries need to be coordinated? If so, how? What problems are created by oil price changes or by loans from private banks to countries? These questions are some of the unresolved issues of open economy macroeconomics. To complete our survey of open economy macroeconomics, we will summarize some of the research being carried out on these topics.

The Mismanaged Float

Countries have generally followed a policy of "leaning against the wind" by resisting exchange rate changes. When exchange rates have appreciated, countries have accumulated dollars to slow the appreciation; when their currencies have depreciated, countries have sold dollars to prop up their home currency. In many ways the attempt to resist exchange rate changes is an attempt to peg exchange rates at existing levels when there is a change in the equilibrium level. The authorities can hold out temporarily but must eventually allow exchange rates to adjust. Many economists assert that this policy of government intervention has been the base cause of problems with the floating exchange rate system.[15] In the years since the collapse of the Bretton Woods system, the U.S. has intervened actively in exchange markets, as have Spain, Italy, the United Kingdom, France, and West Germany among others. Whether these policies are beneficial or not is controversial.[16]

It is claimed that large exchange rate movements can impose costs on countries due to the portfolio shifts that individuals and institutional investors make among assets. Another disadvantage of the large exchange rate movements is said to be the inflationary effect on the countries whose currencies are depreciating. Still another cost of exchange rate fluctuations is that they induce pressures for protection from import-competing industries within a country whose currency is appreciating. Intervention is justified as an attempt to minimize these costs.

Whether intervention minimizes these costs or worsens them is a point of concern.[17] For example, from January, 1974, when Spain allowed the peseta to float, until July, 1977, the Spanish authorities used $5 billion in reserves to buy pesetas. Despite these support purchases, the price of

---

the arguments.

[15] Many of the issues are discussed in Robert Solomon, "Official Intervention in Foreign Exchange Markets: A Survey" (unpublished manuscript, March, 1983).

[16] See Arthur B. Laffer and Marc A. Miles, op. cit., pp. 286-291.

[17] See Robert Solomon, op. cit. See also, Russell S. Boyer, "Optimal Foreign Exchange Market Intervention," *Journal of Political Economy* (December, 1978), pp. 1045-1056; and M. Goldstein, "Have Flexible Exchange Rates Handicapped Macroeconomic Policy?" *Special Papers in International Economics*, No. 14, International Finance Section (Princeton University Press, June, 1980).

the peseta began to decline. Thus, the authorities only delayed the fall in the exchange rate. From June, 1973, through May, 1975, the United Kingdom expended $7.5 billion in reserves to buy pounds in support operations. Nevertheless, the pound began to drop, and by the time the authorities gave up they had increased support operations by another $7.5 billion.[18]

Problems Such As the Third World Debt and Oil Price Changes

While the Great Stagflation of 1974-79 was carefully examined in Chapter 13, we did not look at its effect on other countries. A quick survey of international data points out that while most countries suffered from rising inflation, such as was the case in the U.S., both Japan and West Germany pursued policies that kept their inflation rates below those of the rest of the world. The lesson that comes from this survey is that it is possible to insulate a country from an inflation affecting the rest of the world. By pursuing firm enough domestic monetary policies (which also must be credible) low inflation and a strong currency can be achieved. This result requires that a country float its currency and permit an appreciation of the value of the currency against those currencies of countries where inflation rates are higher. While offsetting inflation, however, this approach could worsen fluctuations of real variables such as output and unemployment.[19]

Another question that arose out of the 1974 oil price shock and from the 1982-83 oil price decline concerns the impact of oil price changes on the world financial system. One thing to keep in mind when discussing international developments is that changes that adversely affect one country will benefit some other country. For example, the oil price rise in 1974 meant that foreign exchange flowed from the oil consuming countries to the oil producing countries. Conversely, the declines in oil prices in 1982-83 meant a decline in the flow of foreign exchange from oil consuming countries to oil producing countries. There is a significant controversy over what the actual impact of these shocks has been.[20] There was a

---

[18] A conference on the international monetary system was held at Columbia University in May, 1983. This was a warm-up for the latest economic summit held in Williamsburg, Virginia later that month. At each conference the main point of discussion was the exchange rate regime. See "Have Currencies Floated Too Long?" *New York Times* (May 8, 1983), p. 1.

[19] The debate over fixed versus flexible exchange rates is continually in the literature. See for example, the textbooks by McKinnon, by Laffer and Miles, or by Dornbusch. See also Dornbusch, "Exchange Rate Economics: Where Do We Stand?" *Brookings Papers on Economics Activity* (1:1980), pp. 143-185; and W. Weber, "Output Variability under Monetary Policy and Exchange Rate Rules," *Journal of Political Economy* (August, 1981), pp. 733-751.

[20] See Laffer and Miles, op. cit., pp. 161-3.

sharp deterioration of the trade balances of oil consumers and an equally sharp improvement for oil producers in 1974 as the oil price rise took place. Consumers could not switch to other energy sources rapidly (the elasticity of demand was very low) and hence the oil producers accumulated significant funds. It did not take very long for the oil producers to begin recirculating these funds, however. By 1975, the terms of trade between the two groups of countries was reversing as oil producers began consuming more of other types of goods and services and investing in the oil consuming countries. The impact of the 1982-83 price decline was essentially the opposite of that described previously. The oil consumers gained initially and the oil producers lost. The LDCs (particularly those betting on oil production for the development of their countries) were forced into de facto bankruptcy in 1980-83. This debt crisis struck a sensitive chord in the developed countries. It was feared that a default by one or more of the debt ridden countries would bankrupt several of the major financial institutions of the developed countries thereby throwing their economies into a tailspin. In addition the decline in the purchasing power of the LDCs affected the developed economies. In 1982, developing countries accounted for more than 40 percent of the U.S. exports and 28 percent of all exports by the 24 industrial countries that make up the Organization for Economic Cooperation and Development (OECD). The IMF along with those commercial banks that had poured approximately $640 billion in short- and long-term loans into the Third World restructured these loans. This, in essence, meant that additional funds were loaned to keep the nations from defaulting.

The Coordination of the Policies of Central Banks

Given the difficulties of the floating exchange rate regime (such as due to mismanaged intervention, to inherent problems with the flexible rate system, or to the lack of monetary discipline), several economists have called for a coordination of monetary policies by the major industrialized countries. We previously discussed the proposals of Professors McKinnon and Mundell. Both agree that it will take an explicit agreement, much like Bretton Woods, for central bank policies to be coordinated. Mundell calls for a return to a gold standard while McKinnon argues for an agreement among Japan, West Germany, and the U.S. to fix a rate of growth in the monetary base for the system as a whole in order to stabilize world prices. "Such a formal tripartite agreement would dramatically signal international investors that they could safely hold yen, marks, or dollars without continually switching among them."[21] A great deal of research is currently

---

[21] McKinnon "How to Coordinate Central Bank Policies," *New York Times* (January 30, 1983).

in progress over whether it is desirable for the major countries to coordinate policies and whether, in fact, they can coordinate policies.[22]

These and several other questions are being discussed concerning the open economy: Are fixed or flexible exchange rates the better system? How are equilibrium exchange rates determined? Why doesn't the purchasing power parity hold in the short run? What causes fluctuations in exchange rates? These are among the many unanswered questions of open economy macroeconomics.[23]

PROBLEMS AND EXERCISES

1. Explain the role of money in the international adjustment process.
2. Discuss the purchasing power parity doctrine.
3. Compare and contrast McKinnon's and Mundell's approaches to international monetary reform. Why have they both called for a change in the flexible exchange rate system?
4. What is the difference between the closed and the open economy in terms of the *IS-LM* framework?
5. Using the *IS-LM* framework, describe the impact of a monetary expansion in the open and in the closed economy. Be sure to make your assumptions of the exchange rate system explicit.
6. Compare and contrast the fixed and the flexible exchange rate systems. Which makes more sense? Why?
7. Utilizing the *AD-AS* framework, compare and contrast the impact of a monetary expansion under the open and the closed economy.
8. What is intervention? Why is it used?

---

[22] See John Taylor, "The Coordination of Monetary Policies" (unpublished manuscript, March, 1983); R. C. Bryant, *Money and Monetary Policies in Interdependent Nations* (Washington, D.C.: The Brookings Institution, 1980).

[23] Rudiger Dornbusch, "PPP Exchange-Rate Rules and Macroeconomic Stability," *Journal of Political Economy* (February, 1982), pp. 158-165; P. Hooper and J. Morton, "Fluctuations in the Dollar: A Model of Nominal and Real Exchange Rate Determination," *Journal of International Money and Finance* (April, 1982), pp. 39-56; and P. J. K. Kouri and J. B. de Macedo, "Exchange Rates and the International Adjustment Process," *Brookings Papers on Economics Activity* (1:1978), pp. 111-157.

_SUGGESTED READINGS

The literature on open economy macroeconomics is expanding at an exponential rate. For several examples of the debate over exchange regimes, see

Warren Weber, "Output Variability under Monetary Policy and Exchange Rate Rules," *Journal of Political Economy* (August, 1981), pp. 733-751.

Betty Daniel, "International Transmission of a Real Shock under Flexible Exchange Rates: A Comment," *Journal of Political Economy* (August, 1981), pp. 813-818.

G. Geoffrey Booth, Fred Kaen, and Peter Koveos, "An Analysis of Foreign Exchange Rates under Two International Monetary Regimes," *Journal of Monetary Economics* (1982), pp. 407-415.

This chapter has assumed that readers are familar with the microeconomics of gains from trade. For brief refreshers, read

Ryan C. Amacher, *Principles of Economics* (Cincinnati, Ohio: South-Western Publishing Company, 1983), Chapter 30.

Robert Paul Thomas, *Macroeconomic Applications* (Belmont, Calif.: Wadsworth Publishing Co., Inc., 1980), Chapter 33.

Each issue of the Quarterly Review of the Federal Reserve Bank of New York contains a discussion of U. S. Treasury and Federal Reserve operations in the foreign exchange markets. Additional overviews on international trade and investment are presented in

Robert Aliber, *The International Monetary Game*, 4th ed. (New York: Basic Books, Inc., Publishers, 1983).

William Branson, "Trends in United States International Trade and Investment since World War II," *The American Economy in Transition*, M. Feldstein, ed. Chicago: University of Chicago Press, 1980), pp. 183-257.

For alternative viewpoints on exchange rate systems see

Rudiger Dornbusch, "Exchange Rate Economics: Where Do We Stand?" *Brookings Papers on Economic Activity* (1: 1980), pp. 143-185.

"Why Floating Exchange Rates Aren't Doing Their Job," *Forbes* (October 2, 1978).

"The IMF and World Economic Stability: An Interview with Richard D. Erb, U. S. Director of the IMF," *Challenge* (September-October, 1981), pp. 22-27.

Robert Triffin, "The American Response to the European Monetary System," *Challenge* (January-February, 1979), pp. 17-25.

Henry C. Wallich, "Evolution of the International Monetary System," *Challenge* (January-February, 1979), pp. 13-17.

The pros and cons of protectionism are reviewed in

Melvyn B. Krauss, "Stagnation and the 'New Protectionism'," *Challenge* (January-February 1978), pp. 40-44.

Franklin R. Root, *International Trade and Investment*, 5th ed. (Cincinnati, Ohio: South-Western Publishing Company, 1984), Chapter 14.

An excellent series of papers on virtually every topic covered in this chapter has been published by the American Enterprise Institute.

Jacob S. Dreyer, Gottfried Haberler, and Thomas D. Willett, eds., *The International Monetary System* (Washington, D.C.: The American Enterprise Institute for Public Policy Research, 1982).

For an extension of the analysis of incomes policies to an open economy setting, see

William J. Boyes and D. E. Schlagenhauf, "Price Controls in an Open Economy," *Journal of Macroeconomics* (Summer, 1981), pp. 391-408.

GLOSSARY

Accelerationist Hypothesis The idea that monetary and fiscal policy can be used to permanently reduce the rate of unemployment only at the cost of accepting an accelerating rate of inflation.

Accord An agreement between the Federal Reserve and the U. S. Treasury concluded in March, 1951. It freed the Federal Reserve from the obligation of pegging interest rates and allowed it to pursue a discretionary monetary policy.

Adaptive Expectations The idea that people form their expectations of economic variables solely on the basis of previous values of those variables.

Adjustable Peg The exchange rate system under the Bretton Woods agreement. Each country agreed to keep the exchange rate between its currency and other currencies within narrow bands. If those bands became indefensible, the pegged exchange rate could be readjusted and new bands set up.

Administered Prices According to Gardiner Means, large corporations in the U. S. economy are not subject to price competition. Instead, they administer prices to maximize their profits. As a consequence, he believes, most prices do not fluctuate as much as would be expected on the basis of shifts in supply and demand.

Administrative Lag The time lapse between the recognition of a problem and when a policy action is undertaken to correct it.

Aggregate Demand *(AD)* A curve showing the demand for the total output of the economy (real GNP) as a function of its price.

Aggregate Supply *(AS)* A curve showing the total supply of output (real GNP) as a function of its price.

All-Saver's Certificate A special type of deposit instrument introduced in 1981. A saver could invest a maximum of $2,000 and receive tax-free interest.

Automatic Stabilizers Institutional structures in the economy which have the effect of dampening business cycle fluctuations. Examples include the progressive income tax, which reduces spending as the economy expands, and unemployment compensation, which helps to maintain consumption during times of high unemployment.

Automatic Transfer System (ATS) Accounts Transactions balances at commercial banks that combine the features of saving and time deposits. These balances earn interest up to the point when a check is written on them. Then funds are automatically transferred to the checking account—hence the name *automatic transfer service accounts*.

Autonomous Independent of national income.

Average Propensity to Consume (APC) The ratio of the level of consumption expenditures to the level of income.

Average Propensity to Save (APS) The ratio of the level of saving to the level of national income (APS = 1 − APC).

Bracket Creep In a progressive tax system, inflation drives individuals into higher tax brackets. As a result, such individuals find themselves paying higher taxes even though their real incomes have not grown.

Bretton Woods The fixed exchange rate system prevailing in the world economy between 1945 and 1971.

Business Cycles Fluctuations in economic activity in which an expansion is followed by a contraction and then another expansion.

Business Fixed Investment Spending by businesses on plant and equipment.

Capital The factor of production comprising produced goods which are used as inputs to further production. It is the stock related to the accumulation of investment flows.

Capital Account That part of the balance of payments statistics that records net changes in a nation's international financial assets and liabilities.

Capital Flows Movements of financial assets across national borders.

Classical Economics The dominant macroeconomic theory prior to the 1930s. It viewed the economy as being basically self-regulating. Consequently, the economy would always be at, or approaching, a state of full employment of resources at stable prices. Thus, there was thought to be no need for government intervention.

Clean Float A floating exchange rate system in which there is absolutely no intervention by national governments.

Commodity Market The market for goods and services. Demand and supply interact in this market to determine the level of output to be produced.

Congressional Budget Office (CBO) The Congress's CEA. The CBO is responsible for economic analysis of the budget and other congressional issues.

Consumer Durables Consumer goods that have a lifetime longer than one year. The consumer derives satisfaction from the services that the goods provide rather than from consuming the goods themselves.

Consumer Installment Credit Credit extended to consumers to facilitate the purchase of durable goods. The credit is usually financed through a fixed number of equal payments.

Consumer Price Index (CPI) An index that measures changes in the price of a fixed "market basket" of consumer goods over time. It is often interpreted as an index of the cost of living.

Consumption The flow of expenditures on goods and services used to satisfy wants and needs during the current period. Household spending.

Contemporaneous Reserve Accounting

(CRA) A system under which a financial institution's required reserves on a certain date depend upon its level of deposit liabilities on the same date.

Contract Based Models Macroeconomic theories that focus on the fact that wage rates applicable to a significant portion of the labor force are set in nominal terms for fixed time periods. While such contracts are in effect, the capacity of the economy to adjust to supply or demand changes is limited.

Council of Economic Advisers (CEA) A group of presidential economic advisers originally set up by the Employment Act of 1946. The chairperson is appointed by the president and confirmed by Congress. The CEA is responsible for the preparation of the annual *Economic Report of the President*.

Credibility Believability. Policymakers are said to have credibility when their statements about policy are believed by most people. Also, a theory of expectation formation suggested by William Fellner.

Cross-Sectional Data Economic data collected on different economic units but at the same point in time.

Currency to Deposit Ratio The ratio of the public's demand for currency to its demand for demand deposits.

Current Account That part of the balance of payments statistics that records all real (as opposed to financial) international transactions that enter a nation's gross national product.

Deficit The situation that occurs when an economic unit (usually the government) spends more in a period than it takes in in revenue.

Demand Deposits Deposits at financial institutions that are payable upon demand. Such deposits are transferable by check.

Demand for Money The demand for the stock of real money balances to be held. The demand for money is usually thought to depend upon the interest rate, the level of income, and other variables.

Demand Management The use of monetary and fiscal policy to affect the level of aggregate demand in the economy. Policymakers attempt to increase demand in order to reduce unemployment or to reduce demand in order to slow the rate of inflation.

Dirty Float A floating exchange rate system in which there is some occasional intervention by national governments.

Disintermediation If financial institutions are restricted in the rate of interest they may pay on deposits, then they may lose deposits during periods of high interest rates. Rather than place funds in a financial institution, individuals and businesses may choose to invest directly in such vehicles as Treasury bills and various types of bonds.

Disposable Income Income remaining after payment of taxes.

Employment Ratio The proportion of the noninstitutionalized population that is employed. It provides an aggregate measure of labor market conditions.

Endogenous Determined within the model. An economic model can be solved to determine the values of its endogenous variables.

Entitlements Government programs from which an individual receives payment if the program's requirements are met. For example, if one meets the requirements for Social Security, one receives monthly payments from the Social Security Administration.

Equation of Exchange An accounting relationship given mathematically as $M \cdot V = P \cdot Q$. In this equation, M is the stock of money, V is the velocity of money (the average number of times per period that the money stock is used to purchase output), P is the price level, and Q is the level of real output.

Equilibrium The situation that occurs in a market when there is no tendency for any variable determined in that market to change. In equilibrium, the plans of demanders are consistent with the plans of suppliers.

Equilibrium Business Cycle Theory The theory that attempts to account for economic fluctuations while assuming that wages and prices are perfectly flexible. Also known as the *New Classical Economics*.

Eurodollars Dollar denominated assets held in financial institutions, called *Eurobanks*, operating outside the U.S. The fact that these banks (or subsidiaries of U.S. banks) are based outside the U.S. has meant that they are exempt from U.S. regulations, particularly reserve requirements.

Excess Demand The situation that exists when demand exceeds supply at a given price level.

Excess Reserves The excess of a financial institution's vault cash and reserves at the Fed over its required reserves.

Excess Supply The situation that exists when supply exceeds demand at a given price level.

Exchange Rate The price of a unit of one country's currency in terms of another country's currency.

Exogenous Determined outside the model under investigation. An exogenous variable affects the model but is not affected by it.

Expectations Forecasts of the future values of an economic variable.

Exports Domestically produced goods and services that are sold to residents of foreign countries.

Fed See Federal Reserve System.

Federal Deposit Insurance Corporation (FDIC) A federally chartered agency that insures deposits at member financial institutions.

Federal Funds Market The market in which financial institutions with deficient reserves may borrow reserves from other financial institutions or from nonfinancial corporations. The reserves are typically in the form of deposits at the Federal Reserve.

Federal Funds Rate The equilibrium interest rate in the federal funds market. It is the rate which financial institutions must pay to borrow in that market.

Federal Housing Administration (FHA) A program set up in the 1930s to attempt to aid individuals in obtaining home mortgages. The FHA subsidized mortgages by offering lower than market interest rates.

Federal Open Market Committee (FOMC) The policymaking arm of the Federal Reserve System. The FOMC directs open market operations—the buying and selling of U.S. Government securities in order to control the U.S. money supply. The FOMC also directs operations in foreign exchange markets.

Federal Reserve System (Fed) The central bank of the United States.

Fine Tuning The idea that policymakers can use monetary and/or fiscal policy to reduce fluctuations in output and employment.

Fiscal Drag An automatic stabilization device originating in the progressive tax system. As nominal incomes expand, individuals are pushed into higher tax brackets and their average tax liability increases. This has a dampening effect on spending.

Fiscal Policy The deliberate manipulation of taxes and government expenditures in order to affect the level of national income, prices, unemployment, and other economic variables.

Fixed (Pegged) Exchange Rates An exchange rate system in which governments buy and sell currency in order to keep the exchange rate within a narrow band of values.

Flat Rate Tax An income tax in which a uniform tax rate is applied to all businesses and individuals.

Flexible (Floating) Exchange Rate An exchange rate that is determined by the forces of supply and demand in the absence of intervention by national governments.

Foreign Exchange A financial asset involving a cash claim held by a resident of one country against a resident of another country.

Foreign Reserves Central government holdings of gold, foreign exchange reserve positions in the International Monetary Fund, and Special Drawing Rights.

Fractional Reserve Banking System A monetary system in which financial institutions keep only a fraction of their deposits in the form of reserves.

Friedman-Phelps Alternative An explanation of the Phillips curve in terms of workers' incorrect price expectations. According to this theory, the short-run Phillips curve presents a trade-off between unemployment and inflation only as long as workers maintain the same price expectations. When expectations change, the short-run Phillips curve shifts. In the long run, the Phillips curve is vertical at the natural rate of unemployment.

Gold Exchange Standard A variation on the gold standard. Under the gold exchange standard a country pegs the value of its currency to the value of the currency of some other country which is on the gold standard.

Gold Standard A monetary system according to which the value of a country's money is legally defined as a fixed quantity of gold. The country's monetary authority agrees to exchange domestic currency for gold at a specified rate.

Great Depression The unusually severe recession that lasted from 1929 until the beginning of World War II.

Gross National Product (GNP) The value, at market prices, of all final goods and services produced in the economy during a given time period. It is a measure of the aggregate production of the economy during that time period.

Gross Private Domestic Investment (GPDI) The total amount of spending by business and households on plant, equipment, inventories, and housing in the domestic economy.

High-Employment Surplus (HES) The surplus (or if negative, the deficit) that the federal government would run on its budget if the economy were at its potential output level. It is used to measure the impact of fiscal policy.

High-Powered Money Another name for the monetary base—the sum of currency in circulation plus reserve deposits at the Fed.

Imports Domestically consumed goods that are produced in foreign countries.

Incomes Policies Policies designed to influence the wage and price setting behavior of firms and unions by exhortation, threat of specific actions or legislation. Often called wage and price controls.

Indexation Adjustment of nominal values of contracts in line with movements in a price index. A fully indexed economy is insulated against the cost of unanticipated inflation.

Individual Retirement Account (IRA) A retirement plan to which an employee may contribute as much as $2,000 per year. Contributions are tax-deductible and interest compounds tax-free.

Information Based Models Macroeconomic theories that focus on the effects of a lack of information on the economy's capacity to adjust to supply and demand shifts.

International Monetary Fund (IMF) An international organization set up to administer the Bretton Woods fixed exchange rate systems. In recent years it has specialized in making loans to financially distressed low income countries.

Inventories Stocks of raw materials, semifinished and finished goods which are maintained by firms. Unintended inventories comprise those goods that firms planned to sell but did not.

Inventory Investment Changes in the stock of raw materials and finished or semifinished goods held by business firms.

Investment The flow of expenditure on additions to the stock of capital. Alternatively, the flow of expenditures on goods that are used as inputs to further stages of production.

Investment Tax Credit (ITC) A reduction in income tax liability offered to businesses that undertake certain forms of investment spending.

Involuntary Unemployment A situation that exists when, at the prevailing wage rate, some people who want jobs cannot find jobs. There is some controversy over whether there is such a thing as involuntary unemployment. If a university professor is laid off and refuses to work except at another university, is this voluntary or involuntary unemployment?

_IS_ Curve A negatively sloped curve showing all combinations of the interest rate and the level of income that are consistent with equilibrium in the goods market.

Keynesianism A macroeconomic theory that predicts that the economy may reach an equilibrium position below the full-employment level of output. The theory postulates a variety of price rigidities and focuses on the use of fiscal policy to return the economy to full employment.

Laffer Curve A relationship purporting to show the connection between marginal tax rates and total tax collections. The curve shows that there are two marginal tax rates consistent with every level of total tax collections.

Lagged Reserve Accounting (LRA) A system under which a financial institution's required reserves on a certain date depend upon its level of deposit liabilities two weeks before.

Law of One Price The idea that arbitrage will compete away all price differences on identical commodities sold in different countries. More precisely, arbitrage will continue until there are no more profits to be made from buying a commodity in the country where its price is low and selling it in the country where its price is high.

Life Cycle Theory *(LCT)* A theory of consumption spending developed by Ando, Brumberg, and Modigliani. The theory is based on the hypothesis that economic units attempt to smooth out consumption over their lifetime despite the fact that income may vary widely.

Liquidity Trap A situation that exists when the demand for real money balances is perfectly interest elastic. In such a situation, a drop in the interest rate will not induce larger money holdings, and therefore the *LM* curve will be horizontal.

***LM* Curve** A positively sloped curve showing all combinations of the interest rate and the level of income that are consistent with equilibrium in the money market.

Long-Run Aggregate Supply Curve In the long run, when workers correctly forecast prices, the supply curve will be vertical at the natural output level. The natural rate of output will be consistent with any rate of inflation.

***M*-1** The sum of currency and coin, traveler's checks of nonbank issuers, demand deposits at commercial banks, NOW and ATS account balances, credit union share draft balances, and demand deposits at mutual savings banks. This monetary aggregate is often taken to represent money in its role as a medium of exchange.

***M*-2** The sum of *M*-1 plus savings and small denomination time deposits at all depository institutions, overnight repurchase agreements, overnight Eurodollars, and money market mutual fund balances. This monetary aggregate is often taken as a measure of money in its role as a store of wealth.

***M*-3** The sum of *M*-2 plus large denomination time deposits at all depository institutions, term repurchase agreements at commercial banks and savings and loan associations, and balances of money market mutual funds of institutions.

Marginal Product *(MP)* The change in output attributable to the last unit of a variable factor of production employed.

Marginal Propensity to Consume (MPC) The ratio of additional consumption expenditure to the change in national income that induced it.

Marginal Propensity to Save (MPS) The ratio of a change in saving to the change in national income which induced it. MPS = 1 − MPC.

Marginal Tax Rate The rate of tax on the last dollar earned.

Monetarism A macroeconomic theory that takes variations in the money supply to be the major cause of economic fluctuations and of changes in the price level.

Monetary Aggregates Various measures of the supply of money in the economy.

Monetary Base The total of currency in circulation plus reserve deposits at the Fed.

Monetary Policy The deliberate manipulation of the money supply and/or interest rates in order to affect the level of national income, prices, unemployment, and other economic variables.

Monetization A situation that occurs when newly issued federal government bonds, issued to finance a budget deficit, are purchased by the Federal Reserve. As a consequence, the economy's money supply is increased.

Money Market The market for real money balances. Demand and supply interact in this market to determine the level of real balances to be held.

Money Market Mutual Funds Mutual funds investing in highly liquid short-term debts of the government or leading corporations. Ordinarily depositors may write checks on their fund balances.

Money Neutrality The situation that exists when real economic variables, such as employment and real output, are not affected by changes in the supply of money.

Multiplier The ratio of the change in income to the change in the autonomous component of aggregate demand which caused it.

National Income and Product Accounts (NIPA) The United States government's official statistics on output, investment, prices, and a variety of other economic variables.

Natural Employment Level of Output The amount of real GNP produced when there is no involuntary unemployment and no misperceptions of prices.

Natural Rate Hypothesis In the long run, there will be a natural rate of employment determined by real economic forces. Policymakers can increase employment above this rate only by accepting accelerating inflation.

Negotiable Order of Withdrawal (NOW) Accounts Transaction balances held at financial institutions from which funds may be transferred using a checklike instrument called a negotiable order of withdrawal. Such deposits may earn interest.

Neoclassical Synthesis The description of the economy characterized by the Friedman-Phelps alternative. In the short run, there are rigidities in the adjustment of wages and prices so that the aggregate supply curve is positively sloped.

Nominal Variables Economic variables expressed in current dollar terms. These variables are not adjusted for inflation.

Off Budget Items Government projects and programs that are not listed on the budget. As such, financing of the projects need not face the annual review which other projects face.

Office of Management and Budget (OMB) The executive branch department responsible for the structure of the federal government's budget.

Official Reserve Transactions Account That part of the balance of payments statistics that shows the net foreign transactions of a nation's central bank, central government Treasury, and exchange stabilization agency.

Okun's Law An empirical relationship discovered by Arthur Okun which says that every one percent increase in the unemployment rate means that real GNP will fall by about three percent.

Old Age and Survivors Insurance (OASI) Along with disability insurance, OASI comprises the social insurance program known as Social Security.

Operational Lag The time between the point when a policy is implemented and the point when it begins to take effect.

Pension Funds Contributions out of current income by employers and employees for the purpose of accumulating retirement income.

Perfect Foresight The situation that exists when all economic units accurately forecast future values of relevant economic variables.

Permanent Income Hypothesis (PIH) A theory of consumption spending developed by Milton Friedman. It postulates that economic units determine their present consumption based on their permanent income—the income which the unit expects to receive over the balance of its lifetime. More formally, permanent income is the current asset value of the lifetime income stream consisting of both labor and property income.

Personal Saving Current disposable income minus expenditures on consumption.

Phillips Curve A curve showing an inverse relationship between the unemployment rate and the rate of inflation.

Political Business Cycle The theory that politicians manipulate the economy to gain reelection. The economy is artificially stimulated prior to election day while adverse reactions set in after the election is over. Hence, business cycle fluctuations are worsened.

Portfolio A collection of assets (both real and financial) held by an individual or a firm.

Potential Output The amount of output (GNP) that could be produced by the economy if all resources were fully employed.

Prime Rate The interest rate charged by commercial banks on loans to their best customers.

Producer Price Index (PPI) An index that measures changes in the price of a fixed basket of raw materials and semifinished goods over time. (The PPI was originally called the Wholesale Price Index.)

Productivity The average output produced, per period, by a unit of a factor of production.

Purchasing Power Parity An extension of the law of one price to a multigood setting. The rate at which two currencies can be exchanged (the exchange rate) should reflect the relative purchasing powers of those currencies.

Quantity Theory of Money A theory of price determination. Using the equation of exchange and assuming full employment and a stable demand for money, the theory asserts that there is a direct and proportional relationship between the stock and the price level.

Random Walk An economic variable is said to follow a random walk when the best forecast of its future value is just the present value; that is, the future value is equal to the present value plus an unpredictable random error.

Rate of Depreciation The rate of decrease in the value of a capital good due to physical deterioriation or to technological obsolescence.

Rational Expectations Hypothesis *(REH)* The idea that people form their expectations regarding future values of economic variables by using all information that is available to them. This means that individuals will not systematically err in forming expectations.

Reaganomics The economic policies advocated by President Ronald Reagan. The policies included tax reductions, investment incentives, and deregulation of industry.

Real Interest Rate The nominal (measured) interest rate corrected for inflation. The real rate is defined as the nominal rate of interest minus the expected rate of inflation.

Real Variables Economic variables measured in physical or constant dollar terms. Alternatively, nominal variables deflated by a price index.

Recognition Lag The time it takes for policymakers to notice a problem that has arisen in the economy.

Regulation *Q* A regulation of the Federal Reserve that sets maximum interest rates which commercial banks may pay on various types of deposits. Under the Depository Institutions Deregulation and Monetary Control Act of 1980, this regulation is being phased out.

Repurchase Agreements *(RPs)* Sales of securities with a simultaneous agreement to repurchase them at a specified future date, usually the following day.

Required Reserves The percentage of a financial institution's deposits that must be held in the form of vault cash or reserves at the Fed.

Reserve to Deposit Ratio The ratio of a financial institution's reserves to its level of deposit liabilities.

Residential Investment Additions to the stock of homes and apartment buldings.

Rules Fixed mechanisms for carrying out macroeconomic policy. Rules obviate the use of discretionary changes in monetary or fiscal policy tools.

Savings and Loan Associations (S&Ls) Financial intermediaries that have tradiitionally obtained funds from depositors and channeled them into mortgage loans to finance the purchase of homes.

Shoe Leather Costs Costs incurred by individuals and businesses in attempting to minimize their holdings of cash. During inflationary times cash balances lose value, and so real resources are devoted to minimizing such balances.

Short-Run Aggregate Supply Curve In the short run, a positively sloped relationship between the supply of output and its price may exist. According to Friedman and Phelps, such a relationship derives from incorrect price expectations on the part of workers. The positive slope of the curve will last only so long as workers misforecast prices. According to others, particularly the contract-based theorists, it is rigidities in the adjustment of wages and prices that cause the supply curve to be positively sloped.

Snake An arrangement of the European Economic Community (EEC) to coordinate member country exchange rates. Exchange rates between member countries can fluctuate only within narrow bands while the overall group exchange rate can vary freely with respect to the U.S. dollar.

Special Drawing Rights (SDRs) A form of international money issued by the International Monetary Fund. SDRs are used by nations as a form of reserves for financing balance of payments deficits.

Stabilization Policy Macroeconomic policy designed to reduce business cycle fluctuations or to reduce the rate of inflation.

Stagflation High rates of unemployment accompanied by high inflation rates or a simultaneously increasing rate of unemployment and inflation.

Stop-and-Go Policies When policymakers shift rapidly between attempts to reduce the unemployment rate and attempts to lower the rate of inflation.

Supply Shocks Events that cause a reduction in the productive capacity of an economy. Such shocks reduce supply either by reducing the availability of factor inputs or by reducing the productivity of those inputs.

Supply-Side Economics An economic theory that focuses on the role of incentives to work and produce as the most important determinants of the level of economic activity. Supply-siders advocate tax cuts, investment incentives, and deregulation as tools to stimulate the productive capacity of the economy.

Suppressed Inflation A situation in which, at existing wages and prices, the aggregate demands for output and labor exceed the corresponding supplies.

Surplus The situation which occurs when an economic unit (usually the government) spends less in a period than it takes in revenue.

Tax Surcharge An additional tax levied on the existing tax structure. Typically, a surcharge is intended to be temporary.

Time Series Data Economic data collected at discrete intervals of time but for the same economic unit.

Tobin's q The ratio of the market value of existing capital to the replacement cost of that capital. According to Tobin, this ratio is an important determinant of the level of investment spending.

Total Product Total output produced in an economy. The total product curve is a positively sloping curve that shows all output levels that can be attained in an economy at a given time using various amounts of labor.

Trade-off Curve Another name for the Phillips curve. Policymakers interpreted the Phillips curve as showing the trade-off between inflation and unemployment. According to this interpretation, any point along the curve could be attained through the use of monetary and fiscal policy.

Treasury Bill (T-Bill) A short-term promissory note issued by the U.S. Treasury. Such notes carry a maturity of less than one year and pay no explicit interest. They are sold at a discount from their face value.

Uncontrollable Budget Those items in the federal government budget that grow over time without explicit action on the part of Congress and the president.

User Cost The implicit rental value of capital services.

Value of the Marginal Product *(VMP)* The marginal physical product of a factor input multiplied by the unit price of the output the factor helps to create. The *VMP* measures the contribution to a firm's revenue arising from the last unit of a productive factor hired.

Velocity A rate at which the stock of money is used to purchase GNP. It is a measure of the speed with which the average dollar changes hands. GNP/*M* = velocity.

Wage and Price Controls *See* Incomes policies.

Wage-Push Inflation Inflation caused by accelerating wage demands by unions and individuals. The higher wages are supposed to be passed along to consumers in the form of higher prices.

Wealth Effects Changes in aggregate demand caused by changes in wealth. Such changes, in turn, arise because of variations in prices or in interest rates.

World Money Supply The sum of the money supplies in each country denominated in a common currency and weighted by the percent of total world trade each country engages in.

AUTHOR INDEX

SUBJECT INDEX